THE
GRAPHICAL PLAYER
2008

John Burnson

Craig Brown
Marc Normandin
Jeff Sackmann

with

John Beamer
Greg Rybarczyk

Shandler Enterprises, LLC

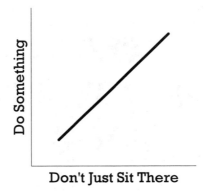

First Edition: November 2007

Published by Shandler Enterprises, LLC, P.O. Box 20303, Roanoke, VA 24018 (540-772-6315)

www.baseballhq.com/gp.shtml

ISBN 1-891566-53-9
Printed in the United States of America

INTRODUCTION

"It doesn't mean much now / It's built for the future"
– The Fixx

In baseball, taking a lead off a base is an anticipatory act. By itself, the move means nothing, and in fact it puts the runner in danger of a pick-off. The benefit of leading off is realized only if the man at the plate puts the ball into play and the runner needs to streak to the next base. As The Fixx would say, it's built for the future.

This book has undergone similar renovation. In the past 12 months, baseball fans have witnessed an explosion of analysis, as more granular – and more affordable – data are made available. No longer must we settle for labels like "home run" or "strikeout" – we can say how far the home run went (and in what direction), or what pitches made up the strikeout (and where they crossed the plate). If you need data for commercial purposes, you can call on Baseball Info Solutions; for casual analysis, you can tap MLB's Enhanced Gameday files. Either way, the data are no hurdle.

Clearly, this is a thrilling time – we're smashing atoms and tracking the stitching. The catch is that our questions for the new data outnumber our answers. We are still in the *descriptive* phase of the investigation – defining terms; forging a lingo; demarcating the areas that need demarcation.

This quandary is especially true of that deepest of arts, pitching. For the first time, each pitcher in this book gets a pitch profile showing a rough distribution of his fastballs, change-ups, and breaking balls. We have ideas about what a "good" profile should look like: being able to throw in the 90's; being able to change speeds effectively; having a sizable repertoire of pitches. But is that enough? Are there better metrics? And do the data hide trends that would aid our forecasts?

For now, we can't say. However, as we run the profiles in future editions – and as we are able to compare pitchers not only to their peers but also to younger versions of themselves – we expect that the answers to our queries will become clearer.

We are on the frontier. The sky is blue, the land is rich, and the vista is long. Bring the family and stake your claim.

The 5th edition of the GRAPHICAL PLAYER packs as many innovations as did the first four editions combined. You get:

- Projected 3-year trends
- Spray charts for hitters
- Pitch profiles for pitchers
- Fielding assessments for hitters
- Line-up profiles for hitters

The headlong pace of power-ups owes to advances in data gathering and desktop processing, and also to the ancient spirit of camaraderie. Most of our statistics were purchased from Baseball Info Solutions. Jeff Sackmann of Minor League Splits (www.MinorLeagueSplits.com) created the projections. Along with Jeff, analysts Craig Brown and Marc Normandin diagnosed the hitters. John Beamer of The Hardball Times (www.HardballTimes.com) marshaled the pitch data. Greg Rybarczyk of Hit Tracker (www.HitTrackerOnline.com) caught the HR.

If you like what you see in this book, you will want to subscribe to **HEATER** (www.HeaterMagazine.com). It's 65 pages of beat-the-pants-off-your-opponents stats published weekly during the regular season. And if you are a fiend for box scores, direct your browser to **The Rundown** (www.HeaterMagazine.com/TheRundown) – it's a free daily PDF of box scores for not just baseball but other sports, all in a compact form perfect for bus or lunch counter.

We've our own illustrations of life: Mom and Dad; Lulu (7 and a disciplined hitter herself), Zoot (3), and Kim (ageless); Ron & the Huston Street Irregulars at BaseballHQ; Dave and David at Hardball Times; creators Ed Brubaker, Brian Stepanek, and John Dufilho; *Eastern Promises*, *Journeyman,* and *New Magnetic Wonder*; the Hero Factory (friends, allies, and co-campaigners); and everyone else who plots their own course.

Finally, thanks to you, for setting our vision in front of yours. Remember– when something seems out of reach, just adjust the axis.   JB

ABOUT THIS BOOK

You will not find a lot of numbers in this book – in part, this book is meant to *complement* lists of figures. Moreover, the portraits in this book affirm trends that are often lost in a too-great attention to details.

You also will not find dollar values. We are more interested in showing the *influences* on player values and their likely ranges. The proliferation of fantasy formats dashes the utility of posted prices, anyway.

What you *will* find is the BIG PICTURE. We have selected those trends and gauges that have the broadest application to baseball watchers. And we have depicted those items in a way that requires neither a magnifying glass nor a master's degree. You need only those two orbs above your nose.

Don't be daunted. If you can follow a hit ball in flight, you can master the graphs in this book.

TABLE OF CONTENTS

THE PITCHERS

In this edition, we cover virtually all pitchers who tossed at least 65 IP in 2007, plus about 80 other pitchers who distinguished themselves in limited play. In all, there are 300 pitchers, listed alphabetically.

Beside each pitcher's name, we indicate whether he was a starting pitcher ("SP") or relief pitcher ("RP"). We classify a pitcher as a starter if he started at least half his games in 2007. Also, we note the pitcher's handedness ("R" or "L").

John Burnson covers the pitchers.

AGE AMONG PEERS

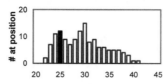

We do not present much personal information about our players – you won't find a player's height or hometown. However, a player's age is a detail of a different caliber. The trick is to phrase the question right. We don't want to know a player's age because we aim to send him a birthday card. Rather, we want to know, "What does his age say about his future?" This question, a chart can handle.

In this chart, the horizontal axis is age; the height of each column is the number of players at that position & age in our pool.

We post separate graphs for starting pitchers (SP) and relief pitchers (RP). The black column is the age of the player in question – thus, this player is 25 years old. Age is figured as of October 1, 2007.

Two forces push players into smaller roles. One is aging, and the attendant shrinking of skills and amplifying of aches; the other is the replenishment of rivals, mostly in the form of rookies. People often grasp the first force but not the second. And yet, all but the keenest players will eventually fall to fiercer (or fresher) faces.

CAREER FORTUNES

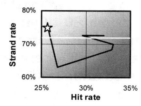

Here, we focus on the role of beneficial bounces & opportune outs. Our targets are **hit rate** (H%, the rate at which catchable balls turn into hits) and **strand rate** (S%, the fraction of runners who get stuck on base). A high hit rate is bad; a high strand rate is good. Hit rate is largely out of a pitcher's control (but not entirely, since ground balls have a higher hit rate than fly balls – remember that H% deals only with potentially catchable balls, so it ignores homers). Strand rate is more loyal – a pitcher tends to strand more runners if he strikes out more batters and sees fewer fly balls (i.e., home runs) and walks. (The place for skill in strand rate is why we use the word "fortunes" instead of "luck.") However, even strand rate is open to an inconvenient homer or bullpen blow-up.

This graph follows a pitcher's hit and strand rates over his career. The blend for the latest season is marked with a star. Rates of 30% for hit rate and 70% for strand rate are ordinary. (Note that strand rate is not independent of hit rate, since more hits means more runners advanced.)

Fortune rises from the shady lower right (high H%, low S%) to the sunny upper left (low H%, high S%). Watch out for points that are unusual for the pitcher or are far from the center; the next year could see a return to normalcy (to the pitcher's detriment or benefit, as the case may be).

A white line runs across the graph; this line is the pitcher's **expected strand rate** (based on his skills) for 2007. An actual strand rate that is well above expectations is cause for reproach.

We can show the interplay of skill and luck by two angles. First, imagine a pitcher with rates of 6 K/9 IP, 3 BB/9 IP, and 1 HR/9 IP. With normal fortunes, his ERA would be 4.40, but it falls to 2.90 with a 25% hit rate and 80% strand rate, and rises to 6.40 with a 35% hit rate and 60% strand rate. If we instead hold fortune constant and ask what skills produce a 4.40 ERA, we find that a pitcher in the lower right has to strike out about half his batters, but a pitcher in the upper left has to strike out hardly anyone.

The upshot: Good luck shields shoddy skills, and bad luck buries good skills.

2

GAME LOG

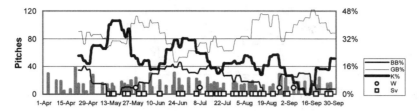

If we aim to understand a pitcher's year, it is imperative that we chart his trends over the season. Thus, the Game Log.

The long axis shows from the full regular season, day by day. Each column is one game. The height of the column is the pitch count, as shown on the left axis. This layout reveals both how often a pitcher threw and how much he was taxed those days. When a game log has a gap (such as for a trip to the DL or the minors), we note the reason.

Running across the graph are our three key gauges: strikeout rate (thick line), walk rate (medium-weight line); and ground-ball rate (thin line). The height of the line indicates its rate per batters faced (BF), as given on the axis to the right. The rates are not one-game figures but rolling rates over several games – three games for starters, five games for relievers.

What do we look for? We like a K% over 16% and a BB% below 8% – these rates equate to the familiar targets of 6 K/9 IP and 3 BB/9 IP. A typical ground-ball rate is 42%; a rate below 32% marks a fly-ball-heavy run of games. All else equal, grounders are preferable: A higher GB% leads to a lower rate of fly balls – and thus home runs – and a higher rate of stranded runners. (Note that GB% moves contrarily to K%, since strikeouts preclude contact.)

Across a season, we esteem a rising strikeout rate and a falling walk rate. More strikeouts means a lesser role for luck on hit balls; fewer walks means fewer riskless at-bats for hitters and less wasted effort. A rising walk rate, or a falling strikeout rate or ground-ball rate, could indicate fatigue.

New for 2008: Pitchers tend to occupy one of three roles: starter, reliever, and closer. To help identify the pitcher's role (and his success in it), we provide two sets of tick marks along the bottom. The circles note when the pitcher got a Win, and the squares say when he got a Save. These marks are especially helpful at tracking movement into and out of the closer's seat.

SIM ERA

This tool digests a pitcher's skills *and* fortunes and shows what should have been. Sim ERA uses data from the online site Retrosheet.org to unfurl a game play by play. The nature and incidence of the simulated plays depend on a pitcher's actual K%, BB%, and GB%. We tabulate the results from 6,000 simulated seasons.

The tall axis shows ERA, proceeding from 5.00 to 2.00 by quarter runs. Note that a part of the curve may be under 2.00 (which is swell) or over 5.00 (which is not). The wide axis is the probability of the pitcher's having that ERA. The bar that extends furthest to the left is the likeliest ERA. The pitcher's actual ERA is in black.

The above graph shows a curve for a slightly above-average pitcher: The likeliest ERA is from 3.50-4.00, though a 5.00 ERA is not unimaginable. But this pitcher's real ERA was 2.25; hence he overachieved. The broad range of outcomes implies a big role for luck – either this guy had relatively few IP or he lacked a burly strikeout rate.

Sim ERA is not symmetrical: Worse results are more likely. Bad pitchers often don't get a chance to get better, but good pitchers always get a chance to get worse.

PITCH PROFILE

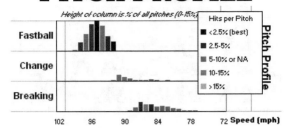

(Note: The pitch data in this book came from Baseball Info Solutions. Here, we describe a simple method for classifying the data found in MLB's publicly available data files; we applied similar rules to the data from BIS.)

For its Enhanced Gameday service, which lets users follow games on the Internet in real time, Major League Baseball collects gobs of pitch data. In late 2006, MLB began posting this data on the web. The files aren't readily readable, but with work, they can be fetched and sifted. And, as you may imagine, they have been.

Much of the analysis to date relates the start speed and horizontal and vertical breaks to pin down the exact type of pitch. For this book, we were more interested in expressing the pitcher's overall palette. Ultimately, we chose to plot our pitch data by four variables: **speed**, **general type**, **frequency**, and **effectiveness**.

Getting the pitch speed is easy – the speed at release is one of the variables in MLB's files. The next task is labeling the pitches. With 300 pitchers to grade, it is not practical to scan the data for each one. By looking at the data for many pitchers, Hardball Times's John Beamer was able to come up with a short routine that sufficed:

1. For each pitcher, find the mean speed of all pitches. Pitches faster than the mean speed are **fastballs**.
2. Find the mean horizontal and vertical breaks of his fastballs; these tell where the fastballs cross home plate. All non-fastballs that fall within 7" left or right and 5" up or down of this area are **change-ups**.
3. Everything else is **breaking balls**.

There was one set of exceptions: pitchers with speeds of greater than 90 mph for at least 75% of their pitches. For them, it was not reliable to use the mean speed of all pitches to determine fastballs; instead, we had to find a proper cut-off by visually inspecting the data.

John Beamer did this work for 10 hurlers: Jonathan Papelbon, J.J. Putz, Mariano Rivera, Alan Embree, Bobby Howry, Brandon Morrow, Scot Shields, Rafael Soriano, Matt Thornton, and Joel Zumaya.

After these steps, we have a bunch of buckets of pitches classified by speed and type for each pitcher. We then calculate how often the pitcher threw each combination; that value is the height of the column in the graph. (Each of the three rows runs in height from 0-15% of recorded pitches.)

The last step is computing effectiveness. In the end, we settled on the rate of *hits allowed per pitch*. This is not a perfect gauge – it doesn't hold called balls against the pitcher, nor does it distinguish hits by their severity. Still, this is an easily graspable measure that works for our purposes. For each pitcher, we put each combination of pitch type and speed in one of five categories, from H/P below 2.5% (best) to over 15% (worst). Combinations with fewer than 20 examples went into the middle bin.

If you use MLB's files, note that the equipment for recording the data was not rolled out to all parks at once, and in fact a number of sites seemed not to have it even by season's end. As a result, some pitchers are lightly represented or even absent.

For reference, here's a collective pitch profile for major-league pitchers in 2007:

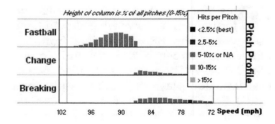

To learn more about MLB's data files, visit www.HardballTimes.com and check out the work of John Beamer and also John Walsh. Chris Constancio assisted with this analysis.

CAREER TRENDS

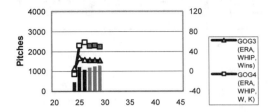

Although generalizations based on age or fortunes have a role in forecasting players, we believe the best guide to a player's future is his past – not just the last X seasons, either. This graph depicts a player's full big-league career.

The long axis shows the pitcher's age. For pitchers, Career Trends run from ages 20 to 45. The tall axis shows two things. The axis on the left shows the number of pitches thrown in the majors, as indicated by the vertical gray bar at each age. We count by "pitches" instead of "innings" because we believe that total pitches is a truer account of a pitcher's load.

The axis on the right tracks GOG (our metric of pitching value), as shown by the two trend lines. A pitcher bears responsibility for five basic outcomes: strikeout, walk, ground ball, fly ball, and line drive. GOG3 figures contributions of these results to three stats – ERA, WHIP, and Wins. GOG4 adds Strikeouts. (We ignore Saves since they are too much a function of role.)

The equations have been adjusted so that a GOG of 0 (for both indicators) denotes a pitcher with the barest acceptable rates (6 K/9 IP, 3 BB/9 IP, and typical GB/FB). Thus, a GOG above 0 signals worthiness.

One quality of GOG is that it does not consider either a pitcher's allowed batting average or his allowed home-run rate. As stated earlier, these rates are driven by other factors (allowed contact for BA, allowed fly balls for HR), and so they should not be held against the pitcher as such.

New for 2008: In past years, we relied on readers' eyes alone to fill in the future, but with this edition, we decided to lend a hand with not one but *three* years of projected trends. The gray triangles and squares project the rate stats – for GOG3 and GOG4, respectively – and the gray columns project pitch count. You can learn more about our projection system in Jeff Sackmann's essay "Working the Seam" later in this book.

PROGNOSIS

2.14 ERA. Accardo took over the closer job from Frasor in May and then held on for dear life. Projections are flat but K% is cascading. We'll take the stairs.   —

We don't enjoy rendering verdicts. Our original mission was to show baseball players *without* words – in fact, this book was partly a rebellion against gassy commentaries. But readers seem to appreciate our observations, so we provide them again. We don't think we are pointing out features you can't see, but maybe we can lead you to the landmarks.

New for 2008: For pitchers, we lead off our analysis with the year's ERA, given in bold.

The indicator on the right says whether we think that the player will be reasonably (or under-) valued ($) or not (—) on Draft Day. Fantasy owners spend a lot of time on becoming better judges of *skill*; however, fantasy leagues are markets, and so it is

equally (or more) crucial to become better judges of *sentiment*. You must have the discipline to set aside your own suspicions and measure the temperature of the wider world. We give our best guess, but you should test the currents in your own seas.

Regarding the projected trends: You will find that many prognoses stand in *opposition* to the projections. This is by design. The forecasts are the rulings of the Cosmic Scoreboard Operator, who sees all players from a great distance, but the system does not make distinctions for in-season trends, fielding, pedigree, or nature of injury. The commentators in this book can, and in so doing, hope to pick out those cases where the All-Seeing Selig's judgment is clouded.

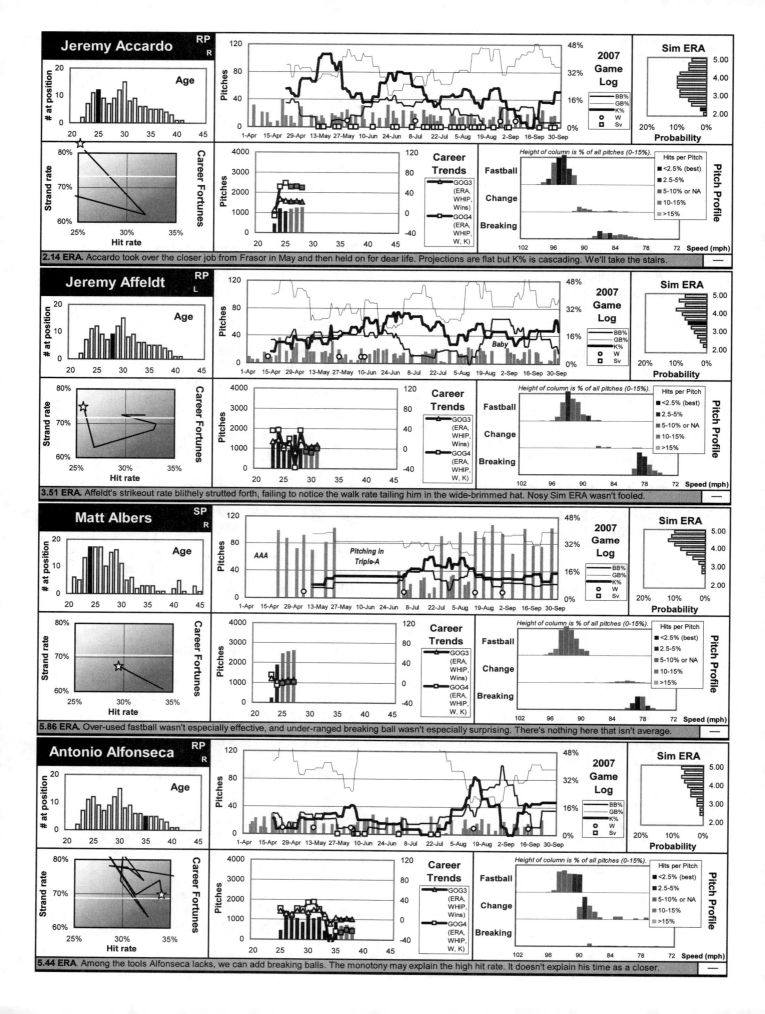

Jeremy Accardo — RP R

2007 Game Log — BB%, GB%, K%, W (○), Sv (□)

Sim ERA / Probability

Age — # at position

Career Fortunes — Strand rate vs. Hit rate

Career Trends — Pitches — GOG3 (ERA, WHIP, Wins), GOG4 (ERA, WHIP, W, K)

Pitch Profile — Height of column is % of all pitches (0-15%). Fastball, Change, Breaking. Hits per Pitch: <2.5% (best), 2.5-5%, 5-10% or NA, 10-15%, >15%. Speed (mph)

2.14 ERA. Accardo took over the closer job from Frasor in May and then held on for dear life. Projections are flat but K% is cascading. We'll take the stairs. —

Jeremy Affeldt — RP L

2007 Game Log — BB%, GB%, K%, W (○), Sv (□) — Baby

Sim ERA / Probability

Age — # at position

Career Fortunes — Strand rate vs. Hit rate

Career Trends — Pitches — GOG3 (ERA, WHIP, Wins), GOG4 (ERA, WHIP, W, K)

Pitch Profile — Height of column is % of all pitches (0-15%). Fastball, Change, Breaking. Hits per Pitch: <2.5% (best), 2.5-5%, 5-10% or NA, 10-15%, >15%. Speed (mph)

3.51 ERA. Affeldt's strikeout rate blithely strutted forth, failing to notice the walk rate tailing him in the wide-brimmed hat. Nosy Sim ERA wasn't fooled. —

Matt Albers — SP R

2007 Game Log — BB%, GB%, K%, W (○), Sv (□) — AAA — Pitching in Triple-A

Sim ERA / Probability

Age — # at position

Career Fortunes — Strand rate vs. Hit rate

Career Trends — Pitches — GOG3 (ERA, WHIP, Wins), GOG4 (ERA, WHIP, W, K)

Pitch Profile — Height of column is % of all pitches (0-15%). Fastball, Change, Breaking. Hits per Pitch: <2.5% (best), 2.5-5%, 5-10% or NA, 10-15%, >15%. Speed (mph)

5.86 ERA. Over-used fastball wasn't especially effective, and under-ranged breaking ball wasn't especially surprising. There's nothing here that isn't average. —

Antonio Alfonseca — RP R

2007 Game Log — BB%, GB%, K%, W (○), Sv (□)

Sim ERA / Probability

Age — # at position

Career Fortunes — Strand rate vs. Hit rate

Career Trends — Pitches — GOG3 (ERA, WHIP, Wins), GOG4 (ERA, WHIP, W, K)

Pitch Profile — Height of column is % of all pitches (0-15%). Fastball, Change, Breaking. Hits per Pitch: <2.5% (best), 2.5-5%, 5-10% or NA, 10-15%, >15%. Speed (mph)

5.44 ERA. Among the tools Alfonseca lacks, we can add breaking balls. The monotony may explain the high hit rate. It doesn't explain his time as a closer. —

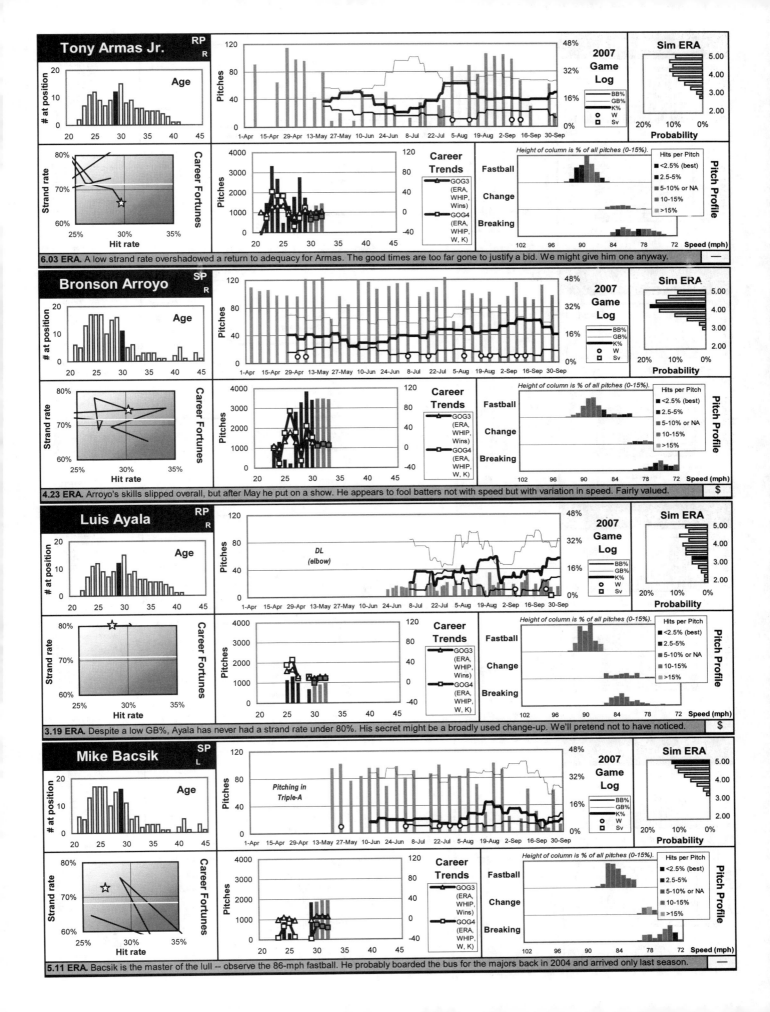

Tony Armas Jr. RP R

2007 Game Log

BB%
GB%
K%
W ○
Sv ☐

Sim ERA

Age

Career Fortunes

Career Trends
GOG3 (ERA, WHIP, Wins)
GOG4 (ERA, WHIP, W, K)

Height of column is % of all pitches (0-15%)

Hits per Pitch
■ <2.5% (best)
■ 2.5-5%
■ 5-10% or NA
■ 10-15%
▨ >15%

Fastball
Change
Breaking

Pitch Profile

6.03 ERA. A low strand rate overshadowed a return to adequacy for Armas. The good times are too far gone to justify a bid. We might give him one anyway. —

Bronson Arroyo SP R

2007 Game Log

BB%
GB%
K%
W ○
Sv ☐

Sim ERA

Age

Career Fortunes

Career Trends
GOG3 (ERA, WHIP, Wins)
GOG4 (ERA, WHIP, W, K)

Height of column is % of all pitches (0-15%)

Hits per Pitch
■ <2.5% (best)
■ 2.5-5%
■ 5-10% or NA
■ 10-15%
▨ >15%

Fastball
Change
Breaking

Pitch Profile

4.23 ERA. Arroyo's skills slipped overall, but after May he put on a show. He appears to fool batters not with speed but with variation in speed. Fairly valued. $

Luis Ayala RP R

DL (elbow)

2007 Game Log

BB%
GB%
K%
W ○
Sv ☐

Sim ERA

Age

Career Fortunes

Career Trends
GOG3 (ERA, WHIP, Wins)
GOG4 (ERA, WHIP, W, K)

Height of column is % of all pitches (0-15%).

Hits per Pitch
■ <2.5% (best)
■ 2.5-5%
■ 5-10% or NA
■ 10-15%
▨ >15%

Fastball
Change
Breaking

Pitch Profile

3.19 ERA. Despite a low GB%, Ayala has never had a strand rate under 80%. His secret might be a broadly used change-up. We'll pretend not to have noticed. $

Mike Bacsik SP L

Pitching in Triple-A

2007 Game Log

BB%
GB%
K%
W ○
Sv ☐

Sim ERA

Age

Career Fortunes

Career Trends
GOG3 (ERA, WHIP, Wins)
GOG4 (ERA, WHIP, W, K)

Height of column is % of all pitches (0-15%).

Hits per Pitch
■ <2.5% (best)
■ 2.5-5%
■ 5-10% or NA
■ 10-15%
▨ >15%

Fastball
Change
Breaking

Pitch Profile

5.11 ERA. Bacsik is the master of the lull -- observe the 86-mph fastball. He probably boarded the bus for the majors back in 2004 and arrived only last season. —

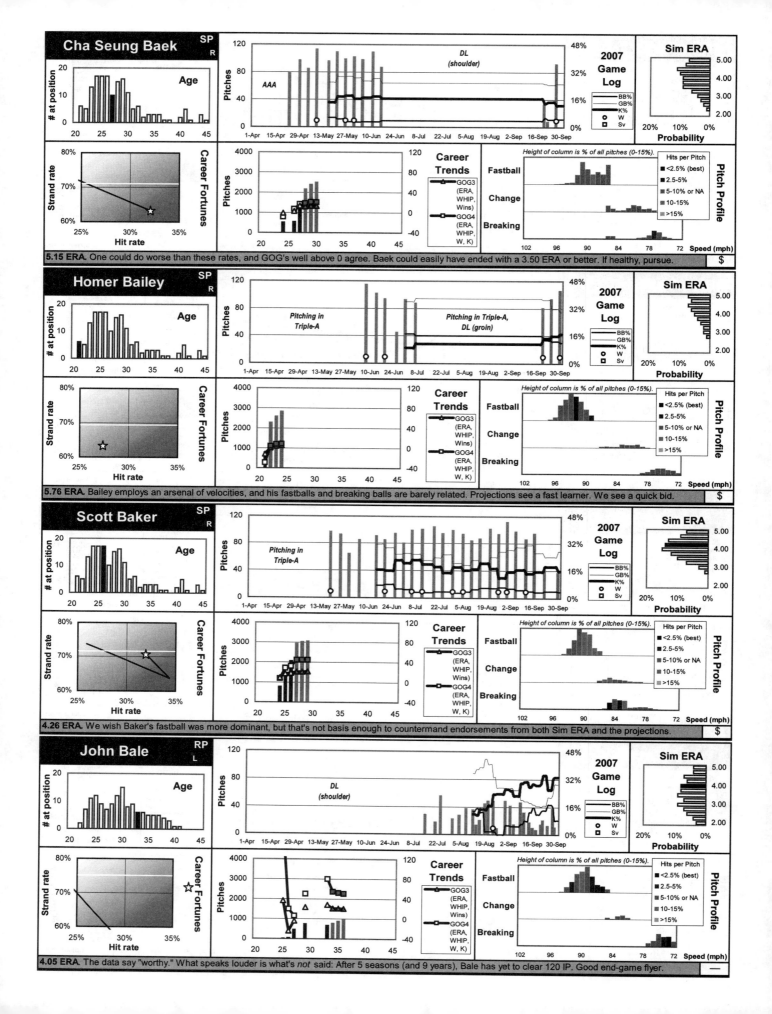

Cha Seung Baek — SP, R

Age

Career Fortunes — Strand rate / Hit rate

Pitches — DL (shoulder), AAA

2007 Game Log — BB%, GB%, K%, W, Sv

Sim ERA — Probability

Career Trends — GOG3 (ERA, WHIP, Wins), GOG4 (ERA, WHIP, W, K)

Pitch Profile — Height of column is % of all pitches (0-15%). Hits per Pitch: <2.5% (best), 2.5-5%, 5-10% or NA, 10-15%, >15%. Fastball, Change, Breaking. Speed (mph)

5.15 ERA. One could do worse than these rates, and GOG's well above 0 agree. Baek could easily have ended with a 3.50 ERA or better. If healthy, pursue. **$**

Homer Bailey — SP, R

Age

Career Fortunes — Strand rate / Hit rate

Pitches — Pitching in Triple-A; Pitching in Triple-A, DL (groin)

2007 Game Log — BB%, GB%, K%, W, Sv

Sim ERA — Probability

Career Trends — GOG3 (ERA, WHIP, Wins), GOG4 (ERA, WHIP, W, K)

Pitch Profile — Height of column is % of all pitches (0-15%). Hits per Pitch: <2.5% (best), 2.5-5%, 5-10% or NA, 10-15%, >15%. Fastball, Change, Breaking. Speed (mph)

5.76 ERA. Bailey employs an arsenal of velocities, and his fastballs and breaking balls are barely related. Projections see a fast learner. We see a quick bid. **$**

Scott Baker — SP, R

Age

Career Fortunes — Strand rate / Hit rate

Pitches — Pitching in Triple-A

2007 Game Log — BB%, GB%, K%, W, Sv

Sim ERA — Probability

Career Trends — GOG3 (ERA, WHIP, Wins), GOG4 (ERA, WHIP, W, K)

Pitch Profile — Height of column is % of all pitches (0-15%). Hits per Pitch: <2.5% (best), 2.5-5%, 5-10% or NA, 10-15%, >15%. Fastball, Change, Breaking. Speed (mph)

4.26 ERA. We wish Baker's fastball was more dominant, but that's not basis enough to countermand endorsements from both Sim ERA and the projections. **$**

John Bale — RP, L

Age

Career Fortunes — Strand rate / Hit rate

Pitches — DL (shoulder)

2007 Game Log — BB%, GB%, K%, W, Sv

Sim ERA — Probability

Career Trends — GOG3 (ERA, WHIP, Wins), GOG4 (ERA, WHIP, W, K)

Pitch Profile — Height of column is % of all pitches (0-15%). Hits per Pitch: <2.5% (best), 2.5-5%, 5-10% or NA, 10-15%, >15%. Fastball, Change, Breaking. Speed (mph)

4.05 ERA. The data say "worthy." What speaks louder is what's *not* said: After 5 seasons (and 9 years), Bale has yet to clear 120 IP. Good end-game flyer. **—**

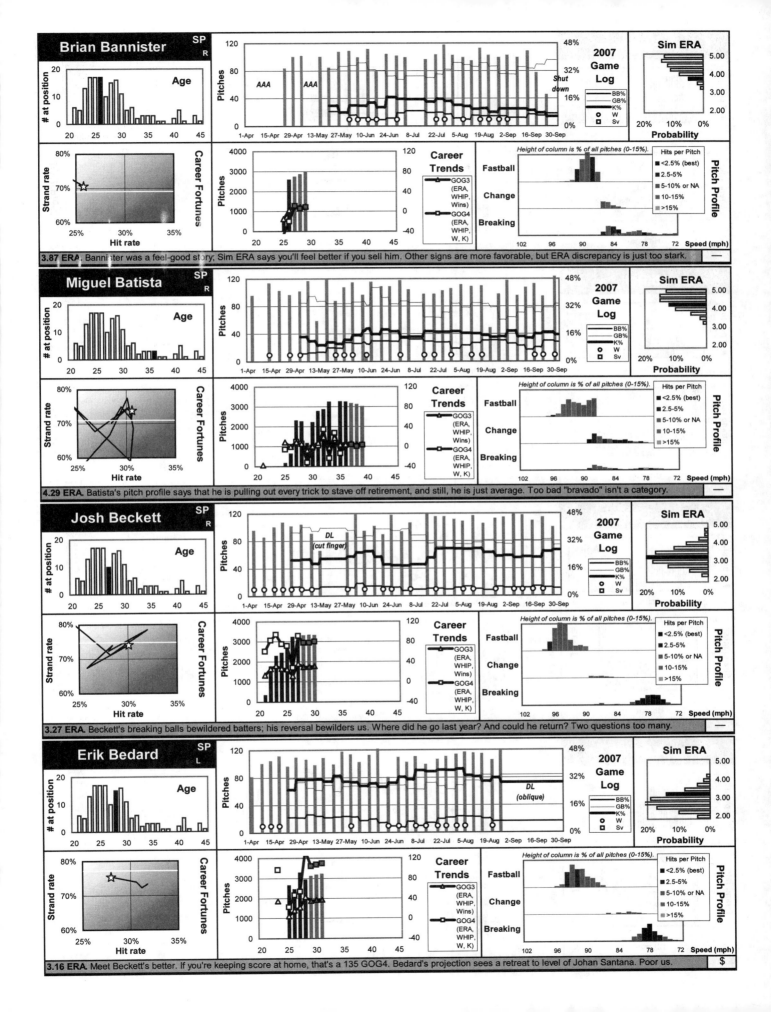

Brian Bannister SP R

2007 Game Log

Sim ERA

AAA   AAA

Shut down

BB%
GB%
K%
W
Sv

Age

Strand rate / Hit rate

Career Trends

GOG3 (ERA, WHIP, Wins)
GOG4 (ERA, WHIP, W, K)

Pitch Profile

Height of column is % of all pitches (0-15%).
Hits per Pitch
<2.5% (best)
2.5-5%
5-10% or NA
10-15%
>15%

Fastball
Change
Breaking

3.87 ERA. Bannister was a feel-good story; Sim ERA says you'll feel better if you sell him. Other signs are more favorable, but ERA discrepancy is just too stark. —

Miguel Batista SP R

2007 Game Log

Sim ERA

BB%
GB%
K%
W
Sv

Age

Strand rate / Hit rate

Career Trends

GOG3 (ERA, WHIP, Wins)
GOG4 (ERA, WHIP, W, K)

Pitch Profile

Height of column is % of all pitches (0-15%).
Hits per Pitch
<2.5% (best)
2.5-5%
5-10% or NA
10-15%
>15%

Fastball
Change
Breaking

4.29 ERA. Batista's pitch profile says that he is pulling out every trick to stave off retirement, and still, he is just average. Too bad "bravado" isn't a category. —

Josh Beckett SP R

2007 Game Log

Sim ERA

DL (cut finger)

BB%
GB%
K%
W
Sv

Age

Strand rate / Hit rate

Career Trends

GOG3 (ERA, WHIP, Wins)
GOG4 (ERA, WHIP, W, K)

Pitch Profile

Height of column is % of all pitches (0-15%).
Hits per Pitch
<2.5% (best)
2.5-5%
5-10% or NA
10-15%
>15%

Fastball
Change
Breaking

3.27 ERA. Beckett's breaking balls bewildered batters; his reversal bewilders us. Where did he go last year? And could he return? Two questions too many. —

Erik Bedard SP L

2007 Game Log

Sim ERA

DL (oblique)

BB%
GB%
K%
W
Sv

Age

Strand rate / Hit rate

Career Trends

GOG3 (ERA, WHIP, Wins)
GOG4 (ERA, WHIP, W, K)

Pitch Profile

Height of column is % of all pitches (0-15%).
Hits per Pitch
<2.5% (best)
2.5-5%
5-10% or NA
10-15%
>15%

Fastball
Change
Breaking

3.16 ERA. Meet Beckett's better. If you're keeping score at home, that's a 135 GOG4. Bedard's projection sees a retreat to level of Johan Santana. Poor us. $

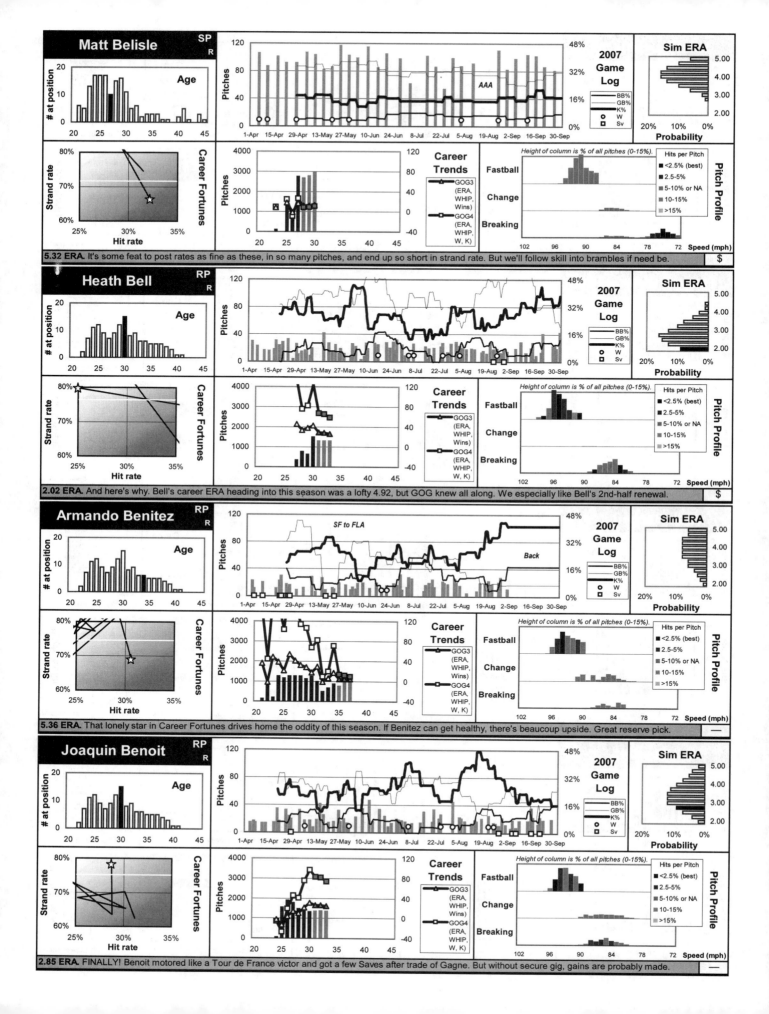

Matt Belisle SP R

Age | # at position | 20 | 25 | 30 | 35 | 40 | 45

Pitches | 120 80 40 0 | 2007 Game Log | AAA | BB% GB% K% W Sv | Sim ERA 5.00 4.00 3.00 2.00 | Probability 20% 10% 0%

1-Apr 15-Apr 29-Apr 13-May 27-May 10-Jun 24-Jun 8-Jul 22-Jul 5-Aug 19-Aug 2-Sep 16-Sep 30-Sep

Strand rate | 80% 70% 60% | Hit rate 25% 30% 35% | Career Fortunes

Pitches | 4000 3000 2000 1000 0 | 20 25 30 35 40 45 | 120 80 40 0 -40 | Career Trends | GOG3 (ERA, WHIP, Wins) GOG4 (ERA, WHIP, W, K)

Height of column is % of all pitches (0-15%). | Hits per Pitch ■ <2.5% (best) ■ 2.5-5% 5-10% or NA 10-15% >15% | Fastball Change Breaking | 102 96 90 84 78 72 Speed (mph) | Pitch Profile

5.32 ERA. It's some feat to post rates as fine as these, in so many pitches, and end up so short in strand rate. But we'll follow skill into brambles if need be. | $

Heath Bell RP R

Age | # at position | 20 | 25 | 30 | 35 | 40 | 45

Pitches | 120 80 40 0 | 2007 Game Log | BB% GB% K% W Sv | Sim ERA 5.00 4.00 3.00 2.00 | Probability 20% 10% 0%

1-Apr 15-Apr 29-Apr 13-May 27-May 10-Jun 24-Jun 8-Jul 22-Jul 5-Aug 19-Aug 2-Sep 16-Sep 30-Sep

Strand rate | 80% 70% 60% | Hit rate 25% 30% 35% | Career Fortunes

Pitches | 4000 3000 2000 1000 0 | 20 25 30 35 40 45 | 120 80 40 0 -40 | Career Trends | GOG3 (ERA, WHIP, Wins) GOG4 (ERA, WHIP, W, K)

Height of column is % of all pitches (0-15%). | Hits per Pitch ■ <2.5% (best) ■ 2.5-5% 5-10% or NA 10-15% >15% | Fastball Change Breaking | 102 96 90 84 78 72 Speed (mph) | Pitch Profile

2.02 ERA. And here's why. Bell's career ERA heading into this season was a lofty 4.92, but GOG knew all along. We especially like Bell's 2nd-half renewal. | $

Armando Benitez RP R

Age | # at position | 20 | 25 | 30 | 35 | 40 | 45

Pitches | 120 80 40 0 | SF to FLA | Back | 2007 Game Log | BB% GB% K% W Sv | Sim ERA 5.00 4.00 3.00 2.00 | Probability 20% 10% 0%

1-Apr 15-Apr 29-Apr 13-May 27-May 10-Jun 24-Jun 8-Jul 22-Jul 5-Aug 19-Aug 2-Sep 16-Sep 30-Sep

Strand rate | 80% 70% 60% | Hit rate 25% 30% 35% | Career Fortunes

Pitches | 4000 3000 2000 1000 0 | 20 25 30 35 40 45 | 120 80 40 0 -40 | Career Trends | GOG3 (ERA, WHIP, Wins) GOG4 (ERA, WHIP, W, K)

Height of column is % of all pitches (0-15%). | Hits per Pitch ■ <2.5% (best) ■ 2.5-5% 5-10% or NA 10-15% >15% | Fastball Change Breaking | 102 96 90 84 78 72 Speed (mph) | Pitch Profile

5.36 ERA. That lonely star in Career Fortunes drives home the oddity of this season. If Benitez can get healthy, there's beaucoup upside. Great reserve pick. | —

Joaquin Benoit RP R

Age | # at position | 20 | 25 | 30 | 35 | 40 | 45

Pitches | 120 80 40 0 | 2007 Game Log | BB% GB% K% W Sv | Sim ERA 5.00 4.00 3.00 2.00 | Probability 20% 10% 0%

1-Apr 15-Apr 29-Apr 13-May 27-May 10-Jun 24-Jun 8-Jul 22-Jul 5-Aug 19-Aug 2-Sep 16-Sep 30-Sep

Strand rate | 80% 70% 60% | Hit rate 25% 30% 35% | Career Fortunes

Pitches | 4000 3000 2000 1000 0 | 20 25 30 35 40 45 | 120 80 40 0 -40 | Career Trends | GOG3 (ERA, WHIP, Wins) GOG4 (ERA, WHIP, W, K)

Height of column is % of all pitches (0-15%). | Hits per Pitch ■ <2.5% (best) ■ 2.5-5% 5-10% or NA 10-15% >15% | Fastball Change Breaking | 102 96 90 84 78 72 Speed (mph) | Pitch Profile

2.85 ERA. FINALLY! Benoit motored like a Tour de France victor and got a few Saves after trade of Gagne. But without secure gig, gains are probably made. | —

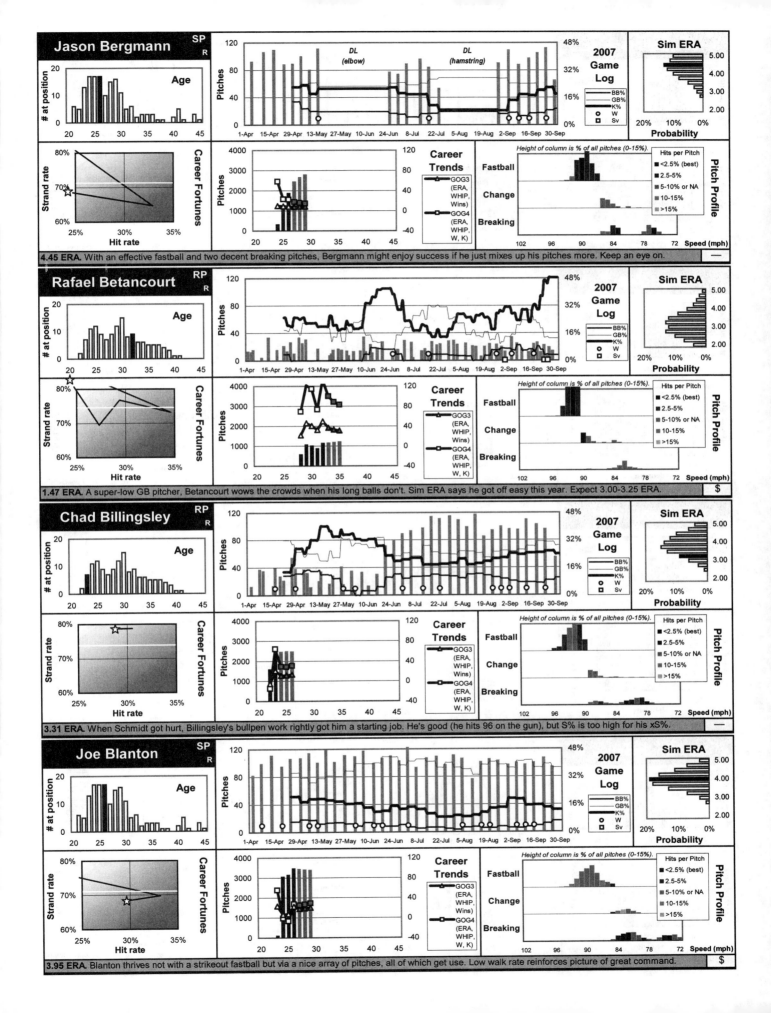

Jason Bergmann SP R

Rafael Betancourt RP R

Chad Billingsley RP R

Joe Blanton SP R

4.45 ERA. With an effective fastball and two decent breaking pitches, Bergmann might enjoy success if he just mixes up his pitches more. Keep an eye on. —

1.47 ERA. A super-low GB pitcher, Betancourt wows the crowds when his long balls don't. Sim ERA says he got off easy this year. Expect 3.00-3.25 ERA. $

3.31 ERA. When Schmidt got hurt, Billingsley's bullpen work rightly got him a starting job. He's good (he hits 96 on the gun), but S% is too high for his xS%. —

3.95 ERA. Blanton thrives not with a strikeout fastball but via a nice array of pitches, all of which get use. Low walk rate reinforces picture of great command. $

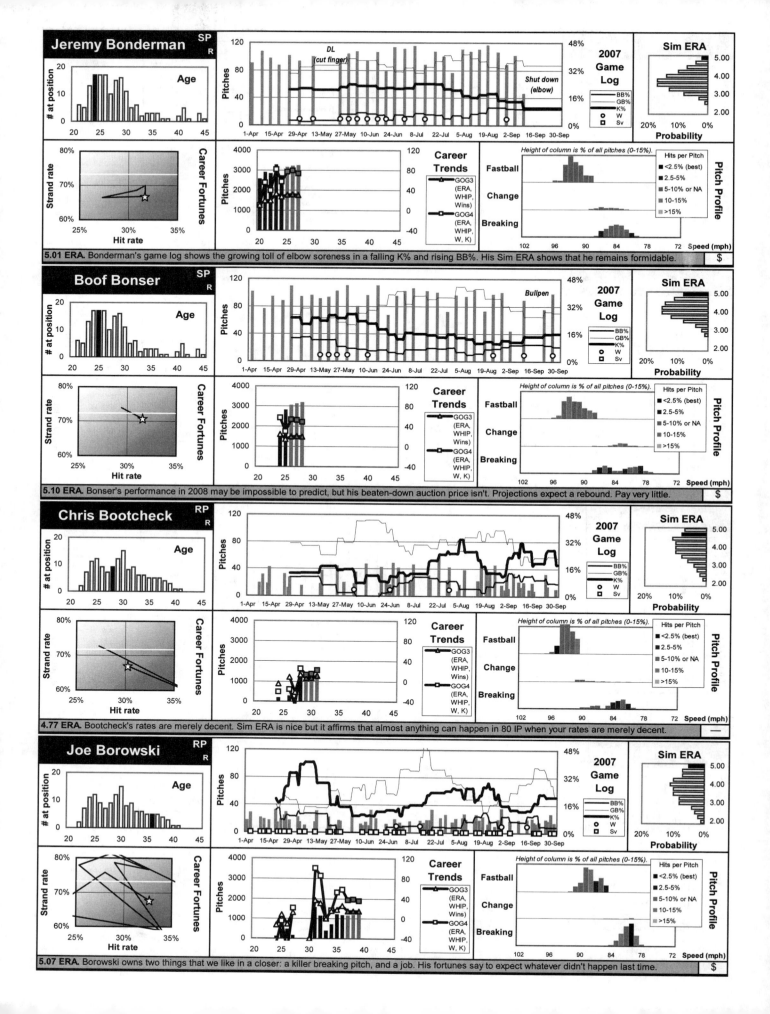

Jeremy Bonderman SP R

Age

DL (cut finger)

Shut down (elbow)

2007 Game Log

BB%
GB%
K%
W
Sv

Sim ERA

Probability

Career Fortunes

Strand rate / Hit rate

Career Trends

GOG3 (ERA, WHIP, Wins)
GOG4 (ERA, WHIP, W, K)

Height of column is % of all pitches (0-15%).

Fastball
Change
Breaking

Hits per Pitch
<2.5% (best)
2.5-5%
5-10% or NA
10-15%
>15%

Pitch Profile

Speed (mph)

5.01 ERA. Bonderman's game log shows the growing toll of elbow soreness in a falling K% and rising BB%. His Sim ERA shows that he remains formidable. $

Boof Bonser SP R

Age

Bullpen

2007 Game Log

BB%
GB%
K%
W
Sv

Sim ERA

Probability

Career Fortunes

Strand rate / Hit rate

Career Trends

GOG3 (ERA, WHIP, Wins)
GOG4 (ERA, WHIP, W, K)

Height of column is % of all pitches (0-15%).

Fastball
Change
Breaking

Hits per Pitch
<2.5% (best)
2.5-5%
5-10% or NA
10-15%
>15%

Pitch Profile

Speed (mph)

5.10 ERA. Bonser's performance in 2008 may be impossible to predict, but his beaten-down auction price isn't. Projections expect a rebound. Pay very little. $

Chris Bootcheck RP R

Age

2007 Game Log

BB%
GB%
K%
W
Sv

Sim ERA

Probability

Career Fortunes

Strand rate / Hit rate

Career Trends

GOG3 (ERA, WHIP, Wins)
GOG4 (ERA, WHIP, W, K)

Height of column is % of all pitches (0-15%).

Fastball
Change
Breaking

Hits per Pitch
<2.5% (best)
2.5-5%
5-10% or NA
10-15%
>15%

Pitch Profile

Speed (mph)

4.77 ERA. Bootcheck's rates are merely decent. Sim ERA is nice but it affirms that almost anything can happen in 80 IP when your rates are merely decent. —

Joe Borowski RP R

Age

2007 Game Log

BB%
GB%
K%
W
Sv

Sim ERA

Probability

Career Fortunes

Strand rate / Hit rate

Career Trends

GOG3 (ERA, WHIP, Wins)
GOG4 (ERA, WHIP, W, K)

Height of column is % of all pitches (0-15%).

Fastball
Change
Breaking

Hits per Pitch
<2.5% (best)
2.5-5%
5-10% or NA
10-15%
>15%

Pitch Profile

Speed (mph)

5.07 ERA. Borowski owns two things that we like in a closer: a killer breaking pitch, and a job. His fortunes say to expect whatever didn't happen last time. $

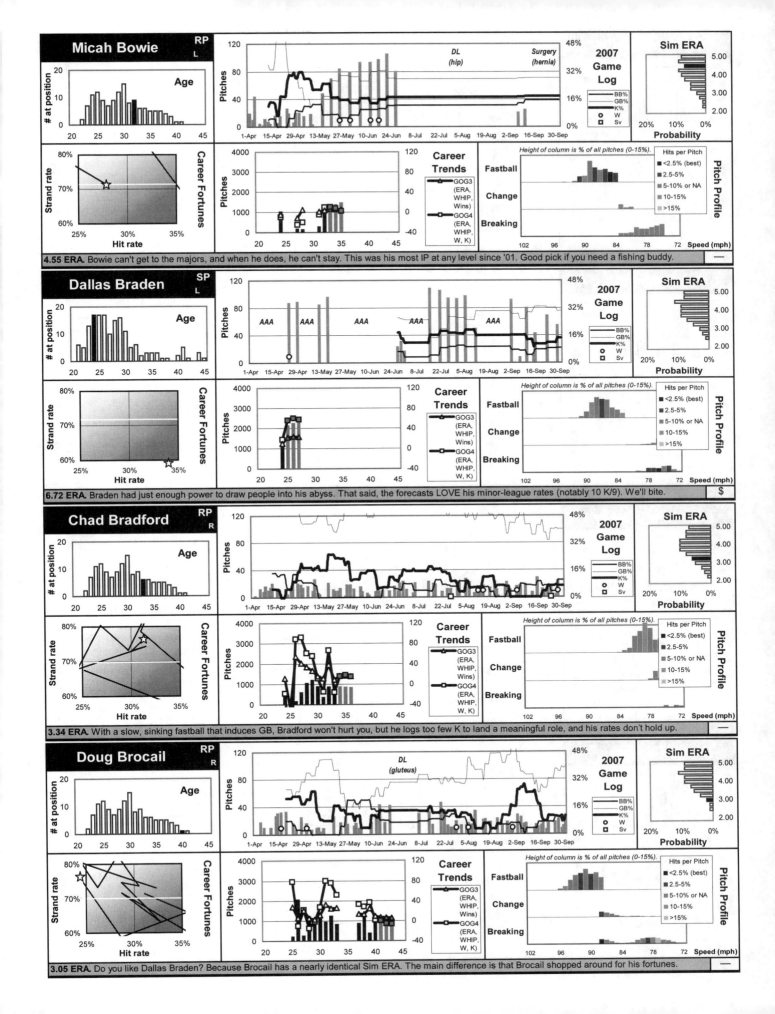

Micah Bowie — RP / L

Age — # at position

DL (hip) — Surgery (hernia)

2007 Game Log — BB% / GB% / K% — W / Sv

Sim ERA — Probability

Strand rate / Hit rate — Career Fortunes

Career Trends — GOG3 (ERA, WHIP, Wins) — GOG4 (ERA, WHIP, W, K)

Height of column is % of all pitches (0-15%). — Hits per Pitch: <2.5% (best), 2.5-5%, 5-10% or NA, 10-15%, >15% — Fastball / Change / Breaking — Pitch Profile — Speed (mph)

4.55 ERA. Bowie can't get to the majors, and when he does, he can't stay. This was his most IP at any level since '01. Good pick if you need a fishing buddy. —

Dallas Braden — SP / L

Age — # at position

AAA   AAA   AAA   AAA   AAA

2007 Game Log — BB% / GB% / K% — W / Sv

Sim ERA — Probability

Strand rate / Hit rate — Career Fortunes

Career Trends — GOG3 (ERA, WHIP, Wins) — GOG4 (ERA, WHIP, W, K)

Height of column is % of all pitches (0-15%). — Hits per Pitch: <2.5% (best), 2.5-5%, 5-10% or NA, 10-15%, >15% — Fastball / Change / Breaking — Pitch Profile — Speed (mph)

6.72 ERA. Braden had just enough power to draw people into his abyss. That said, the forecasts LOVE his minor-league rates (notably 10 K/9). We'll bite. $

Chad Bradford — RP / R

Age — # at position

2007 Game Log — BB% / GB% / K% — W / Sv

Sim ERA — Probability

Strand rate / Hit rate — Career Fortunes

Career Trends — GOG3 (ERA, WHIP, Wins) — GOG4 (ERA, WHIP, W, K)

Height of column is % of all pitches (0-15%). — Hits per Pitch: <2.5% (best), 2.5-5%, 5-10% or NA, 10-15%, >15% — Fastball / Change / Breaking — Pitch Profile — Speed (mph)

3.34 ERA. With a slow, sinking fastball that induces GB, Bradford won't hurt you, but he logs too few K to land a meaningful role, and his rates don't hold up. —

Doug Brocail — RP / R

Age — # at position

DL (gluteus)

2007 Game Log — BB% / GB% / K% — W / Sv

Sim ERA — Probability

Strand rate / Hit rate — Career Fortunes

Career Trends — GOG3 (ERA, WHIP, Wins) — GOG4 (ERA, WHIP, W, K)

Height of column is % of all pitches (0-15%). — Hits per Pitch: <2.5% (best), 2.5-5%, 5-10% or NA, 10-15%, >15% — Fastball / Change / Breaking — Pitch Profile — Speed (mph)

3.05 ERA. Do you like Dallas Braden? Because Brocail has a nearly identical Sim ERA. The main difference is that Brocail shopped around for his fortunes. —

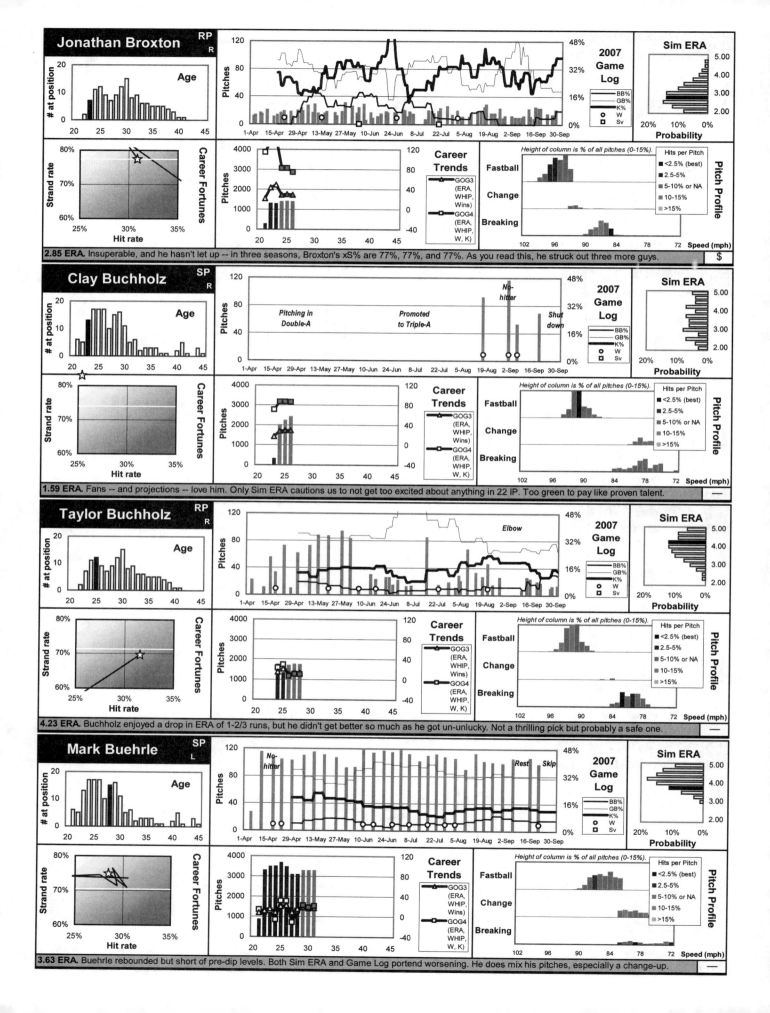

Jonathan Broxton — RP R

Age (# at position)

2007 Game Log — BB%, GB%, K%, W, Sv

Sim ERA — Probability

Career Fortunes — Strand rate vs Hit rate

Career Trends — GOG3 (ERA, WHIP, Wins), GOG4 (ERA, WHIP, W, K)

Pitch Profile — Height of column is % of all pitches (0-15%). Hits per Pitch: <2.5% (best), 2.5-5%, 5-10% or NA, 10-15%, >15%. Fastball, Change, Breaking. Speed (mph)

2.85 ERA. Insuperable, and he hasn't let up -- in three seasons, Broxton's xS% are 77%, 77%, and 77%. As you read this, he struck out three more guys. $

Clay Buchholz — SP R

Age

2007 Game Log — Pitching in Double-A, Promoted to Triple-A, No-hitter, Shut down

Sim ERA — Probability

Career Fortunes — Strand rate vs Hit rate

Career Trends — GOG3 (ERA, WHIP, Wins), GOG4 (ERA, WHIP, W, K)

Pitch Profile — Fastball, Change, Breaking

1.59 ERA. Fans -- and projections -- love him. Only Sim ERA cautions us to not get too excited about anything in 22 IP. Too green to pay like proven talent.   —

Taylor Buchholz — RP R

Age

2007 Game Log — Elbow

Sim ERA — Probability

Career Fortunes — Strand rate vs Hit rate

Career Trends — GOG3 (ERA, WHIP, Wins), GOG4 (ERA, WHIP, W, K)

Pitch Profile — Fastball, Change, Breaking

4.23 ERA. Buchholz enjoyed a drop in ERA of 1-2/3 runs, but he didn't get better so much as he got un-unlucky. Not a thrilling pick but probably a safe one.   —

Mark Buehrle — SP L

Age

2007 Game Log — No-hitter, Rest, Skip

Sim ERA — Probability

Career Fortunes — Strand rate vs Hit rate

Career Trends — GOG3 (ERA, WHIP, Wins), GOG4 (ERA, WHIP, W, K)

Pitch Profile — Fastball, Change, Breaking

3.63 ERA. Buehrle rebounded but short of pre-dip levels. Both Sim ERA and Game Log portend worsening. He does mix his pitches, especially a change-up.   —

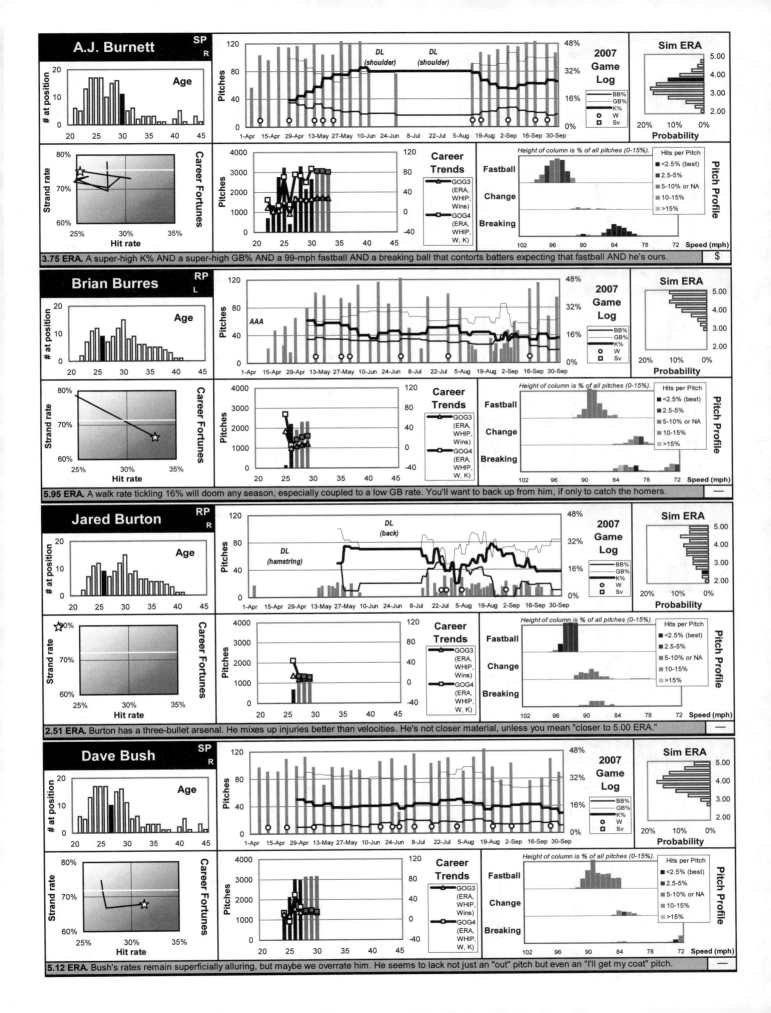

A.J. Burnett — SP R

2007 Game Log — DL (shoulder), DL (shoulder)

Sim ERA

Age — # at position

Career Fortunes — Strand rate / Hit rate

Career Trends — GOG3 (ERA, WHIP, Wins), GOG4 (ERA, WHIP, W, K)

Pitch Profile — Height of column is % of all pitches (0-15%). Hits per Pitch: <2.5% (best), 2.5-5%, 5-10% or NA, 10-15%, >15%

3.75 ERA. A super-high K% AND a super-high GB% AND a 99-mph fastball AND a breaking ball that contorts batters expecting that fastball AND he's ours. $

Brian Burres — RP L

2007 Game Log — AAA

Sim ERA

Age

Career Fortunes

Career Trends — GOG3 (ERA, WHIP, Wins), GOG4 (ERA, WHIP, W, K)

Pitch Profile

5.95 ERA. A walk rate tickling 16% will doom any season, especially coupled to a low GB rate. You'll want to back up from him, if only to catch the homers. —

Jared Burton — RP R

2007 Game Log — DL (back), DL (hamstring)

Sim ERA

Age

Career Fortunes

Career Trends — GOG3 (ERA, WHIP, Wins), GOG4 (ERA, WHIP, W, K)

Pitch Profile

2.51 ERA. Burton has a three-bullet arsenal. He mixes up injuries better than velocities. He's not closer material, unless you mean "closer to 5.00 ERA." —

Dave Bush — SP R

2007 Game Log

Sim ERA

Age

Career Fortunes

Career Trends — GOG3 (ERA, WHIP, Wins), GOG4 (ERA, WHIP, W, K)

Pitch Profile

5.12 ERA. Bush's rates remain superficially alluring, but maybe we overrate him. He seems to lack not just an "out" pitch but even an "I'll get my coat" pitch. —

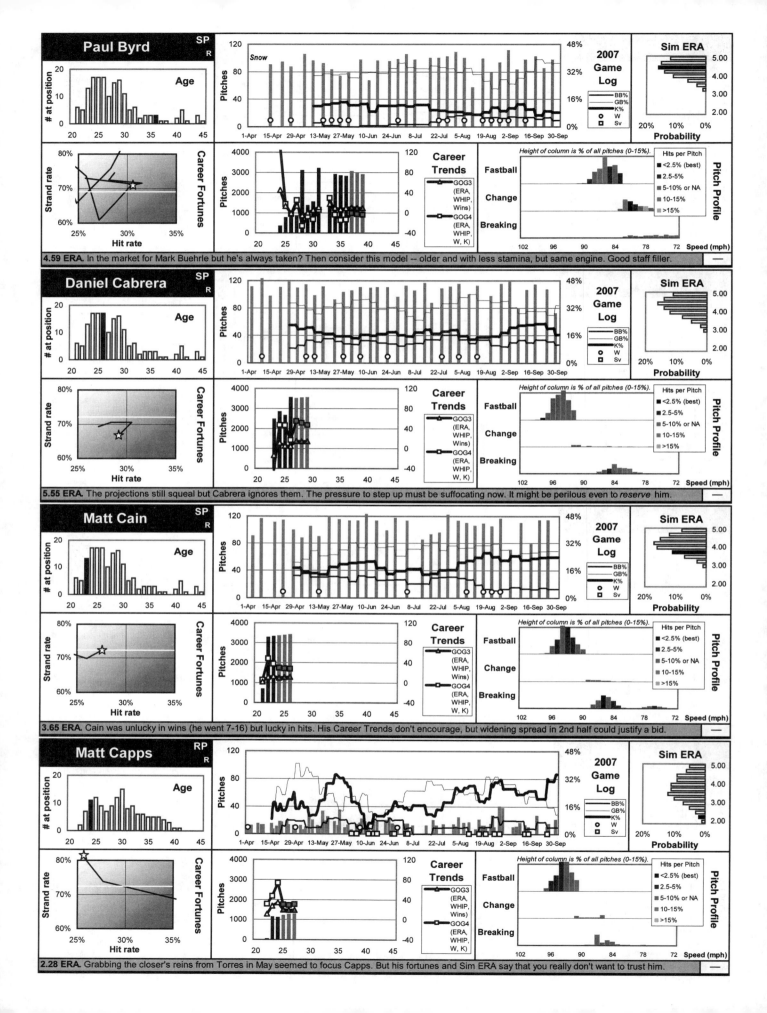

Paul Byrd SP R

Age — # at position (20–45)

2007 Game Log — Pitches, BB%, GB%, K%, W, Sv (1-Apr to 30-Sep). "Snow"

Sim ERA — Probability (20%–0%), 2.00–5.00

Career Fortunes — Strand rate (60%–80%) vs Hit rate (25%–35%)

Career Trends — Pitches (0–4000), GOG3 (ERA, WHIP, Wins), GOG4 (ERA, WHIP, W, K), ages 20–45

Pitch Profile — Height of column is % of all pitches (0-15%). Fastball, Change, Breaking. Hits per Pitch: <2.5% (best), 2.5-5%, 5-10% or NA, 10-15%, >15%. Speed (mph) 102–72.

4.59 ERA. In the market for Mark Buehrle but he's always taken? Then consider this model -- older and with less stamina, but same engine. Good staff filler. —

Daniel Cabrera SP R

5.55 ERA. The projections still squeal but Cabrera ignores them. The pressure to step up must be suffocating now. It might be perilous even to *reserve* him. —

Matt Cain SP R

3.65 ERA. Cain was unlucky in wins (he went 7-16) but lucky in hits. His Career Trends don't encourage, but widening spread in 2nd half could justify a bid. —

Matt Capps RP R

2.28 ERA. Grabbing the closer's reins from Torres in May seemed to focus Capps. But his fortunes and Sim ERA say that you really don't want to trust him. —

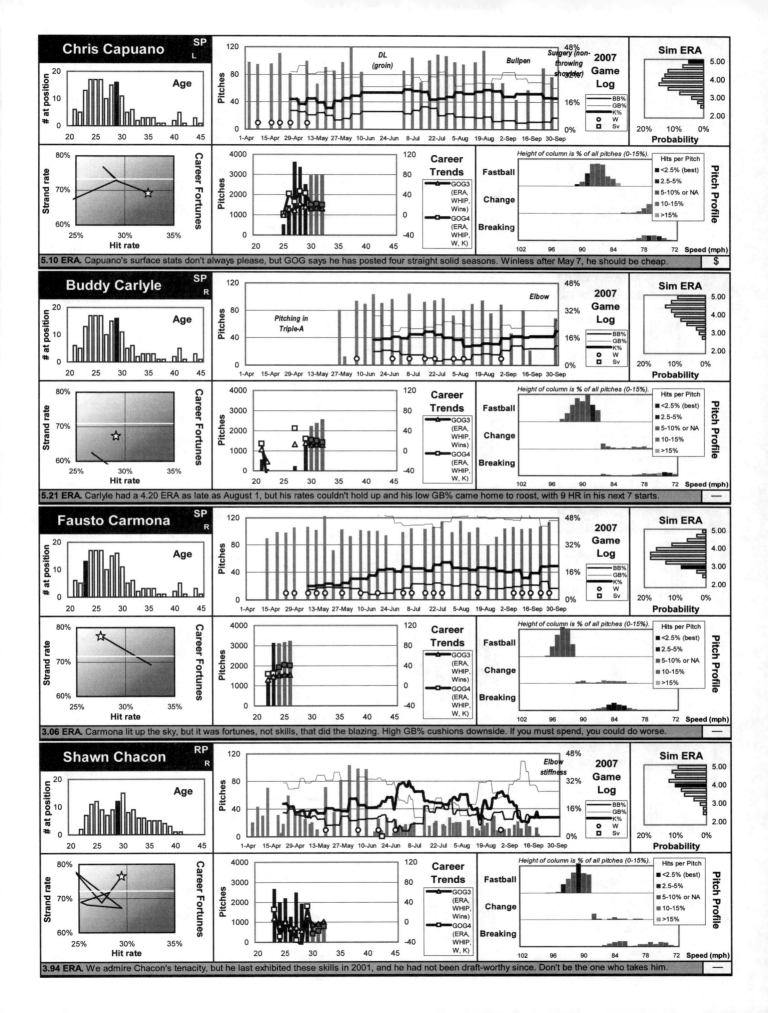

Chris Capuano — SP L

Age — # at position (20–45)

Sim ERA — Probability (20%–0%), 2.00–5.00

2007 Game Log — Pitches (0–120), 48%/16%
- BB%
- GB%
- K%
- ○ W
- □ Sv

DL (groin) · Bullpen · Surgery (non-throwing shoulder)

Career Fortunes — Strand rate (60%–80%) vs Hit rate (25%–35%)

Career Trends — Pitches (0–4000), (−40 to 120)
- GOG3 (ERA, WHIP, Wins)
- GOG4 (ERA, WHIP, W, K)

Pitch Profile — Height of column is % of all pitches (0-15%). Fastball / Change / Breaking, Speed (mph) 102–72
- Hits per Pitch: <2.5% (best), 2.5-5%, 5-10% or NA, 10-15%, >15%

5.10 ERA. Capuano's surface stats don't always please, but GOG says he has posted four straight solid seasons. Winless after May 7, he should be cheap. **$**

Buddy Carlyle — SP R

Age — # at position (20–45)

Sim ERA — Probability (20%–0%), 2.00–5.00

2007 Game Log — Pitches (0–120), 48%/32%/16%
- BB%
- GB%
- K%
- ○ W
- □ Sv

Pitching in Triple-A · Elbow

Career Fortunes — Strand rate (60%–80%) vs Hit rate (25%–35%)

Career Trends — Pitches (0–4000), (−40 to 120)
- GOG3 (ERA, WHIP, Wins)
- GOG4 (ERA, WHIP, W, K)

Pitch Profile — Height of column is % of all pitches (0-15%). Fastball / Change / Breaking, Speed (mph) 102–72
- Hits per Pitch: <2.5% (best), 2.5-5%, 5-10% or NA, 10-15%, >15%

5.21 ERA. Carlyle had a 4.20 ERA as late as August 1, but his rates couldn't hold up and his low GB% came home to roost, with 9 HR in his next 7 starts. **—**

Fausto Carmona — SP R

Age — # at position (20–45)

Sim ERA — Probability (20%–0%), 2.00–5.00

2007 Game Log — Pitches (0–120), 48%/32%/16%
- BB%
- GB%
- K%
- ○ W
- □ Sv

Career Fortunes — Strand rate (60%–80%) vs Hit rate (25%–35%)

Career Trends — Pitches (0–4000), (−40 to 120)
- GOG3 (ERA, WHIP, Wins)
- GOG4 (ERA, WHIP, W, K)

Pitch Profile — Height of column is % of all pitches (0-15%). Fastball / Change / Breaking, Speed (mph) 102–72
- Hits per Pitch: <2.5% (best), 2.5-5%, 5-10% or NA, 10-15%, >15%

3.06 ERA. Carmona lit up the sky, but it was fortunes, not skills, that did the blazing. High GB% cushions downside. If you must spend, you could do worse. **—**

Shawn Chacon — RP R

Age — # at position (20–45)

Sim ERA — Probability (20%–0%), 2.00–5.00

2007 Game Log — Pitches (0–120), 48%/32%/16%
- BB%
- GB%
- K%
- ○ W
- □ Sv

Elbow stiffness

Career Fortunes — Strand rate (60%–80%) vs Hit rate (25%–35%)

Career Trends — Pitches (0–4000), (−40 to 120)
- GOG3 (ERA, WHIP, Wins)
- GOG4 (ERA, WHIP, W, K)

Pitch Profile — Height of column is % of all pitches (0-15%). Fastball / Change / Breaking, Speed (mph) 102–72
- Hits per Pitch: <2.5% (best), 2.5-5%, 5-10% or NA, 10-15%, >15%

3.94 ERA. We admire Chacon's tenacity, but he last exhibited these skills in 2001, and he had not been draft-worthy since. Don't be the one who takes him. **—**

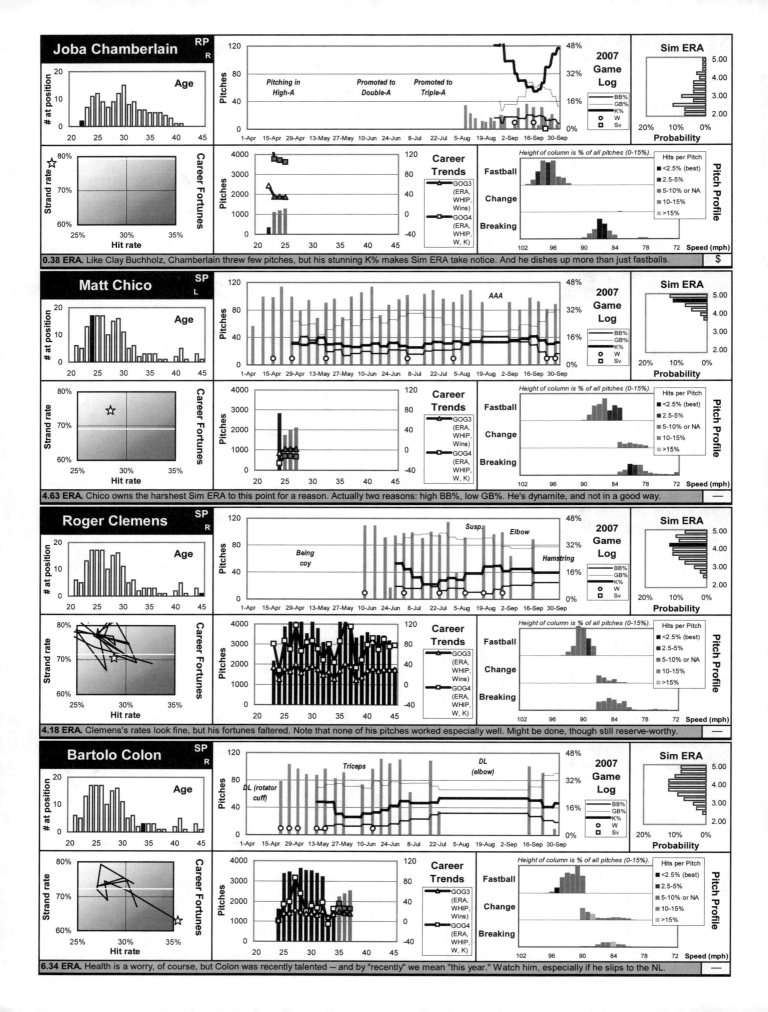

Joba Chamberlain RP R

Age

2007 Game Log

Sim ERA

Strand rate

Career Fortunes

Career Trends
GOG3 (ERA, WHIP, Wins)
GOG4 (ERA, WHIP, W, K)

Pitch Profile
Height of column is % of all pitches (0-15%).
Hits per Pitch
<2.5% (best)
2.5-5%
5-10% or NA
10-15%
>15%
Fastball
Change
Breaking

Pitching in High-A — Promoted to Double-A — Promoted to Triple-A

0.38 ERA. Like Clay Buchholz, Chamberlain threw few pitches, but his stunning K% makes Sim ERA take notice. And he dishes up more than just fastballs. $

Matt Chico SP L

Age

AAA

2007 Game Log

Sim ERA

Strand rate

Career Fortunes

Career Trends
GOG3 (ERA, WHIP, Wins)
GOG4 (ERA, WHIP, W, K)

Pitch Profile
Height of column is % of all pitches (0-15%).
Hits per Pitch
<2.5% (best)
2.5-5%
5-10% or NA
10-15%
>15%
Fastball
Change
Breaking

4.63 ERA. Chico owns the harshest Sim ERA to this point for a reason. Actually two reasons: high BB%, low GB%. He's dynamite, and not in a good way. —

Roger Clemens SP R

Age

2007 Game Log

Sim ERA

Being coy — Susp. — Elbow — Hamstring

Strand rate

Career Fortunes

Career Trends
GOG3 (ERA, WHIP, Wins)
GOG4 (ERA, WHIP, W, K)

Pitch Profile
Height of column is % of all pitches (0-15%).
Hits per Pitch
<2.5% (best)
2.5-5%
5-10% or NA
10-15%
>15%
Fastball
Change
Breaking

4.18 ERA. Clemens's rates look fine, but his fortunes faltered. Note that none of his pitches worked especially well. Might be done, though still reserve-worthy. —

Bartolo Colon SP R

Age

Triceps — DL (elbow)

DL (rotator cuff)

2007 Game Log

Sim ERA

Strand rate

Career Fortunes

Career Trends
GOG3 (ERA, WHIP, Wins)
GOG4 (ERA, WHIP, W, K)

Pitch Profile
Height of column is % of all pitches (0-15%).
Hits per Pitch
<2.5% (best)
2.5-5%
5-10% or NA
10-15%
>15%
Fastball
Change
Breaking

6.34 ERA. Health is a worry, of course, but Colon was recently talented -- and by "recently" we mean "this year." Watch him, especially if he slips to the NL. —

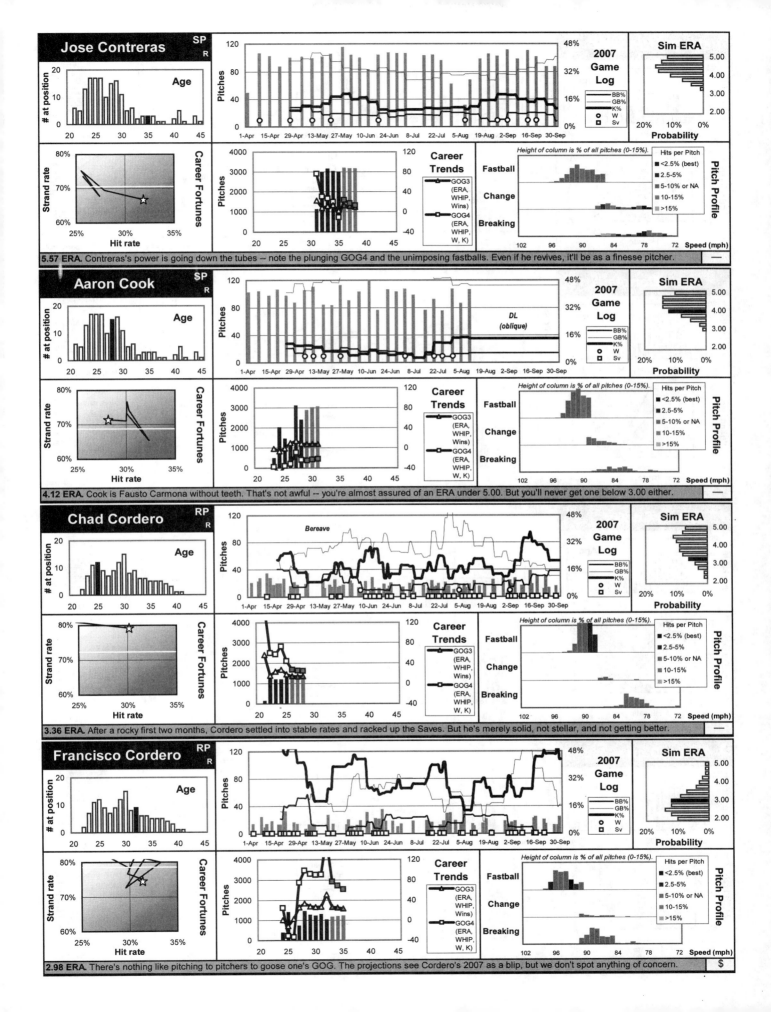

Jose Contreras SP R

Age — # at position — 20 25 30 35 40 45

Pitches — 120 80 40 0 — 1-Apr 15-Apr 29-Apr 13-May 27-May 10-Jun 24-Jun 8-Jul 22-Jul 5-Aug 19-Aug 2-Sep 16-Sep 30-Sep — 48% 32% 16% 0%

2007 Game Log — BB% GB% K% ○ W □ Sv

Sim ERA — 5.00 4.00 3.00 2.00 — 20% 10% 0% Probability

Strand rate — 80% 70% 60% — 25% 30% 35% — Hit rate — Career Fortunes

Pitches — 4000 3000 2000 1000 0 — 20 25 30 35 40 45 — 120 80 40 0 -40 — Career Trends — GOG3 (ERA, WHIP, Wins) GOG4 (ERA, WHIP, W, K)

Height of column is % of all pitches (0-15%). — Hits per Pitch ■ <2.5% (best) ■ 2.5-5% 5-10% or NA 10-15% >15% — Fastball Change Breaking — 102 96 90 84 78 72 Speed (mph) — Pitch Profile

5.57 ERA. Contreras's power is going down the tubes -- note the plunging GOG4 and the unimposing fastballs. Even if he revives, it'll be as a finesse pitcher. — —

Aaron Cook SP R

Age — # at position — 20 25 30 35 40 45

Pitches — 120 80 40 0 — 1-Apr 15-Apr 29-Apr 13-May 27-May 10-Jun 24-Jun 8-Jul 22-Jul 5-Aug 19-Aug 2-Sep 16-Sep 30-Sep — DL (oblique) — 48% 32% 16% 0%

2007 Game Log — BB% GB% K% ○ W □ Sv

Sim ERA — 5.00 4.00 3.00 2.00 — 20% 10% 0% Probability

Strand rate — 80% 70% 60% — 25% 30% 35% — Hit rate — Career Fortunes

Pitches — 4000 3000 2000 1000 0 — 20 25 30 35 40 45 — 120 80 40 0 -40 — Career Trends — GOG3 (ERA, WHIP, Wins) GOG4 (ERA, WHIP, W, K)

Height of column is % of all pitches (0-15%). — Hits per Pitch ■ <2.5% (best) ■ 2.5-5% 5-10% or NA 10-15% >15% — Fastball Change Breaking — 102 96 90 84 78 72 Speed (mph) — Pitch Profile

4.12 ERA. Cook is Fausto Carmona without teeth. That's not awful -- you're almost assured of an ERA under 5.00. But you'll never get one below 3.00 either. — —

Chad Cordero RP R

Age — # at position — 20 25 30 35 40 45

Pitches — 120 80 40 0 — Bereave — 1-Apr 15-Apr 29-Apr 13-May 27-May 10-Jun 24-Jun 8-Jul 22-Jul 5-Aug 19-Aug 2-Sep 16-Sep 30-Sep — 48% 32% 16% 0%

2007 Game Log — BB% GB% K% ○ W □ Sv

Sim ERA — 5.00 4.00 3.00 2.00 — 20% 10% 0% Probability

Strand rate — 80% 70% 60% — 25% 30% 35% — Hit rate — Career Fortunes

Pitches — 4000 3000 2000 1000 0 — 20 25 30 35 40 45 — 120 80 40 0 -40 — Career Trends — GOG3 (ERA, WHIP, Wins) GOG4 (ERA, WHIP, W, K)

Height of column is % of all pitches (0-15%). — Hits per Pitch ■ <2.5% (best) ■ 2.5-5% 5-10% or NA 10-15% >15% — Fastball Change Breaking — 102 96 90 84 78 72 Speed (mph) — Pitch Profile

3.36 ERA. After a rocky first two months, Cordero settled into stable rates and racked up the Saves. But he's merely solid, not stellar, and not getting better. — —

Francisco Cordero RP R

Age — # at position — 20 25 30 35 40 45

Pitches — 120 80 40 0 — 1-Apr 15-Apr 29-Apr 13-May 27-May 10-Jun 24-Jun 8-Jul 22-Jul 5-Aug 19-Aug 2-Sep 16-Sep 30-Sep — 48% 32% 16% 0%

2007 Game Log — BB% GB% K% ○ W □ Sv

Sim ERA — 5.00 4.00 3.00 2.00 — 20% 10% 0% Probability

Strand rate — 80% 70% 60% — 25% 30% 35% — Hit rate — Career Fortunes

Pitches — 4000 3000 2000 1000 0 — 20 25 30 35 40 45 — 120 80 40 0 -40 — Career Trends — GOG3 (ERA, WHIP, Wins) GOG4 (ERA, WHIP, W, K)

Height of column is % of all pitches (0-15%). — Hits per Pitch ■ <2.5% (best) ■ 2.5-5% 5-10% or NA 10-15% >15% — Fastball Change Breaking — 102 96 90 84 78 72 Speed (mph) — Pitch Profile

2.98 ERA. There's nothing like pitching to pitchers to goose one's GOG. The projections see Cordero's 2007 as a blip, but we don't spot anything of concern. — $

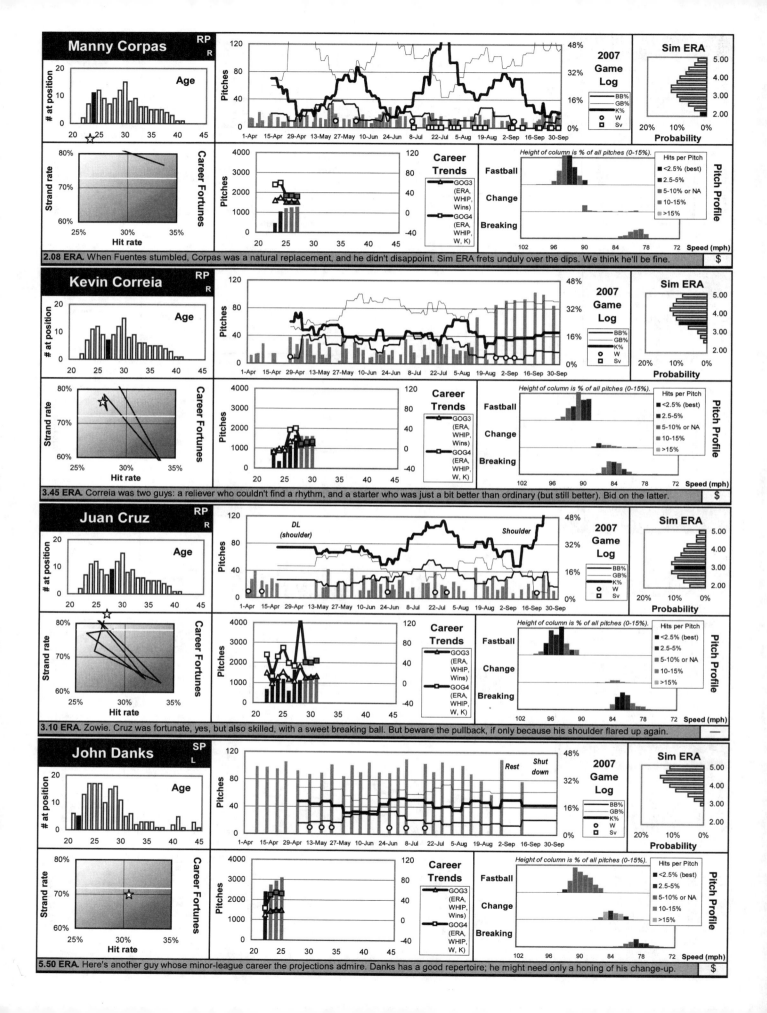

Manny Corpas

RP R

Age

2007 Game Log
- BB%
- GB%
- K%
- ○ W
- □ Sv

Sim ERA

Career Trends
- △ GOG3 (ERA, WHIP, Wins)
- □ GOG4 (ERA, WHIP, W, K)

Career Fortunes

Pitch Profile

Height of column is % of all pitches (0-15%).

Hits per Pitch
- ■ <2.5% (best)
- ■ 2.5-5%
- ■ 5-10% or NA
- ■ 10-15%
- ■ >15%

2.08 ERA. When Fuentes stumbled, Corpas was a natural replacement, and he didn't disappoint. Sim ERA frets unduly over the dips. We think he'll be fine. **$**

Kevin Correia

RP R

Age

2007 Game Log
- BB%
- GB%
- K%
- ○ W
- □ Sv

Sim ERA

Career Trends
- △ GOG3 (ERA, WHIP, Wins)
- □ GOG4 (ERA, WHIP, W, K)

Career Fortunes

Pitch Profile

Height of column is % of all pitches (0-15%).

Hits per Pitch
- ■ <2.5% (best)
- ■ 2.5-5%
- ■ 5-10% or NA
- ■ 10-15%
- ■ >15%

3.45 ERA. Correia was two guys: a reliever who couldn't find a rhythm, and a starter who was just a bit better than ordinary (but still better). Bid on the latter. **$**

Juan Cruz

RP R

Age

DL (shoulder)   Shoulder

2007 Game Log
- BB%
- GB%
- K%
- ○ W
- □ Sv

Sim ERA

Career Trends
- △ GOG3 (ERA, WHIP, Wins)
- □ GOG4 (ERA, WHIP, W, K)

Career Fortunes

Pitch Profile

Height of column is % of all pitches (0-15%).

Hits per Pitch
- ■ <2.5% (best)
- ■ 2.5-5%
- ■ 5-10% or NA
- ■ 10-15%
- ■ >15%

3.10 ERA. Zowie. Cruz was fortunate, yes, but also skilled, with a sweet breaking ball. But beware the pullback, if only because his shoulder flared up again. **—**

John Danks

SP L

Age

Rest   Shut down

2007 Game Log
- BB%
- GB%
- K%
- ○ W
- □ Sv

Sim ERA

Career Trends
- △ GOG3 (ERA, WHIP, Wins)
- □ GOG4 (ERA, WHIP, W, K)

Career Fortunes

Pitch Profile

Height of column is % of all pitches (0-15%).

Hits per Pitch
- ■ <2.5% (best)
- ■ 2.5-5%
- ■ 5-10% or NA
- ■ 10-15%
- ■ >15%

5.50 ERA. Here's another guy whose minor-league career the projections admire. Danks has a good repertoire; he might need only a honing of his change-up. **$**

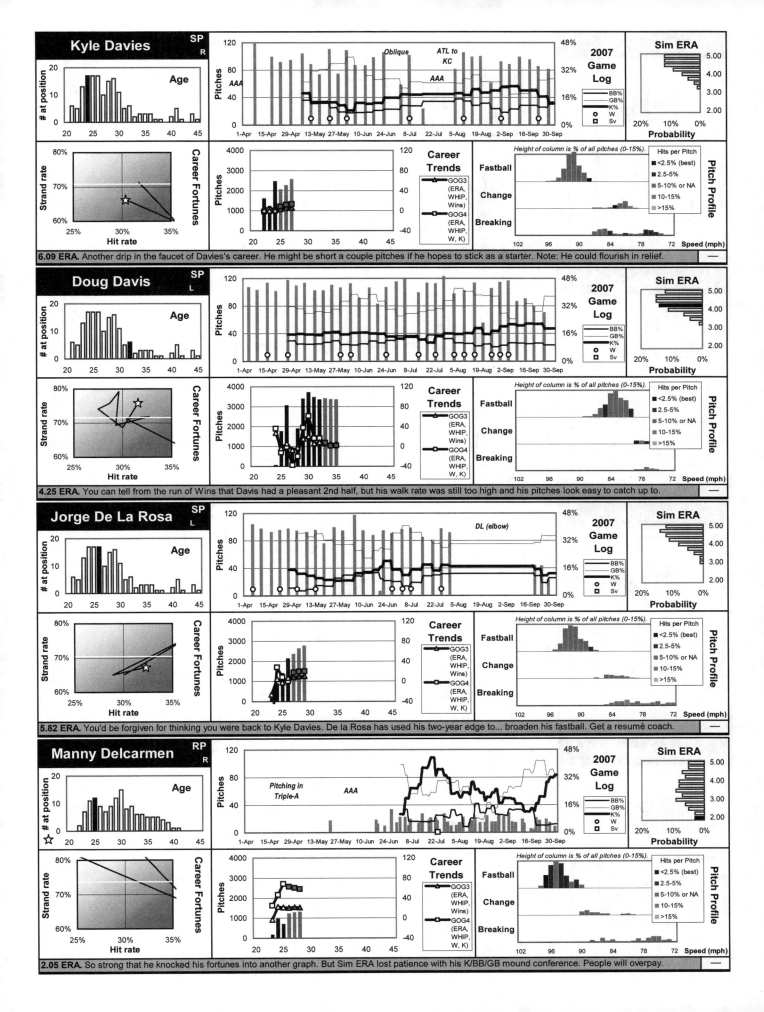

Kyle Davies — SP R

6.09 ERA. Another drip in the faucet of Davies's career. He might be short a couple pitches if he hopes to stick as a starter. Note: He could flourish in relief.

Doug Davis — SP L

4.25 ERA. You can tell from the run of Wins that Davis had a pleasant 2nd half, but his walk rate was still too high and his pitches look easy to catch up to.

Jorge De La Rosa — SP L

5.82 ERA. You'd be forgiven for thinking you were back to Kyle Davies. De la Rosa has used his two-year edge to... broaden his fastball. Get a resumé coach.

Manny Delcarmen — RP R

2.05 ERA. So strong that he knocked his fortunes into another graph. But Sim ERA lost patience with his K/BB/GB mound conference. People will overpay.

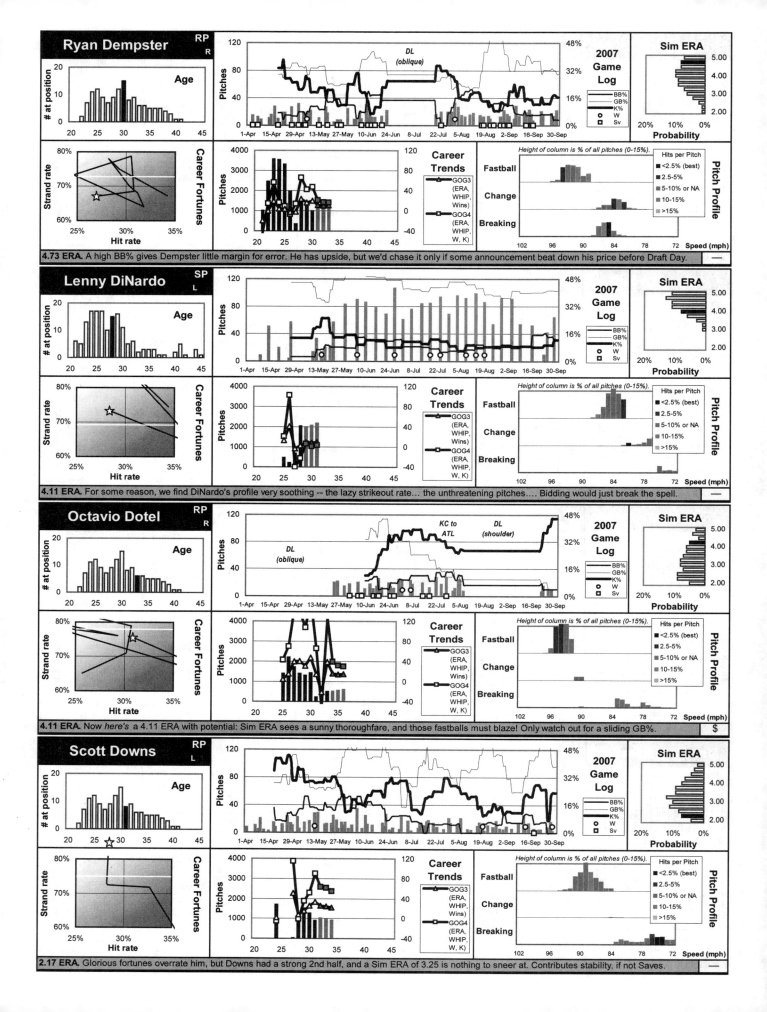

Ryan Dempster RP R

4.73 ERA. A high BB% gives Dempster little margin for error. He has upside, but we'd chase it only if some announcement beat down his price before Draft Day. —

Lenny DiNardo SP L

4.11 ERA. For some reason, we find DiNardo's profile very soothing -- the lazy strikeout rate... the unthreatening pitches.... Bidding would just break the spell. —

Octavio Dotel RP R

4.11 ERA. Now *here's* a 4.11 ERA with potential: Sim ERA sees a sunny thoroughfare, and those fastballs must blaze! Only watch out for a sliding GB%. $

Scott Downs RP L

2.17 ERA. Glorious fortunes overrate him, but Downs had a strong 2nd half, and a Sim ERA of 3.25 is nothing to sneer at. Contributes stability, if not Saves. —

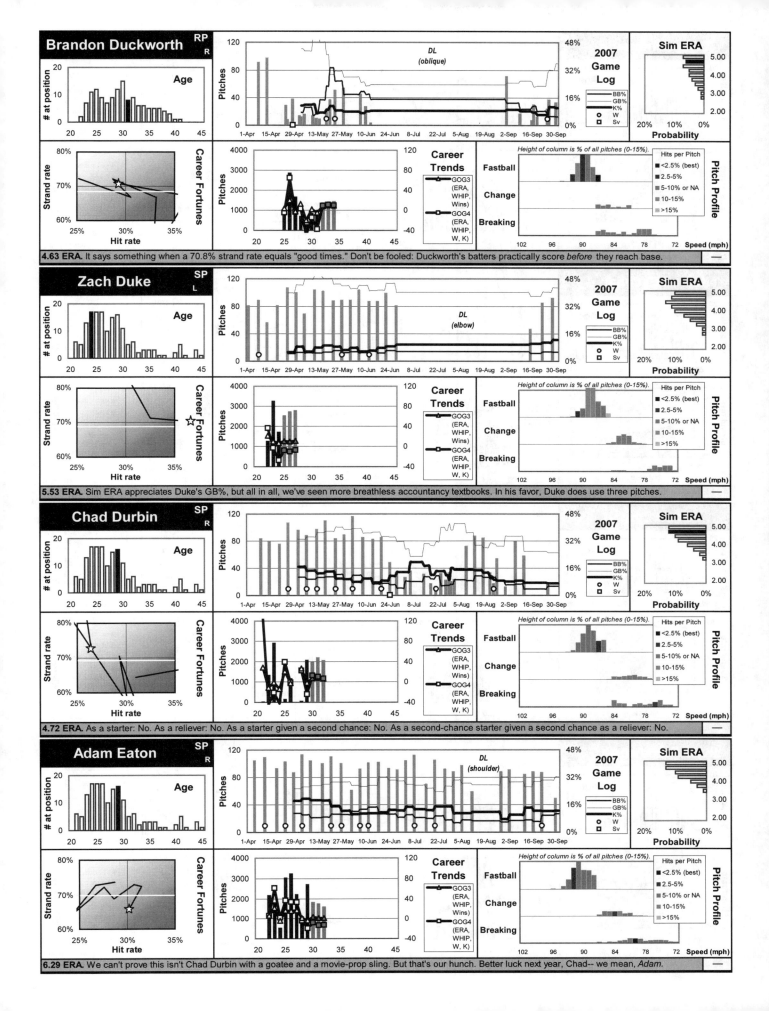

Brandon Duckworth RP R

4.63 ERA. It says something when a 70.8% strand rate equals "good times." Don't be fooled: Duckworth's batters practically score *before* they reach base. —

Zach Duke SP L

5.53 ERA. Sim ERA appreciates Duke's GB%, but all in all, we've seen more breathless accountancy textbooks. In his favor, Duke does use three pitches. —

Chad Durbin SP R

4.72 ERA. As a starter: No. As a reliever: No. As a starter given a second chance: No. As a second-chance starter given a second chance as a reliever: No. —

Adam Eaton SP R

6.29 ERA. We can't prove this isn't Chad Durbin with a goatee and a movie-prop sling. But that's our hunch. Better luck next year, Chad-- we mean, *Adam*. —

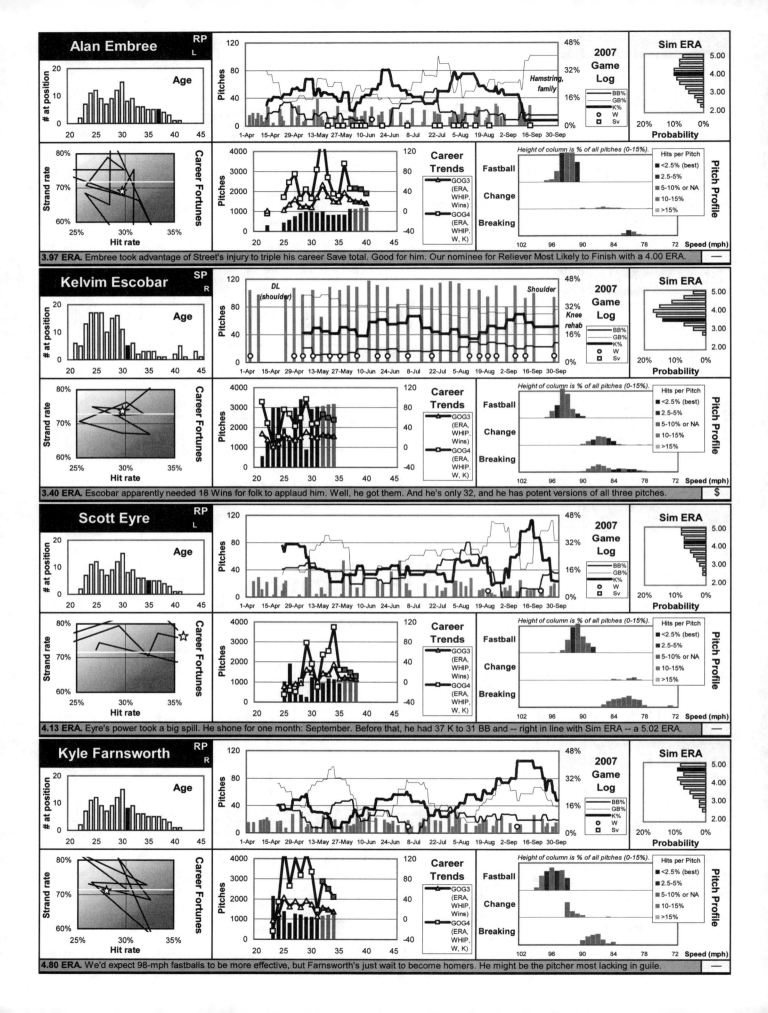

Alan Embree — RP / L

Age | # at position | Pitches | 2007 Game Log | Sim ERA | Career Fortunes | Career Trends | Pitch Profile

Hamstring, family

BB%, GB%, K%, W, Sv

Strand rate / Hit rate

GOG3 (ERA, WHIP, Wins) — GOG4 (ERA, WHIP, W, K)

Height of column is % of all pitches (0-15%). Fastball / Change / Breaking

Hits per Pitch: <2.5% (best), 2.5-5%, 5-10% or NA, 10-15%, >15%

Speed (mph)

3.97 ERA. Embree took advantage of Street's injury to triple his career Save total. Good for him. Our nominee for Reliever Most Likely to Finish with a 4.00 ERA. —

Kelvim Escobar — SP / R

DL (shoulder) — Shoulder — Knee rehab

3.40 ERA. Escobar apparently needed 18 Wins for folk to applaud him. Well, he got them. And he's only 32, and he has potent versions of all three pitches. $

Scott Eyre — RP / L

4.13 ERA. Eyre's power took a big spill. He shone for one month: September. Before that, he had 37 K to 31 BB and -- right in line with Sim ERA -- a 5.02 ERA. —

Kyle Farnsworth — RP / R

4.80 ERA. We'd expect 98-mph fastballs to be more effective, but Farnsworth's just wait to become homers. He might be the pitcher most lacking in guile. —

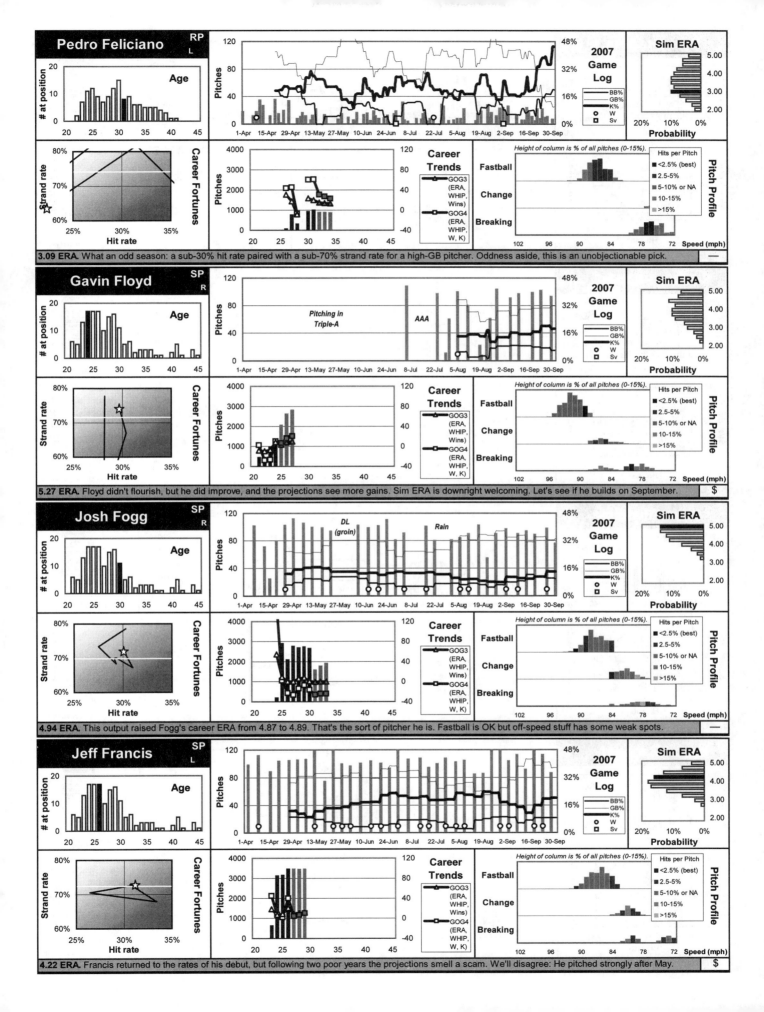

Pedro Feliciano RP L

2007 Game Log
BB%
GB%
K%
W
Sv

Sim ERA

Age

Career Fortunes

Career Trends
GOG3 (ERA, WHIP, Wins)
GOG4 (ERA, WHIP, W, K)

Pitch Profile
Height of column is % of all pitches (0-15%).
Hits per Pitch
<2.5% (best)
2.5-5%
5-10% or NA
10-15%
>15%
Fastball
Change
Breaking

3.09 ERA. What an odd season: a sub-30% hit rate paired with a sub-70% strand rate for a high-GB pitcher. Oddness aside, this is an unobjectionable pick. —

Gavin Floyd SP R

2007 Game Log
BB%
GB%
K%
W
Sv

Sim ERA

Age

Pitching in Triple-A   AAA

Career Fortunes

Career Trends
GOG3 (ERA, WHIP, Wins)
GOG4 (ERA, WHIP, W, K)

Pitch Profile
Height of column is % of all pitches (0-15%).
Hits per Pitch
<2.5% (best)
2.5-5%
5-10% or NA
10-15%
>15%
Fastball
Change
Breaking

5.27 ERA. Floyd didn't flourish, but he did improve, and the projections see more gains. Sim ERA is downright welcoming. Let's see if he builds on September. $

Josh Fogg SP R

2007 Game Log
BB%
GB%
K%
W
Sv

Sim ERA

Age

DL (groin)   Rain

Career Fortunes

Career Trends
GOG3 (ERA, WHIP, Wins)
GOG4 (ERA, WHIP, W, K)

Pitch Profile
Height of column is % of all pitches (0-15%).
Hits per Pitch
<2.5% (best)
2.5-5%
5-10% or NA
10-15%
>15%
Fastball
Change
Breaking

4.94 ERA. This output raised Fogg's career ERA from 4.87 to 4.89. That's the sort of pitcher he is. Fastball is OK but off-speed stuff has some weak spots. —

Jeff Francis SP L

2007 Game Log
BB%
GB%
K%
W
Sv

Sim ERA

Age

Career Fortunes

Career Trends
GOG3 (ERA, WHIP, Wins)
GOG4 (ERA, WHIP, W, K)

Pitch Profile
Height of column is % of all pitches (0-15%).
Hits per Pitch
<2.5% (best)
2.5-5%
5-10% or NA
10-15%
>15%
Fastball
Change
Breaking

4.22 ERA. Francis returned to the rates of his debut, but following two poor years the projections smell a scam. We'll disagree: He pitched strongly after May. $

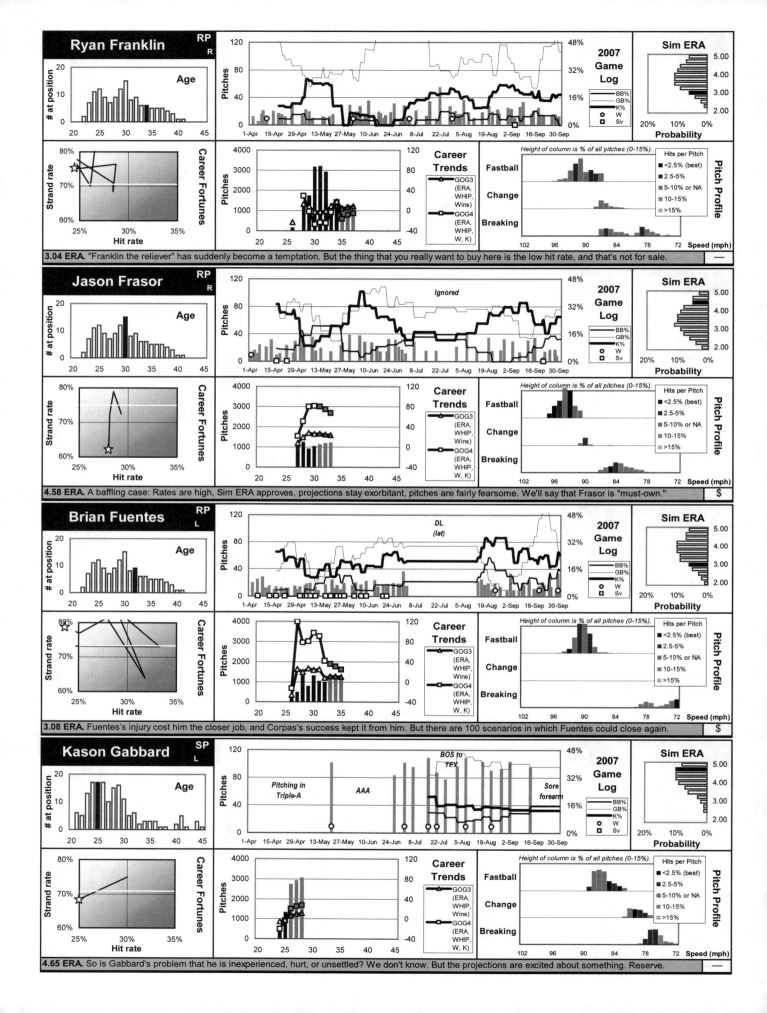

Ryan Franklin — RP R

Age

2007 Game Log
BB%
GB%
K%
○ W
□ Sv

Sim ERA — Probability

Career Fortunes — Strand rate / Hit rate

Career Trends
GOG3 (ERA, WHIP, Wins)
GOG4 (ERA, WHIP, W, K)

Pitch Profile — Height of column is % of all pitches (0-15%). Hits per Pitch: <2.5% (best), 2.5-5%, 5-10% or NA, 10-15%, >15%
Fastball / Change / Breaking — Speed (mph)

3.04 ERA. "Franklin the reliever" has suddenly become a temptation. But the thing that you really want to buy here is the low hit rate, and that's not for sale. —

Jason Frasor — RP R

Age

2007 Game Log — *Ignored*
BB%
GB%
K%
○ W
□ Sv

Sim ERA — Probability

Career Fortunes — Strand rate / Hit rate

Career Trends
GOG3 (ERA, WHIP, Wins)
GOG4 (ERA, WHIP, W, K)

Pitch Profile — Height of column is % of all pitches (0-15%). Hits per Pitch: <2.5% (best), 2.5-5%, 5-10% or NA, 10-15%, >15%
Fastball / Change / Breaking — Speed (mph)

4.58 ERA. A baffling case: Rates are high, Sim ERA approves, projections stay exorbitant, pitches are fairly fearsome. We'll say that Frasor is "must-own." $

Brian Fuentes — RP L

Age

2007 Game Log — DL (lat)
BB%
GB%
K%
○ W
□ Sv

Sim ERA — Probability

Career Fortunes — Strand rate / Hit rate

Career Trends
GOG3 (ERA, WHIP, Wins)
GOG4 (ERA, WHIP, W, K)

Pitch Profile — Height of column is % of all pitches (0-15%). Hits per Pitch: <2.5% (best), 2.5-5%, 5-10% or NA, 10-15%, >15%
Fastball / Change / Breaking — Speed (mph)

3.08 ERA. Fuentes's injury cost him the closer job, and Corpas's success kept it from him. But there are 100 scenarios in which Fuentes could close again. $

Kason Gabbard — SP L

Age

2007 Game Log — Pitching in Triple-A / AAA / BOS to TEX / Sore forearm
BB%
GB%
K%
○ W
□ Sv

Sim ERA — Probability

Career Fortunes — Strand rate / Hit rate

Career Trends
GOG3 (ERA, WHIP, Wins)
GOG4 (ERA, WHIP, W, K)

Pitch Profile — Height of column is % of all pitches (0-15%). Hits per Pitch: <2.5% (best), 2.5-5%, 5-10% or NA, 10-15%, >15%
Fastball / Change / Breaking — Speed (mph)

4.65 ERA. So is Gabbard's problem that he is inexperienced, hurt, or unsettled? We don't know. But the projections are excited about something. Reserve. —

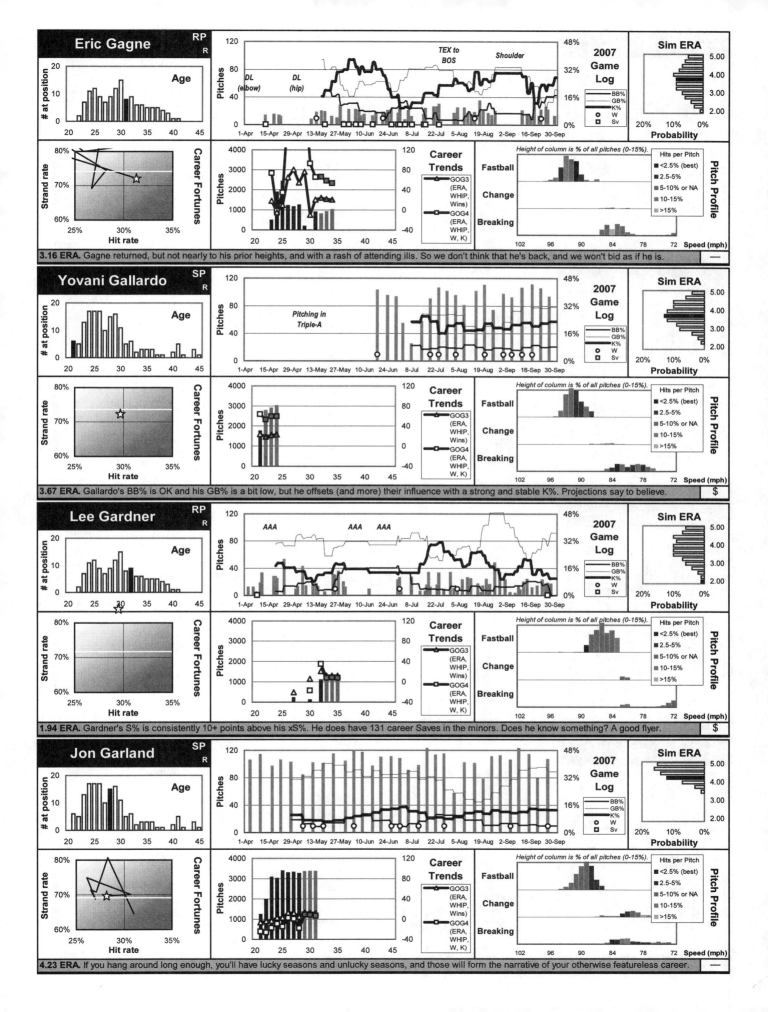

Eric Gagne — RP R

Age — # at position (20–45)

2007 Game Log — Pitches (0–120), 48% scale. Labels: *DL (elbow)*, *DL (hip)*, *TEX to BOS*, *Shoulder*. Legend: BB%, GB%, K%, W, Sv.

Sim ERA — Probability (20%–0%), ERA 2.00–5.00

Career Fortunes — Strand rate (60%–80%) vs Hit rate (25%–35%)

Career Trends — Pitches (0–4000) vs Age (20–45). Legend: GOG3 (ERA, WHIP, Wins), GOG4 (ERA, WHIP, W, K)

Pitch Profile — Height of column is % of all pitches (0–15%). Fastball / Change / Breaking. Speed (mph) 102–72. Hits per Pitch: <2.5% (best), 2.5–5%, 5–10% or NA, 10–15%, >15%

3.16 ERA. Gagne returned, but not nearly to his prior heights, and with a rash of attending ills. So we don't think that he's back, and we won't bid as if he is. —

Yovani Gallardo — SP R

Age — # at position (20–45)

2007 Game Log — *Pitching in Triple-A*. Legend: BB%, GB%, K%, W, Sv.

Sim ERA — Probability (20%–0%), ERA 2.00–5.00

Career Fortunes — Strand rate vs Hit rate

Career Trends — Legend: GOG3 (ERA, WHIP, Wins), GOG4 (ERA, WHIP, W, K)

Pitch Profile — Fastball / Change / Breaking

3.67 ERA. Gallardo's BB% is OK and his GB% is a bit low, but he offsets (and more) their influence with a strong and stable K%. Projections say to believe. $

Lee Gardner — RP R

Age — # at position (20–45)

2007 Game Log — *AAA*, *AAA*, *AAA*. Legend: BB%, GB%, K%, W, Sv.

Sim ERA — Probability, ERA 2.00–5.00

Career Fortunes — Strand rate vs Hit rate

Career Trends — Legend: GOG3 (ERA, WHIP, Wins), GOG4 (ERA, WHIP, W, K)

Pitch Profile — Fastball / Change / Breaking

1.94 ERA. Gardner's S% is consistently 10+ points above his xS%. He does have 131 career Saves in the minors. Does he know something? A good flyer. $

Jon Garland — SP R

Age — # at position (20–45)

2007 Game Log — Legend: BB%, GB%, K%, W, Sv.

Sim ERA — Probability, ERA 2.00–5.00

Career Fortunes — Strand rate vs Hit rate

Career Trends — Legend: GOG3 (ERA, WHIP, Wins), GOG4 (ERA, WHIP, W, K)

Pitch Profile — Fastball / Change / Breaking

4.23 ERA. If you hang around long enough, you'll have lucky seasons and unlucky seasons, and those will form the narrative of your otherwise featureless career. —

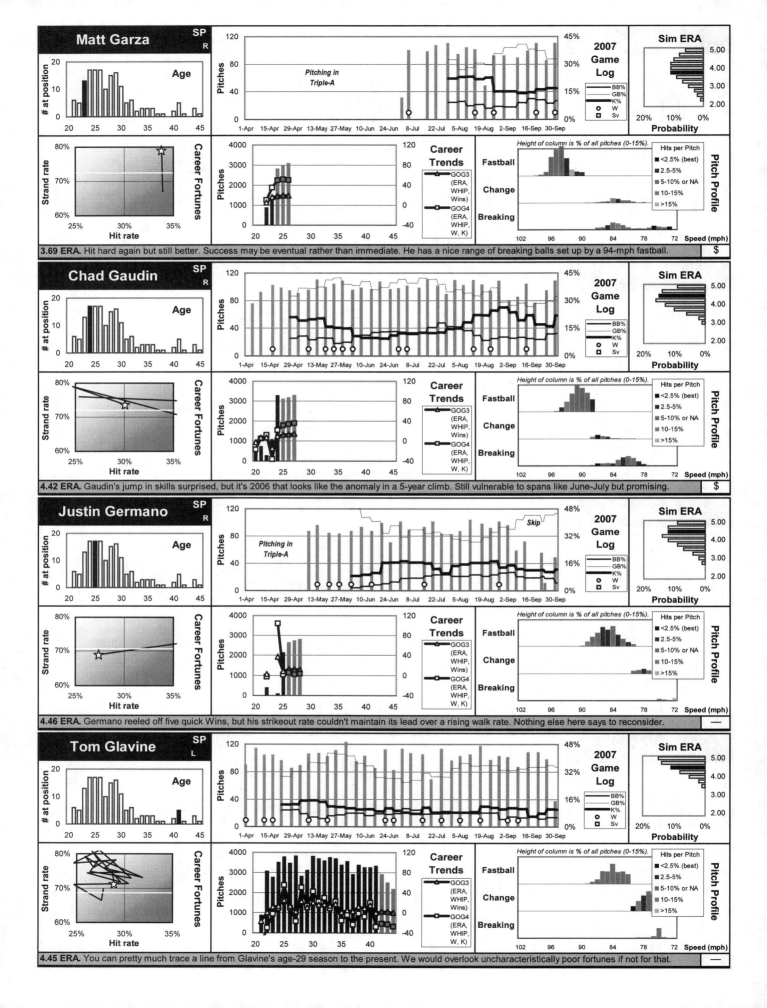

Matt Garza — SP R

Age — # at position

Pitching in Triple-A

2007 Game Log — BB%, GB%, K%, W, Sv

Sim ERA — Probability

Strand rate / Hit rate — **Career Fortunes**

Career Trends — GOG3 (ERA, WHIP, Wins), GOG4 (ERA, WHIP, W, K)

Pitch Profile — Height of column is % of all pitches (0-15%). Hits per Pitch: <2.5% (best), 2.5-5%, 5-10% or NA, 10-15%, >15%. Fastball, Change, Breaking. Speed (mph)

3.69 ERA. Hit hard again but still better. Success may be eventual rather than immediate. He has a nice range of breaking balls set up by a 94-mph fastball. **$**

Chad Gaudin — SP R

Age — # at position

2007 Game Log — BB%, GB%, K%, W, Sv

Sim ERA — Probability

Strand rate / Hit rate — **Career Fortunes**

Career Trends — GOG3 (ERA, WHIP, Wins), GOG4 (ERA, WHIP, W, K)

Pitch Profile — Height of column is % of all pitches (0-15%). Hits per Pitch: <2.5% (best), 2.5-5%, 5-10% or NA, 10-15%, >15%. Fastball, Change, Breaking. Speed (mph)

4.42 ERA. Gaudin's jump in skills surprised, but it's 2006 that looks like the anomaly in a 5-year climb. Still vulnerable to spans like June-July but promising. **$**

Justin Germano — SP R

Age — # at position

Pitching in Triple-A

Skip

2007 Game Log — BB%, GB%, K%, W, Sv

Sim ERA — Probability

Strand rate / Hit rate — **Career Fortunes**

Career Trends — GOG3 (ERA, WHIP, Wins), GOG4 (ERA, WHIP, W, K)

Pitch Profile — Height of column is % of all pitches (0-15%). Hits per Pitch: <2.5% (best), 2.5-5%, 5-10% or NA, 10-15%, >15%. Fastball, Change, Breaking. Speed (mph)

4.46 ERA. Germano reeled off five quick Wins, but his strikeout rate couldn't maintain its lead over a rising walk rate. Nothing else here says to reconsider. **—**

Tom Glavine — SP L

Age — # at position

2007 Game Log — BB%, GB%, K%, W, Sv

Sim ERA — Probability

Strand rate / Hit rate — **Career Fortunes**

Career Trends — GOG3 (ERA, WHIP, Wins), GOG4 (ERA, WHIP, W, K)

Pitch Profile — Height of column is % of all pitches (0-15%). Hits per Pitch: <2.5% (best), 2.5-5%, 5-10% or NA, 10-15%, >15%. Fastball, Change, Breaking. Speed (mph)

4.45 ERA. You can pretty much trace a line from Glavine's age-29 season to the present. We would overlook uncharacteristically poor fortunes if not for that. **—**

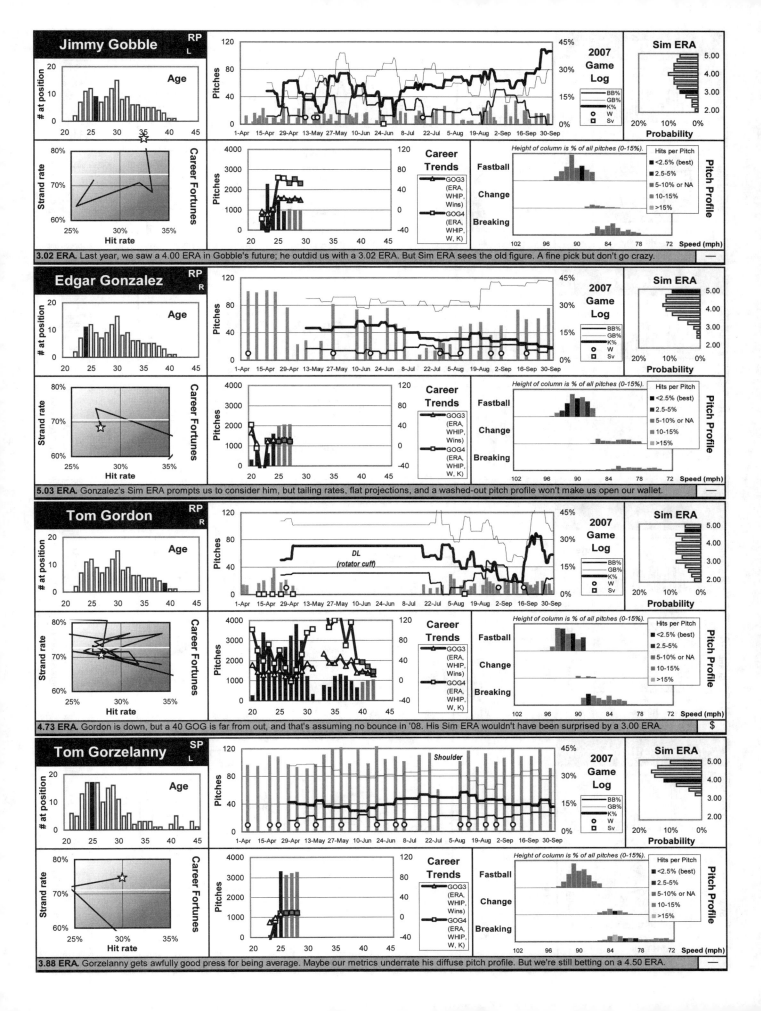

Jimmy Gobble RP L

Age · # at position · Career Fortunes · Strand rate · Hit rate

2007 Game Log · Pitches · BB% · GB% · K% · W · Sv

Sim ERA · Probability

Career Trends · GOG3 (ERA, WHIP, Wins) · GOG4 (ERA, WHIP, W, K)

Height of column is % of all pitches (0-15%). · Fastball · Change · Breaking · Speed (mph) · Pitch Profile · Hits per Pitch: <2.5% (best), 2.5-5%, 5-10% or NA, 10-15%, >15%

3.02 ERA. Last year, we saw a 4.00 ERA in Gobble's future; he outdid us with a 3.02 ERA. But Sim ERA sees the old figure. A fine pick but don't go crazy. — —

Edgar Gonzalez RP R

Age · # at position · Career Fortunes · Strand rate · Hit rate

2007 Game Log · Pitches · BB% · GB% · K% · W · Sv

Sim ERA · Probability

Career Trends · GOG3 (ERA, WHIP, Wins) · GOG4 (ERA, WHIP, W, K)

Height of column is % of all pitches (0-15%). · Fastball · Change · Breaking · Speed (mph) · Pitch Profile

5.03 ERA. Gonzalez's Sim ERA prompts us to consider him, but tailing rates, flat projections, and a washed-out pitch profile won't make us open our wallet. — —

Tom Gordon RP R

Age · # at position · Career Fortunes · Strand rate · Hit rate

2007 Game Log · Pitches · DL (rotator cuff) · BB% · GB% · K% · W · Sv

Sim ERA · Probability

Career Trends · GOG3 (ERA, WHIP, Wins) · GOG4 (ERA, WHIP, W, K)

Height of column is % of all pitches (0-15%). · Fastball · Change · Breaking · Speed (mph) · Pitch Profile

4.73 ERA. Gordon is down, but a 40 GOG is far from out, and that's assuming no bounce in '08. His Sim ERA wouldn't have been surprised by a 3.00 ERA. — $

Tom Gorzelanny SP L

Age · # at position · Career Fortunes · Strand rate · Hit rate

2007 Game Log · Pitches · Shoulder · BB% · GB% · K% · W · Sv

Sim ERA · Probability

Career Trends · GOG3 (ERA, WHIP, Wins) · GOG4 (ERA, WHIP, W, K)

Height of column is % of all pitches (0-15%). · Fastball · Change · Breaking · Speed (mph) · Pitch Profile

3.88 ERA. Gorzelanny gets awfully good press for being average. Maybe our metrics underrate his diffuse pitch profile. But we're still betting on a 4.50 ERA. — —

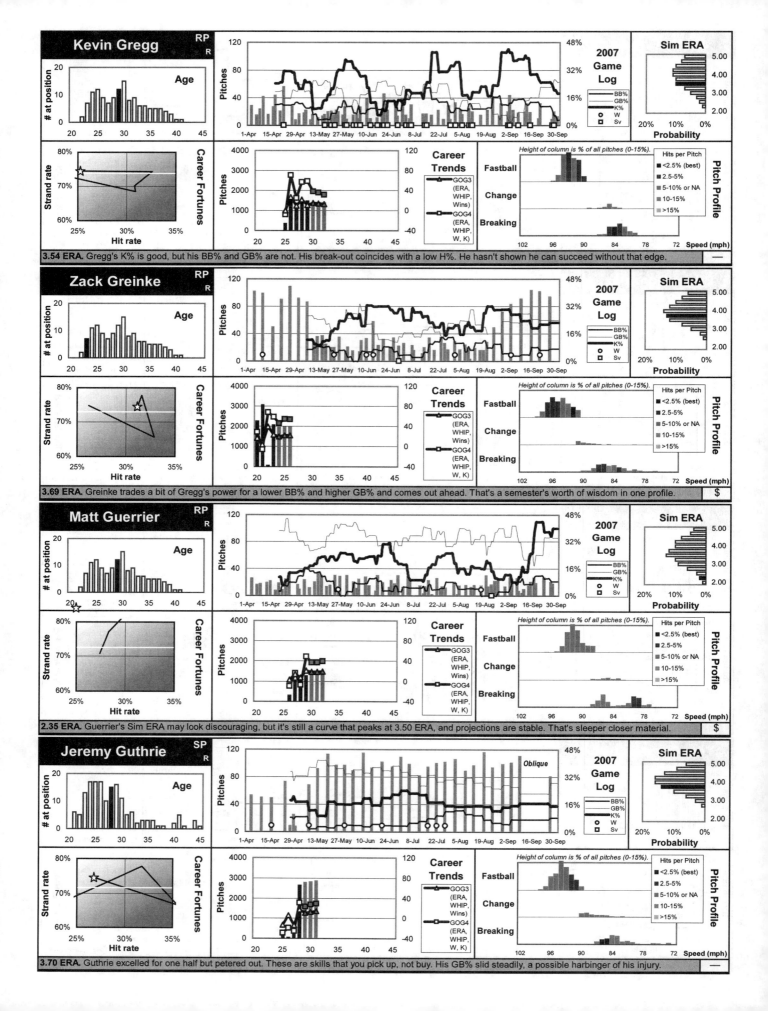

Kevin Gregg RP R

2007 Game Log

Sim ERA

Age

Career Fortunes

Career Trends
GOG3 (ERA, WHIP, Wins)
GOG4 (ERA, WHIP, W, K)

Pitch Profile
Height of column is % of all pitches (0-15%).
Hits per Pitch
<2.5% (best)
2.5-5%
5-10% or NA
10-15%
>15%
Fastball
Change
Breaking

3.54 ERA. Gregg's K% is good, but his BB% and GB% are not. His break-out coincides with a low H%. He hasn't shown he can succeed without that edge. —

Zack Greinke RP R

2007 Game Log

Sim ERA

Age

Career Fortunes

Career Trends
GOG3 (ERA, WHIP, Wins)
GOG4 (ERA, WHIP, W, K)

Pitch Profile
Height of column is % of all pitches (0-15%).
Hits per Pitch
<2.5% (best)
2.5-5%
5-10% or NA
10-15%
>15%
Fastball
Change
Breaking

3.69 ERA. Greinke trades a bit of Gregg's power for a lower BB% and higher GB% and comes out ahead. That's a semester's worth of wisdom in one profile. $

Matt Guerrier RP R

2007 Game Log

Sim ERA

Age

Career Fortunes

Career Trends
GOG3 (ERA, WHIP, Wins)
GOG4 (ERA, WHIP, W, K)

Pitch Profile
Height of column is % of all pitches (0-15%).
Hits per Pitch
<2.5% (best)
2.5-5%
5-10% or NA
10-15%
>15%
Fastball
Change
Breaking

2.35 ERA. Guerrier's Sim ERA may look discouraging, but it's still a curve that peaks at 3.50 ERA, and projections are stable. That's sleeper closer material. $

Jeremy Guthrie SP R

2007 Game Log

Oblique

Sim ERA

Age

Career Fortunes

Career Trends
GOG3 (ERA, WHIP, Wins)
GOG4 (ERA, WHIP, W, K)

Pitch Profile
Height of column is % of all pitches (0-15%).
Hits per Pitch
<2.5% (best)
2.5-5%
5-10% or NA
10-15%
>15%
Fastball
Change
Breaking

3.70 ERA. Guthrie excelled for one half but petered out. These are skills that you pick up, not buy. His GB% slid steadily, a possible harbinger of his injury. —

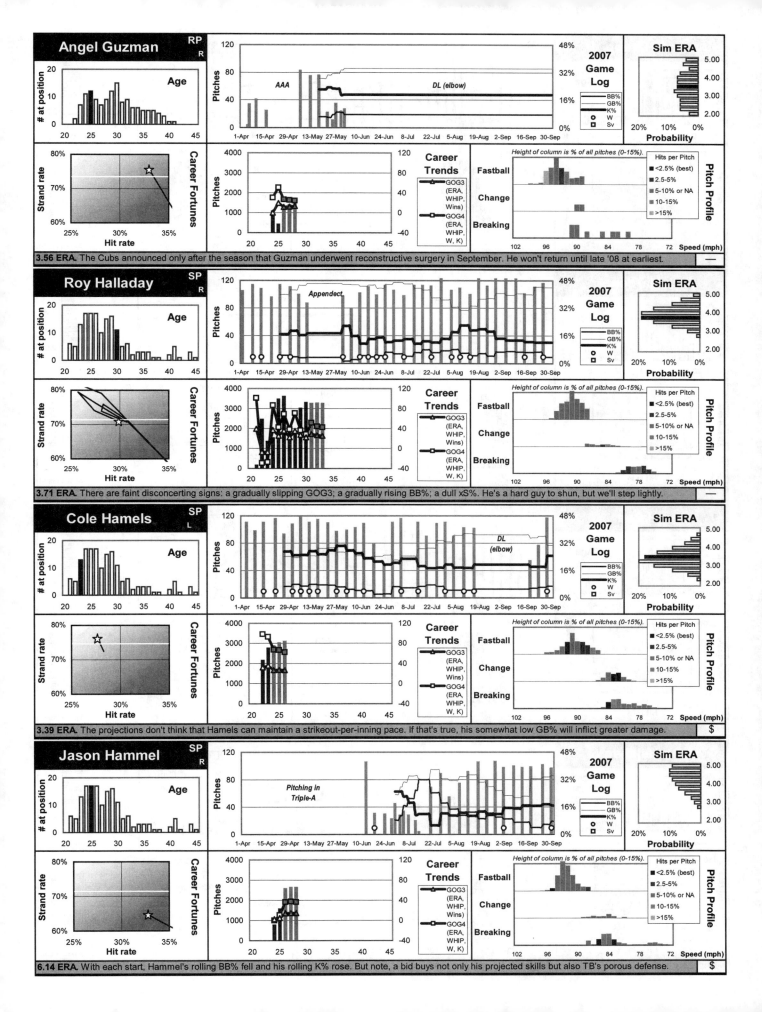

Angel Guzman — RP / R

3.56 ERA. The Cubs announced only after the season that Guzman underwent reconstructive surgery in September. He won't return until late '08 at earliest. — —

Roy Halladay — SP / R

3.71 ERA. There are faint disconcerting signs: a gradually slipping GOG3; a gradually rising BB%; a dull xS%. He's a hard guy to shun, but we'll step lightly. — —

Cole Hamels — SP / L

3.39 ERA. The projections don't think that Hamels can maintain a strikeout-per-inning pace. If that's true, his somewhat low GB% will inflict greater damage. — $

Jason Hammel — SP / R

6.14 ERA. With each start, Hammel's rolling BB% fell and his rolling K% rose. But note, a bid buys not only his projected skills but also TB's porous defense. — $

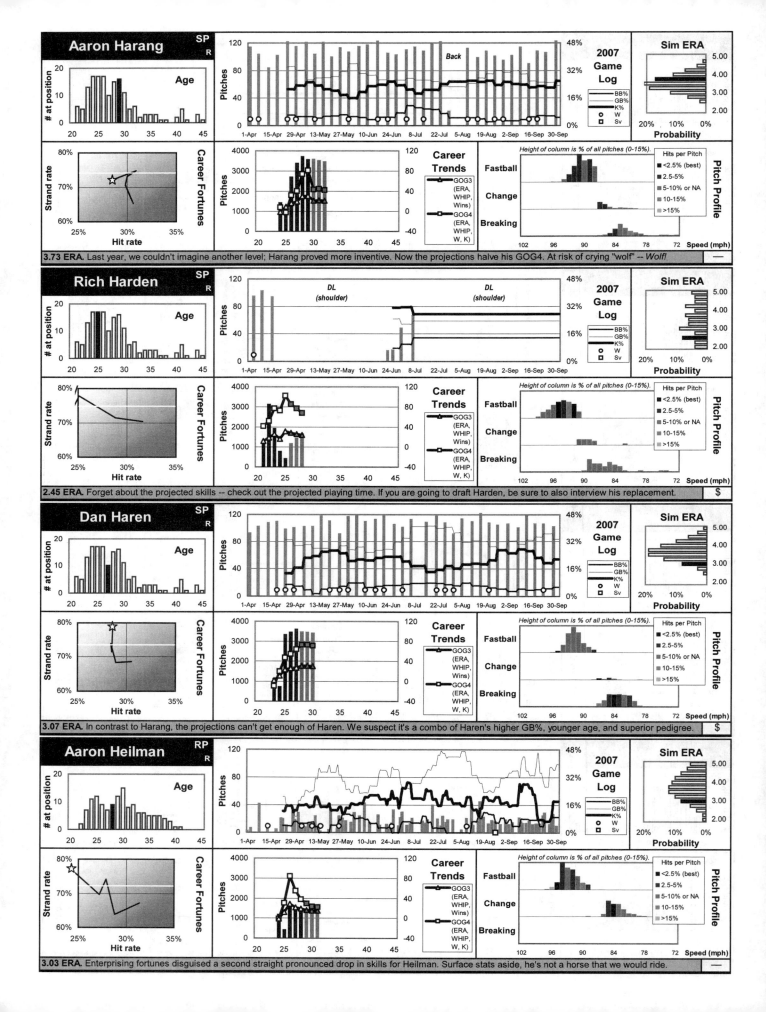

Aaron Harang SP R

3.73 ERA. Last year, we couldn't imagine another level; Harang proved more inventive. Now the projections halve his GOG4. At risk of crying "wolf" -- *Wolf!* —

Rich Harden SP R

2.45 ERA. Forget about the projected skills -- check out the projected playing time. If you are going to draft Harden, be sure to also interview his replacement. $

Dan Haren SP R

3.07 ERA. In contrast to Harang, the projections can't get enough of Haren. We suspect it's a combo of Haren's higher GB%, younger age, and superior pedigree. $

Aaron Heilman RP R

3.03 ERA. Enterprising fortunes disguised a second straight pronounced drop in skills for Heilman. Surface stats aside, he's not a horse that we would ride. —

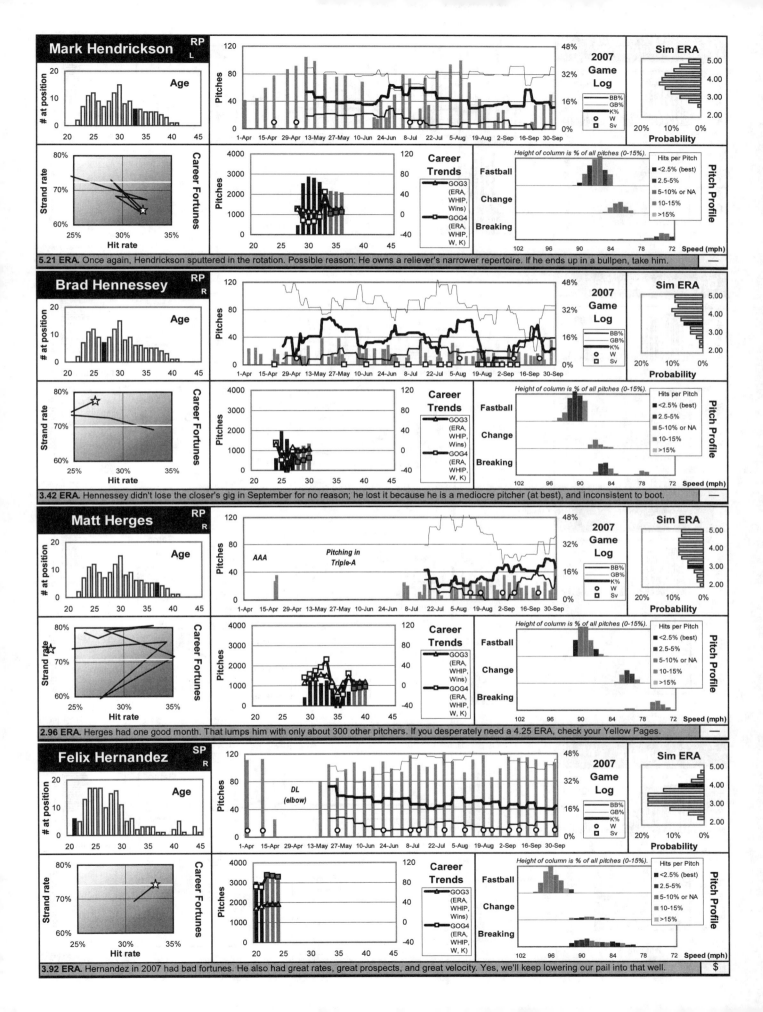

Mark Hendrickson RP L

Age

Career Fortunes

2007 Game Log — BB% / GB% / K% / W / Sv

Sim ERA — Probability

Career Trends — GOG3 (ERA, WHIP, Wins) / GOG4 (ERA, WHIP, W, K)

Pitch Profile — Height of column is % of all pitches (0-15%). — Hits per Pitch: <2.5% (best) / 2.5-5% / 5-10% or NA / 10-15% / >15% — Fastball / Change / Breaking — Speed (mph)

5.21 ERA. Once again, Hendrickson sputtered in the rotation. Possible reason: He owns a reliever's narrower repertoire. If he ends up in a bullpen, take him. — —

Brad Hennessey RP R

Age

Career Fortunes

2007 Game Log — BB% / GB% / K% / W / Sv

Sim ERA — Probability

Career Trends — GOG3 (ERA, WHIP, Wins) / GOG4 (ERA, WHIP, W, K)

Pitch Profile — Height of column is % of all pitches (0-15%). — Hits per Pitch: <2.5% (best) / 2.5-5% / 5-10% or NA / 10-15% / >15% — Fastball / Change / Breaking — Speed (mph)

3.42 ERA. Hennessey didn't lose the closer's gig in September for no reason; he lost it because he is a mediocre pitcher (at best), and inconsistent to boot. — —

Matt Herges RP R

Age

Career Fortunes

2007 Game Log — AAA — Pitching in Triple-A — BB% / GB% / K% / W / Sv

Sim ERA — Probability

Career Trends — GOG3 (ERA, WHIP, Wins) / GOG4 (ERA, WHIP, W, K)

Pitch Profile — Height of column is % of all pitches (0-15%). — Hits per Pitch: <2.5% (best) / 2.5-5% / 5-10% or NA / 10-15% / >15% — Fastball / Change / Breaking — Speed (mph)

2.96 ERA. Herges had one good month. That lumps him with only about 300 other pitchers. If you desperately need a 4.25 ERA, check your Yellow Pages. — —

Felix Hernandez SP R

Age

Career Fortunes

2007 Game Log — DL (elbow) — BB% / GB% / K% / W / Sv

Sim ERA — Probability

Career Trends — GOG3 (ERA, WHIP, Wins) / GOG4 (ERA, WHIP, W, K)

Pitch Profile — Height of column is % of all pitches (0-15%). — Hits per Pitch: <2.5% (best) / 2.5-5% / 5-10% or NA / 10-15% / >15% — Fastball / Change / Breaking — Speed (mph)

3.92 ERA. Hernandez in 2007 had bad fortunes. He also had great rates, great prospects, and great velocity. Yes, we'll keep lowering our pail into that well. — $

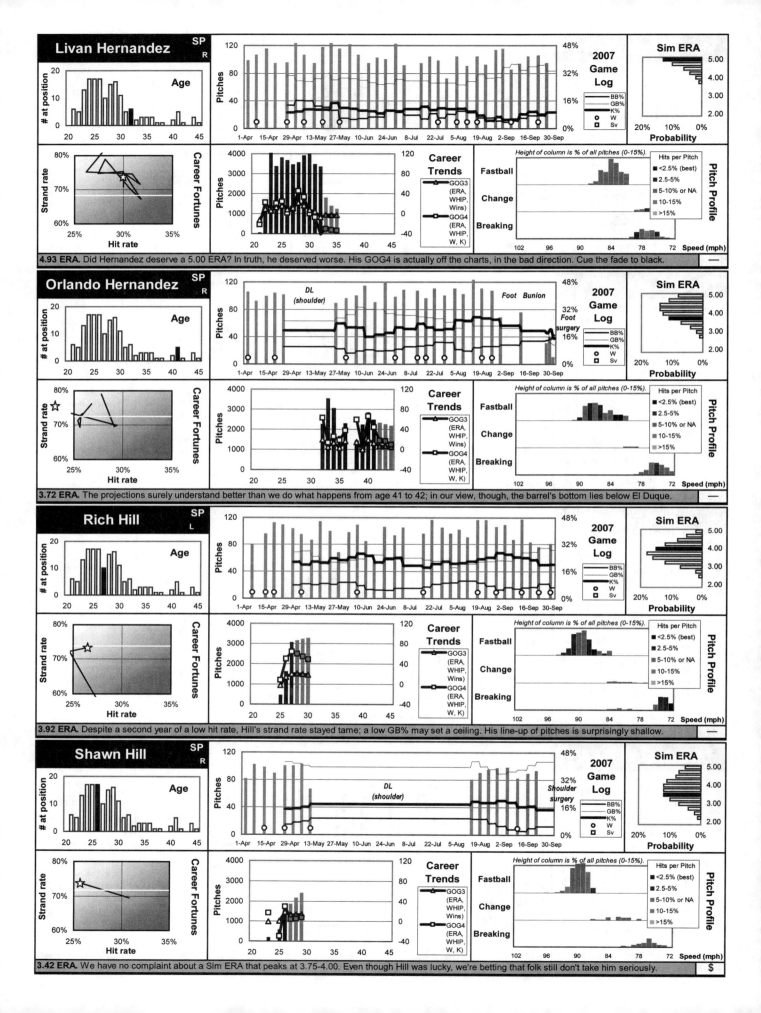

Livan Hernandez — SP R

Age | Career Fortunes | 2007 Game Log | Sim ERA | Career Trends | Pitch Profile

BB%, GB%, K%, W, Sv

GOG3 (ERA, WHIP, Wins) / GOG4 (ERA, WHIP, W, K)

Height of column is % of all pitches (0-15%). Hits per Pitch: <2.5% (best), 2.5-5%, 5-10% or NA, 10-15%, >15%

4.93 ERA. Did Hernandez deserve a 5.00 ERA? In truth, he deserved worse. His GOG4 is actually off the charts, in the bad direction. Cue the fade to black. —

Orlando Hernandez — SP R

DL (shoulder) ... Foot Bunion ... Foot surgery

3.72 ERA. The projections surely understand better than we do what happens from age 41 to 42; in our view, though, the barrel's bottom lies below El Duque. —

Rich Hill — SP L

3.92 ERA. Despite a second year of a low hit rate, Hill's strand rate stayed tame; a low GB% may set a ceiling. His line-up of pitches is surprisingly shallow. —

Shawn Hill — SP R

DL (shoulder) ... Shoulder surgery

3.42 ERA. We have no complaint about a Sim ERA that peaks at 3.75-4.00. Even though Hill was lucky, we're betting that folk still don't take him seriously. $

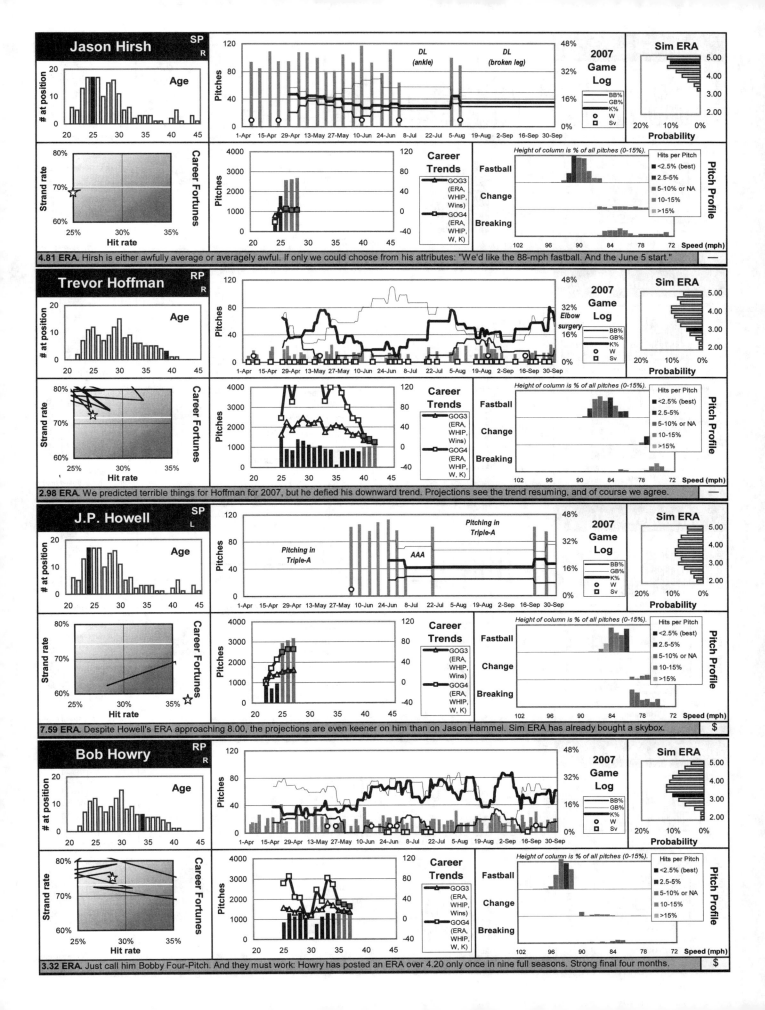

Jason Hirsh SP R

Age
at position

2007 Game Log
BB%
GB%
K%
o W
□ Sv

Sim ERA
Probability

DL (ankle)   DL (broken leg)

Strand rate — Hit rate — Career Fortunes

Career Trends
GOG3 (ERA, WHIP, Wins)
GOG4 (ERA, WHIP, W, K)

Height of column is % of all pitches (0-15%).
Fastball
Change
Breaking
Pitch Profile

Hits per Pitch
<2.5% (best)
2.5-5%
5-10% or NA
10-15%
>15%

Speed (mph)

4.81 ERA. Hirsh is either awfully average or averagely awful. If only we could choose from his attributes: "We'd like the 88-mph fastball. And the June 5 start." —

Trevor Hoffman RP R

Age
at position

2007 Game Log
Elbow surgery
BB%
GB%
K%
o W
□ Sv

Sim ERA
Probability

Strand rate — Hit rate — Career Fortunes

Career Trends
GOG3 (ERA, WHIP, Wins)
GOG4 (ERA, WHIP, W, K)

Height of column is % of all pitches (0-15%).
Fastball
Change
Breaking
Pitch Profile

Hits per Pitch
<2.5% (best)
2.5-5%
5-10% or NA
10-15%
>15%

Speed (mph)

2.98 ERA. We predicted terrible things for Hoffman for 2007, but he defied his downward trend. Projections see the trend resuming, and of course we agree. —

J.P. Howell SP L

Age
at position

2007 Game Log
Pitching in Triple-A   AAA   Pitching in Triple-A
BB%
GB%
K%
o W
□ Sv

Sim ERA
Probability

Strand rate — Hit rate — Career Fortunes

Career Trends
GOG3 (ERA, WHIP, Wins)
GOG4 (ERA, WHIP, W, K)

Height of column is % of all pitches (0-15%).
Fastball
Change
Breaking
Pitch Profile

Hits per Pitch
<2.5% (best)
2.5-5%
5-10% or NA
10-15%
>15%

Speed (mph)

7.59 ERA. Despite Howell's ERA approaching 8.00, the projections are even keener on him than on Jason Hammel. Sim ERA has already bought a skybox. $

Bob Howry RP R

Age
at position

2007 Game Log
BB%
GB%
K%
o W
□ Sv

Sim ERA
Probability

Strand rate — Hit rate — Career Fortunes

Career Trends
GOG3 (ERA, WHIP, Wins)
GOG4 (ERA, WHIP, W, K)

Height of column is % of all pitches (0-15%).
Fastball
Change
Breaking
Pitch Profile

Hits per Pitch
<2.5% (best)
2.5-5%
5-10% or NA
10-15%
>15%

Speed (mph)

3.32 ERA. Just call him Bobby Four-Pitch. And they must work: Howry has posted an ERA over 4.20 only once in nine full seasons. Strong final four months. $

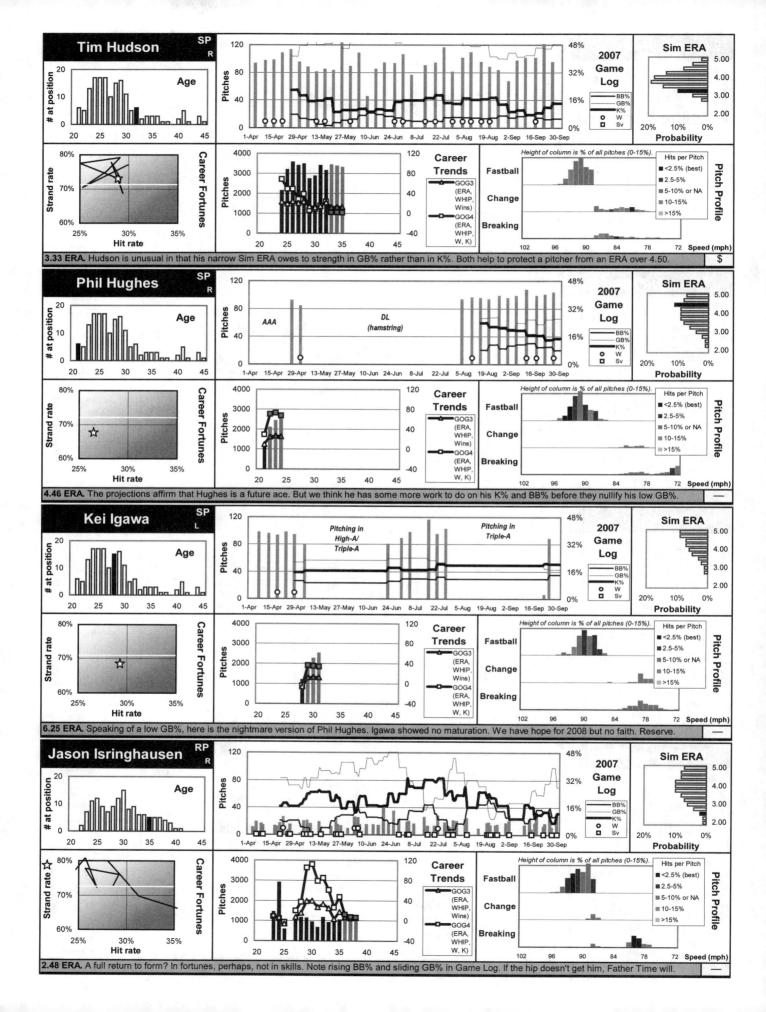

Tim Hudson — SP, R

Age | Pitches | 2007 Game Log | Sim ERA | Career Fortunes | Career Trends | Pitch Profile

3.33 ERA. Hudson is unusual in that his narrow Sim ERA owes to strength in GB% rather than in K%. Both help to protect a pitcher from an ERA over 4.50. **$**

Phil Hughes — SP, R

AAA | DL (hamstring)

4.46 ERA. The projections affirm that Hughes is a future ace. But we think he has some more work to do on his K% and BB% before they nullify his low GB%. **—**

Kei Igawa — SP, L

Pitching in High-A/Triple-A | Pitching in Triple-A

6.25 ERA. Speaking of a low GB%, here is the nightmare version of Phil Hughes. Igawa showed no maturation. We have hope for 2008 but no faith. Reserve. **—**

Jason Isringhausen — RP, R

2.48 ERA. A full return to form? In fortunes, perhaps, not in skills. Note rising BB% and sliding GB% in Game Log. If the hip doesn't get him, Father Time will. **—**

Legend elements: BB%, GB%, K%, W, Sv

Pitch Profile — Height of column is % of all pitches (0-15%). Fastball, Change, Breaking. Speed (mph): 102, 96, 90, 84, 78, 72.

Hits per Pitch: <2.5% (best); 2.5-5%; 5-10% or NA; 10-15%; >15%

Career Trends: GOG3 (ERA, WHIP, Wins); GOG4 (ERA, WHIP, W, K)

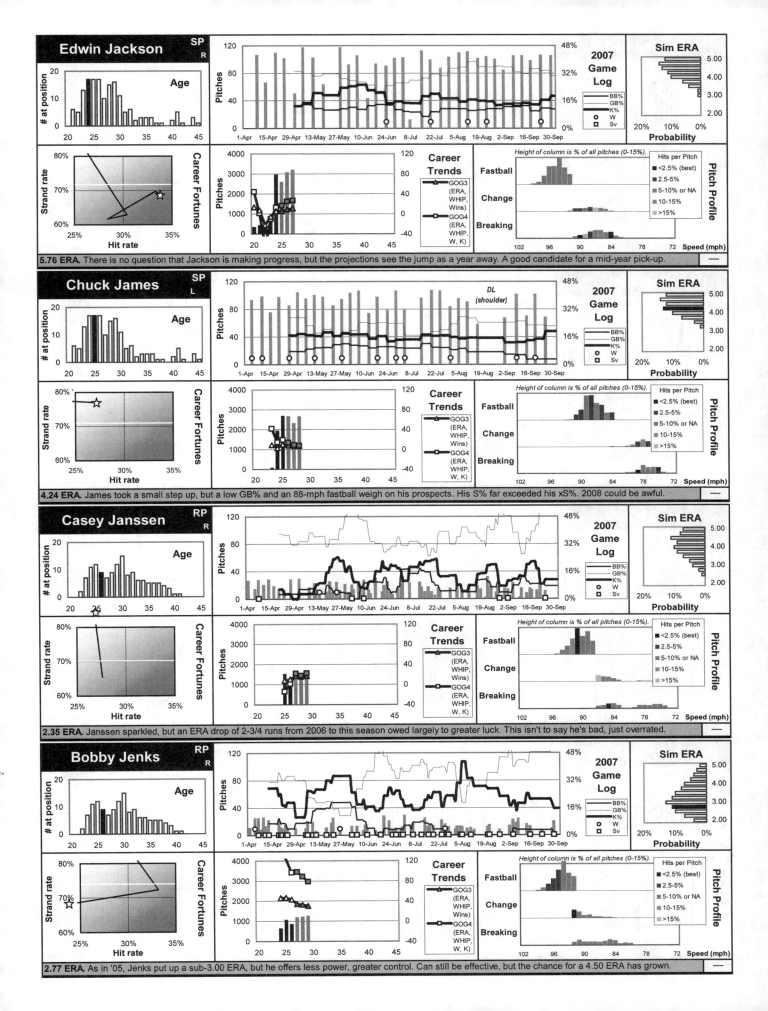

Edwin Jackson SP R

Age

2007 Game Log

BB%
GB%
K%
○ W
□ Sv

Sim ERA
Probability

Career Fortunes

Career Trends
GOG3 (ERA, WHIP, Wins)
GOG4 (ERA, WHIP, W, K)

Pitch Profile
Height of column is % of all pitches (0-15%).
Fastball
Change
Breaking
Hits per Pitch
■ <2.5% (best)
■ 2.5-5%
5-10% or NA
10-15%
>15%

5.76 ERA. There is no question that Jackson is making progress, but the projections see the jump as a year away. A good candidate for a mid-year pick-up. —

Chuck James SP L

Age

DL (shoulder)

2007 Game Log

BB%
GB%
K%
○ W
□ Sv

Sim ERA
Probability

Career Fortunes

Career Trends
GOG3 (ERA, WHIP, Wins)
GOG4 (ERA, WHIP, W, K)

Pitch Profile
Height of column is % of all pitches (0-15%).
Fastball
Change
Breaking
Hits per Pitch
■ <2.5% (best)
■ 2.5-5%
5-10% or NA
10-15%
>15%

4.24 ERA. James took a small step up, but a low GB% and an 88-mph fastball weigh on his prospects. His S% far exceeded his xS%. 2008 could be awful. —

Casey Janssen RP R

Age

2007 Game Log

BB%
GB%
K%
○ W
□ Sv

Sim ERA
Probability

Career Fortunes

Career Trends
GOG3 (ERA, WHIP, Wins)
GOG4 (ERA, WHIP, W, K)

Pitch Profile
Height of column is % of all pitches (0-15%).
Fastball
Change
Breaking
Hits per Pitch
■ <2.5% (best)
■ 2.5-5%
5-10% or NA
10-15%
>15%

2.35 ERA. Janssen sparkled, but an ERA drop of 2-3/4 runs from 2006 to this season owed largely to greater luck. This isn't to say he's bad, just overrated. —

Bobby Jenks RP R

Age

2007 Game Log

BB%
GB%
K%
○ W
□ Sv

Sim ERA
Probability

Career Fortunes

Career Trends
GOG3 (ERA, WHIP, Wins)
GOG4 (ERA, WHIP, W, K)

Pitch Profile
Height of column is % of all pitches (0-15%).
Fastball
Change
Breaking
Hits per Pitch
■ <2.5% (best)
■ 2.5-5%
5-10% or NA
10-15%
>15%

2.77 ERA. As in '05, Jenks put up a sub-3.00 ERA, but he offers less power, greater control. Can still be effective, but the chance for a 4.50 ERA has grown. —

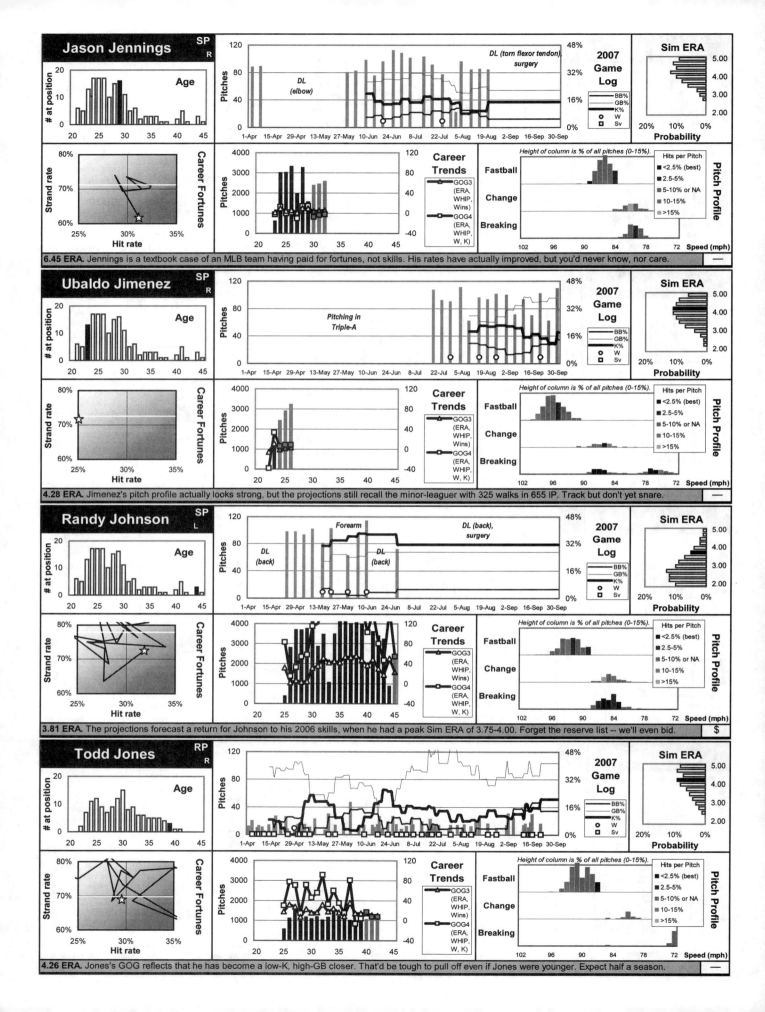

Jason Jennings — SP, R

Age (# at position)

2007 Game Log — Pitches
- DL (elbow)
- DL (torn flexor tendon), surgery
- 48% / 32% / 16% / 0%
- BB%, GB%, K%, W (○), Sv (□)

Sim ERA — 5.00 / 4.00 / 3.00 / 2.00 — Probability (20% 10% 0%)

Career Fortunes — Strand rate (80% 70% 60%) vs Hit rate (25% 30% 35%)

Career Trends — Pitches
- GOG3 (ERA, WHIP, Wins)
- GOG4 (ERA, WHIP, W, K)

Pitch Profile — Height of column is % of all pitches (0-15%).
- Fastball, Change, Breaking
- Hits per Pitch: <2.5% (best), 2.5-5%, 5-10% or NA, 10-15%, >15%
- Speed (mph): 102 96 90 84 78 72

6.45 ERA. Jennings is a textbook case of an MLB team having paid for fortunes, not skills. His rates have actually improved, but you'd never know, nor care. — —

Ubaldo Jimenez — SP, R

Age (# at position)

2007 Game Log — Pitches
- Pitching in Triple-A
- 48% / 32% / 16% / 0%
- BB%, GB%, K%, W (○), Sv (□)

Sim ERA — 5.00 / 4.00 / 3.00 / 2.00 — Probability (20% 10% 0%)

Career Fortunes — Strand rate (80% 70% 60%) vs Hit rate (25% 30% 35%)

Career Trends — Pitches
- GOG3 (ERA, WHIP, Wins)
- GOG4 (ERA, WHIP, W, K)

Pitch Profile — Height of column is % of all pitches (0-15%).
- Fastball, Change, Breaking
- Hits per Pitch: <2.5% (best), 2.5-5%, 5-10% or NA, 10-15%, >15%
- Speed (mph): 102 96 90 84 78 72

4.28 ERA. Jimenez's pitch profile actually looks strong, but the projections still recall the minor-leaguer with 325 walks in 655 IP. Track but don't yet snare. — —

Randy Johnson — SP, L

Age (# at position)

2007 Game Log — Pitches
- DL (back)
- Forearm
- DL (back)
- DL (back), surgery
- 48% / 32% / 16% / 0%
- BB%, GB%, K%, W (○), Sv (□)

Sim ERA — 5.00 / 4.00 / 3.00 / 2.00 — Probability (20% 10% 0%)

Career Fortunes — Strand rate (80% 70% 60%) vs Hit rate (25% 30% 35%)

Career Trends — Pitches
- GOG3 (ERA, WHIP, Wins)
- GOG4 (ERA, WHIP, W, K)

Pitch Profile — Height of column is % of all pitches (0-15%).
- Fastball, Change, Breaking
- Hits per Pitch: <2.5% (best), 2.5-5%, 5-10% or NA, 10-15%, >15%
- Speed (mph): 102 96 90 84 78 72

3.81 ERA. The projections forecast a return for Johnson to his 2006 skills, when he had a peak Sim ERA of 3.75-4.00. Forget the reserve list -- we'll even bid. **$**

Todd Jones — RP, R

Age (# at position)

2007 Game Log — Pitches
- 48% / 32% / 16% / 0%
- BB%, GB%, K%, W (○), Sv (□)

Sim ERA — 5.00 / 4.00 / 3.00 / 2.00 — Probability (20% 10% 0%)

Career Fortunes — Strand rate (80% 70% 60%) vs Hit rate (25% 30% 35%)

Career Trends — Pitches
- GOG3 (ERA, WHIP, Wins)
- GOG4 (ERA, WHIP, W, K)

Pitch Profile — Height of column is % of all pitches (0-15%).
- Fastball, Change, Breaking
- Hits per Pitch: <2.5% (best), 2.5-5%, 5-10% or NA, 10-15%, >15%
- Speed (mph): 102 96 90 84 78 72

4.26 ERA. Jones's GOG reflects that he has become a low-K, high-GB closer. That'd be tough to pull off even if Jones were younger. Expect half a season. — —

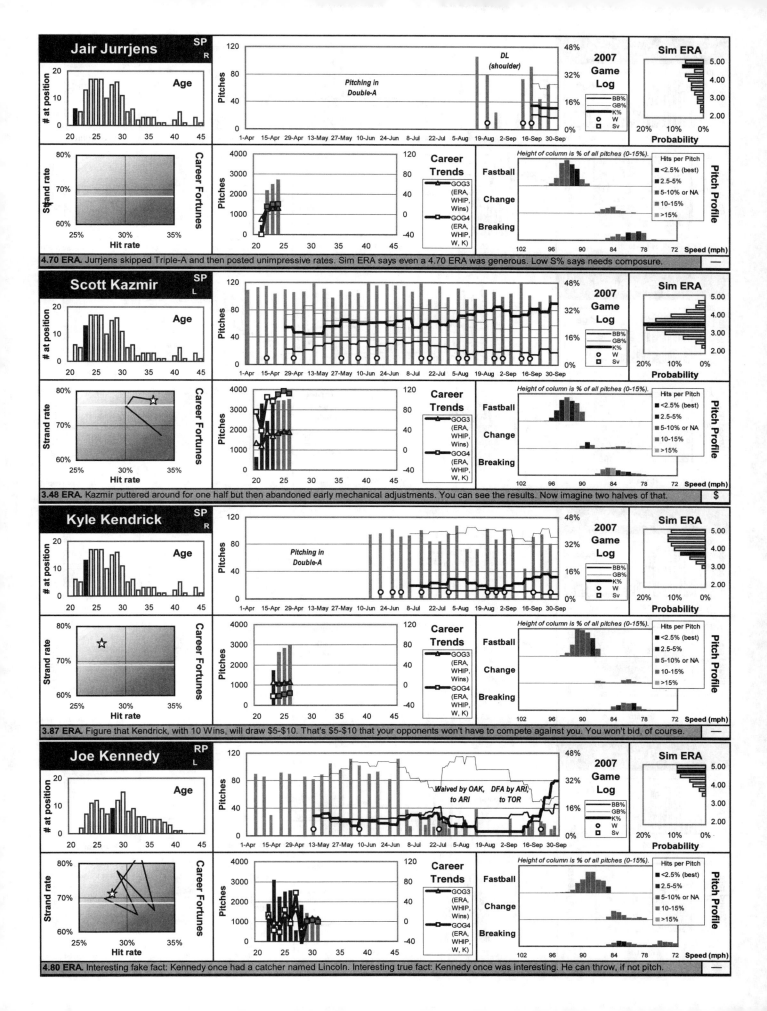

Jair Jurrjens — SP R

4.70 ERA. Jurrjens skipped Triple-A and then posted unimpressive rates. Sim ERA says even a 4.70 ERA was generous. Low S% says needs composure. —

Scott Kazmir — SP L

3.48 ERA. Kazmir puttered around for one half but then abandoned early mechanical adjustments. You can see the results. Now imagine two halves of that. $

Kyle Kendrick — SP R

3.87 ERA. Figure that Kendrick, with 10 Wins, will draw $5-$10. That's $5-$10 that your opponents won't have to compete against you. You won't bid, of course. —

Joe Kennedy — RP L

4.80 ERA. Interesting fake fact: Kennedy once had a catcher named Lincoln. Interesting true fact: Kennedy once was interesting. He can throw, if not pitch. —

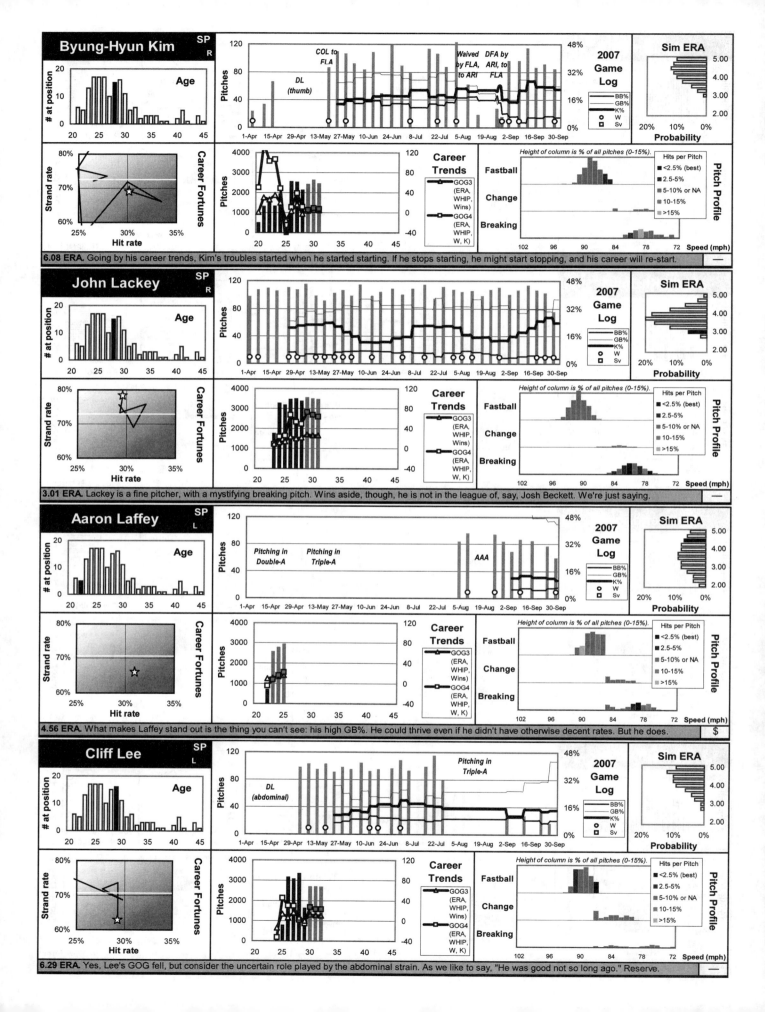

Byung-Hyun Kim SP R

Age — # at position / 20 25 30 35 40 45

Pitches — 2007 Game Log — DL (thumb), COL to FLA, Waived by FLA, DFA by ARI, to ARI to FLA — BB%, GB%, K%, W, Sv — 1-Apr 15-Apr 29-Apr 13-May 27-May 10-Jun 24-Jun 8-Jul 22-Jul 5-Aug 19-Aug 2-Sep 16-Sep 30-Sep

Sim ERA — 5.00 4.00 3.00 2.00 — 20% 10% 0% Probability

Career Fortunes — Strand rate 80% 70% 60% / Hit rate 25% 30% 35%

Career Trends — GOG3 (ERA, WHIP, Wins), GOG4 (ERA, WHIP, W, K) — 20 25 30 35 40 45

Pitch Profile — Height of column is % of all pitches (0-15%). — Fastball, Change, Breaking — Hits per Pitch: <2.5% (best), 2.5-5%, 5-10% or NA, 10-15%, >15% — 102 96 90 84 78 72 Speed (mph)

6.08 ERA. Going by his career trends, Kim's troubles started when he started starting. If he stops starting, he might start stopping, and his career will re-start. —

John Lackey SP R

Age — # at position / 20 25 30 35 40 45

Pitches — 2007 Game Log — BB%, GB%, K%, W, Sv — 1-Apr 15-Apr 29-Apr 13-May 27-May 10-Jun 24-Jun 8-Jul 22-Jul 5-Aug 19-Aug 2-Sep 16-Sep 30-Sep

Sim ERA — 5.00 4.00 3.00 2.00 — 20% 10% 0% Probability

Career Fortunes — Strand rate 80% 70% 60% / Hit rate 25% 30% 35%

Career Trends — GOG3 (ERA, WHIP, Wins), GOG4 (ERA, WHIP, W, K) — 20 25 30 35 40 45

Pitch Profile — Height of column is % of all pitches (0-15%). — Fastball, Change, Breaking — Hits per Pitch: <2.5% (best), 2.5-5%, 5-10% or NA, 10-15%, >15% — 102 96 90 84 78 72 Speed (mph)

3.01 ERA. Lackey is a fine pitcher, with a mystifying breaking pitch. Wins aside, though, he is not in the league of, say, Josh Beckett. We're just saying. —

Aaron Laffey SP L

Age — # at position / 20 25 30 35 40 45

Pitches — 2007 Game Log — Pitching in Double-A, Pitching in Triple-A, AAA — BB%, GB%, K%, W, Sv — 1-Apr 15-Apr 29-Apr 13-May 27-May 10-Jun 24-Jun 8-Jul 22-Jul 5-Aug 19-Aug 2-Sep 16-Sep 30-Sep

Sim ERA — 5.00 4.00 3.00 2.00 — 20% 10% 0% Probability

Career Fortunes — Strand rate 80% 70% 60% / Hit rate 25% 30% 35%

Career Trends — GOG3 (ERA, WHIP, Wins), GOG4 (ERA, WHIP, W, K) — 20 25 30 35 40 45

Pitch Profile — Height of column is % of all pitches (0-15%). — Fastball, Change, Breaking — Hits per Pitch: <2.5% (best), 2.5-5%, 5-10% or NA, 10-15%, >15% — 102 96 90 84 78 72 Speed (mph)

4.56 ERA. What makes Laffey stand out is the thing you can't see: his high GB%. He could thrive even if he didn't have otherwise decent rates. But he does. $

Cliff Lee SP L

Age — # at position / 20 25 30 35 40 45

Pitches — 2007 Game Log — DL (abdominal), Pitching in Triple-A — BB%, GB%, K%, W, Sv — 1-Apr 15-Apr 29-Apr 13-May 27-May 10-Jun 24-Jun 8-Jul 22-Jul 5-Aug 19-Aug 2-Sep 16-Sep 30-Sep

Sim ERA — 5.00 4.00 3.00 2.00 — 20% 10% 0% Probability

Career Fortunes — Strand rate 80% 70% 60% / Hit rate 25% 30% 35%

Career Trends — GOG3 (ERA, WHIP, Wins), GOG4 (ERA, WHIP, W, K) — 20 25 30 35 40 45

Pitch Profile — Height of column is % of all pitches (0-15%). — Fastball, Change, Breaking — Hits per Pitch: <2.5% (best), 2.5-5%, 5-10% or NA, 10-15%, >15% — 102 96 90 84 78 72 Speed (mph)

6.29 ERA. Yes, Lee's GOG fell, but consider the uncertain role played by the abdominal strain. As we like to say, "He was good not so long ago." Reserve. —

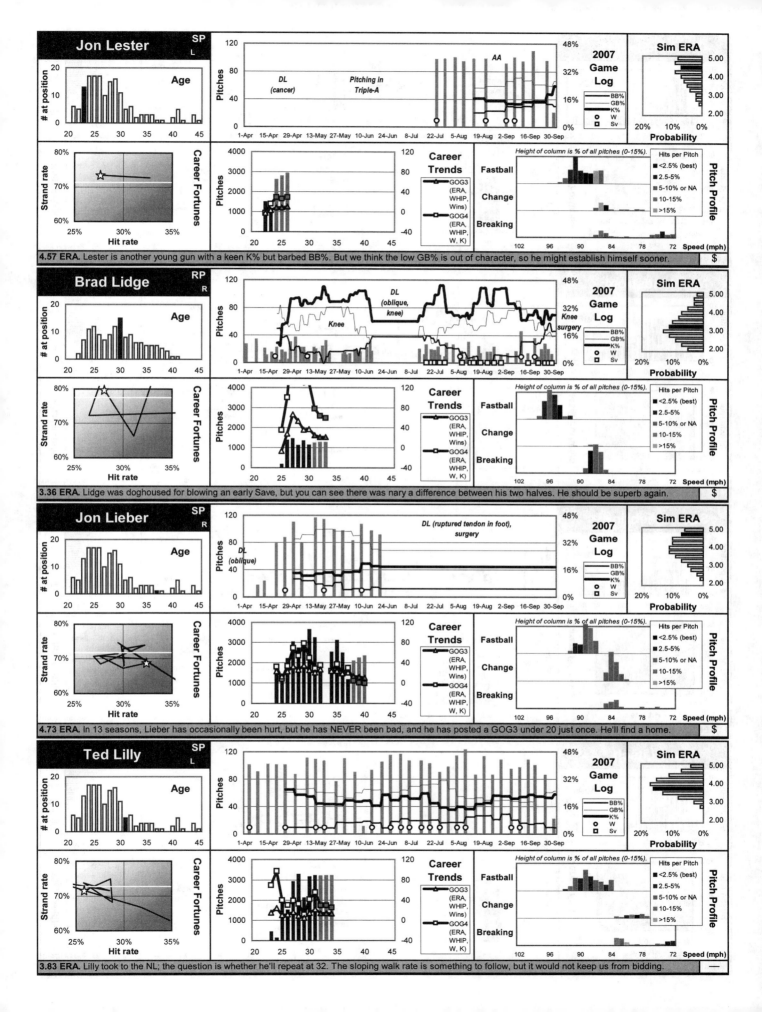

Jon Lester — SP L

Age — # at position

2007 Game Log — Pitches — DL (cancer), Pitching in Triple-A, AA — BB%, GB%, K%, W, Sv

Sim ERA — Probability

Career Fortunes — Strand rate vs Hit rate

Career Trends — Pitches — GOG3 (ERA, WHIP, Wins), GOG4 (ERA, WHIP, W, K)

Pitch Profile — Height of column is % of all pitches (0-15%) — Fastball, Change, Breaking — Hits per Pitch: <2.5% (best), 2.5-5%, 5-10% or NA, 10-15%, >15% — Speed (mph)

4.57 ERA. Lester is another young gun with a keen K% but barbed BB%. But we think the low GB% is out of character, so he might establish himself sooner. **$**

Brad Lidge — RP R

Age — # at position

2007 Game Log — Pitches — DL (oblique, knee), Knee, Knee surgery — BB%, GB%, K%, W, Sv

Sim ERA — Probability

Career Fortunes — Strand rate vs Hit rate

Career Trends — Pitches — GOG3 (ERA, WHIP, Wins), GOG4 (ERA, WHIP, W, K)

Pitch Profile — Height of column is % of all pitches (0-15%) — Fastball, Change, Breaking — Hits per Pitch: <2.5% (best), 2.5-5%, 5-10% or NA, 10-15%, >15% — Speed (mph)

3.36 ERA. Lidge was doghoused for blowing an early Save, but you can see there was nary a difference between his two halves. He should be superb again. **$**

Jon Lieber — SP R

Age — # at position

2007 Game Log — Pitches — DL (oblique), DL (ruptured tendon in foot), surgery — BB%, GB%, K%, W, Sv

Sim ERA — Probability

Career Fortunes — Strand rate vs Hit rate

Career Trends — Pitches — GOG3 (ERA, WHIP, Wins), GOG4 (ERA, WHIP, W, K)

Pitch Profile — Height of column is % of all pitches (0-15%) — Fastball, Change, Breaking — Hits per Pitch: <2.5% (best), 2.5-5%, 5-10% or NA, 10-15%, >15% — Speed (mph)

4.73 ERA. In 13 seasons, Lieber has occasionally been hurt, but he has NEVER been bad, and he has posted a GOG3 under 20 just once. He'll find a home. **$**

Ted Lilly — SP L

Age — # at position

2007 Game Log — Pitches — BB%, GB%, K%, W, Sv

Sim ERA — Probability

Career Fortunes — Strand rate vs Hit rate

Career Trends — Pitches — GOG3 (ERA, WHIP, Wins), GOG4 (ERA, WHIP, W, K)

Pitch Profile — Height of column is % of all pitches (0-15%) — Fastball, Change, Breaking — Hits per Pitch: <2.5% (best), 2.5-5%, 5-10% or NA, 10-15%, >15% — Speed (mph)

3.83 ERA. Lilly took to the NL; the question is whether he'll repeat at 32. The sloping walk rate is something to follow, but it would not keep us from bidding. **—**

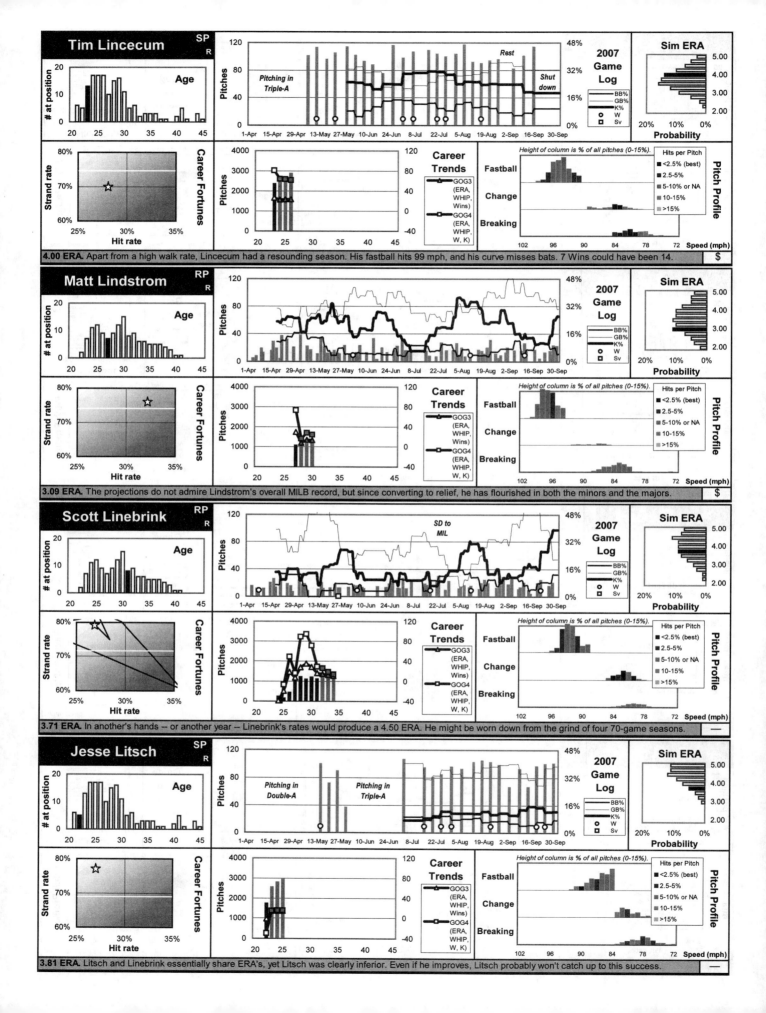

Tim Lincecum SP R

Age

2007 Game Log

Pitching in Triple-A

Rest

Shut down

BB%
GB%
K%
W
Sv

Sim ERA

Probability

Strand rate
Hit rate

Career Fortunes

Career Trends

GOG3 (ERA, WHIP, Wins)
GOG4 (ERA, WHIP, W, K)

Pitch Profile

Height of column is % of all pitches (0-15%).

Fastball
Change
Breaking

Hits per Pitch
<2.5% (best)
2.5-5%
5-10% or NA
10-15%
>15%

Speed (mph)

4.00 ERA. Apart from a high walk rate, Lincecum had a resounding season. His fastball hits 99 mph, and his curve misses bats. 7 Wins could have been 14. $

Matt Lindstrom RP R

Age

2007 Game Log

BB%
GB%
K%
W
Sv

Sim ERA

Probability

Strand rate
Hit rate

Career Fortunes

Career Trends

GOG3 (ERA, WHIP, Wins)
GOG4 (ERA, WHIP, W, K)

Pitch Profile

Height of column is % of all pitches (0-15%).

Fastball
Change
Breaking

Hits per Pitch
<2.5% (best)
2.5-5%
5-10% or NA
10-15%
>15%

Speed (mph)

3.09 ERA. The projections do not admire Lindstrom's overall MILB record, but since converting to relief, he has flourished in both the minors and the majors. $

Scott Linebrink RP R

Age

2007 Game Log

SD to MIL

BB%
GB%
K%
W
Sv

Sim ERA

Probability

Strand rate
Hit rate

Career Fortunes

Career Trends

GOG3 (ERA, WHIP, Wins)
GOG4 (ERA, WHIP, W, K)

Pitch Profile

Height of column is % of all pitches (0-15%).

Fastball
Change
Breaking

Hits per Pitch
<2.5% (best)
2.5-5%
5-10% or NA
10-15%
>15%

Speed (mph)

3.71 ERA. In another's hands -- or another year -- Linebrink's rates would produce a 4.50 ERA. He might be worn down from the grind of four 70-game seasons. —

Jesse Litsch SP R

Age

2007 Game Log

Pitching in Double-A

Pitching in Triple-A

BB%
GB%
K%
W
Sv

Sim ERA

Probability

Strand rate
Hit rate

Career Fortunes

Career Trends

GOG3 (ERA, WHIP, Wins)
GOG4 (ERA, WHIP, W, K)

Pitch Profile

Height of column is % of all pitches (0-15%).

Fastball
Change
Breaking

Hits per Pitch
<2.5% (best)
2.5-5%
5-10% or NA
10-15%
>15%

Speed (mph)

3.81 ERA. Litsch and Linebrink essentially share ERA's, yet Litsch was clearly inferior. Even if he improves, Litsch probably won't catch up to this success. —

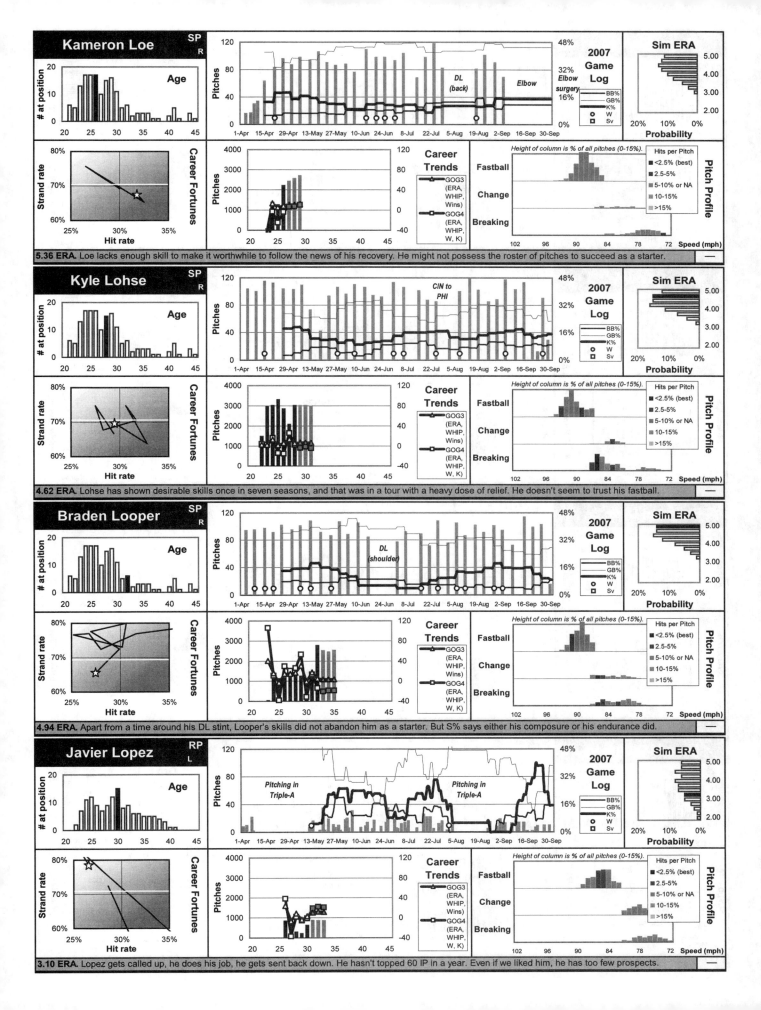

Kameron Loe SP R

Age

Career Fortunes

2007 Game Log — BB% / GB% / K% / W / Sv

Sim ERA — Probability

Career Trends — GOG3 (ERA, WHIP, Wins) / GOG4 (ERA, WHIP, W, K)

Pitch Profile — Height of column is % of all pitches (0-15%). Hits per Pitch: <2.5% (best) / 2.5-5% / 5-10% or NA / 10-15% / >15%. Fastball / Change / Breaking. Speed (mph)

DL (back) — Elbow — Elbow surgery

5.36 ERA. Loe lacks enough skill to make it worthwhile to follow the news of his recovery. He might not possess the roster of pitches to succeed as a starter.

Kyle Lohse SP R

Age

Career Fortunes

2007 Game Log

Sim ERA

Career Trends

Pitch Profile — Height of column is % of all pitches (0-15%).

CIN to PHI

4.62 ERA. Lohse has shown desirable skills once in seven seasons, and that was in a tour with a heavy dose of relief. He doesn't seem to trust his fastball.

Braden Looper SP R

Age

Career Fortunes

2007 Game Log

Sim ERA

Career Trends

Pitch Profile — Height of column is % of all pitches (0-15%).

DL (shoulder)

4.94 ERA. Apart from a time around his DL stint, Looper's skills did not abandon him as a starter. But S% says either his composure or his endurance did.

Javier Lopez RP L

Age

Career Fortunes

2007 Game Log

Sim ERA

Career Trends

Pitch Profile — Height of column is % of all pitches (0-15%).

Pitching in Triple-A — Pitching in Triple-A

3.10 ERA. Lopez gets called up, he does his job, he gets sent back down. He hasn't topped 60 IP in a year. Even if we liked him, he has too few prospects.

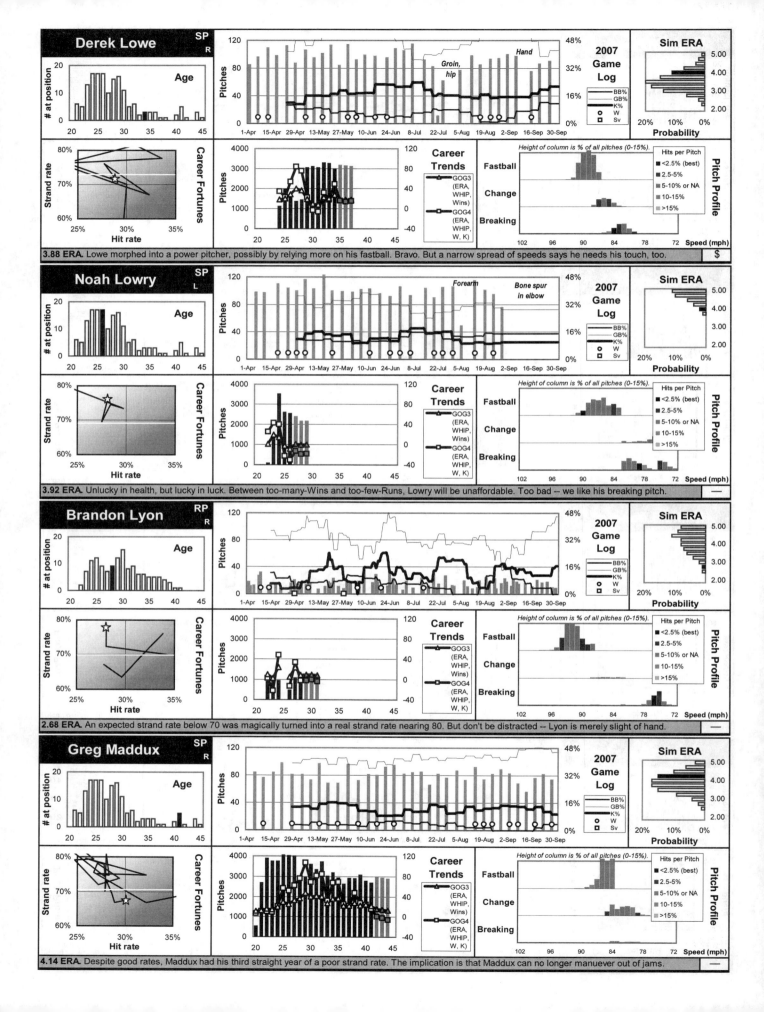

Derek Lowe SP R

Age

Career Fortunes

Strand rate / Hit rate

Pitches / 2007 Game Log — BB%, GB%, K%, W, Sv

Career Trends — GOG3 (ERA, WHIP, Wins), GOG4 (ERA, WHIP, W, K)

Sim ERA / Probability

Pitch Profile — Fastball, Change, Breaking. Height of column is % of all pitches (0-15%). Hits per Pitch: <2.5% (best), 2.5-5%, 5-10% or NA, 10-15%, >15%

Groin, hip / Hand

3.88 ERA. Lowe morphed into a power pitcher, possibly by relying more on his fastball. Bravo. But a narrow spread of speeds says he needs his touch, too. $

Noah Lowry SP L

Forearm / Bone spur in elbow

3.92 ERA. Unlucky in health, but lucky in luck. Between too-many-Wins and too-few-Runs, Lowry will be unaffordable. Too bad -- we like his breaking pitch. —

Brandon Lyon RP R

2.68 ERA. An expected strand rate below 70 was magically turned into a real strand rate nearing 80. But don't be distracted -- Lyon is merely slight of hand. —

Greg Maddux SP R

4.14 ERA. Despite good rates, Maddux had his third straight year of a poor strand rate. The implication is that Maddux can no longer manuever out of jams. —

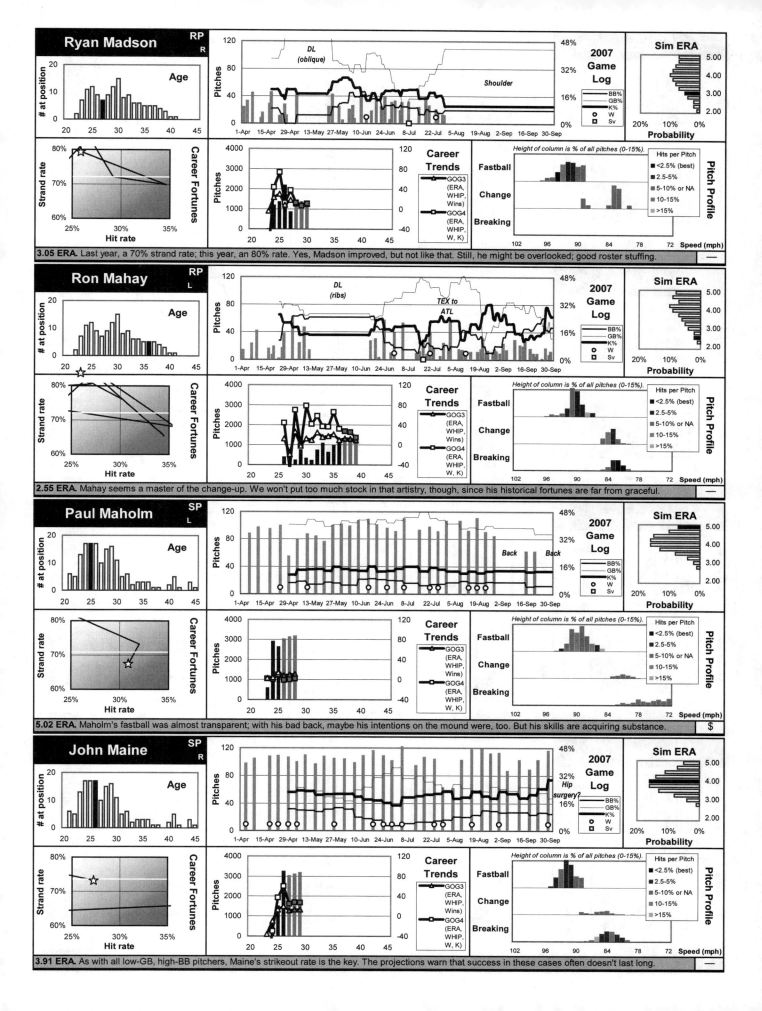

Ryan Madson RP R

3.05 ERA. Last year, a 70% strand rate; this year, an 80% rate. Yes, Madson improved, but not like that. Still, he might be overlooked; good roster stuffing. —

Ron Mahay RP L

2.55 ERA. Mahay seems a master of the change-up. We won't put too much stock in that artistry, though, since his historical fortunes are far from graceful. —

Paul Maholm SP L

5.02 ERA. Maholm's fastball was almost transparent; with his bad back, maybe his intentions on the mound were, too. But his skills are acquiring substance. $

John Maine SP R

3.91 ERA. As with all low-GB, high-BB pitchers, Maine's strikeout rate is the key. The projections warn that success in these cases often doesn't last long. —

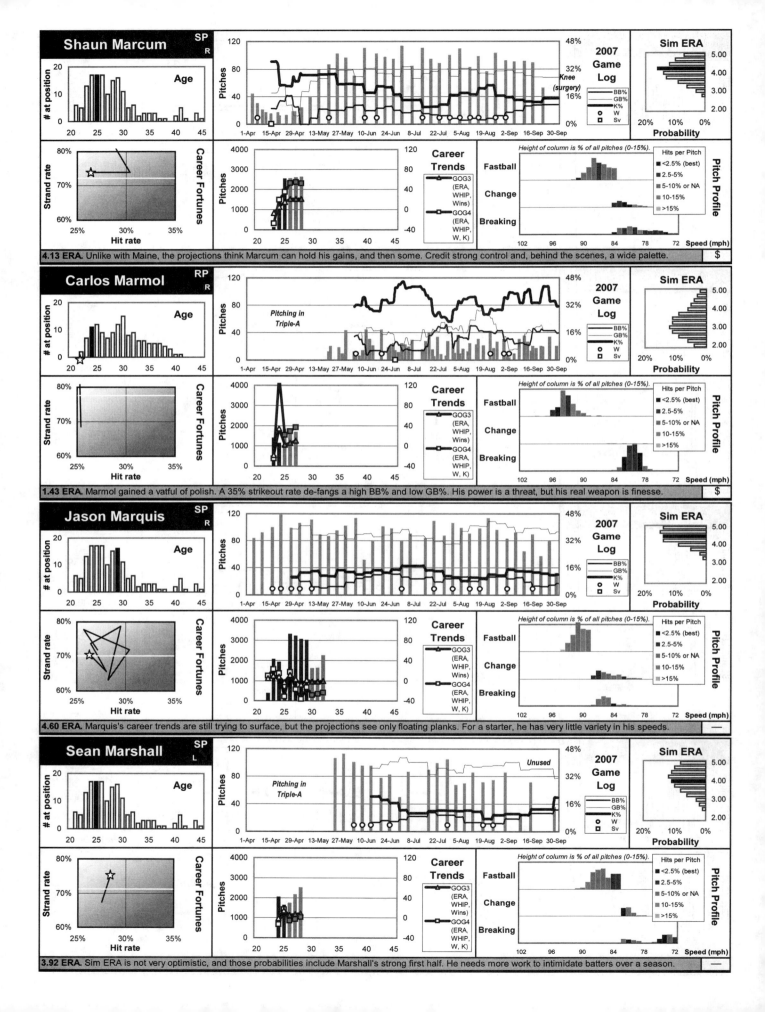

Shaun Marcum SP R

Age — # at position (20-45)

Sim ERA — Probability (20%-0%), 5.00-2.00

2007 Game Log — Pitches, BB%, GB%, K%, W, Sv — Knee (surgery)

Career Fortunes — Strand rate vs Hit rate

Career Trends — Pitches — GOG3 (ERA, WHIP, Wins), GOG4 (ERA, WHIP, W, K)

Pitch Profile — Height of column is % of all pitches (0-15%). Hits per Pitch: <2.5% (best), 2.5-5%, 5-10% or NA, 10-15%, >15% — Fastball, Change, Breaking — Speed (mph)

4.13 ERA. Unlike with Maine, the projections think Marcum can hold his gains, and then some. Credit strong control and, behind the scenes, a wide palette. $

Carlos Marmol RP R

Pitching in Triple-A

1.43 ERA. Marmol gained a vatful of polish. A 35% strikeout rate de-fangs a high BB% and low GB%. His power is a threat, but his real weapon is finesse. $

Jason Marquis SP R

4.60 ERA. Marquis's career trends are still trying to surface, but the projections see only floating planks. For a starter, he has very little variety in his speeds. —

Sean Marshall SP L

Pitching in Triple-A — Unused

3.92 ERA. Sim ERA is not very optimistic, and those probabilities include Marshall's strong first half. He needs more work to intimidate batters over a season. —

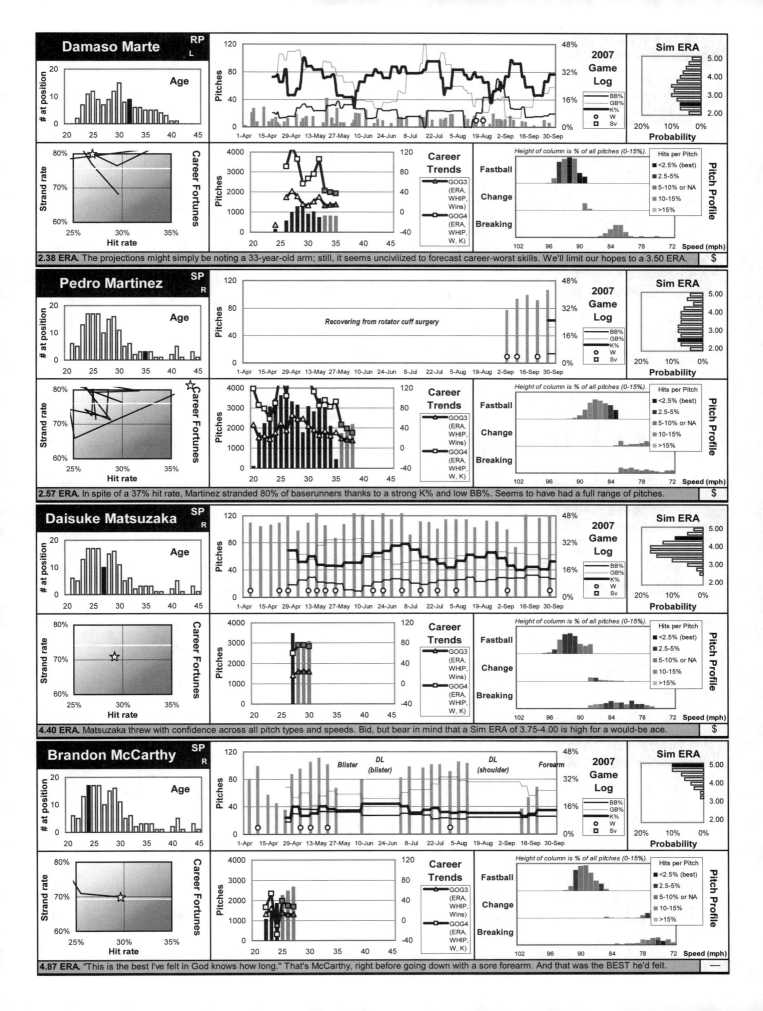

Damaso Marte RP L

Age

Strand rate / Hit rate — Career Fortunes

2007 Game Log — BB%, GB%, K%, W, Sv

Career Trends — GOG3 (ERA, WHIP, Wins), GOG4 (ERA, WHIP, W, K)

Sim ERA / Probability

Pitch Profile — Height of column is % of all pitches (0-15%). Hits per Pitch: <2.5% (best), 2.5-5%, 5-10% or NA, 10-15%, >15%. Fastball, Change, Breaking. Speed (mph)

2.38 ERA. The projections might simply be noting a 33-year-old arm; still, it seems uncivilized to forecast career-worst skills. We'll limit our hopes to a 3.50 ERA. $

Pedro Martinez SP R

Age

Strand rate / Hit rate — Career Fortunes

2007 Game Log — Recovering from rotator cuff surgery

Career Trends

Sim ERA / Probability

Pitch Profile

2.57 ERA. In spite of a 37% hit rate, Martinez stranded 80% of baserunners thanks to a strong K% and low BB%. Seems to have had a full range of pitches. $

Daisuke Matsuzaka SP R

Age

Strand rate / Hit rate — Career Fortunes

2007 Game Log

Career Trends

Sim ERA / Probability

Pitch Profile

4.40 ERA. Matsuzaka threw with confidence across all pitch types and speeds. Bid, but bear in mind that a Sim ERA of 3.75-4.00 is high for a would-be ace. $

Brandon McCarthy SP R

Age

Strand rate / Hit rate — Career Fortunes

2007 Game Log — Blister, DL (blister), DL (shoulder), Forearm

Career Trends

Sim ERA / Probability

Pitch Profile

4.87 ERA. "This is the best I've felt in God knows how long." That's McCarthy, right before going down with a sore forearm. And that was the BEST he'd felt. —

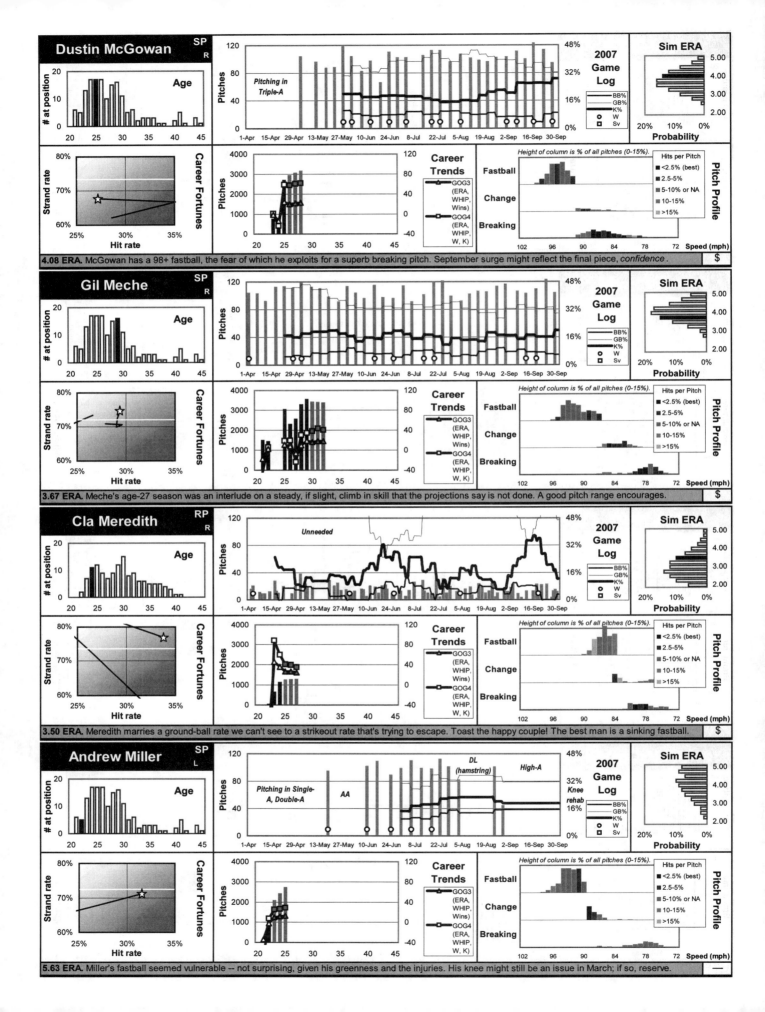

Dustin McGowan SP R

Age

Strand rate / Hit rate — Career Fortunes

Pitches — 2007 Game Log — BB%, GB%, K%, W, Sv

Sim ERA — Probability

Career Trends — GOG3 (ERA, WHIP, Wins); GOG4 (ERA, WHIP, W, K)

Height of column is % of all pitches (0-15%). Fastball, Change, Breaking — Pitch Profile — Hits per Pitch: <2.5% (best), 2.5-5%, 5-10% or NA, 10-15%, >15% — Speed (mph)

4.08 ERA. McGowan has a 98+ fastball, the fear of which he exploits for a superb breaking pitch. September surge might reflect the final piece, *confidence*. **$**

Gil Meche SP R

Age

Pitching in Triple-A

Strand rate / Hit rate — Career Fortunes

Pitches — 2007 Game Log — BB%, GB%, K%, W, Sv

Sim ERA — Probability

Career Trends — GOG3 (ERA, WHIP, Wins); GOG4 (ERA, WHIP, W, K)

Height of column is % of all pitches (0-15%). Fastball, Change, Breaking — Pitch Profile — Hits per Pitch — Speed (mph)

3.67 ERA. Meche's age-27 season was an interlude on a steady, if slight, climb in skill that the projections say is not done. A good pitch range encourages. **$**

Cla Meredith RP R

Age

Unneeded

Strand rate / Hit rate — Career Fortunes

Pitches — 2007 Game Log — BB%, GB%, K%, W, Sv

Sim ERA — Probability

Career Trends — GOG3 (ERA, WHIP, Wins); GOG4 (ERA, WHIP, W, K)

Height of column is % of all pitches (0-15%). Fastball, Change, Breaking — Pitch Profile — Hits per Pitch — Speed (mph)

3.50 ERA. Meredith marries a ground-ball rate we can't see to a strikeout rate that's trying to escape. Toast the happy couple! The best man is a sinking fastball. **$**

Andrew Miller SP L

Age

Pitching in Single-A, Double-A — AA — DL (hamstring) — High-A — Knee rehab

Strand rate / Hit rate — Career Fortunes

Pitches — 2007 Game Log — BB%, GB%, K%, W, Sv

Sim ERA — Probability

Career Trends — GOG3 (ERA, WHIP, Wins); GOG4 (ERA, WHIP, W, K)

Height of column is % of all pitches (0-15%). Fastball, Change, Breaking — Pitch Profile — Hits per Pitch — Speed (mph)

5.63 ERA. Miller's fastball seemed vulnerable -- not surprising, given his greenness and the injuries. His knee might still be an issue in March; if so, reserve. **—**

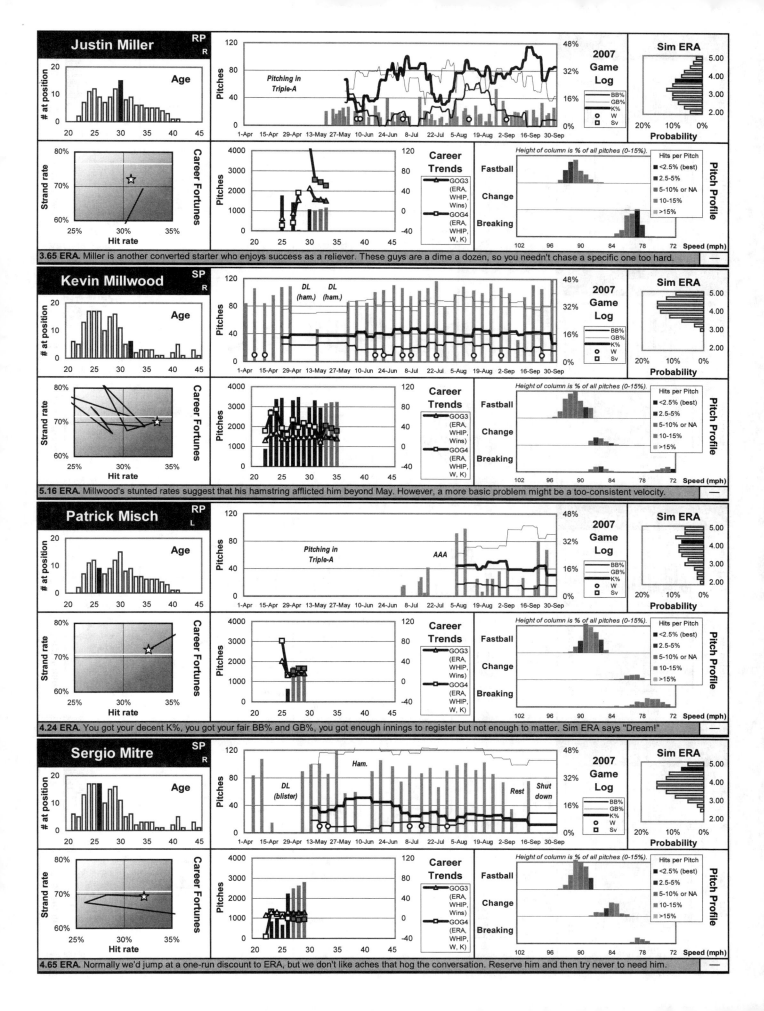

Justin Miller RP R

Pitching in Triple-A

2007 Game Log
BB%
GB%
K%
○ W
□ Sv

Sim ERA

Career Trends
GOG3 (ERA, WHIP, Wins)
GOG4 (ERA, WHIP, W, K)

Pitch Profile
Height of column is % of all pitches (0-15%).
Hits per Pitch
■ <2.5% (best)
■ 2.5-5%
▨ 5-10% or NA
▨ 10-15%
▨ >15%
Fastball
Change
Breaking

3.65 ERA. Miller is another converted starter who enjoys success as a reliever. These guys are a dime a dozen, so you needn't chase a specific one too hard. —

Kevin Millwood SP R

DL (ham.) DL (ham.)

2007 Game Log
BB%
GB%
K%
○ W
□ Sv

Sim ERA

Career Trends
GOG3 (ERA, WHIP, Wins)
GOG4 (ERA, WHIP, W, K)

Pitch Profile
Height of column is % of all pitches (0-15%).
Hits per Pitch
■ <2.5% (best)
■ 2.5-5%
▨ 5-10% or NA
▨ 10-15%
▨ >15%
Fastball
Change
Breaking

5.16 ERA. Millwood's stunted rates suggest that his hamstring afflicted him beyond May. However, a more basic problem might be a too-consistent velocity. —

Patrick Misch RP L

Pitching in Triple-A AAA

2007 Game Log
BB%
GB%
K%
○ W
□ Sv

Sim ERA

Career Trends
GOG3 (ERA, WHIP, Wins)
GOG4 (ERA, WHIP, W, K)

Pitch Profile
Height of column is % of all pitches (0-15%).
Hits per Pitch
■ <2.5% (best)
■ 2.5-5%
▨ 5-10% or NA
▨ 10-15%
▨ >15%
Fastball
Change
Breaking

4.24 ERA. You got your decent K%, you got your fair BB% and GB%, you got enough innings to register but not enough to matter. Sim ERA says "Dream!" —

Sergio Mitre SP R

DL (blister) Ham. Rest Shut down

2007 Game Log
BB%
GB%
K%
○ W
□ Sv

Sim ERA

Career Trends
GOG3 (ERA, WHIP, Wins)
GOG4 (ERA, WHIP, W, K)

Pitch Profile
Height of column is % of all pitches (0-15%).
Hits per Pitch
■ <2.5% (best)
■ 2.5-5%
▨ 5-10% or NA
▨ 10-15%
▨ >15%
Fastball
Change
Breaking

4.65 ERA. Normally we'd jump at a one-run discount to ERA, but we don't like aches that hog the conversation. Reserve him and then try never to need him. —

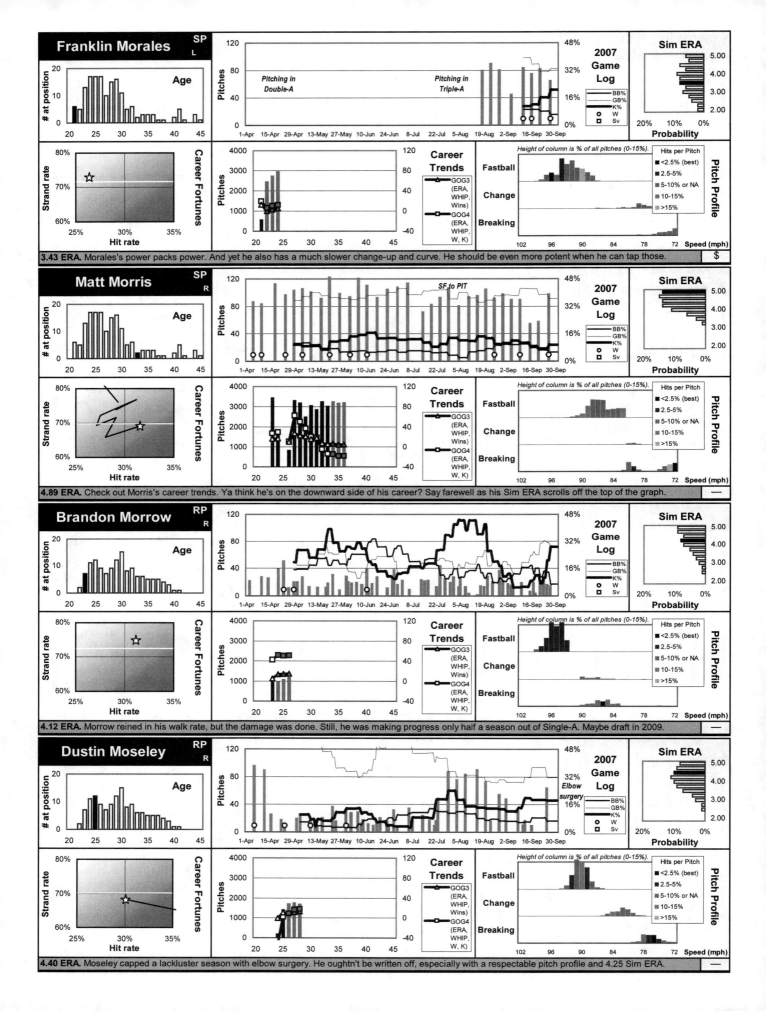

Franklin Morales SP L

3.43 ERA. Morales's power packs power. And yet he also has a much slower change-up and curve. He should be even more potent when he can tap those. **$**

Matt Morris SP R

4.89 ERA. Check out Morris's career trends. Ya think he's on the downward side of his career? Say farewell as his Sim ERA scrolls off the top of the graph. **—**

Brandon Morrow RP R

4.12 ERA. Morrow reined in his walk rate, but the damage was done. Still, he was making progress only half a season out of Single-A. Maybe draft in 2009. **—**

Dustin Moseley RP R

4.40 ERA. Moseley capped a lackluster season with elbow surgery. He oughtn't be written off, especially with a respectable pitch profile and 4.25 Sim ERA. **—**

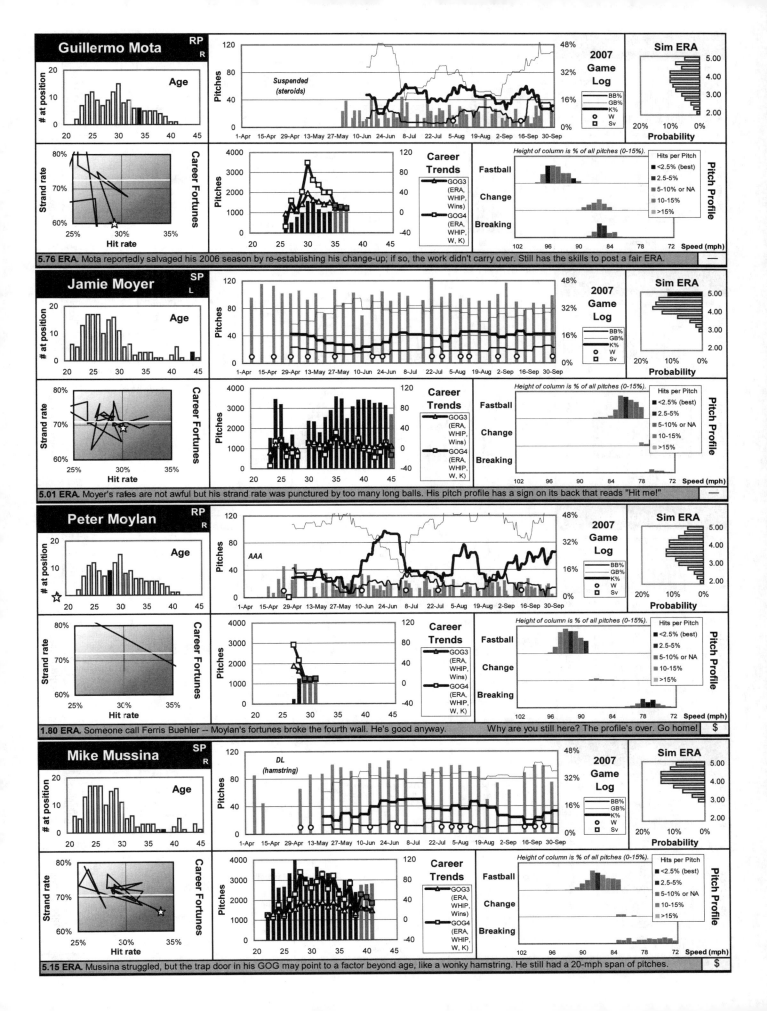

Guillermo Mota RP R

Age

2007 Game Log

Sim ERA

Suspended (steroids)

BB%
GB%
K%
○ W
□ Sv

Career Fortunes

Strand rate / Hit rate

Career Trends

GOG3 (ERA, WHIP, Wins)
GOG4 (ERA, WHIP, W, K)

Height of column is % of all pitches (0-15%)

Fastball
Change
Breaking

Hits per Pitch
■ <2.5% (best)
■ 2.5-5%
■ 5-10% or NA
■ 10-15%
■ >15%

Pitch Profile

Speed (mph)

5.76 ERA. Mota reportedly salvaged his 2006 season by re-establishing his change-up; if so, the work didn't carry over. Still has the skills to post a fair ERA. —

Jamie Moyer SP L

Age

2007 Game Log

Sim ERA

BB%
GB%
K%
○ W
□ Sv

Career Fortunes

Strand rate / Hit rate

Career Trends

GOG3 (ERA, WHIP, Wins)
GOG4 (ERA, WHIP, W, K)

Height of column is % of all pitches (0-15%)

Fastball
Change
Breaking

Hits per Pitch
■ <2.5% (best)
■ 2.5-5%
■ 5-10% or NA
■ 10-15%
■ >15%

Pitch Profile

Speed (mph)

5.01 ERA. Moyer's rates are not awful but his strand rate was punctured by too many long balls. His pitch profile has a sign on its back that reads "Hit me!" —

Peter Moylan RP R

Age

2007 Game Log

Sim ERA

AAA

BB%
GB%
K%
○ W
□ Sv

Career Fortunes

Strand rate / Hit rate

Career Trends

GOG3 (ERA, WHIP, Wins)
GOG4 (ERA, WHIP, W, K)

Height of column is % of all pitches (0-15%)

Fastball
Change
Breaking

Hits per Pitch
■ <2.5% (best)
■ 2.5-5%
■ 5-10% or NA
■ 10-15%
■ >15%

Pitch Profile

Speed (mph)

1.80 ERA. Someone call Ferris Buehler -- Moylan's fortunes broke the fourth wall. He's good anyway. Why are you still here? The profile's over. Go home! $

Mike Mussina SP R

Age

2007 Game Log

Sim ERA

DL (hamstring)

BB%
GB%
K%
○ W
□ Sv

Career Fortunes

Strand rate / Hit rate

Career Trends

GOG3 (ERA, WHIP, Wins)
GOG4 (ERA, WHIP, W, K)

Height of column is % of all pitches (0-15%)

Fastball
Change
Breaking

Hits per Pitch
■ <2.5% (best)
■ 2.5-5%
■ 5-10% or NA
■ 10-15%
■ >15%

Pitch Profile

Speed (mph)

5.15 ERA. Mussina struggled, but the trap door in his GOG may point to a factor beyond age, like a wonky hamstring. He still had a 20-mph span of pitches. $

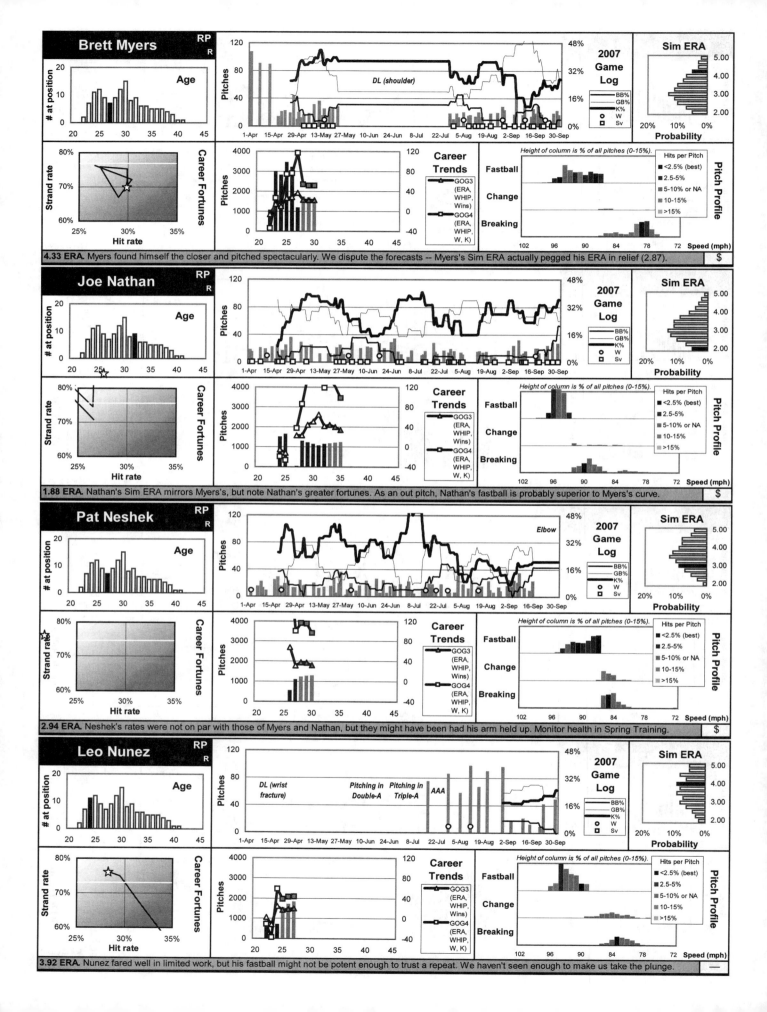

Brett Myers RP R

Age

at position

Sim ERA

2007 Game Log

BB%
GB%
K%
W
Sv

DL (shoulder)

Strand rate — Hit rate — Career Fortunes

Career Trends
GOG3 (ERA, WHIP, Wins)
GOG4 (ERA, WHIP, W, K)

Pitch Profile
Height of column is % of all pitches (0-15%).
Fastball
Change
Breaking

Hits per Pitch
<2.5% (best)
2.5-5%
5-10% or NA
10-15%
>15%

Speed (mph)

4.33 ERA. Myers found himself the closer and pitched spectacularly. We dispute the forecasts -- Myers's Sim ERA actually pegged his ERA in relief (2.87). $

Joe Nathan RP R

Age

Sim ERA

2007 Game Log

BB%
GB%
K%
W
Sv

Strand rate — Hit rate — Career Fortunes

Career Trends
GOG3 (ERA, WHIP, Wins)
GOG4 (ERA, WHIP, W, K)

Pitch Profile
Height of column is % of all pitches (0-15%).
Fastball
Change
Breaking

Hits per Pitch
<2.5% (best)
2.5-5%
5-10% or NA
10-15%
>15%

Speed (mph)

1.88 ERA. Nathan's Sim ERA mirrors Myers's, but note Nathan's greater fortunes. As an out pitch, Nathan's fastball is probably superior to Myers's curve. $

Pat Neshek RP R

Age

Sim ERA

2007 Game Log

BB%
GB%
K%
W
Sv

Elbow

Strand rate — Hit rate — Career Fortunes

Career Trends
GOG3 (ERA, WHIP, Wins)
GOG4 (ERA, WHIP, W, K)

Pitch Profile
Height of column is % of all pitches (0-15%).
Fastball
Change
Breaking

Hits per Pitch
<2.5% (best)
2.5-5%
5-10% or NA
10-15%
>15%

Speed (mph)

2.94 ERA. Neshek's rates were not on par with those of Myers and Nathan, but they might have been had his arm held up. Monitor health in Spring Training. $

Leo Nunez RP R

Age

Sim ERA

2007 Game Log

BB%
GB%
K%
W
Sv

DL (wrist fracture)   Pitching in Double-A   Pitching in Triple-A   AAA

Strand rate — Hit rate — Career Fortunes

Career Trends
GOG3 (ERA, WHIP, Wins)
GOG4 (ERA, WHIP, W, K)

Pitch Profile
Height of column is % of all pitches (0-15%).
Fastball
Change
Breaking

Hits per Pitch
<2.5% (best)
2.5-5%
5-10% or NA
10-15%
>15%

Speed (mph)

3.92 ERA. Nunez fared well in limited work, but his fastball might not be potent enough to trust a repeat. We haven't seen enough to make us take the plunge. —

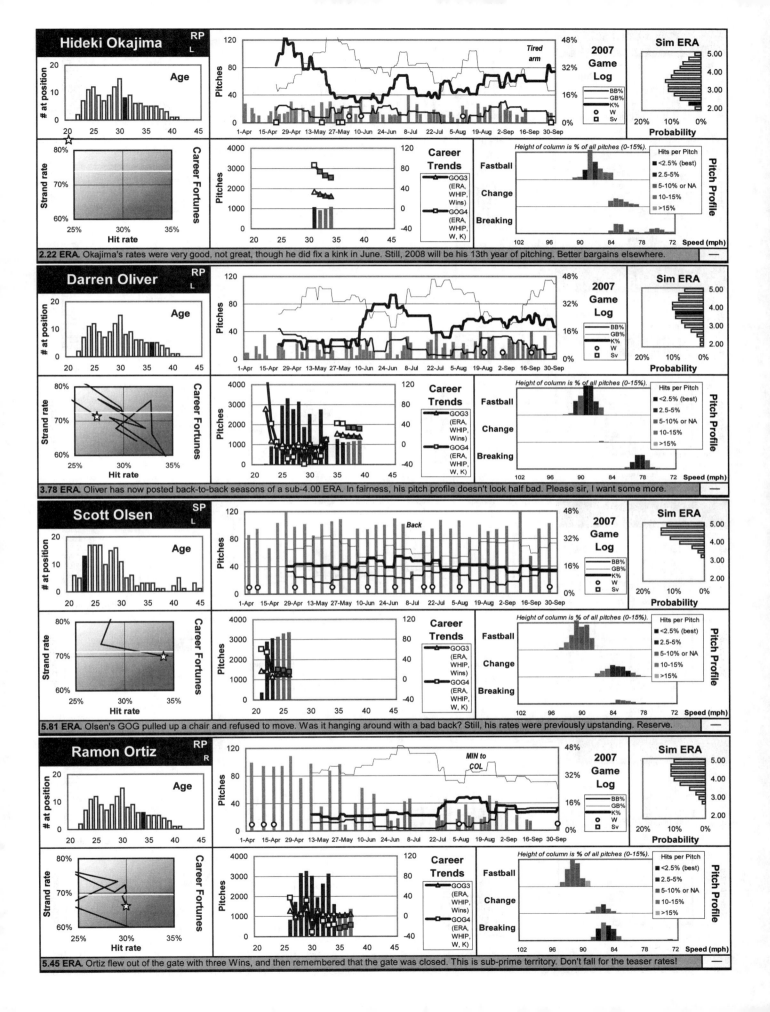

Hideki Okajima RP L

Age | Career Fortunes | 2007 Game Log | Sim ERA | Career Trends | Pitch Profile

2.22 ERA. Okajima's rates were very good, not great, though he did fix a kink in June. Still, 2008 will be his 13th year of pitching. Better bargains elsewhere. —

Darren Oliver RP L

3.78 ERA. Oliver has now posted back-to-back seasons of a sub-4.00 ERA. In fairness, his pitch profile doesn't look half bad. Please sir, I want some more. —

Scott Olsen SP L

5.81 ERA. Olsen's GOG pulled up a chair and refused to move. Was it hanging around with a bad back? Still, his rates were previously upstanding. Reserve. —

Ramon Ortiz RP R

5.45 ERA. Ortiz flew out of the gate with three Wins, and then remembered that the gate was closed. This is sub-prime territory. Don't fall for the teaser rates! —

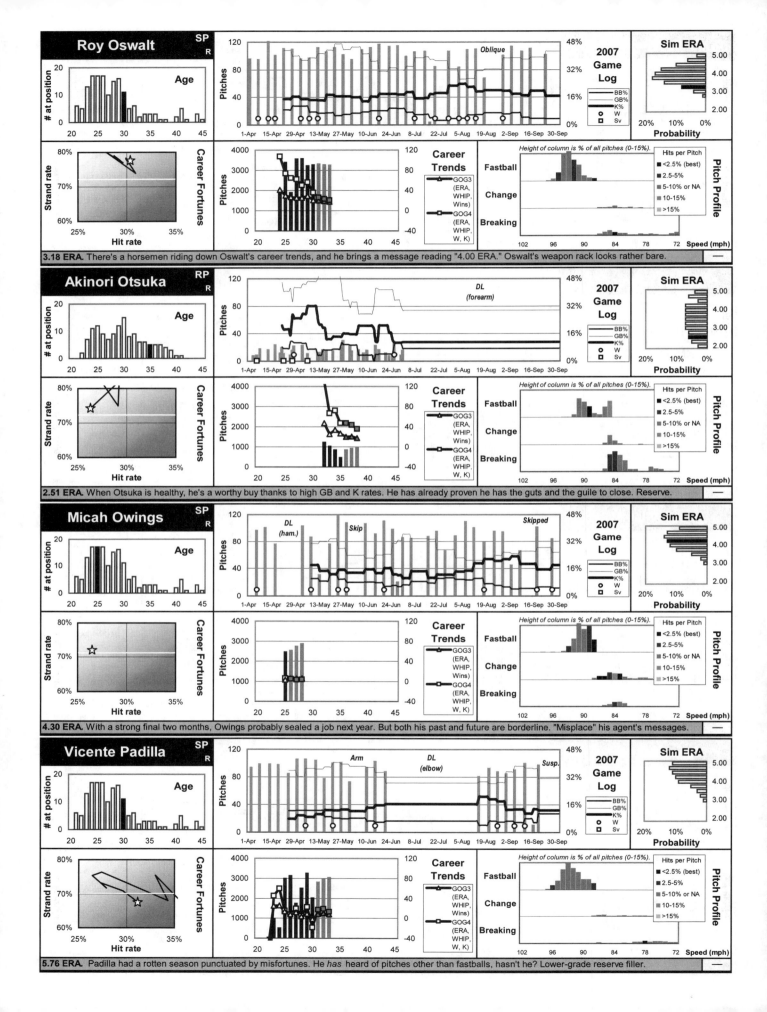

Roy Oswalt — SP / R

2007 Game Log — Oblique
Sim ERA
Career Fortunes — Strand rate / Hit rate
Career Trends — GOG3 (ERA, WHIP, Wins), GOG4 (ERA, WHIP, W, K)
Pitch Profile — Fastball, Change, Breaking. Height of column is % of all pitches (0-15%). Hits per Pitch: <2.5% (best), 2.5-5%, 5-10% or NA, 10-15%, >15%

3.18 ERA. There's a horsemen riding down Oswalt's career trends, and he brings a message reading "4.00 ERA." Oswalt's weapon rack looks rather bare.

Akinori Otsuka — RP / R

2007 Game Log — DL (forearm)
Sim ERA

2.51 ERA. When Otsuka is healthy, he's a worthy buy thanks to high GB and K rates. He has already proven he has the guts and the guile to close. Reserve.

Micah Owings — SP / R

2007 Game Log — DL (ham.), Skip, Skipped
Sim ERA

4.30 ERA. With a strong final two months, Owings probably sealed a job next year. But both his past and future are borderline. "Misplace" his agent's messages.

Vicente Padilla — SP / R

2007 Game Log — Arm, DL (elbow), Susp.
Sim ERA

5.76 ERA. Padilla had a rotten season punctuated by misfortunes. He *has* heard of pitches other than fastballs, hasn't he? Lower-grade reserve filler.

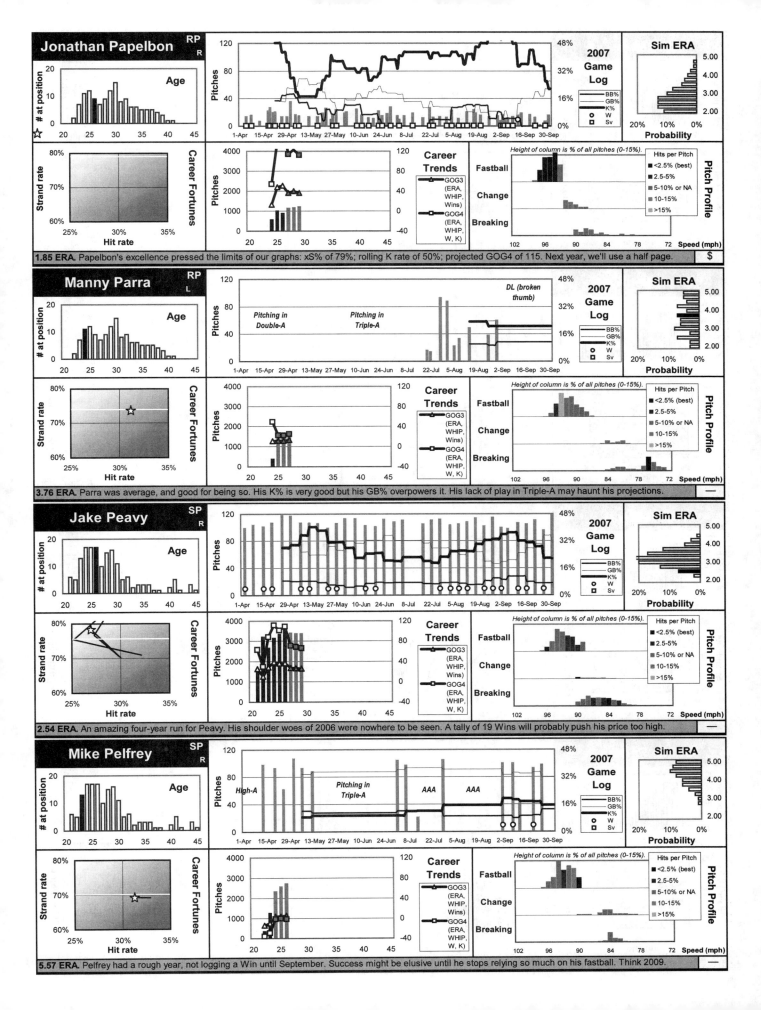

Jonathan Papelbon RP R

Age

at position

Pitches / 2007 Game Log / Sim ERA

BB% / GB% / K% / W / Sv

Strand rate / Hit rate / Career Fortunes

Career Trends / GOG3 (ERA, WHIP, Wins) / GOG4 (ERA, WHIP, W, K)

Pitch Profile — Height of column is % of all pitches (0-15%).
Fastball / Change / Breaking
Hits per Pitch: <2.5% (best) / 2.5-5% / 5-10% or NA / 10-15% / >15%
Speed (mph)

1.85 ERA. Papelbon's excellence pressed the limits of our graphs: xS% of 79%; rolling K rate of 50%; projected GOG4 of 115. Next year, we'll use a half page. $

Manny Parra RP L

Age

Pitches / 2007 Game Log / Sim ERA

DL (broken thumb)
Pitching in Double-A / Pitching in Triple-A

BB% / GB% / K% / W / Sv

Strand rate / Hit rate / Career Fortunes

Career Trends / GOG3 (ERA, WHIP, Wins) / GOG4 (ERA, WHIP, W, K)

Pitch Profile — Height of column is % of all pitches (0-15%).
Fastball / Change / Breaking
Hits per Pitch: <2.5% (best) / 2.5-5% / 5-10% or NA / 10-15% / >15%
Speed (mph)

3.76 ERA. Parra was average, and good for being so. His K% is very good but his GB% overpowers it. His lack of play in Triple-A may haunt his projections. —

Jake Peavy SP R

Age

Pitches / 2007 Game Log / Sim ERA

BB% / GB% / K% / W / Sv

Strand rate / Hit rate / Career Fortunes

Career Trends / GOG3 (ERA, WHIP, Wins) / GOG4 (ERA, WHIP, W, K)

Pitch Profile — Height of column is % of all pitches (0-15%).
Fastball / Change / Breaking
Hits per Pitch: <2.5% (best) / 2.5-5% / 5-10% or NA / 10-15% / >15%
Speed (mph)

2.54 ERA. An amazing four-year run for Peavy. His shoulder woes of 2006 were nowhere to be seen. A tally of 19 Wins will probably push his price too high. —

Mike Pelfrey SP R

Age

Pitches / 2007 Game Log / Sim ERA

High-A / Pitching in Triple-A / AAA / AAA

BB% / GB% / K% / W / Sv

Strand rate / Hit rate / Career Fortunes

Career Trends / GOG3 (ERA, WHIP, Wins) / GOG4 (ERA, WHIP, W, K)

Pitch Profile — Height of column is % of all pitches (0-15%).
Fastball / Change / Breaking
Hits per Pitch: <2.5% (best) / 2.5-5% / 5-10% or NA / 10-15% / >15%
Speed (mph)

5.57 ERA. Pelfrey had a rough year, not logging a Win until September. Success might be elusive until he stops relying so much on his fastball. Think 2009. —

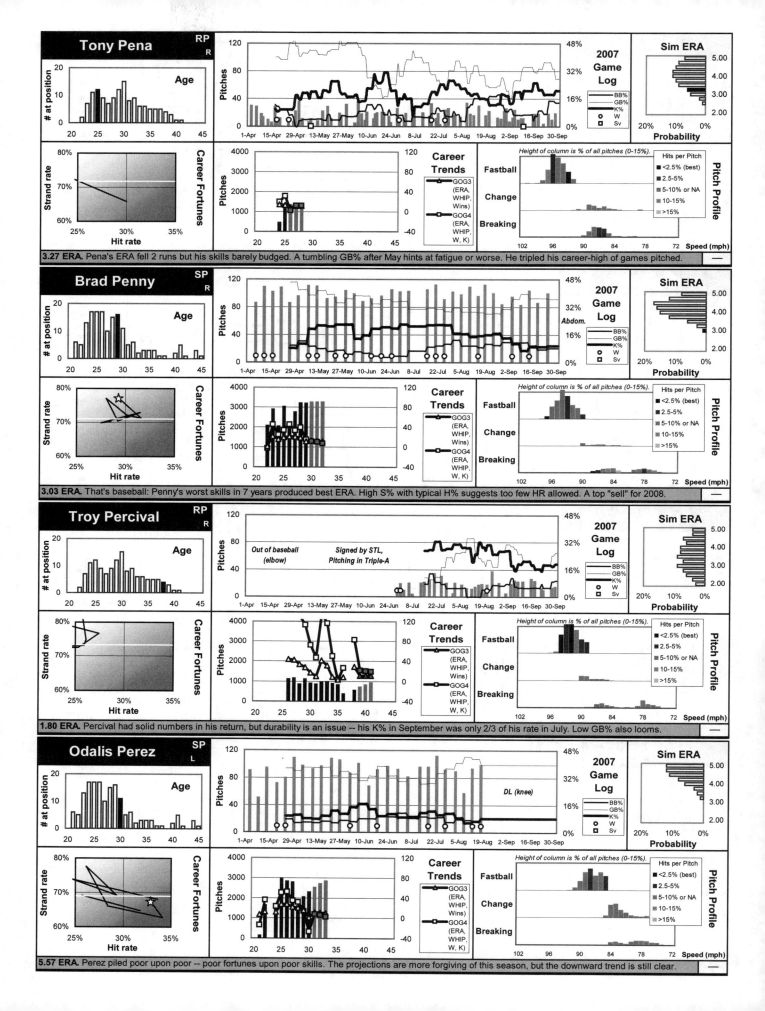

Tony Pena
RP / R

Age — # at position

Pitches — 2007 Game Log — BB%, GB%, K%, W, Sv

Sim ERA — Probability

Strand rate / **Hit rate** — Career Fortunes

Career Trends — GOG3 (ERA, WHIP, Wins), GOG4 (ERA, WHIP, W, K)

Pitch Profile — Height of column is % of all pitches (0-15%). Hits per Pitch: <2.5% (best), 2.5-5%, 5-10% or NA, 10-15%, >15%. Fastball, Change, Breaking — Speed (mph)

3.27 ERA. Pena's ERA fell 2 runs but his skills barely budged. A tumbling GB% after May hints at fatigue or worse. He tripled his career-high of games pitched.

Brad Penny
SP / R

Age — # at position

Pitches — 2007 Game Log — *Abdom.* — BB%, GB%, K%, W, Sv

Sim ERA — Probability

Strand rate / **Hit rate** — Career Fortunes

Career Trends — GOG3 (ERA, WHIP, Wins), GOG4 (ERA, WHIP, W, K)

Pitch Profile — Height of column is % of all pitches (0-15%). Hits per Pitch: <2.5% (best), 2.5-5%, 5-10% or NA, 10-15%, >15%. Fastball, Change, Breaking — Speed (mph)

3.03 ERA. That's baseball: Penny's worst skills in 7 years produced best ERA. High S% with typical H% suggests too few HR allowed. A top "sell" for 2008.

Troy Percival
RP / R

Age — # at position

Pitches — 2007 Game Log — *Out of baseball (elbow)* — *Signed by STL, Pitching in Triple-A* — BB%, GB%, K%, W, Sv

Sim ERA — Probability

Strand rate / **Hit rate** — Career Fortunes

Career Trends — GOG3 (ERA, WHIP, Wins), GOG4 (ERA, WHIP, W, K)

Pitch Profile — Height of column is % of all pitches (0-15%). Hits per Pitch: <2.5% (best), 2.5-5%, 5-10% or NA, 10-15%, >15%. Fastball, Change, Breaking — Speed (mph)

1.80 ERA. Percival had solid numbers in his return, but durability is an issue -- his K% in September was only 2/3 of his rate in July. Low GB% also looms.

Odalis Perez
SP / L

Age — # at position

Pitches — 2007 Game Log — *DL (knee)* — BB%, GB%, K%, W, Sv

Sim ERA — Probability

Strand rate / **Hit rate** — Career Fortunes

Career Trends — GOG3 (ERA, WHIP, Wins), GOG4 (ERA, WHIP, W, K)

Pitch Profile — Height of column is % of all pitches (0-15%). Hits per Pitch: <2.5% (best), 2.5-5%, 5-10% or NA, 10-15%, >15%. Fastball, Change, Breaking — Speed (mph)

5.57 ERA. Perez piled poor upon poor -- poor fortunes upon poor skills. The projections are more forgiving of this season, but the downward trend is still clear.

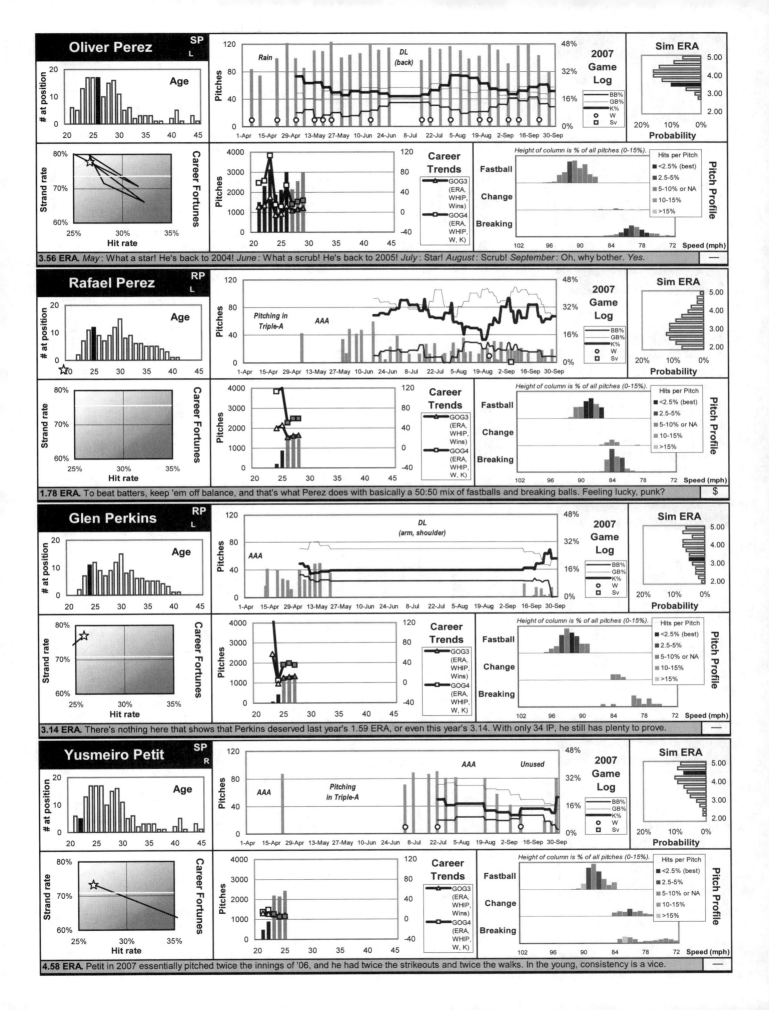

Oliver Perez SP L

at position — Age
Sim ERA
2007 Game Log
BB% GB% K% W Sv

Strand rate — Career Fortunes
Hit rate
Career Trends
GOG3 (ERA, WHIP, Wins)
GOG4 (ERA, WHIP, W, K)

Pitch Profile
Height of column is % of all pitches (0-15%)
Hits per Pitch: <2.5% (best), 2.5-5%, 5-10% or NA, 10-15%, >15%
Fastball / Change / Breaking
Speed (mph)

3.56 ERA. *May*: What a star! He's back to 2004! *June*: What a scrub! He's back to 2005! *July*: Star! *August*: Scrub! *September*: Oh, why bother. *Yes.* —

Rafael Perez RP L

at position — Age
Sim ERA
2007 Game Log

Strand rate — Career Fortunes
Career Trends
Pitch Profile

1.78 ERA. To beat batters, keep 'em off balance, and that's what Perez does with basically a 50:50 mix of fastballs and breaking balls. Feeling lucky, punk? $

Glen Perkins RP L

at position — Age
Sim ERA
2007 Game Log

Strand rate — Career Fortunes
Career Trends
Pitch Profile

3.14 ERA. There's nothing here that shows that Perkins deserved last year's 1.59 ERA, or even this year's 3.14. With only 34 IP, he still has plenty to prove. —

Yusmeiro Petit SP R

at position — Age
Sim ERA
2007 Game Log

Strand rate — Career Fortunes
Career Trends
Pitch Profile

4.58 ERA. Petit in 2007 essentially pitched twice the innings of '06, and he had twice the strikeouts and twice the walks. In the young, consistency is a vice. —

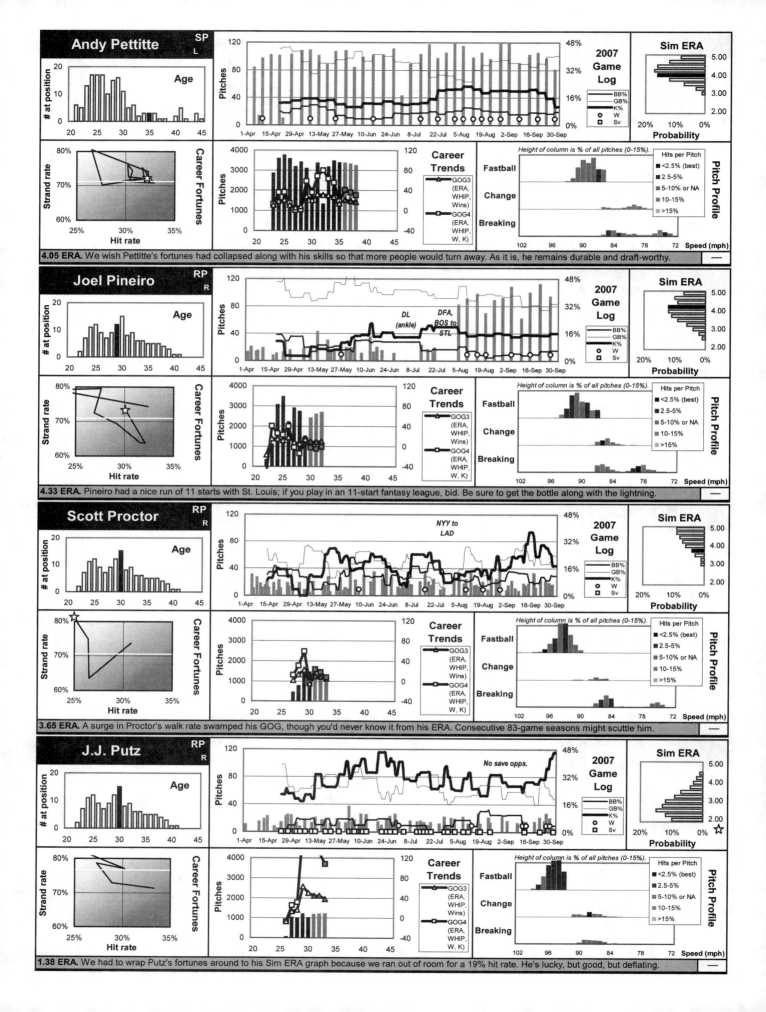

Andy Pettitte SP L

4.05 ERA. We wish Pettitte's fortunes had collapsed along with his skills so that more people would turn away. As it is, he remains durable and draft-worthy. —

Joel Pineiro RP R

4.33 ERA. Pineiro had a nice run of 11 starts with St. Louis; if you play in an 11-start fantasy league, bid. Be sure to get the bottle along with the lightning. —

Scott Proctor RP R

3.65 ERA. A surge in Proctor's walk rate swamped his GOG, though you'd never know it from his ERA. Consecutive 83-game seasons might scuttle him. —

J.J. Putz RP R

1.38 ERA. We had to wrap Putz's fortunes around to his Sim ERA graph because we ran out of room for a 19% hit rate. He's lucky, but good, but deflating. —

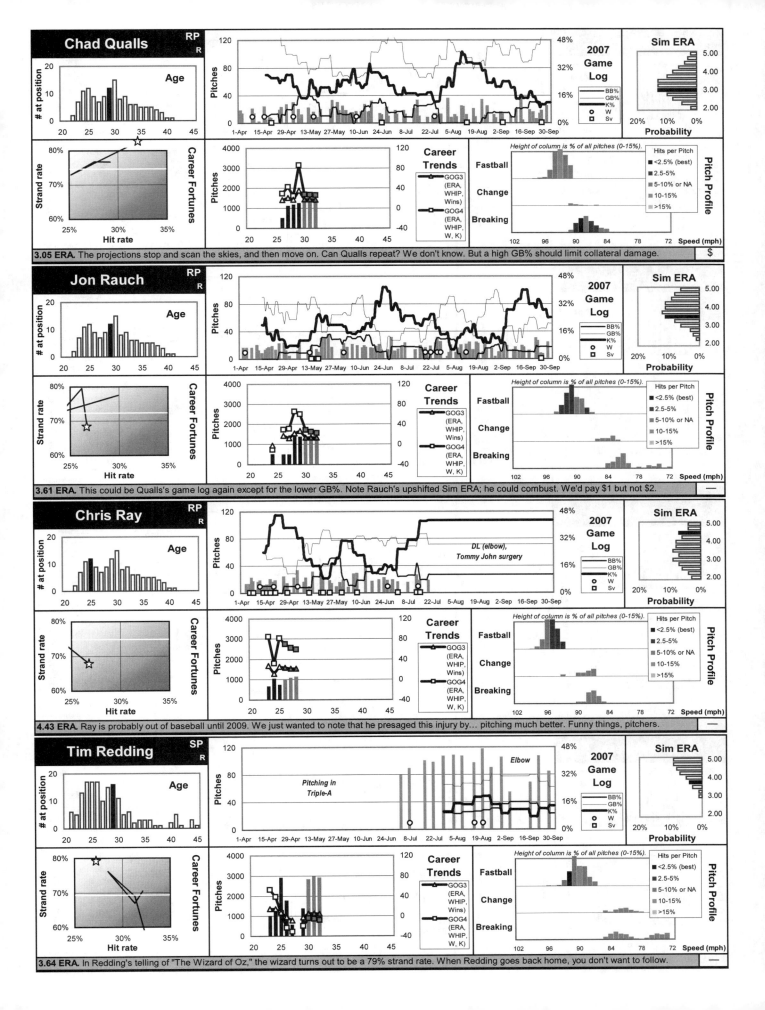

Chad Qualls — RP, R

3.05 ERA. The projections stop and scan the skies, and then move on. Can Qualls repeat? We don't know. But a high GB% should limit collateral damage. $

Jon Rauch — RP, R

3.61 ERA. This could be Qualls's game log again except for the lower GB%. Note Rauch's upshifted Sim ERA; he could combust. We'd pay $1 but not $2. —

Chris Ray — RP, R

DL (elbow), Tommy John surgery

4.43 ERA. Ray is probably out of baseball until 2009. We just wanted to note that he presaged this injury by… pitching much better. Funny things, pitchers. —

Tim Redding — SP, R

Pitching in Triple-A

Elbow

3.64 ERA. In Redding's telling of "The Wizard of Oz," the wizard turns out to be a 79% strand rate. When Redding goes back home, you don't want to follow. —

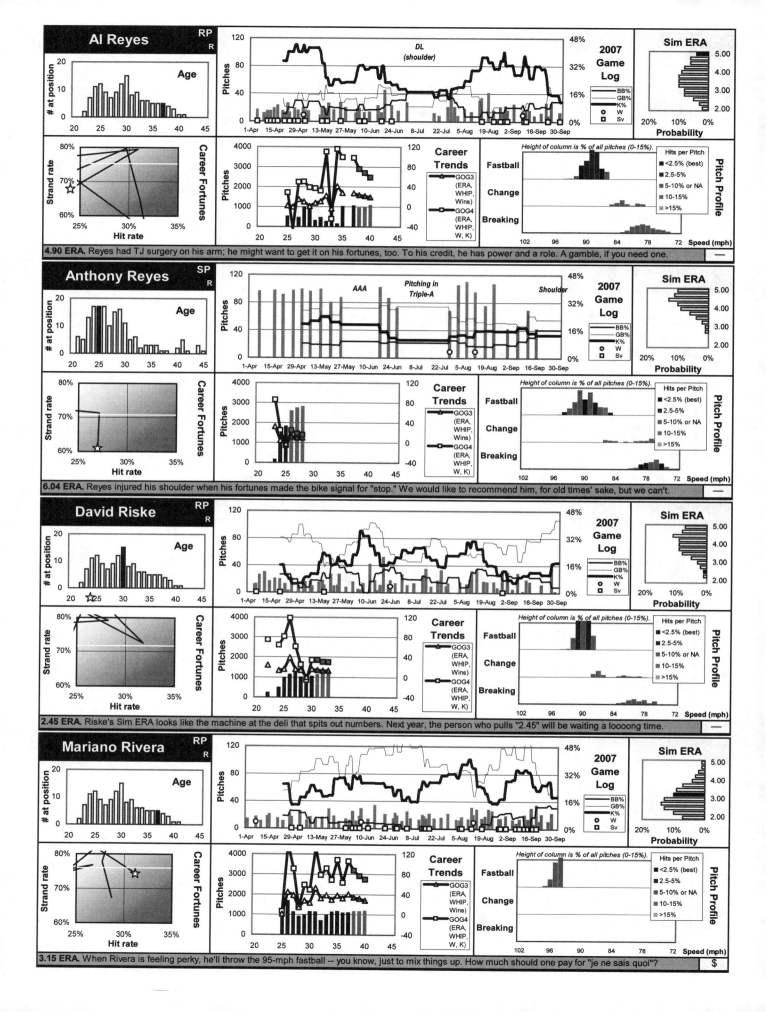

Al Reyes — RP R

4.90 ERA. Reyes had TJ surgery on his arm; he might want to get it on his fortunes, too. To his credit, he has power and a role. A gamble, if you need one. —

Anthony Reyes — SP R

6.04 ERA. Reyes injured his shoulder when his fortunes made the bike signal for "stop." We would like to recommend him, for old times' sake, but we can't. —

David Riske — RP R

2.45 ERA. Riske's Sim ERA looks like the machine at the deli that spits out numbers. Next year, the person who pulls "2.45" will be waiting a looooong time. —

Mariano Rivera — RP R

3.15 ERA. When Rivera is feeling perky, he'll throw the 95-mph fastball -- you know, just to mix things up. How much should one pay for "je ne sais quoi"? $

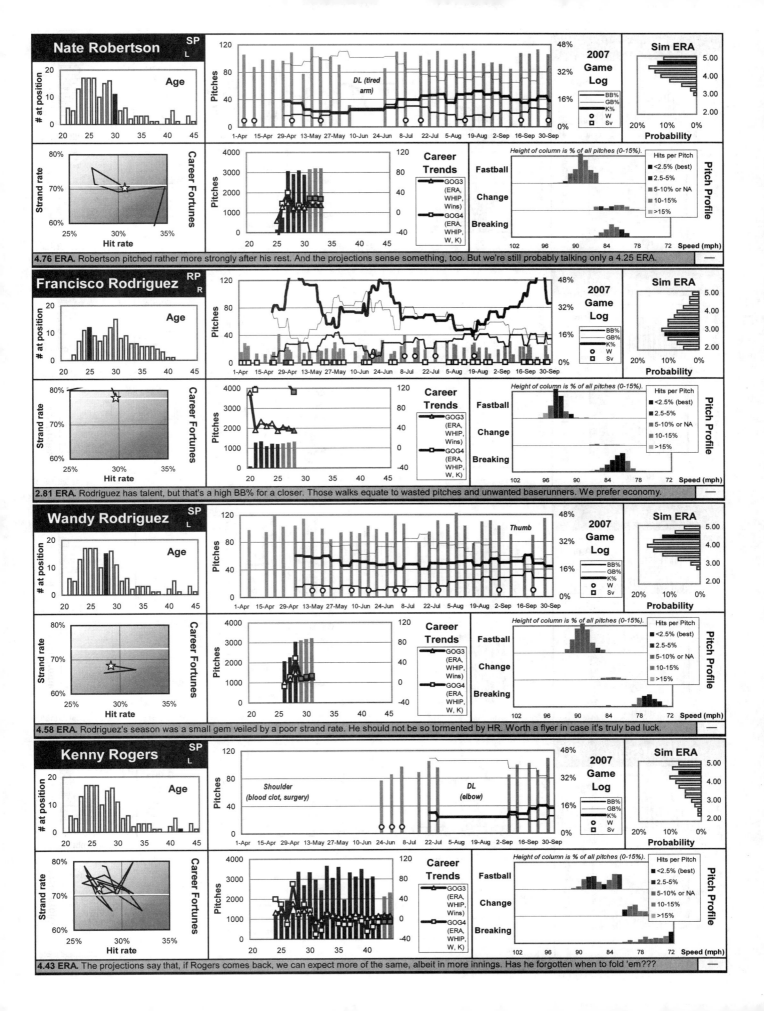

Nate Robertson SP L

4.76 ERA. Robertson pitched rather more strongly after his rest. And the projections sense something, too. But we're still probably talking only a 4.25 ERA. —

Francisco Rodriguez RP R

2.81 ERA. Rodriguez has talent, but that's a high BB% for a closer. Those walks equate to wasted pitches and unwanted baserunners. We prefer economy. —

Wandy Rodriguez SP L

4.58 ERA. Rodriguez's season was a small gem veiled by a poor strand rate. He should not be so tormented by HR. Worth a flyer in case it's truly bad luck. —

Kenny Rogers SP L

4.43 ERA. The projections say that, if Rogers comes back, we can expect more of the same, albeit in more innings. Has he forgotten when to fold 'em??? —

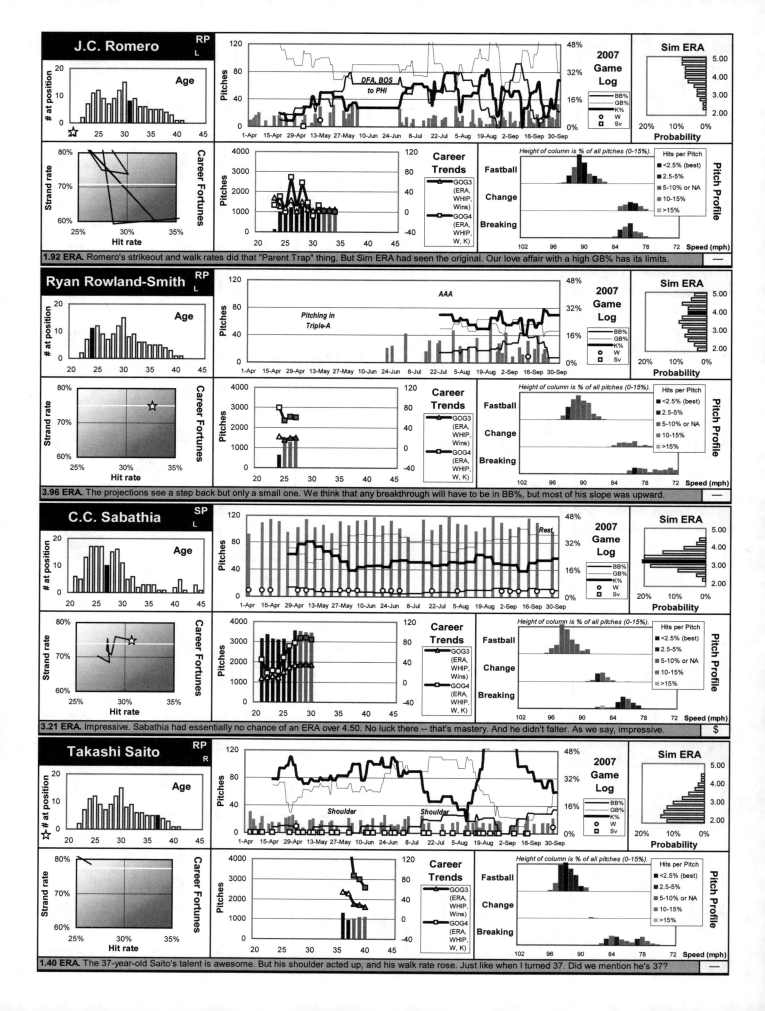

J.C. Romero RP L

Age

at position

Strand rate / Hit rate / Career Fortunes

Pitches / 2007 Game Log (BB%, GB%, K%, W, Sv) — DFA, BOS to PHI

Sim ERA / Probability

Career Trends — GOG3 (ERA, WHIP, Wins) / GOG4 (ERA, WHIP, W, K)

Pitch Profile — Height of column is % of all pitches (0-15%). Hits per Pitch: <2.5% (best), 2.5-5%, 5-10% or NA, 10-15%, >15%. Fastball, Change, Breaking / Speed (mph)

1.92 ERA. Romero's strikeout and walk rates did that "Parent Trap" thing. But Sim ERA had seen the original. Our love affair with a high GB% has its limits. —

Ryan Rowland-Smith RP L

Age

at position

Pitches / 2007 Game Log — Pitching in Triple-A — AAA

Sim ERA / Probability

Strand rate / Hit rate / Career Fortunes

Career Trends — GOG3 (ERA, WHIP, Wins) / GOG4 (ERA, WHIP, W, K)

Pitch Profile — Height of column is % of all pitches (0-15%). Hits per Pitch: <2.5% (best), 2.5-5%, 5-10% or NA, 10-15%, >15%. Fastball, Change, Breaking / Speed (mph)

3.96 ERA. The projections see a step back but only a small one. We think that any breakthrough will have to be in BB%, but most of his slope was upward. —

C.C. Sabathia SP L

Age

at position

Pitches / 2007 Game Log — Rest

Sim ERA / Probability

Strand rate / Hit rate / Career Fortunes

Career Trends — GOG3 (ERA, WHIP, Wins) / GOG4 (ERA, WHIP, W, K)

Pitch Profile — Height of column is % of all pitches (0-15%). Hits per Pitch: <2.5% (best), 2.5-5%, 5-10% or NA, 10-15%, >15%. Fastball, Change, Breaking / Speed (mph)

3.21 ERA. Impressive. Sabathia had essentially no chance of an ERA over 4.50. No luck there -- that's mastery. And he didn't falter. As we say, impressive. $

Takashi Saito RP R

Age

at position

Pitches / 2007 Game Log — Shoulder — Shoulder

Sim ERA / Probability

Strand rate / Hit rate / Career Fortunes

Career Trends — GOG3 (ERA, WHIP, Wins) / GOG4 (ERA, WHIP, W, K)

Pitch Profile — Height of column is % of all pitches (0-15%). Hits per Pitch: <2.5% (best), 2.5-5%, 5-10% or NA, 10-15%, >15%. Fastball, Change, Breaking / Speed (mph)

1.40 ERA. The 37-year-old Saito's talent is awesome. But his shoulder acted up, and his walk rate rose. Just like when I turned 37. Did we mention he's 37? —

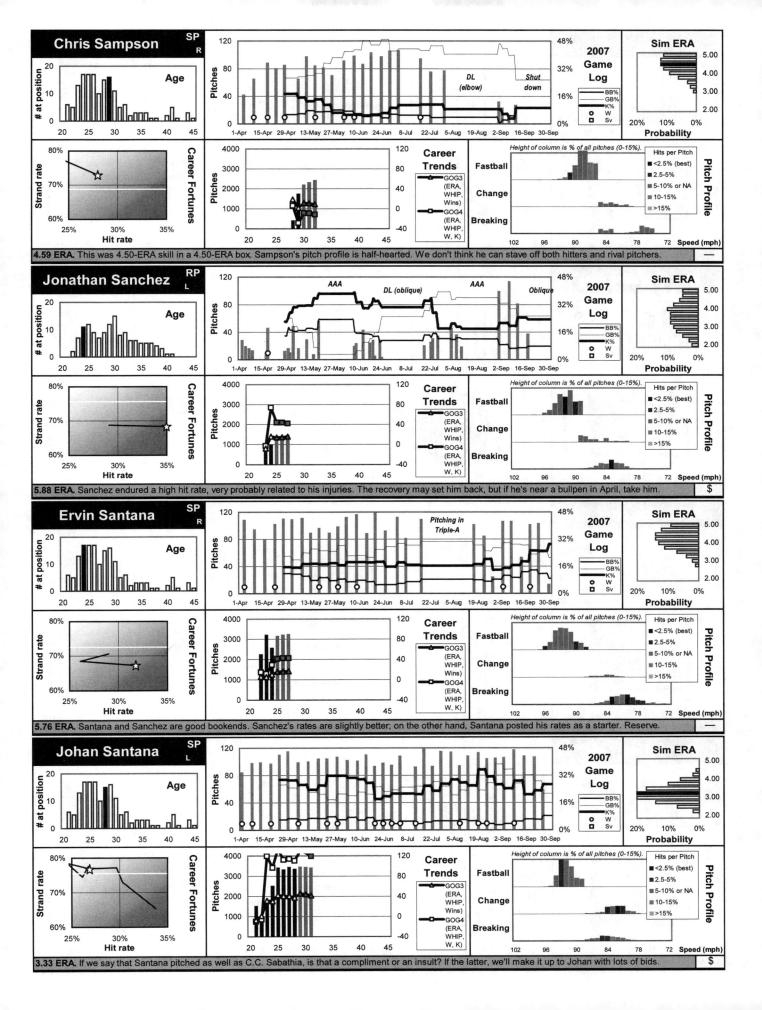

Chris Sampson — SP R

2007 Game Log

Sim ERA

Career Trends — GOG3 (ERA, WHIP, Wins), GOG4 (ERA, WHIP, W, K)

Pitch Profile — Height of column is % of all pitches (0-15%). Hits per Pitch: <2.5% (best), 2.5-5%, 5-10% or NA, 10-15%, >15%

DL (elbow) — Shut down

4.59 ERA. This was 4.50-ERA skill in a 4.50-ERA box. Sampson's pitch profile is half-hearted. We don't think he can stave off both hitters and rival pitchers. —

Jonathan Sanchez — RP L

AAA — DL (oblique) — AAA — Oblique

2007 Game Log

Sim ERA

5.88 ERA. Sanchez endured a high hit rate, very probably related to his injuries. The recovery may set him back, but if he's near a bullpen in April, take him. $

Ervin Santana — SP R

Pitching in Triple-A

2007 Game Log

Sim ERA

5.76 ERA. Santana and Sanchez are good bookends. Sanchez's rates are slightly better; on the other hand, Santana posted his rates as a starter. Reserve. —

Johan Santana — SP L

2007 Game Log

Sim ERA

3.33 ERA. If we say that Santana pitched as well as C.C. Sabathia, is that a compliment or an insult? If the latter, we'll make it up to Johan with lots of bids. $

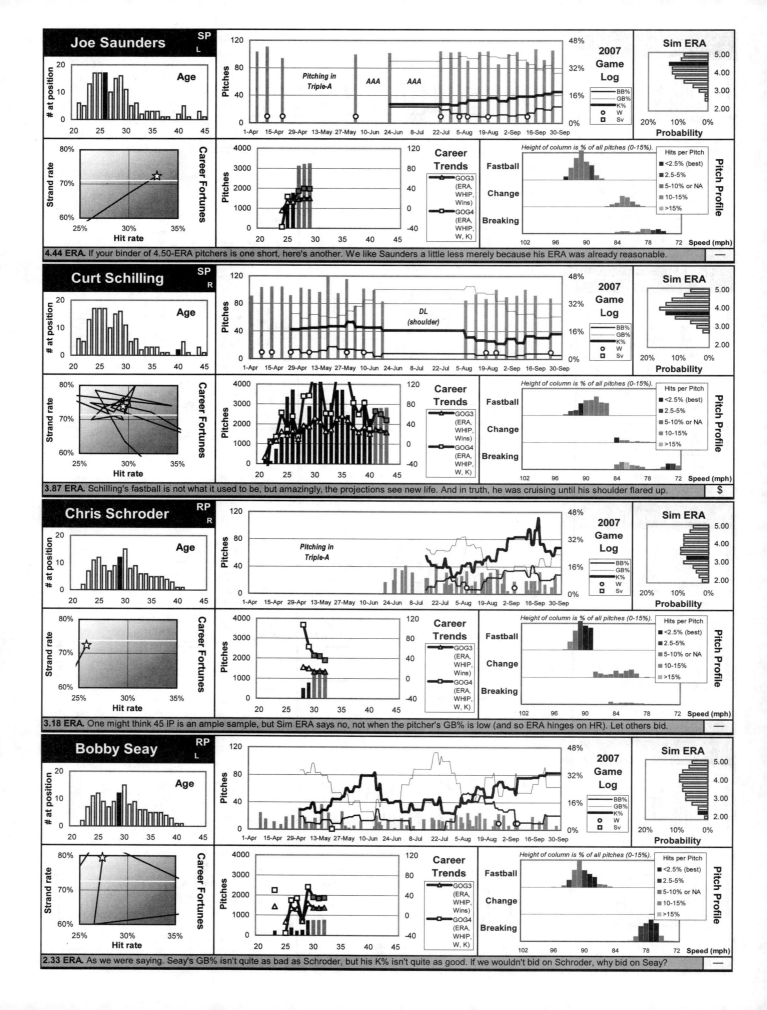

Joe Saunders — SP L

Age — # at position (20–45)

2007 Game Log — Pitches (0–120), BB%, GB%, K%, W, Sv (0%–48%)
Pitching in Triple-A — AAA — AAA

Sim ERA — Probability (20% 10% 0%)

Career Fortunes — Strand rate (60%–80%) vs Hit rate (25%–35%)

Career Trends — Pitches, GOG3 (ERA, WHIP, Wins), GOG4 (ERA, WHIP, W, K)

Pitch Profile — Height of column is % of all pitches (0-15%). Hits per Pitch: <2.5% (best), 2.5-5%, 5-10% or NA, 10-15%, >15%. Fastball, Change, Breaking — Speed (mph) 102 96 90 84 78 72

4.44 ERA. If your binder of 4.50-ERA pitchers is one short, here's another. We like Saunders a little less merely because his ERA was already reasonable. —

Curt Schilling — SP R

Age — # at position (20–45)

2007 Game Log — Pitches (0–120), BB%, GB%, K%, W, Sv
DL (shoulder)

Sim ERA — Probability

Career Fortunes — Strand rate vs Hit rate

Career Trends — GOG3 (ERA, WHIP, Wins), GOG4 (ERA, WHIP, W, K)

Pitch Profile — Fastball, Change, Breaking

3.87 ERA. Schilling's fastball is not what it used to be, but amazingly, the projections see new life. And in truth, he was cruising until his shoulder flared up. $

Chris Schroder — RP R

Age — # at position (20–45)

2007 Game Log — Pitches, BB%, GB%, K%, W, Sv
Pitching in Triple-A

Sim ERA — Probability

Career Fortunes — Strand rate vs Hit rate

Career Trends — GOG3 (ERA, WHIP, Wins), GOG4 (ERA, WHIP, W, K)

Pitch Profile — Fastball, Change, Breaking

3.18 ERA. One might think 45 IP is an ample sample, but Sim ERA says no, not when the pitcher's GB% is low (and so ERA hinges on HR). Let others bid. —

Bobby Seay — RP L

Age — # at position (20–45)

2007 Game Log — Pitches, BB%, GB%, K%, W, Sv

Sim ERA — Probability

Career Fortunes — Strand rate vs Hit rate

Career Trends — GOG3 (ERA, WHIP, Wins), GOG4 (ERA, WHIP, W, K)

Pitch Profile — Fastball, Change, Breaking

2.33 ERA. As we were saying. Seay's GB% isn't quite as bad as Schroder, but his K% isn't quite as good. If we wouldn't bid on Schroder, why bid on Seay? —

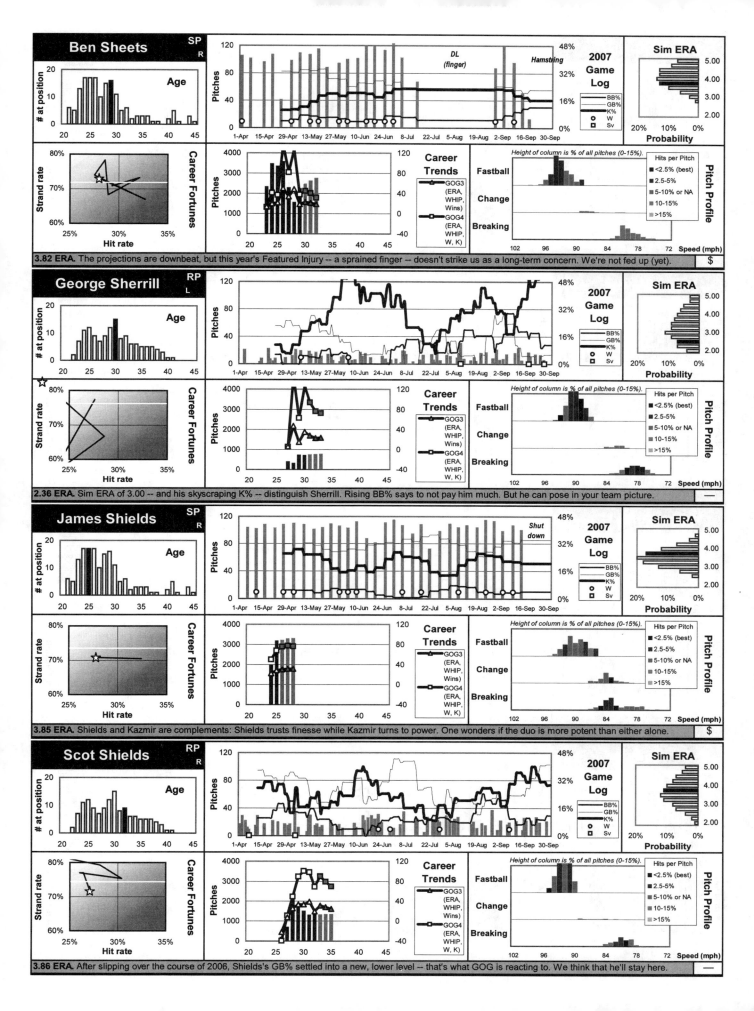

Ben Sheets — SP R

3.82 ERA. The projections are downbeat, but this year's Featured Injury -- a sprained finger -- doesn't strike us as a long-term concern. We're not fed up (yet). $

George Sherrill — RP L

2.36 ERA. Sim ERA of 3.00 -- and his skyscraping K% -- distinguish Sherrill. Rising BB% says to not pay him much. But he can pose in your team picture. —

James Shields — SP R

3.85 ERA. Shields and Kazmir are complements: Shields trusts finesse while Kazmir turns to power. One wonders if the duo is more potent than either alone. $

Scot Shields — RP R

3.86 ERA. After slipping over the course of 2006, Shields's GB% settled into a new, lower level -- that's what GOG is reacting to. We think that he'll stay here. —

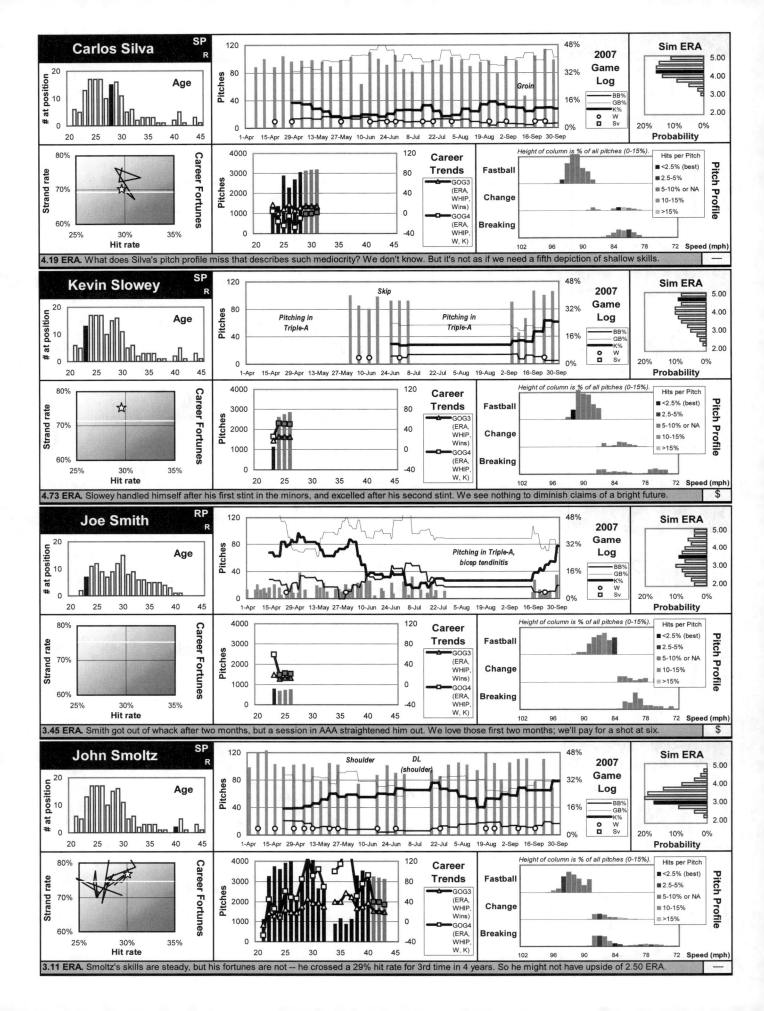

Carlos Silva SP R

Age — # at position

Career Fortunes — Strand rate / Hit rate

2007 Game Log — Pitches — BB%, GB%, K%, W, Sv

Sim ERA — Probability

Career Trends — GOG3 (ERA, WHIP, Wins), GOG4 (ERA, WHIP, W, K)

Pitch Profile — Height of column is % of all pitches (0-15%). Hits per Pitch: <2.5% (best), 2.5-5%, 5-10% or NA, 10-15%, >15%. Fastball, Change, Breaking — Speed (mph)

Groin

4.19 ERA. What does Silva's pitch profile miss that describes such mediocrity? We don't know. But it's not as if we need a fifth depiction of shallow skills. —

Kevin Slowey SP R

Skip

Pitching in Triple-A

Pitching in Triple-A

4.73 ERA. Slowey handled himself after his first stint in the minors, and excelled after his second stint. We see nothing to diminish claims of a bright future. $

Joe Smith RP R

Pitching in Triple-A, bicep tendinitis

3.45 ERA. Smith got out of whack after two months, but a session in AAA straightened him out. We love those first two months; we'll pay for a shot at six. $

John Smoltz SP R

Shoulder

DL (shoulder)

3.11 ERA. Smoltz's skills are steady, but his fortunes are not -- he crossed a 29% hit rate for 3rd time in 4 years. So he might not have upside of 2.50 ERA. —

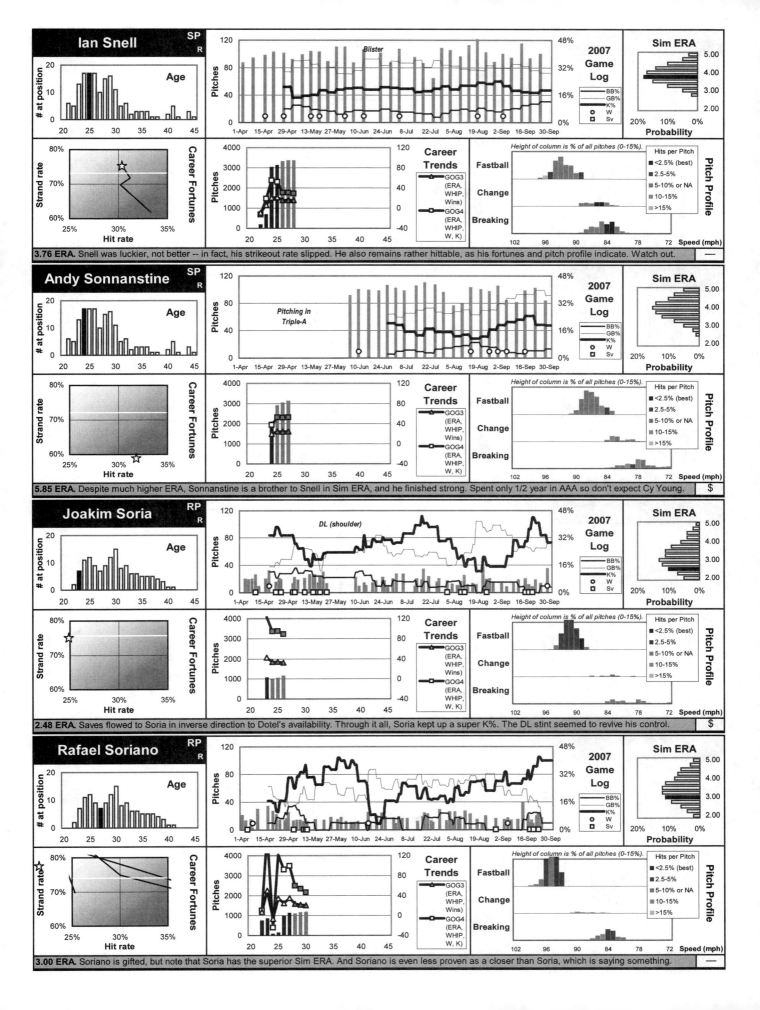

Ian Snell SP R

2007 Game Log

Sim ERA

Career Fortunes

Career Trends — GOG3 (ERA, WHIP, Wins) / GOG4 (ERA, WHIP, W, K)

Pitch Profile — Height of column is % of all pitches (0-15%). Hits per Pitch: <2.5% (best), 2.5-5%, 5-10% or NA, 10-15%, >15%

Blister

3.76 ERA. Snell was luckier, not better -- in fact, his strikeout rate slipped. He also remains rather hittable, as his fortunes and pitch profile indicate. Watch out. —

Andy Sonnanstine SP R

Pitching in Triple-A

5.85 ERA. Despite much higher ERA, Sonnanstine is a brother to Snell in Sim ERA, and he finished strong. Spent only 1/2 year in AAA so don't expect Cy Young. $

Joakim Soria RP R

DL (shoulder)

2.48 ERA. Saves flowed to Soria in inverse direction to Dotel's availability. Through it all, Soria kept up a super K%. The DL stint seemed to revive his control. $

Rafael Soriano RP R

3.00 ERA. Soriano is gifted, but note that Soria has the superior Sim ERA. And Soriano is even less proven as a closer than Soria, which is saying something. —

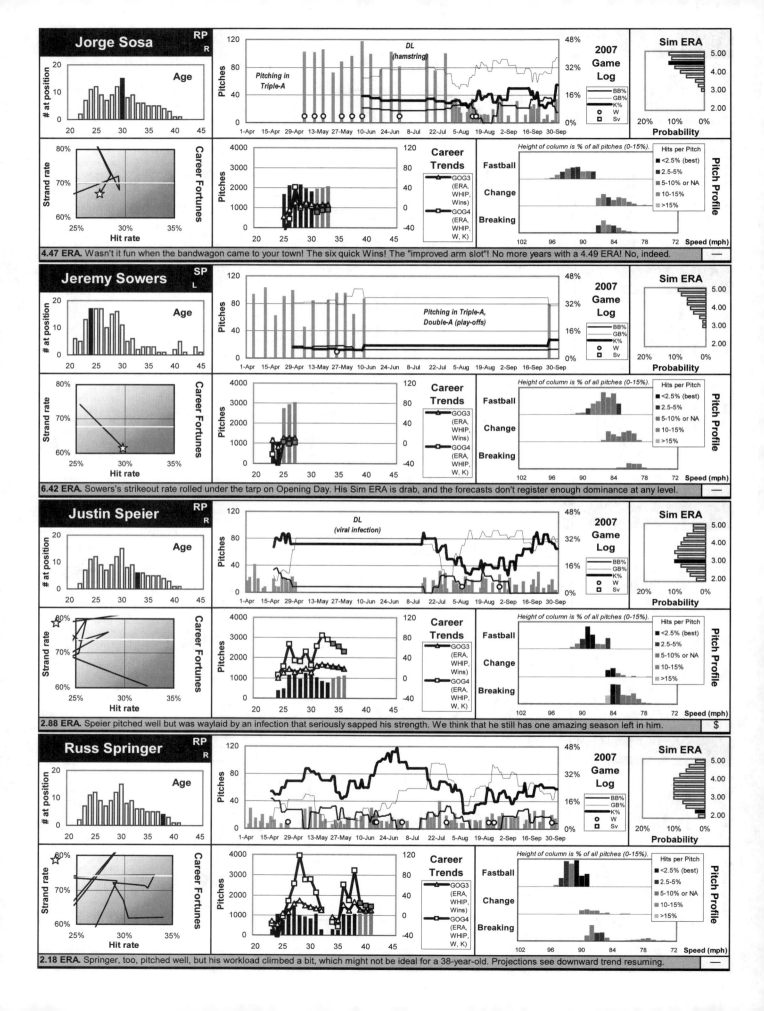

Jorge Sosa — RP (R)

Age (# at position, x-axis 20–45)

2007 Game Log — Pitches, BB%, GB%, K%, W, Sv; *Pitching in Triple-A*; *DL (hamstring)*

Sim ERA — Probability (20%, 10%, 0%); 2.00–5.00

Career Fortunes — Strand rate vs Hit rate

Career Trends — Pitches; GOG3 (ERA, WHIP, Wins), GOG4 (ERA, WHIP, W, K)

Pitch Profile — Height of column is % of all pitches (0–15%). Hits per Pitch: <2.5% (best), 2.5–5%, 5–10% or NA, 10–15%, >15%. Fastball, Change, Breaking; Speed (mph) 102–72

4.47 ERA. Wasn't it fun when the bandwagon came to your town! The six quick Wins! The "improved arm slot"! No more years with a 4.49 ERA! No, indeed. —

Jeremy Sowers — SP (L)

Age (# at position, x-axis 20–45)

2007 Game Log — *Pitching in Triple-A, Double-A (play-offs)*; BB%, GB%, K%, W, Sv

Sim ERA — Probability

Career Fortunes — Strand rate vs Hit rate

Career Trends — GOG3 (ERA, WHIP, Wins), GOG4 (ERA, WHIP, W, K)

Pitch Profile — Height of column is % of all pitches (0–15%). Fastball, Change, Breaking

6.42 ERA. Sowers's strikeout rate rolled under the tarp on Opening Day. His Sim ERA is drab, and the forecasts don't register enough dominance at any level. —

Justin Speier — RP (R)

Age (# at position, x-axis 20–45)

2007 Game Log — *DL (viral infection)*; BB%, GB%, K%, W, Sv

Sim ERA — Probability

Career Fortunes — Strand rate vs Hit rate

Career Trends — GOG3 (ERA, WHIP, Wins), GOG4 (ERA, WHIP, W, K)

Pitch Profile — Height of column is % of all pitches (0–15%). Fastball, Change, Breaking

2.88 ERA. Speier pitched well but was waylaid by an infection that seriously sapped his strength. We think that he still has one amazing season left in him. $

Russ Springer — RP (R)

Age (# at position, x-axis 20–45)

2007 Game Log — BB%, GB%, K%, W, Sv

Sim ERA — Probability

Career Fortunes — Strand rate vs Hit rate

Career Trends — GOG3 (ERA, WHIP, Wins), GOG4 (ERA, WHIP, W, K)

Pitch Profile — Height of column is % of all pitches (0–15%). Fastball, Change, Breaking

2.18 ERA. Springer, too, pitched well, but his workload climbed a bit, which might not be ideal for a 38-year-old. Projections see downward trend resuming. —

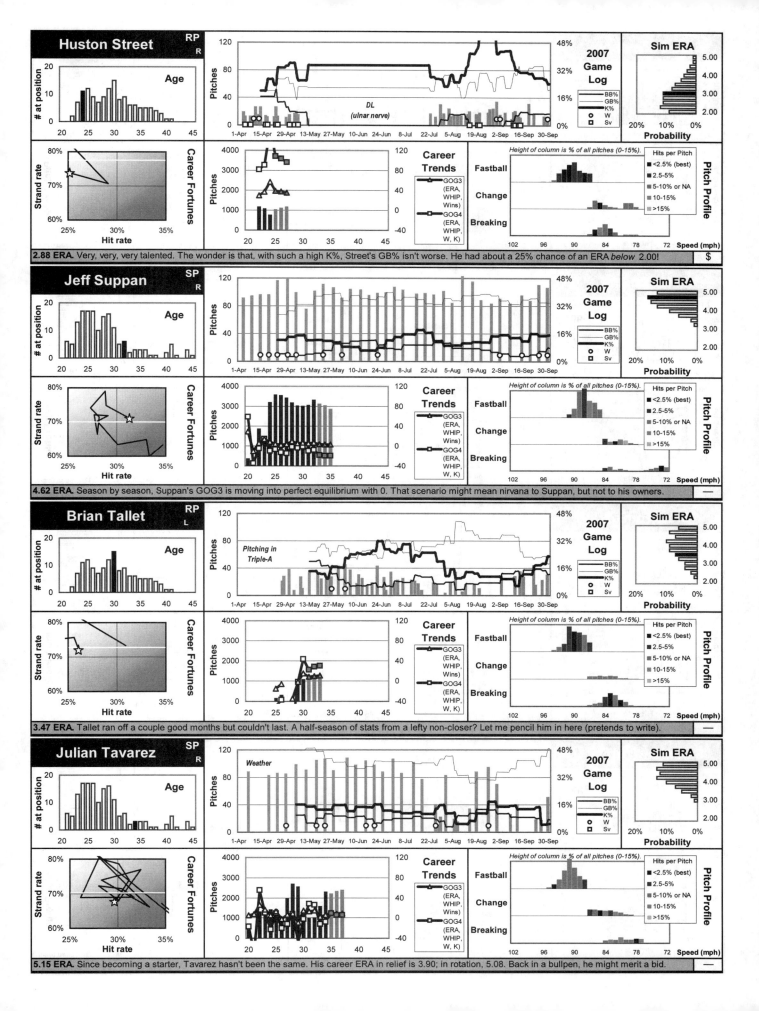

Huston Street — RP, R

Age | # at position
2007 Game Log | Pitches | BB%, GB%, K%, W, Sv
Sim ERA | Probability
Career Fortunes | Strand rate vs Hit rate
Career Trends | Pitches | GOG3 (ERA, WHIP, Wins), GOG4 (ERA, WHIP, W, K)
Pitch Profile | Height of column is % of all pitches (0-15%). | Hits per Pitch: <2.5% (best), 2.5-5%, 5-10% or NA, 10-15%, >15% | Fastball, Change, Breaking | Speed (mph)

DL (ulnar nerve)

2.88 ERA. Very, very, very talented. The wonder is that, with such a high K%, Street's GB% isn't worse. He had about a 25% chance of an ERA *below* 2.00! $

Jeff Suppan — SP, R

4.62 ERA. Season by season, Suppan's GOG3 is moving into perfect equilibrium with 0. That scenario might mean nirvana to Suppan, but not to his owners. —

Brian Tallet — RP, L

Pitching in Triple-A

3.47 ERA. Tallet ran off a couple good months but couldn't last. A half-season of stats from a lefty non-closer? Let me pencil him in here (pretends to write). —

Julian Tavarez — SP, R

Weather

5.15 ERA. Since becoming a starter, Tavarez hasn't been the same. His career ERA in relief is 3.90; in rotation, 5.08. Back in a bullpen, he might merit a bid. —

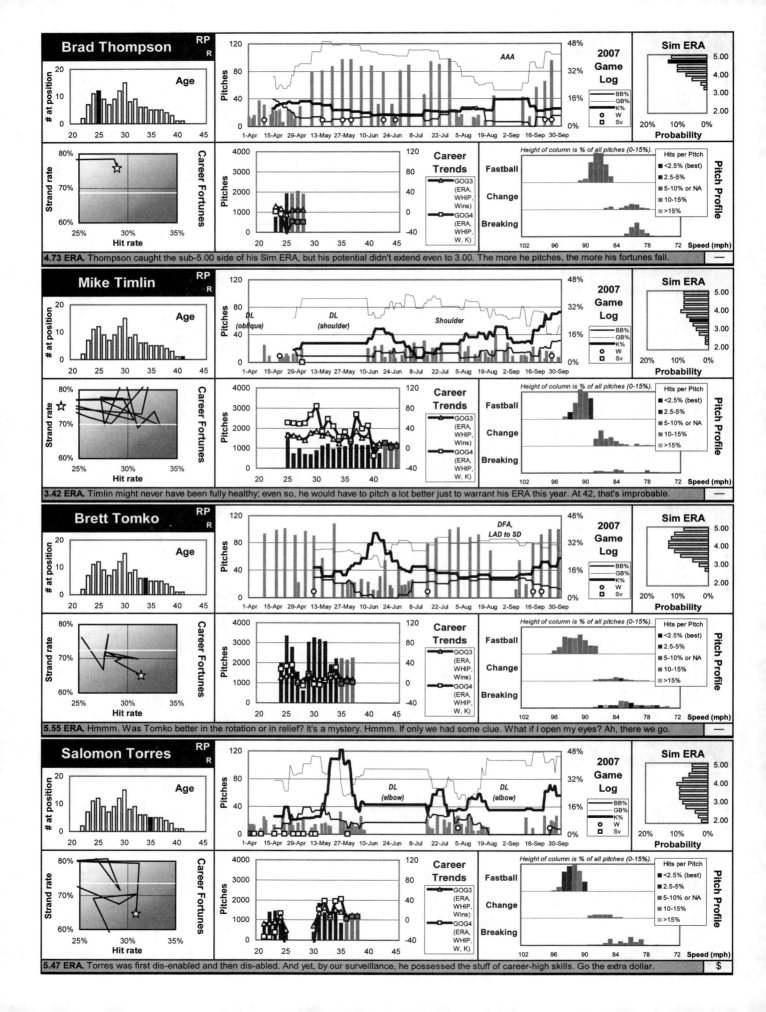

Brad Thompson RP R

Age

Career Fortunes

2007 Game Log

BB%
GB%
K%
W
Sv

Sim ERA

AAA

Pitch Profile

Height of column is % of all pitches (0-15%).
Hits per Pitch
<2.5% (best)
2.5-5%
5-10% or NA
10-15%
>15%

Fastball
Change
Breaking

4.73 ERA. Thompson caught the sub-5.00 side of his Sim ERA, but his potential didn't extend even to 3.00. The more he pitches, the more his fortunes fall. —

Mike Timlin RP R

Age

Career Fortunes

2007 Game Log

DL (oblique)
DL (shoulder)
Shoulder

Sim ERA

Career Trends
GOG3 (ERA, WHIP, Wins)
GOG4 (ERA, WHIP, W, K)

Pitch Profile

Fastball
Change
Breaking

3.42 ERA. Timlin might never have been fully healthy; even so, he would have to pitch a lot better just to warrant his ERA this year. At 42, that's improbable. —

Brett Tomko RP R

Age

Career Fortunes

2007 Game Log

DFA, LAD to SD

Sim ERA

Career Trends
GOG3 (ERA, WHIP, Wins)
GOG4 (ERA, WHIP, W, K)

Pitch Profile

Fastball
Change
Breaking

5.55 ERA. Hmmm. Was Tomko better in the rotation or in relief? It's a mystery. Hmmm. If only we had some clue. What if I open my eyes? Ah, there we go. —

Salomon Torres RP R

Age

Career Fortunes

2007 Game Log

DL (elbow)
DL (elbow)

Sim ERA

Career Trends
GOG3 (ERA, WHIP, Wins)
GOG4 (ERA, WHIP, W, K)

Pitch Profile

Fastball
Change
Breaking

5.47 ERA. Torres was first dis-enabled and then dis-abled. And yet, by our surveillance, he possessed the stuff of career-high skills. Go the extra dollar. $

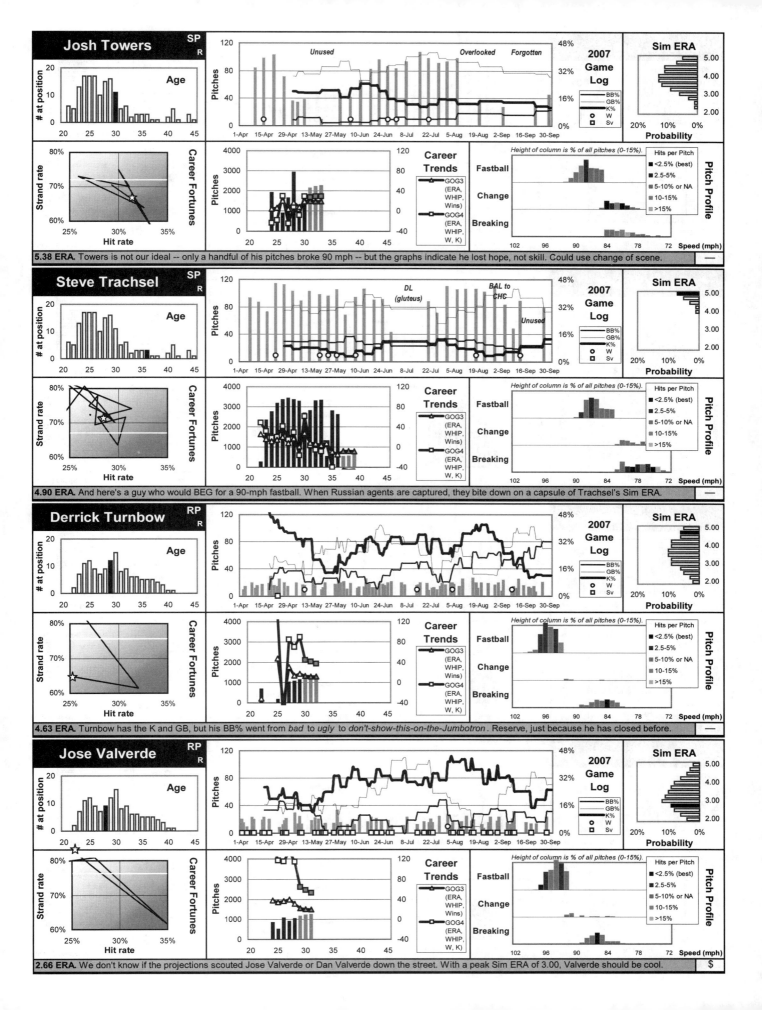

Josh Towers — SP / R

Age (# at position)

2007 Game Log — *Unused ... Overlooked ... Forgotten*
BB%, GB%, K%, W, Sv

Sim ERA — Probability

Career Fortunes — Strand rate vs Hit rate

Career Trends — GOG3 (ERA, WHIP, Wins), GOG4 (ERA, WHIP, W, K)

Pitch Profile — Height of column is % of all pitches (0-15%). Fastball, Change, Breaking. Hits per Pitch: <2.5% (best), 2.5-5%, 5-10% or NA, 10-15%, >15%. Speed (mph) 102–72

5.38 ERA. Towers is not our ideal -- only a handful of his pitches broke 90 mph -- but the graphs indicate he lost hope, not skill. Could use change of scene. —

Steve Trachsel — SP / R

Age

2007 Game Log — *DL (gluteus) ... BAL to CHC ... Unused*
BB%, GB%, K%, W, Sv

Sim ERA — Probability

Career Fortunes

Career Trends — GOG3 (ERA, WHIP, Wins), GOG4 (ERA, WHIP, W, K)

Pitch Profile — Height of column is % of all pitches (0-15%). Fastball, Change, Breaking. Hits per Pitch: <2.5% (best), 2.5-5%, 5-10% or NA, 10-15%, >15%.

4.90 ERA. And here's a guy who would BEG for a 90-mph fastball. When Russian agents are captured, they bite down on a capsule of Trachsel's Sim ERA. —

Derrick Turnbow — RP / R

Age

2007 Game Log — BB%, GB%, K%, W, Sv

Sim ERA — Probability

Career Fortunes

Career Trends — GOG3 (ERA, WHIP, Wins), GOG4 (ERA, WHIP, W, K)

Pitch Profile — Height of column is % of all pitches (0-15%). Fastball, Change, Breaking. Hits per Pitch: <2.5% (best), 2.5-5%, 5-10% or NA, 10-15%, >15%.

4.63 ERA. Turnbow has the K and GB, but his BB% went from *bad* to *ugly* to *don't-show-this-on-the-Jumbotron*. Reserve, just because he has closed before. —

Jose Valverde — RP / R

Age

2007 Game Log — BB%, GB%, K%, W, Sv

Sim ERA — Probability

Career Fortunes

Career Trends — GOG3 (ERA, WHIP, Wins), GOG4 (ERA, WHIP, W, K)

Pitch Profile — Height of column is % of all pitches (0-15%). Fastball, Change, Breaking. Hits per Pitch: <2.5% (best), 2.5-5%, 5-10% or NA, 10-15%, >15%.

2.66 ERA. We don't know if the projections scouted Jose Valverde or Dan Valverde down the street. With a peak Sim ERA of 3.00, Valverde should be cool. $

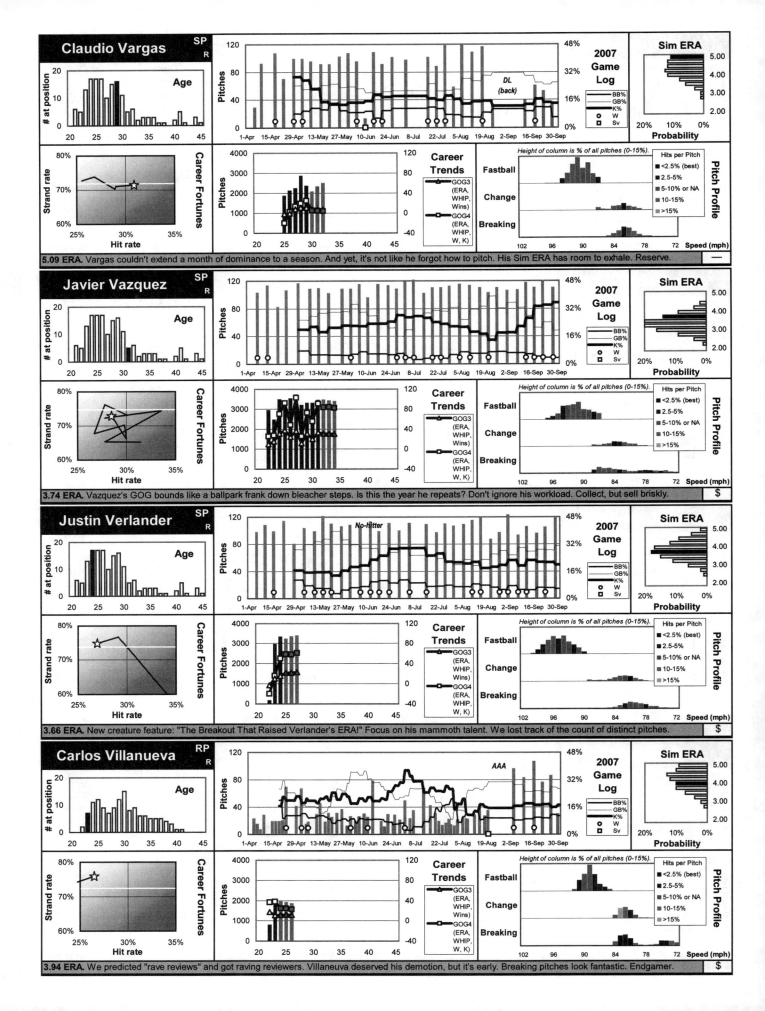

Claudio Vargas SP R

Age
at position

Strand rate / Hit rate — Career Fortunes

Pitches — Career Trends

2007 Game Log

Sim ERA

Pitch Profile

DL (back)

BB%
GB%
K%
○ W
□ Sv

Height of column is % of all pitches (0-15%).
Fastball / Change / Breaking

Hits per Pitch
■ <2.5% (best)
■ 2.5-5%
■ 5-10% or NA
■ 10-15%
▦ >15%

GOG3 (ERA, WHIP, Wins)
GOG4 (ERA, WHIP, W, K)

5.09 ERA. Vargas couldn't extend a month of dominance to a season. And yet, it's not like he forgot how to pitch. His Sim ERA has room to exhale. Reserve. —

Javier Vazquez SP R

Age
at position

Strand rate / Hit rate — Career Fortunes

Pitches — Career Trends

2007 Game Log

Sim ERA

Pitch Profile

BB%
GB%
K%
○ W
□ Sv

GOG3 (ERA, WHIP, Wins)
GOG4 (ERA, WHIP, W, K)

Height of column is % of all pitches (0-15%).
Fastball / Change / Breaking

Hits per Pitch
■ <2.5% (best)
■ 2.5-5%
■ 5-10% or NA
■ 10-15%
▦ >15%

3.74 ERA. Vazquez's GOG bounds like a ballpark frank down bleacher steps. Is this the year he repeats? Don't ignore his workload. Collect, but sell briskly. $

Justin Verlander SP R

Age
at position

No-Hitter

Strand rate / Hit rate — Career Fortunes

Pitches — Career Trends

2007 Game Log

Sim ERA

Pitch Profile

BB%
GB%
K%
○ W
□ Sv

GOG3 (ERA, WHIP, Wins)
GOG4 (ERA, WHIP, W, K)

Height of column is % of all pitches (0-15%).
Fastball / Change / Breaking

Hits per Pitch
■ <2.5% (best)
■ 2.5-5%
■ 5-10% or NA
■ 10-15%
▦ >15%

3.66 ERA. New creature feature: "The Breakout That Raised Verlander's ERA!" Focus on his mammoth talent. We lost track of the count of distinct pitches. $

Carlos Villanueva RP R

Age
at position

AAA

Strand rate / Hit rate — Career Fortunes

Pitches — Career Trends

2007 Game Log

Sim ERA

Pitch Profile

BB%
GB%
K%
○ W
□ Sv

GOG3 (ERA, WHIP, Wins)
GOG4 (ERA, WHIP, W, K)

Height of column is % of all pitches (0-15%).
Fastball / Change / Breaking

Hits per Pitch
■ <2.5% (best)
■ 2.5-5%
■ 5-10% or NA
■ 10-15%
▦ >15%

3.94 ERA. We predicted "rave reviews" and got raving reviewers. Villanueva deserved his demotion, but it's early. Breaking pitches look fantastic. Endgamer. $

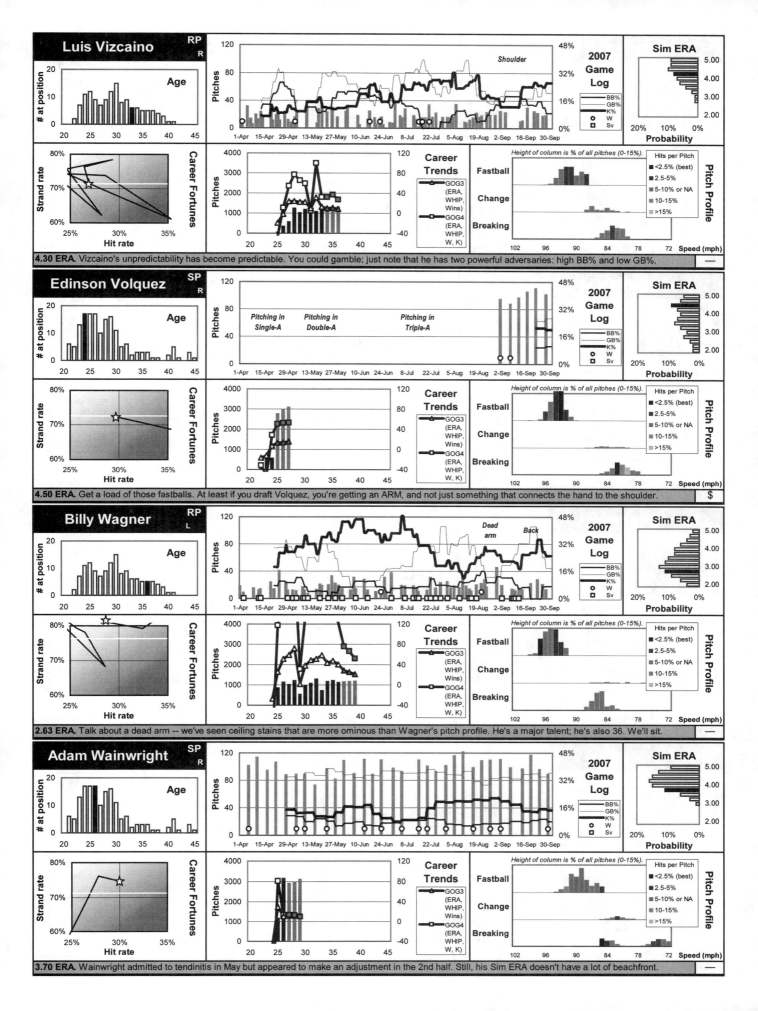

Luis Vizcaino — RP / R

2007 Game Log

Sim ERA

Age

Career Fortunes — Strand rate / Hit rate

GOG3 (ERA, WHIP, Wins)
GOG4 (ERA, WHIP, W, K)

Pitch Profile — Height of column is % of all pitches (0-15%).

Hits per Pitch
■ <2.5% (best)
■ 2.5-5%
■ 5-10% or NA
■ 10-15%
■ >15%

Fastball / Change / Breaking

Shoulder

BB% / GB% / K% / W / Sv

4.30 ERA. Vizcaino's unpredictability has become predictable. You could gamble; just note that he has two powerful adversaries: high BB% and low GB%. —

Edinson Volquez — SP / R

2007 Game Log

Sim ERA

Age

Pitching in Single-A   Pitching in Double-A   Pitching in Triple-A

Career Fortunes — Strand rate / Hit rate

GOG3 (ERA, WHIP, Wins)
GOG4 (ERA, WHIP, W, K)

Pitch Profile — Height of column is % of all pitches (0-15%).

Fastball / Change / Breaking

4.50 ERA. Get a load of those fastballs. At least if you draft Volquez, you're getting an ARM, and not just something that connects the hand to the shoulder. $

Billy Wagner — RP / L

2007 Game Log

Sim ERA

Age

Dead arm   Back

Career Fortunes — Strand rate / Hit rate

GOG3 (ERA, WHIP, Wins)
GOG4 (ERA, WHIP, W, K)

Pitch Profile — Height of column is % of all pitches (0-15%).

Fastball / Change / Breaking

2.63 ERA. Talk about a dead arm -- we've seen ceiling stains that are more ominous than Wagner's pitch profile. He's a major talent; he's also 36. We'll sit. —

Adam Wainwright — SP / R

2007 Game Log

Sim ERA

Age

Career Trends — Strand rate / Hit rate

GOG3 (ERA, WHIP, Wins)
GOG4 (ERA, WHIP, W, K)

Pitch Profile — Height of column is % of all pitches (0-15%).

Fastball / Change / Breaking

3.70 ERA. Wainwright admitted to tendinitis in May but appeared to make an adjustment in the 2nd half. Still, his Sim ERA doesn't have a lot of beachfront. —

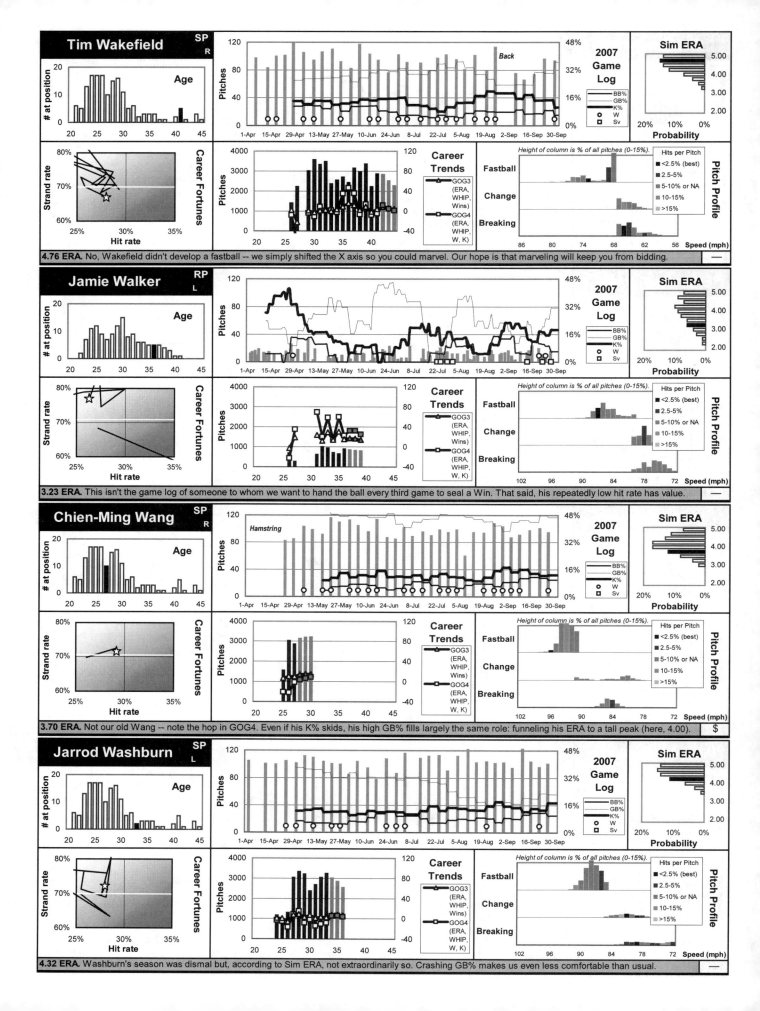

Tim Wakefield — SP / R

at position | Age | 20 15 10 5 0 | 20 25 30 35 40 45

Pitches — 2007 Game Log — 120 80 40 0 | 48% 32% 16% 0% | *Back* | BB% GB% K% ○ W □ Sv | 1-Apr 15-Apr 29-Apr 13-May 27-May 10-Jun 24-Jun 8-Jul 22-Jul 5-Aug 19-Aug 2-Sep 16-Sep 30-Sep

Sim ERA — Probability — 5.00 4.00 3.00 2.00 | 20% 10% 0%

Strand rate 80% 70% 60% — Hit rate 25% 30% 35% — Career Fortunes

Pitches 4000 3000 2000 1000 0 | 120 80 40 0 -40 | Career Trends | GOG3 (ERA, WHIP, Wins) / GOG4 (ERA, WHIP, W, K) | 20 25 30 35 40 45

Pitch Profile — Fastball / Change / Breaking — Height of column is % of all pitches (0-15%). — Hits per Pitch: <2.5% (best) / 2.5-5% / 5-10% or NA / 10-15% / >15% — Speed (mph) 86 80 74 68 62 56

4.76 ERA. No, Wakefield didn't develop a fastball -- we simply shifted the X axis so you could marvel. Our hope is that marveling will keep you from bidding. —

Jamie Walker — RP / L

at position | Age | 20 15 10 5 0 | 20 25 30 35 40 45

Pitches — 2007 Game Log — 120 80 40 0 | 48% 32% 16% 0% | BB% GB% K% ○ W □ Sv | 1-Apr 15-Apr 29-Apr 13-May 27-May 10-Jun 24-Jun 8-Jul 22-Jul 5-Aug 19-Aug 2-Sep 16-Sep 30-Sep

Sim ERA — Probability — 5.00 4.00 3.00 2.00 | 20% 10% 0%

Strand rate 80% 70% 60% — Hit rate 25% 30% 35% — Career Fortunes

Pitches 4000 3000 2000 1000 0 | 120 80 40 0 -40 | Career Trends | GOG3 (ERA, WHIP, Wins) / GOG4 (ERA, WHIP, W, K) | 20 25 30 35 40 45

Pitch Profile — Fastball / Change / Breaking — Height of column is % of all pitches (0-15%). — Hits per Pitch: <2.5% (best) / 2.5-5% / 5-10% or NA / 10-15% / >15% — Speed (mph) 102 96 90 84 78 72

3.23 ERA. This isn't the game log of someone to whom we want to hand the ball every third game to seal a Win. That said, his repeatedly low hit rate has value. —

Chien-Ming Wang — SP / R

at position | Age | 20 15 10 5 0 | 20 25 30 35 40 45

Pitches — 2007 Game Log — 120 80 40 0 | 48% 32% 16% 0% | *Hamstring* | BB% GB% K% ○ W □ Sv | 1-Apr 15-Apr 29-Apr 13-May 27-May 10-Jun 24-Jun 8-Jul 22-Jul 5-Aug 19-Aug 2-Sep 16-Sep 30-Sep

Sim ERA — Probability — 5.00 4.00 3.00 2.00 | 20% 10% 0%

Strand rate 80% 70% 60% — Hit rate 25% 30% 35% — Career Fortunes

Pitches 4000 3000 2000 1000 0 | 120 80 40 0 -40 | Career Trends | GOG3 (ERA, WHIP, Wins) / GOG4 (ERA, WHIP, W, K) | 20 25 30 35 40 45

Pitch Profile — Fastball / Change / Breaking — Height of column is % of all pitches (0-15%). — Hits per Pitch: <2.5% (best) / 2.5-5% / 5-10% or NA / 10-15% / >15% — Speed (mph) 102 96 90 84 78 72

3.70 ERA. Not our old Wang -- note the hop in GOG4. Even if his K% skids, his high GB% fills largely the same role: funneling his ERA to a tall peak (here, 4.00). $

Jarrod Washburn — SP / L

at position | Age | 20 15 10 5 0 | 20 25 30 35 40 45

Pitches — 2007 Game Log — 120 80 40 0 | 48% 32% 16% 0% | BB% GB% K% ○ W □ Sv | 1-Apr 15-Apr 29-Apr 13-May 27-May 10-Jun 24-Jun 8-Jul 22-Jul 5-Aug 19-Aug 2-Sep 16-Sep 30-Sep

Sim ERA — Probability — 5.00 4.00 3.00 2.00 | 20% 10% 0%

Strand rate 80% 70% 60% — Hit rate 25% 30% 35% — Career Fortunes

Pitches 4000 3000 2000 1000 0 | 120 80 40 0 -40 | Career Trends | GOG3 (ERA, WHIP, Wins) / GOG4 (ERA, WHIP, W, K) | 20 25 30 35 40 45

Pitch Profile — Fastball / Change / Breaking — Height of column is % of all pitches (0-15%). — Hits per Pitch: <2.5% (best) / 2.5-5% / 5-10% or NA / 10-15% / >15% — Speed (mph) 102 96 90 84 78 72

4.32 ERA. Washburn's season was dismal but, according to Sim ERA, not extraordinarily so. Crashing GB% makes us even less comfortable than usual. —

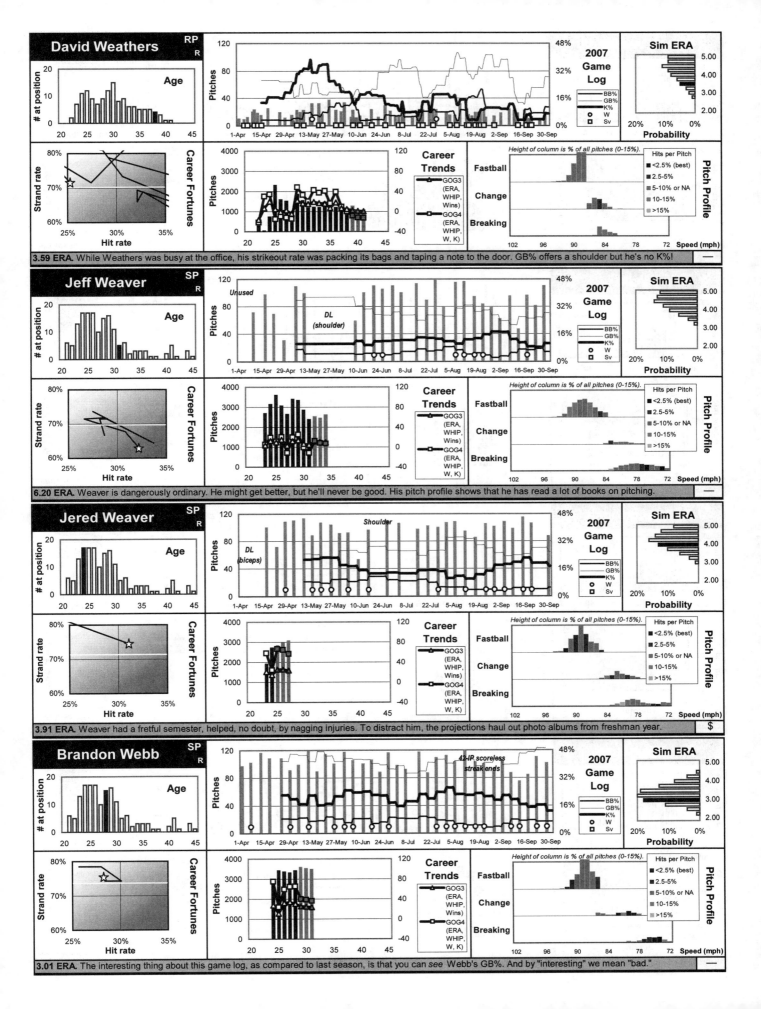

David Weathers — RP (R)

3.59 ERA. While Weathers was busy at the office, his strikeout rate was packing its bags and taping a note to the door. GB% offers a shoulder but he's no K%! — —

Jeff Weaver — SP (R)

6.20 ERA. Weaver is dangerously ordinary. He might get better, but he'll never be good. His pitch profile shows that he has read a lot of books on pitching. — —

Jered Weaver — SP (R)

3.91 ERA. Weaver had a fretful semester, helped, no doubt, by nagging injuries. To distract him, the projections haul out photo albums from freshman year. — $

Brandon Webb — SP (R)

3.01 ERA. The interesting thing about this game log, as compared to last season, is that you can *see* Webb's GB%. And by "interesting" we mean "bad." — —

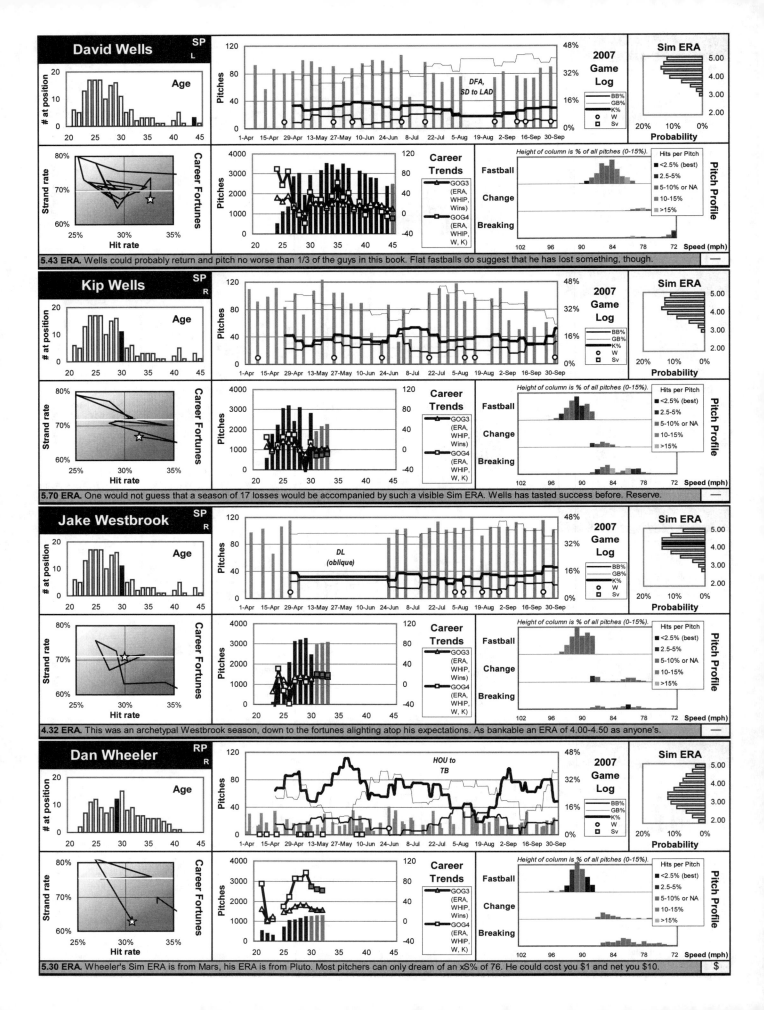

David Wells SP L

Age

Strand rate / Hit rate — Career Fortunes

2007 Game Log — BB%, GB%, K%, W, Sv

Sim ERA — Probability

Career Trends — GOG3 (ERA, WHIP, Wins), GOG4 (ERA, WHIP, W, K)

Pitch Profile — Height of column is % of all pitches (0-15%). Hits per Pitch: <2.5% (best), 2.5-5%, 5-10% or NA, 10-15%, >15%. Fastball, Change, Breaking. Speed (mph)

DFA, SD to LAD

5.43 ERA. Wells could probably return and pitch no worse than 1/3 of the guys in this book. Flat fastballs do suggest that he has lost something, though. —

Kip Wells SP R

Age

2007 Game Log

Sim ERA — Probability

Career Fortunes

Career Trends — GOG3 (ERA, WHIP, Wins), GOG4 (ERA, WHIP, W, K)

Pitch Profile — Height of column is % of all pitches (0-15%). Hits per Pitch: <2.5% (best), 2.5-5%, 5-10% or NA, 10-15%, >15%. Fastball, Change, Breaking. Speed (mph)

5.70 ERA. One would not guess that a season of 17 losses would be accompanied by such a visible Sim ERA. Wells has tasted success before. Reserve. —

Jake Westbrook SP R

Age

2007 Game Log

Sim ERA — Probability

Career Fortunes

Career Trends — GOG3 (ERA, WHIP, Wins), GOG4 (ERA, WHIP, W, K)

DL (oblique)

Pitch Profile — Height of column is % of all pitches (0-15%). Hits per Pitch: <2.5% (best), 2.5-5%, 5-10% or NA, 10-15%, >15%. Fastball, Change, Breaking. Speed (mph)

4.32 ERA. This was an archetypal Westbrook season, down to the fortunes alighting atop his expectations. As bankable an ERA of 4.00-4.50 as anyone's. —

Dan Wheeler RP R

Age

2007 Game Log

Sim ERA — Probability

HOU to TB

Career Fortunes

Career Trends — GOG3 (ERA, WHIP, Wins), GOG4 (ERA, WHIP, W, K)

Pitch Profile — Height of column is % of all pitches (0-15%). Hits per Pitch: <2.5% (best), 2.5-5%, 5-10% or NA, 10-15%, >15%. Fastball, Change, Breaking. Speed (mph)

5.30 ERA. Wheeler's Sim ERA is from Mars, his ERA is from Pluto. Most pitchers can only dream of an xS% of 76. He could cost you $1 and net you $10. $

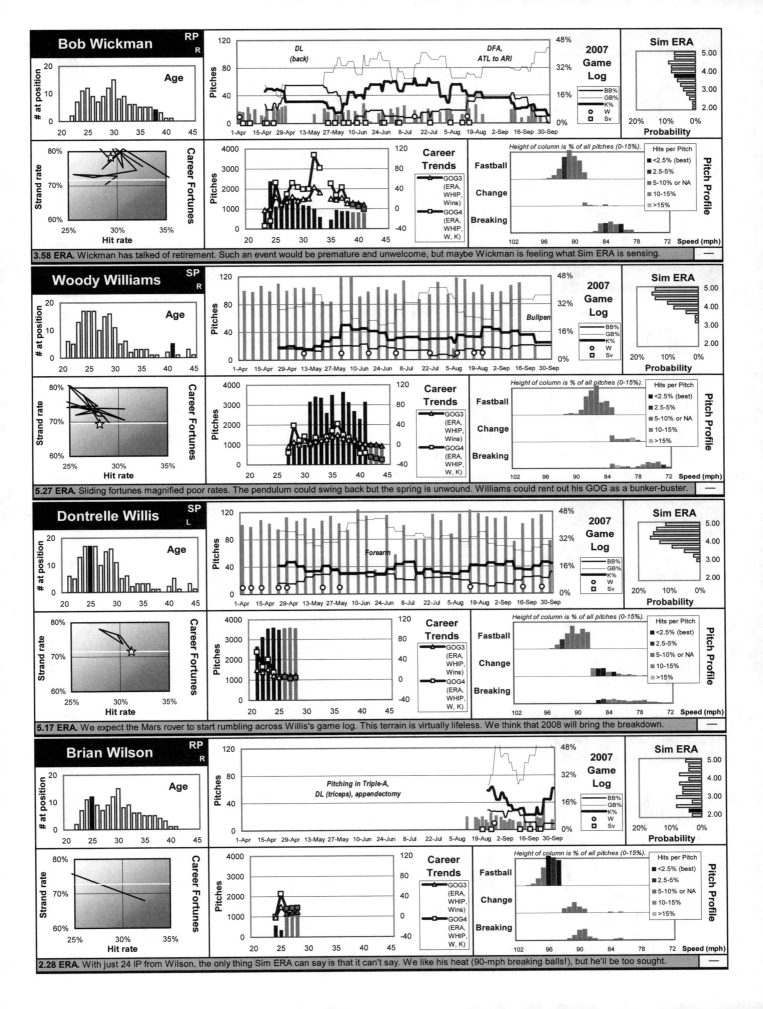

Bob Wickman — RP / R

3.58 ERA. Wickman has talked of retirement. Such an event would be premature and unwelcome, but maybe Wickman is feeling what Sim ERA is sensing.

DL (back)
DFA, ATL to ARI

Woody Williams — SP / R

5.27 ERA. Sliding fortunes magnified poor rates. The pendulum could swing back but the spring is unwound. Williams could rent out his GOG as a bunker-buster.

Bullpen

Dontrelle Willis — SP / L

5.17 ERA. We expect the Mars rover to start rumbling across Willis's game log. This terrain is virtually lifeless. We think that 2008 will bring the breakdown.

Forearm

Brian Wilson — RP / R

2.28 ERA. With just 24 IP from Wilson, the only thing Sim ERA can say is that it can't say. We like his heat (90-mph breaking balls!), but he'll be too sought.

Pitching in Triple-A, DL (triceps), appendectomy

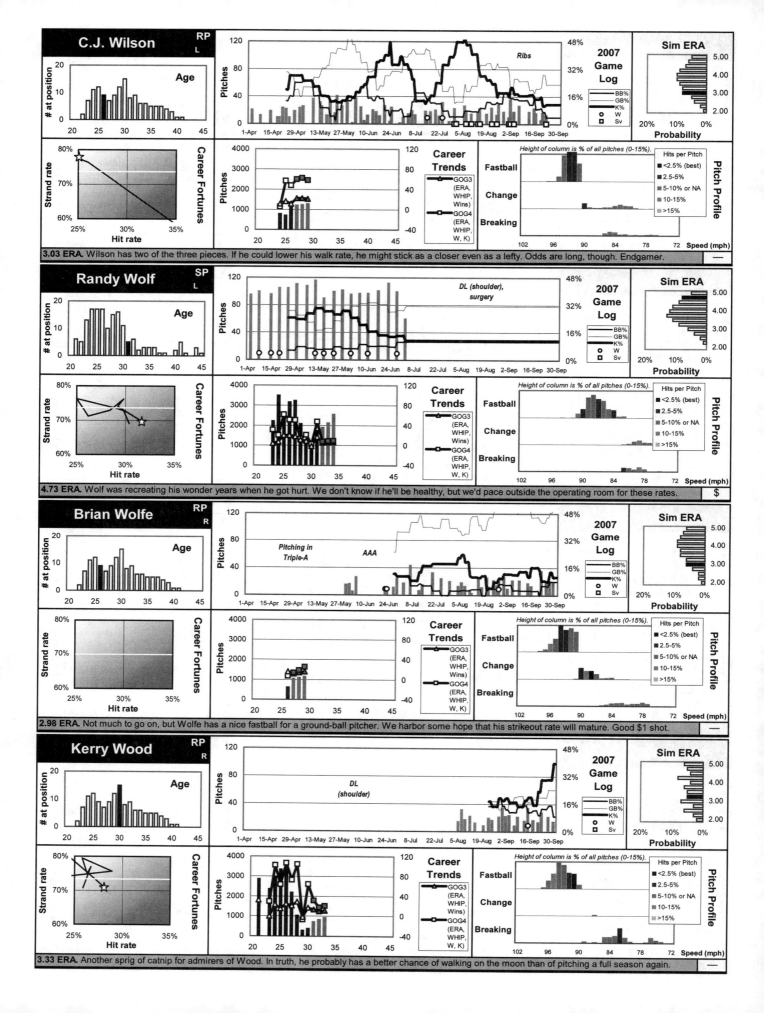

C.J. Wilson RP L

3.03 ERA. Wilson has two of the three pieces. If he could lower his walk rate, he might stick as a closer even as a lefty. Odds are long, though. Endgamer. — —

Randy Wolf SP L

4.73 ERA. Wolf was recreating his wonder years when he got hurt. We don't know if he'll be healthy, but we'd pace outside the operating room for these rates. $

Brian Wolfe RP R

2.98 ERA. Not much to go on, but Wolfe has a nice fastball for a ground-ball pitcher. We harbor some hope that his strikeout rate will mature. Good $1 shot. — —

Kerry Wood RP R

3.33 ERA. Another sprig of catnip for admirers of Wood. In truth, he probably has a better chance of walking on the moon than of pitching a full season again. — —

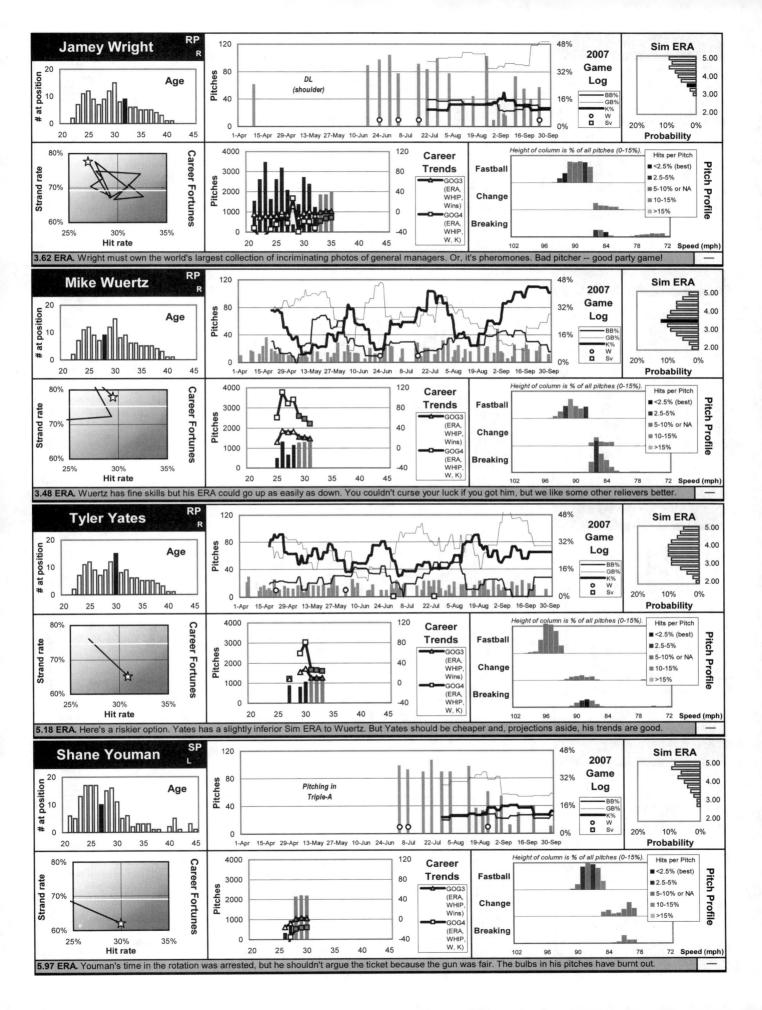

Jamey Wright — RP / R

2007 Game Log
- BB%
- GB%
- K%
- W (○)
- Sv (□)

DL (shoulder)

Sim ERA

Age

Career Fortunes — Strand rate / Hit rate

Career Trends
- GOG3 (ERA, WHIP, Wins)
- GOG4 (ERA, WHIP, W, K)

Pitch Profile — Height of column is % of all pitches (0-15%).
- Fastball
- Change
- Breaking

Hits per Pitch:
- <2.5% (best)
- 2.5-5%
- 5-10% or NA
- 10-15%
- >15%

3.62 ERA. Wright must own the world's largest collection of incriminating photos of general managers. Or, it's pheromones. Bad pitcher -- good party game! —

Mike Wuertz — RP / R

2007 Game Log
- BB%
- GB%
- K%
- W (○)
- Sv (□)

Sim ERA

Age

Career Fortunes — Strand rate / Hit rate

Career Trends
- GOG3 (ERA, WHIP, Wins)
- GOG4 (ERA, WHIP, W, K)

Pitch Profile — Height of column is % of all pitches (0-15%).
- Fastball
- Change
- Breaking

Hits per Pitch:
- <2.5% (best)
- 2.5-5%
- 5-10% or NA
- 10-15%
- >15%

3.48 ERA. Wuertz has fine skills but his ERA could go up as easily as down. You couldn't curse your luck if you got him, but we like some other relievers better. —

Tyler Yates — RP / R

2007 Game Log
- BB%
- GB%
- K%
- W (○)
- Sv (□)

Sim ERA

Age

Career Fortunes — Strand rate / Hit rate

Career Trends
- GOG3 (ERA, WHIP, Wins)
- GOG4 (ERA, WHIP, W, K)

Pitch Profile — Height of column is % of all pitches (0-15%).
- Fastball
- Change
- Breaking

Hits per Pitch:
- <2.5% (best)
- 2.5-5%
- 5-10% or NA
- 10-15%
- >15%

5.18 ERA. Here's a riskier option. Yates has a slightly inferior Sim ERA to Wuertz. But Yates should be cheaper and, projections aside, his trends are good. —

Shane Youman — SP / L

2007 Game Log
- BB%
- GB%
- K%
- W (○)
- Sv (□)

Pitching in Triple-A

Sim ERA

Age

Career Fortunes — Strand rate / Hit rate

Career Trends
- GOG3 (ERA, WHIP, Wins)
- GOG4 (ERA, WHIP, W, K)

Pitch Profile — Height of column is % of all pitches (0-15%).
- Fastball
- Change
- Breaking

Hits per Pitch:
- <2.5% (best)
- 2.5-5%
- 5-10% or NA
- 10-15%
- >15%

5.97 ERA. Youman's time in the rotation was arrested, but he shouldn't argue the ticket because the gun was fair. The bulbs in his pitches have burnt out. —

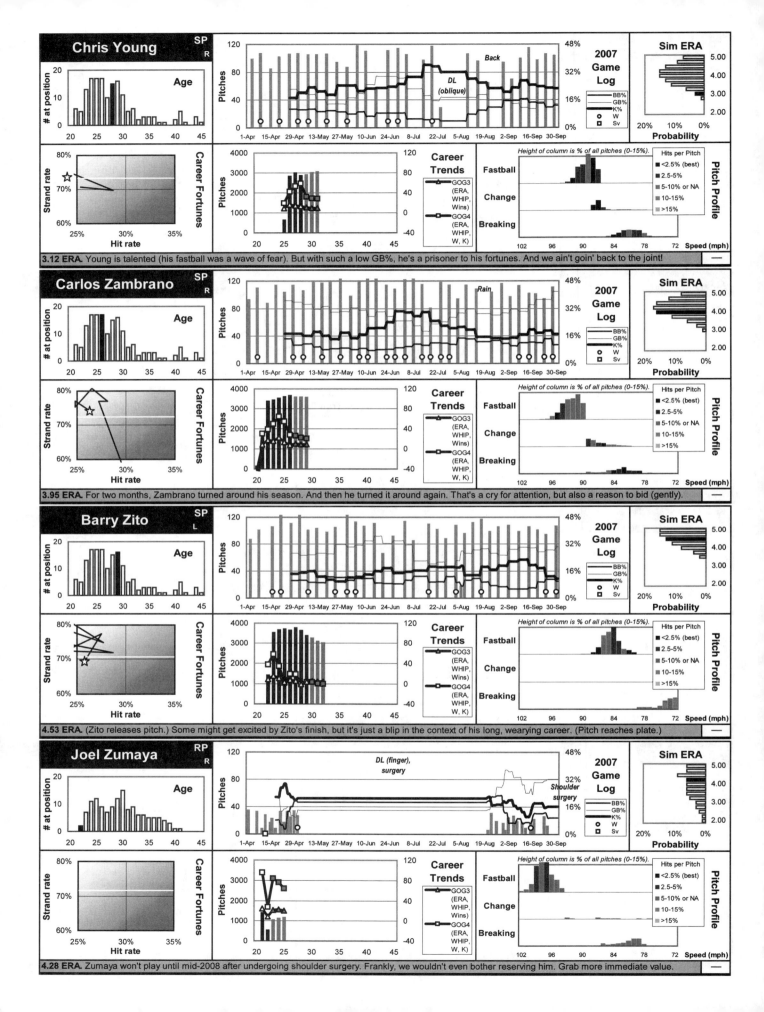

Chris Young SP R

3.12 ERA. Young is talented (his fastball was a wave of fear). But with such a low GB%, he's a prisoner to his fortunes. And we ain't goin' back to the joint! —

Carlos Zambrano SP R

3.95 ERA. For two months, Zambrano turned around his season. And then he turned it around again. That's a cry for attention, but also a reason to bid (gently). —

Barry Zito SP L

4.53 ERA. (Zito releases pitch.) Some might get excited by Zito's finish, but it's just a blip in the context of his long, wearying career. (Pitch reaches plate.) —

Joel Zumaya RP R

4.28 ERA. Zumaya won't play until mid-2008 after undergoing shoulder surgery. Frankly, we wouldn't even bother reserving him. Grab more immediate value. —

THE HITTERS

In this edition, we cover 456 hitters who made a dent in the big leagues in 2007. In general, a hitter needed at least 80 AB to be eligible, though we made exceptions for stand-out rookies. To the right of the hitter's name, we give the position at which he played the most games in 2007. We also note his handedness ("R," "L," or both for switch-hitters).

Craig Brown covers Bobby Abreu to Curtis Granderson.

Marc Normandin covers Shawn Green to Lastings Milledge.

Jeff Sackmann covers Damian Miller to Ben Zobrist.

AGE AMONG PEERS

As with the pitchers, we plot age by position for the hitters in this book. Again, age runs along the bottom, and the number of players along the side.

Not surprisingly, different spots have different spreads. Long-time readers of the book may detect that the graphs skew a bit younger than last year's. This observation exemplifies a drift that has been identified by Dave Studeman of The Hardball Times, among others: Since 2004, the average major-league age has fallen by six months.

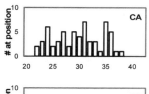
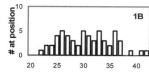
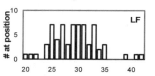
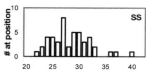
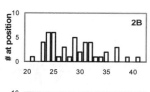
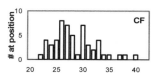
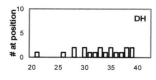
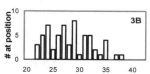
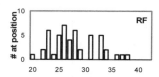

PRODUCTION

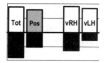

This graph shows the hitter's productivity by rate (OPS) and tenure (PA). The white and gray columns indicate OPS, from 0.000-1.000. The hitter's OPS in 2007 is white and marked **Tot**. His rates versus right- and left-handed hurlers (**vRH** and **vLH**) are also white. The OPS of *other* players at the hitter's main position is gray and marked **Pos**.

The black columns traveling downward indicate playing time, from 0-750 PA. The columns under **Tot**, **vRH**, and **vLH** are *this hitter's* playing time over which he posted that OPS. The one under **Pos** is the *average* playing time for other hitters at this spot.

Thus, you can tell at a glance if the hitter was better or worse than his peers in 2007 and if he was in a platoon, or should have been. In the graph accompanying this text, the hitter was better than his peers overall, better against RH'ers than against LH'ers, and better against both types of pitchers than were his peers overall.

GAMES PLAYED BY POSITION

1B		
3B	28	
2B	25	
SS	7	
C		
LF		
CF		
RF		

Revised for 2008: This diagram tells the hitter's jobs in 2007. Spots where the hitter played have reverse text and are shaded. The shade grows darker as the count of games crosses certain customary thresholds: 1 game; 5 games; 10 games; and (darkest) 20 games. For reference, we also give the actual count of games played.

To the right of the count might appear 1-3 gloves, either white or black. These icons indicate the fielding skill of the hitter in 2007. Fielding skill is an important factor – even in fantasy baseball – because some hitters get more play than they otherwise deserve because they are good fielders, and some sluggers have less-secure jobs because they are poor fielders. You can learn more about our approach to defense in the essay "White Gloves, Black Gloves" at the back of the book, where you will also find ratings of teams by defense.

GAME LOG

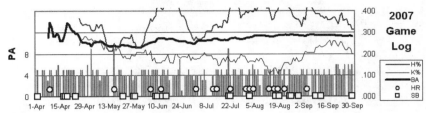

2007 Game Log

H%
K%
BA
○ HR
□ SB

PA

.400 .300 .200 .100 .000

8
4
0

1-Apr 15-Apr 29-Apr 13-May 27-May 10-Jun 24-Jun 8-Jul 22-Jul 5-Aug 19-Aug 2-Sep 16-Sep 30-Sep

The common focus in baseball guides on 1st-half/2nd-half splits can lead us to forget that a season consists not of two huge increments but of 162 small ones. And seasons can hang on single days. So we do, too.

This graph shows when, and to what extent, a hitter played in 2007. It runs day by day from Opening Day to the final regular-season game. Each gray column is one game; the height is the number of plate appearances, as marked on the left.

The three lines track three key rates: *hit rate* (the medium-weight line); *strikeout rate* (the thin line); and *batting average* (the thick line). The height of a line gives its rate, as shown on the right axis. The line for BA is *season-to-date*, so the rightmost endpoint is the hitter's final BA. The lines for K% and H% are *20-game rolling rates*, so that you can spot those mid-course adjustments that we mentioned.

Note that BA ($^H/_{AB}$) is the product of H% ($^H/_{(AB-K)}$) and contact rate ($^{(AB-K)}/_{AB}$), the latter of which is the counterpart of strike-out rate ($^K/_{AB}$). Thus, we have split BA into (1) how often the hitter put a ball in play and (2) what happened when he did.

The league K rate is 21%. A rate under 10% marks a contact hitter and is usually good for BA (but not necessarily power); a rate over 30% marks a free swinger and is usually bad for BA (and all else). For H%, the average is 33%; a rate of 37% is strong (higher rates can be touched but not held).

New for 2008: A batter's season is often defined by certain spans – months where he clubbed 10 home runs, weeks where he stole 7 bases. To evoke those stretches, we offer two sets of tick marks along the bottom. The circles denote those occasions when the hitter swatted a home run; the squares tell when he swiped a base. The same symbols are used in Career Trends.

LINEUP PROFILE

#1

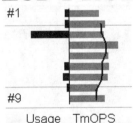

#9

Usage   TmOPS

New for 2008: In many fantasy leagues, owners are tasked with reeling in Runs and RBI. The hitch is that both stats are highly dependent on the context in which the hitter hits. This graph supplies the context.

The black bars to the left show where and how often the hitter appeared in the starting line-up, from the lead-off spot at the top of the graph to the #9 spot at the bottom. (Games in which the batter did not start were not considered.) This hitter got most of his appearances at the #3 spot; he also got play in the first two spots and after the #5 spot.

The gray bars to the right give the OPS of the starting line-up *in those games that the hitter started* (and including his stats). Thus, a hitter who started sporadically may have gotten different support than his team produced overall. This hitter was lucky to bat often in front of a prodigious #4 hitter; later batters were strong, too. His Run total was probably inflated, and might be again.

The black line snaking down the right side is the average OPS by spot for the hitter's league. If the batter played in both leagues in 2007, we give the line for the league where he wrapped up the season.

83

CAREER TRENDS

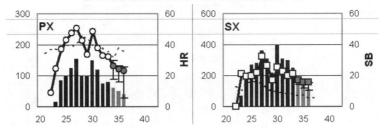

Power and speed are distinct skills – and distinctly prized by fantasy GM's – so we plot them separately. In both cases, the wide axis marks the hitter's age, from 20-42. The black columns represent a counting stat – either HR or SB – with values as shown on the left axis. The accompanying line denotes the underlying rate – either PX or SX – as given on the right axis.

For our power index (PX), we went with Isolated Slugging Percentage (defined as Slugging Percentage - Batting Average). As for speed, we wanted to put a player's ability in terms dear to fantasy owners – namely, stolen bases – so we turned to the man who has the biggest responsibility for sending him: his manager. Speed Index (SX) is just an estimate of the rate at which a hitter tries to steal (successfully or not).

In both graphs, the dashed line running across the body is the *average* rate at each age for other players at the hitter's main position. Thus, you can easily compare a hitter's PX and SX to his peers. The facing page gives career trends by position.

New for 2008: In past years, we relied on readers' eyes alone to fill in the future, but with this edition, we have decided to help with not one but *three* years of projected trends. The gray circles and squares project rate stats, and the gray columns project counting stats. You will also find high and low error bars that mark the 80th and 20th percentiles, respectively, of the hitter's forecast (where higher percentiles are better). You can learn more about our projection system in Jeff Sackmann's essay "Working the Seam" later in this book.

SPRAY CHART

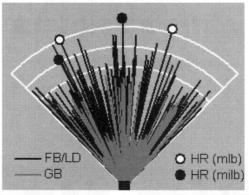

— FB/LD
— GB
○ HR (mlb)
● HR (milb)

New for 2008: A hitter's job may be to hit, but typical numerical stats offer remarkably little insight into a hitter's ways beyond counts of particular events like home runs.

This graph compiles a season's worth of a hitter's batted balls, both hits and outs. Here you can tell whether the hitter tended to swing up or down, whether he favored a field, and whether he had power alleys.

The graph overlays two categories of data. First, we distinguish between balls hit onto the ground and those hit in the air.

The paths of fly balls and liners are shown in black; superimposed on those are the paths of ground balls in gray. (Note: These are not the true trajectories but lines from home plate to the ball's final resting spot.)

We also distinguish between power exhibited in the minors and power exhibited in the majors. Big-league homers are marked by white circles, whereas minor-league homers are noted by black circles.

The white arcs in the outfield depict distances of 300', 350', and 400'.

CAREER TRENDS BY POSITION

Here are the graphs for Power Index and Speed Index for all nine hitting positions. In each graph, the wide axis is age, from 20 to 42. The gray column is a counting stat, either HR or SB, as shown on the right axis. The dashed line is the associated rate, either PX or SX, as shown on the left axis. Our source data is the careers of the 456 hitters in this book. For PX, we show rates only for those ages at which we have at least 1,000 total at-bats; for SX, the threshold is 250 total trips to first base.

Note: These graphs do not show what players *will* do at each age — rather, they show what players *must* do to fend off each year's new crop of rookies and keep their jobs. ("Must" is too strong a word, since these numbers are only averages, but you get our gist.) It's not that 39-year-old second basemen *will* hit 20 HR — it's that 39-year-old second basemen *must* hit 20 HR, or they won't be second basemen. Likewise, it's not that all 21-year-old third baseman hit 10 HR; it's that only those 21-year-old third basemen who can hit 10 HR in the majors stick around. Check the profiles to see if your players can meet these demands.

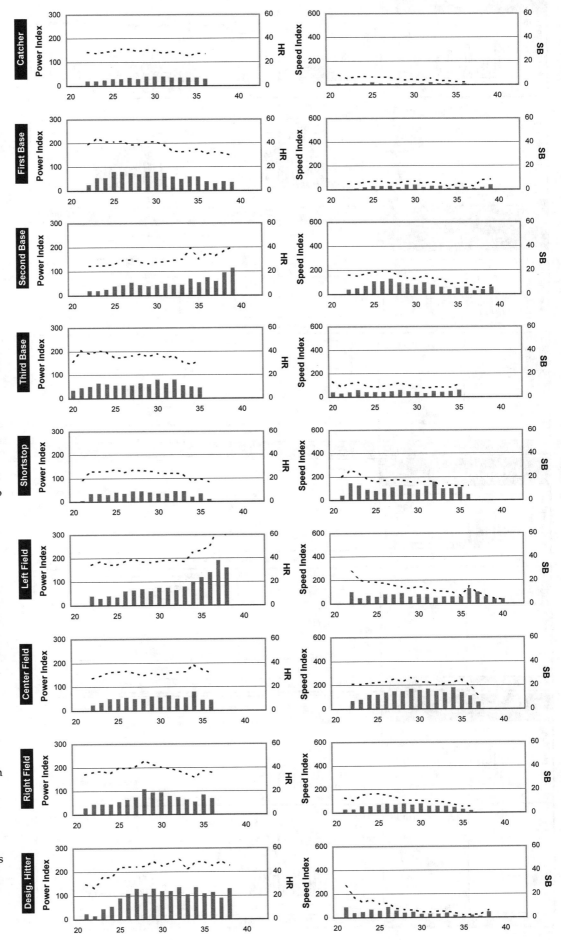

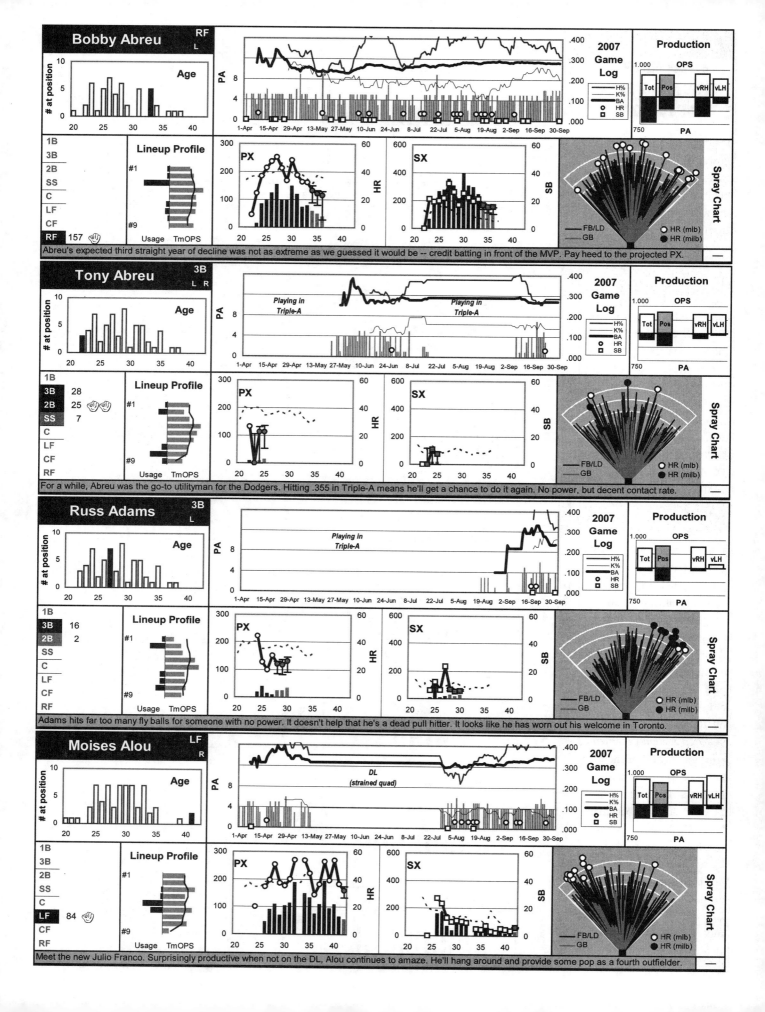

Bobby Abreu — RF, L

Age — # at position

2007 Game Log

H%, K%, BA, HR (○), SB (□)

PA / .400 .300 .200 .100 .000

Production — OPS — Tot, Pos, vRH, vLH — 1.000 / 750 — PA

Lineup Profile — #1 ... #9 — Usage, TmOPS

Positions: 1B, 3B, 2B, SS, C, LF, CF, **RF 157**

PX — HR / SX — SB

Spray Chart — FB/LD, GB, HR (mlb) ○, HR (milb) ●

Abreu's expected third straight year of decline was not as extreme as we guessed it would be -- credit batting in front of the MVP. Pay heed to the projected PX.

Tony Abreu — 3B, L R

Age — # at position

2007 Game Log

Playing in Triple-A ... *Playing in Triple-A*

H%, K%, BA, HR (○), SB (□)

PA / .400 .300 .200 .100 .000

Production — OPS — Tot, Pos, vRH, vLH — 1.000 / 750 — PA

Lineup Profile — #1 ... #9 — Usage, TmOPS

Positions: 1B, **3B 28**, **2B 25**, **SS 7**, C, LF, CF, RF

PX — HR / SX — SB

Spray Chart — FB/LD, GB, HR (mlb) ○, HR (milb) ●

For a while, Abreu was the go-to utilityman for the Dodgers. Hitting .355 in Triple-A means he'll get a chance to do it again. No power, but decent contact rate.

Russ Adams — 3B, L

Age — # at position

2007 Game Log

Playing in Triple-A

H%, K%, BA, HR (○), SB (□)

PA / .400 .300 .200 .100 .000

Production — OPS — Tot, Pos, vRH, vLH — 1.000 / 750 — PA

Lineup Profile — #1 ... #9 — Usage, TmOPS

Positions: 1B, **3B 16**, **2B 2**, SS, C, LF, CF, RF

PX — HR / SX — SB

Spray Chart — FB/LD, GB, HR (mlb) ○, HR (milb) ●

Adams hits far too many fly balls for someone with no power. It doesn't help that he's a dead pull hitter. It looks like he has worn out his welcome in Toronto.

Moises Alou — LF, R

Age — # at position

2007 Game Log

DL (strained quad)

H%, K%, BA, HR (○), SB (□)

PA / .400 .300 .200 .100 .000

Production — OPS — Tot, Pos, vRH, vLH — 1.000 / 750 — PA

Lineup Profile — #1 ... #9 — Usage, TmOPS

Positions: 1B, 3B, 2B, SS, C, **LF 84**, CF, RF

PX — HR / SX — SB

Spray Chart — FB/LD, GB, HR (mlb) ○, HR (milb) ●

Meet the new Julio Franco. Surprisingly productive when not on the DL, Alou continues to amaze. He'll hang around and provide some pop as a fourth outfielder.

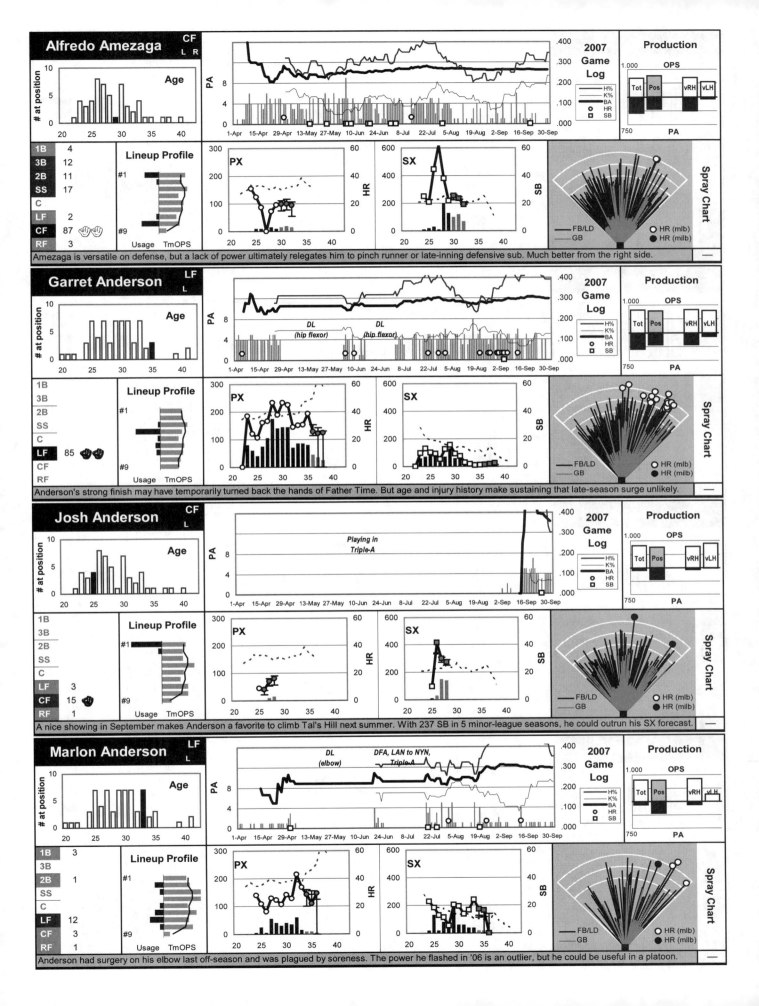

Alfredo Amezaga — CF — L R

Age | PA | 2007 Game Log | Production — OPS

1B 4
3B 12
2B 11
SS 17
C
LF 2
CF 87
RF 3

Lineup Profile — #1 ... #9 — Usage — TmOPS

PX | SX | Spray Chart — FB/LD — GB — HR (mlb) — HR (milb)

Amezaga is versatile on defense, but a lack of power ultimately relegates him to pinch runner or late-inning defensive sub. Much better from the right side. —

Garret Anderson — LF — L

Age | PA | 2007 Game Log | Production — OPS

DL (hip flexor)   DL (hip flexor)

1B
3B
2B
SS
C
LF 85
CF
RF

Lineup Profile — #1 ... #9 — Usage — TmOPS

PX | SX | Spray Chart — FB/LD — GB — HR (mlb) — HR (milb)

Anderson's strong finish may have temporarily turned back the hands of Father Time. But age and injury history make sustaining that late-season surge unlikely. —

Josh Anderson — CF — L

Age | PA | 2007 Game Log | Production — OPS

Playing in Triple-A

1B
3B
2B
SS
C
LF 3
CF 15
RF 1

Lineup Profile — #1 ... #9 — Usage — TmOPS

PX | SX | Spray Chart — FB/LD — GB — HR (mlb) — HR (milb)

A nice showing in September makes Anderson a favorite to climb Tal's Hill next summer. With 237 SB in 5 minor-league seasons, he could outrun his SX forecast. —

Marlon Anderson — LF — L

Age | PA | 2007 Game Log | Production — OPS

DL (elbow)   DFA, LAN to NYN, Triple-A

1B 3
3B
2B 1
SS
C
LF 12
CF 3
RF 1

Lineup Profile — #1 ... #9 — Usage — TmOPS

PX | SX | Spray Chart — FB/LD — GB — HR (mlb) — HR (milb)

Anderson had surgery on his elbow last off-season and was plagued by soreness. The power he flashed in '06 is an outlier, but he could be useful in a platoon. —

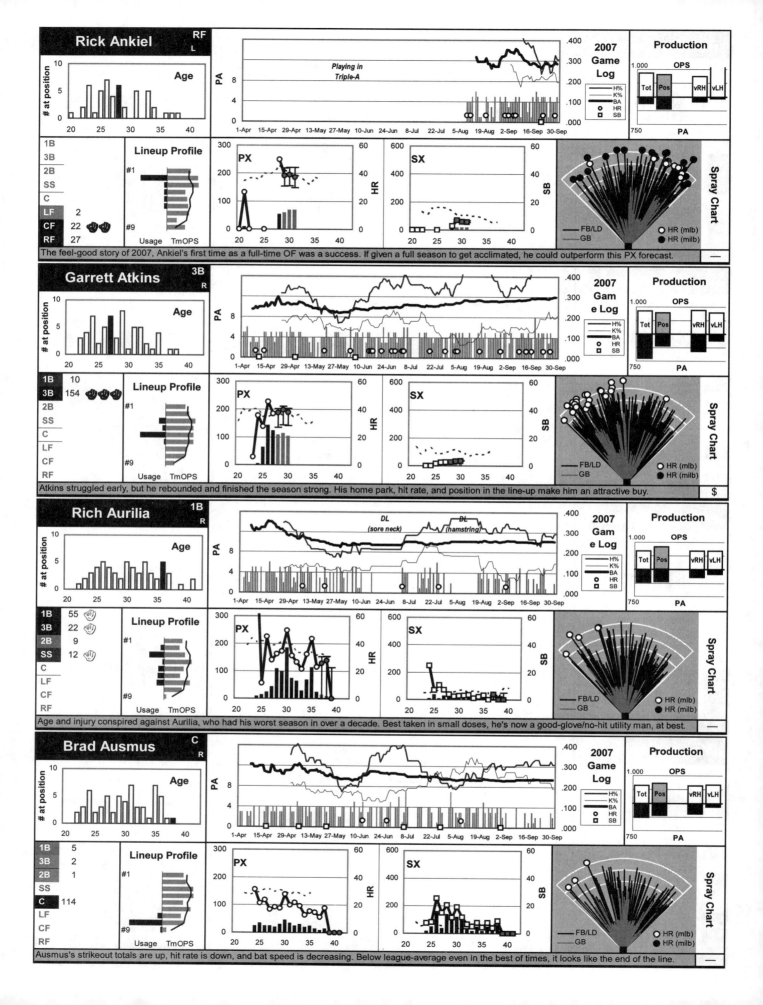

Rick Ankiel RF / L

Age

PA — 2007 Game Log
Playing in Triple-A
H% / K% / BA / HR / SB

Production — OPS (Tot, Pos, vRH, vLH) PA

1B / 3B / 2B / SS / C / LF 2 / CF 22 / RF 27

Lineup Profile (#1 ... #9, Usage, TmOPS)

PX / HR
SX / SB
Spray Chart — FB/LD, GB, HR (mlb), HR (milb)

The feel-good story of 2007, Ankiel's first time as a full-time OF was a success. If given a full season to get acclimated, he could outperform this PX forecast. —

Garrett Atkins 3B / R

Age

PA — 2007 Game Log
H% / K% / BA / HR / SB

Production — OPS (Tot, Pos, vRH, vLH) PA

1B 10 / 3B 154 / 2B / SS / C / LF / CF / RF

Lineup Profile (#1 ... #9, Usage, TmOPS)

PX / HR
SX / SB
Spray Chart — FB/LD, GB, HR (mlb), HR (milb)

Atkins struggled early, but he rebounded and finished the season strong. His home park, hit rate, and position in the line-up make him an attractive buy. $

Rich Aurilia 1B / R

Age

PA — 2007 Game Log
DL (sore neck) / DL (hamstring)
H% / K% / BA / HR / SB

Production — OPS (Tot, Pos, vRH, vLH) PA

1B 55 / 3B 22 / 2B 9 / SS 12 / C / LF / CF / RF

Lineup Profile (#1 ... #9, Usage, TmOPS)

PX / HR
SX / SB
Spray Chart — FB/LD, GB, HR (mlb), HR (milb)

Age and injury conspired against Aurilia, who had his worst season in over a decade. Best taken in small doses, he's now a good-glove/no-hit utility man, at best. —

Brad Ausmus C / R

Age

PA — 2007 Game Log
H% / K% / BA / HR / SB

Production — OPS (Tot, Pos, vRH, vLH) PA

1B 5 / 3B 2 / 2B 1 / SS / C 114 / LF / CF / RF

Lineup Profile (#1 ... #9, Usage, TmOPS)

PX / HR
SX / SB
Spray Chart — FB/LD, GB, HR (mlb), HR (milb)

Ausmus's strikeout totals are up, hit rate is down, and bat speed is decreasing. Below league-average even in the best of times, it looks like the end of the line. —

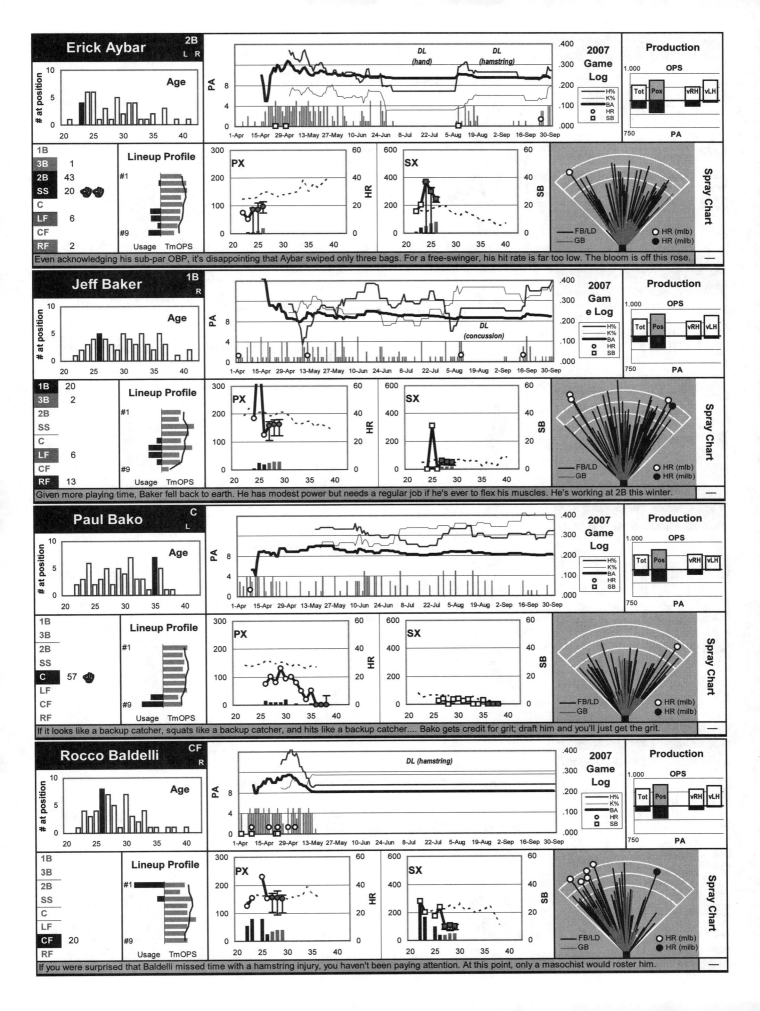

Erick Aybar — 2B — L R

Age

PA / 2007 Game Log
.400 / .300 / .200 / .100 / .000
H% / K% / BA / HR / SB

DL (hand)   DL (hamstring)

Production — OPS
1.000 / 750
Tot / Pos / vRH / vLH
PA

Pos	#
1B	
3B	1
2B	43
SS	20
C	
LF	6
CF	
RF	2

Lineup Profile — #1 ... #9 — Usage / TmOPS

PX — HR

SX — SB

Spray Chart — FB/LD / GB / HR (mlb) / HR (milb)

Even acknowledging his sub-par OBP, it's disappointing that Aybar swiped only three bags. For a free-swinger, his hit rate is far too low. The bloom is off this rose. —

Jeff Baker — 1B — R

Age

PA / 2007 Game Log
.400 / .300 / .200 / .100 / .000
H% / K% / BA / HR / SB

DL (concussion)

Production — OPS
1.000 / 750
Tot / Pos / vRH / vLH
PA

Pos	#
1B	20
3B	2
2B	
SS	
C	
LF	6
CF	
RF	13

Lineup Profile — #1 ... #9 — Usage / TmOPS

PX — HR

SX — SB

Spray Chart — FB/LD / GB / HR (mlb) / HR (milb)

Given more playing time, Baker fell back to earth. He has modest power but needs a regular job if he's ever to flex his muscles. He's working at 2B this winter. —

Paul Bako — C — L

Age

PA / 2007 Game Log
.400 / .300 / .200 / .100 / .000
H% / K% / BA / HR / SB

Production — OPS
1.000 / 750
Tot / Pos / vRH / vLH
PA

Pos	#
1B	
3B	
2B	
SS	
C	57
LF	
CF	
RF	

Lineup Profile — #1 ... #9 — Usage / TmOPS

PX — HR

SX — SB

Spray Chart — FB/LD / GB / HR (mlb) / HR (milb)

If it looks like a backup catcher, squats like a backup catcher, and hits like a backup catcher.... Bako gets credit for grit; draft him and you'll just get the grit. —

Rocco Baldelli — CF — R

Age

PA / 2007 Game Log
.400 / .300 / .200 / .100 / .000
H% / K% / BA / HR / SB

DL (hamstring)

Production — OPS
1.000 / 750
Tot / Pos / vRH / vLH
PA

Pos	#
1B	
3B	
2B	
SS	
C	
LF	
CF	20
RF	

Lineup Profile — #1 ... #9 — Usage / TmOPS

PX — HR

SX — SB

Spray Chart — FB/LD / GB / HR (mlb) / HR (milb)

If you were surprised that Baldelli missed time with a hamstring injury, you haven't been paying attention. At this point, only a masochist would roster him. —

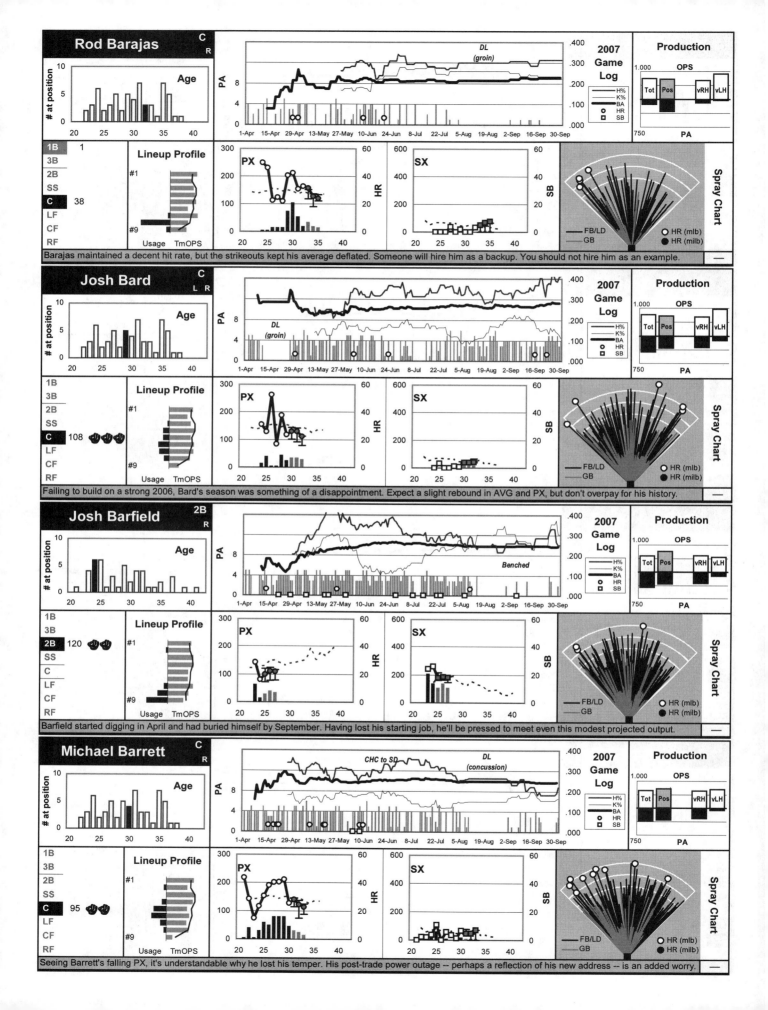

Rod Barajas C R

Barajas maintained a decent hit rate, but the strikeouts kept his average deflated. Someone will hire him as a backup. You should not hire him as an example.

Josh Bard C L R

Failing to build on a strong 2006, Bard's season was something of a disappointment. Expect a slight rebound in AVG and PX, but don't overpay for his history.

Josh Barfield 2B R

Barfield started digging in April and had buried himself by September. Having lost his starting job, he'll be pressed to meet even this modest projected output.

Michael Barrett C R

Seeing Barrett's falling PX, it's understandable why he lost his temper. His post-trade power outage -- perhaps a reflection of his new address -- is an added worry.

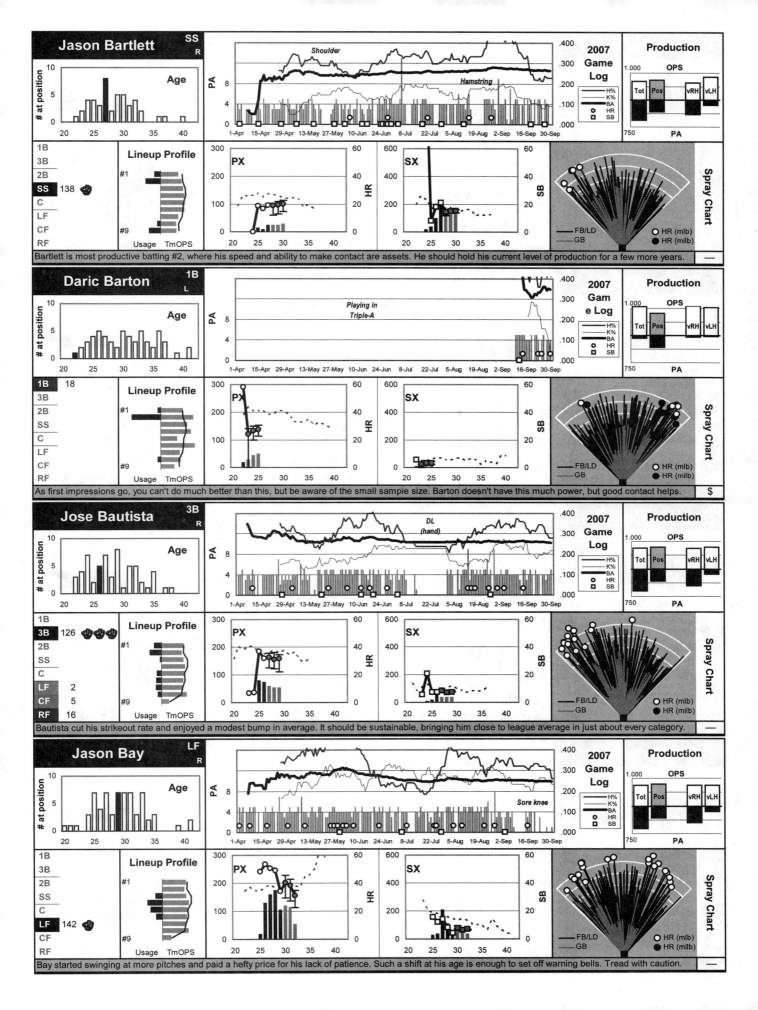

Jason Bartlett SS R

Bartlett is most productive batting #2, where his speed and ability to make contact are assets. He should hold his current level of production for a few more years. —

Daric Barton 1B L

As first impressions go, you can't do much better than this, but be aware of the small sample size. Barton doesn't have this much power, but good contact helps. $

Jose Bautista 3B R

Bautista cut his strikeout rate and enjoyed a modest bump in average. It should be sustainable, bringing him close to league average in just about every category. —

Jason Bay LF R

Bay started swinging at more pitches and paid a hefty price for his lack of patience. Such a shift at his age is enough to set off warning bells. Tread with caution. —

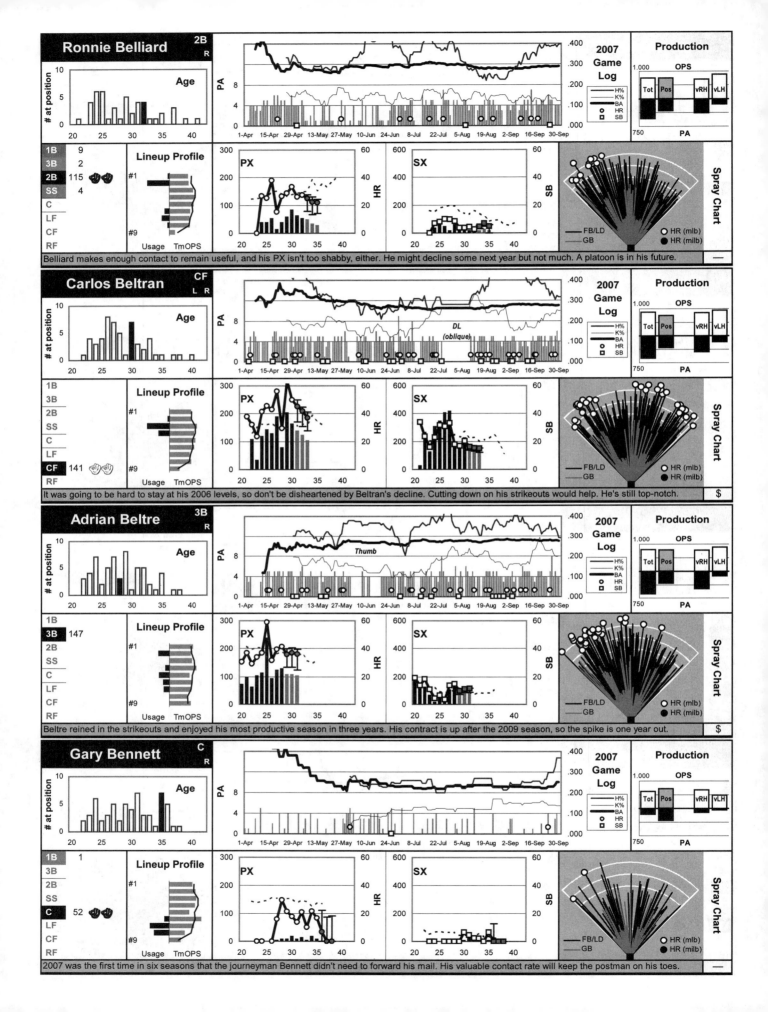

Ronnie Belliard — 2B / R

Age (# at position)

1B	9
3B	2
2B	115
SS	4
C	
LF	
CF	
RF	

Lineup Profile — Usage / TmOPS — #1 ... #9

PX · HR · SX · SB

2007 Game Log: H% · K% · BA · HR · SB

Production — OPS — Tot · Pos · vRH · vLH — PA

Spray Chart — FB/LD · GB · HR (mlb) · HR (milb)

Belliard makes enough contact to remain useful, and his PX isn't too shabby, either. He might decline some next year but not much. A platoon is in his future. — —

Carlos Beltran — CF / L R

Age (# at position)

1B	
3B	
2B	
SS	
C	
LF	
CF	141
RF	

Lineup Profile — Usage / TmOPS — #1 ... #9

PX · HR · SX · SB

2007 Game Log: H% · K% · BA · HR · SB — DL (oblique)

Production — OPS — Tot · Pos · vRH · vLH — PA

Spray Chart — FB/LD · GB · HR (mlb) · HR (milb)

It was going to be hard to stay at his 2006 levels, so don't be disheartened by Beltran's decline. Cutting down on his strikeouts would help. He's still top-notch. — $

Adrian Beltre — 3B / R

Age (# at position)

1B	
3B	147
2B	
SS	
C	
LF	
CF	
RF	

Lineup Profile — Usage / TmOPS — #1 ... #9

PX · HR · SX · SB

2007 Game Log: H% · K% · BA · HR · SB — Thumb

Production — OPS — Tot · Pos · vRH · vLH — PA

Spray Chart — FB/LD · GB · HR (mlb) · HR (milb)

Beltre reined in the strikeouts and enjoyed his most productive season in three years. His contract is up after the 2009 season, so the spike is one year out. — $

Gary Bennett — C / R

Age (# at position)

1B	1
3B	
2B	
SS	
C	52
LF	
CF	
RF	

Lineup Profile — Usage / TmOPS — #1 ... #9

PX · HR · SX · SB

2007 Game Log: H% · K% · BA · HR · SB

Production — OPS — Tot · Pos · vRH · vLH — PA

Spray Chart — FB/LD · GB · HR (mlb) · HR (milb)

2007 was the first time in six seasons that the journeyman Bennett didn't need to forward his mail. His valuable contact rate will keep the postman on his toes. — —

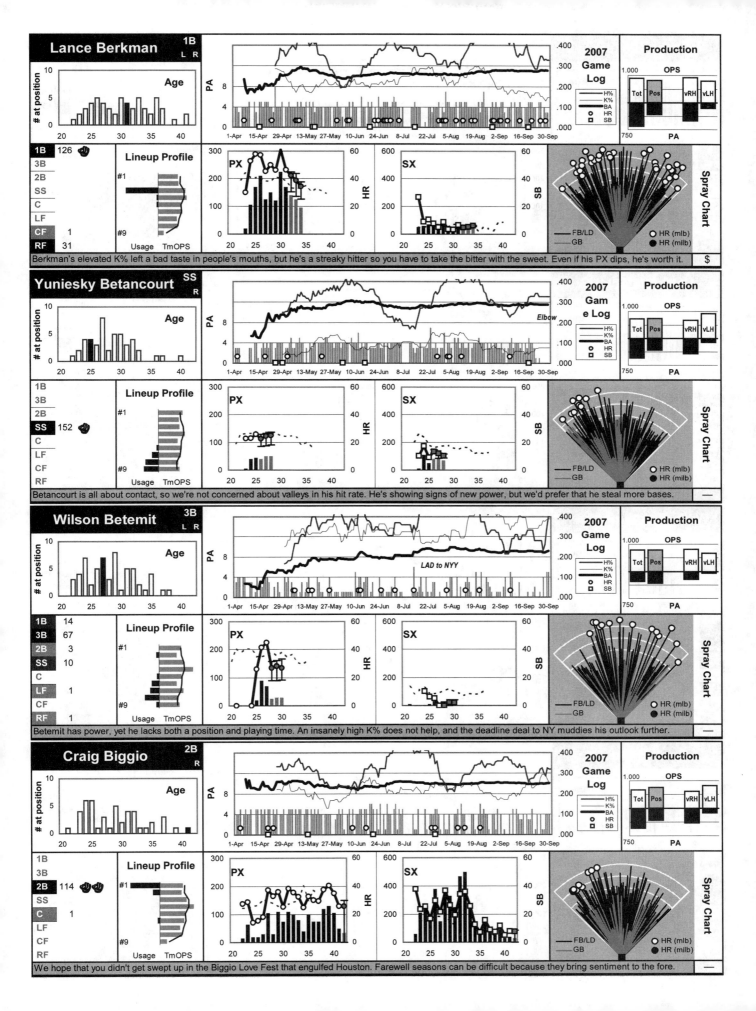

Lance Berkman 1B
L R

Age · # at position

1B 126
3B
2B
SS
C
LF
CF 1
RF 31

Lineup Profile · #1 ... #9 · Usage TmOPS

PA · 2007 Game Log · H% K% BA HR SB · 1-Apr 15-Apr 29-Apr 13-May 27-May 10-Jun 24-Jun 8-Jul 22-Jul 5-Aug 19-Aug 2-Sep 16-Sep 30-Sep

Production · OPS · 1.000 · Tot Pos vRH vLH · 750 · PA

PX · HR · **SX** · SB · FB/LD GB · HR (mlb) HR (milb) · Spray Chart

Berkman's elevated K% left a bad taste in people's mouths, but he's a streaky hitter so you have to take the bitter with the sweet. Even if his PX dips, he's worth it. $

Yuniesky Betancourt SS
R

Age · # at position

1B
3B
2B
SS 152
C
LF
CF
RF

Lineup Profile · #1 ... #9 · Usage TmOPS

PA · 2007 Game Log · Elbow · H% K% BA HR SB · 1-Apr 15-Apr 29-Apr 13-May 27-May 10-Jun 24-Jun 8-Jul 22-Jul 5-Aug 19-Aug 2-Sep 16-Sep 30-Sep

Production · OPS · 1.000 · Tot Pos vRH vLH · 750 · PA

PX · HR · **SX** · SB · FB/LD GB · HR (mlb) HR (milb) · Spray Chart

Betancourt is all about contact, so we're not concerned about valleys in his hit rate. He's showing signs of new power, but we'd prefer that he steal more bases. —

Wilson Betemit 3B
L R

Age · # at position

1B 14
3B 67
2B 3
SS 10
C
LF 1
CF
RF 1

Lineup Profile · #1 ... #9 · Usage TmOPS

PA · 2007 Game Log · LAD to NYY · H% K% BA HR · 1-Apr 15-Apr 29-Apr 13-May 27-May 10-Jun 24-Jun 8-Jul 22-Jul 5-Aug 19-Aug 2-Sep 16-Sep 30-Sep

Production · OPS · 1.000 · Tot Pos vRH vLH · 750 · PA

PX · HR · **SX** · SB · FB/LD GB · HR (mlb) HR (milb) · Spray Chart

Betemit has power, yet he lacks both a position and playing time. An insanely high K% does not help, and the deadline deal to NY muddies his outlook further. —

Craig Biggio 2B
R

Age · # at position

1B
3B
2B 114
SS
C 1
LF
CF
RF

Lineup Profile · #1 ... #9 · Usage TmOPS

PA · 2007 Game Log · H% K% BA HR SB · 1-Apr 15-Apr 29-Apr 13-May 27-May 10-Jun 24-Jun 8-Jul 22-Jul 5-Aug 19-Aug 2-Sep 16-Sep 30-Sep

Production · OPS · 1.000 · Tot Pos vRH vLH · 750 · PA

PX · HR · **SX** · SB · FB/LD GB · HR (mlb) HR (milb) · Spray Chart

We hope that you didn't get swept up in the Biggio Love Fest that engulfed Houston. Farewell seasons can be difficult because they bring sentiment to the fore. —

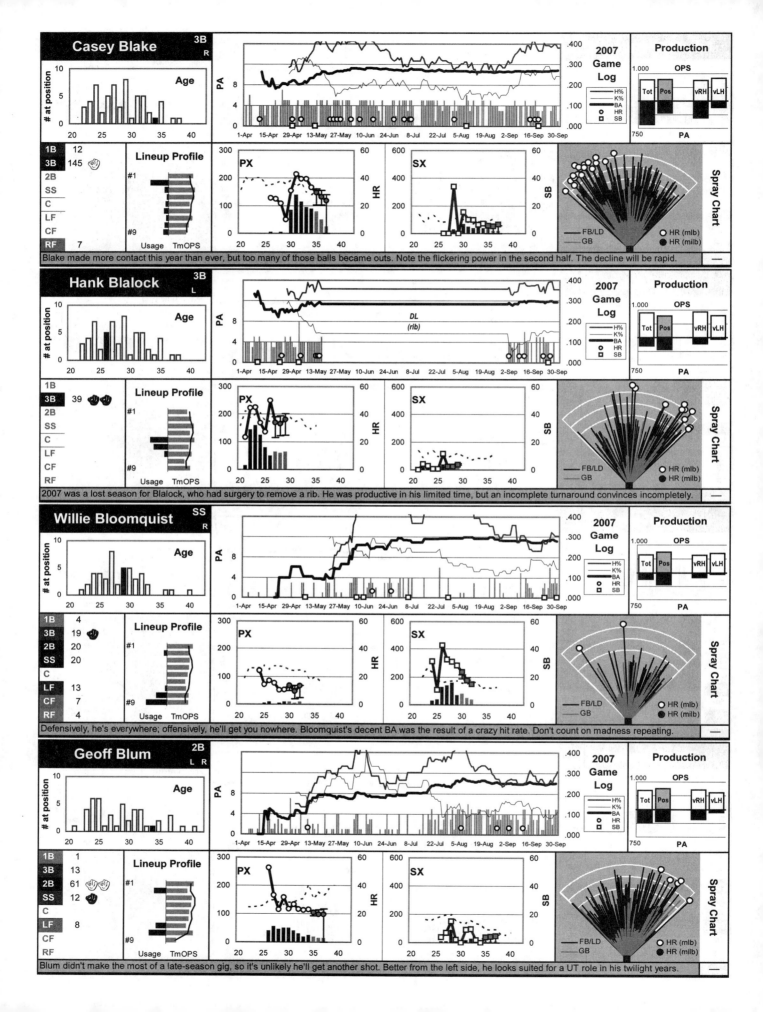

Casey Blake — 3B, R

Age / PA / 2007 Game Log (H%, K%, BA, HR, SB) / Production OPS (Tot, Pos, vRH, vLH) / PA

Position	#
1B	12
3B	145
2B	
SS	
C	
LF	
CF	
RF	7

Lineup Profile — #1 ... #9, Usage, TmOPS

PX / SX / Spray Chart (FB/LD, GB, HR (mlb), HR (milb))

Blake made more contact this year than ever, but too many of those balls became outs. Note the flickering power in the second half. The decline will be rapid.

Hank Blalock — 3B, L

Age / PA / 2007 Game Log / DL (rib) / Production OPS (Tot, Pos, vRH, vLH) / PA

Position	#
1B	
3B	39
2B	
SS	
C	
LF	
CF	
RF	

Lineup Profile — #1 ... #9, Usage, TmOPS

PX / SX / Spray Chart

2007 was a lost season for Blalock, who had surgery to remove a rib. He was productive in his limited time, but an incomplete turnaround convinces incompletely.

Willie Bloomquist — SS, R

Age / PA / 2007 Game Log / Production OPS (Tot, Pos, vRH, vLH) / PA

Position	#
1B	4
3B	19
2B	20
SS	20
C	
LF	13
CF	7
RF	4

Lineup Profile — #1 ... #9, Usage, TmOPS

PX / SX / Spray Chart

Defensively, he's everywhere; offensively, he'll get you nowhere. Bloomquist's decent BA was the result of a crazy hit rate. Don't count on madness repeating.

Geoff Blum — 2B, L R

Age / PA / 2007 Game Log / Production OPS (Tot, Pos, vRH, vLH) / PA

Position	#
1B	1
3B	13
2B	61
SS	12
C	
LF	8
CF	
RF	

Lineup Profile — #1 ... #9, Usage, TmOPS

PX / SX / Spray Chart

Blum didn't make the most of a late-season gig, so it's unlikely he'll get another shot. Better from the left side, he looks suited for a UT role in his twilight years.

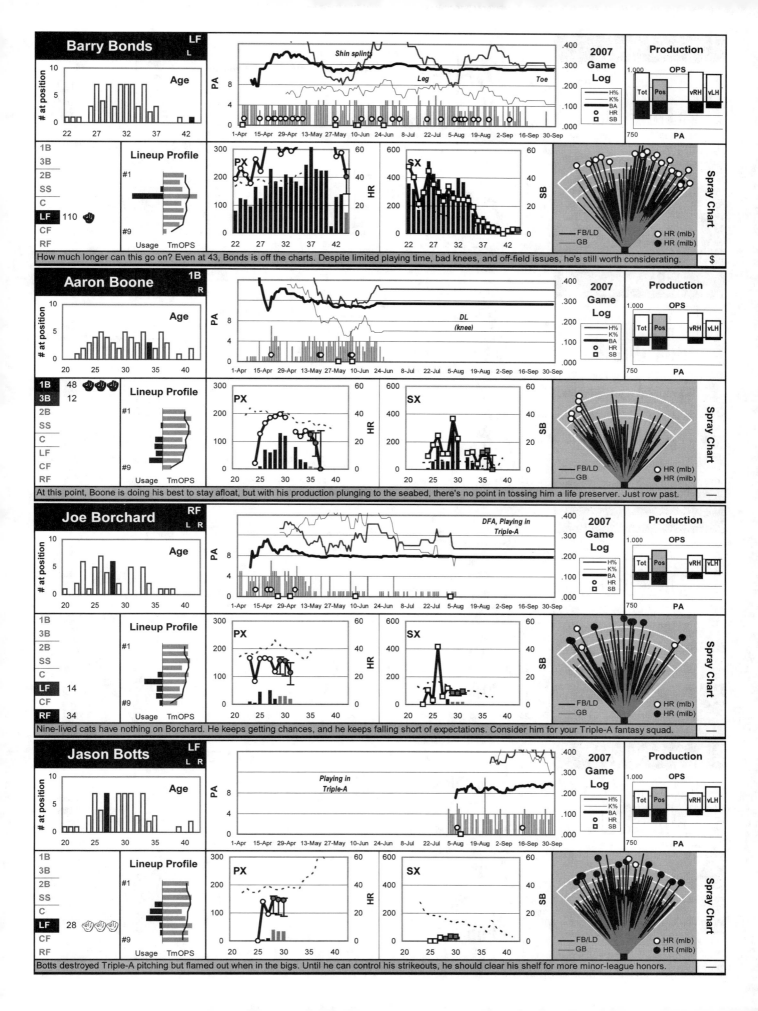

Barry Bonds — LF / L

Shin splints

Leg

Toe

2007 Game Log
- H%
- K%
- BA
- ○ HR
- □ SB

Production — OPS
Tot | Pos | vRH | vLH

1B
3B
2B
SS
C
LF 110
CF
RF

Lineup Profile #1 ... #9 Usage TmOPS

PX — HR

SX — SB

Spray Chart
FB/LD
GB
○ HR (mlb)
● HR (milb)

How much longer can this go on? Even at 43, Bonds is off the charts. Despite limited playing time, bad knees, and off-field issues, he's still worth considering. **$**

Aaron Boone — 1B / R

DL (knee)

2007 Game Log
- H%
- K%
- BA
- ○ HR
- □ SB

Production — OPS
Tot | Pos | vRH | vLH

1B 48
3B 12
2B
SS
C
LF
CF
RF

Lineup Profile #1 ... #9 Usage TmOPS

PX — HR

SX — SB

Spray Chart
FB/LD
GB
○ HR (mlb)
● HR (milb)

At this point, Boone is doing his best to stay afloat, but with his production plunging to the seabed, there's no point in tossing him a life preserver. Just row past. **—**

Joe Borchard — RF / L R

DFA, Playing in Triple-A

2007 Game Log
- H%
- K%
- BA
- ○ HR
- □ SB

Production — OPS
Tot | Pos | vRH | vLH

1B
3B
2B
SS
C
LF 14
CF
RF 34

Lineup Profile #1 ... #9 Usage TmOPS

PX — HR

SX — SB

Spray Chart
FB/LD
GB
○ HR (mlb)
● HR (milb)

Nine-lived cats have nothing on Borchard. He keeps getting chances, and he keeps falling short of expectations. Consider him for your Triple-A fantasy squad. **—**

Jason Botts — LF / L R

Playing in Triple-A

2007 Game Log
- H%
- K%
- BA
- ○ HR
- □ SB

Production — OPS
Tot | Pos | vRH | vLH

1B
3B
2B
SS
C
LF 28
CF
RF

Lineup Profile #1 ... #9 Usage TmOPS

PX — HR

SX — SB

Spray Chart
FB/LD
GB
○ HR (mlb)
● HR (milb)

Botts destroyed Triple-A pitching but flamed out when in the bigs. Until he can control his strikeouts, he should clear his shelf for more minor-league honors. **—**

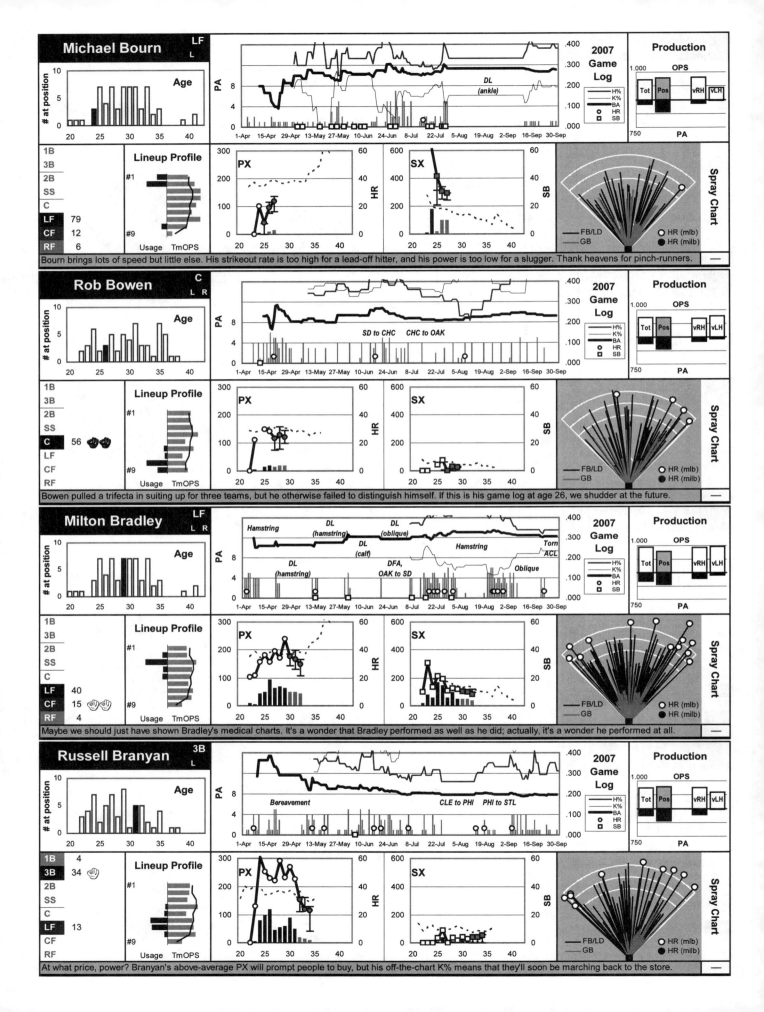

Michael Bourn — LF / L

Age (# at position): 20–40

2007 Game Log — H%, K%, BA, HR, SB
DL (ankle)

Production — OPS / PA: Tot, Pos, vRH, vLH

LF 79
CF 12
RF 6

Lineup Profile — #1 ... #9, Usage, TmOPS

PX / HR

SX / SB
FB/LD, GB, HR (mlb), HR (milb)

Spray Chart

Bourn brings lots of speed but little else. His strikeout rate is too high for a lead-off hitter, and his power is too low for a slugger. Thank heavens for pinch-runners. —

Rob Bowen — C / L R

Age (# at position): 20–40

2007 Game Log — H%, K%, BA, HR, SB
SD to CHC   CHC to OAK

Production — OPS / PA: Tot, Pos, vRH, vLH

C 56

Lineup Profile — #1 ... #9, Usage, TmOPS

PX / HR

SX / SB
FB/LD, GB, HR (mlb), HR (milb)

Spray Chart

Bowen pulled a trifecta in suiting up for three teams, but he otherwise failed to distinguish himself. If this is his game log at age 26, we shudder at the future. —

Milton Bradley — LF / L R

Age (# at position): 20–40

2007 Game Log — H%, K%, BA, HR, SB
Hamstring   DL (hamstring)   DL (oblique)
DL (calf)   Hamstring   Torn ACL
DL (hamstring)   DFA, OAK to SD   Oblique

Production — OPS / PA: Tot, Pos, vRH, vLH

LF 40
CF 15
RF 4

Lineup Profile — #1 ... #9, Usage, TmOPS

PX / HR

SX / SB
FB/LD, GB, HR (mlb), HR (milb)

Spray Chart

Maybe we should just have shown Bradley's medical charts. It's a wonder that Bradley performed as well as he did; actually, it's a wonder he performed at all. —

Russell Branyan — 3B / L

Age (# at position): 20–40

2007 Game Log — H%, K%, BA, HR, SB
Bereavement   CLE to PHI   PHI to STL

Production — OPS / PA: Tot, Pos, vRH, vLH

1B 4
3B 34
LF 13

Lineup Profile — #1 ... #9, Usage, TmOPS

PX / HR

SX / SB
FB/LD, GB, HR (mlb), HR (milb)

Spray Chart

At what price, power? Branyan's above-average PX will prompt people to buy, but his off-the-chart K% means that they'll soon be marching back to the store. —

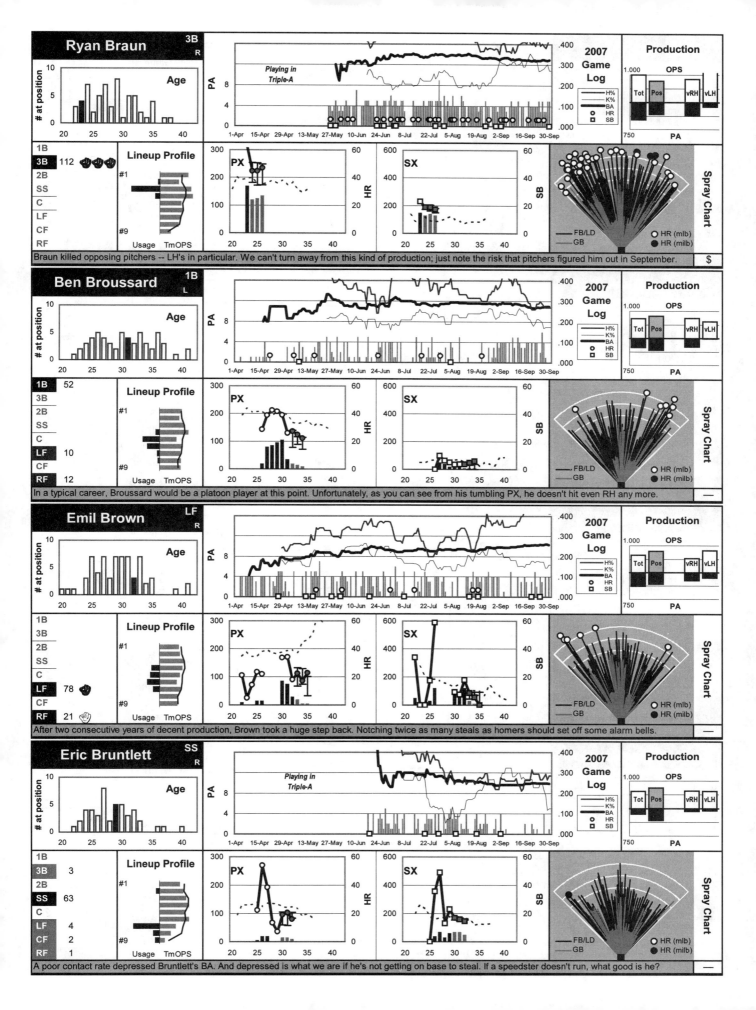

Ryan Braun — 3B / R

Age

PA — Playing in Triple-A

2007 Game Log
- H%
- K%
- BA
- HR ○
- SB □

Production — OPS
Tot | Pos | vRH | vLH — PA

1B
3B 112
2B
SS
C
LF
CF
RF

Lineup Profile — #1 ... #9 — Usage / TmOPS

PX | SX | Spray Chart
FB/LD — GB — HR (mlb) ○ — HR (milb) ●

Braun killed opposing pitchers -- LH's in particular. We can't turn away from this kind of production; just note the risk that pitchers figured him out in September. $

Ben Broussard — 1B / L

Age

PA

2007 Game Log
- H%
- K%
- BA
- HR ○
- SB □

Production — OPS
Tot | Pos | vRH | vLH — PA

1B 52
3B
2B
SS
C
LF 10
CF
RF 12

Lineup Profile — #1 ... #9 — Usage / TmOPS

PX | SX | Spray Chart
FB/LD — GB — HR (mlb) ○ — HR (milb) ●

In a typical career, Broussard would be a platoon player at this point. Unfortunately, as you can see from his tumbling PX, he doesn't hit even RH any more. —

Emil Brown — LF / R

Age

PA

2007 Game Log
- H%
- K%
- BA
- HR ○
- SB □

Production — OPS
Tot | Pos | vRH | vLH — PA

1B
3B
2B
SS
C
LF 78
CF
RF 21

Lineup Profile — #1 ... #9 — Usage / TmOPS

PX | SX | Spray Chart
FB/LD — GB — HR (mlb) ○ — HR (milb) ●

After two consecutive years of decent production, Brown took a huge step back. Notching twice as many steals as homers should set off some alarm bells. —

Eric Bruntlett — SS / R

Age

PA — Playing in Triple-A

2007 Game Log
- H%
- K%
- BA
- HR ○
- SB □

Production — OPS
Tot | Pos | vRH | vLH — PA

1B
3B 3
2B
SS 63
C
LF 4
CF 2
RF 1

Lineup Profile — #1 ... #9 — Usage / TmOPS

PX | SX | Spray Chart
FB/LD — GB — HR (mlb) ○ — HR (milb) ●

A poor contact rate depressed Bruntlett's BA. And depressed is what we are if he's not getting on base to steal. If a speedster doesn't run, what good is he? —

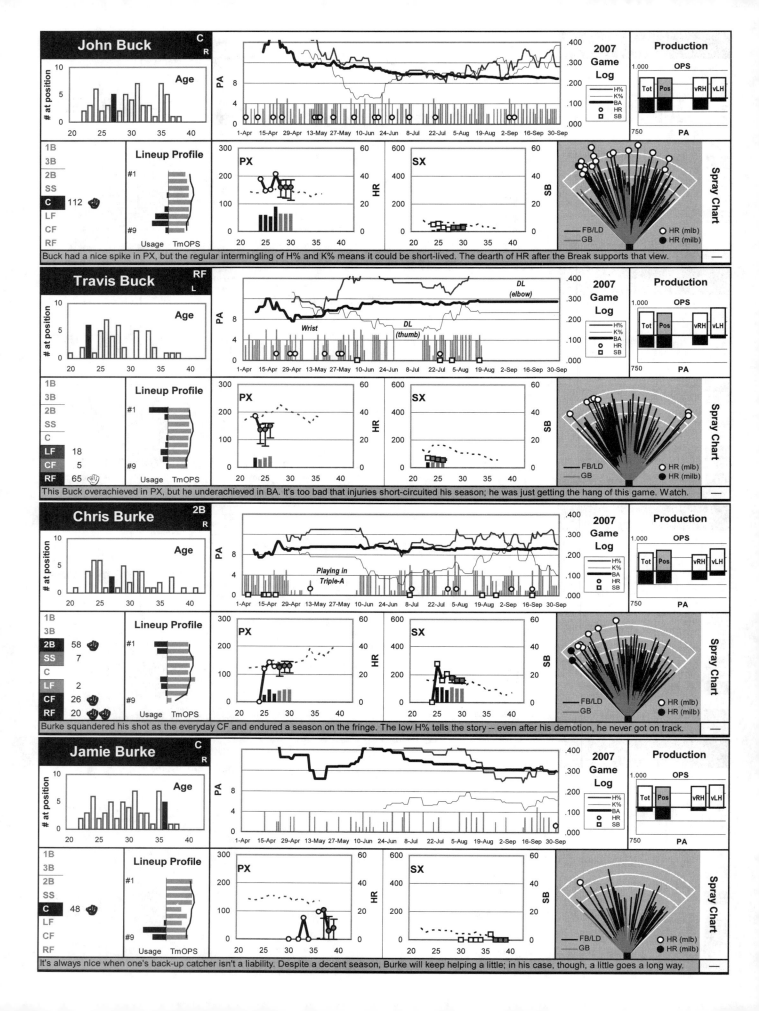

John Buck C R

2007 Game Log

Production

C 112

Buck had a nice spike in PX, but the regular intermingling of H% and K% means it could be short-lived. The dearth of HR after the Break supports that view. —

Travis Buck RF L

2007 Game Log

Production

LF 18
CF 5
RF 65

This Buck overachieved in PX, but he underachieved in BA. It's too bad that injuries short-circuited his season; he was just getting the hang of this game. Watch. —

Chris Burke 2B R

2007 Game Log

Production

Playing in Triple-A

2B 58
SS 7
LF 2
CF 26
RF 20

Burke squandered his shot as the everyday CF and endured a season on the fringe. The low H% tells the story -- even after his demotion, he never got on track. —

Jamie Burke C R

2007 Game Log

Production

C 48

It's always nice when one's back-up catcher isn't a liability. Despite a decent season, Burke will keep helping a little; in his case, though, a little goes a long way. —

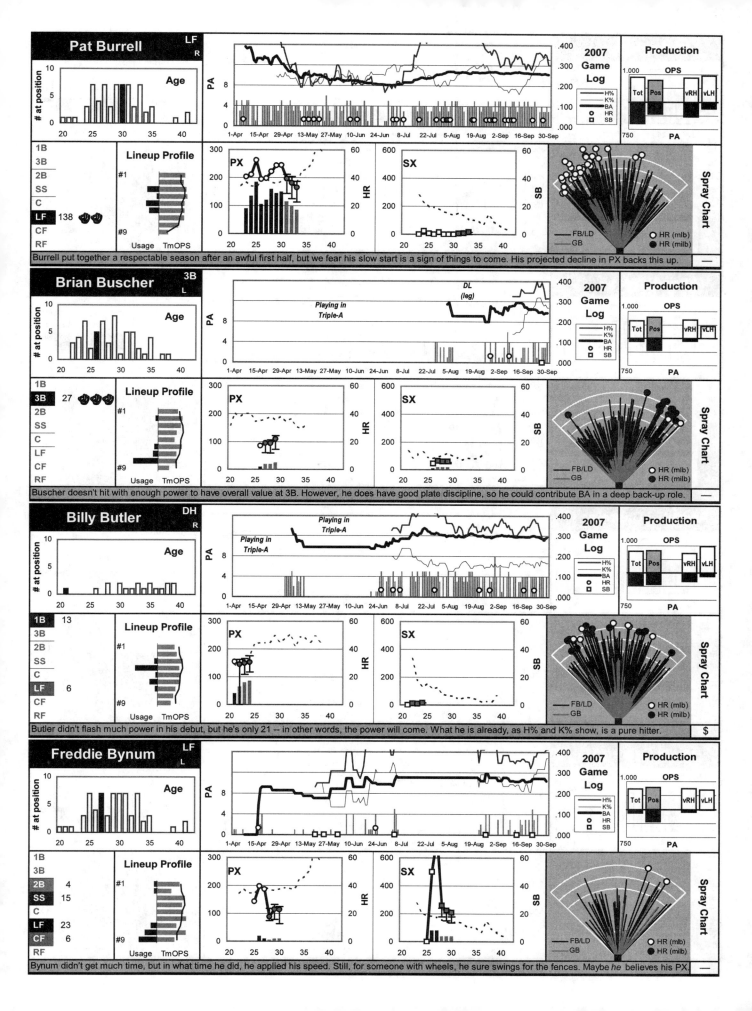

Pat Burrell — LF, R

Age · # at position

2007 Game Log · PA · .400 / .300 / .200 / .100 / .000 · H% · K% · BA · ○ HR · □ SB

1-Apr 15-Apr 29-Apr 13-May 27-May 10-Jun 24-Jun 8-Jul 22-Jul 5-Aug 19-Aug 2-Sep 16-Sep 30-Sep

Production · OPS · 1.000 · Tot · Pos · vRH · vLH · 750 · PA

1B · 3B · 2B · SS · C · **LF 138** · CF · RF

Lineup Profile · #1 ... #9 · Usage · TmOPS

PX · HR · SX · SB · **Spray Chart** · FB/LD · GB · ○ HR (mlb) · ● HR (milb)

Burrell put together a respectable season after an awful first half, but we fear his slow start is a sign of things to come. His projected decline in PX backs this up. — —

Brian Buscher — 3B, L

Age · # at position

2007 Game Log · PA · .400 / .300 / .200 / .100 / .000 · Playing in Triple-A · DL (leg) · H% · K% · BA · ○ HR · □ SB

1-Apr 15-Apr 29-Apr 13-May 27-May 10-Jun 24-Jun 8-Jul 5-Aug 19-Aug 2-Sep 16-Sep 30-Sep

Production · OPS · 1.000 · Tot · Pos · vRH · vLH · 750 · PA

1B · **3B 27** · 2B · SS · C · LF · CF · RF

Lineup Profile · #1 ... #9 · Usage · TmOPS

PX · HR · SX · SB · **Spray Chart** · FB/LD · GB · ○ HR (mlb) · ● HR (milb)

Buscher doesn't hit with enough power to have overall value at 3B. However, he does have good plate discipline, so he could contribute BA in a deep back-up role. — —

Billy Butler — DH, R

Age · # at position

2007 Game Log · PA · .400 / .300 / .200 / .100 / .000 · Playing in Triple-A · Playing in Triple-A · H% · K% · BA · ○ HR · □ SB

1-Apr 15-Apr 29-Apr 13-May 27-May 10-Jun 24-Jun 8-Jul 22-Jul 5-Aug 19-Aug 2-Sep 16-Sep 30-Sep

Production · OPS · 1.000 · Tot · Pos · vRH · vLH · 750 · PA

1B 13 · 3B · 2B · SS · C · **LF 6** · CF · RF

Lineup Profile · #1 ... #9 · Usage · TmOPS

PX · HR · SX · SB · **Spray Chart** · FB/LD · GB · ○ HR (mlb) · ● HR (milb)

Butler didn't flash much power in his debut, but he's only 21 -- in other words, the power will come. What he is already, as H% and K% show, is a pure hitter. $

Freddie Bynum — LF, L

Age · # at position

2007 Game Log · PA · .400 / .300 / .200 / .100 / .000 · H% · K% · BA · ○ HR · □ SB

1-Apr 15-Apr 29-Apr 13-May 27-May 10-Jun 24-Jun 8-Jul 22-Jul 5-Aug 19-Aug 2-Sep 16-Sep 30-Sep

Production · OPS · 1.000 · Tot · Pos · vRH · vLH · 750 · PA

1B · 3B · **2B 4** · **SS 15** · C · **LF 23** · **CF 6** · RF

Lineup Profile · #1 ... #9 · Usage · TmOPS

PX · HR · SX · SB · **Spray Chart** · FB/LD · GB · ○ HR (mlb) · ● HR (milb)

Bynum didn't get much time, but in what time he did, he applied his speed. Still, for someone with wheels, he sure swings for the fences. Maybe *he* believes his PX. — —

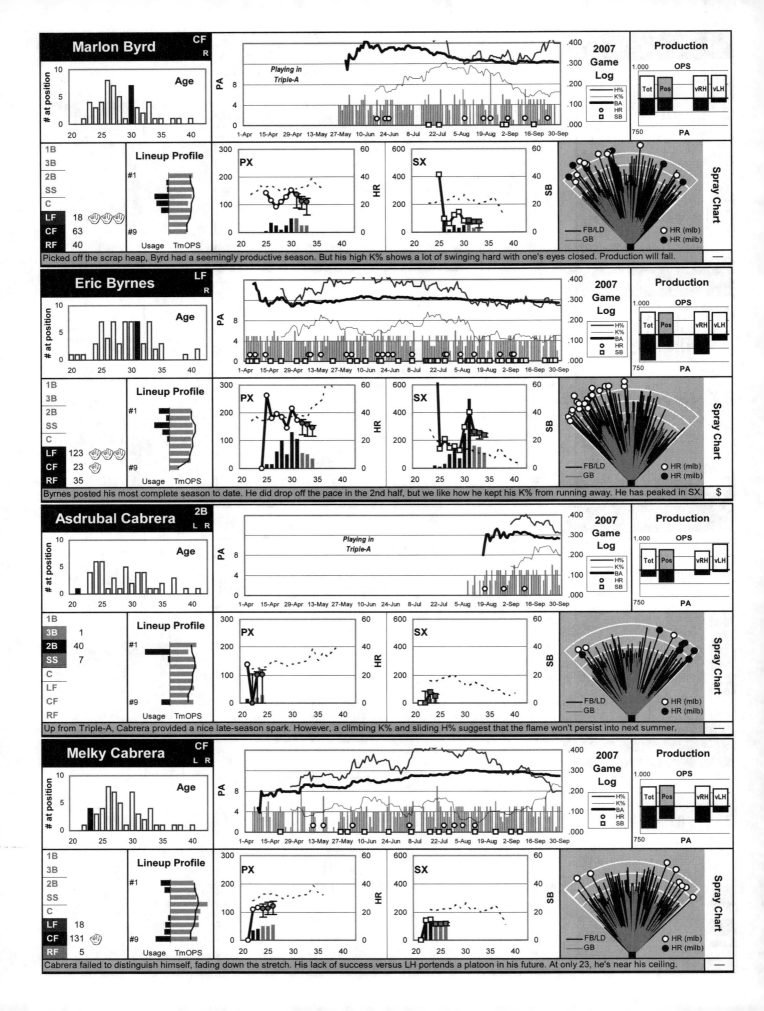

Marlon Byrd — CF / R

Age | # at position

Lineup Profile — Usage / TmOPS
- LF 18
- CF 63
- RF 40

2007 Game Log — PA / BA, H%, K%, HR, SB

Production — OPS: Tot, Pos, vRH, vLH / PA

PX | HR | SX | SB | Spray Chart (FB/LD, GB, HR (mlb), HR (milb))

Playing in Triple-A

Picked off the scrap heap, Byrd had a seemingly productive season. But his high K% shows a lot of swinging hard with one's eyes closed. Production will fall. —

Eric Byrnes — LF / R

Age | # at position

Lineup Profile — Usage / TmOPS
- LF 123
- CF 23
- RF 35

2007 Game Log — PA / BA, H%, K%, HR, SB

Production — OPS: Tot, Pos, vRH, vLH / PA

PX | HR | SX | SB | Spray Chart

Byrnes posted his most complete season to date. He did drop off the pace in the 2nd half, but we like how he kept his K% from running away. He has peaked in SX. $

Asdrubal Cabrera — 2B / L R

Age | # at position

Lineup Profile — Usage / TmOPS
- 3B 1
- 2B 40
- SS 7

2007 Game Log — PA / BA, H%, K%, HR, SB

Production — OPS: Tot, Pos, vRH, vLH / PA

PX | HR | SX | SB | Spray Chart

Playing in Triple-A

Up from Triple-A, Cabrera provided a nice late-season spark. However, a climbing K% and sliding H% suggest that the flame won't persist into next summer. —

Melky Cabrera — CF / L R

Age | # at position

Lineup Profile — Usage / TmOPS
- LF 18
- CF 131
- RF 5

2007 Game Log — PA / BA, H%, K%, HR, SB

Production — OPS: Tot, Pos, vRH, vLH / PA

PX | HR | SX | SB | Spray Chart

Cabrera failed to distinguish himself, fading down the stretch. His lack of success versus LH portends a platoon in his future. At only 23, he's near his ceiling. —

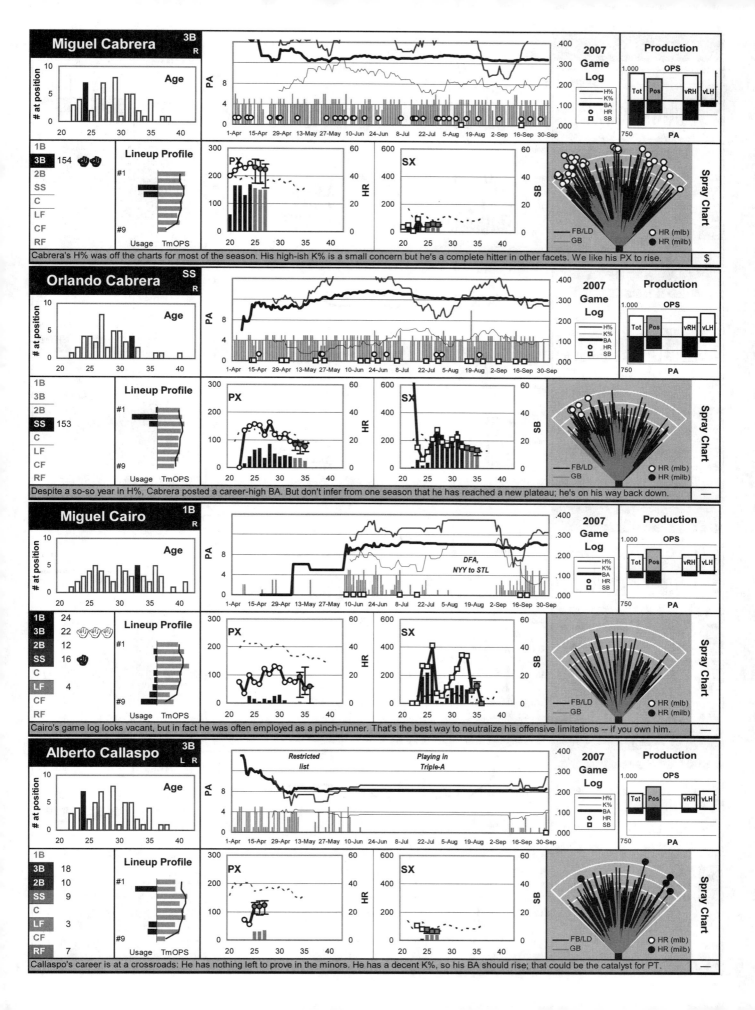

Miguel Cabrera — 3B / R

Cabrera's H% was off the charts for most of the season. His high-ish K% is a small concern but he's a complete hitter in other facets. We like his PX to rise. $

3B 154

Orlando Cabrera — SS / R

Despite a so-so year in H%, Cabrera posted a career-high BA. But don't infer from one season that he has reached a new plateau; he's on his way back down.   —

SS 153

Miguel Cairo — 1B / R

Cairo's game log looks vacant, but in fact he was often employed as a pinch-runner. That's the best way to neutralize his offensive limitations -- if you own him.   —

1B	24
3B	22
2B	12
SS	16
LF	4

DFA, NYY to STL

Alberto Callaspo — 3B / L R

Callaspo's career is at a crossroads: He has nothing left to prove in the minors. He has a decent K%, so his BA should rise; that could be the catalyst for PT.   —

3B	18
2B	10
SS	9
LF	3
RF	7

Restricted list *Playing in Triple-A*

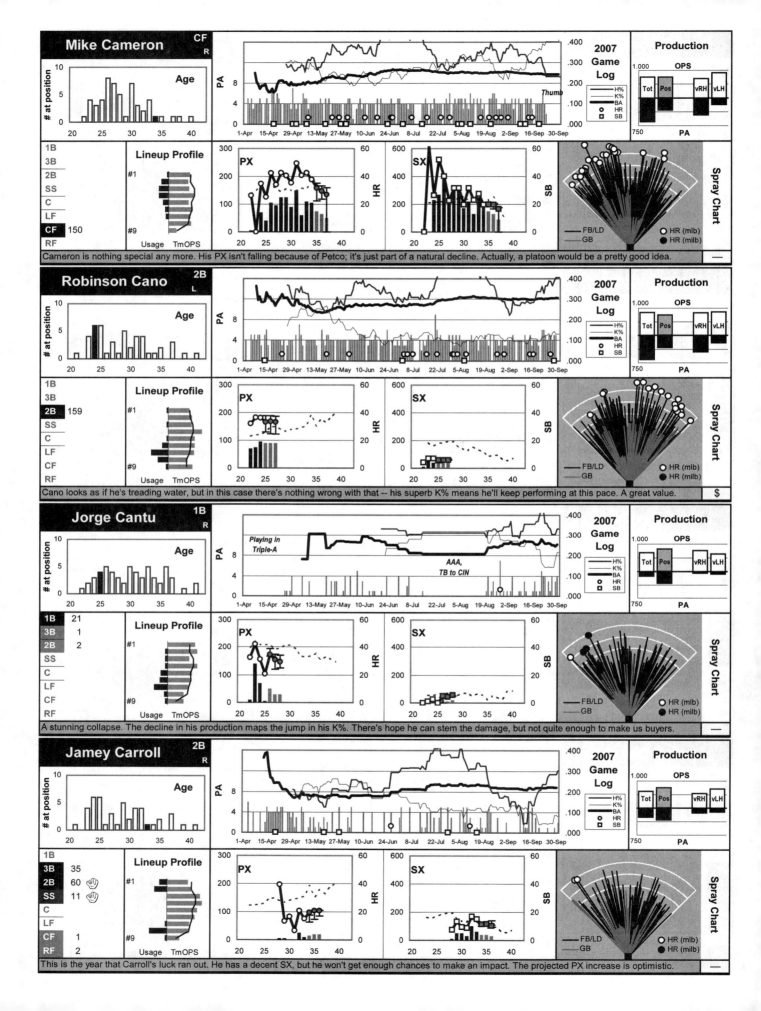

Mike Cameron — CF, R

Age (# at position)

2007 Game Log — H%, K%, BA, HR, SB — *Thumb*

Production — OPS: Tot, Pos, vRH, vLH

Position	
1B	
3B	
2B	
SS	
C	
LF	
CF	150
RF	

Lineup Profile — #1 ... #9, Usage, TmOPS

PX / HR — **SX** / SB

Spray Chart — FB/LD, GB, HR (mlb), HR (milb)

Cameron is nothing special any more. His PX isn't falling because of Petco; it's just part of a natural decline. Actually, a platoon would be a pretty good idea. — —

Robinson Cano — 2B, L

Age (# at position)

2007 Game Log — H%, K%, BA, HR, SB

Production — OPS: Tot, Pos, vRH, vLH

Position	
1B	
3B	
2B	159
SS	
C	
LF	
CF	
RF	

Lineup Profile — #1 ... #9, Usage, TmOPS

PX / HR — **SX** / SB

Spray Chart — FB/LD, GB, HR (mlb), HR (milb)

Cano looks as if he's treading water, but in this case there's nothing wrong with that -- his superb K% means he'll keep performing at this pace. A great value. — $

Jorge Cantu — 1B, R

Age (# at position)

2007 Game Log — H%, K%, BA, HR, SB — *Playing in Triple-A* — *AAA, TB to CIN*

Production — OPS: Tot, Pos, vRH, vLH

Position	
1B	21
3B	1
2B	2
SS	
C	
LF	
CF	
RF	

Lineup Profile — #1 ... #9, Usage, TmOPS

PX / HR — **SX** / SB

Spray Chart — FB/LD, GB, HR (mlb), HR (milb)

A stunning collapse. The decline in his production maps the jump in his K%. There's hope he can stem the damage, but not quite enough to make us buyers. — —

Jamey Carroll — 2B, R

Age (# at position)

2007 Game Log — H%, K%, BA, HR, SB

Production — OPS: Tot, Pos, vRH, vLH

Position	
1B	
3B	35
2B	60
SS	11
C	
LF	
CF	1
RF	2

Lineup Profile — #1 ... #9, Usage, TmOPS

PX / HR — **SX** / SB

Spray Chart — FB/LD, GB, HR (mlb), HR (milb)

This is the year that Carroll's luck ran out. He has a decent SX, but he won't get enough chances to make an impact. The projected PX increase is optimistic. — —

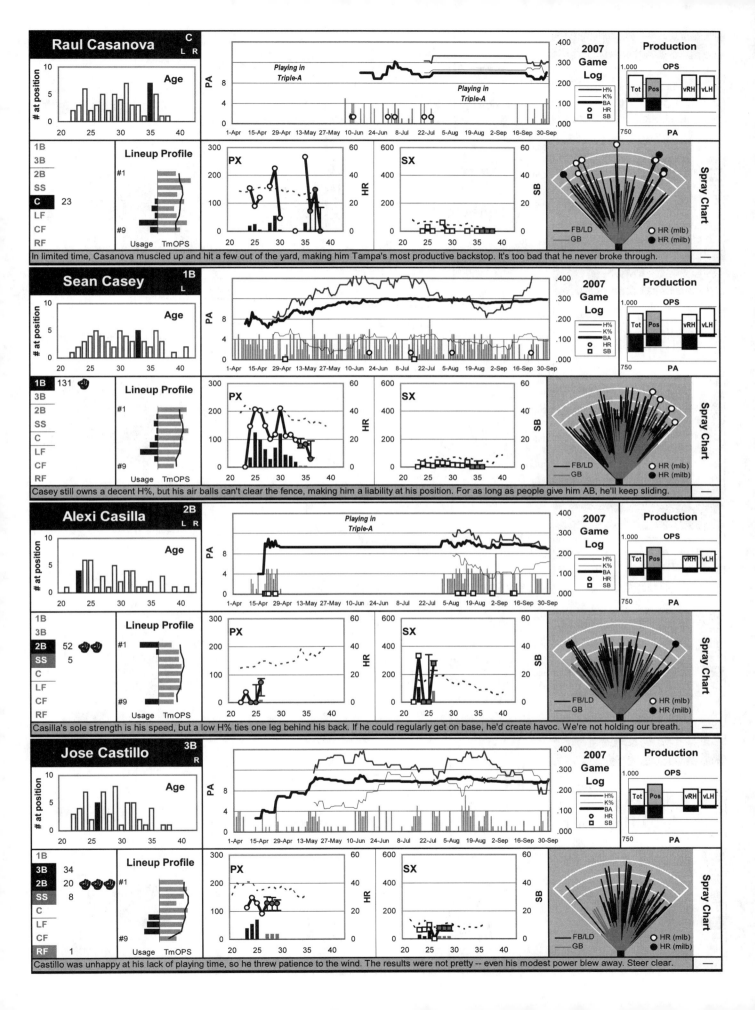

Raul Casanova — C L R

Age

PA / 2007 Game Log (H%, K%, BA, HR, SB)
Playing in Triple-A
Playing in Triple-A

Production — OPS (Tot, Pos, vRH, vLH) / PA

Lineup Profile

1B
3B
2B
SS
C   23
LF
CF
RF

Usage   TmOPS

PX / HR
SX / SB

Spray Chart — FB/LD, GB, HR (mlb), HR (milb)

In limited time, Casanova muscled up and hit a few out of the yard, making him Tampa's most productive backstop. It's too bad that he never broke through.   —

Sean Casey — 1B L

Age

PA / 2007 Game Log (H%, K%, BA, HR, SB)

Production — OPS (Tot, Pos, vRH, vLH) / PA

Lineup Profile

1B   131
3B
2B
SS
C
LF
CF
RF

Usage   TmOPS

PX / HR
SX / SB

Spray Chart — FB/LD, GB, HR (mlb), HR (milb)

Casey still owns a decent H%, but his air balls can't clear the fence, making him a liability at his position. For as long as people give him AB, he'll keep sliding.   —

Alexi Casilla — 2B L R

Age

PA / 2007 Game Log (H%, K%, BA, HR, SB)
Playing in Triple-A

Production — OPS (Tot, Pos, vRH, vLH) / PA

Lineup Profile

1B
3B
2B   52
SS   5
C
LF
CF
RF

Usage   TmOPS

PX / HR
SX / SB

Spray Chart — FB/LD, GB, HR (mlb), HR (milb)

Casilla's sole strength is his speed, but a low H% ties one leg behind his back. If he could regularly get on base, he'd create havoc. We're not holding our breath.   —

Jose Castillo — 3B R

Age

PA / 2007 Game Log (H%, K%, BA, HR, SB)

Production — OPS (Tot, Pos, vRH, vLH) / PA

Lineup Profile

1B
3B   34
2B   20
SS   8
C
LF
CF
RF   1

Usage   TmOPS

PX / HR
SX / SB

Spray Chart — FB/LD, GB, HR (mlb), HR (milb)

Castillo was unhappy at his lack of playing time, so he threw patience to the wind. The results were not pretty -- even his modest power blew away. Steer clear.   —

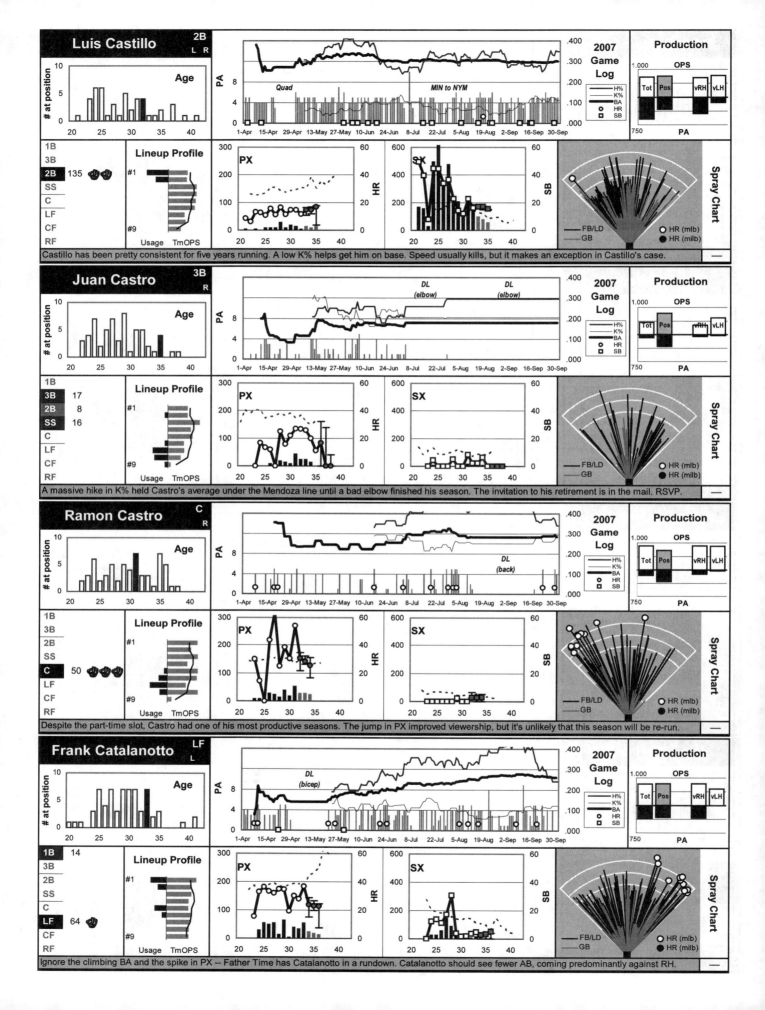

Luis Castillo 2B
L R

Castillo has been pretty consistent for five years running. A low K% helps get him on base. Speed usually kills, but it makes an exception in Castillo's case.

Juan Castro 3B
R

A massive hike in K% held Castro's average under the Mendoza line until a bad elbow finished his season. The invitation to his retirement is in the mail. RSVP.

Ramon Castro C
R

Despite the part-time slot, Castro had one of his most productive seasons. The jump in PX improved viewership, but it's unlikely that this season will be re-run.

Frank Catalanotto LF
L

Ignore the climbing BA and the spike in PX -- Father Time has Catalanotto in a rundown. Catalanotto should see fewer AB, coming predominantly against RH.

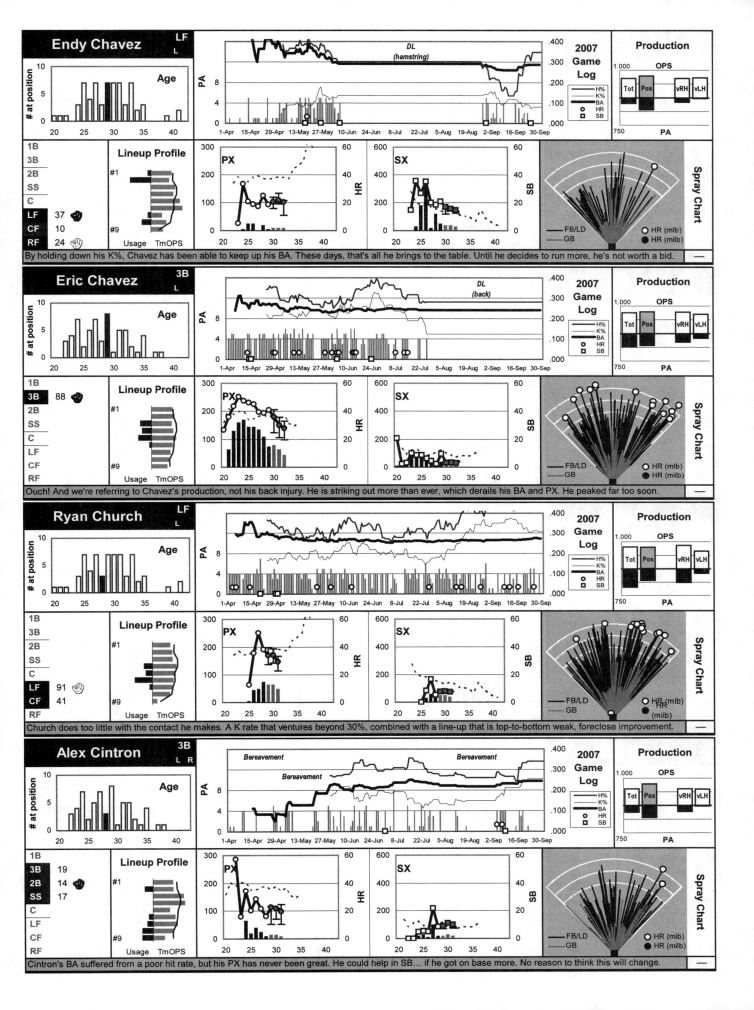

Endy Chavez — LF, L

Age / # at position

PA / 2007 Game Log — DL (hamstring)

Legend: H% / K% / BA / ○ HR / □ SB

Production — OPS: Tot, Pos, vRH, vLH / PA

1B, 3B, 2B, SS, C, **LF 37**, **CF 10**, **RF 24**

Lineup Profile #1 ... #9 / Usage TmOPS

PX / HR

SX / SB

Spray Chart — FB/LD, GB, ○ HR (mlb), ● HR (milb)

By holding down his K%, Chavez has been able to keep up his BA. These days, that's all he brings to the table. Until he decides to run more, he's not worth a bid. — —

Eric Chavez — 3B, L

Age / # at position

PA / 2007 Game Log — DL (back)

Legend: H% / K% / BA / ○ HR / □ SB

Production — OPS: Tot, Pos, vRH, vLH / PA

1B, **3B 88**, 2B, SS, C, LF, CF, RF

Lineup Profile #1 ... #9 / Usage TmOPS

PX / HR

SX / SB

Spray Chart — FB/LD, GB, ○ HR (mlb), ● HR (milb)

Ouch! And we're referring to Chavez's production, not his back injury. He is striking out more than ever, which derails his BA and PX. He peaked far too soon. — —

Ryan Church — LF, L

Age / # at position

PA / 2007 Game Log

Legend: H% / K% / BA / ○ HR / □ SB

Production — OPS: Tot, Pos, vRH, vLH / PA

1B, 3B, 2B, SS, C, **LF 91**, **CF 41**, RF

Lineup Profile #1 ... #9 / Usage TmOPS

PX / HR

SX / SB

Spray Chart — FB/LD, GB, ○ HR (mlb), ● (milb)

Church does too little with the contact he makes. A K rate that ventures beyond 30%, combined with a line-up that is top-to-bottom weak, foreclose improvement. — —

Alex Cintron — 3B, L R

Age / # at position

PA / 2007 Game Log — Bereavement, Bereavement, Bereavement

Legend: H% / K% / BA / ○ HR / □ SB

Production — OPS: Tot, Pos, vRH, vLH / PA

1B, **3B 19**, **2B 14**, **SS 17**, C, LF, CF, RF

Lineup Profile #1 ... #9 / Usage TmOPS

PX / HR

SX / SB

Spray Chart — FB/LD, GB, ○ HR (mlb), ● HR (milb)

Cintron's BA suffered from a poor hit rate, but his PX has never been great. He could help in SB... if he got on base more. No reason to think this will change. — —

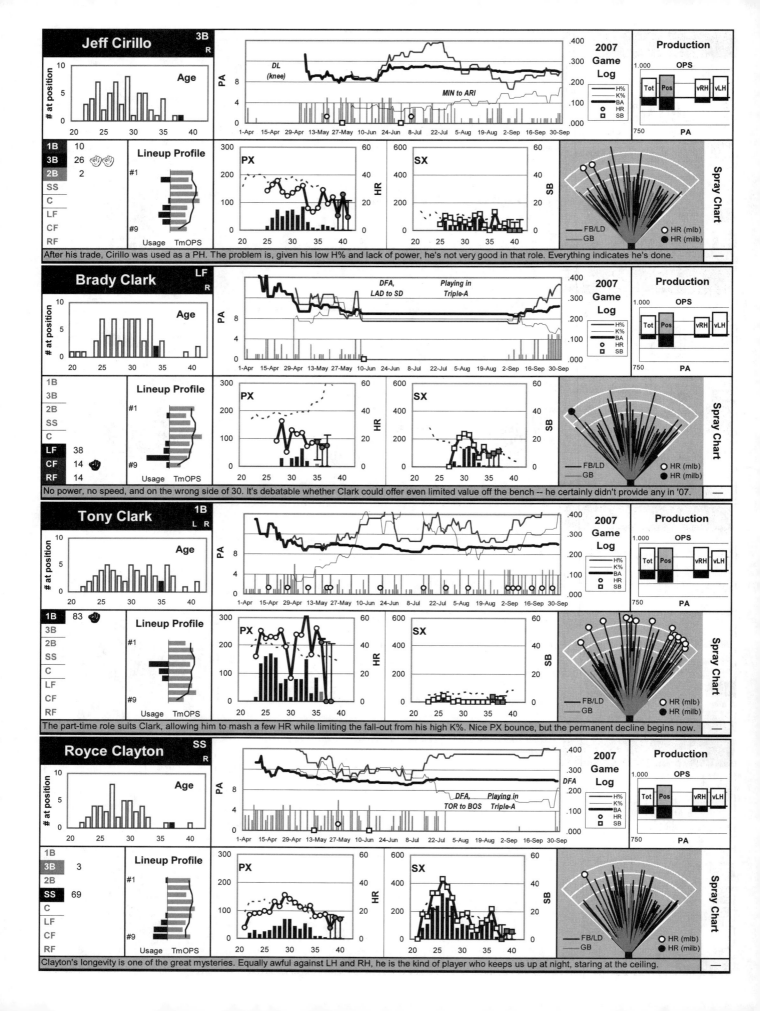

Jeff Cirillo — 3B, R

Age — # at position
2007 Game Log — PA, DL (knee), MIN to ARI, H%, K%, BA, HR (○), SB (□)
Production — OPS: Tot, Pos, vRH, vLH

1B	10
3B	26
2B	2

Lineup Profile — #1 to #9, Usage, TmOPS

PX, SX, Spray Chart — FB/LD, GB, HR (mlb) ○, HR (milb) ●

After his trade, Cirillo was used as a PH. The problem is, given his low H% and lack of power, he's not very good in that role. Everything indicates he's done. —

Brady Clark — LF, R

Age — # at position
2007 Game Log — PA, DFA LAD to SD, Playing in Triple-A, H%, K%, BA, HR (○), SB (□)
Production — OPS: Tot, Pos, vRH, vLH

LF	38
CF	14
RF	14

Lineup Profile — #1 to #9, Usage, TmOPS

PX, SX, Spray Chart — FB/LD, GB, HR (mlb) ○, HR (milb) ●

No power, no speed, and on the wrong side of 30. It's debatable whether Clark could offer even limited value off the bench -- he certainly didn't provide any in '07. —

Tony Clark — 1B, L R

Age — # at position
2007 Game Log — PA, H%, K%, BA, HR (○), SB (□)
Production — OPS: Tot, Pos, vRH, vLH

| 1B | 83 |

Lineup Profile — #1 to #9, Usage, TmOPS

PX, SX, Spray Chart — FB/LD, GB, HR (mlb) ○, HR (milb) ●

The part-time role suits Clark, allowing him to mash a few HR while limiting the fall-out from his high K%. Nice PX bounce, but the permanent decline begins now. —

Royce Clayton — SS, R

Age — # at position
2007 Game Log — PA, DFA, Playing in Triple-A, TOR to BOS, DFA, H%, K%, BA, HR (○), SB (□)
Production — OPS: Tot, Pos, vRH, vLH

| 3B | 3 |
| SS | 69 |

Lineup Profile — #1 to #9, Usage, TmOPS

PX, SX, Spray Chart — FB/LD, GB, HR (mlb) ○, HR (milb) ●

Clayton's longevity is one of the great mysteries. Equally awful against LH and RH, he is the kind of player who keeps us up at night, staring at the ceiling. —

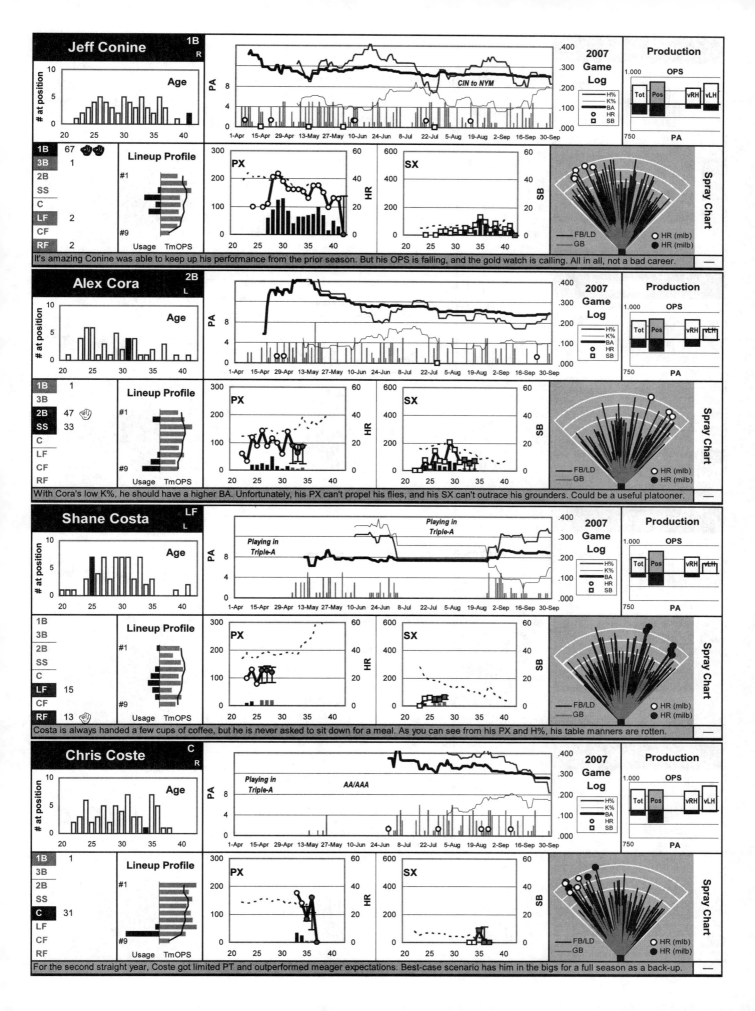

Jeff Conine — 1B / R

It's amazing Conine was able to keep up his performance from the prior season. But his OPS is falling, and the gold watch is calling. All in all, not a bad career.

Alex Cora — 2B / L

With Cora's low K%, he should have a higher BA. Unfortunately, his PX can't propel his flies, and his SX can't outrace his grounders. Could be a useful platooner.

Shane Costa — LF / L

Costa is always handed a few cups of coffee, but he is never asked to sit down for a meal. As you can see from his PX and H%, his table manners are rotten.

Chris Coste — C / R

For the second straight year, Coste got limited PT and outperformed meager expectations. Best-case scenario has him in the bigs for a full season as a back-up.

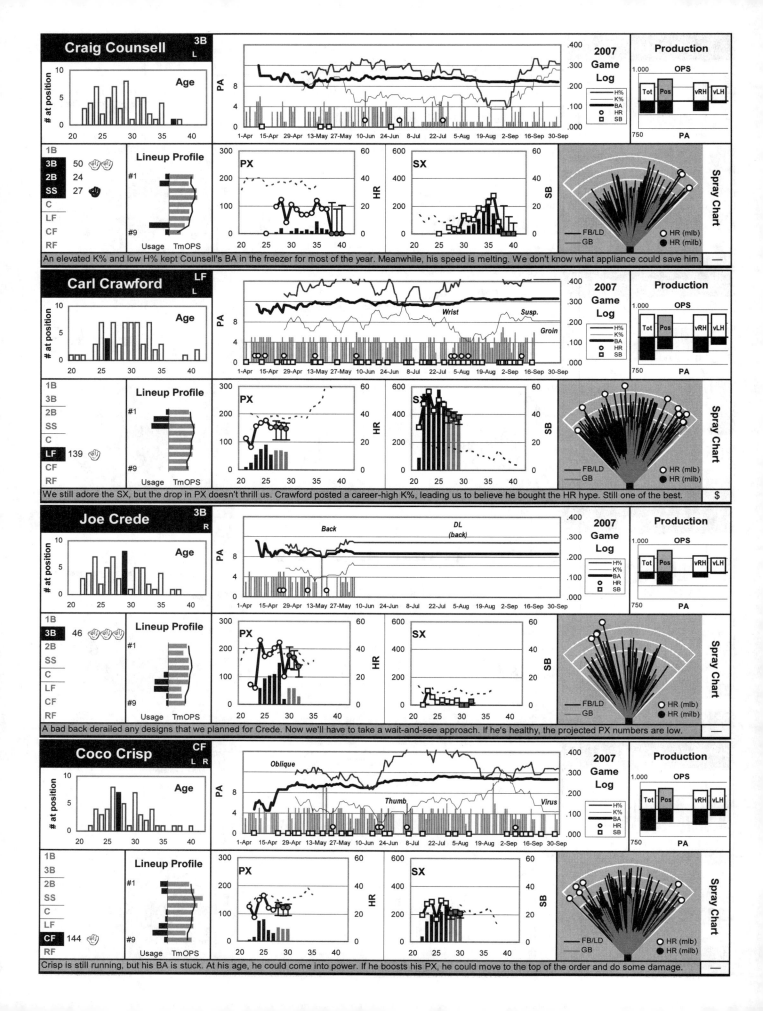

Craig Counsell — 3B — L

Age — # at position

2007 Game Log — H% / K% / BA / HR (o) / SB (□)

Production — OPS — Tot / Pos / vRH / vLH

1B	
3B	50
2B	24
SS	27
C	
LF	
CF	
RF	

Lineup Profile — #1 ... #9 — Usage / TmOPS

PX — HR
SX — SB

Spray Chart — FB/LD / GB — HR (mlb) (○) / HR (milb) (●)

An elevated K% and low H% kept Counsell's BA in the freezer for most of the year. Meanwhile, his speed is melting. We don't know what appliance could save him. — —

Carl Crawford — LF — L

Age — # at position

2007 Game Log — Wrist — Susp. — Groin — H% / K% / BA / HR (o) / SB (□)

Production — OPS — Tot / Pos / vRH / vLH

1B	
3B	
2B	
SS	
C	
LF	139
CF	
RF	

Lineup Profile — #1 ... #9 — Usage / TmOPS

PX — HR
SX — SB

Spray Chart — FB/LD / GB — HR (mlb) (○) / HR (milb) (●)

We still adore the SX, but the drop in PX doesn't thrill us. Crawford posted a career-high K%, leading us to believe he bought the HR hype. Still one of the best. — $

Joe Crede — 3B — R

Age — # at position

2007 Game Log — Back — DL (back) — H% / K% / BA / HR (o) / SB (□)

Production — OPS — Tot / Pos / vRH / vLH

1B	
3B	46
2B	
SS	
C	
LF	
CF	
RF	

Lineup Profile — #1 ... #9 — Usage / TmOPS

PX — HR
SX — SB

Spray Chart — FB/LD / GB — HR (mlb) (○) / HR (milb) (●)

A bad back derailed any designs that we planned for Crede. Now we'll have to take a wait-and-see approach. If he's healthy, the projected PX numbers are low. — —

Coco Crisp — CF — L R

Age — # at position

2007 Game Log — Oblique — Thumb — Virus — H% / K% / BA / HR (o) / SB (□)

Production — OPS — Tot / Pos / vRH / vLH

1B	
3B	
2B	
SS	
C	
LF	
CF	144
RF	

Lineup Profile — #1 ... #9 — Usage / TmOPS

PX — HR
SX — SB

Spray Chart — FB/LD / GB — HR (mlb) (○) / HR (milb) (●)

Crisp is still running, but his BA is stuck. At his age, he could come into power. If he boosts his PX, he could move to the top of the order and do some damage. — —

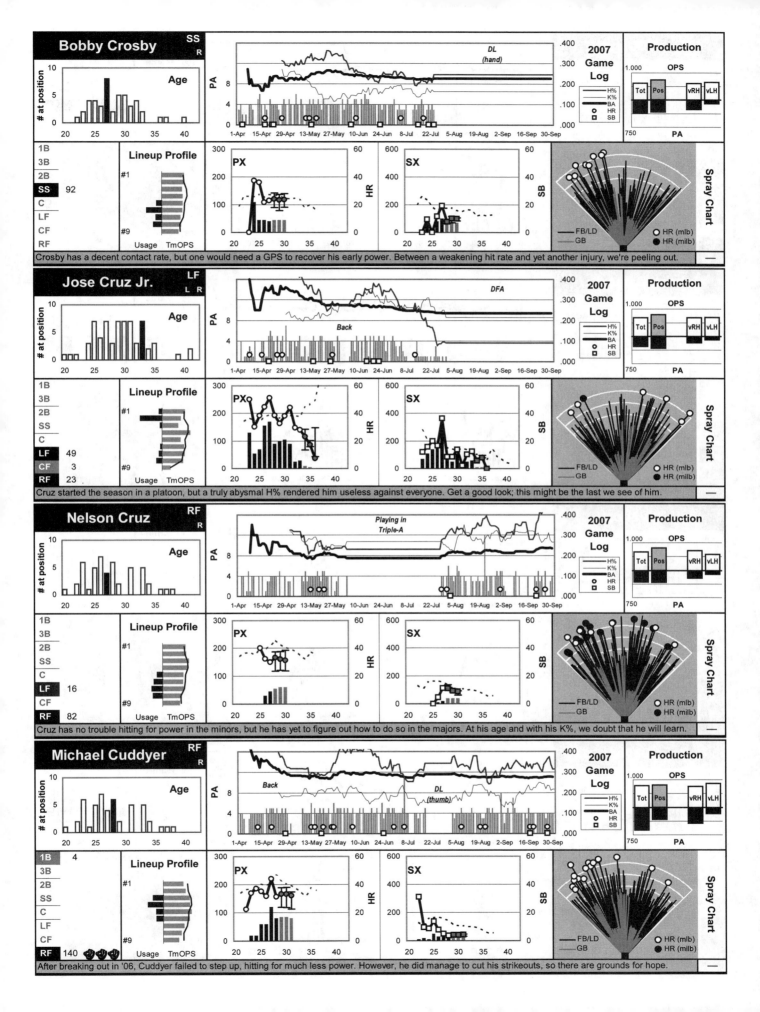

Bobby Crosby — SS / R

Age (# at position)

DL (hand)

2007 Game Log — H%, K%, BA, HR (○), SB (□)

Production — OPS: Tot, Pos, vRH, vLH (PA)

Pos	
1B	
3B	
2B	
SS	92
C	
LF	
CF	
RF	

Lineup Profile (#1 … #9, Usage, TmOPS)

PX / HR — **SX** / SB — **Spray Chart** (FB/LD, GB, HR (mlb) ○, HR (milb) ●)

Crosby has a decent contact rate, but one would need a GPS to recover his early power. Between a weakening hit rate and yet another injury, we're peeling out. —

Jose Cruz Jr. — LF / L R

Age (# at position)

DFA, Back

2007 Game Log — H%, K%, BA, HR (○), SB (□)

Production — OPS: Tot, Pos, vRH, vLH (PA)

Pos	
1B	
3B	
2B	
SS	
C	
LF	49
CF	3
RF	23

Lineup Profile (#1 … #9, Usage, TmOPS)

PX / HR — **SX** / SB — **Spray Chart** (FB/LD, GB, HR (mlb) ○, HR (milb) ●)

Cruz started the season in a platoon, but a truly abysmal H% rendered him useless against everyone. Get a good look; this might be the last we see of him. —

Nelson Cruz — RF / R

Age (# at position)

Playing in Triple-A

2007 Game Log — H%, K%, BA, HR (○), SB (□)

Production — OPS: Tot, Pos, vRH, vLH (PA)

Pos	
1B	
3B	
2B	
SS	
C	
LF	16
CF	
RF	82

Lineup Profile (#1 … #9, Usage, TmOPS)

PX / HR — **SX** / SB — **Spray Chart** (FB/LD, GB, HR (mlb) ○, HR (milb) ●)

Cruz has no trouble hitting for power in the minors, but he has yet to figure out how to do so in the majors. At his age and with his K%, we doubt that he will learn. —

Michael Cuddyer — RF / R

Age (# at position)

Back, DL (thumb)

2007 Game Log — H%, K%, BA, HR (○), SB (□)

Production — OPS: Tot, Pos, vRH, vLH (PA)

Pos	
1B	4
3B	
2B	
SS	
C	
LF	
CF	
RF	140

Lineup Profile (#1 … #9, Usage, TmOPS)

PX / HR — **SX** / SB — **Spray Chart** (FB/LD, GB, HR (mlb) ○, HR (milb) ●)

After breaking out in '06, Cuddyer failed to step up, hitting for much less power. However, he did manage to cut his strikeouts, so there are grounds for hope. —

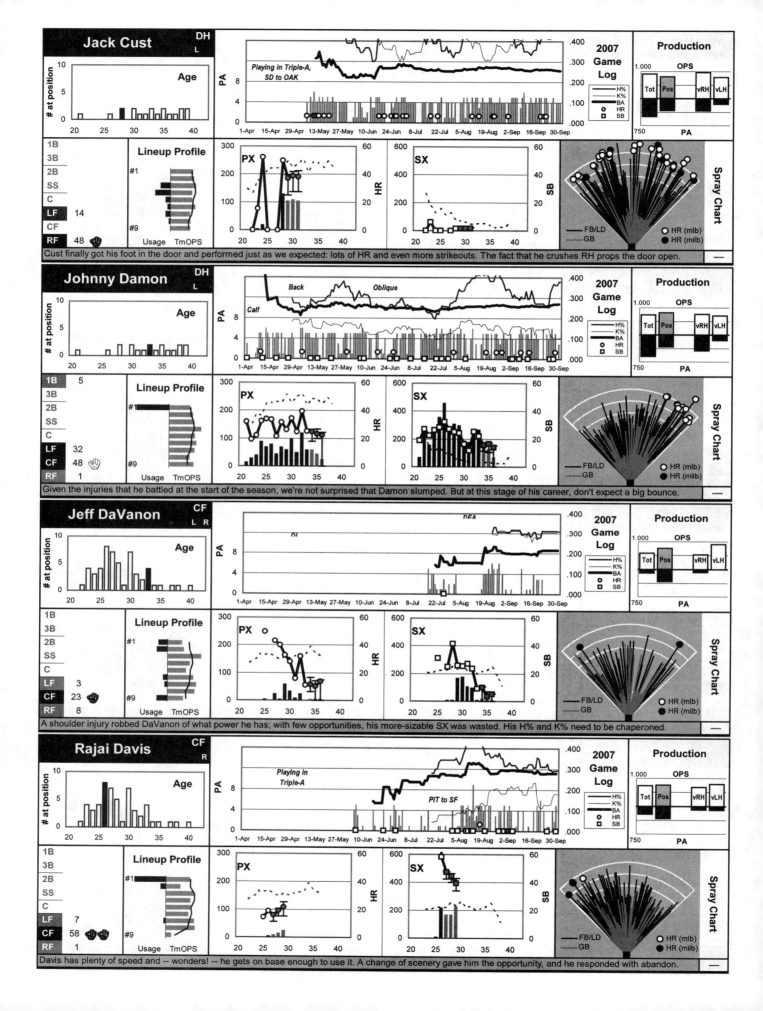

Jack Cust — DH / L

Age · # at position (0–10)

2007 Game Log · .400 / .300 / .200 / .100 / .000
Playing in Triple-A, SD to OAK
H% / K% / BA / HR ○ / SB □
1-Apr 15-Apr 29-Apr 13-May 27-May 10-Jun 24-Jun 8-Jul 22-Jul 5-Aug 19-Aug 2-Sep 16-Sep 30-Sep

Production · OPS · Tot / Pos / vRH / vLH · PA

Position usage: LF 14 · RF 48

Lineup Profile · #1 ... #9 · Usage / TmOPS

PX · **SX** · **Spray Chart**
FB/LD · GB · HR (mlb) ○ · HR (milb) ●

Cust finally got his foot in the door and performed just as we expected: lots of HR and even more strikeouts. The fact that he crushes RH props the door open. —

Johnny Damon — DH / L

Age · # at position (0–10)

2007 Game Log · .400 / .300 / .200 / .100 / .000
Back · Oblique · Calf
H% / K% / BA / HR ○ / SB □
1-Apr 15-Apr 29-Apr 13-May 27-May 10-Jun 24-Jun 8-Jul 22-Jul 5-Aug 19-Aug 2-Sep 16-Sep 30-Sep

Production · OPS · Tot / Pos / vRH / vLH · PA

Position usage: 1B 5 · LF 32 · CF 48 · RF 1

Lineup Profile · #1 ... #9 · Usage / TmOPS

PX · **SX** · **Spray Chart**
FB/LD · GB · HR (mlb) ○ · HR (milb) ●

Given the injuries that he battled at the start of the season, we're not surprised that Damon slumped. But at this stage of his career, don't expect a big bounce. —

Jeff DaVanon — CF / L R

Age · # at position (0–10)

2007 Game Log · .400 / .300 / .200 / .100 / .000
DL · DL
H% / K% / BA / HR ○ / SB □
1-Apr 15-Apr 29-Apr 13-May 27-May 10-Jun 24-Jun 8-Jul 22-Jul 5-Aug 19-Aug 2-Sep 16-Sep 30-Sep

Production · OPS · Tot / Pos / vRH / vLH · PA

Position usage: LF 3 · CF 23 · RF 8

Lineup Profile · #1 ... #9 · Usage / TmOPS

PX · **SX** · **Spray Chart**
FB/LD · GB · HR (mlb) ○ · HR (milb) ●

A shoulder injury robbed DaVanon of what power he has; with few opportunities, his more-sizable SX was wasted. His H% and K% need to be chaperoned. —

Rajai Davis — CF / R

Age · # at position (0–10)

2007 Game Log · .400 / .300 / .200 / .100 / .000
Playing in Triple-A
PIT to SF
H% / K% / BA / HR ○ / SB □
1-Apr 15-Apr 29-Apr 13-May 27-May 10-Jun 24-Jun 8-Jul 22-Jul 5-Aug 19-Aug 2-Sep 16-Sep 30-Sep

Production · OPS · Tot / Pos / vRH / vLH · PA

Position usage: LF 7 · CF 58 · RF 1

Lineup Profile · #1 ... #9 · Usage / TmOPS

PX · **SX** · **Spray Chart**
FB/LD · GB · HR (mlb) ○ · HR (milb) ●

Davis has plenty of speed and -- wonders! -- he gets on base enough to use it. A change of scenery gave him the opportunity, and he responded with abandon. —

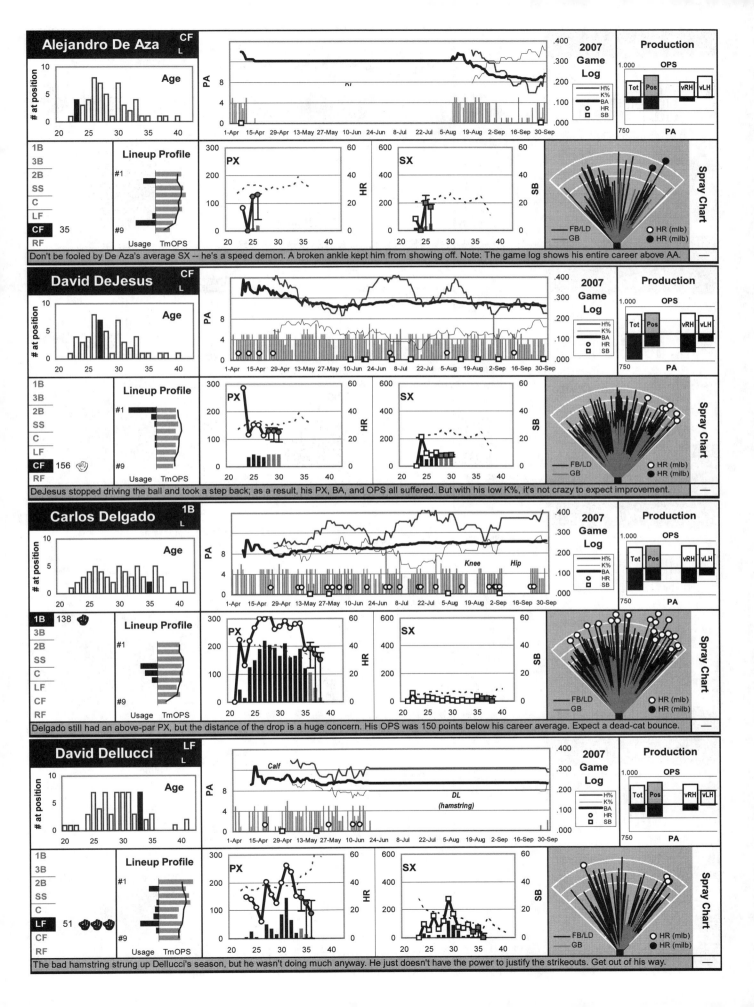

Alejandro De Aza — CF, L
Age · PA · 2007 Game Log · H% K% BA HR SB · Production OPS 1.000 750 · Tot Pos vRH vLH · PA
Lineup Profile · #1 #9 · Usage TmOPS · CF 35 · PX HR · SX SB · FB/LD GB · HR (mlb) HR (milb) · Spray Chart
Don't be fooled by De Aza's average SX -- he's a speed demon. A broken ankle kept him from showing off. Note: The game log shows his entire career above AA.

David DeJesus — CF, L
Age · PA · 2007 Game Log · H% K% BA HR SB · Production OPS 1.000 750 · Tot Pos vRH vLH · PA
Lineup Profile · #1 #9 · Usage TmOPS · CF 156 · PX HR · SX SB · FB/LD GB · HR (mlb) HR (milb) · Spray Chart
DeJesus stopped driving the ball and took a step back; as a result, his PX, BA, and OPS all suffered. But with his low K%, it's not crazy to expect improvement.

Carlos Delgado — 1B, L
Age · PA · 2007 Game Log · H% K% BA HR SB · Knee · Hip · Production OPS 1.000 750 · Tot Pos vRH vLH · PA
1B 138 · Lineup Profile · #1 #9 · Usage TmOPS · PX HR · SX SB · FB/LD GB · HR (mlb) HR (milb) · Spray Chart
Delgado still had an above-par PX, but the distance of the drop is a huge concern. His OPS was 150 points below his career average. Expect a dead-cat bounce.

David Dellucci — LF, L
Age · PA · 2007 Game Log · Calf · DL (hamstring) · H% K% BA HR SB · Production OPS 1.000 750 · Tot Pos vRH vLH · PA
Lineup Profile · #1 #9 · Usage TmOPS · LF 51 · PX HR · SX SB · FB/LD GB · HR (mlb) HR (milb) · Spray Chart
The bad hamstring strung up Dellucci's season, but he wasn't doing much anyway. He just doesn't have the power to justify the strikeouts. Get out of his way.

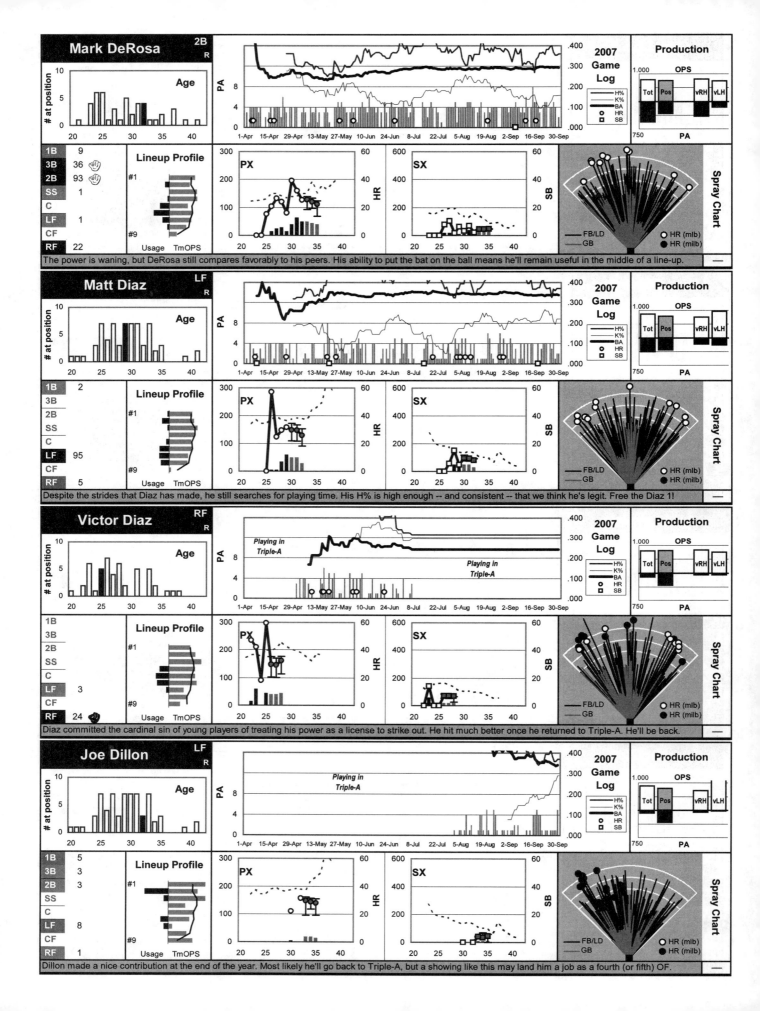

Mark DeRosa 2B R

Age

1B 9
3B 36
2B 93
SS 1
C
LF 1
CF
RF 22

Lineup Profile

2007 Game Log

H%
K%
BA
HR
SB

Production
OPS
Tot Pos vRH vLH
PA

PX / HR
SX / SB

FB/LD
GB
HR (mlb)
HR (milb)

Spray Chart

The power is waning, but DeRosa still compares favorably to his peers. His ability to put the bat on the ball means he'll remain useful in the middle of a line-up. —

Matt Diaz LF R

Age

1B 2
3B
2B
SS
C
LF 95
CF
RF 5

Lineup Profile

2007 Game Log

H%
K%
BA
HR
SB

Production
OPS
Tot Pos vRH vLH
PA

PX / HR
SX / SB

FB/LD
GB
HR (mlb)
HR (milb)

Spray Chart

Despite the strides that Diaz has made, he still searches for playing time. His H% is high enough -- and consistent -- that we think he's legit. Free the Diaz 1! —

Victor Diaz RF R

Age

Playing in Triple-A

Playing in Triple-A

1B
3B
2B
SS
C
LF 3
CF
RF 24

Lineup Profile

2007 Game Log

H%
K%
BA
HR
SB

Production
OPS
Tot Pos vRH vLH
PA

PX / HR
SX / SB

FB/LD
GB
HR (mlb)
HR (milb)

Spray Chart

Diaz committed the cardinal sin of young players of treating his power as a license to strike out. He hit much better once he returned to Triple-A. He'll be back. —

Joe Dillon LF R

Age

Playing in Triple-A

1B 5
3B 3
2B 3
SS
C
LF 8
CF
RF 1

Lineup Profile

2007 Game Log

H%
K%
BA
HR
SB

Production
OPS
Tot Pos vRH vLH
PA

PX / HR
SX / SB

FB/LD
GB
HR (mlb)
HR (milb)

Spray Chart

Dillon made a nice contribution at the end of the year. Most likely he'll go back to Triple-A, but a showing like this may land him a job as a fourth (or fifth) OF. —

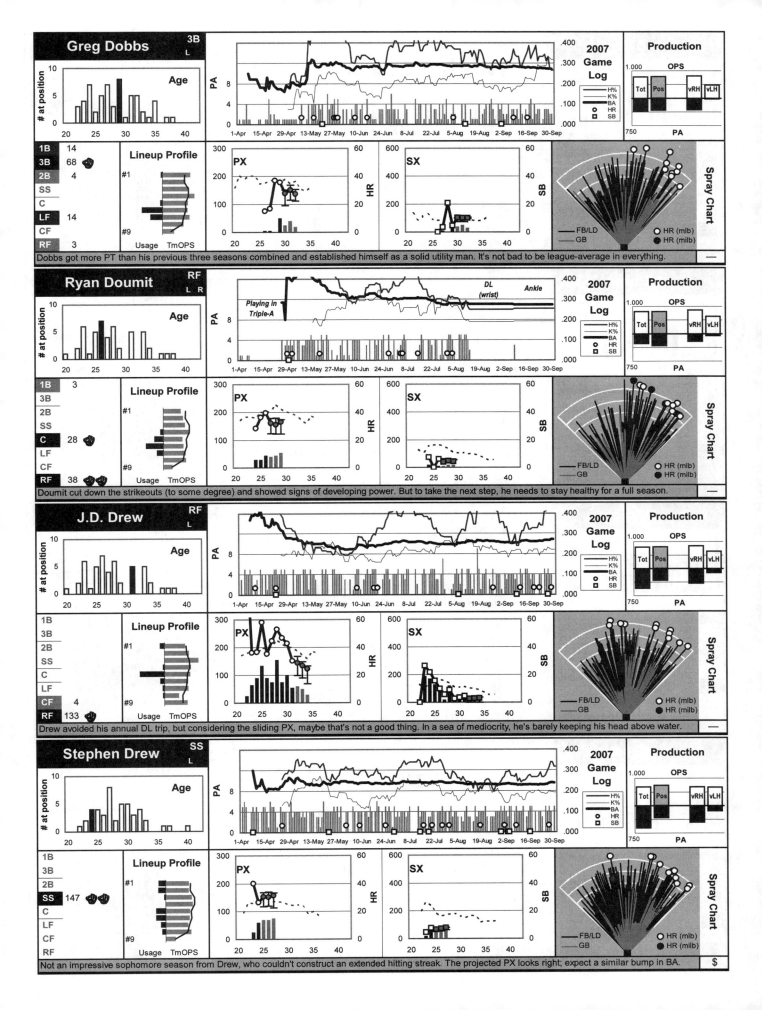

Greg Dobbs 3B L

1B	14
3B	68
2B	4
SS	
C	
LF	14
CF	
RF	3

Dobbs got more PT than his previous three seasons combined and established himself as a solid utility man. It's not bad to be league-average in everything. —

Ryan Doumit RF L R

1B	3
3B	
2B	
SS	
C	28
LF	
CF	
RF	38

Doumit cut down the strikeouts (to some degree) and showed signs of developing power. But to take the next step, he needs to stay healthy for a full season. —

J.D. Drew RF L

1B	
3B	
2B	
SS	
C	
LF	
CF	4
RF	133

Drew avoided his annual DL trip, but considering the sliding PX, maybe that's not a good thing. In a sea of mediocrity, he's barely keeping his head above water. —

Stephen Drew SS L

1B	
3B	
2B	
SS	147
C	
LF	
CF	
RF	

Not an impressive sophomore season from Drew, who couldn't construct an extended hitting streak. The projected PX looks right; expect a similar bump in BA. $

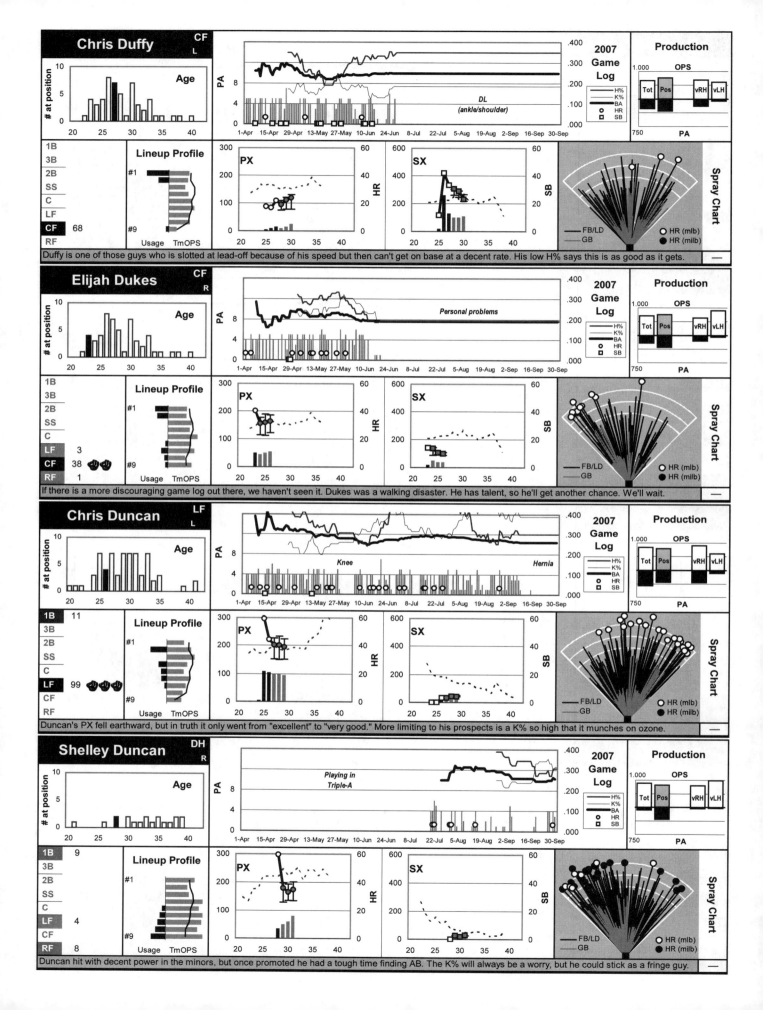

Chris Duffy CF L

at position | Age
20 25 30 35 40

1B / 3B / 2B / SS / C / LF / **CF 68** / RF

Lineup Profile — #1 ... #9 — Usage · TmOPS

PA · 2007 Game Log · DL (ankle/shoulder)
1-Apr 15-Apr 29-Apr 13-May 27-May 10-Jun 24-Jun 8-Jul 22-Jul 5-Aug 19-Aug 2-Sep 16-Sep 30-Sep
.400 .300 .200 .100 .000
H% / K% / BA / HR / SB

PX · HR
20 25 30 35 40

SX · SB
20 25 30 35 40

Production — OPS
1.000 · Tot Pos vRH vLH · 750 · PA

Spray Chart — FB/LD · GB · HR (mlb) · HR (milb)

Duffy is one of those guys who is slotted at lead-off because of his speed but then can't get on base at a decent rate. His low H% says this is as good as it gets. —

Elijah Dukes CF R

at position | Age
20 25 30 35 40

1B / 3B / 2B / SS / C / **LF 3** / **CF 38** / **RF 1**

Lineup Profile — #1 ... #9 — Usage · TmOPS

PA · 2007 Game Log · Personal problems
1-Apr 15-Apr 29-Apr 13-May 27-May 10-Jun 24-Jun 8-Jul 22-Jul 5-Aug 19-Aug 2-Sep 16-Sep 30-Sep
.400 .300 .200 .100 .000
H% / K% / BA / HR / SB

PX · HR
20 25 30 35 40

SX · SB
20 25 30 35 40

Production — OPS
1.000 · Tot Pos vRH vLH · 750 · PA

Spray Chart — FB/LD · GB · HR (mlb) · HR (milb)

If there is a more discouraging game log out there, we haven't seen it. Dukes was a walking disaster. He has talent, so he'll get another chance. We'll wait. —

Chris Duncan LF L

at position | Age
20 25 30 35 40

1B 11 / 3B / 2B / SS / C / **LF 99** / CF / RF

Lineup Profile — #1 ... #9 — Usage · TmOPS

PA · 2007 Game Log · Knee · Hernia
1-Apr 15-Apr 29-Apr 13-May 27-May 10-Jun 24-Jun 8-Jul 22-Jul 5-Aug 19-Aug 2-Sep 16-Sep 30-Sep
.400 .300 .200 .100 .000
H% / K% / BA / HR / SB

PX · HR
20 25 30 35 40

SX · SB
20 25 30 35 40

Production — OPS
1.000 · Tot Pos vRH vLH · 750 · PA

Spray Chart — FB/LD · GB · HR (mlb) · HR (milb)

Duncan's PX fell earthward, but in truth it only went from "excellent" to "very good." More limiting to his prospects is a K% so high that it munches on ozone. —

Shelley Duncan DH R

at position | Age
20 25 30 35 40

1B 9 / 3B / 2B / SS / C / **LF 4** / CF / **RF 8**

Lineup Profile — #1 ... #9 — Usage · TmOPS

PA · 2007 Game Log · Playing in Triple-A
1-Apr 15-Apr 29-Apr 13-May 27-May 10-Jun 24-Jun 8-Jul 22-Jul 5-Aug 19-Aug 2-Sep 16-Sep 30-Sep
.400 .300 .200 .100 .000
H% / K% / BA / HR / SB

PX · HR
20 25 30 35 40

SX · SB
20 25 30 35 40

Production — OPS
1.000 · Tot Pos vRH vLH · 750 · PA

Spray Chart — FB/LD · GB · HR (mlb) · HR (milb)

Duncan hit with decent power in the minors, but once promoted he had a tough time finding AB. The K% will always be a worry, but he could stick as a fringe guy. —

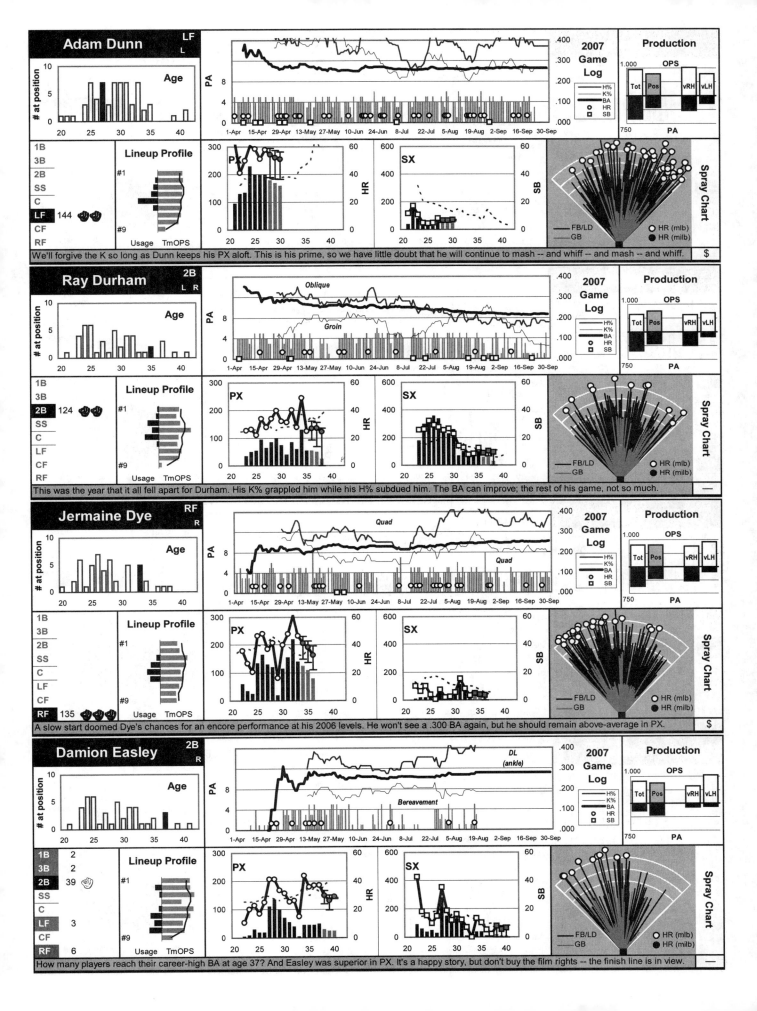

Adam Dunn — LF / L

2007 Game Log

Production — OPS

LF 144

Lineup Profile — Usage / TmOPS

We'll forgive the K so long as Dunn keeps his PX aloft. This is his prime, so we have little doubt that he will continue to mash -- and whiff -- and mash -- and whiff. $

Ray Durham — 2B / L R

2007 Game Log

Oblique   Groin

Production — OPS

2B 124

Lineup Profile — Usage / TmOPS

This was the year that it all fell apart for Durham. His K% grappled him while his H% subdued him. The BA can improve; the rest of his game, not so much. —

Jermaine Dye — RF / R

2007 Game Log

Quad   Quad

Production — OPS

RF 135

Lineup Profile — Usage / TmOPS

A slow start doomed Dye's chances for an encore performance at his 2006 levels. He won't see a .300 BA again, but he should remain above-average in PX. $

Damion Easley — 2B / R

2007 Game Log

DL (ankle)   Bereavement

Production — OPS

1B 2
3B 2
2B 39
LF 3
RF 6

Lineup Profile — Usage / TmOPS

How many players reach their career-high BA at age 37? And Easley was superior in PX. It's a happy story, but don't buy the film rights -- the finish line is in view. —

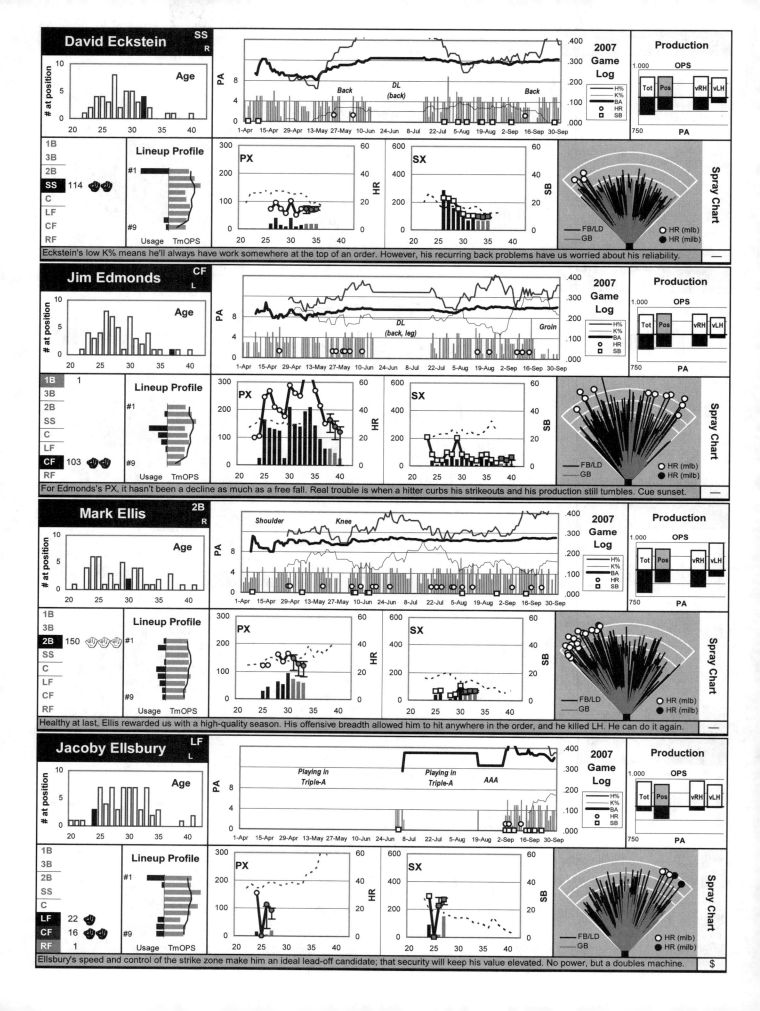

David Eckstein SS R

Age

2007 Game Log

Production — OPS
Tot | Pos | vRH | vLH

1B
3B
2B
SS 114
C
LF
CF
RF

Lineup Profile
#1
#9
Usage TmOPS

PX HR
SX SB

Spray Chart
FB/LD
GB
HR (mlb)
HR (milb)

Eckstein's low K% means he'll always have work somewhere at the top of an order. However, his recurring back problems have us worried about his reliability. —

Jim Edmonds CF L

Age

2007 Game Log

Production — OPS
Tot | Pos | vRH | vLH

1B 1
3B
2B
SS
C
LF
CF 103
RF

Lineup Profile
#1
#9
Usage TmOPS

PX HR
SX SB

Spray Chart
FB/LD
GB
HR (mlb)
HR (milb)

For Edmonds's PX, it hasn't been a decline as much as a free fall. Real trouble is when a hitter curbs his strikeouts and his production still tumbles. Cue sunset. —

Mark Ellis 2B R

Age

2007 Game Log

Production — OPS
Tot | Pos | vRH | vLH

1B
3B
2B 150
SS
C
LF
CF
RF

Lineup Profile
#1
#9
Usage TmOPS

PX HR
SX SB

Spray Chart
FB/LD
GB
HR (mlb)
HR (milb)

Healthy at last, Ellis rewarded us with a high-quality season. His offensive breadth allowed him to hit anywhere in the order, and he killed LH. He can do it again. —

Jacoby Ellsbury LF L

Age

2007 Game Log

Production — OPS
Tot | Pos | vRH | vLH

1B
3B
2B
SS
C
LF 22
CF 16
RF 1

Lineup Profile
#1
#9
Usage TmOPS

PX HR
SX SB

Spray Chart
FB/LD
GB
HR (mlb)
HR (milb)

Ellsbury's speed and control of the strike zone make him an ideal lead-off candidate; that security will keep his value elevated. No power, but a doubles machine. $

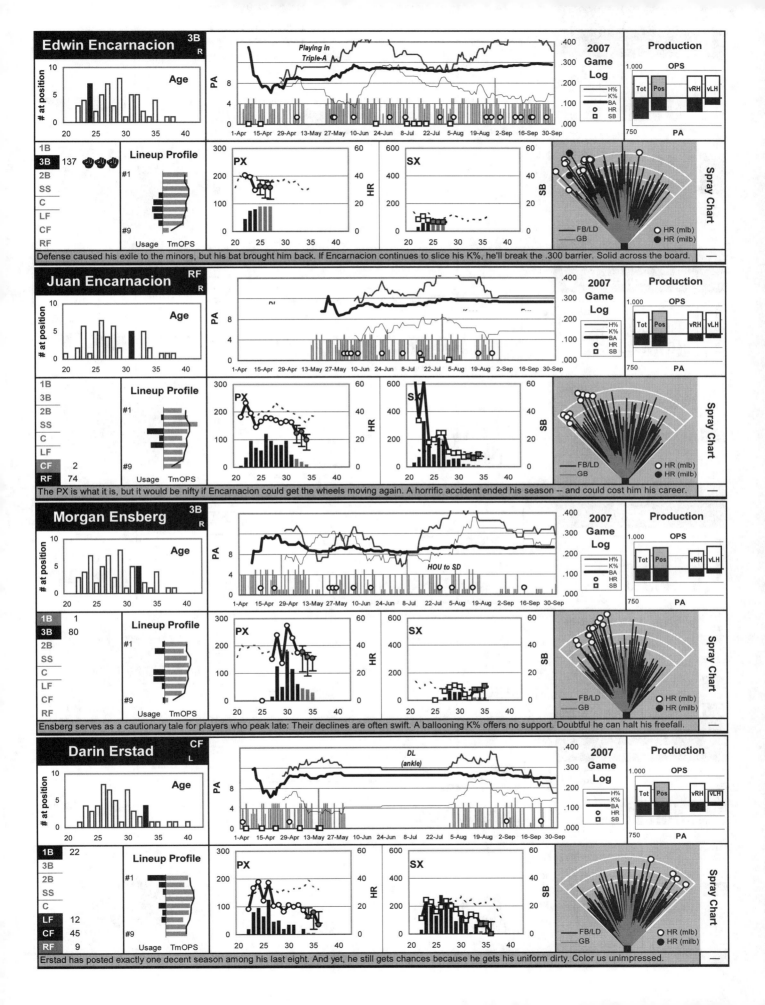

Edwin Encarnacion — 3B, R

Age

Playing in Triple-A

2007 Game Log
H% / K% / BA / HR / SB

Production — OPS
Tot / Pos / vRH / vLH — PA

3B 137

Lineup Profile — #1 ... #9 — Usage / TmOPS

PX

SX

Spray Chart
FB/LD / GB — HR (mlb) / HR (milb)

Defense caused his exile to the minors, but his bat brought him back. If Encarnacion continues to slice his K%, he'll break the .300 barrier. Solid across the board. —

Juan Encarnacion — RF, R

Age

DL

2007 Game Log
H% / K% / BA / HR / SB

Production — OPS
Tot / Pos / vRH / vLH — PA

CF 2
RF 74

Lineup Profile — #1 ... #9 — Usage / TmOPS

PX

SX

Spray Chart
FB/LD / GB — HR (mlb) / HR (milb)

The PX is what it is, but it would be nifty if Encarnacion could get the wheels moving again. A horrific accident ended his season -- and could cost him his career. —

Morgan Ensberg — 3B, R

Age

HOU to SD

2007 Game Log
H% / K% / BA / HR / SB

Production — OPS
Tot / Pos / vRH / vLH — PA

1B 1
3B 80

Lineup Profile — #1 ... #9 — Usage / TmOPS

PX

SX

Spray Chart
FB/LD / GB — HR (mlb) / HR (milb)

Ensberg serves as a cautionary tale for players who peak late: Their declines are often swift. A ballooning K% offers no support. Doubtful he can halt his freefall. —

Darin Erstad — CF, L

Age

DL (ankle)

2007 Game Log
H% / K% / BA / HR / SB

Production — OPS
Tot / Pos / vRH / vLH — PA

1B 22
LF 12
CF 45
RF 9

Lineup Profile — #1 ... #9 — Usage / TmOPS

PX

SX

Spray Chart
FB/LD / GB — HR (mlb) / HR (milb)

Erstad has posted exactly one decent season among his last eight. And yet, he still gets chances because he gets his uniform dirty. Color us unimpressed. —

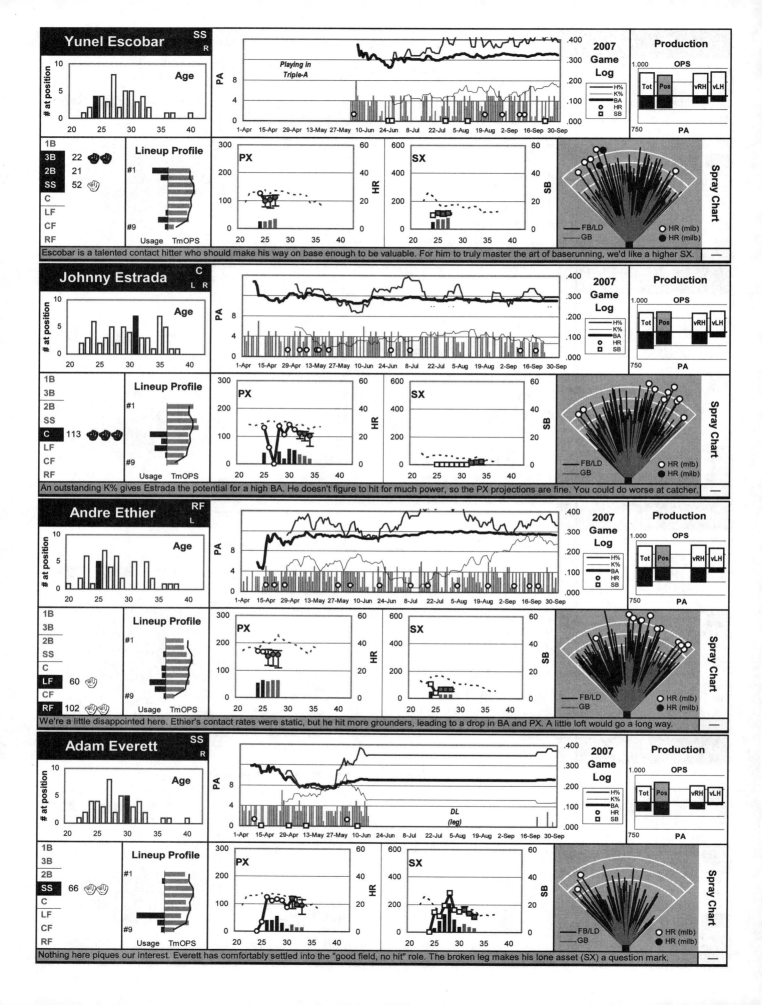

Yunel Escobar — SS / R

Age (# at position)

2007 Game Log — PA, H%, K%, BA, HR, SB
Playing in Triple-A

Production — OPS: Tot, Pos, vRH, vLH (PA)

Position		
1B		
3B	22	
2B	21	
SS	52	
C		
LF		
CF		
RF		

Lineup Profile (#1–#9, Usage, TmOPS)

PX — HR
SX — SB
Spray Chart — FB/LD, GB, HR (mlb), HR (milb)

Escobar is a talented contact hitter who should make his way on base enough to be valuable. For him to truly master the art of baserunning, we'd like a higher SX. —

Johnny Estrada — C / L R

Age (# at position)

2007 Game Log — PA, H%, K%, BA, HR, SB

Production — OPS: Tot, Pos, vRH, vLH (PA)

Position		
1B		
3B		
2B		
SS		
C	113	
LF		
CF		
RF		

Lineup Profile (#1–#9, Usage, TmOPS)

PX — HR
SX — SB
Spray Chart — FB/LD, GB, HR (mlb), HR (milb)

An outstanding K% gives Estrada the potential for a high BA. He doesn't figure to hit for much power, so the PX projections are fine. You could do worse at catcher. —

Andre Ethier — RF / L

Age (# at position)

2007 Game Log — PA, H%, K%, BA, HR, SB

Production — OPS: Tot, Pos, vRH, vLH (PA)

Position		
1B		
3B		
2B		
SS		
C		
LF	60	
CF		
RF	102	

Lineup Profile (#1–#9, Usage, TmOPS)

PX — HR
SX — SB
Spray Chart — FB/LD, GB, HR (mlb), HR (milb)

We're a little disappointed here. Ethier's contact rates were static, but he hit more grounders, leading to a drop in BA and PX. A little loft would go a long way. —

Adam Everett — SS / R

Age (# at position)

2007 Game Log — PA, H%, K%, BA, HR, SB
DL (leg)

Production — OPS: Tot, Pos, vRH, vLH (PA)

Position		
1B		
3B		
2B		
SS	66	
C		
LF		
CF		
RF		

Lineup Profile (#1–#9, Usage, TmOPS)

PX — HR
SX — SB
Spray Chart — FB/LD, GB, HR (mlb), HR (milb)

Nothing here piques our interest. Everett has comfortably settled into the "good field, no hit" role. The broken leg makes his lone asset (SX) a question mark.

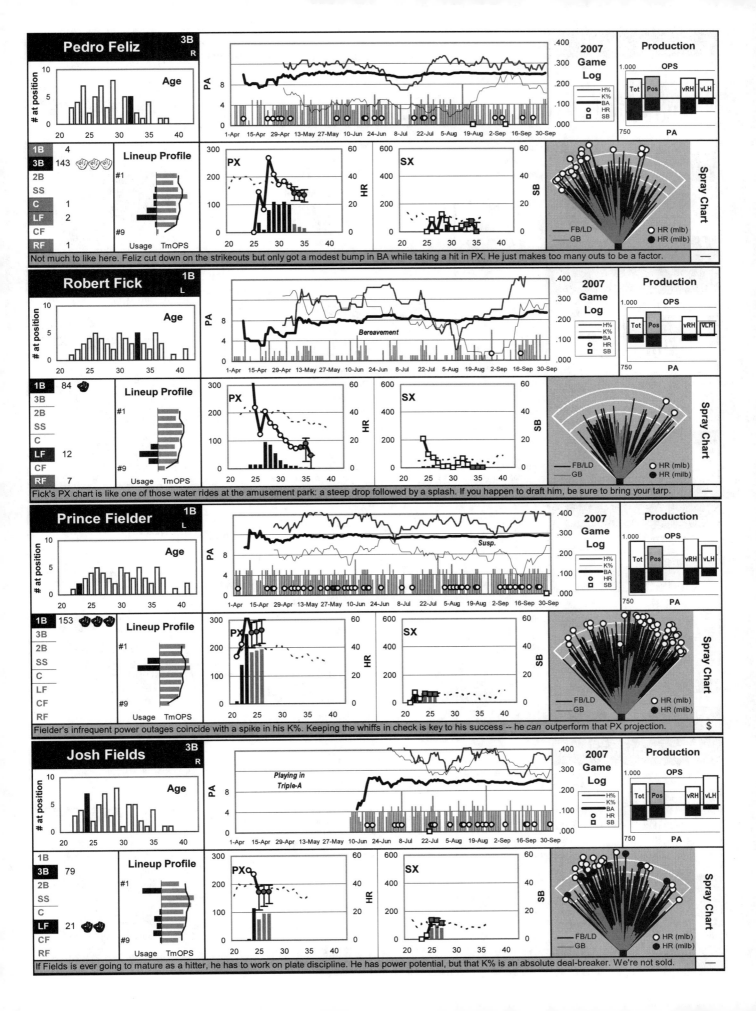

Pedro Feliz 3B R

at position / Age

1B 4
3B 143
2B
SS
C 1
LF 2
CF
RF 1

Lineup Profile
#1
#9
Usage TmOPS

PX HR
SX SB

2007 Game Log
H%
K%
BA
○ HR
□ SB

Production
OPS
Tot | Pos | vRH | vLH
PA

Spray Chart
— FB/LD
— GB
○ HR (mlb)
● HR (milb)

Not much to like here. Feliz cut down on the strikeouts but only got a modest bump in BA while taking a hit in PX. He just makes too many outs to be a factor. —

Robert Fick 1B L

at position / Age

1B 84
3B
2B
SS
C
LF 12
CF
RF 7

Lineup Profile
#1
#9
Usage TmOPS

PX HR
SX SB

Bereavement

2007 Game Log
H%
K%
BA
○ HR
□ SB

Production
OPS
Tot | Pos | vRH | vLH
PA

Spray Chart
— FB/LD
— GB
○ HR (mlb)
● HR (milb)

Fick's PX chart is like one of those water rides at the amusement park: a steep drop followed by a splash. If you happen to draft him, be sure to bring your tarp. —

Prince Fielder 1B L

at position / Age

1B 153
3B
2B
SS
C
LF
CF
RF

Lineup Profile
#1
#9
Usage TmOPS

PX HR
SX SB

Susp.

2007 Game Log
H%
K%
BA
○ HR
□ SB

Production
OPS
Tot | Pos | vRH | vLH
PA

Spray Chart
— FB/LD
— GB
○ HR (mlb)
● HR (milb)

Fielder's infrequent power outages coincide with a spike in his K%. Keeping the whiffs in check is key to his success -- he *can* outperform that PX projection. $

Josh Fields 3B R

at position / Age

1B
3B 79
2B
SS
C
LF 21
CF
RF

Lineup Profile
#1
#9
Usage TmOPS

Playing in Triple-A

PX HR
SX SB

2007 Game Log
H%
K%
BA
○ HR
□ SB

Production
OPS
Tot | Pos | vRH | vLH
PA

Spray Chart
— FB/LD
— GB
○ HR (mlb)
● HR (milb)

If Fields is ever going to mature as a hitter, he has to work on plate discipline. He has power potential, but that K% is an absolute deal-breaker. We're not sold. —

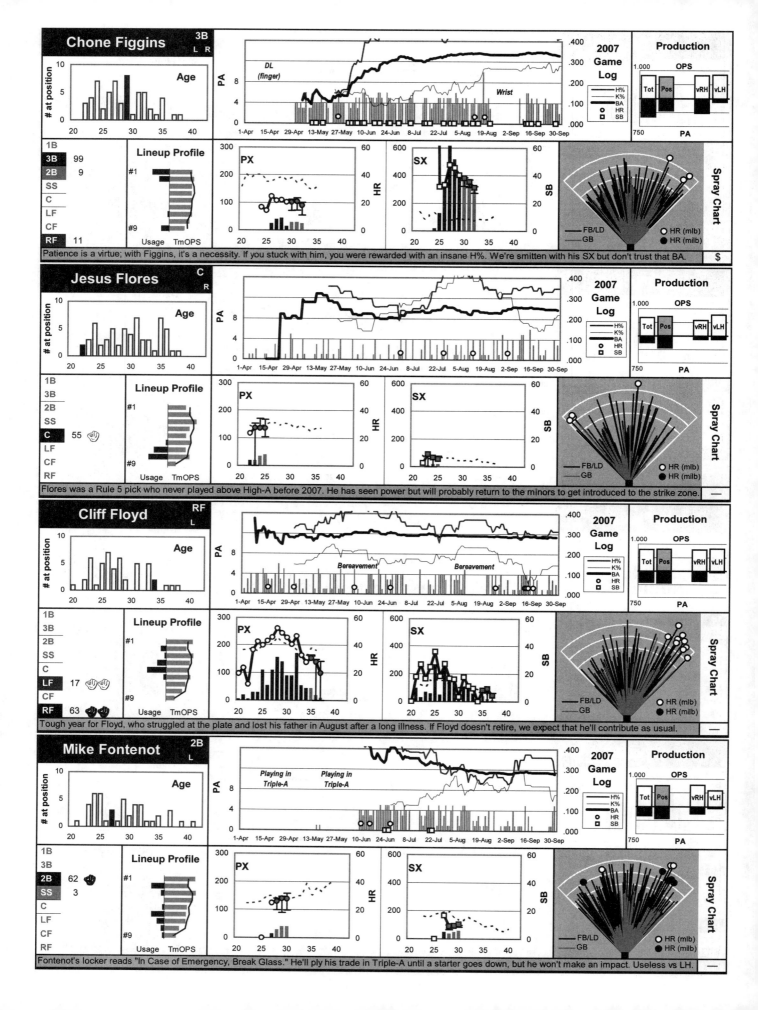

Chone Figgins — 3B (L/R)

2007 Game Log · DL (finger) · Wrist
H% · K% · BA · HR · SB

Production — OPS (Tot, Pos, vRH, vLH) · PA

Age · # at position

1B · **3B** 99 · **2B** 9 · SS · C · LF · CF · **RF** 11

Lineup Profile (#1 ... #9) · Usage · TmOPS

PX · SX · HR · SB · Spray Chart · FB/LD · GB · HR (mlb) · HR (milb)

Patience is a virtue; with Figgins, it's a necessity. If you stuck with him, you were rewarded with an insane H%. We're smitten with his SX but don't trust that BA. · $

Jesus Flores — C (R)

2007 Game Log
H% · K% · BA · HR · SB

Production — OPS (Tot, Pos, vRH, vLH) · PA

Age · # at position

1B · 3B · 2B · SS · **C** 55 · LF · CF · RF

Lineup Profile (#1 ... #9) · Usage · TmOPS

PX · SX · HR · SB · Spray Chart · FB/LD · GB · HR (mlb) · HR (milb)

Flores was a Rule 5 pick who never played above High-A before 2007. He has seen power but will probably return to the minors to get introduced to the strike zone. · —

Cliff Floyd — RF (L)

2007 Game Log · Bereavement · Bereavement
H% · K% · BA · HR · SB

Production — OPS (Tot, Pos, vRH, vLH) · PA

Age · # at position

1B · 3B · 2B · SS · C · **LF** 17 · CF · **RF** 63

Lineup Profile (#1 ... #9) · Usage · TmOPS

PX · SX · HR · SB · Spray Chart · FB/LD · GB · HR (mlb) · HR (milb)

Tough year for Floyd, who struggled at the plate and lost his father in August after a long illness. If Floyd doesn't retire, we expect that he'll contribute as usual. · —

Mike Fontenot — 2B (L)

2007 Game Log · Playing in Triple-A · Playing in Triple-A
H% · K% · BA · HR · SB

Production — OPS (Tot, Pos, vRH, vLH) · PA

Age · # at position

1B · 3B · **2B** 62 · **SS** 3 · C · LF · CF · RF

Lineup Profile (#1 ... #9) · Usage · TmOPS

PX · SX · HR · SB · Spray Chart · FB/LD · GB · HR (mlb) · HR (milb)

Fontenot's locker reads "In Case of Emergency, Break Glass." He'll ply his trade in Triple-A until a starter goes down, but he won't make an impact. Useless vs LH. · —

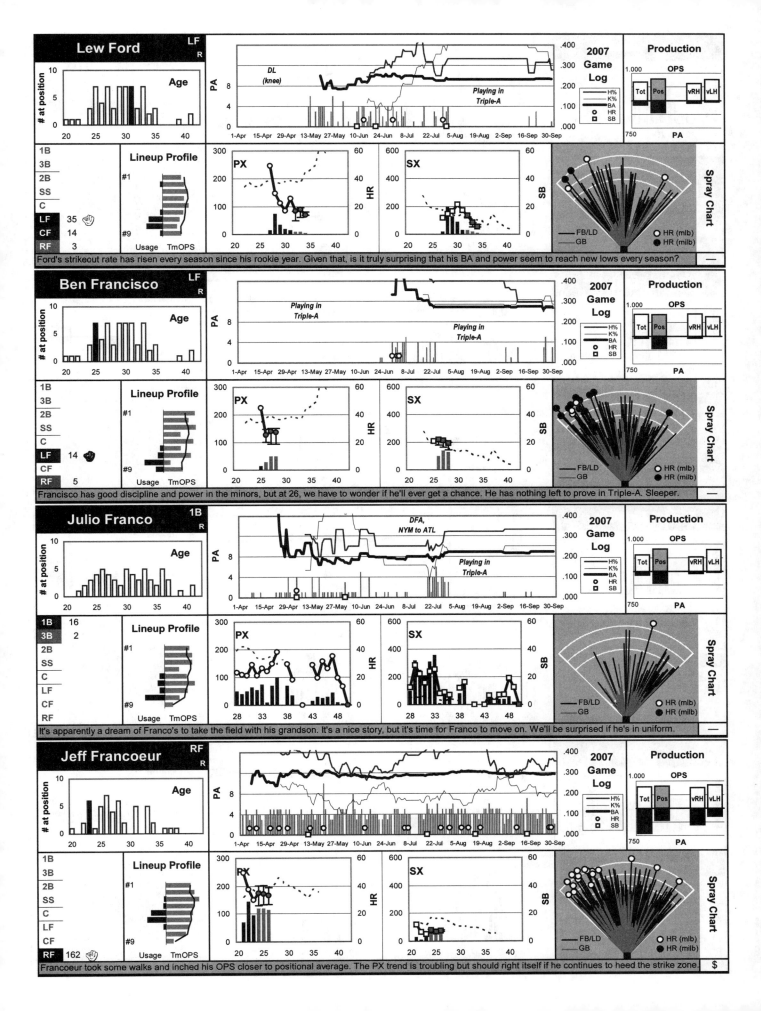

Lew Ford — LF, R

Age

at position

2007 Game Log
DL (knee)
Playing in Triple-A
H%
K%
BA
○ HR
□ SB

Production — OPS
Tot | Pos | vRH | vLH
PA

1B	
3B	
2B	
SS	
C	
LF	35
CF	14
RF	3

Lineup Profile
#1 ... #9
Usage TmOPS

PX / HR
SX / SB

FB/LD
GB
○ HR (mlb)
● HR (milb)

Spray Chart

Ford's strikeout rate has risen every season since his rookie year. Given that, is it truly surprising that his BA and power seem to reach new lows every season? —

Ben Francisco — LF, R

Age

at position

2007 Game Log
Playing in Triple-A
Playing in Triple-A
H%
K%
BA
○ HR
□ SB

Production — OPS
Tot | Pos | vRH | vLH
PA

1B	
3B	
2B	
SS	
C	
LF	14
CF	
RF	5

Lineup Profile
#1 ... #9
Usage TmOPS

PX / HR
SX / SB

FB/LD
GB
○ HR (mlb)
● HR (milb)

Spray Chart

Francisco has good discipline and power in the minors, but at 26, we have to wonder if he'll ever get a chance. He has nothing left to prove in Triple-A. Sleeper. —

Julio Franco — 1B, R

Age

at position

2007 Game Log
DFA, NYM to ATL
Playing in Triple-A
H%
K%
BA
○ HR
□ SB

Production — OPS
Tot | Pos | vRH | vLH
PA

1B	16
3B	2
2B	
SS	
C	
LF	
CF	
RF	

Lineup Profile
#1 ... #9
Usage TmOPS

PX / HR
SX / SB

FB/LD
GB
○ HR (mlb)
● HR (milb)

Spray Chart

It's apparently a dream of Franco's to take the field with his grandson. It's a nice story, but it's time for Franco to move on. We'll be surprised if he's in uniform. —

Jeff Francoeur — RF, R

Age

at position

2007 Game Log
H%
K%
BA
○ HR
□ SB

Production — OPS
Tot | Pos | vRH | vLH
PA

1B	
3B	
2B	
SS	
C	
LF	
CF	
RF	162

Lineup Profile
#1 ... #9
Usage TmOPS

PX / HR
SX / SB

FB/LD
GB
○ HR (mlb)
● HR (milb)

Spray Chart

Francoeur took some walks and inched his OPS closer to positional average. The PX trend is troubling but should right itself if he continues to heed the strike zone. $

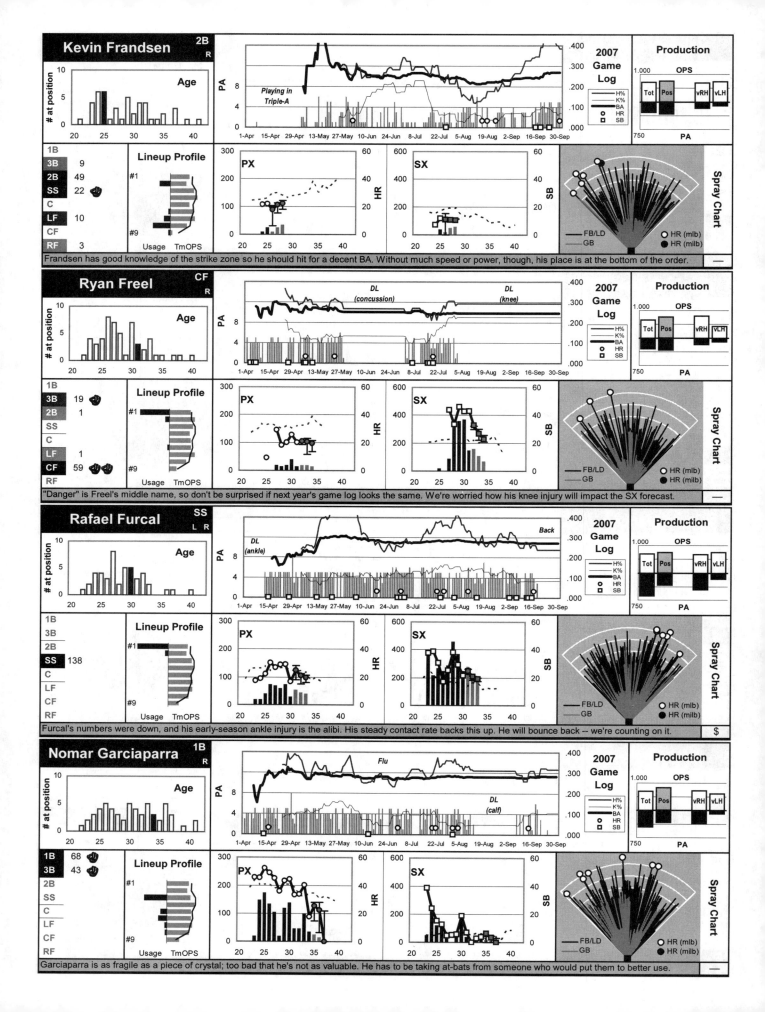

Kevin Frandsen — 2B, R

Age | PA | 2007 Game Log | Production — OPS

Position breakdown:
- 1B
- 3B — 9
- 2B — 49
- SS — 22
- C
- LF — 10
- CF
- RF — 3

Lineup Profile (#1 to #9, Usage / TmOPS)

PX | SX | Spray Chart
- FB/LD
- GB
- HR (mlb)
- HR (milb)

Playing in Triple-A

H%, K%, BA, HR, SB

Frandsen has good knowledge of the strike zone so he should hit for a decent BA. Without much speed or power, though, his place is at the bottom of the order. — —

Ryan Freel — CF, R

Age | PA | 2007 Game Log | Production — OPS

Position breakdown:
- 1B
- 3B — 19
- 2B — 1
- SS
- C
- LF — 1
- CF — 59
- RF

Lineup Profile (#1 to #9, Usage / TmOPS)

PX | SX | Spray Chart

DL (concussion) | DL (knee)

"Danger" is Freel's middle name, so don't be surprised if next year's game log looks the same. We're worried how his knee injury will impact the SX forecast. — —

Rafael Furcal — SS, L R

Age | PA | 2007 Game Log | Production — OPS

Position breakdown:
- 1B
- 3B
- 2B
- SS — 138
- C
- LF
- CF
- RF

Lineup Profile (#1 to #9, Usage / TmOPS)

PX | SX | Spray Chart

DL (ankle) | Back

Furcal's numbers were down, and his early-season ankle injury is the alibi. His steady contact rate backs this up. He will bounce back -- we're counting on it. — $

Nomar Garciaparra — 1B, R

Age | PA | 2007 Game Log | Production — OPS

Position breakdown:
- 1B — 68
- 3B — 43
- 2B
- SS
- C
- LF
- CF
- RF

Lineup Profile (#1 to #9, Usage / TmOPS)

PX | SX | Spray Chart

Flu | DL (calf)

Garciaparra is as fragile as a piece of crystal; too bad that he's not as valuable. He has to be taking at-bats from someone who would put them to better use. — —

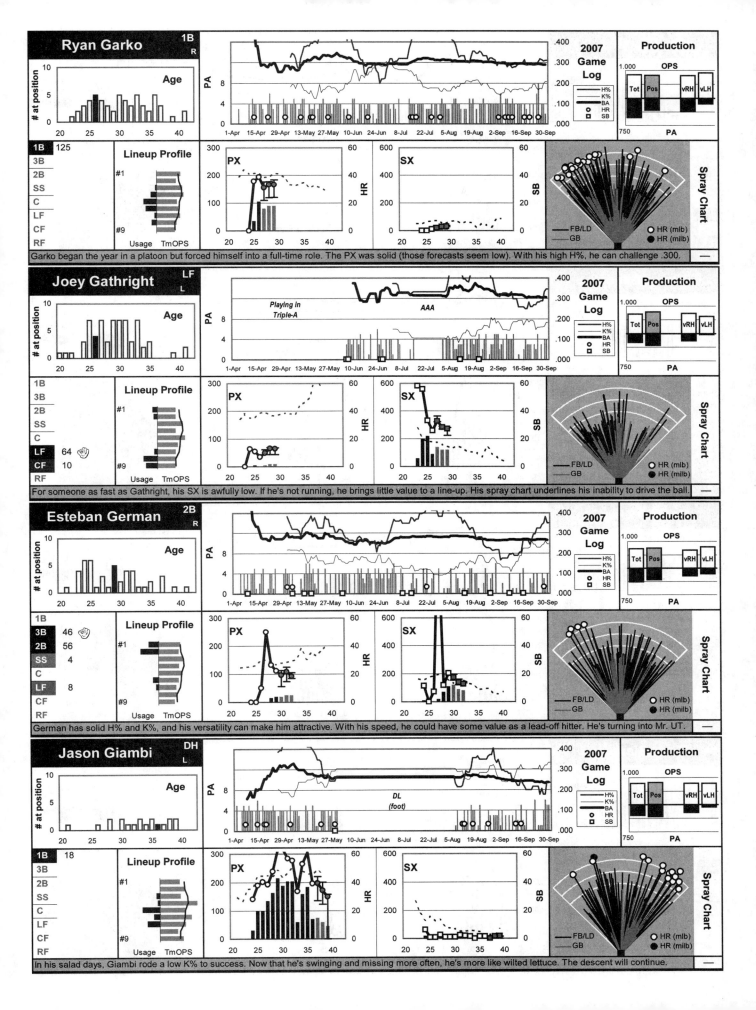

Ryan Garko — 1B / R

1B 125

Garko began the year in a platoon but forced himself into a full-time role. The PX was solid (those forecasts seem low). With his high H%, he can challenge .300.

Joey Gathright — LF / L

Playing in Triple-A   AAA

LF 64
CF 10

For someone as fast as Gathright, his SX is awfully low. If he's not running, he brings little value to a line-up. His spray chart underlines his inability to drive the ball.

Esteban German — 2B / R

3B 46
2B 56
SS 4
LF 8

German has solid H% and K%, and his versatility can make him attractive. With his speed, he could have some value as a lead-off hitter. He's turning into Mr. UT.

Jason Giambi — DH / L

DL (foot)

1B 18

In his salad days, Giambi rode a low K% to success. Now that he's swinging and missing more often, he's more like wilted lettuce. The descent will continue.

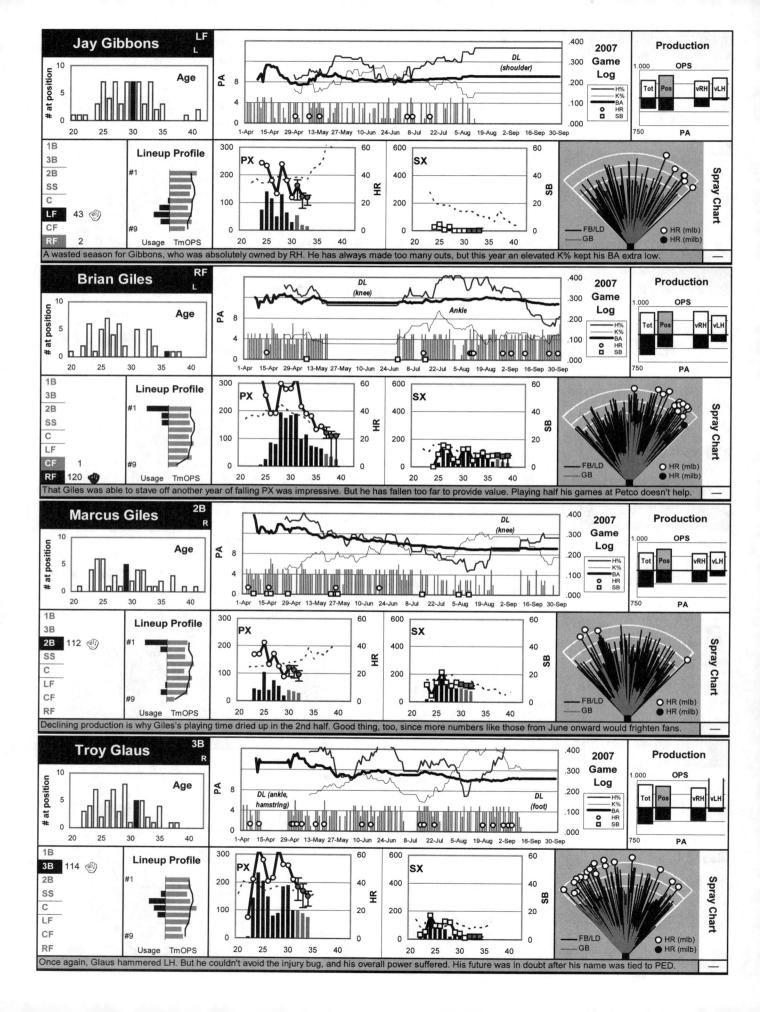

Jay Gibbons — LF / L

Age (# at position)

2007 Game Log — PA, DL (shoulder)
- H%
- K%
- BA
- ○ HR
- □ SB

Production — OPS: Tot, Pos, vRH, vLH — PA

Positions: 1B, 3B, 2B, SS, C, **LF 43**, CF, **RF 2**

Lineup Profile — #1 to #9, Usage, TmOPS

PX — HR
SX — SB
Spray Chart — FB/LD, GB, ○ HR (mlb), ● HR (milb)

A wasted season for Gibbons, who was absolutely owned by RH. He has always made too many outs, but this year an elevated K% kept his BA extra low.

Brian Giles — RF / L

Age (# at position)

2007 Game Log — PA, DL (knee), Ankle
- H%
- K%
- BA
- ○ HR
- □ SB

Production — OPS: Tot, Pos, vRH, vLH — PA

Positions: 1B, 3B, 2B, SS, C, LF, **CF 1**, **RF 120**

Lineup Profile — #1 to #9, Usage, TmOPS

PX — HR
SX — SB
Spray Chart — FB/LD, GB, ○ HR (mlb), ● HR (milb)

That Giles was able to stave off another year of falling PX was impressive. But he has fallen too far to provide value. Playing half his games at Petco doesn't help.

Marcus Giles — 2B / R

Age (# at position)

2007 Game Log — PA, DL (knee)
- H%
- K%
- BA
- ○ HR
- □ SB

Production — OPS: Tot, Pos, vRH, vLH — PA

Positions: 1B, 3B, **2B 112**, SS, C, LF, CF, RF

Lineup Profile — #1 to #9, Usage, TmOPS

PX — HR
SX — SB
Spray Chart — FB/LD, GB, ○ HR (mlb), ● HR (milb)

Declining production is why Giles's playing time dried up in the 2nd half. Good thing, too, since more numbers like those from June onward would frighten fans.

Troy Glaus — 3B / R

Age (# at position)

2007 Game Log — PA, DL (ankle, hamstring), DL (foot)
- H%
- K%
- BA
- ○ HR
- □ SB

Production — OPS: Tot, Pos, vRH, vLH — PA

Positions: 1B, **3B 114**, 2B, SS, C, LF, CF, RF

Lineup Profile — #1 to #9, Usage, TmOPS

PX — HR
SX — SB
Spray Chart — FB/LD, GB, ○ HR (mlb), ● HR (milb)

Once again, Glaus hammered LH. But he couldn't avoid the injury bug, and his overall power suffered. His future was in doubt after his name was tied to PED.

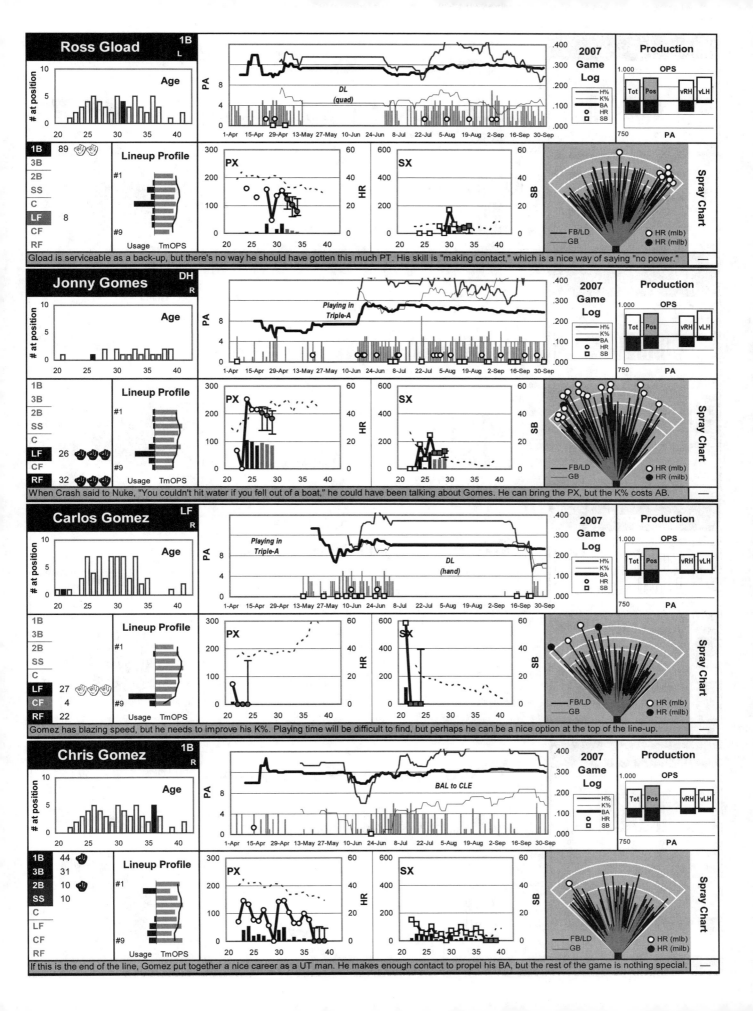

Ross Gload 1B L

Age

PA / 2007 Game Log — H%, K%, BA, HR, SB — DL (quad)

Production — OPS: Tot, Pos, vRH, vLH — PA

1B 89
3B
2B
SS
C
LF 8
CF
RF

Lineup Profile — #1 ... #9 — Usage, TmOPS

PX — HR
SX — SB

Spray Chart — FB/LD, GB — HR (mlb), HR (milb)

Gload is serviceable as a back-up, but there's no way he should have gotten this much PT. His skill is "making contact," which is a nice way of saying "no power." —

Jonny Gomes DH R

Age

PA / 2007 Game Log — Playing in Triple-A — H%, K%, BA, HR, SB

Production — OPS: Tot, Pos, vRH, vLH — PA

1B
3B
2B
SS
C
LF 26
CF
RF 32

Lineup Profile — #1 ... #9 — Usage, TmOPS

PX — HR
SX — SB

Spray Chart — FB/LD, GB — HR (mlb), HR (milb)

When Crash said to Nuke, "You couldn't hit water if you fell out of a boat," he could have been talking about Gomes. He can bring the PX, but the K% costs AB. —

Carlos Gomez LF R

Age

PA / 2007 Game Log — Playing in Triple-A — H%, K%, BA, HR, SB — DL (hand)

Production — OPS: Tot, Pos, vRH, vLH — PA

1B
3B
2B
SS
C
LF 27
CF 4
RF 22

Lineup Profile — #1 ... #9 — Usage, TmOPS

PX — HR
SX — SB

Spray Chart — FB/LD, GB — HR (mlb), HR (milb)

Gomez has blazing speed, but he needs to improve his K%. Playing time will be difficult to find, but perhaps he can be a nice option at the top of the line-up. —

Chris Gomez 1B R

Age

PA / 2007 Game Log — BAL to CLE — H%, K%, BA, HR, SB

Production — OPS: Tot, Pos, vRH, vLH — PA

1B 44
3B 31
2B 10
SS 10
C
LF
CF
RF

Lineup Profile — #1 ... #9 — Usage, TmOPS

PX — HR
SX — SB

Spray Chart — FB/LD, GB — HR (mlb), HR (milb)

If this is the end of the line, Gomez put together a nice career as a UT man. He makes enough contact to propel his BA, but the rest of the game is nothing special. —

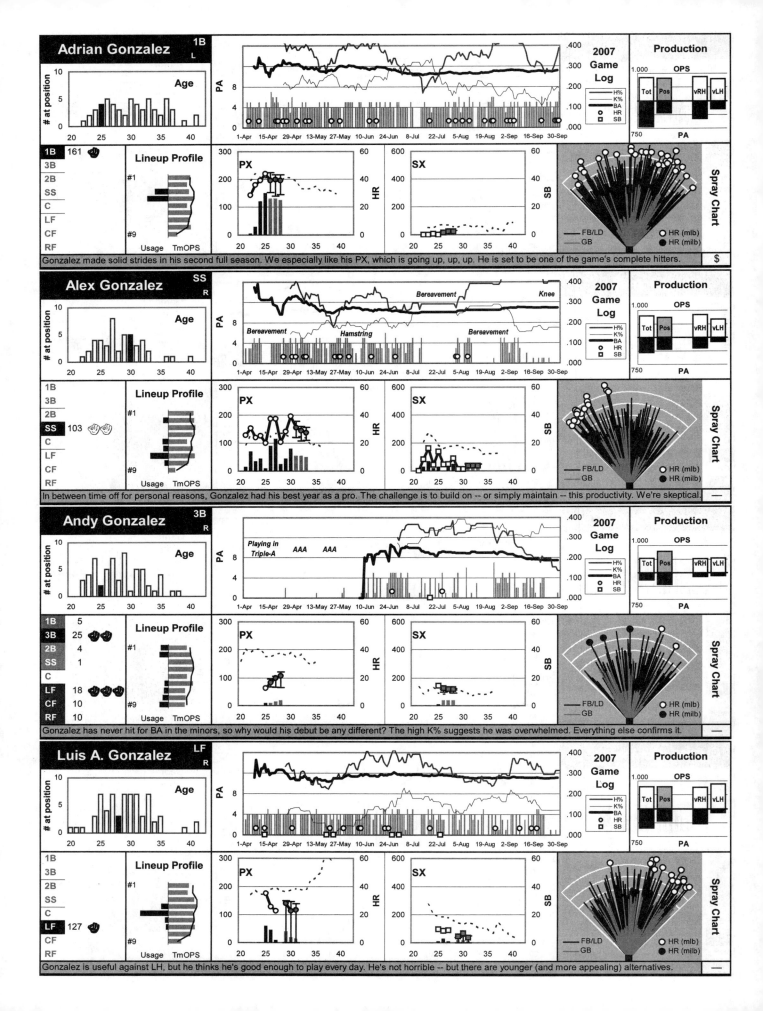

Adrian Gonzalez — 1B / L

Age — # at position

2007 Game Log — PA

.400 / .300 / .200 / .100 / .000

Legend: H% / K% / BA / HR (○) / SB (□)

1-Apr 15-Apr 29-Apr 13-May 27-May 10-Jun 24-Jun 8-Jul 22-Jul 5-Aug 19-Aug 2-Sep 16-Sep 30-Sep

Production — OPS — 1.000 / 750 — Tot / Pos / vRH / vLH — PA

Lineup Profile — #1 ... #9 — Usage / TmOPS

Pos	#
1B	161
3B	
2B	
SS	
C	
LF	
CF	
RF	

PX (HR) — SX (SB)

Spray Chart — FB/LD / GB — HR (mlb) ○ / HR (milb) ●

Gonzalez made solid strides in his second full season. We especially like his PX, which is going up, up, up. He is set to be one of the game's complete hitters. $

Alex Gonzalez — SS / R

Age — # at position

2007 Game Log — PA

Bereavement / Knee / Bereavement / Hamstring / Bereavement

Legend: H% / K% / BA / HR (○) / SB (□)

1-Apr 15-Apr 29-Apr 13-May 27-May 10-Jun 24-Jun 8-Jul 22-Jul 5-Aug 19-Aug 2-Sep 16-Sep 30-Sep

Production — OPS — 1.000 / 750 — Tot / Pos / vRH / vLH — PA

Lineup Profile — #1 ... #9 — Usage / TmOPS

Pos	#
1B	
3B	
2B	
SS	103
C	
LF	
CF	
RF	

PX (HR) — SX (SB)

Spray Chart — FB/LD / GB — HR (mlb) ○ / HR (milb) ●

In between time off for personal reasons, Gonzalez had his best year as a pro. The challenge is to build on -- or simply maintain -- this productivity. We're skeptical. —

Andy Gonzalez — 3B / R

Age — # at position

2007 Game Log — PA

Playing in Triple-A   AAA   AAA

.400 / .300 / .200 / .100 / .000

Legend: H% / K% / BA / HR (○) / SB (□)

1-Apr 15-Apr 29-Apr 13-May 27-May 10-Jun 24-Jun 8-Jul 22-Jul 5-Aug 19-Aug 2-Sep 16-Sep 30-Sep

Production — OPS — 1.000 / 750 — Tot / Pos / vRH / vLH — PA

Lineup Profile — #1 ... #9 — Usage / TmOPS

Pos	#
1B	5
3B	25
2B	4
SS	1
C	
LF	18
CF	10
RF	10

PX (HR) — SX (SB)

Spray Chart — FB/LD / GB — HR (mlb) ○ / HR (milb) ●

Gonzalez has never hit for BA in the minors, so why would his debut be any different? The high K% suggests he was overwhelmed. Everything else confirms it. —

Luis A. Gonzalez — LF / R

Age — # at position

2007 Game Log — PA

.400 / .300 / .200 / .100 / .000

Legend: H% / K% / BA / HR (○) / SB (□)

1-Apr 15-Apr 29-Apr 13-May 27-May 10-Jun 24-Jun 8-Jul 22-Jul 5-Aug 19-Aug 2-Sep 16-Sep 30-Sep

Production — OPS — 1.000 / 750 — Tot / Pos / vRH / vLH — PA

Lineup Profile — #1 ... #9 — Usage / TmOPS

Pos	#
1B	
3B	
2B	
SS	
C	
LF	127
CF	
RF	

PX (HR) — SX (SB)

Spray Chart — FB/LD / GB — HR (mlb) ○ / HR (milb) ●

Gonzalez is useful against LH, but he thinks he's good enough to play every day. He's not horrible -- but there are younger (and more appealing) alternatives. —

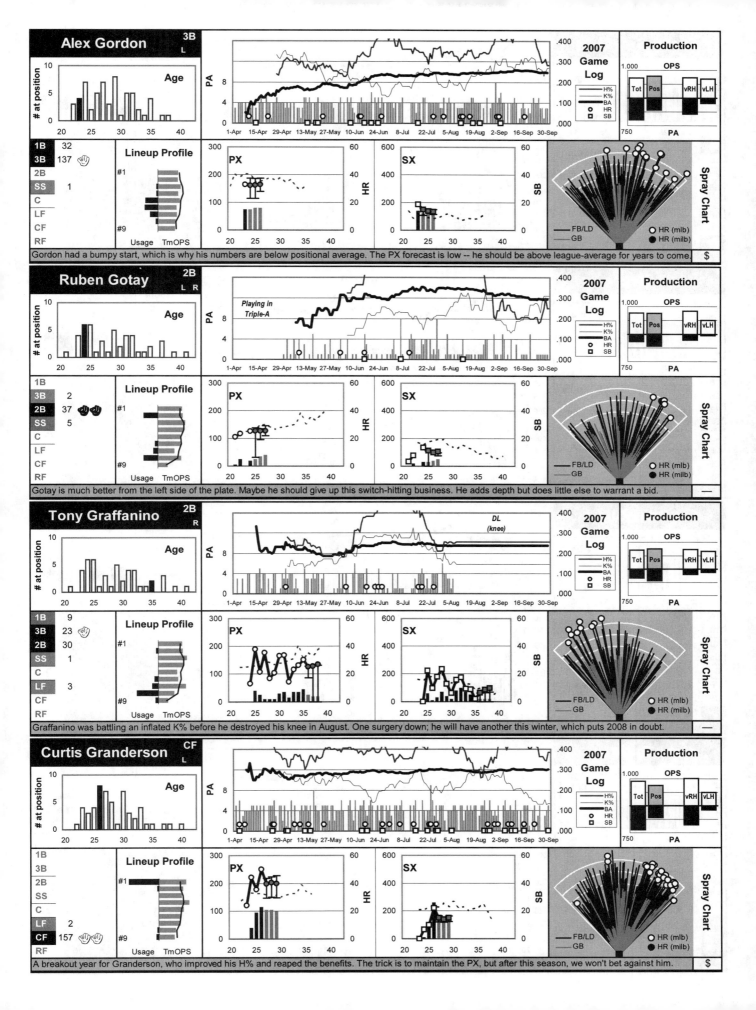

Alex Gordon 3B L

at position / Age

2007 Game Log

Production — OPS / PA

1B	32
3B	137
2B	
SS	1
C	
LF	
CF	
RF	

Lineup Profile — Usage / TmOPS

PX / HR — SX / SB — Spray Chart

H% / K% / BA / HR / SB

FB/LD / GB — HR (mlb) / HR (milb)

Gordon had a bumpy start, which is why his numbers are below positional average. The PX forecast is low -- he should be above league-average for years to come. $

Ruben Gotay 2B L R

at position / Age

Playing in Triple-A

2007 Game Log

Production — OPS / PA

1B	
3B	2
2B	37
SS	5
C	
LF	
CF	
RF	

Lineup Profile — Usage / TmOPS

PX / HR — SX / SB — Spray Chart

FB/LD / GB — HR (mlb) / HR (milb)

Gotay is much better from the left side of the plate. Maybe he should give up this switch-hitting business. He adds depth but does little else to warrant a bid. —

Tony Graffanino 2B R

at position / Age

DL (knee)

2007 Game Log

Production — OPS / PA

1B	9
3B	23
2B	30
SS	1
C	
LF	3
CF	
RF	

Lineup Profile — Usage / TmOPS

PX / HR — SX / SB — Spray Chart

FB/LD / GB — HR (mlb) / HR (milb)

Graffanino was battling an inflated K% before he destroyed his knee in August. One surgery down; he will have another this winter, which puts 2008 in doubt. —

Curtis Granderson CF L

at position / Age

2007 Game Log

Production — OPS / PA

1B	
3B	
2B	
SS	
C	
LF	2
CF	157
RF	

Lineup Profile — Usage / TmOPS

PX / HR — SX / SB — Spray Chart

FB/LD / GB — HR (mlb) / HR (milb)

A breakout year for Granderson, who improved his H% and reaped the benefits. The trick is to maintain the PX, but after this season, we won't bet against him. $

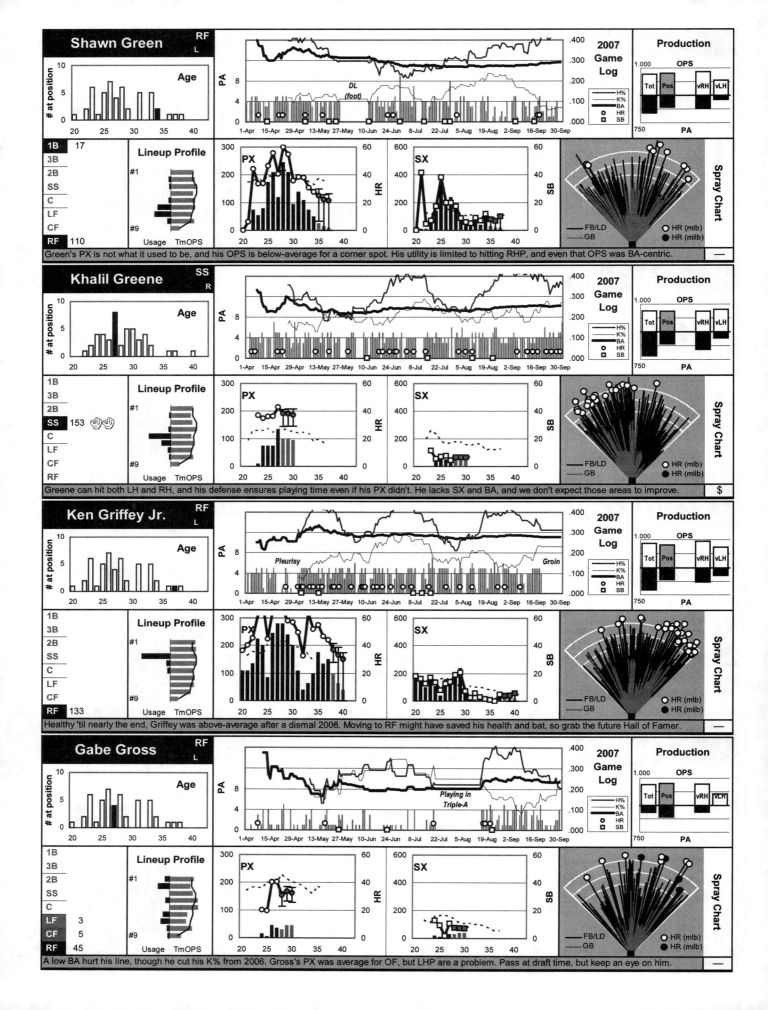

Shawn Green — RF / L

1B 17
3B
2B
SS
C
LF
RF 110

2007 Game Log

Production — OPS

Green's PX is not what it used to be, and his OPS is below-average for a corner spot. His utility is limited to hitting RHP, and even that OPS was BA-centric. — —

Khalil Greene — SS / R

1B
3B
2B
SS 153
C
LF
RF

2007 Game Log

Production — OPS

Greene can hit both LH and RH, and his defense ensures playing time even if his PX didn't. He lacks SX and BA, and we don't expect those areas to improve. — $

Ken Griffey Jr. — RF / L

1B
3B
2B
SS
C
LF
CF
RF 133

2007 Game Log
Pleurisy   Groin

Production — OPS

Healthy 'til nearly the end, Griffey was above-average after a dismal 2006. Moving to RF might have saved his health and bat, so grab the future Hall of Famer. — —

Gabe Gross — RF / L

1B
3B
2B
SS
C
LF 3
CF 5
RF 45

2007 Game Log
Playing in Triple-A

Production — OPS

A low BA hurt his line, though he cut his K% from 2006. Gross's PX was average for OF, but LHP are a problem. Pass at draft time, but keep an eye on him. — —

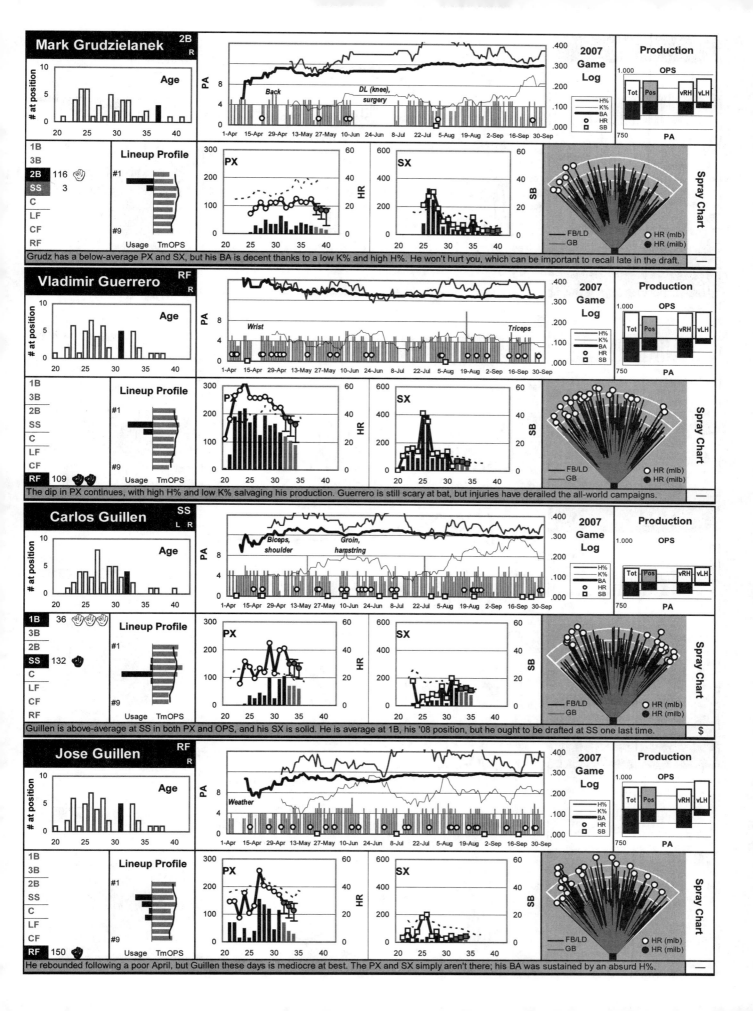

Mark Grudzielanek 2B R

Age | PA | 2007 Game Log | Production OPS

Back | DL (knee), surgery

1B / 3B / 2B 116 / SS 3 / C / LF / CF / RF

Lineup Profile | #1 ... #9 | Usage | TmOPS

PX | SX | Spray Chart

FB/LD / GB | HR (mlb) / HR (milb)

Grudz has a below-average PX and SX, but his BA is decent thanks to a low K% and high H%. He won't hurt you, which can be important to recall late in the draft. | —

Vladimir Guerrero RF R

Age | PA | 2007 Game Log | Production OPS

Wrist | *Triceps*

1B / 3B / 2B / SS / C / LF / CF / RF 109

Lineup Profile | #1 ... #9 | Usage | TmOPS

PX | SX | Spray Chart

FB/LD / GB | HR (mlb) / HR (milb)

The dip in PX continues, with high H% and low K% salvaging his production. Guerrero is still scary at bat, but injuries have derailed the all-world campaigns. | —

Carlos Guillen SS L R

Age | PA | 2007 Game Log | Production OPS

Biceps, shoulder | *Groin, hamstring*

1B 36 / 3B / 2B / SS 132 / C / LF / CF / RF

Lineup Profile | #1 ... #9 | Usage | TmOPS

PX | SX | Spray Chart

FB/LD / GB | HR (mlb) / HR (milb)

Guillen is above-average at SS in both PX and OPS, and his SX is solid. He is average at 1B, his '08 position, but he ought to be drafted at SS one last time. | $

Jose Guillen RF R

Age | PA | 2007 Game Log | Production OPS

Weather

1B / 3B / 2B / SS / C / LF / CF / RF 150

Lineup Profile | #1 ... #9 | Usage | TmOPS

PX | SX | Spray Chart

FB/LD / GB | HR (mlb) / HR (milb)

He rebounded following a poor April, but Guillen these days is mediocre at best. The PX and SX simply aren't there; his BA was sustained by an absurd H%. | —

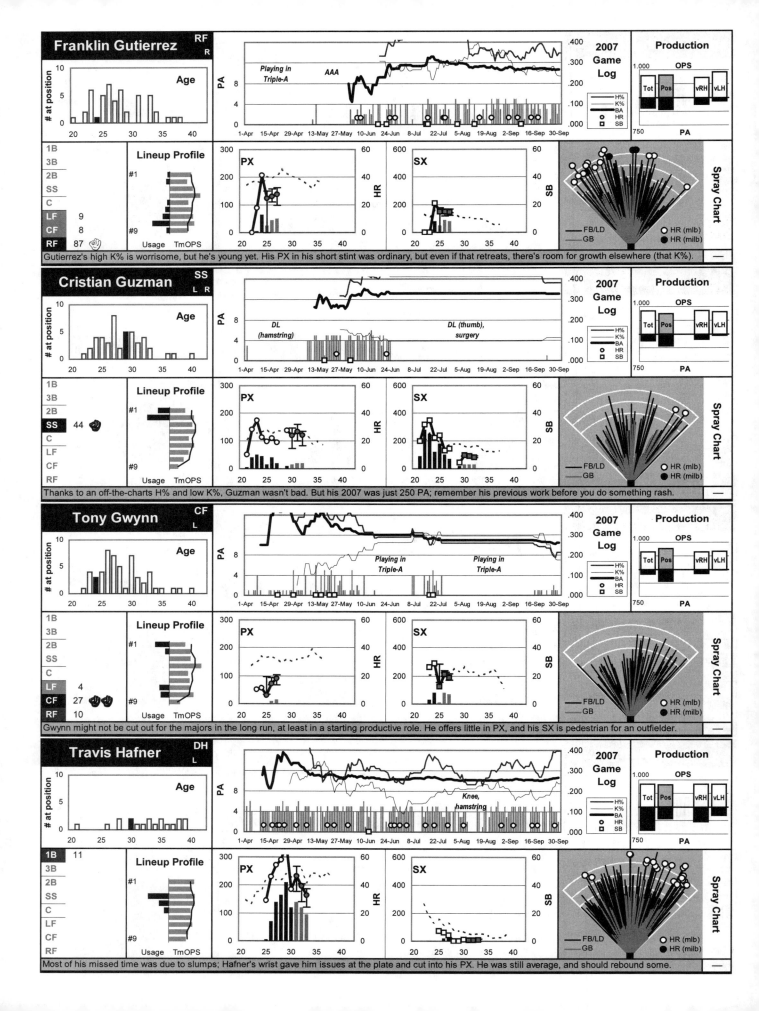

Franklin Gutierrez RF R

Age

PA / 2007 Game Log

Production OPS

H% / K% / BA / HR / SB

1B
3B
2B
SS
C
LF 9
CF 8
RF 87

Lineup Profile
#1
#9
Usage TmOPS

PX / SX / Spray Chart

Playing in Triple-A / AAA

FB/LD — GB
○ HR (mlb) ● HR (milb)

Gutierrez's high K% is worrisome, but he's young yet. His PX in his short stint was ordinary, but even if that retreats, there's room for growth elsewhere (that K%). —

Cristian Guzman SS L R

Age

PA / 2007 Game Log

Production OPS
Tot Pos vRH vLH

1B
3B
2B
SS 44
C
LF
CF
RF

Lineup Profile
#1
#9
Usage TmOPS

PX / SX / Spray Chart

DL (hamstring) / DL (thumb), surgery

FB/LD — GB
○ HR (mlb) ● HR (milb)

Thanks to an off-the-charts H% and low K%, Guzman wasn't bad. But his 2007 was just 250 PA; remember his previous work before you do something rash. —

Tony Gwynn CF L

Age

PA / 2007 Game Log

Production OPS
Tot Pos vRH vLH

1B
3B
2B
SS
C
LF 4
CF 27
RF 10

Lineup Profile
#1
#9
Usage TmOPS

PX / SX / Spray Chart

Playing in Triple-A / Playing in Triple-A

FB/LD — GB
○ HR (mlb) ● HR (milb)

Gwynn might not be cut out for the majors in the long run, at least in a starting productive role. He offers little in PX, and his SX is pedestrian for an outfielder. —

Travis Hafner DH L

Age

PA / 2007 Game Log

Production OPS
Tot Pos vRH vLH

1B 11
3B
2B
SS
C
LF
CF
RF

Lineup Profile
#1
#9
Usage TmOPS

PX / SX / Spray Chart

Knee, hamstring

FB/LD — GB
○ HR (mlb) ● HR (milb)

Most of his missed time was due to slumps; Hafner's wrist gave him issues at the plate and cut into his PX. He was still average, and should rebound some. —

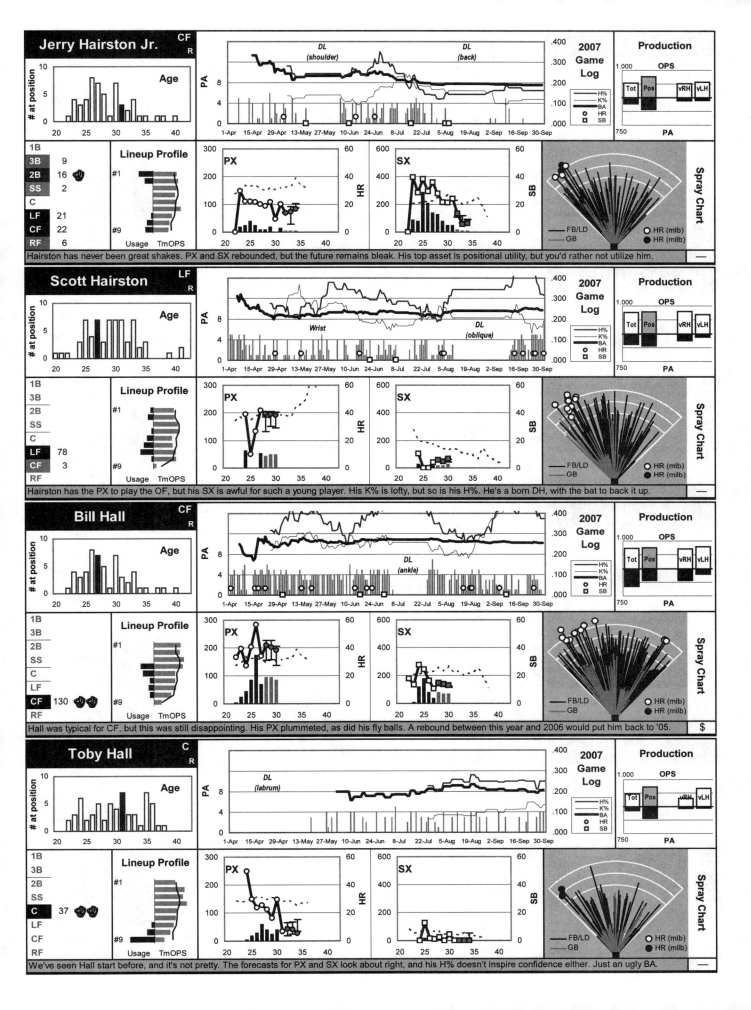

Jerry Hairston Jr. CF R

Age (# at position)

PA — 2007 Game Log — H%, K%, BA, HR, SB

DL (shoulder)   DL (back)

Production OPS — Tot, Pos, vRH, vLH

1B	
3B	9
2B	16
SS	2
C	
LF	21
CF	22
RF	6

Lineup Profile #1 to #9, Usage, TmOPS

PX / HR   **SX** / SB   **Spray Chart** (FB/LD, GB, HR (mlb), HR (milb))

Hairston has never been great shakes. PX and SX rebounded, but the future remains bleak. His top asset is positional utility, but you'd rather not utilize him. —

Scott Hairston LF R

Age (# at position)

PA — 2007 Game Log — H%, K%, BA, HR, SB

Wrist   DL (oblique)

Production OPS — Tot, Pos, vRH, vLH

1B	
3B	
2B	
SS	
C	
LF	78
CF	3
RF	

Lineup Profile #1 to #9, Usage, TmOPS

PX / HR   **SX** / SB   **Spray Chart** (FB/LD, GB, HR (mlb), HR (milb))

Hairston has the PX to play the OF, but his SX is awful for such a young player. His K% is lofty, but so is his H%. He's a born DH, with the bat to back it up. —

Bill Hall CF R

Age (# at position)

PA — 2007 Game Log — H%, K%, BA, HR, SB

DL (ankle)

Production OPS — Tot, Pos, vRH, vLH

1B	
3B	
2B	
SS	
C	
LF	
CF	130
RF	

Lineup Profile #1 to #9, Usage, TmOPS

PX / HR   **SX** / SB   **Spray Chart** (FB/LD, GB, HR (mlb), HR (milb))

Hall was typical for CF, but this was still disappointing. His PX plummeted, as did his fly balls. A rebound between this year and 2006 would put him back to '05. $

Toby Hall C R

Age (# at position)

PA — 2007 Game Log — H%, K%, BA, HR, SB

DL (labrum)

Production OPS — Tot, Pos, vRH, vLH

1B	
3B	
2B	
SS	
C	37
LF	
CF	
RF	

Lineup Profile #1 to #9, Usage, TmOPS

PX / HR   **SX** / SB   **Spray Chart** (FB/LD, GB, HR (mlb), HR (milb))

We've seen Hall start before, and it's not pretty. The forecasts for PX and SX look about right, and his H% doesn't inspire confidence either. Just an ugly BA. —

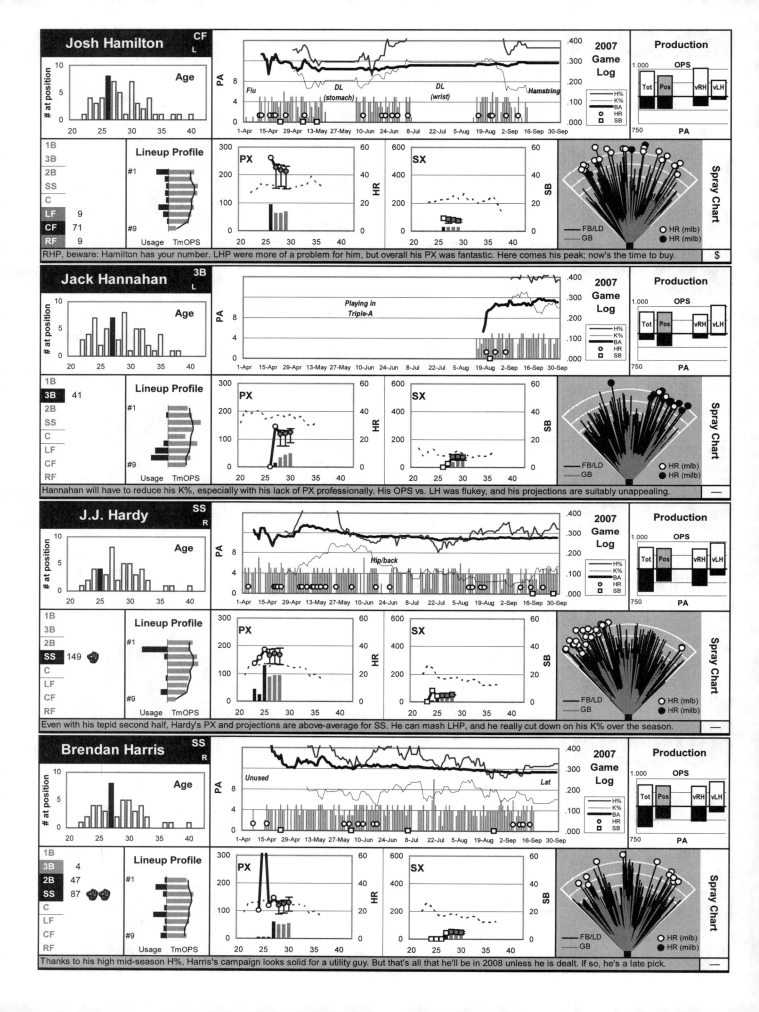

Josh Hamilton — CF / L

2007 Game Log

Flu | DL (stomach) | DL (wrist) | Hamstring

Legend: H%, K%, BA, HR, SB

Production — OPS: Tot, Pos, vRH, vLH

Age

Lineup Profile (#1 – #9), Usage, TmOPS

LF 9
CF 71
RF 9

PX / SX / Spray Chart (FB/LD, GB, HR (mlb), HR (milb))

RHP, beware: Hamilton has your number. LHP were more of a problem for him, but overall his PX was fantastic. Here comes his peak; now's the time to buy. **$**

Jack Hannahan — 3B / L

2007 Game Log

Playing in Triple-A

Legend: H%, K%, BA, HR, SB

Production — OPS: Tot, Pos, vRH, vLH

Age

Lineup Profile (#1 – #9), Usage, TmOPS

3B 41

PX / SX / Spray Chart (FB/LD, GB, HR (mlb), HR (milb))

Hannahan will have to reduce his K%, especially with his lack of PX professionally. His OPS vs. LH was flukey, and his projections are suitably unappealing. **—**

J.J. Hardy — SS / R

2007 Game Log

Hip/back

Legend: H%, K%, BA, HR, SB

Production — OPS: Tot, Pos, vRH, vLH

Age

Lineup Profile (#1 – #9), Usage, TmOPS

SS 149

PX / SX / Spray Chart (FB/LD, GB, HR (mlb), HR (milb))

Even with his tepid second half, Hardy's PX and projections are above-average for SS. He can mash LHP, and he really cut down on his K% over the season. **—**

Brendan Harris — SS / R

2007 Game Log

Unused | Lat

Legend: H%, K%, BA, HR, SB

Production — OPS: Tot, Pos, vRH, vLH

Age

Lineup Profile (#1 – #9), Usage, TmOPS

3B 4
2B 47
SS 87

PX / SX / Spray Chart (FB/LD, GB, HR (mlb), HR (milb))

Thanks to his high mid-season H%, Harris's campaign looks solid for a utility guy. But that's all that he'll be in 2008 unless he is dealt. If so, he's a late pick. **—**

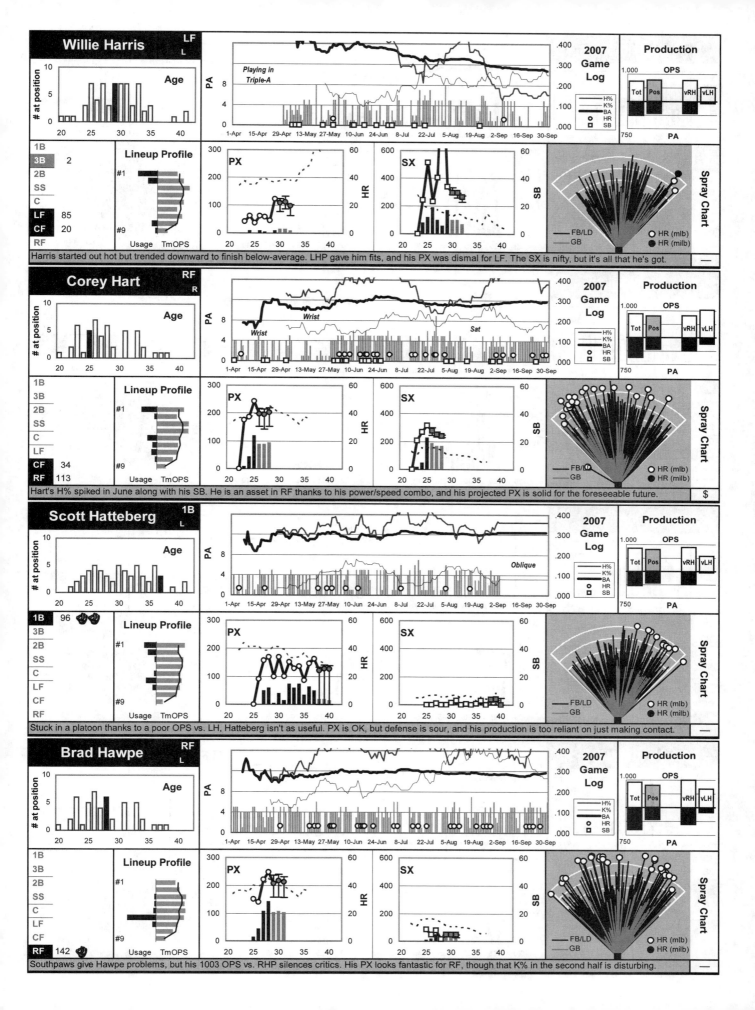

Willie Harris — LF, L

Age — # at position

PA / 2007 Game Log
Playing in Triple-A

Legend: H%, K%, BA, HR (○), SB (□)

Production — OPS
Tot, Pos, vRH, vLH / PA

Lineup positions:
3B 2
LF 85
CF 20

Lineup Profile — #1 ... #9 — Usage / TmOPS

PX — HR
SX — SB

Spray Chart — FB/LD, GB, HR (mlb) ○, HR (milb) ●

Harris started out hot but trended downward to finish below-average. LHP gave him fits, and his PX was dismal for LF. The SX is nifty, but it's all that he's got. — —

Corey Hart — RF, R

Age — # at position

PA / 2007 Game Log
Wrist ... Wrist ... Sat

Legend: H%, K%, BA, HR (○), SB (□)

Production — OPS
Tot, Pos, vRH, vLH / PA

Lineup positions:
CF 34
RF 113

Lineup Profile — #1 ... #9 — Usage / TmOPS

PX — HR
SX — SB

Spray Chart — FB/LD, GB, HR (mlb) ○, HR (milb) ●

Hart's H% spiked in June along with his SB. He is an asset in RF thanks to his power/speed combo, and his projected PX is solid for the foreseeable future. — $

Scott Hatteberg — 1B, L

Age — # at position

PA / 2007 Game Log
Oblique

Legend: H%, K%, BA, HR (○), SB (□)

Production — OPS
Tot, Pos, vRH, vLH / PA

Lineup positions:
1B 96

Lineup Profile — #1 ... #9 — Usage / TmOPS

PX — HR
SX — SB

Spray Chart — FB/LD, GB, HR (mlb) ○, HR (milb) ●

Stuck in a platoon thanks to a poor OPS vs. LH, Hatteberg isn't as useful. PX is OK, but defense is sour, and his production is too reliant on just making contact. — —

Brad Hawpe — RF, L

Age — # at position

PA / 2007 Game Log

Legend: H%, K%, BA, HR (○), SB (□)

Production — OPS
Tot, Pos, vRH, vLH / PA

Lineup positions:
RF 142

Lineup Profile — #1 ... #9 — Usage / TmOPS

PX — HR
SX — SB

Spray Chart — FB/LD, GB, HR (mlb) ○, HR (milb) ●

Southpaws give Hawpe problems, but his 1003 OPS vs. RHP silences critics. His PX looks fantastic for RF, though that K% in the second half is disturbing. — —

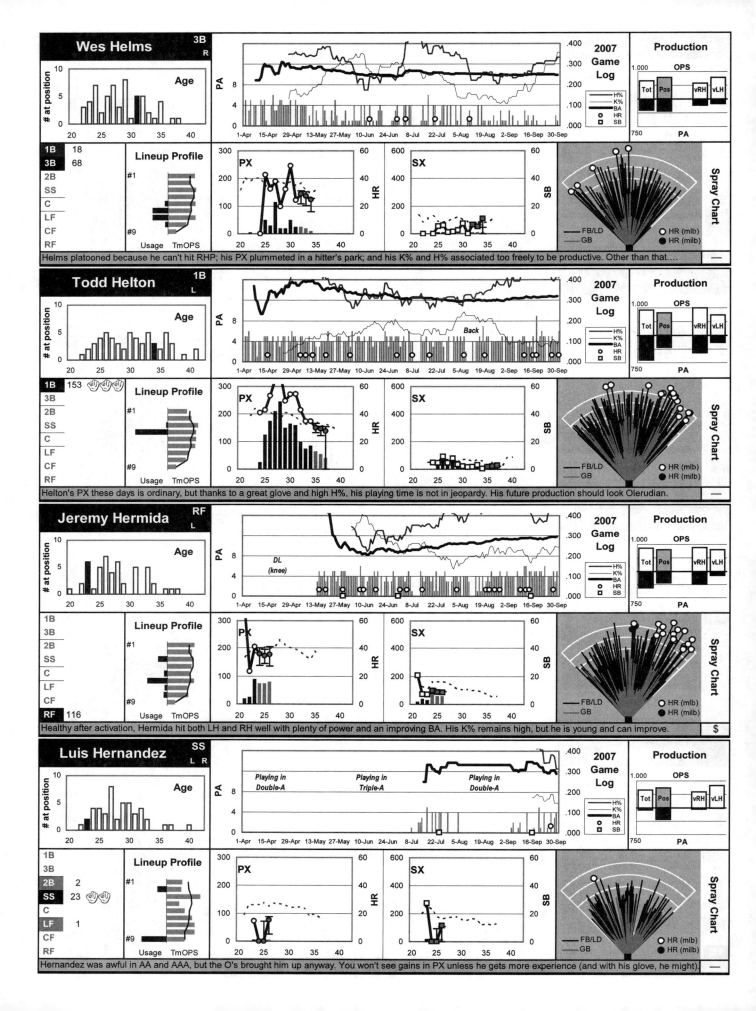

Wes Helms — 3B — R

1B	18
3B	68
2B	
SS	
C	
LF	
CF	
RF	

2007 Game Log

Production — OPS: Tot, Pos, vRH, vLH — PA

Spray Chart — HR (mlb), HR (milb), FB/LD, GB

Helms platooned because he can't hit RHP; his PX plummeted in a hitter's park; and his K% and H% associated too freely to be productive. Other than that…   —

Todd Helton — 1B — L

1B	153
3B	
2B	
SS	
C	
LF	
CF	
RF	

2007 Game Log

Back

Production — OPS: Tot, Pos, vRH, vLH — PA

Spray Chart — HR (mlb), HR (milb), FB/LD, GB

Helton's PX these days is ordinary, but thanks to a great glove and high H%, his playing time is not in jeopardy. His future production should look Olerudian.   —

Jeremy Hermida — RF — L

1B	
3B	
2B	
SS	
C	
LF	
CF	
RF	116

2007 Game Log

DL (knee)

Production — OPS: Tot, Pos, vRH, vLH — PA

Spray Chart — HR (mlb), HR (milb), FB/LD, GB

Healthy after activation, Hermida hit both LH and RH well with plenty of power and an improving BA. His K% remains high, but he is young and can improve. $

Luis Hernandez — SS — L R

1B	
3B	
2B	2
SS	23
C	
LF	1
CF	
RF	

2007 Game Log

Playing in Double-A   Playing in Triple-A   Playing in Double-A

Production — OPS: Tot, Pos, vRH, vLH — PA

Spray Chart — HR (mlb), HR (milb), FB/LD, GB

Hernandez was awful in AA and AAA, but the O's brought him up anyway. You won't see gains in PX unless he gets more experience (and with his glove, he might).   —

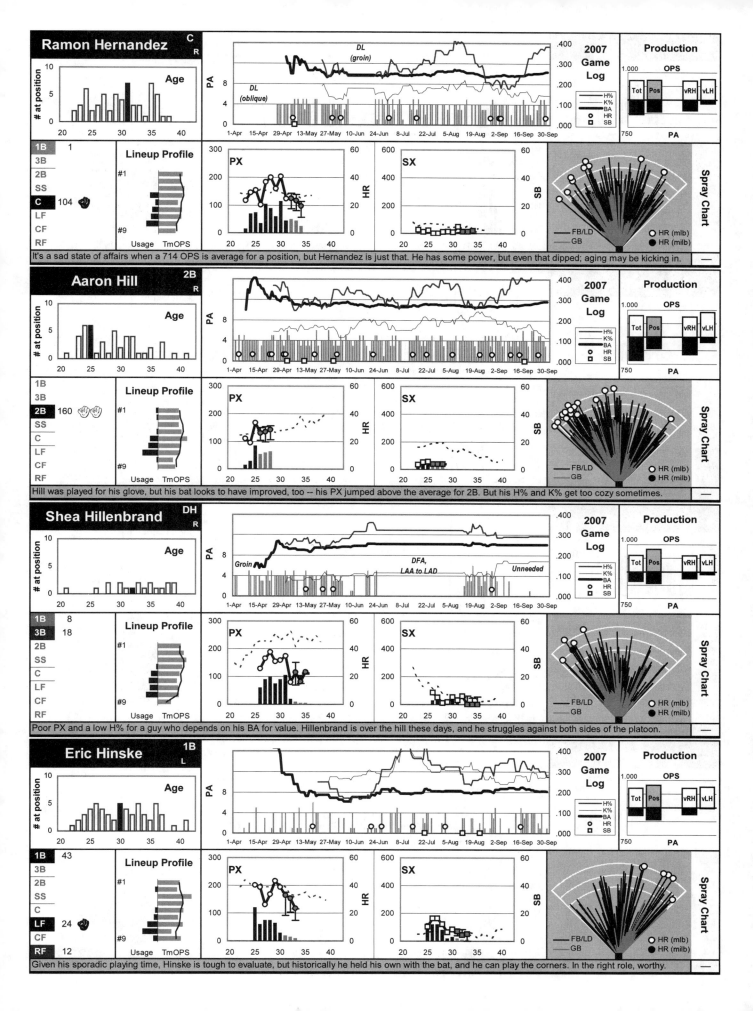

Ramon Hernandez — C, R — Age

2007 Game Log — Production — OPS — PA

DL (groin) · DL (oblique)

H% · K% · BA · HR · SB

1B 1 · 3B · 2B · SS · C 104 · LF · CF · RF

Lineup Profile — #1 ... #9 — Usage · TmOPS

PX · SX · HR · SB — Spray Chart — FB/LD · GB — HR (mlb) · HR (milb)

It's a sad state of affairs when a 714 OPS is average for a position, but Hernandez is just that. He has some power, but even that dipped; aging may be kicking in.

Aaron Hill — 2B, R — Age

2007 Game Log — Production — OPS — PA

H% · K% · BA · HR · SB

1B · 3B · 2B 160 · SS · C · LF · CF · RF

Lineup Profile — #1 ... #9 — Usage · TmOPS

PX · SX · HR · SB — Spray Chart — FB/LD · GB — HR (mlb) · HR (milb)

Hill was played for his glove, but his bat looks to have improved, too -- his PX jumped above the average for 2B. But his H% and K% get too cozy sometimes.

Shea Hillenbrand — DH, R — Age

2007 Game Log — Production — OPS — PA

Groin · DFA, LAA to LAD · Unneeded

H% · K% · BA · HR · SB

1B 8 · 3B 18 · 2B · SS · C · LF · CF · RF

Lineup Profile — #1 ... #9 — Usage · TmOPS

PX · SX · HR · SB — Spray Chart — FB/LD · GB — HR (mlb) · HR (milb)

Poor PX and a low H% for a guy who depends on his BA for value. Hillenbrand is over the hill these days, and he struggles against both sides of the platoon.

Eric Hinske — 1B, L — Age

2007 Game Log — Production — OPS — PA

H% · K% · BA · HR · SB

1B 43 · 3B · 2B · SS · C · LF 24 · CF · RF 12

Lineup Profile — #1 ... #9 — Usage · TmOPS

PX · SX · HR · SB — Spray Chart — FB/LD · GB — HR (mlb) · HR (milb)

Given his sporadic playing time, Hinske is tough to evaluate, but historically he held his own with the bat, and he can play the corners. In the right role, worthy.

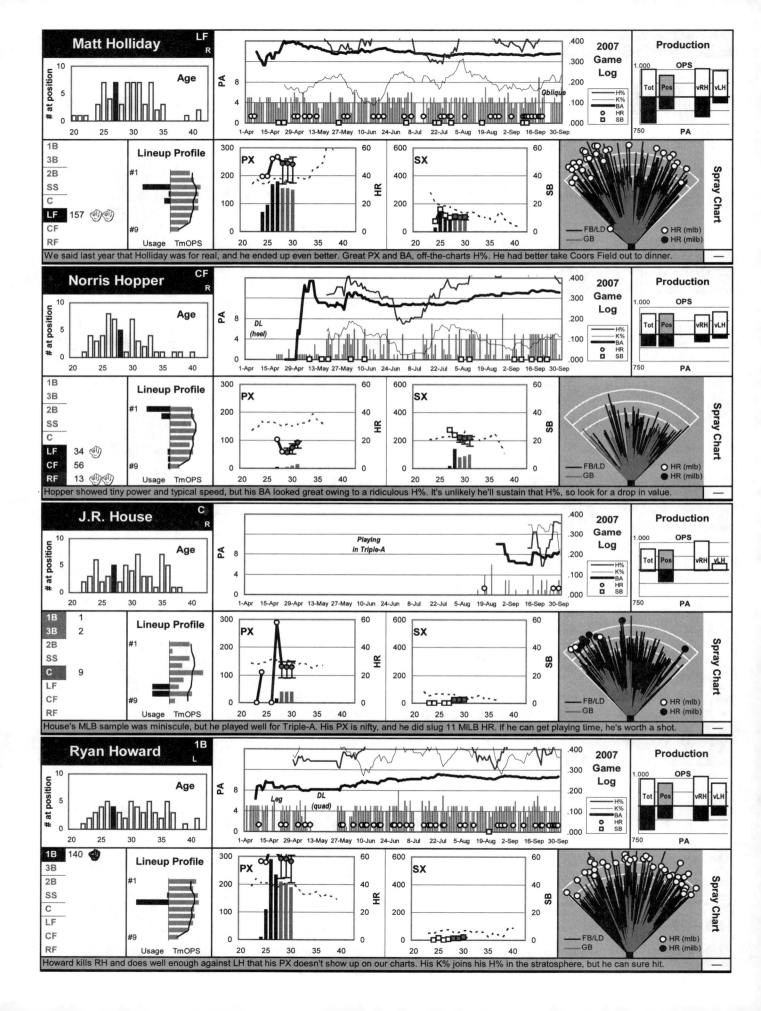

Matt Holliday — LF / R

2007 Game Log

Production — OPS

We said last year that Holliday was for real, and he ended up even better. Great PX and BA, off-the-charts H%. He had better take Coors Field out to dinner.

LF 157

Norris Hopper — CF / R

2007 Game Log

Production — OPS

Hopper showed tiny power and typical speed, but his BA looked great owing to a ridiculous H%. It's unlikely he'll sustain that H%, so look for a drop in value.

LF 34   CF 56   RF 13

J.R. House — C / R

2007 Game Log

Playing in Triple-A

Production — OPS

House's MLB sample was miniscule, but he played well for Triple-A. His PX is nifty, and he did slug 11 MILB HR. If he can get playing time, he's worth a shot.

1B 1   3B 2   C 9

Ryan Howard — 1B / L

2007 Game Log

Leg   *DL (quad)*

Production — OPS

Howard kills RH and does well enough against LH that his PX doesn't show up on our charts. His K% joins his H% in the stratosphere, but he can sure hit.

1B 140

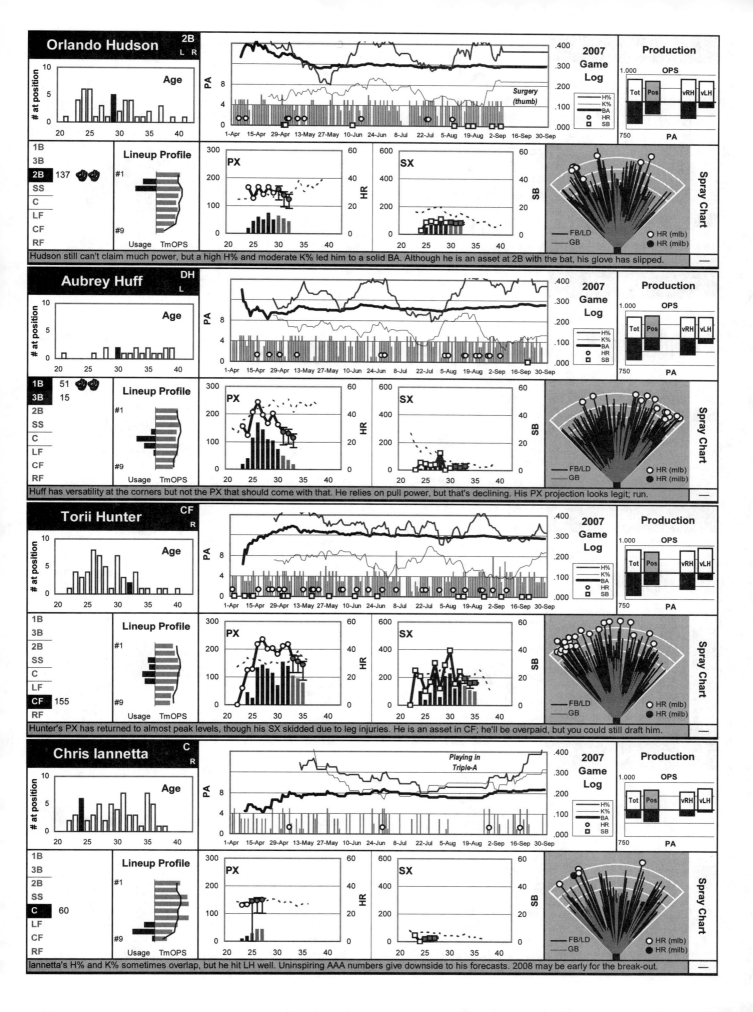

Orlando Hudson — 2B (L R)

2007 Game Log — Surgery (thumb)

Production — OPS

Positions: 2B 137

Hudson still can't claim much power, but a high H% and moderate K% led him to a solid BA. Although he is an asset at 2B with the bat, his glove has slipped.

Aubrey Huff — DH (L)

2007 Game Log

Production — OPS

Positions: 1B 51, 3B 15

Huff has versatility at the corners but not the PX that should come with that. He relies on pull power, but that's declining. His PX projection looks legit; run.

Torii Hunter — CF (R)

2007 Game Log

Production — OPS

Positions: CF 155

Hunter's PX has returned to almost peak levels, though his SX skidded due to leg injuries. He is an asset in CF; he'll be overpaid, but you could still draft him.

Chris Iannetta — C (R)

2007 Game Log — Playing in Triple-A

Production — OPS

Positions: C 60

Iannetta's H% and K% sometimes overlap, but he hit LH well. Uninspiring AAA numbers give downside to his forecasts. 2008 may be early for the break-out.

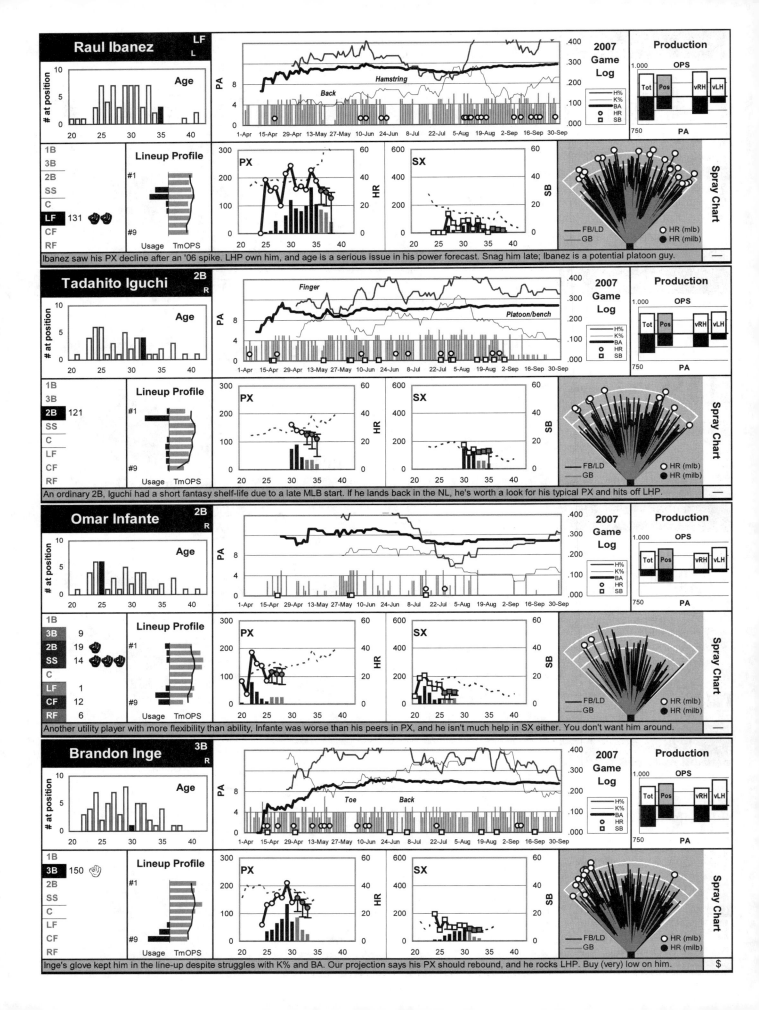

Raul Ibanez — LF, L

Age

1B, 3B, 2B, SS, C, **LF** 131, CF, RF

Lineup Profile — #1 ... #9 — Usage — TmOPS

PX / HR — SX / SB

2007 Game Log — H%, K%, BA, HR, SB

PA — Hamstring, Back

.400 .300 .200 .100 .000

Production — OPS 1.000 — Tot, Pos, vRH, vLH — 750 — PA

Spray Chart — FB/LD, GB — HR (mlb), HR (milb)

Ibanez saw his PX decline after an '06 spike. LHP own him, and age is a serious issue in his power forecast. Snag him late; Ibanez is a potential platoon guy. —

Tadahito Iguchi — 2B, R

Age

1B, 3B, **2B** 121, SS, C, LF, CF, RF

Lineup Profile — #1 ... #9 — Usage — TmOPS

PX / HR — SX / SB

2007 Game Log — H%, K%, BA, HR, SB — Finger — Platoon/bench

.400 .300 .200 .100 .000

Production — OPS 1.000 — Tot, Pos, vRH, vLH — 750 — PA

Spray Chart — FB/LD, GB — HR (mlb), HR (milb)

An ordinary 2B, Iguchi had a short fantasy shelf-life due to a late MLB start. If he lands back in the NL, he's worth a look for his typical PX and hits off LHP. —

Omar Infante — 2B, R

Age

1B, **3B** 9, **2B** 19, **SS** 14, C, **LF** 1, **CF** 12, **RF** 6

Lineup Profile — #1 ... #9 — Usage — TmOPS

PX / HR — SX / SB

2007 Game Log — H%, K%, BA, HR, SB

.400 .300 .200 .100 .000

Production — OPS 1.000 — Tot, Pos, vRH, vLH — 750 — PA

Spray Chart — FB/LD, GB — HR (mlb), HR (milb)

Another utility player with more flexibility than ability, Infante was worse than his peers in PX, and he isn't much help in SX either. You don't want him around. —

Brandon Inge — 3B, R

Age

1B, **3B** 150, 2B, SS, C, LF, CF, RF

Lineup Profile — #1 ... #9 — Usage — TmOPS

PX / HR — SX / SB

2007 Game Log — H%, K%, BA, HR, SB — Toe — Back

.400 .300 .200 .100 .000

Production — OPS 1.000 — Tot, Pos, vRH, vLH — 750 — PA

Spray Chart — FB/LD, GB — HR (mlb), HR (milb)

Inge's glove kept him in the line-up despite struggles with K% and BA. Our projection says his PX should rebound, and he rocks LHP. Buy (very) low on him. $

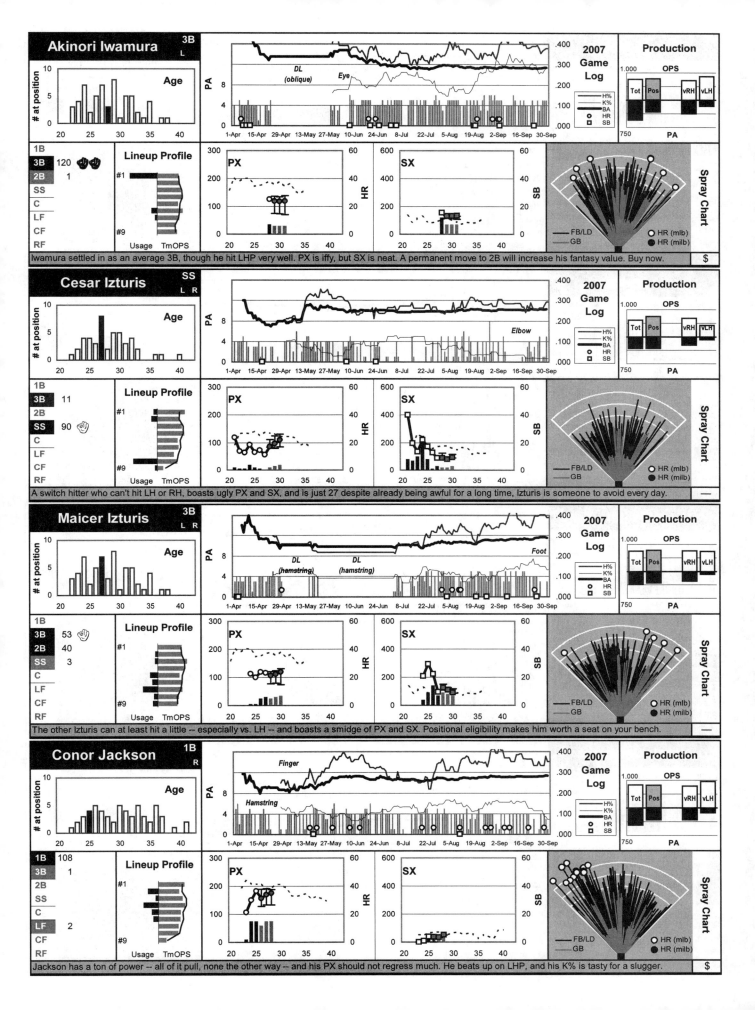

Akinori Iwamura 3B L

at position · Age · PA · 2007 Game Log · Production · OPS · Spray Chart

DL (oblique) · Eye

H% · K% · BA · HR · SB

1B
3B 120
2B 1
SS
C
LF
CF
RF

Lineup Profile · #1 · #9 · Usage · TmOPS

PX · HR · SX · SB · FB/LD · GB · HR (mlb) · HR (milb)

Iwamura settled in as an average 3B, though he hit LHP very well. PX is iffy, but SX is neat. A permanent move to 2B will increase his fantasy value. Buy now. $

Cesar Izturis SS L R

Elbow

1B
3B 11
2B
SS 90
C
LF
CF
RF

A switch hitter who can't hit LH or RH, boasts ugly PX and SX, and is just 27 despite already being awful for a long time, Izturis is someone to avoid every day. —

Maicer Izturis 3B L R

DL (hamstring) · DL (hamstring) · Foot

1B
3B 53
2B 40
SS 3
C
LF
CF
RF

The other Izturis can at least hit a little -- especially vs. LH -- and boasts a smidge of PX and SX. Positional eligibility makes him worth a seat on your bench. —

Conor Jackson 1B R

Finger · Hamstring

1B 108
3B 1
2B
SS
C
LF 2
CF
RF

Jackson has a ton of power -- all of it pull, none the other way -- and his PX should not regress much. He beats up on LHP, and his K% is tasty for a slugger. $

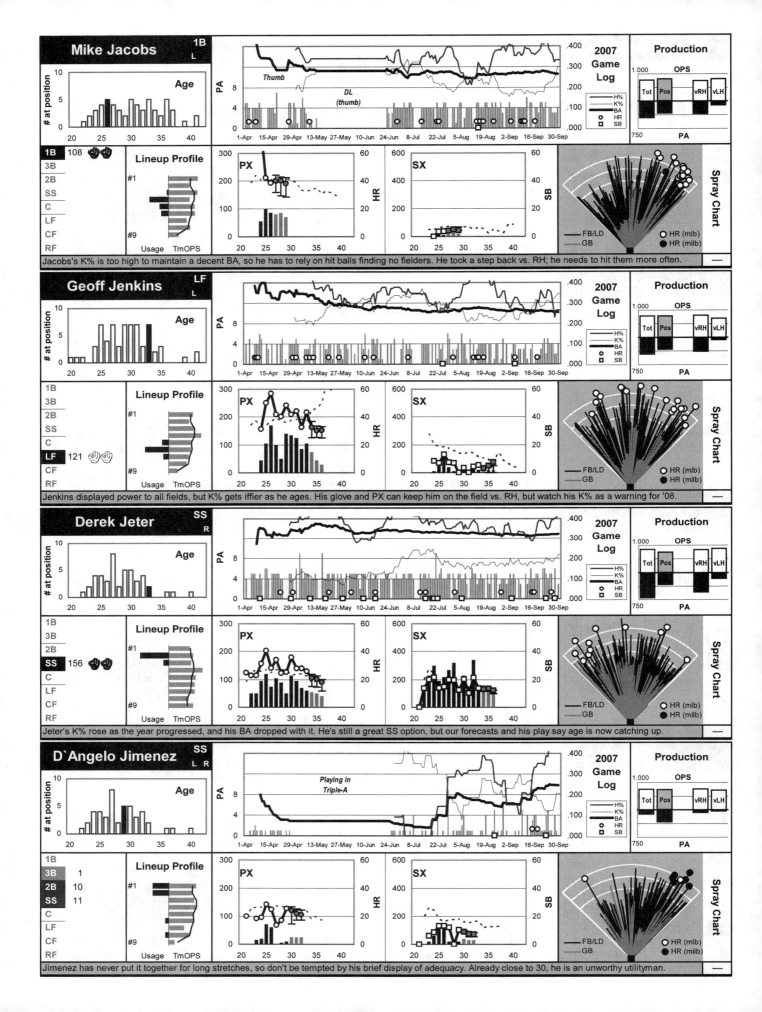

Mike Jacobs — 1B, L

Jacobs's K% is too high to maintain a decent BA, so he has to rely on hit balls finding no fielders. He took a step back vs. RH; he needs to hit them more often.

Geoff Jenkins — LF, L

Jenkins displayed power to all fields, but K% gets iffier as he ages. His glove and PX can keep him on the field vs. RH, but watch his K% as a warning for '08.

Derek Jeter — SS, R

Jeter's K% rose as the year progressed, and his BA dropped with it. He's still a great SS option, but our forecasts and his play say age is now catching up.

D`Angelo Jimenez — SS, L R

Jimenez has never put it together for long stretches, so don't be tempted by his brief display of adequacy. Already close to 30, he is an unworthy utilityman.

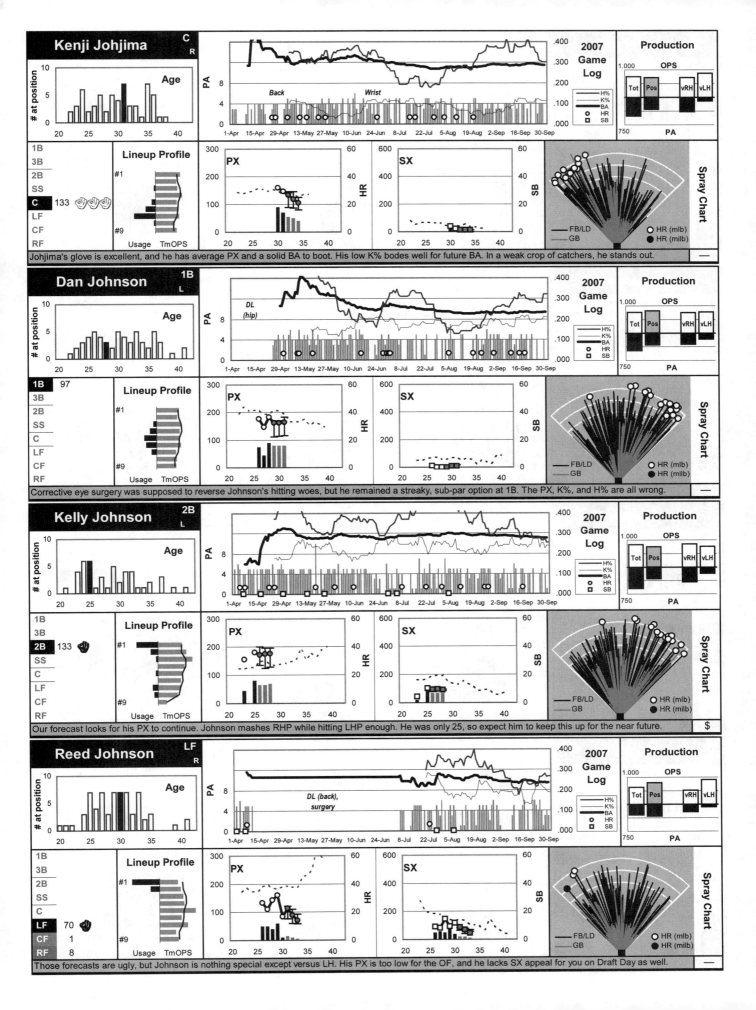

Kenji Johjima — C, R

Age

PA — 2007 Game Log
.400 / .300 / .200 / .100 / .000

Back   Wrist

H% / K% / BA / HR / SB

Production — OPS
Tot / Pos / vRH / vLH
1.000 / 750 — PA

Lineup Profile
#1 ... #9
Usage   TmOPS

C 133

PX   HR
SX   SB
FB/LD / GB   HR (mlb) / HR (milb)
Spray Chart

Johjima's glove is excellent, and he has average PX and a solid BA to boot. His low K% bodes well for future BA. In a weak crop of catchers, he stands out.   —

Dan Johnson — 1B, L

Age

DL (hip)

PA — 2007 Game Log
.400 / .300 / .200 / .100 / .000

H% / K% / BA / HR / SB

Production — OPS
Tot / Pos / vRH / vLH
1.000 / 750 — PA

1B 97

Lineup Profile
#1 ... #9
Usage   TmOPS

PX   HR
SX   SB
FB/LD / GB   HR (mlb) / HR (milb)
Spray Chart

Corrective eye surgery was supposed to reverse Johnson's hitting woes, but he remained a streaky, sub-par option at 1B. The PX, K%, and H% are all wrong.   —

Kelly Johnson — 2B, L

Age

PA — 2007 Game Log
.400 / .300 / .200 / .100 / .000

H% / K% / BA / HR / SB

Production — OPS
Tot / Pos / vRH / vLH
1.000 / 750 — PA

2B 133

Lineup Profile
#1 ... #9
Usage   TmOPS

PX   HR
SX   SB
FB/LD / GB   HR (mlb) / HR (milb)
Spray Chart

Our forecast looks for his PX to continue. Johnson mashes RHP while hitting LHP enough. He was only 25, so expect him to keep this up for the near future. $

Reed Johnson — LF, R

Age

DL (back), surgery

PA — 2007 Game Log
.400 / .300 / .200 / .100 / .000

H% / K% / BA / HR / SB

Production — OPS
Tot / Pos / vRH / vLH
1.000 / 750 — PA

LF 70
CF 1
RF 8

Lineup Profile
#1 ... #9
Usage   TmOPS

PX   HR
SX   SB
FB/LD / GB   HR (mlb) / HR (milb)
Spray Chart

Those forecasts are ugly, but Johnson is nothing special except versus LH. His PX is too low for the OF, and he lacks SX appeal for you on Draft Day as well.   —

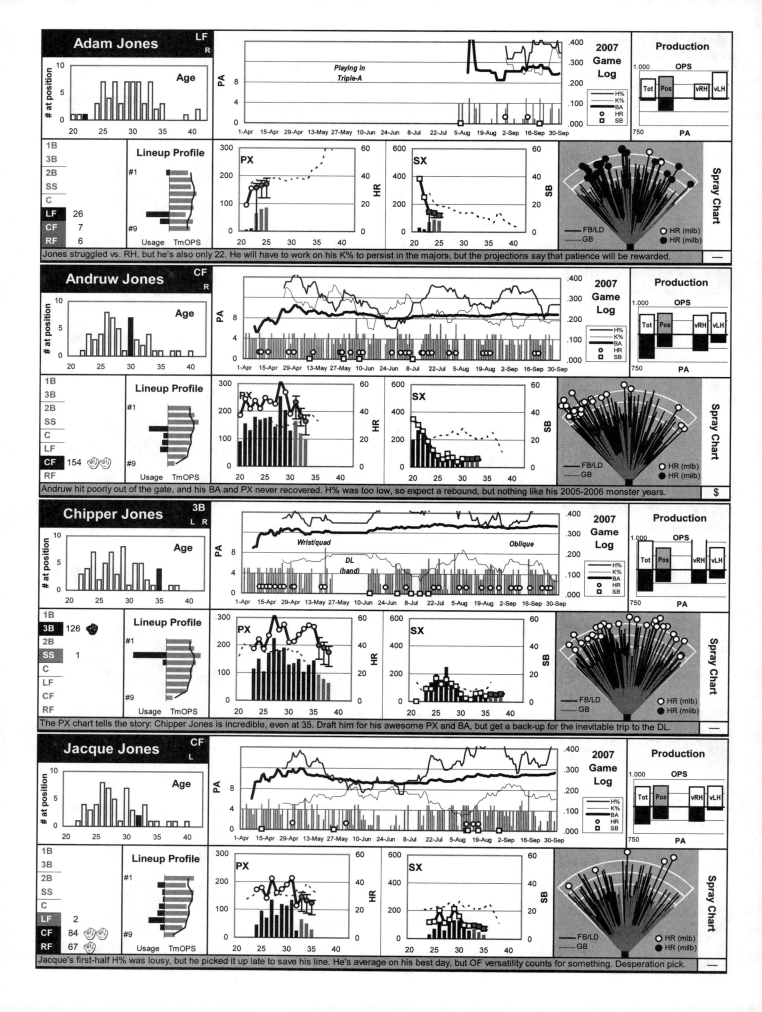

Adam Jones — LF / R

Age (# at position)

2007 Game Log
- H%
- K%
- BA
- HR (○)
- SB (□)

Playing in Triple-A

Production — OPS
- Tot, Pos, vRH, vLH
- PA

Lineup Profile (#1 ... #9) — Usage / TmOPS

Position	#
1B	
3B	
2B	
SS	
C	
LF	26
CF	7
RF	6

PX / HR

SX / SB

Spray Chart
- FB/LD
- GB
- HR (mlb) ○
- HR (milb) ●

Jones struggled vs. RH, but he's also only 22. He will have to work on his K% to persist in the majors, but the projections say that patience will be rewarded. — —

Andruw Jones — CF / R

Age (# at position)

2007 Game Log
- H%
- K%
- BA
- HR (○)
- SB (□)

Production — OPS
- Tot, Pos, vRH, vLH
- PA

Lineup Profile — Usage / TmOPS

Position	#
1B	
3B	
2B	
SS	
C	
LF	
CF	154
RF	

PX / HR

SX / SB

Spray Chart
- FB/LD
- GB
- HR (mlb) ○
- HR (milb) ●

Andruw hit poorly out of the gate, and his BA and PX never recovered. H% was too low, so expect a rebound, but nothing like his 2005-2006 monster years. — $

Chipper Jones — 3B / L R

Age (# at position)

2007 Game Log
- H%
- K%
- BA
- HR (○)
- SB (□)

Wrist/quad   Oblique
DL (hand)

Production — OPS
- Tot, Pos, vRH, vLH
- PA

Lineup Profile — Usage / TmOPS

Position	#
1B	
3B	126
2B	
SS	1
C	
LF	
CF	
RF	

PX / HR

SX / SB

Spray Chart
- FB/LD
- GB
- HR (mlb) ○
- HR (milb) ●

The PX chart tells the story: Chipper Jones is incredible, even at 35. Draft him for his awesome PX and BA, but get a back-up for the inevitable trip to the DL. — —

Jacque Jones — CF / L

Age (# at position)

2007 Game Log
- H%
- K%
- BA
- HR (○)
- SB (□)

Production — OPS
- Tot, Pos, vRH, vLH
- PA

Lineup Profile — Usage / TmOPS

Position	#
1B	
3B	
2B	
SS	
C	
LF	2
CF	84
RF	67

PX / HR

SX / SB

Spray Chart
- FB/LD
- GB
- HR (mlb) ○
- HR (milb) ●

Jacque's first-half H% was lousy, but he picked it up late to save his line. He's average on his best day, but OF versatility counts for something. Desperation pick. — —

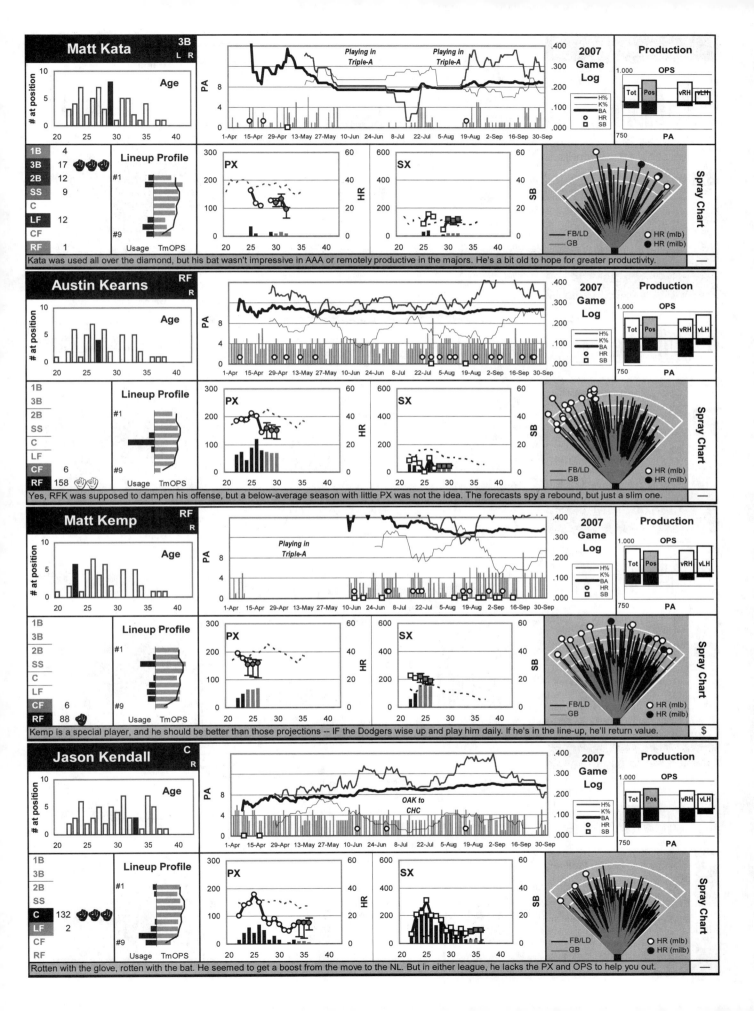

Matt Kata 3B L R

Age / # at position

1B	4
3B	17
2B	12
SS	9
C	
LF	12
CF	
RF	1

Lineup Profile — Usage / TmOPS

2007 Game Log — H%, K%, BA, HR, SB

Production — OPS — Tot, Pos, vRH, vLH — PA

PX / **SX** / **Spray Chart** — FB/LD, GB, HR (mlb), HR (milb)

Kata was used all over the diamond, but his bat wasn't impressive in AAA or remotely productive in the majors. He's a bit old to hope for greater productivity. — —

Austin Kearns RF R

Age / # at position

1B	
3B	
2B	
SS	
C	
LF	
CF	6
RF	158

Lineup Profile — Usage / TmOPS

2007 Game Log — H%, K%, BA, HR, SB

Production — OPS — Tot, Pos, vRH, vLH — PA

PX / **SX** / **Spray Chart** — FB/LD, GB, HR (mlb), HR (milb)

Yes, RFK was supposed to dampen his offense, but a below-average season with little PX was not the idea. The forecasts spy a rebound, but just a slim one. — —

Matt Kemp RF R

Age / # at position

1B	
3B	
2B	
SS	
C	
LF	
CF	6
RF	88

Lineup Profile — Usage / TmOPS

2007 Game Log — H%, K%, BA, HR, SB

Production — OPS — Tot, Pos, vRH, vLH — PA

PX / **SX** / **Spray Chart** — FB/LD, GB, HR (mlb), HR (milb)

Kemp is a special player, and he should be better than those projections -- IF the Dodgers wise up and play him daily. If he's in the line-up, he'll return value. — $

Jason Kendall C R

Age / # at position

1B	
3B	
2B	
SS	
C	132
LF	2
CF	
RF	

Lineup Profile — Usage / TmOPS

2007 Game Log — H%, K%, BA, HR, SB — OAK to CHC

Production — OPS — Tot, Pos, vRH, vLH — PA

PX / **SX** / **Spray Chart** — FB/LD, GB, HR (mlb), HR (milb)

Rotten with the glove, rotten with the bat. He seemed to get a boost from the move to the NL. But in either league, he lacks the PX and OPS to help you out. — —

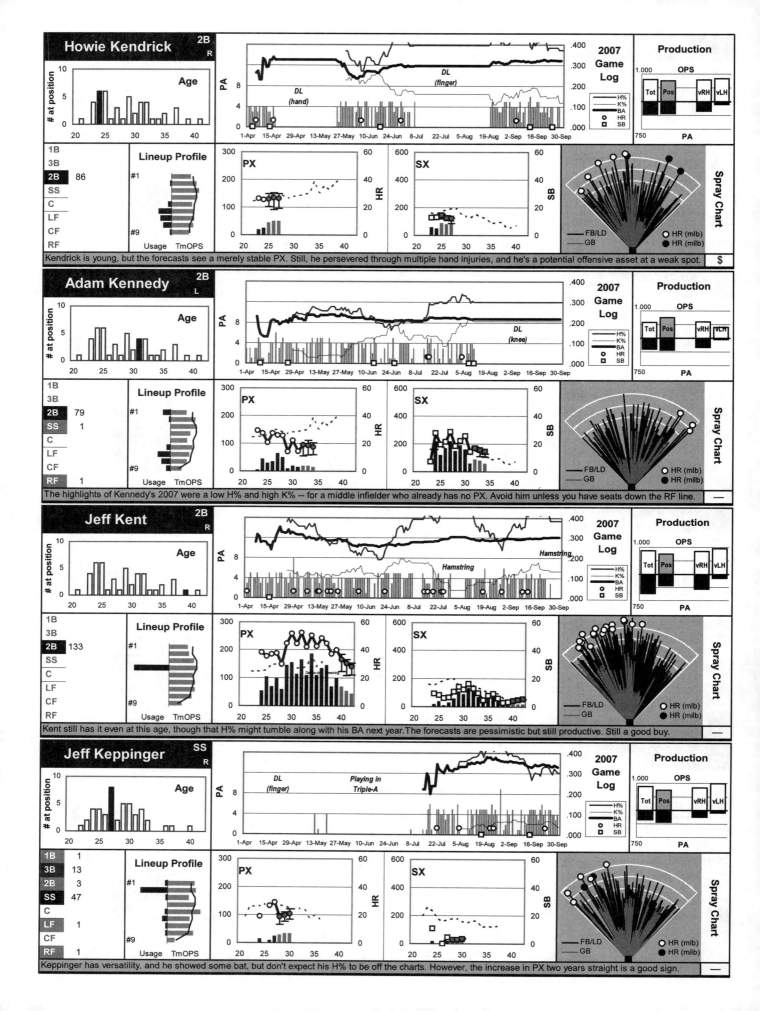

Howie Kendrick 2B R

Age

2B 86

Lineup Profile

PX / HR

SX / SB

2007 Game Log

Production — OPS / PA

Spray Chart

Kendrick is young, but the forecasts see a merely stable PX. Still, he persevered through multiple hand injuries, and he's a potential offensive asset at a weak spot. $

Adam Kennedy 2B L

Age

2B 79
SS 1
RF 1

Lineup Profile

PX / HR

SX / SB

2007 Game Log

Production — OPS / PA

Spray Chart

The highlights of Kennedy's 2007 were a low H% and high K% -- for a middle infielder who already has no PX. Avoid him unless you have seats down the RF line. —

Jeff Kent 2B R

Age

2B 133

Lineup Profile

PX / HR

SX / SB

2007 Game Log

Production — OPS / PA

Spray Chart

Kent still has it even at this age, though that H% might tumble along with his BA next year. The forecasts are pessimistic but still productive. Still a good buy. —

Jeff Keppinger SS R

Age

1B 1
3B 13
2B 3
SS 47
LF 1
CF
RF 1

Lineup Profile

PX / HR

SX / SB

2007 Game Log

Production — OPS / PA

Spray Chart

Keppinger has versatility, and he showed some bat, but don't expect his H% to be off the charts. However, the increase in PX two years straight is a good sign. —

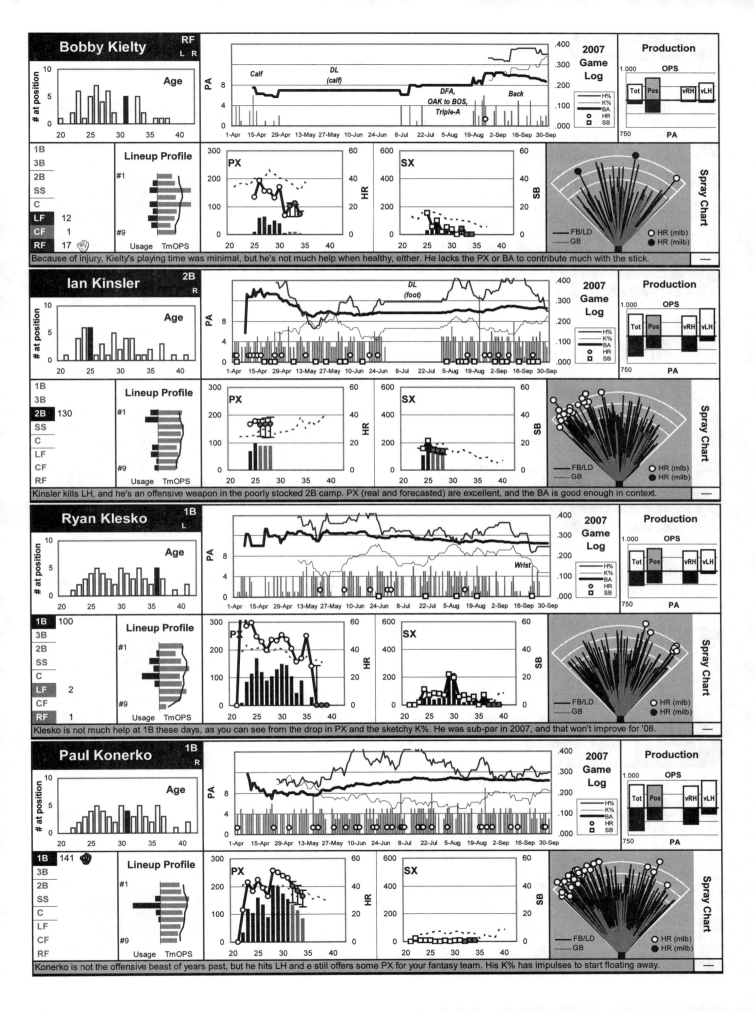

Bobby Kielty RF · L R

Age

PA

.400 .300 .200 .100 .000

2007 Game Log

Calf · DL (calf) · DFA, OAK to BOS, Triple-A · Back

H% K% BA HR SB

Production

OPS — Tot | Pos | vRH | vLH — PA

1B	
3B	
2B	
SS	
C	
LF	12
CF	1
RF	17

Lineup Profile — #1 ... #9 — Usage TmOPS

PX · HR

SX · SB

FB/LD · GB · HR (mlb) · HR (milb)

Spray Chart

Because of injury, Kielty's playing time was minimal, but he's not much help when healthy, either. He lacks the PX or BA to contribute much with the stick.

Ian Kinsler 2B · R

Age

PA

.400 .300 .200 .100 .000

2007 Game Log

DL (foot)

H% K% BA HR SB

Production

OPS — Tot | Pos | vRH | vLH — PA

1B	
3B	
2B	130
SS	
C	
LF	
CF	
RF	

Lineup Profile — #1 ... #9 — Usage TmOPS

PX · HR

SX · SB

FB/LD · GB · HR (mlb) · HR (milb)

Spray Chart

Kinsler kills LH, and he's an offensive weapon in the poorly stocked 2B camp. PX (real and forecasted) are excellent, and the BA is good enough in context.

Ryan Klesko 1B · L

Age

PA

.400 .300 .200 .100 .000

2007 Game Log

Wrist

H% K% BA HR SB

Production

OPS — Tot | Pos | vRH | vLH — PA

1B	100
3B	
2B	
SS	
C	
LF	2
CF	
RF	1

Lineup Profile — #1 ... #9 — Usage TmOPS

PX · HR

SX · SB

FB/LD · GB · HR (mlb) · HR (milb)

Spray Chart

Klesko is not much help at 1B these days, as you can see from the drop in PX and the sketchy K%. He was sub-par in 2007, and that won't improve for '08.

Paul Konerko 1B · R

Age

PA

.400 .300 .200 .100 .000

2007 Game Log

H% K% BA HR SB

Production

OPS — Tot | Pos | vRH | vLH — PA

1B	141
3B	
2B	
SS	
C	
LF	
CF	
RF	

Lineup Profile — #1 ... #9 — Usage TmOPS

PX · HR

SX · SB

FB/LD · GB · HR (mlb) · HR (milb)

Spray Chart

Konerko is not the offensive beast of years past, but he hits LH and e still offers some PX for your fantasy team. His K% has impulses to start floating away.

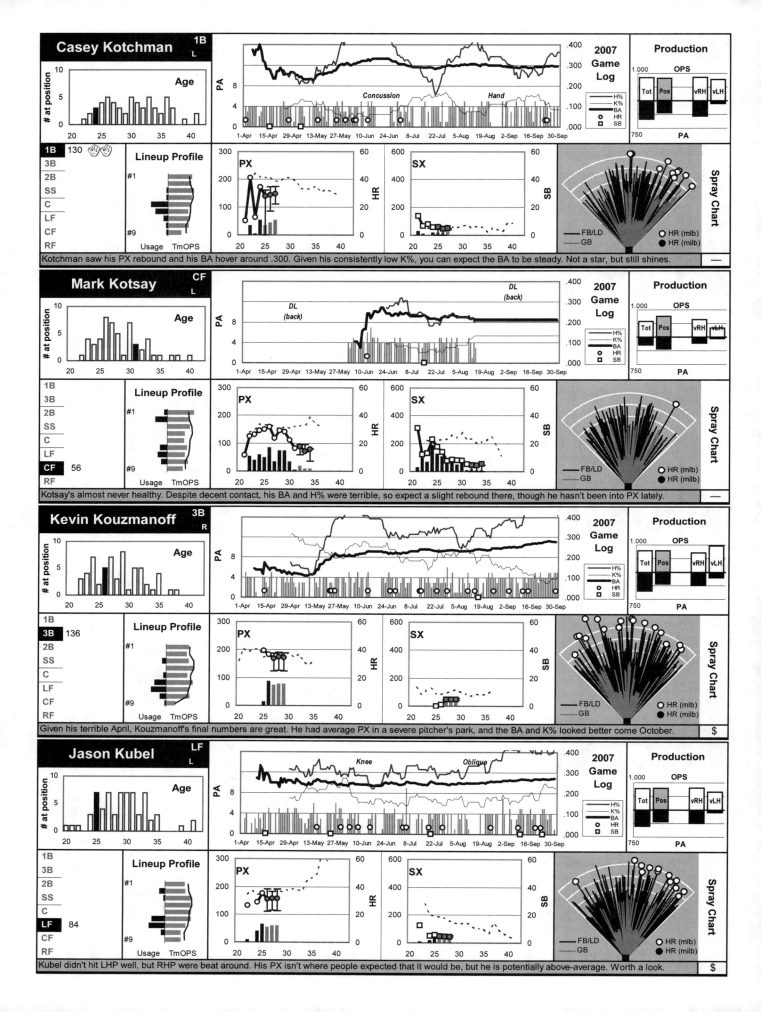

Casey Kotchman 1B L

Age / # at position

2007 Game Log — .400 .300 .200 .100 .000

H% K% BA HR SB — Concussion — Hand

Production — OPS 1.000 — Tot Pos vRH vLH — PA 750

1B 130

3B
2B
SS
C
LF
CF
RF

Lineup Profile — #1 ... #9 — Usage TmOPS

PX — HR
SX — SB

Spray Chart — FB/LD GB — ○ HR (mlb) ● HR (milb)

Kotchman saw his PX rebound and his BA hover around .300. Given his consistently low K%, you can expect the BA to be steady. Not a star, but still shines. —

Mark Kotsay CF L

Age / # at position

2007 Game Log — DL (back) ... DL (back) — H% K% BA HR SB

Production — OPS — Tot Pos vRH vLH — PA 750

1B
3B
2B
SS
C
LF
CF 56
RF

Lineup Profile — #1 ... #9 — Usage TmOPS

PX — HR
SX — SB

Spray Chart — FB/LD GB — ○ HR (mlb) ● HR (milb)

Kotsay's almost never healthy. Despite decent contact, his BA and H% were terrible, so expect a slight rebound there, though he hasn't been into PX lately. —

Kevin Kouzmanoff 3B R

Age / # at position

2007 Game Log — .400 .300 .200 .100 .000 — H% K% BA HR SB

Production — OPS 1.000 — Tot Pos vRH vLH — PA 750

1B
3B 136
2B
SS
C
LF
CF
RF

Lineup Profile — #1 ... #9 — Usage TmOPS

PX — HR
SX — SB

Spray Chart — FB/LD GB — ○ HR (mlb) ● HR (milb)

Given his terrible April, Kouzmanoff's final numbers are great. He had average PX in a severe pitcher's park, and the BA and K% looked better come October. $

Jason Kubel LF L

Age / # at position

2007 Game Log — .400 .300 .200 .100 .000 — Knee ... Oblique — H% K% BA HR SB

Production — OPS 1.000 — Tot Pos vRH vLH — PA 750

1B
3B
2B
SS
C
LF 84
CF
RF

Lineup Profile — #1 ... #9 — Usage TmOPS

PX — HR
SX — SB

Spray Chart — FB/LD GB — ○ HR (mlb) ● HR (milb)

Kubel didn't hit LHP well, but RHP were beat around. His PX isn't where people expected that it would be, but he is potentially above-average. Worth a look. $

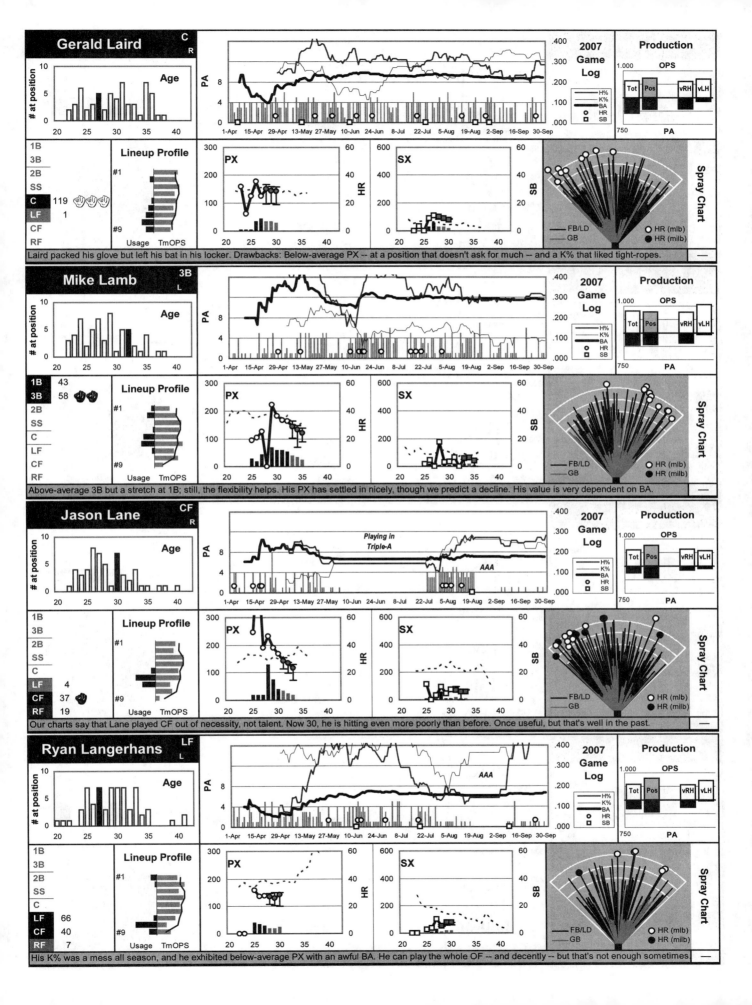

Gerald Laird — C, R

Age | **# at position**

2007 Game Log
- H%
- K%
- BA
- ○ HR
- □ SB

Production — OPS
Tot | Pos | vRH | vLH

Lineup Profile — #1 ... #9 — Usage / TmOPS

1B / 3B / 2B / SS / C 119 / LF 1 / CF / RF

PX | SX | Spray Chart
FB/LD / GB — ○ HR (mlb) / ● HR (milb)

Laird packed his glove but left his bat in his locker. Drawbacks: Below-average PX -- at a position that doesn't ask for much -- and a K% that liked tight-ropes.

Mike Lamb — 3B, L

Age | **# at position**

2007 Game Log
- H%
- K%
- BA
- ○ HR
- □ SB

Production — OPS
Tot | Pos | vRH | vLH

Lineup Profile — #1 ... #9 — Usage / TmOPS

1B 43 / 3B 58 / 2B / SS / C / LF / CF / RF

PX | SX | Spray Chart
FB/LD / GB — ○ HR (mlb) / ● HR (milb)

Above-average 3B but a stretch at 1B; still, the flexibility helps. His PX has settled in nicely, though we predict a decline. His value is very dependent on BA.

Jason Lane — CF, R

Age | **# at position**

2007 Game Log
Playing in Triple-A
AAA
- H%
- K%
- BA
- ○ HR
- □ SB

Production — OPS
Tot | Pos | vRH | vLH

Lineup Profile — #1 ... #9 — Usage / TmOPS

1B / 3B / 2B / SS / C / LF 4 / CF 37 / RF 19

PX | SX | Spray Chart
FB/LD / GB — ○ HR (mlb) / ● HR (milb)

Our charts say that Lane played CF out of necessity, not talent. Now 30, he is hitting even more poorly than before. Once useful, but that's well in the past.

Ryan Langerhans — LF, L

Age | **# at position**

2007 Game Log
AAA
- H%
- K%
- BA
- ○ HR
- □ SB

Production — OPS
Tot | Pos | vRH | vLH

Lineup Profile — #1 ... #9 — Usage / TmOPS

1B / 3B / 2B / SS / C / LF 66 / CF 40 / RF 7

PX | SX | Spray Chart
FB/LD / GB — ○ HR (mlb) / ● HR (milb)

His K% was a mess all season, and he exhibited below-average PX with an awful BA. He can play the whole OF -- and decently -- but that's not enough sometimes.

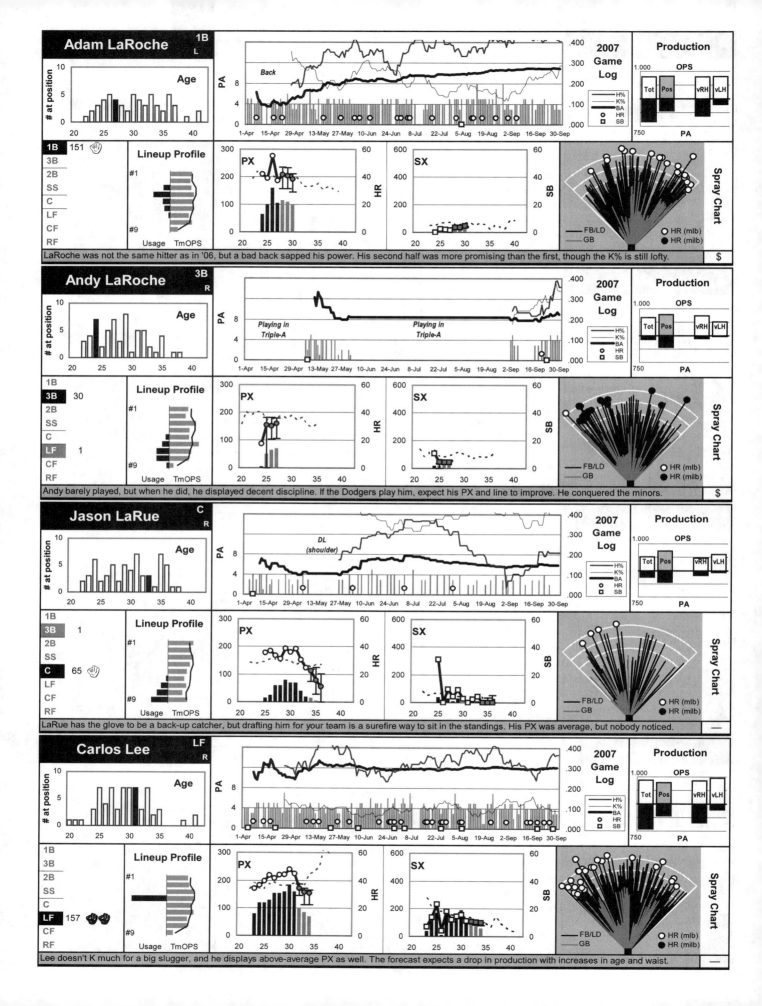

Adam LaRoche — 1B (L)

at position — Age

PA — 2007 Game Log — Back — H% / K% / BA / HR / SB

Production — OPS (1.000 / 750) — Tot, Pos, vRH, vLH — PA

Positions: 1B 151, 3B, 2B, SS, C, LF, CF, RF

Lineup Profile — #1 ... #9 — Usage / TmOPS

PX — HR — SX — SB — FB/LD, GB — HR (mlb), HR (milb) — Spray Chart

LaRoche was not the same hitter as in '06, but a bad back sapped his power. His second half was more promising than the first, though the K% is still lofty. — $

Andy LaRoche — 3B (R)

at position — Age

PA — 2007 Game Log — Playing in Triple-A — Playing in Triple-A — H% / K% / BA / HR / SB

Production — OPS (1.000 / 750) — Tot, Pos, vRH, vLH — PA

Positions: 1B, 3B 30, 2B, SS, C, LF 1, CF, RF

Lineup Profile — #1 ... #9 — Usage / TmOPS

PX — HR — SX — SB — FB/LD, GB — HR (mlb), HR (milb) — Spray Chart

Andy barely played, but when he did, he displayed decent discipline. If the Dodgers play him, expect his PX and line to improve. He conquered the minors. — $

Jason LaRue — C (R)

at position — Age

PA — 2007 Game Log — DL (shoulder) — H% / K% / BA / HR / SB

Production — OPS (1.000 / 750) — Tot, Pos, vRH, vLH — PA

Positions: 1B, 3B 1, 2B, SS, C 65, LF, CF, RF

Lineup Profile — #1 ... #9 — Usage / TmOPS

PX — HR — SX — SB — FB/LD, GB — HR (mlb), HR (milb) — Spray Chart

LaRue has the glove to be a back-up catcher, but drafting him for your team is a surefire way to sit in the standings. His PX was average, but nobody noticed. — —

Carlos Lee — LF (R)

at position — Age

PA — 2007 Game Log — H% / K% / BA / HR / SB

Production — OPS (1.000 / 750) — Tot, Pos, vRH, vLH — PA

Positions: 1B, 3B, 2B, SS, C, LF 157, CF, RF

Lineup Profile — #1 ... #9 — Usage / TmOPS

PX — HR — SX — SB — FB/LD, GB — HR (mlb), HR (milb) — Spray Chart

Lee doesn't K much for a big slugger, and he displays above-average PX as well. The forecast expects a drop in production with increases in age and waist. — —

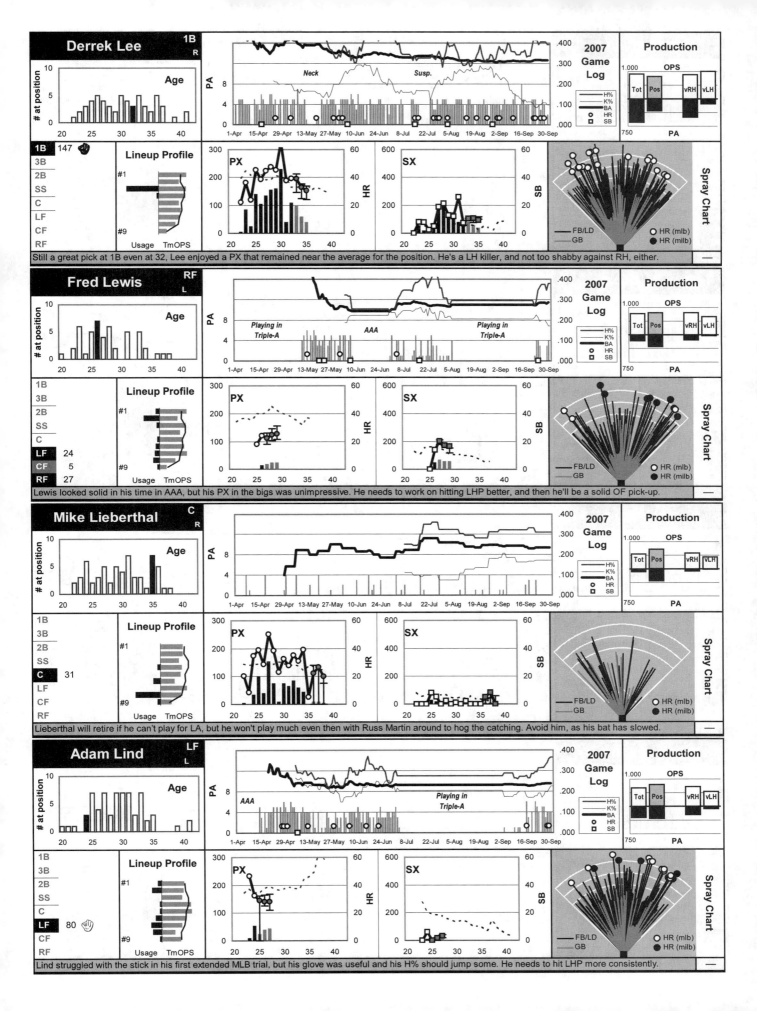

Derrek Lee 1B R

Still a great pick at 1B even at 32, Lee enjoyed a PX that remained near the average for the position. He's a LH killer, and not too shabby against RH, either.

Fred Lewis RF L

Lewis looked solid in his time in AAA, but his PX in the bigs was unimpressive. He needs to work on hitting LHP better, and then he'll be a solid OF pick-up.

Mike Lieberthal C R

Lieberthal will retire if he can't play for LA, but he won't play much even then with Russ Martin around to hog the catching. Avoid him, as his bat has slowed.

Adam Lind LF L

Lind struggled with the stick in his first extended MLB trial, but his glove was useful and his H% should jump some. He needs to hit LHP more consistently.

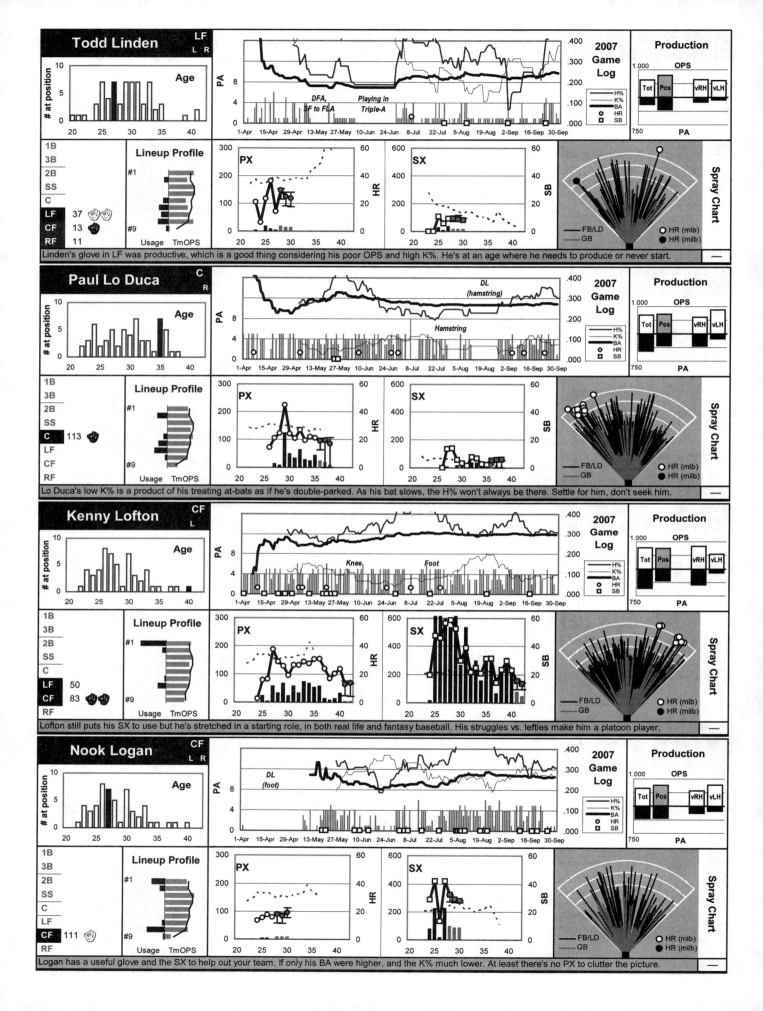

Todd Linden — LF / L R

Age — # at position: LF 37, CF 13, RF 11

2007 Game Log
DFA, SF to FLA — Playing in Triple-A
H%, K%, BA, HR, SB

Production — OPS: Tot, Pos, vRH, vLH — PA

Lineup Profile — Usage / TmOPS — #1 ... #9

PX / SX / Spray Chart — FB/LD, GB — HR (mlb), HR (milb)

Linden's glove in LF was productive, which is a good thing considering his poor OPS and high K%. He's at an age where he needs to produce or never start.

Paul Lo Duca — C R

Age — # at position: C 113

2007 Game Log
DL (hamstring) — Hamstring
H%, K%, BA, HR, SB

Production — OPS: Tot, Pos, vRH, vLH — PA

Lineup Profile — Usage / TmOPS — #1 ... #9

PX / SX / Spray Chart — FB/LD, GB — HR (mlb), HR (milb)

Lo Duca's low K% is a product of his treating at-bats as if he's double-parked. As his bat slows, the H% won't always be there. Settle for him, don't seek him.

Kenny Lofton — CF / L

Age — # at position: LF 50, CF 83

2007 Game Log
Knee — Foot
H%, K%, BA, HR, SB

Production — OPS: Tot, Pos, vRH, vLH — PA

Lineup Profile — Usage / TmOPS — #1 ... #9

PX / SX / Spray Chart — FB/LD, GB — HR (mlb), HR (milb)

Lofton still puts his SX to use but he's stretched in a starting role, in both real life and fantasy baseball. His struggles vs. lefties make him a platoon player.

Nook Logan — CF / L R

Age — # at position: CF 111

2007 Game Log
DL (foot)
H%, K%, BA, HR, SB

Production — OPS: Tot, Pos, vRH, vLH — PA

Lineup Profile — Usage / TmOPS — #1 ... #9

PX / SX / Spray Chart — FB/LD, GB — HR (mlb), HR (milb)

Logan has a useful glove and the SX to help out your team. If only his BA were higher, and the K% much lower. At least there's no PX to clutter the picture.

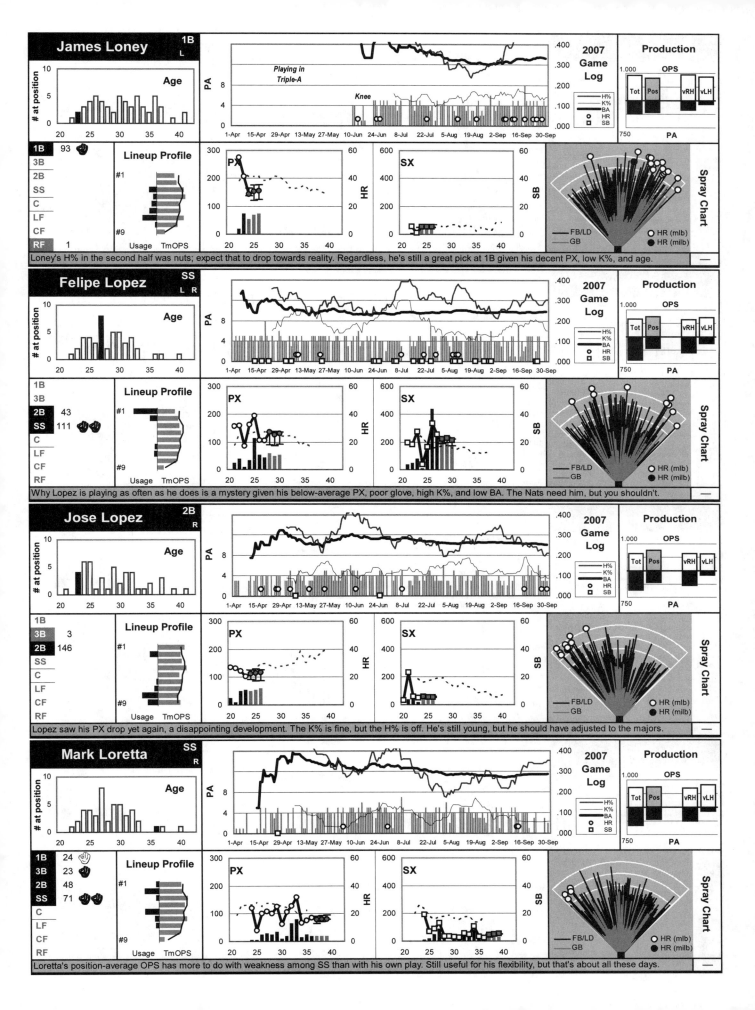

James Loney 1B L

at position — Age

1B 93
3B
2B
SS
C
LF
CF
RF 1

Lineup Profile
#1
#9
Usage TmOPS

PA — *Playing in Triple-A* — *Knee*

2007 Game Log — H% K% BA — HR SB

.400 .300 .200 .100 .000

1-Apr 15-Apr 29-Apr 13-May 27-May 10-Jun 24-Jun 8-Jul 22-Jul 5-Aug 19-Aug 2-Sep 16-Sep 30-Sep

Production — OPS — Tot Pos vRH vLH — PA

PX — HR
SX — SB
20 25 30 35 40

Spray Chart — FB/LD GB — HR (mlb) HR (milb)

Loney's H% in the second half was nuts; expect that to drop towards reality. Regardless, he's still a great pick at 1B given his decent PX, low K%, and age.

Felipe Lopez SS L R

at position — Age

1B
3B
2B 43
SS 111
C
LF
CF
RF

Lineup Profile
#1
#9
Usage TmOPS

PA

2007 Game Log — H% K% BA — HR SB

.400 .300 .200 .100 .000

1-Apr 15-Apr 29-Apr 13-May 27-May 10-Jun 24-Jun 8-Jul 22-Jul 5-Aug 19-Aug 2-Sep 16-Sep 30-Sep

Production — OPS — Tot Pos vRH vLH — PA

PX — HR
SX — SB
20 25 30 35 40

Spray Chart — FB/LD GB — HR (mlb) HR (milb)

Why Lopez is playing as often as he does is a mystery given his below-average PX, poor glove, high K%, and low BA. The Nats need him, but you shouldn't.

Jose Lopez 2B R

at position — Age

1B
3B 3
2B 146
SS
C
LF
CF
RF

Lineup Profile
#1
#9
Usage TmOPS

PA

2007 Game Log — H% K% BA — HR SB

.400 .300 .200 .100 .000

1-Apr 15-Apr 29-Apr 13-May 27-May 10-Jun 24-Jun 8-Jul 22-Jul 5-Aug 19-Aug 2-Sep 16-Sep 30-Sep

Production — OPS — Tot Pos vRH vLH — PA

PX — HR
SX — SB
20 25 30 35 40

Spray Chart — FB/LD GB — HR (mlb) HR (milb)

Lopez saw his PX drop yet again, a disappointing development. The K% is fine, but the H% is off. He's still young, but he should have adjusted to the majors.

Mark Loretta SS R

at position — Age

1B 24
3B 23
2B 48
SS 71
C
LF
CF
RF

Lineup Profile
#1
#9
Usage TmOPS

PA

2007 Game Log — H% K% BA — HR SB

.400 .300 .200 .100 .000

1-Apr 15-Apr 29-Apr 13-May 27-May 10-Jun 24-Jun 8-Jul 22-Jul 5-Aug 19-Aug 2-Sep 16-Sep 30-Sep

Production — OPS — Tot Pos vRH vLH — PA

PX — HR
SX — SB
20 25 30 35 40

Spray Chart — FB/LD GB — HR (mlb) HR (milb)

Loretta's position-average OPS has more to do with weakness among SS than with his own play. Still useful for his flexibility, but that's about all these days.

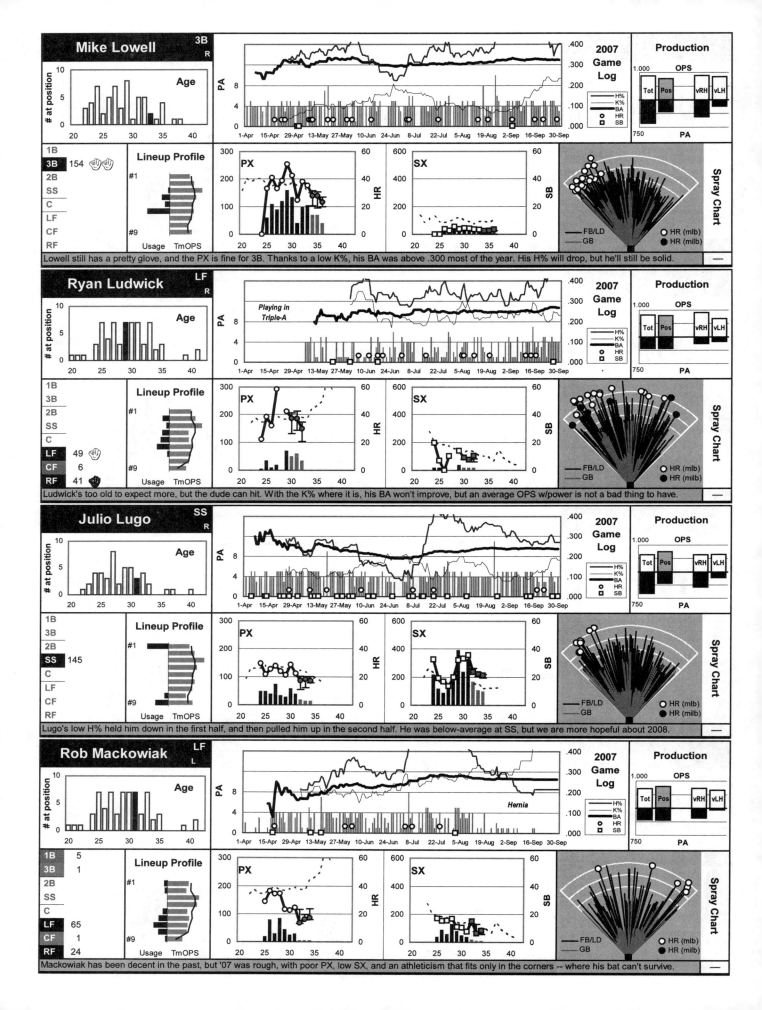

Mike Lowell 3B R

at position | Age

2007 Game Log

Production — OPS

1B
3B 154
2B
SS
C
LF
CF
RF

Lineup Profile

PX | SX | Spray Chart

Lowell still has a pretty glove, and the PX is fine for 3B. Thanks to a low K%, his BA was above .300 most of the year. His H% will drop, but he'll still be solid.

Ryan Ludwick LF R

at position | Age

Playing in Triple-A

2007 Game Log

Production — OPS

1B
3B
2B
SS
C
LF 49
CF 6
RF 41

Lineup Profile

PX | SX | Spray Chart

Ludwick's too old to expect more, but the dude can hit. With the K% where it is, his BA won't improve, but an average OPS w/power is not a bad thing to have.

Julio Lugo SS R

at position | Age

2007 Game Log

Production — OPS

1B
3B
2B
SS 145
C
LF
CF
RF

Lineup Profile

PX | SX | Spray Chart

Lugo's low H% held him down in the first half, and then pulled him up in the second half. He was below-average at SS, but we are more hopeful about 2008.

Rob Mackowiak LF L

at position | Age

Hernia

2007 Game Log

Production — OPS

1B 5
3B 1
2B
SS
C
LF 65
CF 1
RF 24

Lineup Profile

PX | SX | Spray Chart

Mackowiak has been decent in the past, but '07 was rough, with poor PX, low SX, and an athleticism that fits only in the corners -- where his bat can't survive.

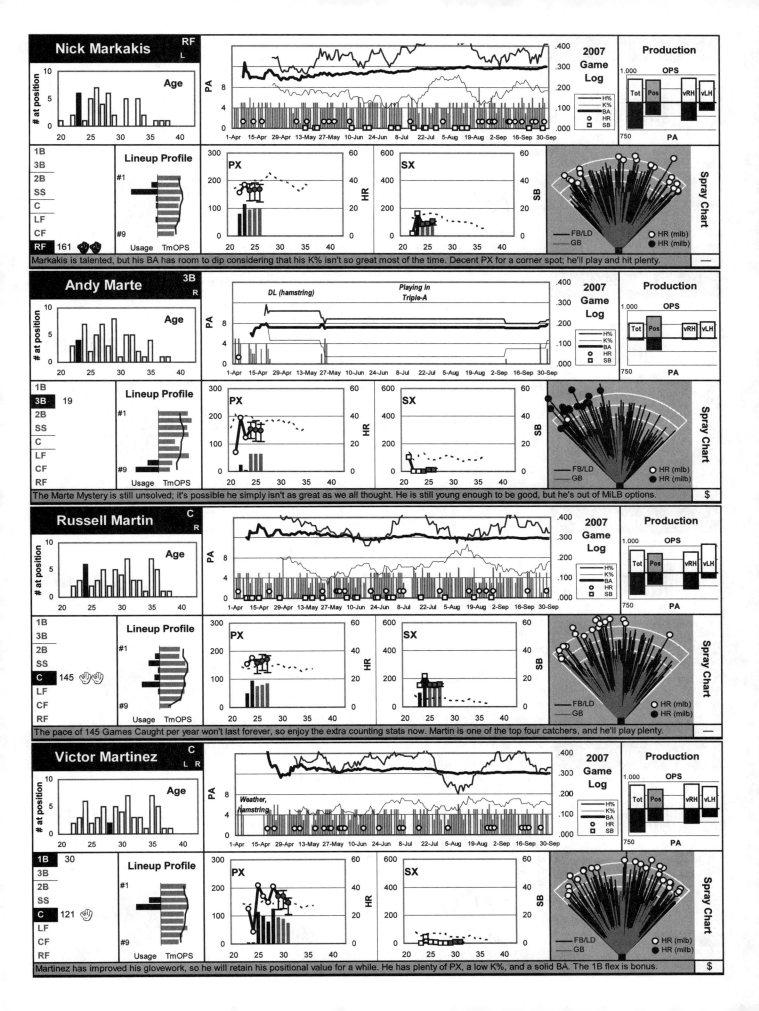

Nick Markakis RF L

Age

1B
3B
2B
SS
C
LF
CF
RF 161

Lineup Profile
#1
#9
Usage TmOPS

PX

SX

2007 Game Log
H%
K%
BA
○ HR
□ SB

Production
OPS
Tot Pos vRH vLH
PA

Spray Chart
FB/LD
GB
○ HR (mlb)
● HR (milb)

Markakis is talented, but his BA has room to dip considering that his K% isn't so great most of the time. Decent PX for a corner spot; he'll play and hit plenty. —

Andy Marte 3B R

Age

1B
3B 19
2B
SS
C
LF
CF
RF

Lineup Profile
#1
#9
Usage TmOPS

DL (hamstring)   Playing in Triple-A

PX

SX

2007 Game Log
H%
K%
BA
○ HR
SB

Production
OPS
Tot Pos vRH vLH
PA

Spray Chart
FB/LD
GB
○ HR (mlb)
● HR (milb)

The Marte Mystery is still unsolved; it's possible he simply isn't as great as we all thought. He is still young enough to be good, but he's out of MiLB options. $

Russell Martin C R

Age

1B
3B
2B
SS
C 145
LF
CF
RF

Lineup Profile
#1
#9
Usage TmOPS

PX

SX

2007 Game Log
H%
K%
BA
○ HR
□ SB

Production
OPS
Tot Pos vRH vLH
PA

Spray Chart
FB/LD
GB
○ HR (mlb)
● HR (milb)

The pace of 145 Games Caught per year won't last forever, so enjoy the extra counting stats now. Martin is one of the top four catchers, and he'll play plenty. —

Victor Martinez C L R

Age

1B 30
3B
2B
SS
C 121
LF
CF
RF

Lineup Profile
#1
#9
Usage TmOPS

Weather, hamstring

PX

SX

2007 Game Log
H%
K%
BA
○ HR
□ SB

Production
OPS
Tot Pos vRH vLH
PA

Spray Chart
FB/LD
GB
○ HR (mlb)
● HR (milb)

Martinez has improved his glovework, so he will retain his positional value for a while. He has plenty of PX, a low K%, and a solid BA. The 1B flex is bonus. $

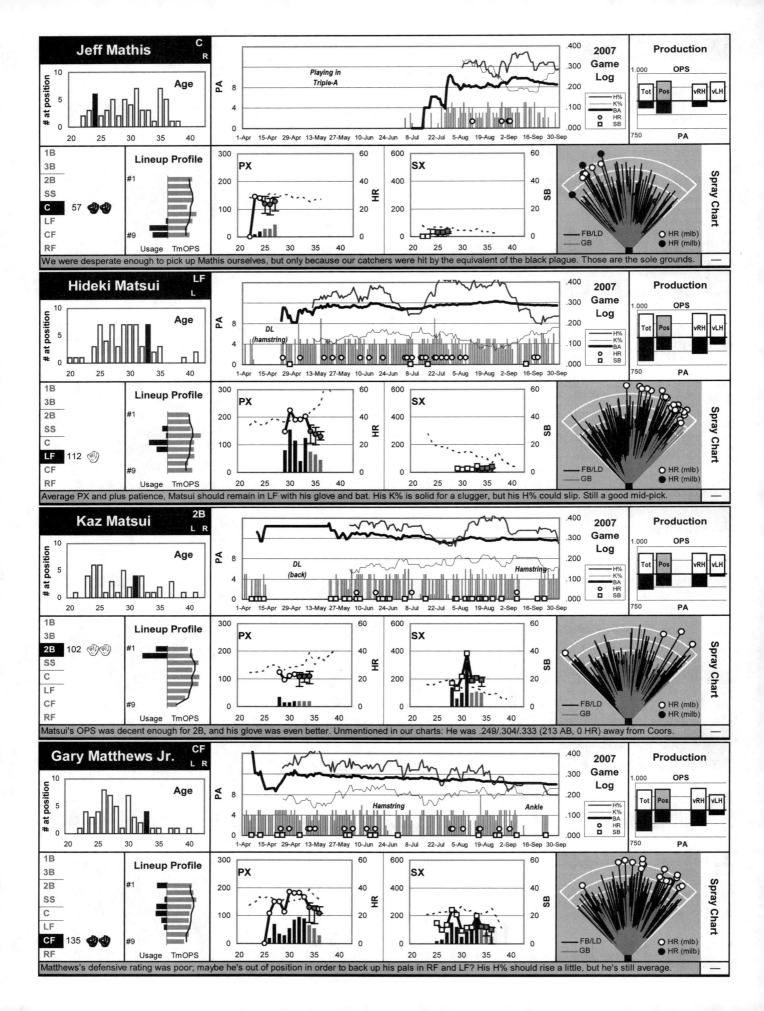

Jeff Mathis — C, R

Age | # at position

2007 Game Log — Playing in Triple-A

H% / K% / BA / HR (○) / SB (□)

Production — OPS: Tot, Pos, vRH, vLH

1B / 3B / 2B / SS / **C 57** / LF / CF / RF

Lineup Profile — #1 ... #9 — Usage / TmOPS

PX / **SX** / **Spray Chart** — FB/LD, GB, HR (mlb) ○, HR (milb) ●

We were desperate enough to pick up Mathis ourselves, but only because our catchers were hit by the equivalent of the black plague. Those are the sole grounds. — —

Hideki Matsui — LF, L

Age | # at position

2007 Game Log — DL (hamstring)

H% / K% / BA / HR (○) / SB (□)

Production — OPS: Tot, Pos, vRH, vLH

1B / 3B / 2B / SS / C / **LF 112** / CF / RF

Lineup Profile — #1 ... #9 — Usage / TmOPS

PX / **SX** / **Spray Chart** — FB/LD, GB, HR (mlb) ○, HR (milb) ●

Average PX and plus patience, Matsui should remain in LF with his glove and bat. His K% is solid for a slugger, but his H% could slip. Still a good mid-pick. — —

Kaz Matsui — 2B, L R

Age | # at position

2007 Game Log — DL (back) ... Hamstring

H% / K% / BA / HR (○) / SB (□)

Production — OPS: Tot, Pos, vRH, vLH

1B / 3B / **2B 102** / SS / C / LF / CF / RF

Lineup Profile — #1 ... #9 — Usage / TmOPS

PX / **SX** / **Spray Chart** — FB/LD, GB, HR (mlb) ○, HR (milb) ●

Matsui's OPS was decent enough for 2B, and his glove was even better. Unmentioned in our charts: He was .249/.304/.333 (213 AB, 0 HR) away from Coors. — —

Gary Matthews Jr. — CF, L R

Age | # at position

2007 Game Log — Hamstring ... Ankle

H% / K% / BA / HR (○) / SB (□)

Production — OPS: Tot, Pos, vRH, vLH

1B / 3B / 2B / SS / C / LF / **CF 135** / RF

Lineup Profile — #1 ... #9 — Usage / TmOPS

PX / **SX** / **Spray Chart** — FB/LD, GB, HR (mlb) ○, HR (milb) ●

Matthews's defensive rating was poor; maybe he's out of position in order to back up his pals in RF and LF? His H% should rise a little, but he's still average. — —

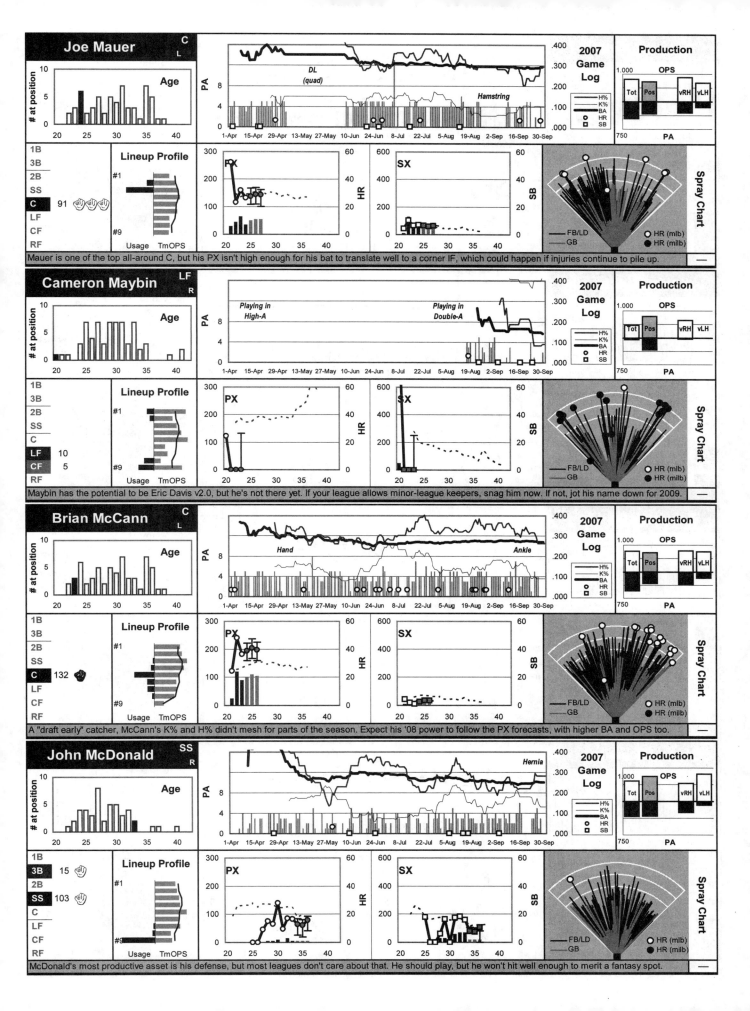

Joe Mauer — C, L

Age (# at position)

2007 Game Log — DL (quad), Hamstring

H%, K%, BA, HR, SB

Production — OPS: Tot, Pos, vRH, vLH — PA

Positions: 1B, 3B, 2B, SS, **C 91**, LF, CF, RF

Lineup Profile — #1 ... #9 — Usage, TmOPS

PX, **SX**, **Spray Chart** — FB/LD, GB — HR (mlb), HR (milb)

Mauer is one of the top all-around C, but his PX isn't high enough for his bat to translate well to a corner IF, which could happen if injuries continue to pile up. — —

Cameron Maybin — LF, R

Age (# at position)

2007 Game Log — Playing in High-A, Playing in Double-A

H%, K%, BA, HR, SB

Production — OPS: Tot, Pos, vRH, vLH — PA

Positions: 1B, 3B, 2B, SS, C, **LF 10**, **CF 5**, RF

Lineup Profile — #1 ... #9 — Usage, TmOPS

PX, **SX**, **Spray Chart** — FB/LD, GB — HR (mlb), HR (milb)

Maybin has the potential to be Eric Davis v2.0, but he's not there yet. If your league allows minor-league keepers, snag him now. If not, jot his name down for 2009. — —

Brian McCann — C, L

Age (# at position)

2007 Game Log — Hand, Ankle

H%, K%, BA, HR, SB

Production — OPS: Tot, Pos, vRH, vLH — PA

Positions: 1B, 3B, 2B, SS, **C 132**, LF, CF, RF

Lineup Profile — #1 ... #9 — Usage, TmOPS

PX, **SX**, **Spray Chart** — FB/LD, GB — HR (mlb), HR (milb)

A "draft early" catcher, McCann's K% and H% didn't mesh for parts of the season. Expect his '08 power to follow the PX forecasts, with higher BA and OPS too. — —

John McDonald — SS, R

Age (# at position)

2007 Game Log — Hernia

H%, K%, BA, HR, SB

Production — OPS: Tot, Pos, vRH, vLH — PA

Positions: 1B, **3B 15**, 2B, **SS 103**, C, LF, CF, RF

Lineup Profile — #1 ... #9 — Usage, TmOPS

PX, **SX**, **Spray Chart** — FB/LD, GB — HR (mlb), HR (milb)

McDonald's most productive asset is his defense, but most leagues don't care about that. He should play, but he won't hit well enough to merit a fantasy spot. — —

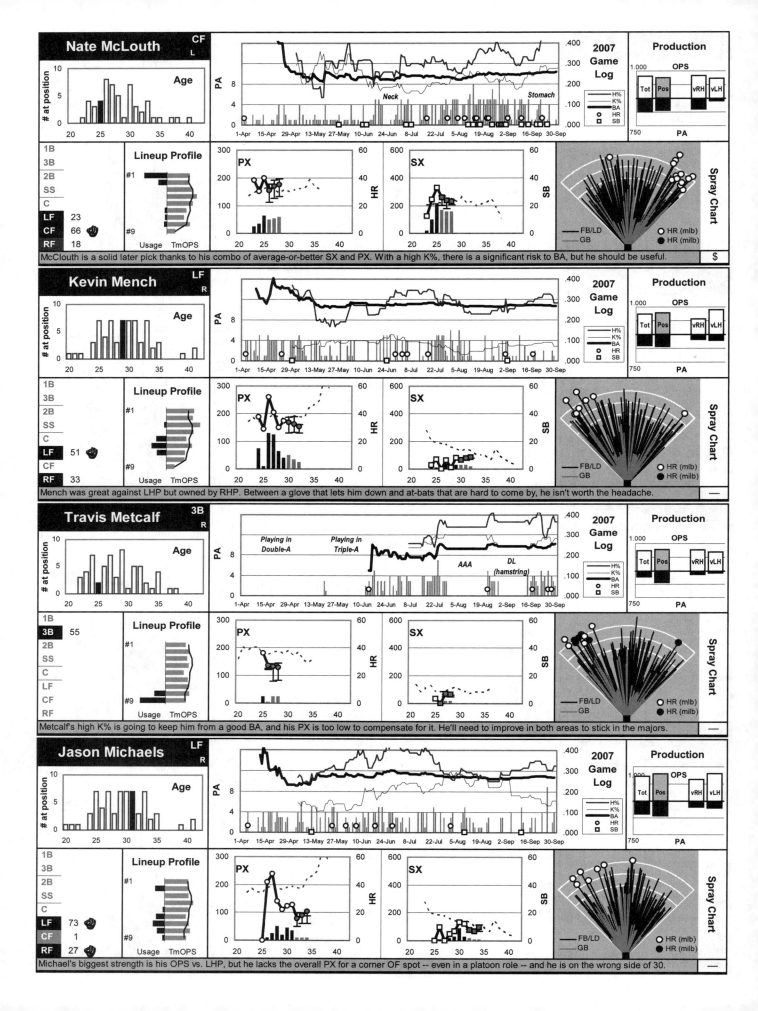

Nate McLouth — CF / L

Age

Lineup Profile: #1 ... #9 — Usage / TmOPS

Positions: LF 23 / CF 66 / RF 18

2007 Game Log — H%, K%, BA, HR, SB

Production — OPS: Tot, Pos, vRH, vLH

PX / SX / Spray Chart — FB/LD, GB, HR (mlb), HR (milb)

Neck ... Stomach

McClouth is a solid later pick thanks to his combo of average-or-better SX and PX. With a high K%, there is a significant risk to BA, but he should be useful. — $

Kevin Mench — LF / R

Age

Lineup Profile: #1 ... #9 — Usage / TmOPS

Positions: LF 51 / CF / RF 33

2007 Game Log — H%, K%, BA, HR, SB

Production — OPS: Tot, Pos, vRH, vLH

PX / SX / Spray Chart — FB/LD, GB, HR (mlb), HR (milb)

Mench was great against LHP but owned by RHP. Between a glove that lets him down and at-bats that are hard to come by, he isn't worth the headache. — —

Travis Metcalf — 3B / R

Age

Lineup Profile: #1 ... #9 — Usage / TmOPS

Positions: 3B 55

2007 Game Log — H%, K%, BA, HR, SB

Playing in Double-A ... Playing in Triple-A ... AAA ... DL (hamstring)

Production — OPS: Tot, Pos, vRH, vLH

PX / SX / Spray Chart — FB/LD, GB, HR (mlb), HR (milb)

Metcalf's high K% is going to keep him from a good BA, and his PX is too low to compensate for it. He'll need to improve in both areas to stick in the majors. — —

Jason Michaels — LF / R

Age

Lineup Profile: #1 ... #9 — Usage / TmOPS

Positions: LF 73 / CF 1 / RF 27

2007 Game Log — H%, K%, BA, HR, SB

Production — OPS: Tot, Pos, vRH, vLH

PX / SX / Spray Chart — FB/LD, GB, HR (mlb), HR (milb)

Michael's biggest strength is his OPS vs. LHP, but he lacks the overall PX for a corner OF spot -- even in a platoon role -- and he is on the wrong side of 30. — —

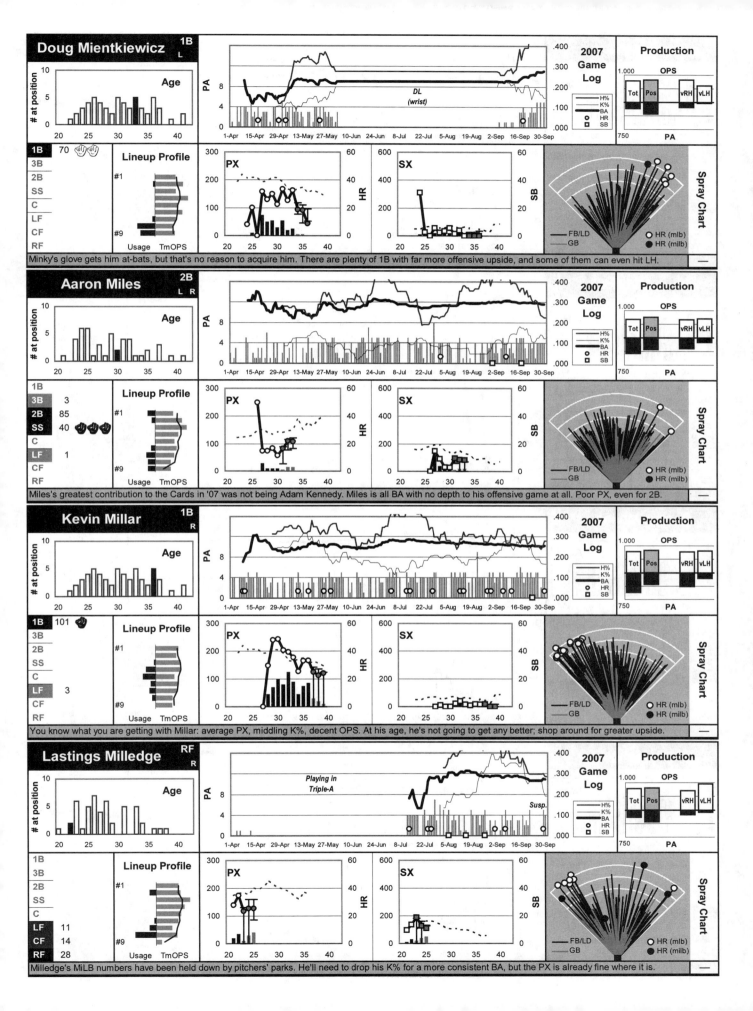

Doug Mientkiewicz — 1B, L

Age / **# at position**

2007 Game Log — DL (wrist)

Production — OPS: Tot, Pos, vRH, vLH / PA

1B 70

Lineup Profile — #1 ... #9 — Usage / TmOPS

PX / **HR** **SX** / **SB** **Spray Chart** — FB/LD, GB, HR (mlb), HR (milb)

Minky's glove gets him at-bats, but that's no reason to acquire him. There are plenty of 1B with far more offensive upside, and some of them can even hit LH.

Aaron Miles — 2B, L R

Age / **# at position**

2007 Game Log

Production — OPS: Tot, Pos, vRH, vLH / PA

3B 3
2B 85
SS 40
LF 1

Lineup Profile — #1 ... #9 — Usage / TmOPS

PX / **HR** **SX** / **SB** **Spray Chart** — FB/LD, GB, HR (mlb), HR (milb)

Miles's greatest contribution to the Cards in '07 was not being Adam Kennedy. Miles is all BA with no depth to his offensive game at all. Poor PX, even for 2B.

Kevin Millar — 1B, R

Age / **# at position**

2007 Game Log

Production — OPS: Tot, Pos, vRH, vLH / PA

1B 101
LF 3

Lineup Profile — #1 ... #9 — Usage / TmOPS

PX / **HR** **SX** / **SB** **Spray Chart** — FB/LD, GB, HR (mlb), HR (milb)

You know what you are getting with Millar: average PX, middling K%, decent OPS. At his age, he's not going to get any better; shop around for greater upside.

Lastings Milledge — RF, R

Age / **# at position**

2007 Game Log — Playing in Triple-A — Susp.

Production — OPS: Tot, Pos, vRH, vLH / PA

LF 11
CF 14
RF 28

Lineup Profile — #1 ... #9 — Usage / TmOPS

PX / **HR** **SX** / **SB** **Spray Chart** — FB/LD, GB, HR (mlb), HR (milb)

Milledge's MiLB numbers have been held down by pitchers' parks. He'll need to drop his K% for a more consistent BA, but the PX is already fine where it is.

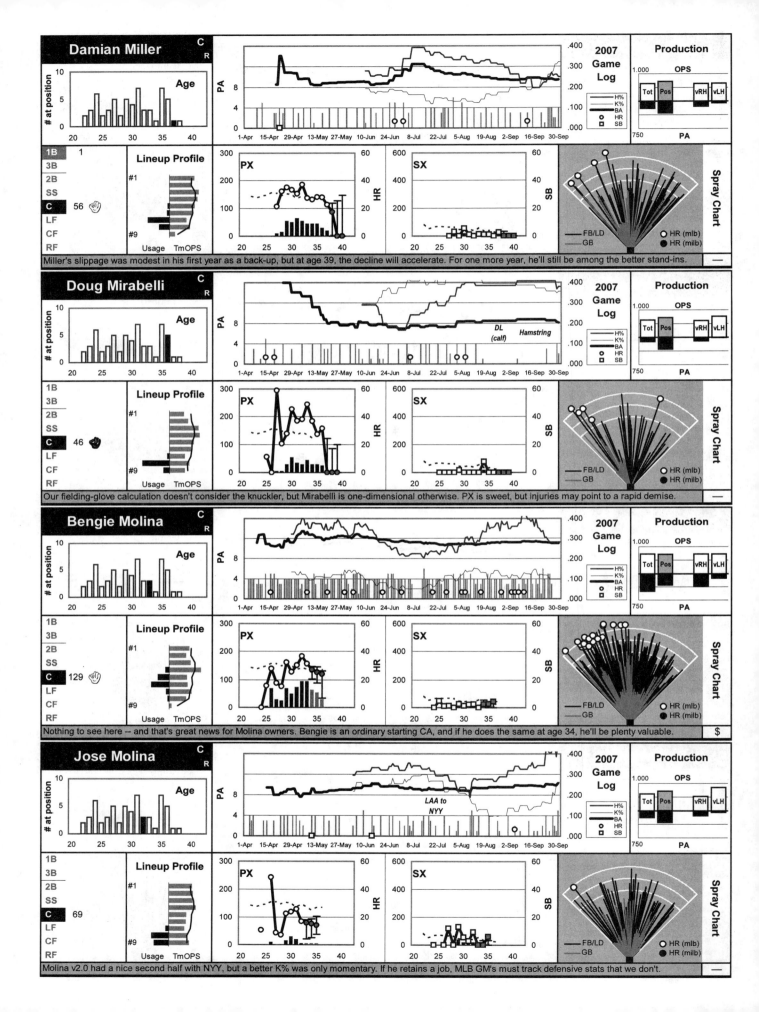

Damian Miller C R

Miller's slippage was modest in his first year as a back-up, but at age 39, the decline will accelerate. For one more year, he'll still be among the better stand-ins. —

Doug Mirabelli C R

Our fielding-glove calculation doesn't consider the knuckler, but Mirabelli is one-dimensional otherwise. PX is sweet, but injuries may point to a rapid demise. —

Bengie Molina C R

Nothing to see here -- and that's great news for Molina owners. Bengie is an ordinary starting CA, and if he does the same at age 34, he'll be plenty valuable. $

Jose Molina C R

Molina v2.0 had a nice second half with NYY, but a better K% was only momentary. If he retains a job, MLB GM's must track defensive stats that we don't. —

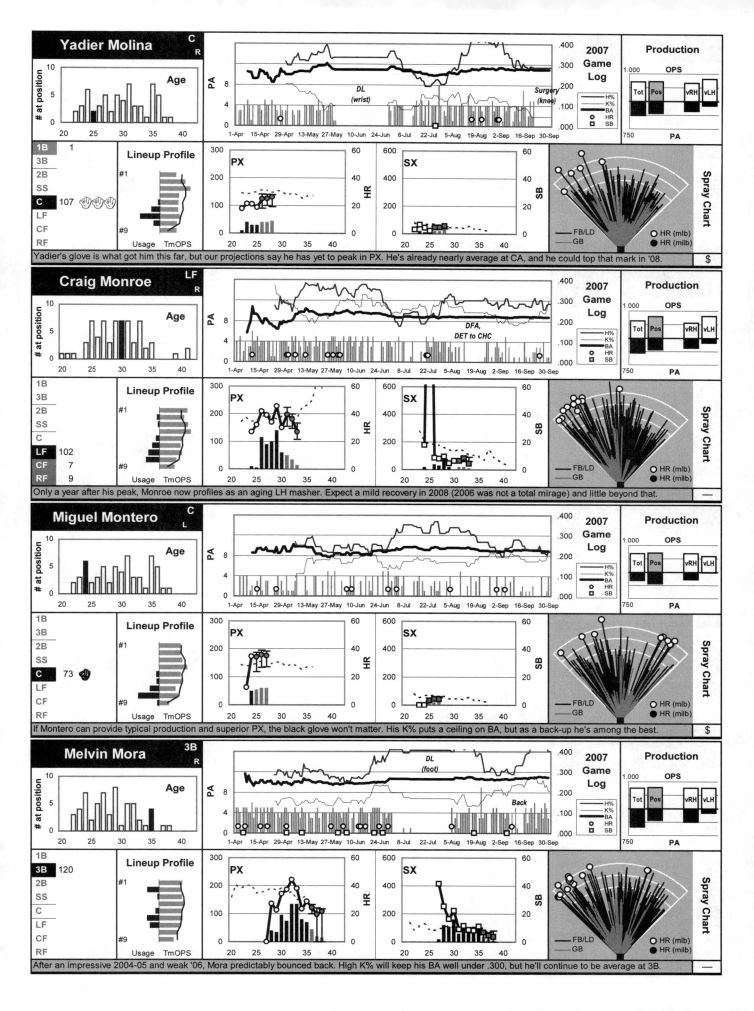

Yadier Molina C R

at position / Age / PA / 2007 Game Log / Production / OPS / Lineup Profile / PX / HR / SX / SB / Spray Chart

DL (wrist) · Surgery (knee)

H% · K% · BA · HR · SB

Tot · Pos · vRH · vLH

1B 1
3B
2B
SS
C 107
LF
CF
RF

FB/LD · GB · HR (mlb) · HR (milb)

Yadier's glove is what got him this far, but our projections say he has yet to peak in PX. He's already nearly average at CA, and he could top that mark in '08. $

Craig Monroe LF R

DFA, DET to CHC

1B
3B
2B
SS
C
LF 102
CF 7
RF 9

Only a year after his peak, Monroe now profiles as an aging LH masher. Expect a mild recovery in 2008 (2006 was not a total mirage) and little beyond that. —

Miguel Montero C L

1B
3B
2B
SS
C 73
LF
CF
RF

If Montero can provide typical production and superior PX, the black glove won't matter. His K% puts a ceiling on BA, but as a back-up he's among the best. $

Melvin Mora 3B R

DL (foot) · Back

1B
3B 120
2B
SS
C
LF
CF
RF

After an impressive 2004-05 and weak '06, Mora predictably bounced back. High K% will keep his BA well under .300, but he'll continue to be average at 3B. —

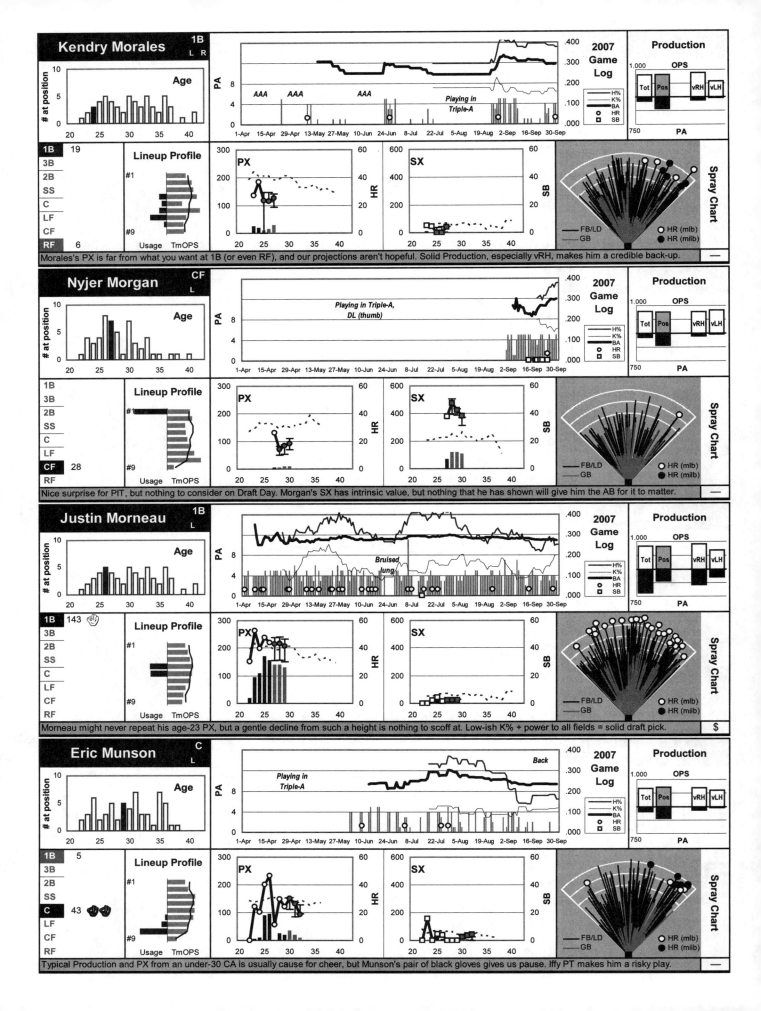

Kendry Morales 1B · L R

Age — # at position

2007 Game Log · AAA AAA AAA · Playing in Triple-A · H% K% BA HR SB · .400 .300 .200 .100 .000

Production · OPS 1.000 · Tot Pos vRH vLH · PA · 750

1B 19 · 3B · 2B · SS · C · LF · CF · RF 6

Lineup Profile · #1 #9 · Usage TmOPS

PX · SX · Spray Chart · FB/LD GB · HR (mlb) HR (milb)

Morales's PX is far from what you want at 1B (or even RF), and our projections aren't hopeful. Solid Production, especially vRH, makes him a credible back-up. —

Nyjer Morgan CF · L

Age — # at position

Playing in Triple-A, DL (thumb) · H% K% BA HR SB · .400 Game Log 2007

Production · OPS 1.000 · Tot Pos vRH vLH · PA · 750

1B · 3B · 2B · SS · C · LF · CF 28 · RF

Lineup Profile · #1 #9 · Usage TmOPS

PX · SX · Spray Chart · FB/LD GB · HR (mlb) HR (milb)

Nice surprise for PIT, but nothing to consider on Draft Day. Morgan's SX has intrinsic value, but nothing that he has shown will give him the AB for it to matter. —

Justin Morneau 1B · L

Age — # at position

Bruised lung · H% K% BA HR SB · 2007 Game Log · .400 .300 .200 .100 .000

Production · OPS 1.000 · Tot Pos vRH vLH · PA · 750

1B 143 · 3B · 2B · SS · C · LF · CF · RF

Lineup Profile · #1 #9 · Usage TmOPS

PX · SX · Spray Chart · FB/LD GB · HR (mlb) HR (milb)

Morneau might never repeat his age-23 PX, but a gentle decline from such a height is nothing to scoff at. Low-ish K% + power to all fields = solid draft pick. $

Eric Munson C · L

Age — # at position

Playing in Triple-A · Back · H% K% BA HR SB · 2007 Game Log · .400 .300 .200 .100 .000

Production · OPS 1.000 · Tot Pos vRH vLH · PA · 750

1B 5 · 3B · 2B · SS · C 43 · LF · CF · RF

Lineup Profile · #1 #9 · Usage TmOPS

PX · SX · Spray Chart · FB/LD GB · HR (mlb) HR (milb)

Typical Production and PX from an under-30 CA is usually cause for cheer, but Munson's pair of black gloves gives us pause. Iffy PT makes him a risky play. —

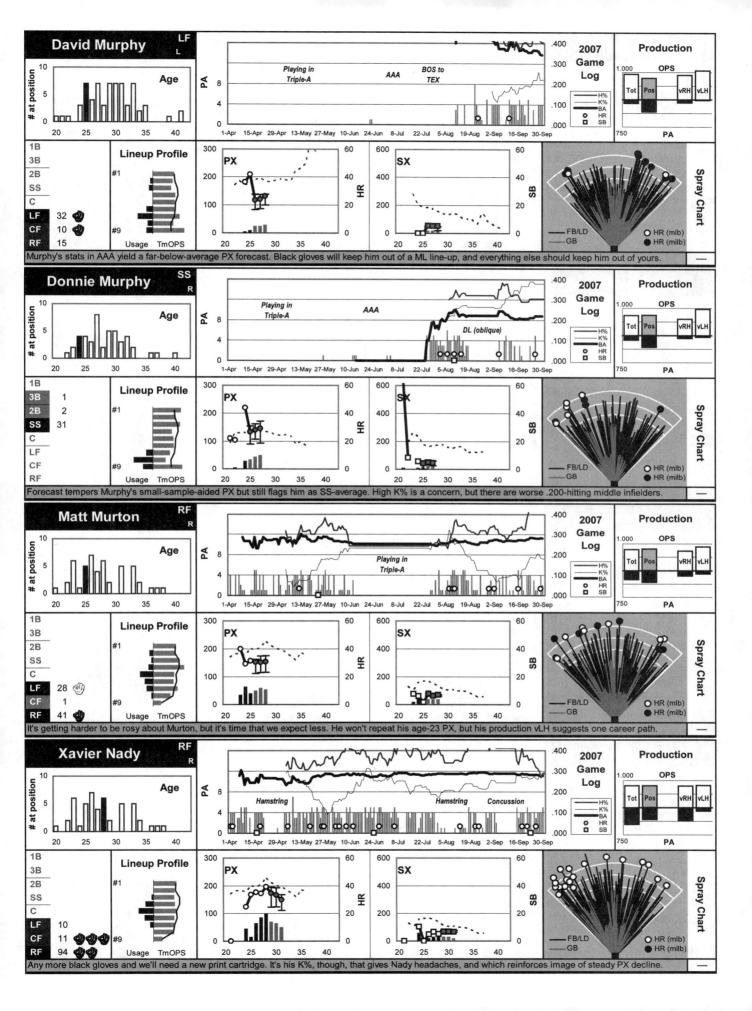

David Murphy — LF / L

Age | PA | 2007 Game Log | Production (OPS)

Playing in Triple-A — AAA — BOS to TEX

LF 32 | CF 10 | RF 15

Lineup Profile — Usage / TmOPS — #1 ... #9

PX | SX | Spray Chart

Murphy's stats in AAA yield a far-below-average PX forecast. Black gloves will keep him out of a ML line-up, and everything else should keep him out of yours.

Donnie Murphy — SS / R

Playing in Triple-A — AAA — DL (oblique)

3B 1 | 2B 2 | SS 31

Forecast tempers Murphy's small-sample-aided PX but still flags him as SS-average. High K% is a concern, but there are worse .200-hitting middle infielders.

Matt Murton — RF / R

Playing in Triple-A

LF 28 | CF 1 | RF 41

It's getting harder to be rosy about Murton, but it's time that we expect less. He won't repeat his age-23 PX, but his production vLH suggests one career path.

Xavier Nady — RF / R

Hamstring — Hamstring — Concussion

LF 10 | CF 11 | RF 94

Any more black gloves and we'll need a new print cartridge. It's his K%, though, that gives Nady headaches, and which reinforces image of steady PX decline.

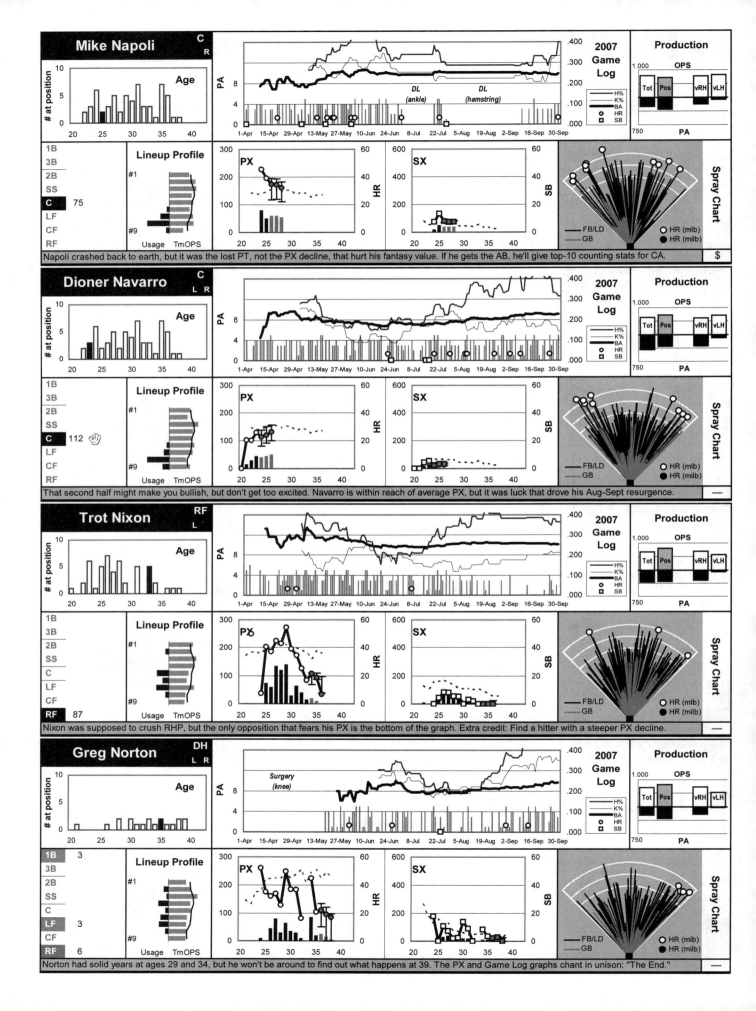

Mike Napoli — C / R

Napoli crashed back to earth, but it was the lost PT, not the PX decline, that hurt his fantasy value. If he gets the AB, he'll give top-10 counting stats for CA. $

Dioner Navarro — C / L R

That second half might make you bullish, but don't get too excited. Navarro is within reach of average PX, but it was luck that drove his Aug-Sept resurgence. —

Trot Nixon — RF / L

Nixon was supposed to crush RHP, but the only opposition that fears his PX is the bottom of the graph. Extra credit: Find a hitter with a steeper PX decline. —

Greg Norton — DH / L R

Norton had solid years at ages 29 and 34, but he won't be around to find out what happens at 39. The PX and Game Log graphs chant in unison: "The End." —

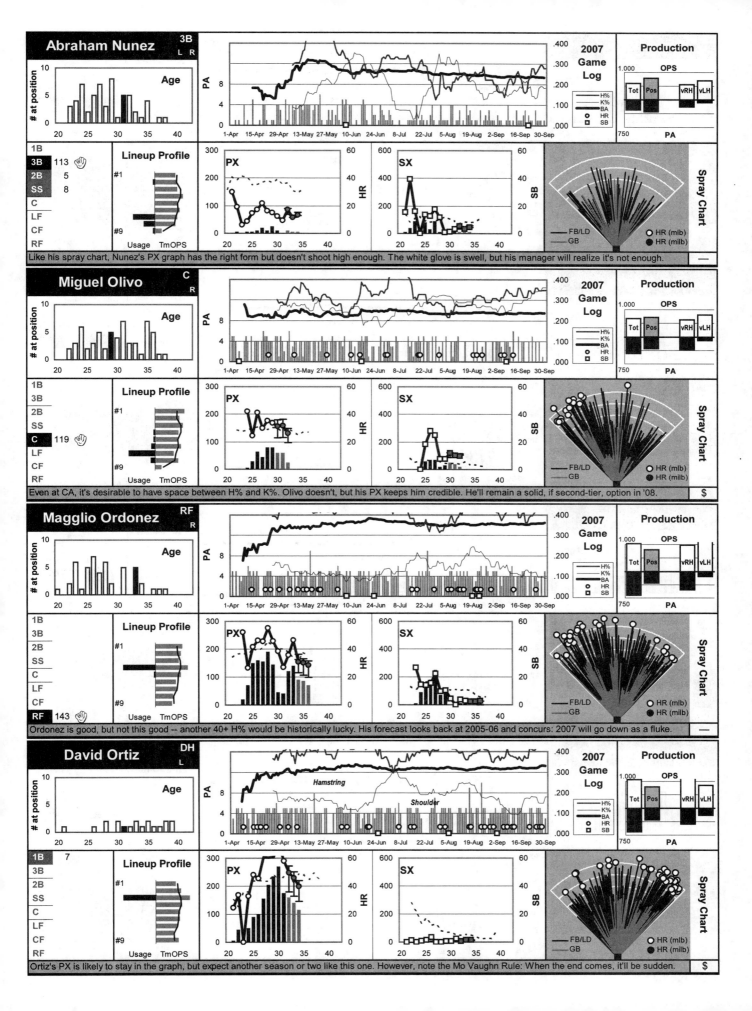

Abraham Nunez 3B
L R

2007 Game Log

Production

Like his spray chart, Nunez's PX graph has the right form but doesn't shoot high enough. The white glove is swell, but his manager will realize it's not enough. —

1B	
3B	113
2B	5
SS	8
C	
LF	
CF	
RF	

Miguel Olivo C
R

2007 Game Log

Production

Even at CA, it's desirable to have space between H% and K%. Olivo doesn't, but his PX keeps him credible. He'll remain a solid, if second-tier, option in '08. $

1B	
3B	
2B	
SS	
C	119
LF	
CF	
RF	

Magglio Ordonez RF
R

2007 Game Log

Production

Ordonez is good, but not this good -- another 40+ H% would be historically lucky. His forecast looks back at 2005-06 and concurs: 2007 will go down as a fluke. —

1B	
3B	
2B	
SS	
C	
LF	
CF	
RF	143

David Ortiz DH
L

2007 Game Log

Production

Ortiz's PX is likely to stay in the graph, but expect another season or two like this one. However, note the Mo Vaughn Rule: When the end comes, it'll be sudden. $

1B	7
3B	
2B	
SS	
C	
LF	
CF	
RF	

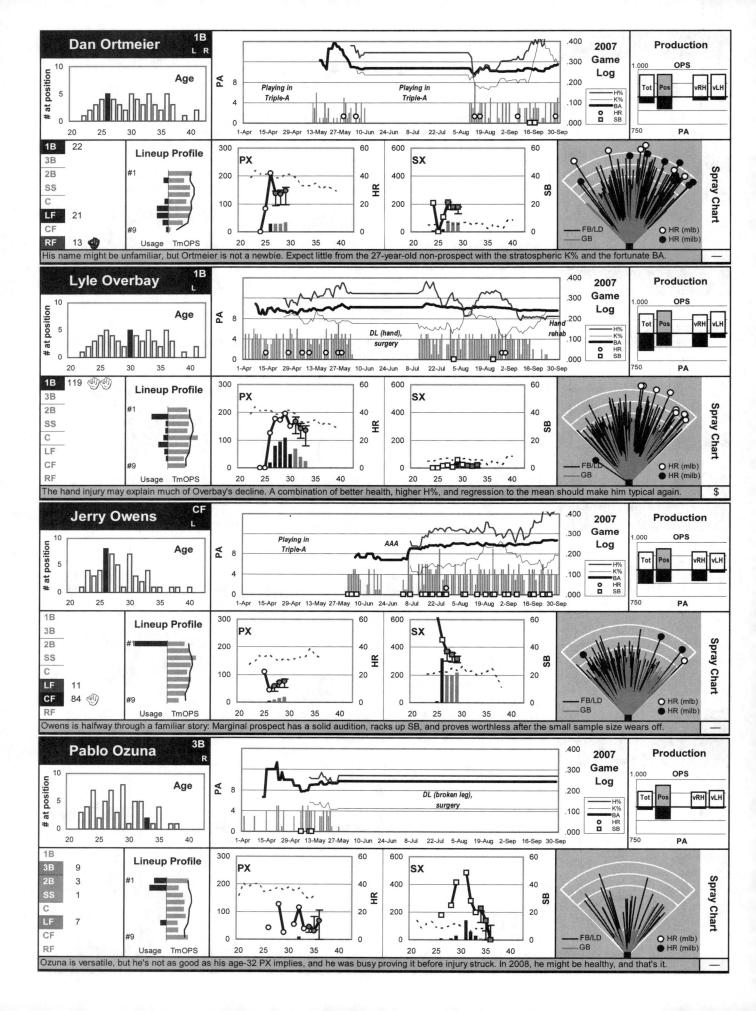

Dan Ortmeier 1B
L R

at position | Age
2007 Game Log
Playing in Triple-A ... *Playing in Triple-A*
H%, K%, BA, HR (○), SB (□)

Production
OPS — Tot, Pos, vRH, vLH
PA

1B	22
3B	
2B	
SS	
C	
LF	21
CF	
RF	13

Lineup Profile — #1 ... #9 — Usage, TmOPS

PX — HR
SX — SB

Spray Chart — FB/LD, GB, ○ HR (mlb), ● HR (milb)

His name might be unfamiliar, but Ortmeier is not a newbie. Expect little from the 27-year-old non-prospect with the stratospheric K% and the fortunate BA. —

Lyle Overbay 1B
L

at position | Age
2007 Game Log
DL (hand), surgery ... *Hand rehab*
H%, K%, BA, HR (○), SB (□)

Production
OPS — Tot, Pos, vRH, vLH
PA

1B	119
3B	
2B	
SS	
C	
LF	
CF	
RF	

Lineup Profile — #1 ... #9 — Usage, TmOPS

PX — HR
SX — SB

Spray Chart — FB/LD, GB, ○ HR (mlb), ● HR (milb)

The hand injury may explain much of Overbay's decline. A combination of better health, higher H%, and regression to the mean should make him typical again. $

Jerry Owens CF
L

at position | Age
2007 Game Log
Playing in Triple-A ... *AAA*
H%, K%, BA, HR (○), SB (□)

Production
OPS — Tot, Pos, vRH, vLH
PA

1B	
3B	
2B	
SS	
C	
LF	11
CF	84
RF	

Lineup Profile — #1 ... #9 — Usage, TmOPS

PX — HR
SX — SB

Spray Chart — FB/LD, GB, ○ HR (mlb), ● HR (milb)

Owens is halfway through a familiar story: Marginal prospect has a solid audition, racks up SB, and proves worthless after the small sample size wears off. —

Pablo Ozuna 3B
R

at position | Age
2007 Game Log
DL (broken leg), surgery
H%, K%, BA, HR (○), SB (□)

Production
OPS — Tot, Pos, vRH, vLH
PA

1B	
3B	9
2B	3
SS	1
C	
LF	7
CF	
RF	

Lineup Profile — #1 ... #9 — Usage, TmOPS

PX — HR
SX — SB

Spray Chart — FB/LD, GB, ○ HR (mlb), ● HR (milb)

Ozuna is versatile, but he's not as good as his age-32 PX implies, and he was busy proving it before injury struck. In 2008, he might be healthy, and that's it. —

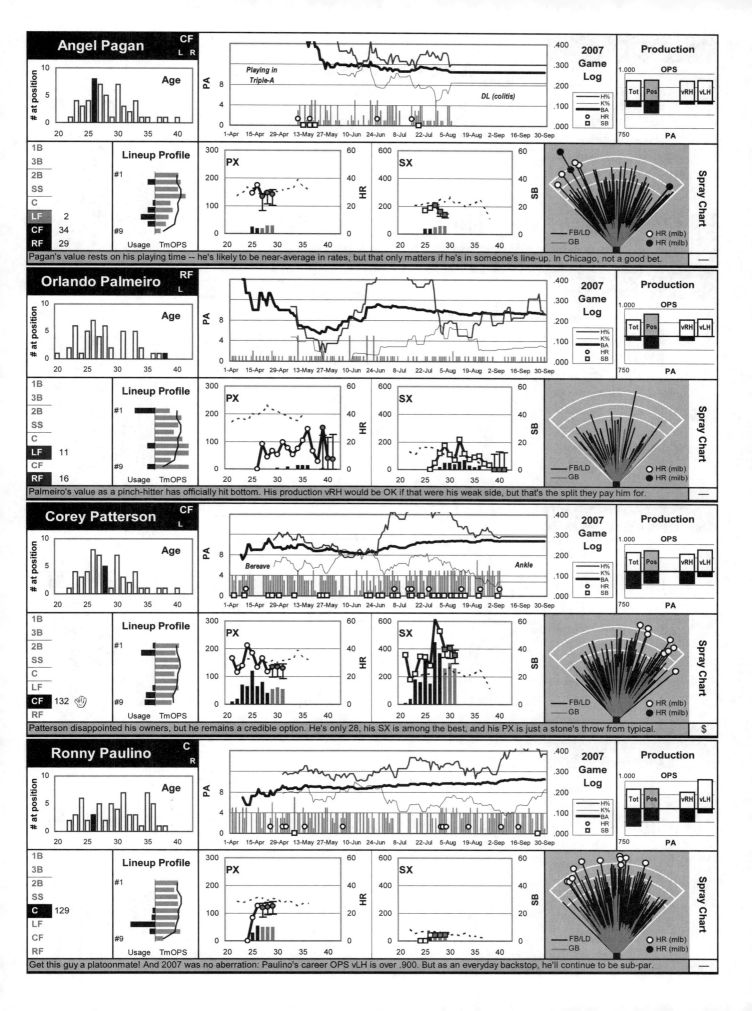

Angel Pagan — CF / L R

Age

Playing in Triple-A

DL (colitis)

2007 Game Log

Production — OPS — Tot Pos vRH vLH — PA

H% / K% / BA / HR (○) / SB (□)

at position — 1B 3B 2B SS C / LF 2 / CF 34 / RF 29

Lineup Profile — #1 ... #9 — Usage — TmOPS

PX / HR
SX / SB
FB/LD — GB — HR (mlb ○) HR (milb ●)

Spray Chart

Pagan's value rests on his playing time -- he's likely to be near-average in rates, but that only matters if he's in someone's line-up. In Chicago, not a good bet. — —

Orlando Palmeiro — RF / L

Age

2007 Game Log

Production — OPS — Tot Pos vRH vLH — PA

at position — 1B 3B 2B SS C / LF 11 / CF / RF 16

Lineup Profile — #1 ... #9 — Usage — TmOPS

PX / HR
SX / SB
FB/LD — GB — HR (mlb ○) HR (milb ●)

Spray Chart

Palmeiro's value as a pinch-hitter has officially hit bottom. His production vRH would be OK if that were his weak side, but that's the split they pay him for. — —

Corey Patterson — CF / L

Age

Bereave   Ankle

2007 Game Log

Production — OPS — Tot Pos vRH vLH — PA

at position — 1B 3B 2B SS C / LF / CF 132 / RF

Lineup Profile — #1 ... #9 — Usage — TmOPS

PX / HR
SX / SB
FB/LD — GB — HR (mlb ○) HR (milb ●)

Spray Chart

Patterson disappointed his owners, but he remains a credible option. He's only 28, his SX is among the best, and his PX is just a stone's throw from typical. — $

Ronny Paulino — C / R

Age

2007 Game Log

Production — OPS — Tot Pos vRH vLH — PA

at position — 1B 3B 2B SS / C 129 / LF CF RF

Lineup Profile — #1 ... #9 — Usage — TmOPS

PX / HR
SX / SB
FB/LD — GB — HR (mlb ○) HR (milb ●)

Spray Chart

Get this guy a platonmate! And 2007 was no aberration: Paulino's career OPS vLH is over .900. But as an everyday backstop, he'll continue to be sub-par. — —

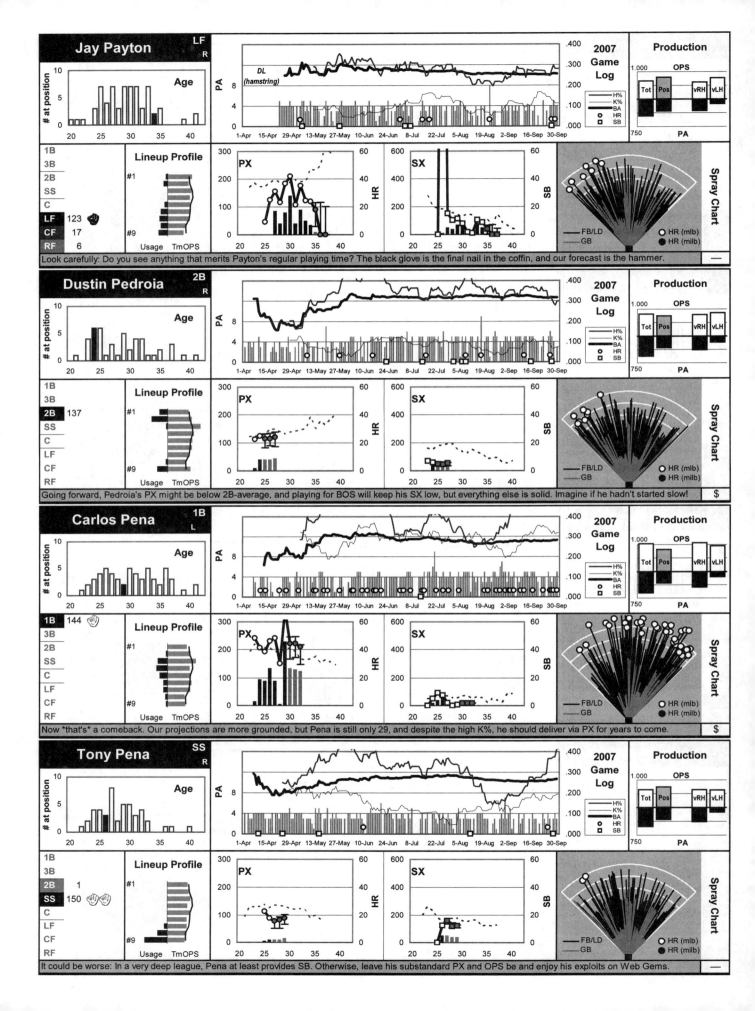

Jay Payton — LF / R

Age | # at position
1B, 3B, 2B, SS, C, **LF 123**, CF 17, RF 6
Lineup Profile — #1 ... #9 — Usage / TmOPS
PA | 2007 Game Log | DL (hamstring) | H% / K% / BA | HR / SB
PX | SX | HR | SB
Production — OPS | Tot / Pos / vRH / vLH | PA
Spray Chart — FB/LD / GB — HR (mlb) / HR (milb)

Look carefully: Do you see anything that merits Payton's regular playing time? The black glove is the final nail in the coffin, and our forecast is the hammer. | —

Dustin Pedroia — 2B / R

Age | # at position
1B, 3B, **2B 137**, SS, C, LF, CF, RF
Lineup Profile — #1 ... #9 — Usage / TmOPS
PA | 2007 Game Log | H% / K% / BA | HR / SB
PX | SX | HR | SB
Production — OPS | Tot / Pos / vRH / vLH | PA
Spray Chart — FB/LD / GB — HR (mlb) / HR (milb)

Going forward, Pedroia's PX might be below 2B-average, and playing for BOS will keep his SX low, but everything else is solid. Imagine if he hadn't started slow! | $

Carlos Pena — 1B / L

Age | # at position
1B 144, 3B, 2B, SS, C, LF, CF, RF
Lineup Profile — #1 ... #9 — Usage / TmOPS
PA | 2007 Game Log | H% / K% / BA | HR / SB
PX | SX | HR | SB
Production — OPS | Tot / Pos / vRH / vLH | PA
Spray Chart — FB/LD / GB — HR (mlb) / HR (milb)

Now *that's* a comeback. Our projections are more grounded, but Pena is still only 29, and despite the high K%, he should deliver via PX for years to come. | $

Tony Pena — SS / R

Age | # at position
1B, 3B, **2B 1**, **SS 150**, C, LF, CF, RF
Lineup Profile — #1 ... #9 — Usage / TmOPS
PA | 2007 Game Log | H% / K% / BA | HR / SB
PX | SX | HR | SB
Production — OPS | Tot / Pos / vRH / vLH | PA
Spray Chart — FB/LD / GB — HR (mlb) / HR (milb)

It could be worse: In a very deep league, Pena at least provides SB. Otherwise, leave his substandard PX and OPS be and enjoy his exploits on Web Gems. | —

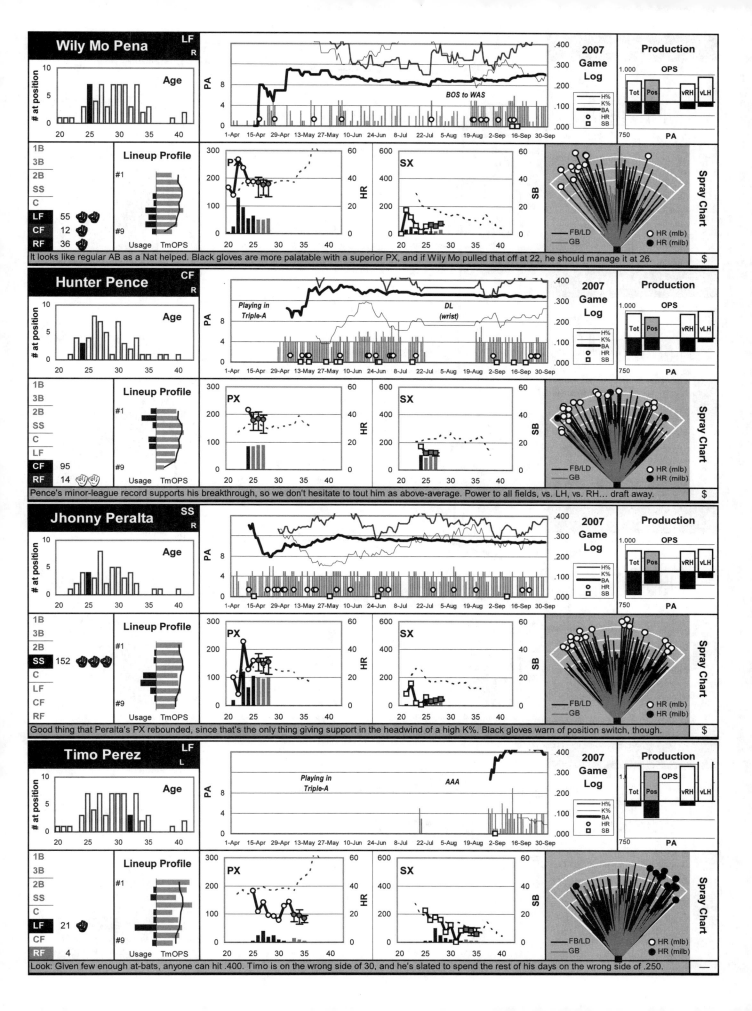

Wily Mo Pena — LF / R

Age | # at position

2007 Game Log

BOS to WAS

Production — OPS | Tot | Pos | vRH | vLH | PA

H% / K% / BA / HR ○ / SB □

Position	#	
1B		
3B		
2B		
SS		
C		
LF	55	
CF	12	
RF	36	

Lineup Profile #1 ... #9 — Usage / TmOPS

PX | SX | **Spray Chart**

FB/LD / GB — HR (mlb) ○ / HR (milb) ●

It looks like regular AB as a Nat helped. Black gloves are more palatable with a superior PX, and if Wily Mo pulled that off at 22, he should manage it at 26. | $

Hunter Pence — CF / R

Playing in Triple-A | DL (wrist)

2007 Game Log

Production — OPS | Tot | Pos | vRH | vLH | PA

Position	#	
1B		
3B		
2B		
SS		
C		
LF		
CF	95	
RF	14	

Lineup Profile #1 ... #9 — Usage / TmOPS

PX | SX | **Spray Chart**

FB/LD / GB — HR (mlb) ○ / HR (milb) ●

Pence's minor-league record supports his breakthrough, so we don't hesitate to tout him as above-average. Power to all fields, vs. LH, vs. RH… draft away. | $

Jhonny Peralta — SS / R

2007 Game Log

Production — OPS | Tot | Pos | vRH | vLH | PA

Position	#	
1B		
3B		
2B		
SS	152	
C		
LF		
CF		
RF		

Lineup Profile #1 ... #9 — Usage / TmOPS

PX | SX | **Spray Chart**

FB/LD / GB — HR (mlb) ○ / HR (milb) ●

Good thing that Peralta's PX rebounded, since that's the only thing giving support in the headwind of a high K%. Black gloves warn of position switch, though. | $

Timo Perez — LF / L

Playing in Triple-A | AAA

2007 Game Log

Production — OPS | Tot | Pos | vRH | vLH | PA

Position	#	
1B		
3B		
2B		
SS		
C		
LF	21	
CF		
RF	4	

Lineup Profile #1 ... #9 — Usage / TmOPS

PX | SX | **Spray Chart**

FB/LD / GB — HR (mlb) ○ / HR (milb) ●

Look: Given few enough at-bats, anyone can hit .400. Timo is on the wrong side of 30, and he's slated to spend the rest of his days on the wrong side of .250. | —

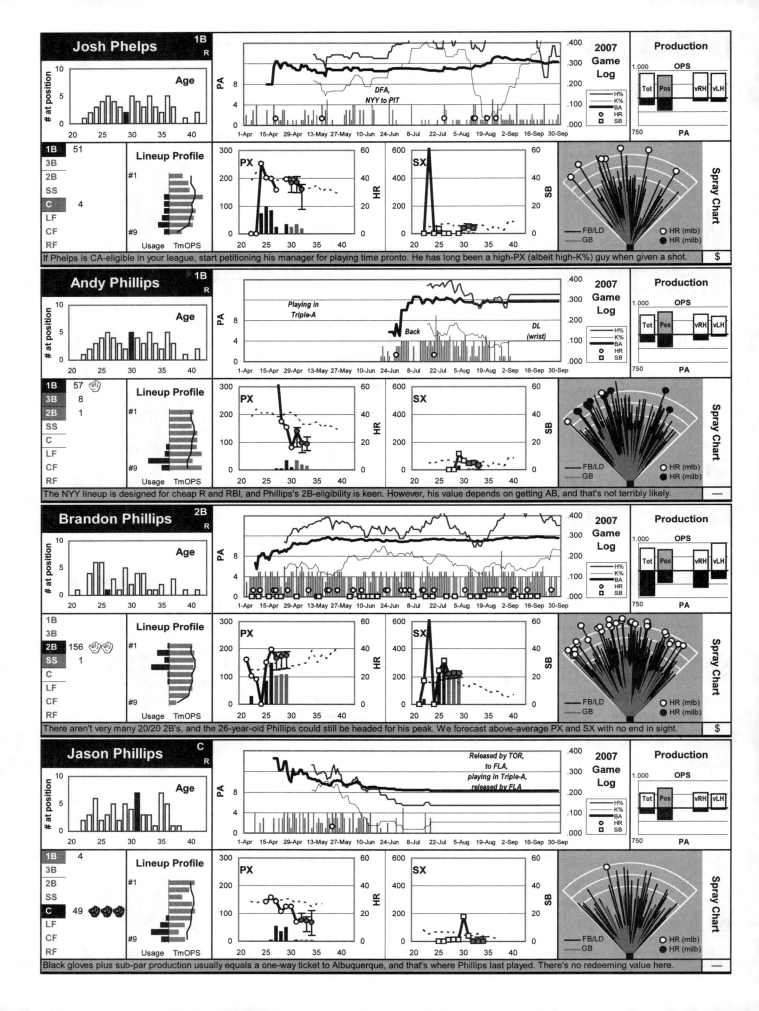

Josh Phelps — 1B — R

Age — # at position: 20 25 30 35 40

2007 Game Log

DFA,
NYY to PIT

.400 / .300 / .200 / .100 / .000

H% / K% / BA / HR / SB

Production — OPS
Tot / Pos / vRH / vLH — PA

1B	51
3B	
2B	
SS	
C	4
LF	
CF	
RF	

Lineup Profile — #1 ... #9 — Usage / TmOPS

PX / HR
SX / SB

Spray Chart — FB/LD, GB — HR (mlb), HR (milb)

If Phelps is CA-eligible in your league, start petitioning his manager for playing time pronto. He has long been a high-PX (albeit high-K%) guy when given a shot. — $

Andy Phillips — 1B — R

Age

2007 Game Log

Playing in
Triple-A

Back

DL
(wrist)

Production — OPS

1B	57
3B	8
2B	1
SS	
C	
LF	
CF	
RF	

Lineup Profile

PX / HR
SX / SB

Spray Chart

The NYY lineup is designed for cheap R and RBI, and Phillips's 2B-eligibility is keen. However, his value depends on getting AB, and that's not terribly likely. — —

Brandon Phillips — 2B — R

Age

2007 Game Log

Production — OPS

1B	
3B	
2B	156
SS	1
C	
LF	
CF	
RF	

Lineup Profile

PX / HR
SX / SB

Spray Chart

There aren't very many 20/20 2B's, and the 26-year-old Phillips could still be headed for his peak. We forecast above-average PX and SX with no end in sight. — $

Jason Phillips — C — R

Age

2007 Game Log

Released by TOR,
to FLA,
playing in Triple-A,
released by FLA

Production — OPS

1B	4
3B	
2B	
SS	
C	49
LF	
CF	
RF	

Lineup Profile

PX / HR
SX / SB

Spray Chart

Black gloves plus sub-par production usually equals a one-way ticket to Albuquerque, and that's where Phillips last played. There's no redeeming value here. — —

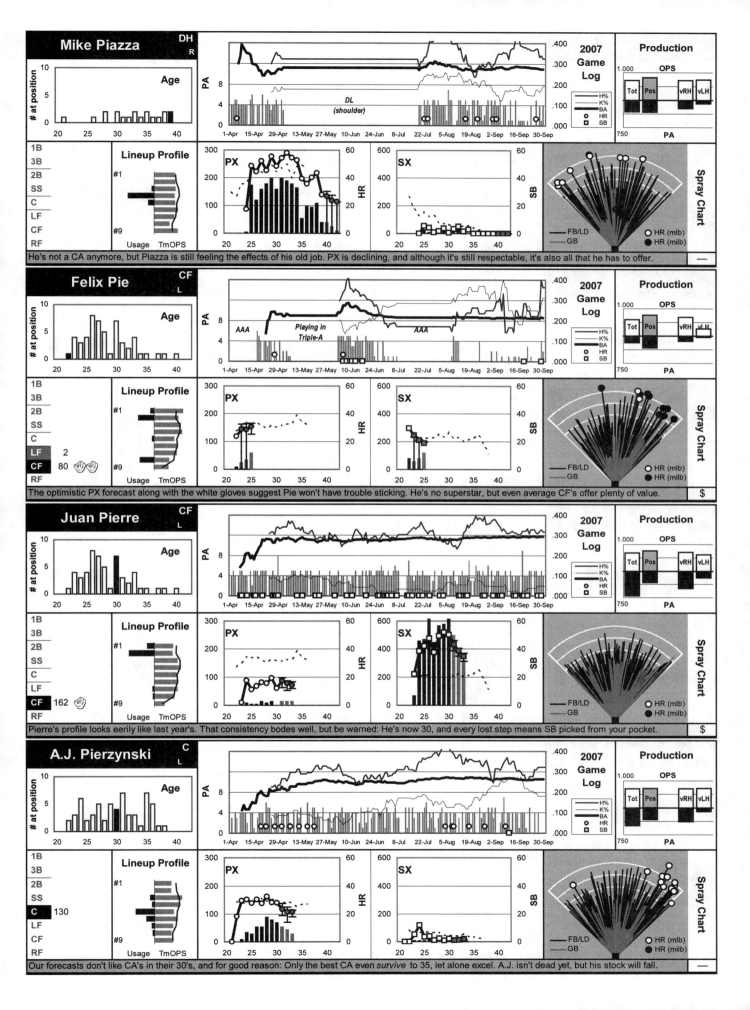

Mike Piazza — DH / R

Age | **PA** | **2007 Game Log** | **Production** | **OPS**

DL (shoulder)

H% / K% / BA / HR / SB

OPS: Tot, Pos, vRH, vLH — PA

Lineup Profile — #1 ... #9 — Usage / TmOPS

PX / **SX** — HR / SB

Spray Chart — FB/LD, GB, HR (mlb), HR (milb)

He's not a CA anymore, but Piazza is still feeling the effects of his old job. PX is declining, and although it's still respectable, it's also all that he has to offer. — —

Felix Pie — CF / L

Age | **PA** | **2007 Game Log** | **Production** | **OPS**

AAA — Playing in Triple-A — AAA

H% / K% / BA / HR / SB

OPS: Tot, Pos, vRH, vLH — PA

Lineup Profile — #1 ... #9 — Usage / TmOPS

LF 2
CF 80

PX / **SX** — HR / SB

Spray Chart — FB/LD, GB, HR (mlb), HR (milb)

The optimistic PX forecast along with the white gloves suggest Pie won't have trouble sticking. He's no superstar, but even average CF's offer plenty of value. — $

Juan Pierre — CF / L

Age | **PA** | **2007 Game Log** | **Production** | **OPS**

H% / K% / BA / HR / SB

OPS: Tot, Pos, vRH, vLH — PA

Lineup Profile — #1 ... #9 — Usage / TmOPS

CF 162

PX / **SX** — HR / SB

Spray Chart — FB/LD, GB, HR (mlb), HR (milb)

Pierre's profile looks eerily like last year's. That consistency bodes well, but be warned: He's now 30, and every lost step means SB picked from your pocket. — $

A.J. Pierzynski — C / L

Age | **PA** | **2007 Game Log** | **Production** | **OPS**

H% / K% / BA / HR / SB

OPS: Tot, Pos, vRH, vLH — PA

Lineup Profile — #1 ... #9 — Usage / TmOPS

C 130

PX / **SX** — HR / SB

Spray Chart — FB/LD, GB, HR (mlb), HR (milb)

Our forecasts don't like CA's in their 30's, and for good reason: Only the best CA even survive to 35, let alone excel. A.J. isn't dead yet, but his stock will fall. — —

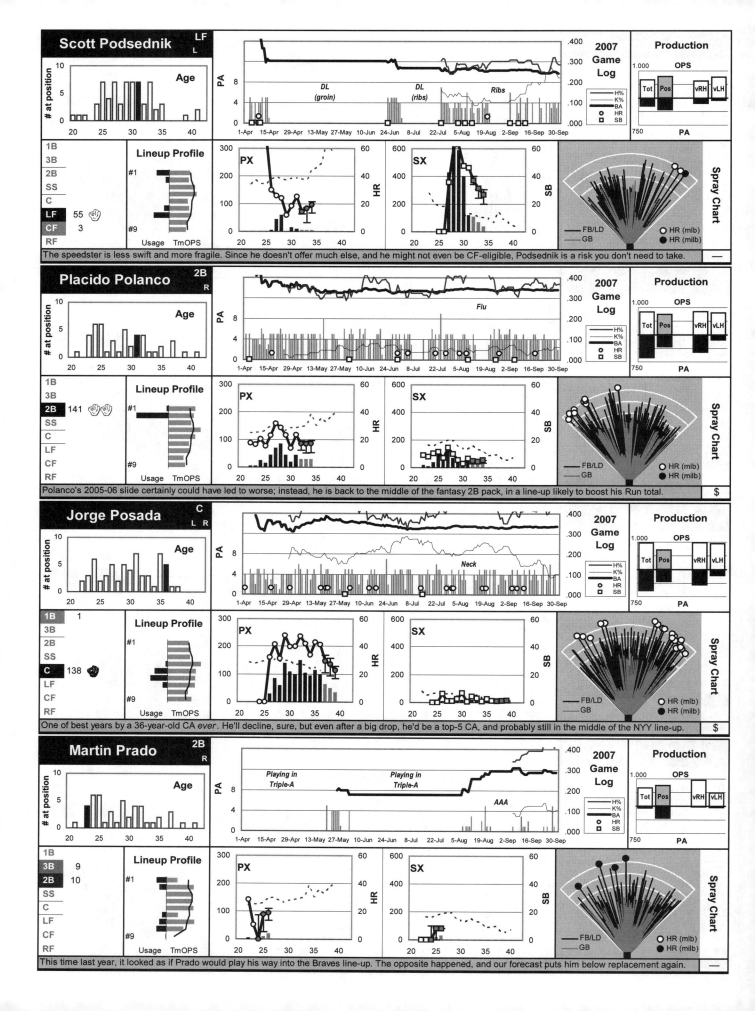

Scott Podsednik — LF, L

Age | PA | 2007 Game Log | Production OPS

Positions: LF 55, CF 3

Lineup Profile — Usage / TmOPS — #1 ... #9

PX | SX | HR | SB

H% / K% / BA / HR / SB

PA: Tot / Pos / vRH / vLH

DL (groin) | DL (ribs) | Ribs

Spray Chart — FB/LD, GB, HR (mlb), HR (milb)

The speedster is less swift and more fragile. Since he doesn't offer much else, and he might not even be CF-eligible, Podsednik is a risk you don't need to take. — —

Placido Polanco — 2B, R

Age | PA | 2007 Game Log | Production OPS

Positions: 2B 141

Lineup Profile — Usage / TmOPS — #1 ... #9

PX | SX | HR | SB

H% / K% / BA / HR / SB

Flu

PA: Tot / Pos / vRH / vLH

Spray Chart — FB/LD, GB, HR (mlb), HR (milb)

Polanco's 2005-06 slide certainly could have led to worse; instead, he is back to the middle of the fantasy 2B pack, in a line-up likely to boost his Run total. — $

Jorge Posada — C, L R

Age | PA | 2007 Game Log | Production OPS

Positions: 1B 1, C 138

Lineup Profile — Usage / TmOPS — #1 ... #9

PX | SX | HR | SB

H% / K% / BA / HR / SB

Neck

PA: Tot / Pos / vRH / vLH

Spray Chart — FB/LD, GB, HR (mlb), HR (milb)

One of best years by a 36-year-old CA *ever*. He'll decline, sure, but even after a big drop, he'd be a top-5 CA, and probably still in the middle of the NYY line-up. — $

Martin Prado — 2B, R

Age | PA | 2007 Game Log | Production OPS

Positions: 3B 9, 2B 10

Lineup Profile — Usage / TmOPS — #1 ... #9

PX | SX | HR | SB

H% / K% / BA / HR / SB

Playing in Triple-A | Playing in Triple-A | AAA

PA: Tot / Pos / vRH / vLH

Spray Chart — FB/LD, GB, HR (mlb), HR (milb)

This time last year, it looked as if Prado would play his way into the Braves line-up. The opposite happened, and our forecast puts him below replacement again. — —

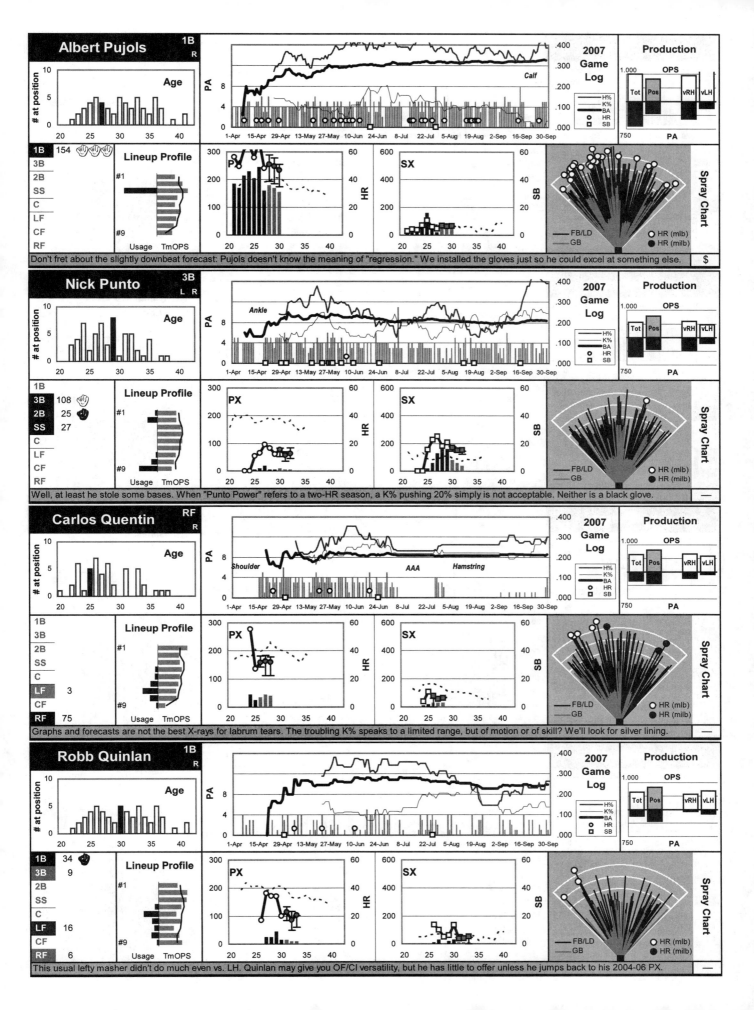

Albert Pujols — 1B / R

Age — # at position

PA — 2007 Game Log — *Calf*

H%, K%, BA, ○ HR, □ SB

Production — OPS — Tot, Pos, vRH, vLH — PA

1B	154
3B	
2B	
SS	
C	
LF	
CF	
RF	

Lineup Profile — #1 ... #9 — Usage / TmOPS

PX — HR — **SX** — SB

Spray Chart — FB/LD, GB, ○ HR (mlb), ● HR (milb)

Don't fret about the slightly downbeat forecast: Pujols doesn't know the meaning of "regression." We installed the gloves just so he could excel at something else. **$**

Nick Punto — 3B / L R

Age — # at position

PA — 2007 Game Log — *Ankle*

H%, K%, BA, ○ HR, □ SB

Production — OPS — Tot, Pos, vRH, vLH — PA

1B	
3B	108
2B	25
SS	27
C	
LF	
CF	
RF	

Lineup Profile — #1 ... #9 — Usage / TmOPS

PX — HR — **SX** — SB

Spray Chart — FB/LD, GB, ○ HR (mlb), ● HR (milb)

Well, at least he stole some bases. When "Punto Power" refers to a two-HR season, a K% pushing 20% simply is not acceptable. Neither is a black glove. **—**

Carlos Quentin — RF / R

Age — # at position

PA — 2007 Game Log — *Shoulder* ... *AAA* ... *Hamstring*

H%, K%, BA, ○ HR, □ SB

Production — OPS — Tot, Pos, vRH, vLH — PA

1B	
3B	
2B	
SS	
C	
LF	3
CF	
RF	75

Lineup Profile — #1 ... #9 — Usage / TmOPS

PX — HR — **SX** — SB

Spray Chart — FB/LD, GB, ○ HR (mlb), ● HR (milb)

Graphs and forecasts are not the best X-rays for labrum tears. The troubling K% speaks to a limited range, but of motion or of skill? We'll look for silver lining. **—**

Robb Quinlan — 1B / R

Age — # at position

PA — 2007 Game Log

H%, K%, BA, ○ HR, □ SB

Production — OPS — Tot, Pos, vRH, vLH — PA

1B	34
3B	9
2B	
SS	
C	
LF	16
CF	
RF	6

Lineup Profile — #1 ... #9 — Usage / TmOPS

PX — HR — **SX** — SB

Spray Chart — FB/LD, GB, ○ HR (mlb), ● HR (milb)

This usual lefty masher didn't do much even vs. LH. Quinlan may give you OF/CI versatility, but he has little to offer unless he jumps back to his 2004-06 PX. **—**

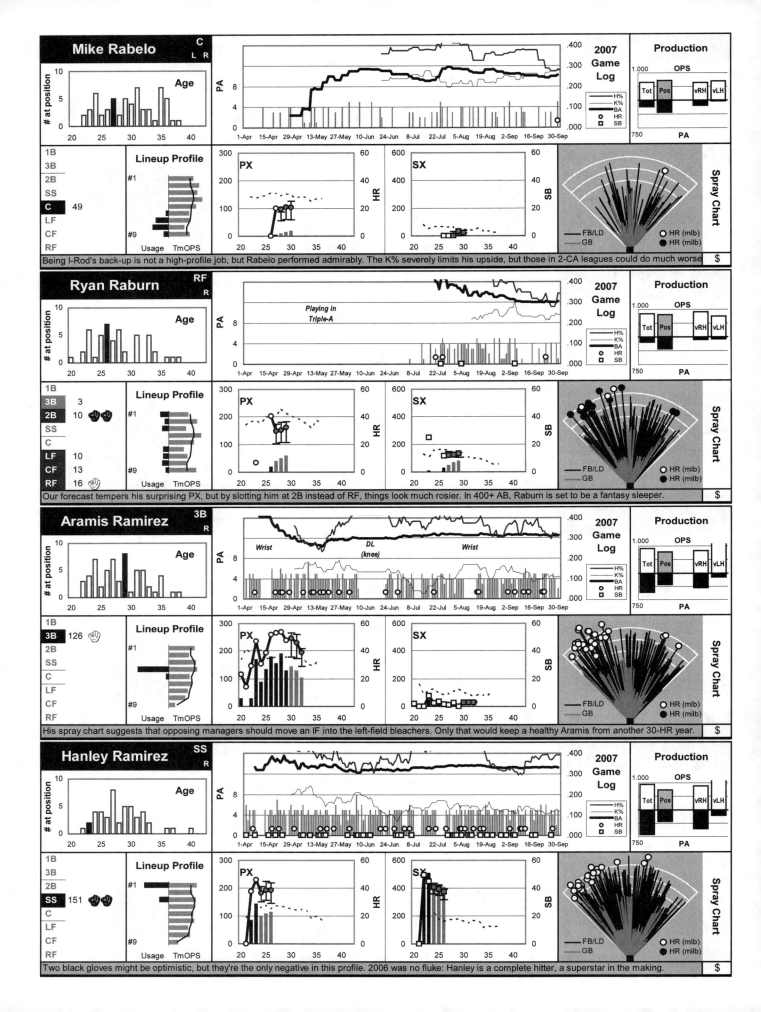

Mike Rabelo C L R

Age

at position

1B
3B
2B
SS
C 49
LF
CF
RF

Lineup Profile
#1
#9
Usage TmOPS

PX
SX

2007 Game Log
H%
K%
BA
○ HR
□ SB

Production
OPS
1.000
Tot Pos vRH vLH
750
PA

Spray Chart
— FB/LD
— GB
○ HR (mlb)
● HR (milb)

Being I-Rod's back-up is not a high-profile job, but Rabelo performed admirably. The K% severely limits his upside, but those in 2-CA leagues could do much worse $

Ryan Raburn RF R

Age

at position

1B
3B 3
2B 10
SS
C
LF 10
CF 13
RF 16

Playing in Triple-A

Lineup Profile
#1
#9
Usage TmOPS

PX
SX

2007 Game Log
H%
K%
BA
○ HR
□ SB

Production
OPS
1.000
Tot Pos vRH vLH
750
PA

Spray Chart
— FB/LD
— GB
○ HR (mlb)
● HR (milb)

Our forecast tempers his surprising PX, but by slotting him at 2B instead of RF, things look much rosier. In 400+ AB, Raburn is set to be a fantasy sleeper. $

Aramis Ramirez 3B R

Age

at position

1B
3B 126
2B
SS
C
LF
CF
RF

Wrist   DL (knee)   Wrist

Lineup Profile
#1
#9
Usage TmOPS

PX
SX

2007 Game Log
H%
K%
BA
○ HR
□ SB

Production
OPS
1.000
Tot Pos vRH vLH
750
PA

Spray Chart
— FB/LD
— GB
○ HR (mlb)
● HR (milb)

His spray chart suggests that opposing managers should move an IF into the left-field bleachers. Only that would keep a healthy Aramis from another 30-HR year. $

Hanley Ramirez SS R

Age

at position

1B
3B
2B
SS 151
C
LF
CF
RF

Lineup Profile
#1
#9
Usage TmOPS

PX
SX

2007 Game Log
H%
K%
BA
○ HR
□ SB

Production
OPS
1.000
Tot Pos vRH vLH
750
PA

Spray Chart
— FB/LD
— GB
○ HR (mlb)
● HR (milb)

Two black gloves might be optimistic, but they're the only negative in this profile. 2006 was no fluke: Hanley is a complete hitter, a superstar in the making. $

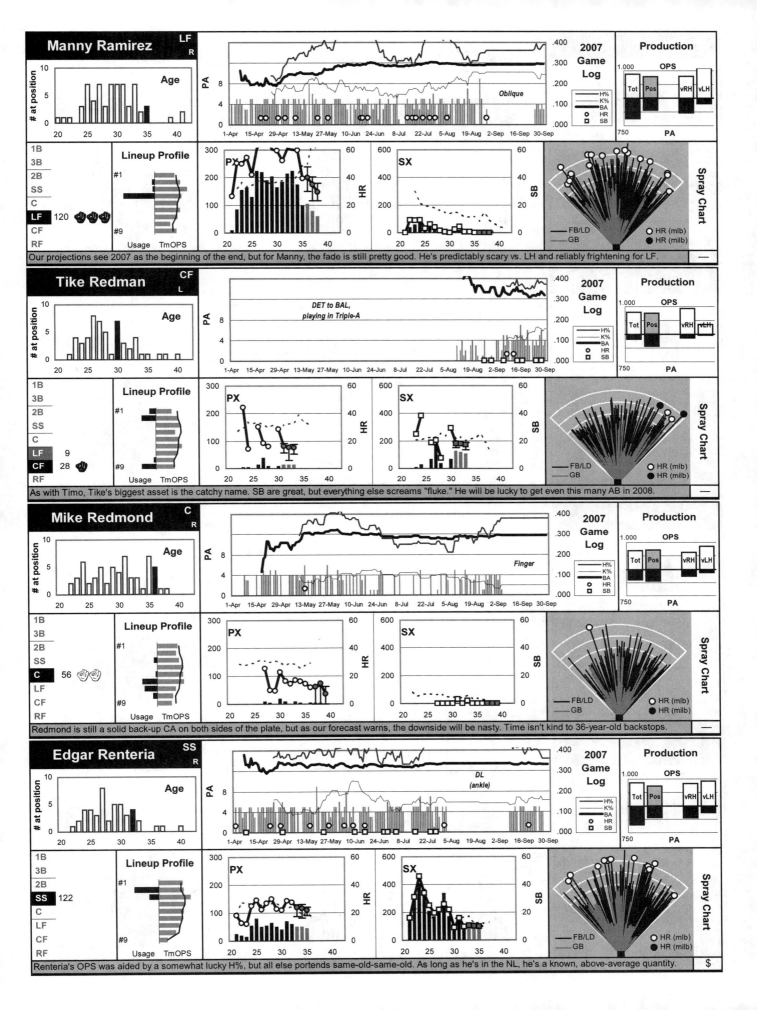

Manny Ramirez — LF / R

Age | **PA** | **2007 Game Log** | **Production — OPS**

Oblique

H% / K% / BA / HR / SB

Tot / Pos / vRH / vLH

Lineup Profile #1 ... #9 — Usage / TmOPS

LF 120

PX | **SX** | **Spray Chart**

FB/LD — GB — HR (mlb) / HR (milb)

Our projections see 2007 as the beginning of the end, but for Manny, the fade is still pretty good. He's predictably scary vs. LH and reliably frightening for LF. —

Tike Redman — CF / L

Age | **PA** | **2007 Game Log** | **Production — OPS**

DET to BAL, playing in Triple-A

Tot / Pos / vRH / vLH

Lineup Profile #1 ... #9 — Usage / TmOPS

LF 9
CF 28

PX | **SX** | **Spray Chart**

FB/LD — GB — HR (mlb) / HR (milb)

As with Timo, Tike's biggest asset is the catchy name. SB are great, but everything else screams "fluke." He will be lucky to get even this many AB in 2008. —

Mike Redmond — C / R

Age | **PA** | **2007 Game Log** | **Production — OPS**

Finger

Tot / Pos / vRH / vLH

Lineup Profile #1 ... #9 — Usage / TmOPS

C 56

PX | **SX** | **Spray Chart**

FB/LD — GB — HR (mlb) / HR (milb)

Redmond is still a solid back-up CA on both sides of the plate, but as our forecast warns, the downside will be nasty. Time isn't kind to 36-year-old backstops. —

Edgar Renteria — SS / R

Age | **PA** | **2007 Game Log** | **Production — OPS**

DL (ankle)

Tot / Pos / vRH / vLH

Lineup Profile #1 ... #9 — Usage / TmOPS

SS 122

PX | **SX** | **Spray Chart**

FB/LD — GB — HR (mlb) / HR (milb)

Renteria's OPS was aided by a somewhat lucky H%, but all else portends same-old-same-old. As long as he's in the NL, he's a known, above-average quantity. $

Jose Reyes — SS — L R

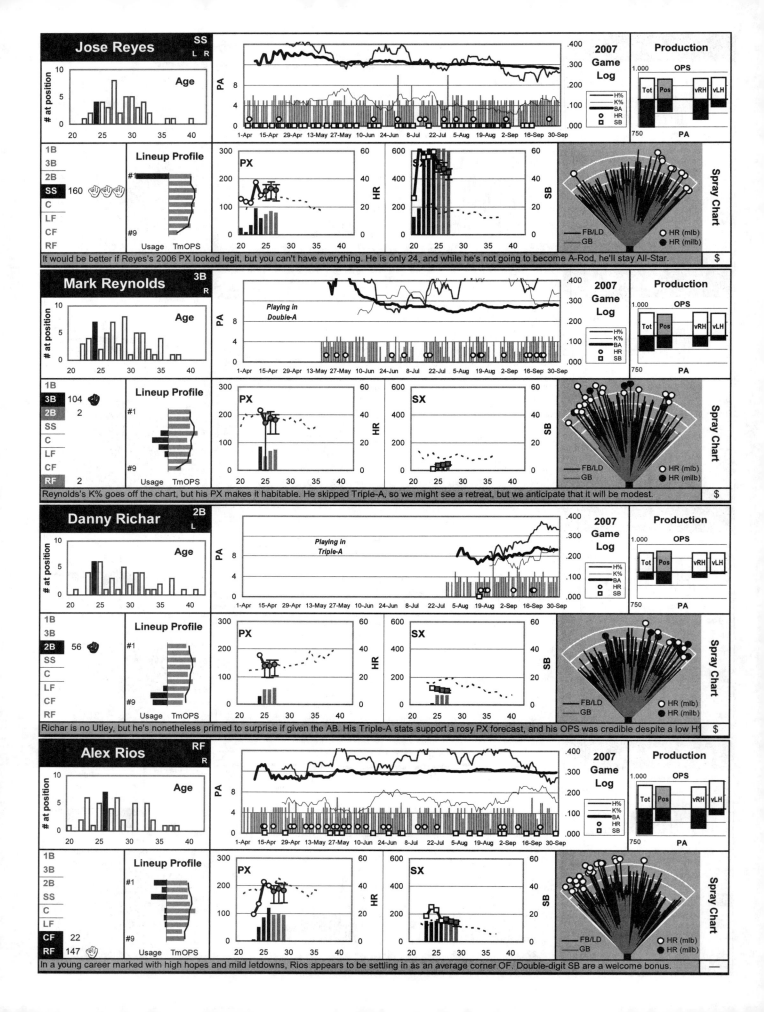

Age — # at position

2007 Game Log — PA / BA — H%, K%, BA, HR, SB

Production — OPS — Tot, Pos, vRH, vLH — PA

Positions: 1B, 3B, 2B, **SS 160**, C, LF, CF, RF

Lineup Profile — #1 ... #9 — Usage / TmOPS

PX — HR

SB — FB/LD, GB — HR (mlb), HR (milb)

Spray Chart

It would be better if Reyes's 2006 PX looked legit, but you can't have everything. He is only 24, and while he's not going to become A-Rod, he'll stay All-Star. $

Mark Reynolds — 3B — R

Age — # at position

Playing in Double-A

2007 Game Log — H%, K%, BA, HR, SB

Production — OPS — Tot, Pos, vRH, vLH — PA

Positions: 1B, **3B 104**, 2B 2, SS, C, LF, CF, RF 2

Lineup Profile — #1 ... #9 — Usage / TmOPS

PX — HR

SX — SB — FB/LD, GB — HR (mlb), HR (milb)

Spray Chart

Reynolds's K% goes off the chart, but his PX makes it habitable. He skipped Triple-A, so we might see a retreat, but we anticipate that it will be modest. $

Danny Richar — 2B — L

Age — # at position

Playing in Triple-A

2007 Game Log — H%, K%, BA, HR, SB

Production — OPS — Tot, Pos, vRH, vLH — PA

Positions: 1B, 3B, **2B 56**, SS, C, LF, CF, RF

Lineup Profile — #1 ... #9 — Usage / TmOPS

PX — HR

SX — SB — FB/LD, GB — HR (mlb), HR (milb)

Spray Chart

Richar is no Utley, but he's nonetheless primed to surprise if given the AB. His Triple-A stats support a rosy PX forecast, and his OPS was credible despite a low H% $

Alex Rios — RF — R

Age — # at position

2007 Game Log — H%, K%, BA, HR, SB

Production — OPS — Tot, Pos, vRH, vLH — PA

Positions: 1B, 3B, 2B, SS, C, LF, **CF 22**, **RF 147**

Lineup Profile — #1 ... #9 — Usage / TmOPS

PX — HR

SX — SB — FB/LD, GB — HR (mlb), HR (milb)

Spray Chart

In a young career marked with high hopes and mild letdowns, Rios appears to be settling in as an average corner OF. Double-digit SB are a welcome bonus. —

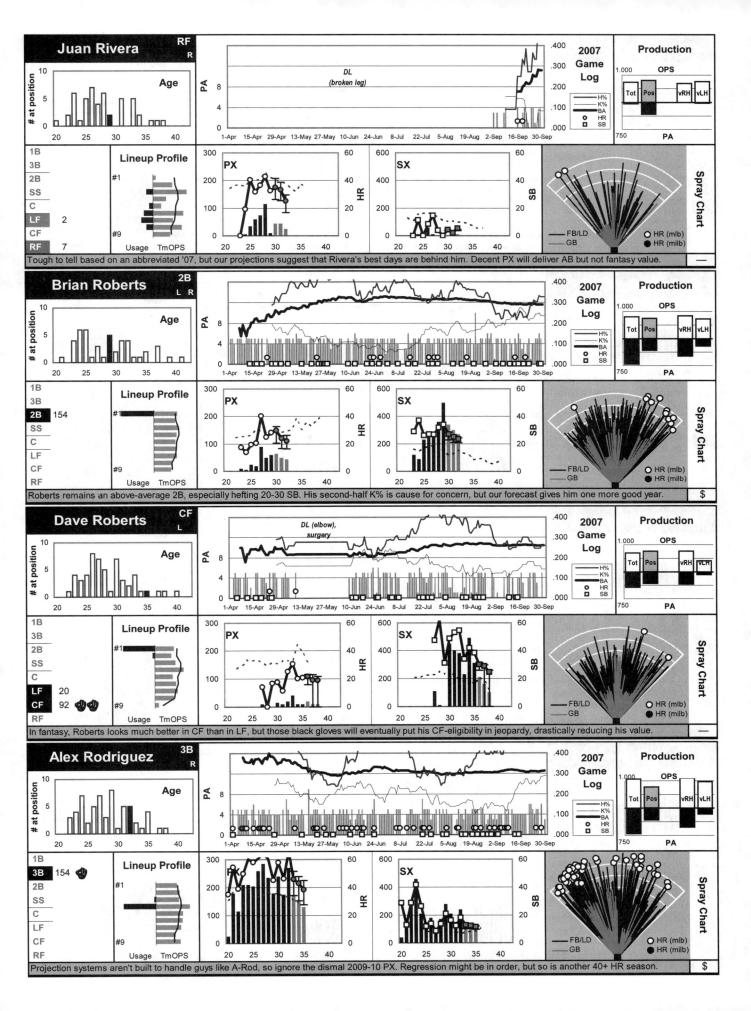

Juan Rivera — RF / R — Age

2007 Game Log — PA — DL (broken leg)

Production — OPS — 1.000 — Tot, Pos, vRH, vLH — PA — .750

Lineup Profile — #1 ... #9 — Usage — TmOPS

1B, 3B, 2B, SS, C, LF 2, CF, RF 7

PX — HR; SX — SB

H%, K%, BA, ○ HR, □ SB

Spray Chart — FB/LD, GB — ○ HR (mlb), ● HR (milb)

Tough to tell based on an abbreviated '07, but our projections suggest that Rivera's best days are behind him. Decent PX will deliver AB but not fantasy value. — —

Brian Roberts — 2B — L R — Age

2007 Game Log

Production — OPS — Tot, Pos, vRH, vLH

Lineup Profile — #1 ... #9 — Usage — TmOPS

1B, 3B, 2B 154, SS, C, LF, CF, RF

PX; SX

Spray Chart — FB/LD, GB — ○ HR (mlb), ● HR (milb)

Roberts remains an above-average 2B, especially hefting 20-30 SB. His second-half K% is cause for concern, but our forecast gives him one more good year. — $

Dave Roberts — CF — L — Age

2007 Game Log — DL (elbow), surgery

Production — OPS — Tot, Pos, vRH, vLH

Lineup Profile — #1 ... #9 — Usage — TmOPS

1B, 3B, 2B, SS, C, LF 20, CF 92, RF

PX; SX

Spray Chart — FB/LD, GB — ○ HR (mlb), ● HR (milb)

In fantasy, Roberts looks much better in CF than in LF, but those black gloves will eventually put his CF-eligibility in jeopardy, drastically reducing his value. — —

Alex Rodriguez — 3B — R — Age

2007 Game Log

Production — OPS — Tot, Pos, vRH, vLH

Lineup Profile — #1 ... #9 — Usage — TmOPS

1B, 3B 154, 2B, SS, C, LF, CF, RF

PX; SX

Spray Chart — FB/LD, GB — ○ HR (mlb), ● HR (milb)

Projection systems aren't built to handle guys like A-Rod, so ignore the dismal 2009-10 PX. Regression might be in order, but so is another 40+ HR season. — $

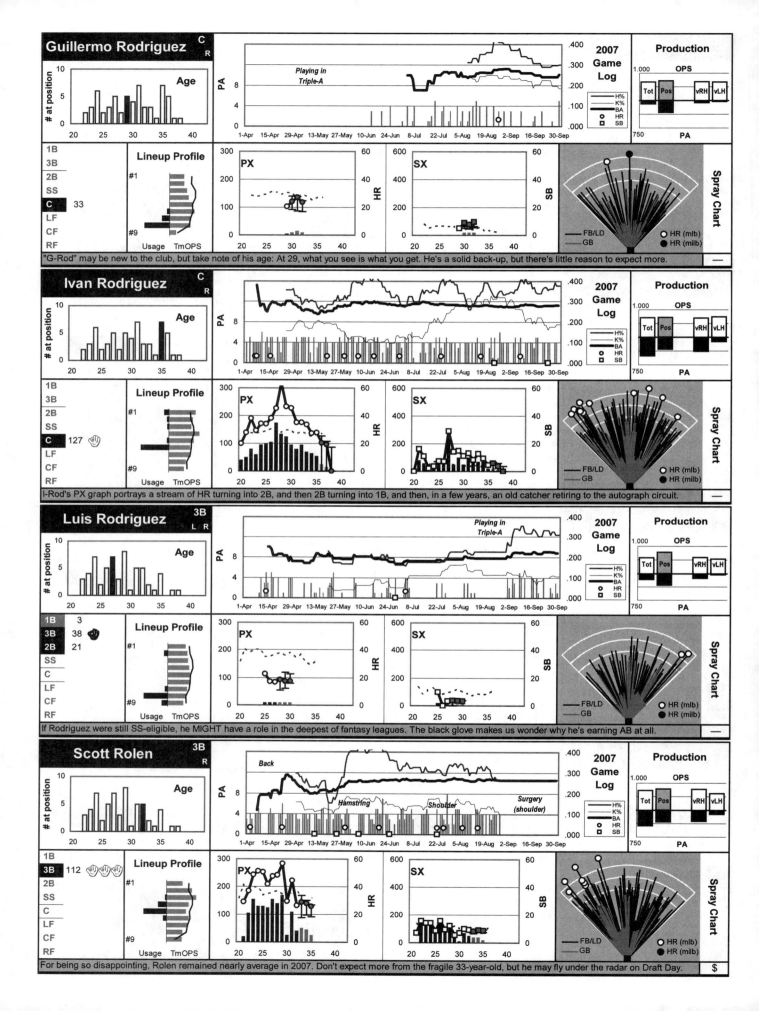

Guillermo Rodriguez (C, R)

Age

at position

PA

2007 Game Log

Playing in Triple-A

H%
K%
BA
HR
SB

Production — OPS

Tot | Pos | vRH | vLH

PA

Lineup Profile

1B
3B
2B
SS
C 33
LF
CF
RF

#1
#9

Usage   TmOPS

PX   HR

SX   SB

FB/LD
GB
HR (mlb)
HR (milb)

Spray Chart

"G-Rod" may be new to the club, but take note of his age: At 29, what you see is what you get. He's a solid back-up, but there's little reason to expect more.   —

Ivan Rodriguez (C, R)

Age

at position

PA

2007 Game Log

H%
K%
BA
HR
SB

Production — OPS

Tot | Pos | vRH | vLH

PA

Lineup Profile

1B
3B
2B
SS
C 127
LF
CF
RF

#1
#9

Usage   TmOPS

PX   HR

SX   SB

FB/LD
GB
HR (mlb)
HR (milb)

Spray Chart

I-Rod's PX graph portrays a stream of HR turning into 2B, and then 2B turning into 1B, and then, in a few years, an old catcher retiring to the autograph circuit.   —

Luis Rodriguez (3B, L R)

Age

at position

PA

2007 Game Log

Playing in Triple-A

H%
K%
BA
HR
SB

Production — OPS

Tot | Pos | vRH | vLH

PA

Lineup Profile

1B 3
3B 38
2B 21
SS
C
LF
CF
RF

#1
#9

Usage   TmOPS

PX   HR

SX   SB

FB/LD
GB
HR (mlb)
HR (milb)

Spray Chart

If Rodriguez were still SS-eligible, he MIGHT have a role in the deepest of fantasy leagues. The black glove makes us wonder why he's earning AB at all.   —

Scott Rolen (3B, R)

Age

at position

PA

2007 Game Log

Back
Hamstring
Shoulder
Surgery (shoulder)

H%
K%
BA
HR
SB

Production — OPS

Tot | Pos | vRH | vLH

PA

Lineup Profile

1B
3B 112
2B
SS
C
LF
CF
RF

#1
#9

Usage   TmOPS

PX   HR

SX   SB

FB/LD
GB
HR (mlb)
HR (milb)

Spray Chart

For being so disappointing, Rolen remained nearly average in 2007. Don't expect more from the fragile 33-year-old, but he may fly under the radar on Draft Day. $

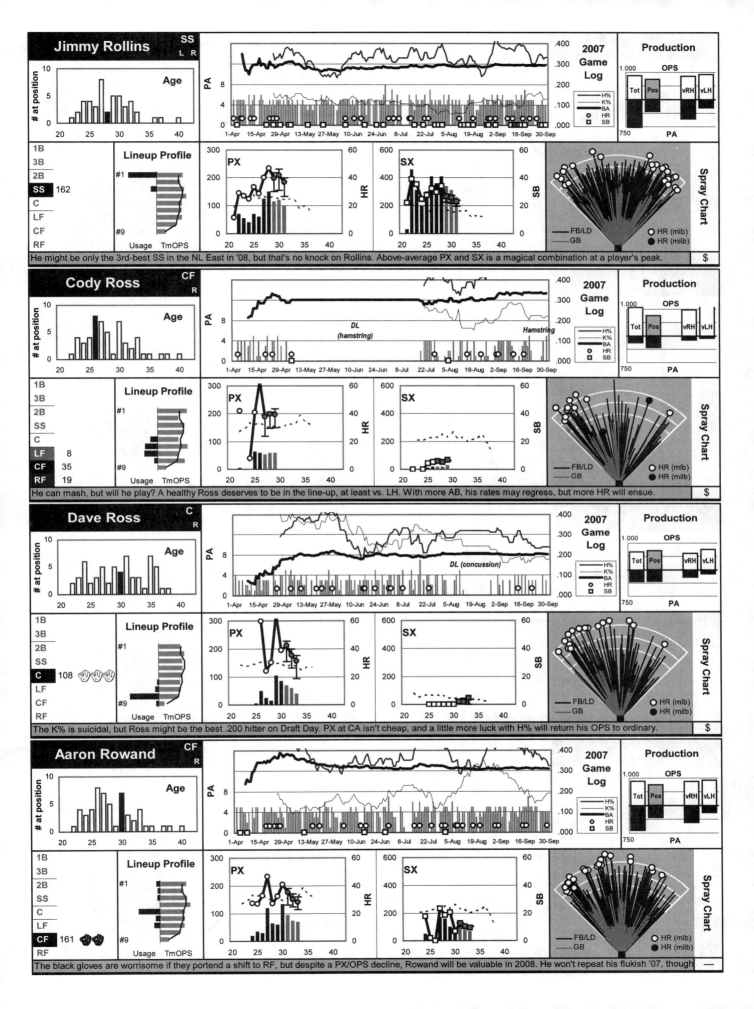

Jimmy Rollins SS L R

Age · PA · 2007 Game Log · Production · OPS · Spray Chart

Lineup Profile · PX · SX

1B 3B 2B SS 162 C LF CF RF · #1 ... #9 · Usage TmOPS

He might be only the 3rd-best SS in the NL East in '08, but that's no knock on Rollins. Above-average PX and SX is a magical combination at a player's peak. $

Cody Ross CF R

Age · PA · 2007 Game Log · Production · OPS · Spray Chart

DL (hamstring) · Hamstring

Lineup Profile · PX · SX

1B 3B 2B SS C LF 8 CF 35 RF 19 · #1 ... #9 · Usage TmOPS

He can mash, but will he play? A healthy Ross deserves to be in the line-up, at least vs. LH. With more AB, his rates may regress, but more HR will ensue. $

Dave Ross C R

Age · PA · 2007 Game Log · Production · OPS · Spray Chart

DL (concussion)

Lineup Profile · PX · SX

1B 3B 2B SS C 108 LF CF RF · #1 ... #9 · Usage TmOPS

The K% is suicidal, but Ross might be the best .200 hitter on Draft Day. PX at CA isn't cheap, and a little more luck with H% will return his OPS to ordinary. $

Aaron Rowand CF R

Age · PA · 2007 Game Log · Production · OPS · Spray Chart

Lineup Profile · PX · SX

1B 3B 2B SS C LF CF 161 RF · #1 ... #9 · Usage TmOPS

The black gloves are worrisome if they portend a shift to RF, but despite a PX/OPS decline, Rowand will be valuable in 2008. He won't repeat his flukish '07, though. —

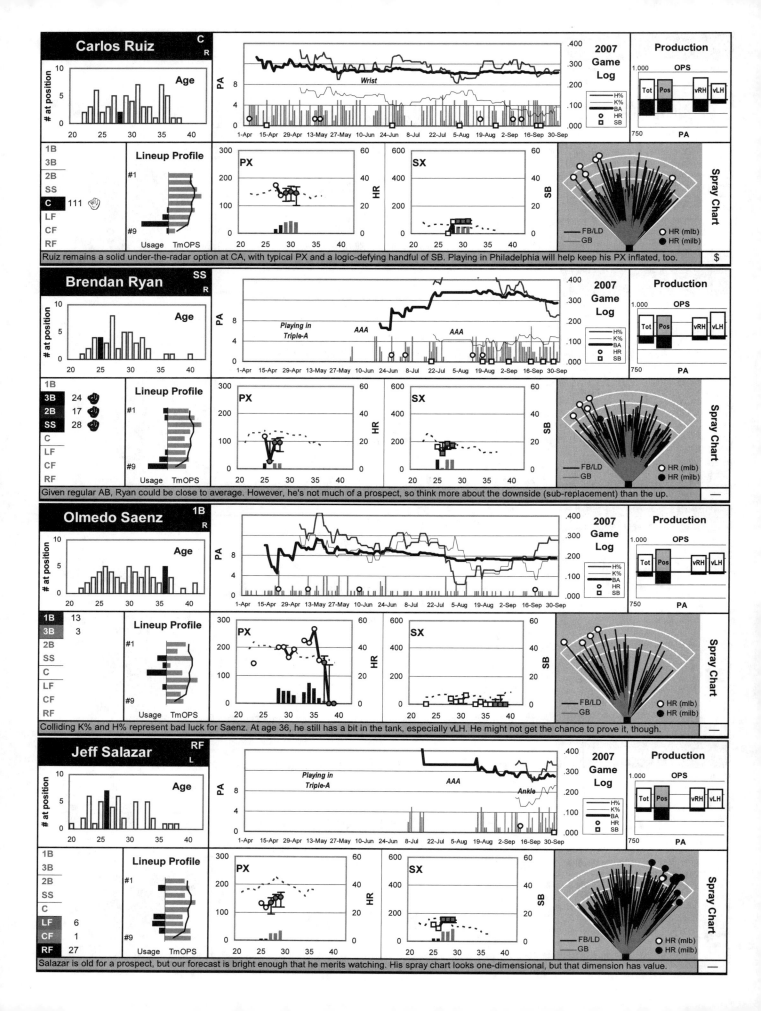

Carlos Ruiz — C, R

Age | # at position

2007 Game Log — PA, .400/.300/.200/.100/.000 — Wrist — H%, K%, BA, HR, SB

Production — OPS — 1.000 / 750 — Tot, Pos, vRH, vLH — PA

Positions: 1B, 3B, 2B, SS, **C 111**, LF, CF, RF

Lineup Profile — #1 ... #9 — Usage, TmOPS

PX — HR — SX — SB

Spray Chart — FB/LD, GB — HR (mlb) ○, HR (milb) ●

Ruiz remains a solid under-the-radar option at CA, with typical PX and a logic-defying handful of SB. Playing in Philadelphia will help keep his PX inflated, too. $

Brendan Ryan — SS, R

Age | # at position

2007 Game Log — Playing in Triple-A — AAA — AAA — H%, K%, BA, HR, SB

Production — OPS — 1.000 / 750 — Tot, Pos, vRH, vLH — PA

Positions: 1B, **3B 24**, **2B 17**, **SS 28**, C, LF, CF, RF

Lineup Profile — #1 ... #9 — Usage, TmOPS

PX — HR — SX — SB

Spray Chart — FB/LD, GB — HR (mlb) ○, HR (milb) ●

Given regular AB, Ryan could be close to average. However, he's not much of a prospect, so think more about the downside (sub-replacement) than the up. —

Olmedo Saenz — 1B, R

Age | # at position

2007 Game Log — H%, K%, BA, HR, SB

Production — OPS — 1.000 / 750 — Tot, Pos, vRH, vLH — PA

Positions: **1B 13**, **3B 3**, 2B, SS, C, LF, CF, RF

Lineup Profile — #1 ... #9 — Usage, TmOPS

PX — HR — SX — SB

Spray Chart — FB/LD, GB — HR (mlb) ○, HR (milb) ●

Colliding K% and H% represent bad luck for Saenz. At age 36, he still has a bit in the tank, especially vLH. He might not get the chance to prove it, though. —

Jeff Salazar — RF, L

Age | # at position

2007 Game Log — Playing in Triple-A — AAA — Ankle — H%, K%, BA, HR, SB

Production — OPS — 1.000 / 750 — Tot, Pos, vRH, vLH — PA

Positions: 1B, 3B, 2B, SS, C, **LF 6**, **CF 1**, **RF 27**

Lineup Profile — #1 ... #9 — Usage, TmOPS

PX — HR — SX — SB

Spray Chart — FB/LD, GB — HR (mlb) ○, HR (milb) ●

Salazar is old for a prospect, but our forecast is bright enough that he merits watching. His spray chart looks one-dimensional, but that dimension has value. —

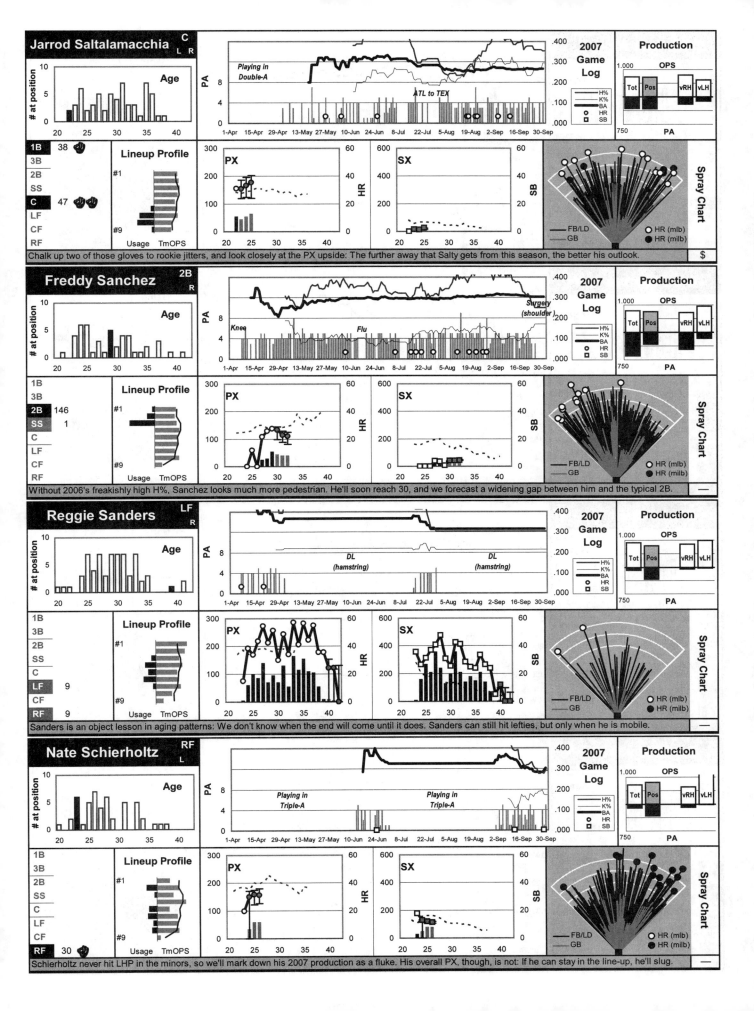

Jarrod Saltalamacchia C L R

Age · # at position

PA — Playing in Double-A — ATL to TEX

2007 Game Log — H% · K% · BA · ○ HR · □ SB

Production — OPS — Tot · Pos · vRH · vLH — PA

1B 38
3B
2B
SS
C 47
LF
CF
RF

Lineup Profile — #1 ... #9 — Usage · TmOPS

PX · HR
SX · SB
Spray Chart — FB/LD · GB — ○ HR (mlb) · ● HR (milb)

Chalk up two of those gloves to rookie jitters, and look closely at the PX upside: The further away that Salty gets from this season, the better his outlook. — $

Freddy Sanchez 2B R

Age · # at position

PA — Knee · Flu · Surgery (shoulder)

2007 Game Log — H% · K% · BA · ○ HR · □ SB

Production — OPS — Tot · Pos · vRH · vLH — PA

1B
3B
2B 146
SS 1
C
LF
CF
RF

Lineup Profile — #1 ... #9 — Usage · TmOPS

PX · HR
SX · SB
Spray Chart — FB/LD · GB — ○ HR (mlb) · ● HR (milb)

Without 2006's freakishly high H%, Sanchez looks much more pedestrian. He'll soon reach 30, and we forecast a widening gap between him and the typical 2B. — —

Reggie Sanders LF R

Age · # at position

PA — DL (hamstring) · DL (hamstring)

2007 Game Log — H% · K% · BA · ○ HR · □ SB

Production — OPS — Tot · Pos · vRH · vLH — PA

1B
3B
2B
SS
C
LF 9
CF
RF 9

Lineup Profile — #1 ... #9 — Usage · TmOPS

PX · HR
SX · SB
Spray Chart — FB/LD · GB — ○ HR (mlb) · ● HR (milb)

Sanders is an object lesson in aging patterns: We don't know when the end will come until it does. Sanders can still hit lefties, but only when he is mobile. — —

Nate Schierholtz RF L

Age · # at position

PA — Playing in Triple-A · Playing in Triple-A

2007 Game Log — H% · K% · BA · ○ HR · □ SB

Production — OPS — Tot · Pos · vRH · vLH — PA

1B
3B
2B
SS
C
LF
CF
RF 30

Lineup Profile — #1 ... #9 — Usage · TmOPS

PX · HR
SX · SB
Spray Chart — FB/LD · GB — ○ HR (mlb) · ● HR (milb)

Schierholtz never hit LHP in the minors, so we'll mark down his 2007 production as a fluke. His overall PX, though, is not: If he can stay in the line-up, he'll slug. — —

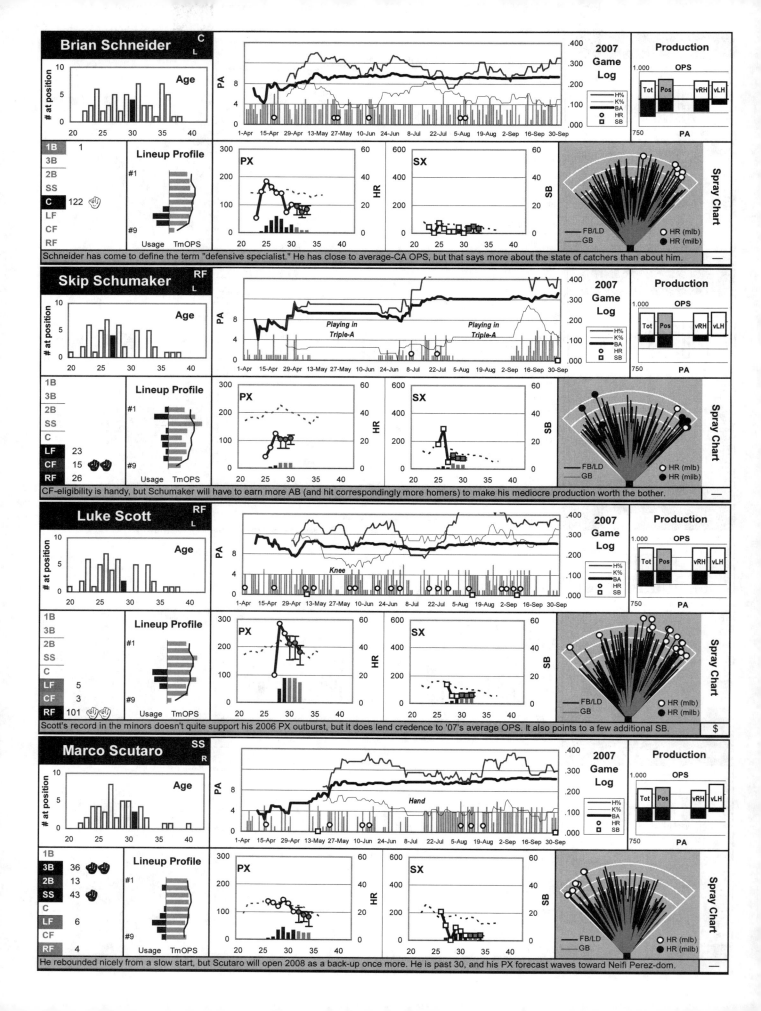

Brian Schneider
C
L

Age | # at position (20–40)

2007 Game Log — PA / H% / K% / BA / ○ HR / □ SB — (.400 / .300 / .200 / .100 / .000), dates 1-Apr to 30-Sep

Production — OPS: Tot, Pos, vRH, vLH (1.000 / .750), PA

Position	
1B	1
3B	
2B	
SS	
C	122
LF	
CF	
RF	

Lineup Profile (#1 to #9) — Usage / TmOPS

PX (0–300, HR 0–60), **SX** (0–600, SB 0–60)

Spray Chart — FB/LD, GB, ○ HR (mlb), ● HR (milb)

Schneider has come to define the term "defensive specialist." He has close to average-CA OPS, but that says more about the state of catchers than about him. — —

Skip Schumaker
RF
L

Age | # at position (20–40)

2007 Game Log — *Playing in Triple-A* (×2), PA / H% / K% / BA / ○ HR / □ SB, dates 1-Apr to 30-Sep

Production — OPS: Tot, Pos, vRH, vLH (1.000 / .750), PA

Position	
1B	
3B	
2B	
SS	
C	
LF	23
CF	15
RF	26

Lineup Profile (#1 to #9) — Usage / TmOPS

PX, **SX**

Spray Chart — FB/LD, GB, ○ HR (mlb), ● HR (milb)

CF-eligibility is handy, but Schumaker will have to earn more AB (and hit correspondingly more homers) to make his mediocre production worth the bother. — —

Luke Scott
RF
L

Age | # at position (20–40)

2007 Game Log — *Knee*, PA / H% / K% / BA / ○ HR / □ SB, dates 1-Apr to 30-Sep

Production — OPS: Tot, Pos, vRH, vLH (1.000 / .750), PA

Position	
1B	
3B	
2B	
SS	
C	
LF	5
CF	3
RF	101

Lineup Profile (#1 to #9) — Usage / TmOPS

PX, **SX**

Spray Chart — FB/LD, GB, ○ HR (mlb), ● HR (milb)

Scott's record in the minors doesn't quite support his 2006 PX outburst, but it does lend credence to '07's average OPS. It also points to a few additional SB. — $

Marco Scutaro
SS
R

Age | # at position (20–40)

2007 Game Log — *Hand*, PA / H% / K% / BA / ○ HR / □ SB, dates 1-Apr to 30-Sep

Production — OPS: Tot, Pos, vRH, vLH (1.000 / .750), PA

Position	
1B	
3B	36
2B	13
SS	43
C	
LF	6
CF	
RF	4

Lineup Profile (#1 to #9) — Usage / TmOPS

PX, **SX**

Spray Chart — FB/LD, GB, ○ HR (mlb), ● HR (milb)

He rebounded nicely from a slow start, but Scutaro will open 2008 as a back-up once more. He is past 30, and his PX forecast waves toward Neifi Perez-dom. — —

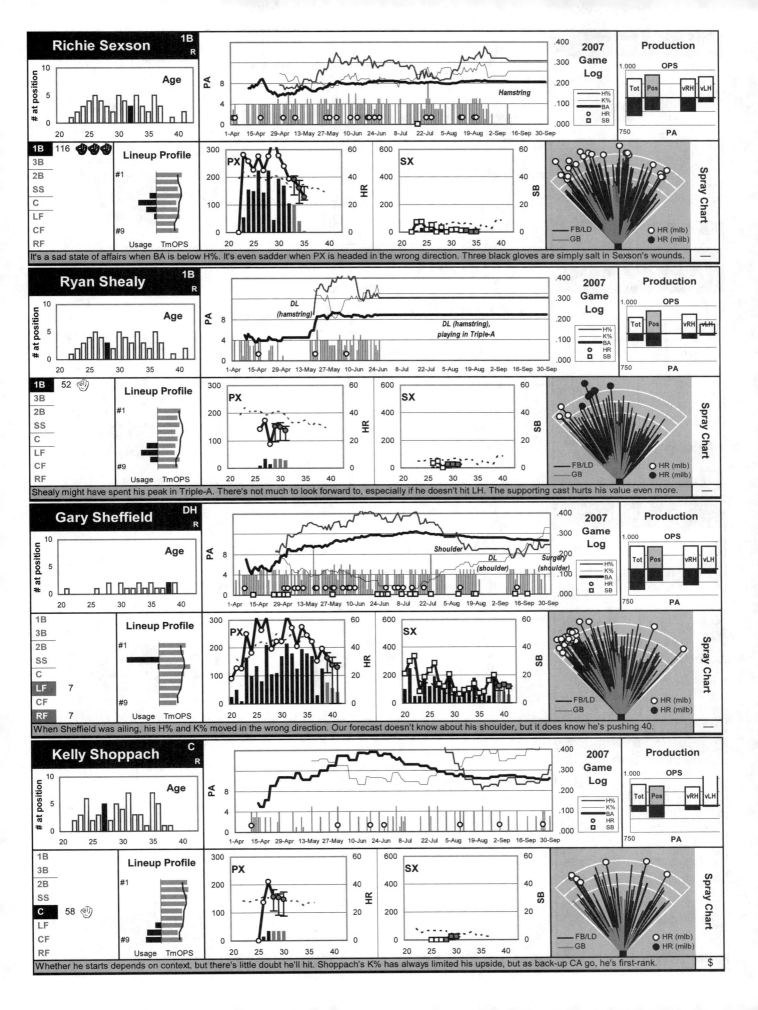

Richie Sexson   1B / R

It's a sad state of affairs when BA is below H%. It's even sadder when PX is headed in the wrong direction. Three black gloves are simply salt in Sexson's wounds.

Ryan Shealy   1B / R

Shealy might have spent his peak in Triple-A. There's not much to look forward to, especially if he doesn't hit LH. The supporting cast hurts his value even more.

Gary Sheffield   DH / R

When Sheffield was ailing, his H% and K% moved in the wrong direction. Our forecast doesn't know about his shoulder, but it does know he's pushing 40.

Kelly Shoppach   C / R

Whether he starts depends on context, but there's little doubt he'll hit. Shoppach's K% has always limited his upside, but as back-up CA go, he's first-rank.

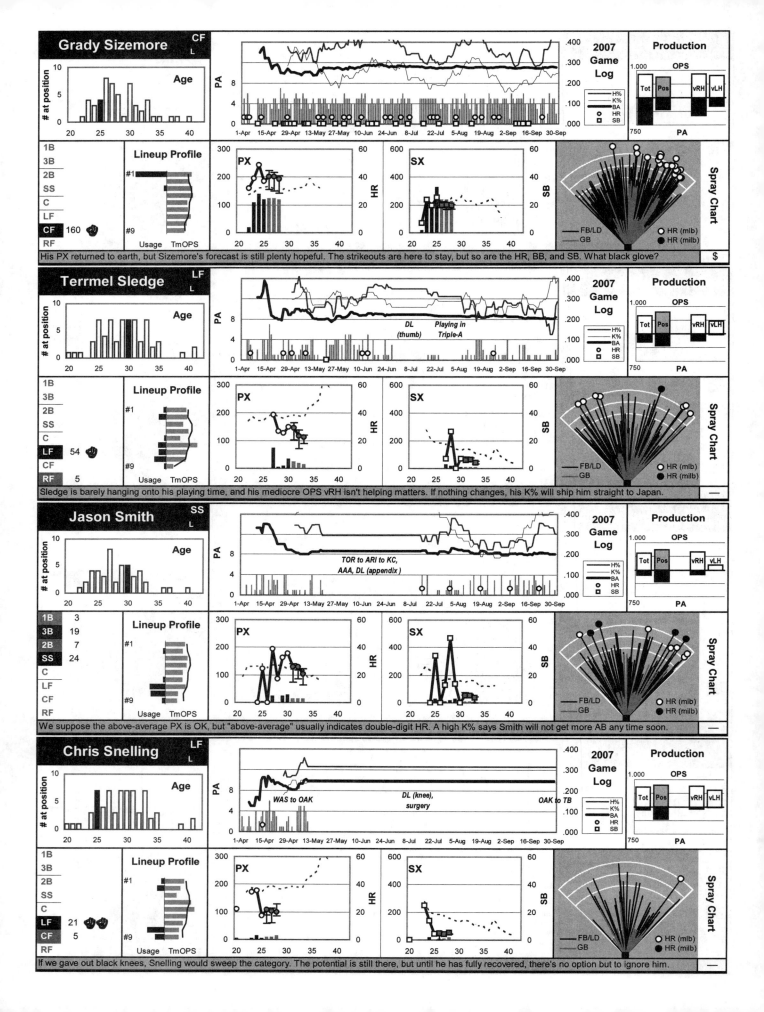

Grady Sizemore CF L

Age

2007 Game Log

Production — OPS

1B
3B
2B
SS
C
LF
CF 160
RF

Lineup Profile

#1
#9
Usage TmOPS

PX

SX

Spray Chart
FB/LD
GB
HR (mlb) ○
HR (milb) ●

His PX returned to earth, but Sizemore's forecast is still plenty hopeful. The strikeouts are here to stay, but so are the HR, BB, and SB. What black glove? | $

Terrmel Sledge LF L

Age

DL (thumb)   Playing in Triple-A

2007 Game Log

Production — OPS

1B
3B
2B
SS
C
LF 54
CF
RF 5

Lineup Profile

#1
#9
Usage TmOPS

PX

SX

Spray Chart
FB/LD
GB
HR (mlb) ○
HR (milb) ●

Sledge is barely hanging onto his playing time, and his mediocre OPS vRH isn't helping matters. If nothing changes, his K% will ship him straight to Japan. | —

Jason Smith SS L

Age

TOR to ARI to KC, AAA, DL (appendix)

2007 Game Log

Production — OPS

1B 3
3B 19
2B 7
SS 24
C
LF
CF
RF

Lineup Profile

#1
#9
Usage TmOPS

PX

SX

Spray Chart
FB/LD
GB
HR (mlb) ○
HR (milb) ●

We suppose the above-average PX is OK, but "above-average" usually indicates double-digit HR. A high K% says Smith will not get more AB any time soon. | —

Chris Snelling LF L

Age

WAS to OAK   DL (knee), surgery   OAK to TB

2007 Game Log

Production — OPS

1B
3B
2B
SS
C
LF 21
CF 5
RF

Lineup Profile

#1
#9
Usage TmOPS

PX

SX

Spray Chart
FB/LD
GB
HR (mlb) ○
HR (milb) ●

If we gave out black knees, Snelling would sweep the category. The potential is still there, but until he has fully recovered, there's no option but to ignore him. | —

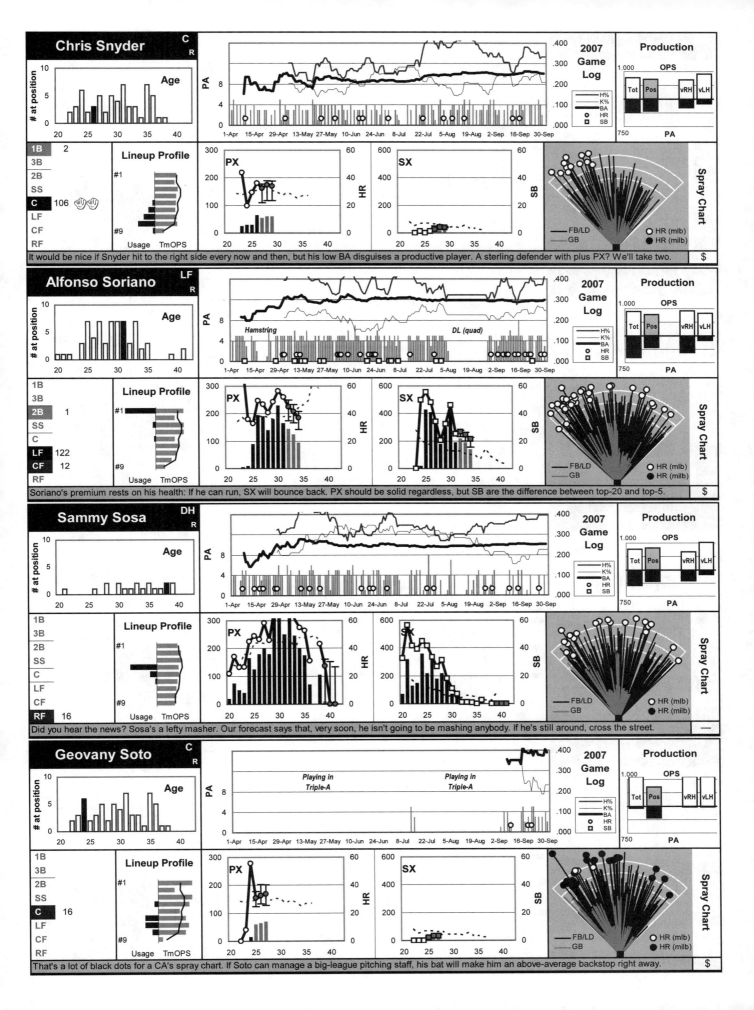

Chris Snyder C R

Age

2007 Game Log

Production — OPS

1B 2
3B
2B
SS
C 106
LF
CF
RF

Lineup Profile
#1
#9
Usage TmOPS

PX

SX

Spray Chart
FB/LD
GB
O HR (mlb)
● HR (milb)

It would be nice if Snyder hit to the right side every now and then, but his low BA disguises a productive player. A sterling defender with plus PX? We'll take two. $

Alfonso Soriano LF R

Age

2007 Game Log

Hamstring   *DL (quad)*

Production — OPS

1B
3B
2B 1
SS
C
LF 122
CF 12
RF

Lineup Profile
#1
#9
Usage TmOPS

PX

SX

Spray Chart
FB/LD
GB
O HR (mlb)
● HR (milb)

Soriano's premium rests on his health: If he can run, SX will bounce back. PX should be solid regardless, but SB are the difference between top-20 and top-5. $

Sammy Sosa DH R

Age

2007 Game Log

Production — OPS

1B
3B
2B
SS
C
LF
CF
RF 16

Lineup Profile
#1
#9
Usage TmOPS

PX

SX

Spray Chart
FB/LD
GB
O HR (mlb)
● HR (milb)

Did you hear the news? Sosa's a lefty masher. Our forecast says that, very soon, he isn't going to be mashing anybody. If he's still around, cross the street. —

Geovany Soto C R

Age

2007 Game Log

Playing in Triple-A   *Playing in Triple-A*

Production — OPS

1B
3B
2B
SS
C 16
LF
CF
RF

Lineup Profile
#1
#9
Usage TmOPS

PX

SX

Spray Chart
FB/LD
GB
O HR (mlb)
● HR (milb)

That's a lot of black dots for a CA's spray chart. If Soto can manage a big-league pitching staff, his bat will make him an above-average backstop right away. $

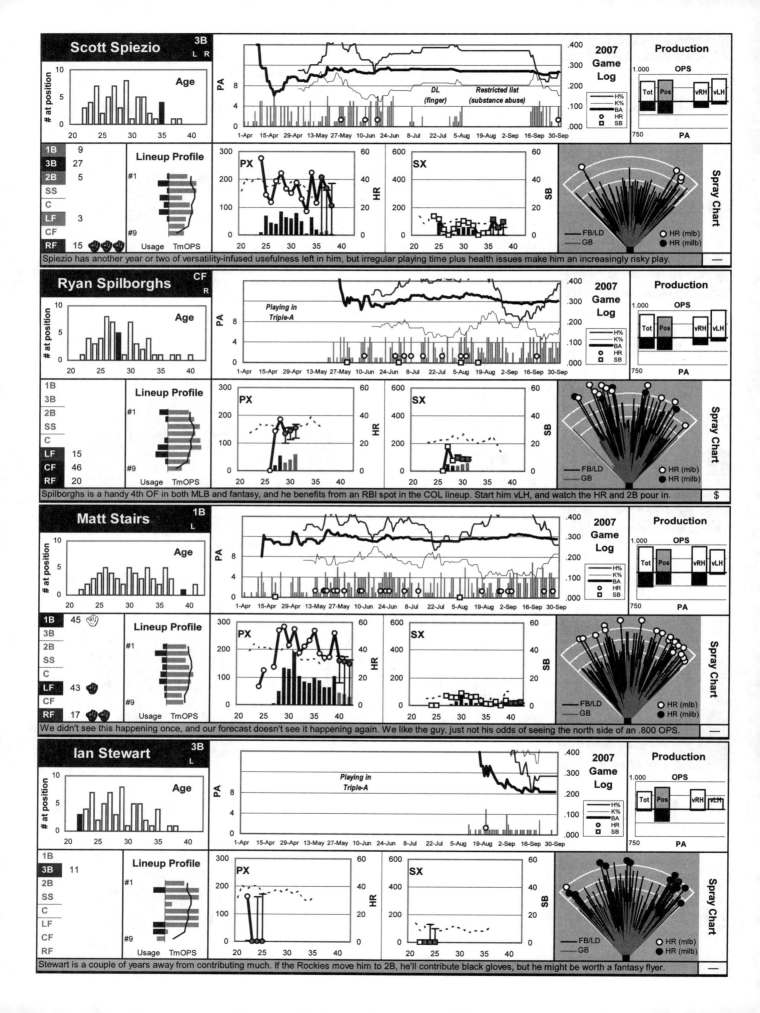

Scott Spiezio — 3B (L R)

at position | Age
1B 9
3B 27
2B 5
SS
C
LF 3
CF
RF 15

2007 Game Log — H% / K% / BA / HR / SB
DL (finger) Restricted list (substance abuse)

Production — OPS: Tot, Pos, vRH, vLH | PA

Lineup Profile — #1 ... #9 — Usage / TmOPS

PX / HR — SX / SB — Spray Chart — FB/LD, GB, HR (mlb), HR (milb)

Spiezio has another year or two of versatility-infused usefulness left in him, but irregular playing time plus health issues make him an increasingly risky play. —

Ryan Spilborghs — CF (R)

at position | Age
1B
3B
2B
SS
C
LF 15
CF 46
RF 20

2007 Game Log — Playing in Triple-A — H% / K% / BA / HR / SB

Production — OPS: Tot, Pos, vRH, vLH | PA

Lineup Profile — #1 ... #9 — Usage / TmOPS

PX / HR — SX / SB — Spray Chart — FB/LD, GB, HR (mlb), HR (milb)

Spilborghs is a handy 4th OF in both MLB and fantasy, and he benefits from an RBI spot in the COL lineup. Start him vLH, and watch the HR and 2B pour in. $

Matt Stairs — 1B (L)

at position | Age
1B 45
3B
2B
SS
C
LF 43
CF
RF 17

2007 Game Log — H% / K% / BA / HR / SB

Production — OPS: Tot, Pos, vRH, vLH | PA

Lineup Profile — #1 ... #9 — Usage / TmOPS

PX / HR — SX / SB — Spray Chart — FB/LD, GB, HR (mlb), HR (milb)

We didn't see this happening once, and our forecast doesn't see it happening again. We like the guy, just not his odds of seeing the north side of an .800 OPS. —

Ian Stewart — 3B (L)

at position | Age
1B
3B 11
2B
SS
C
LF
CF
RF

2007 Game Log — Playing in Triple-A — H% / K% / BA / HR / SB

Production — OPS: Tot, Pos, vRH, vLH | PA

Lineup Profile — #1 ... #9 — Usage / TmOPS

PX / HR — SX / SB — Spray Chart — FB/LD, GB, HR (mlb), HR (milb)

Stewart is a couple of years away from contributing much. If the Rockies move him to 2B, he'll contribute black gloves, but he might be worth a fantasy flyer. —

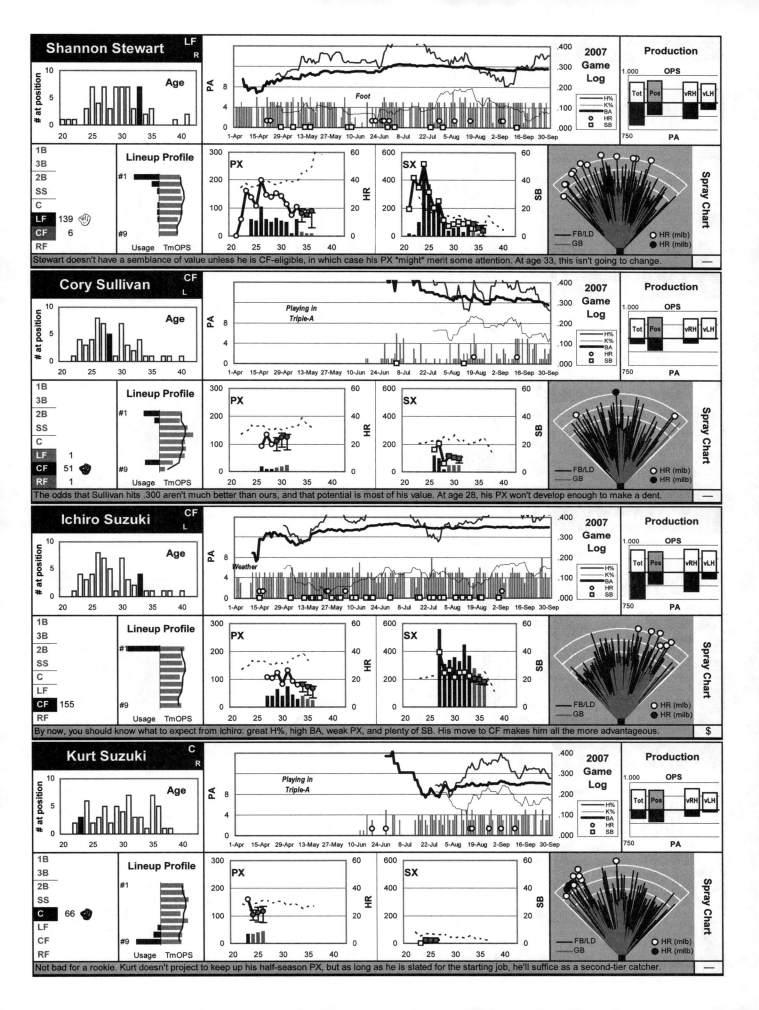

Shannon Stewart — LF / R

Age · # at position · PA · 2007 Game Log · Production · OPS · Lineup Profile · Spray Chart

Positions: 1B, 3B, 2B, SS, C, LF 139, CF 6, RF

PX · SX · HR · SB

H% · K% · BA · HR · SB · Foot

Tot · Pos · vRH · vLH · PA

FB/LD · GB · HR (mlb) · HR (milb)

Stewart doesn't have a semblance of value unless he is CF-eligible, in which case his PX *might* merit some attention. At age 33, this isn't going to change. —

Cory Sullivan — CF / L

Playing in Triple-A

Positions: 1B, 3B, 2B, SS, C, LF 1, CF 51, RF 1

The odds that Sullivan hits .300 aren't much better than ours, and that potential is most of his value. At age 28, his PX won't develop enough to make a dent. —

Ichiro Suzuki — CF / L

Weather

Positions: CF 155

By now, you should know what to expect from Ichiro: great H%, high BA, weak PX, and plenty of SB. His move to CF makes him all the more advantageous. $

Kurt Suzuki — C / R

Playing in Triple-A

Positions: C 66

Not bad for a rookie. Kurt doesn't project to keep up his half-season PX, but as long as he is slated for the starting job, he'll suffice as a second-tier catcher. —

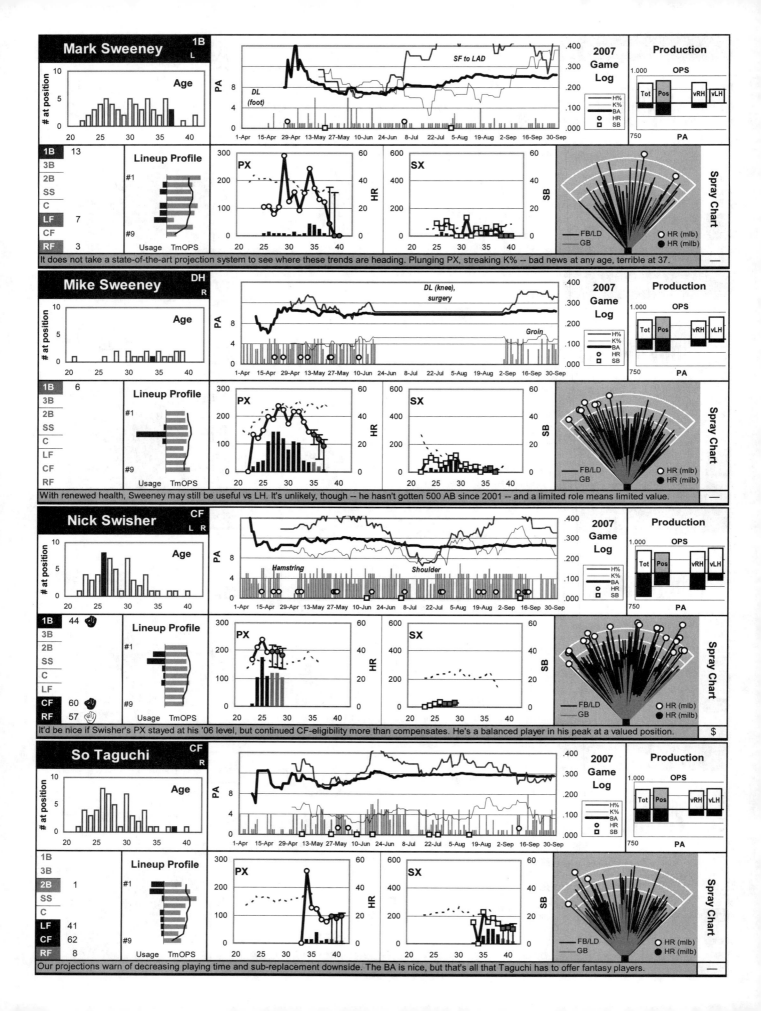

Mark Sweeney 1B L

Age | PA | 2007 Game Log | Production OPS

1B 13 / 3B / 2B / SS / C / LF 7 / CF / RF 3

Lineup Profile — Usage / TmOPS — #1 ... #9

SF to LAD — DL (foot)

H% / K% / BA / HR / SB

PX — HR | SX — SB | Spray Chart — FB/LD, GB, HR (mlb), HR (milb)

It does not take a state-of-the-art projection system to see where these trends are heading. Plunging PX, streaking K% -- bad news at any age, terrible at 37. —

Mike Sweeney DH R

Age | PA | 2007 Game Log | Production OPS

1B 6 / 3B / 2B / SS / C / LF / CF / RF

Lineup Profile — Usage / TmOPS — #1 ... #9

DL (knee), surgery — Groin

H% / K% / BA / HR / SB

PX — HR | SX — SB | Spray Chart — FB/LD, GB, HR (mlb), HR (milb)

With renewed health, Sweeney may still be useful vs LH. It's unlikely, though -- he hasn't gotten 500 AB since 2001 -- and a limited role means limited value. —

Nick Swisher CF L R

Age | PA | 2007 Game Log | Production OPS

1B 44 / 3B / 2B / SS / C / LF / CF 60 / RF 57

Lineup Profile — Usage / TmOPS — #1 ... #9

Hamstring — Shoulder

H% / K% / BA / HR / SB

PX — HR | SX — SB | Spray Chart — FB/LD, GB, HR (mlb), HR (milb)

It'd be nice if Swisher's PX stayed at his '06 level, but continued CF-eligibility more than compensates. He's a balanced player in his peak at a valued position. $

So Taguchi CF R

Age | PA | 2007 Game Log | Production OPS

1B / 3B / 2B 1 / SS / C / LF 41 / CF 62 / RF 8

Lineup Profile — Usage / TmOPS — #1 ... #9

H% / K% / BA / HR / SB

PX — HR | SX — SB | Spray Chart — FB/LD, GB, HR (mlb), HR (milb)

Our projections warn of decreasing playing time and sub-replacement downside. The BA is nice, but that's all that Taguchi has to offer fantasy players. —

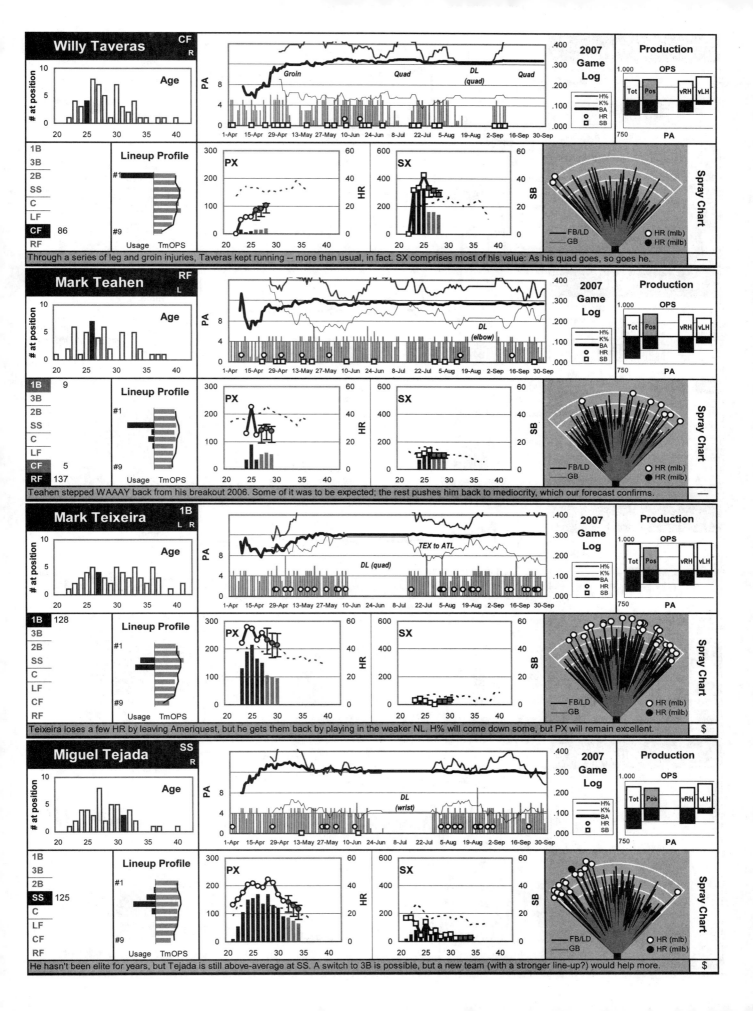

Willy Taveras CF R

Age
at position

2007 Game Log
Production
OPS
Tot | Pos | vRH | vLH
PA

Groin   Quad   DL (quad)   Quad

H%
K%
BA
○ HR
□ SB

1B
3B
2B
SS
C
LF
CF 86
RF

Lineup Profile
#1
#9
Usage TmOPS

PX
HR

SX
SB

Spray Chart
FB/LD
GB
○ HR (mlb)
● HR (milb)

Through a series of leg and groin injuries, Taveras kept running -- more than usual, in fact. SX comprises most of his value: As his quad goes, so goes he. | —

Mark Teahen RF L

Age
at position

2007 Game Log
Production
OPS
Tot | Pos | vRH | vLH
PA

DL (elbow)

H%
K%
BA
○ HR
□ SB

1B 9
3B
2B
SS
C
LF
CF 5
RF 137

Lineup Profile
#1
#9
Usage TmOPS

PX
HR

SX
SB

Spray Chart
FB/LD
GB
○ HR (mlb)
● HR (milb)

Teahen stepped WAAAY back from his breakout 2006. Some of it was to be expected; the rest pushes him back to mediocrity, which our forecast confirms. | —

Mark Teixeira 1B L R

Age
at position

2007 Game Log
Production
OPS
Tot | Pos | vRH | vLH
PA

DL (quad)   TEX to ATL

H%
K%
BA
○ HR
□ SB

1B 128
3B
2B
SS
C
LF
CF
RF

Lineup Profile
#1
#9
Usage TmOPS

PX
HR

SX
SB

Spray Chart
FB/LD
GB
○ HR (mlb)
● HR (milb)

Teixeira loses a few HR by leaving Ameriquest, but he gets them back by playing in the weaker NL. H% will come down some, but PX will remain excellent. | $

Miguel Tejada SS R

Age
at position

2007 Game Log
Production
OPS
Tot | Pos | vRH | vLH
PA

DL (wrist)

H%
K%
BA
○ HR
□ SB

1B
3B
2B
SS 125
C
LF
CF
RF

Lineup Profile
#1
#9
Usage TmOPS

PX
HR

SX
SB

Spray Chart
FB/LD
GB
○ HR (mlb)
● HR (milb)

He hasn't been elite for years, but Tejada is still above-average at SS. A switch to 3B is possible, but a new team (with a stronger line-up?) would help more. | $

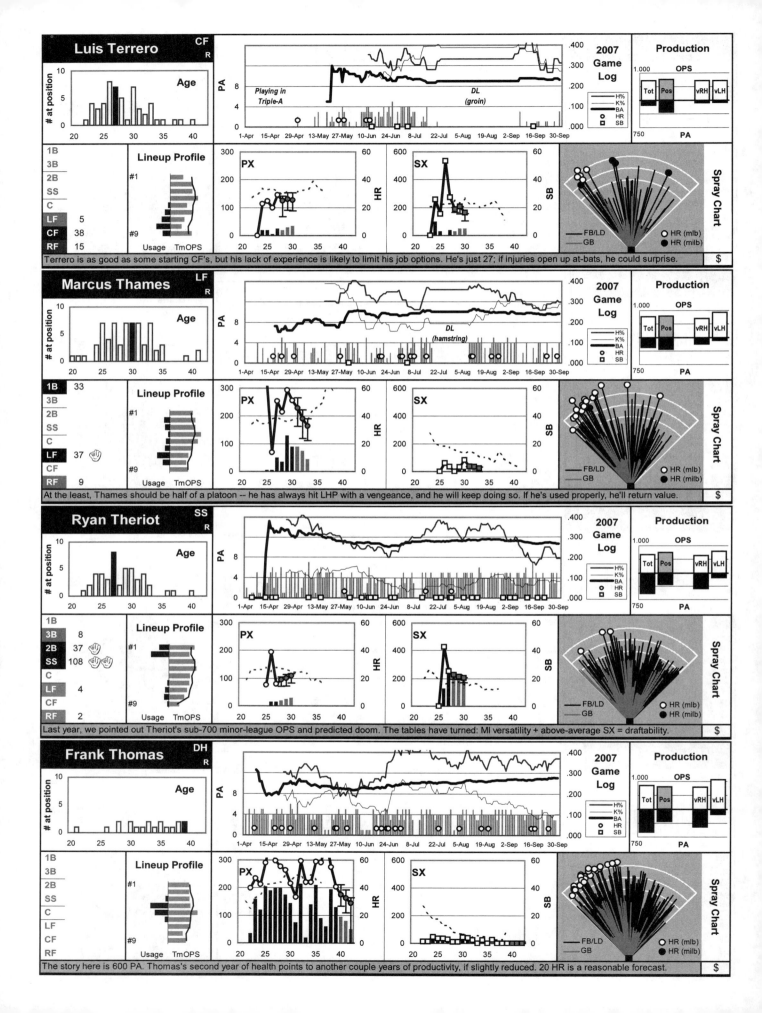

Luis Terrero — CF, R

Age | # at position (20–40)

2007 Game Log | PA / .400 .300 .200 .100 .000 — H%, K%, BA, HR (○), SB (□)
- *Playing in Triple-A*
- *DL (groin)*

Production — OPS (1.000 / 750): Tot, Pos, vRH, vLH | PA

Position usage:
- LF 5
- CF 38
- RF 15

Lineup Profile (#1 to #9) — Usage / TmOPS

PX (20–40, 0–300 / 0–60 HR) — FB/LD, GB
SX (20–40, 0–600 / 0–60 SB)

Spray Chart — FB/LD, GB; HR (mlb) ○, HR (milb) ●

Terrero is as good as some starting CF's, but his lack of experience is likely to limit his job options. He's just 27; if injuries open up at-bats, he could surprise. — $

Marcus Thames — LF, R

Age | # at position (20–40)

2007 Game Log | .400 .300 .200 .100 .000 — H%, K%, BA, HR (○), SB (□)
- *DL (hamstring)*

Production — OPS: Tot, Pos, vRH, vLH | PA

Position usage:
- 1B 33
- LF 37
- RF 9

Lineup Profile — Usage / TmOPS

PX | **SX**

Spray Chart — HR (mlb) ○, HR (milb) ●

At the least, Thames should be half of a platoon -- he has always hit LHP with a vengeance, and he will keep doing so. If he's used properly, he'll return value. — $

Ryan Theriot — SS, R

Age | # at position (20–40)

2007 Game Log | .400 .300 .200 .100 .000 — H%, K%, BA, HR (○), SB (□)

Production — OPS: Tot, Pos, vRH, vLH | PA

Position usage:
- 3B 8
- 2B 37
- SS 108
- LF 4
- RF 2

Lineup Profile — Usage / TmOPS

PX | **SX**

Spray Chart — HR (mlb) ○, HR (milb) ●

Last year, we pointed out Theriot's sub-700 minor-league OPS and predicted doom. The tables have turned: MI versatility + above-average SX = draftability. — $

Frank Thomas — DH, R

Age | # at position (20–40)

2007 Game Log | .400 .300 .200 .100 .000 — H%, K%, BA, HR (○), SB (□)

Production — OPS: Tot, Pos, vRH, vLH | PA

Position usage: 1B, 3B, 2B, SS, C, LF, CF, RF

Lineup Profile — Usage / TmOPS

PX | **SX**

Spray Chart — HR (mlb) ○, HR (milb) ●

The story here is 600 PA. Thomas's second year of health points to another couple years of productivity, if slightly reduced. 20 HR is a reasonable forecast. — $

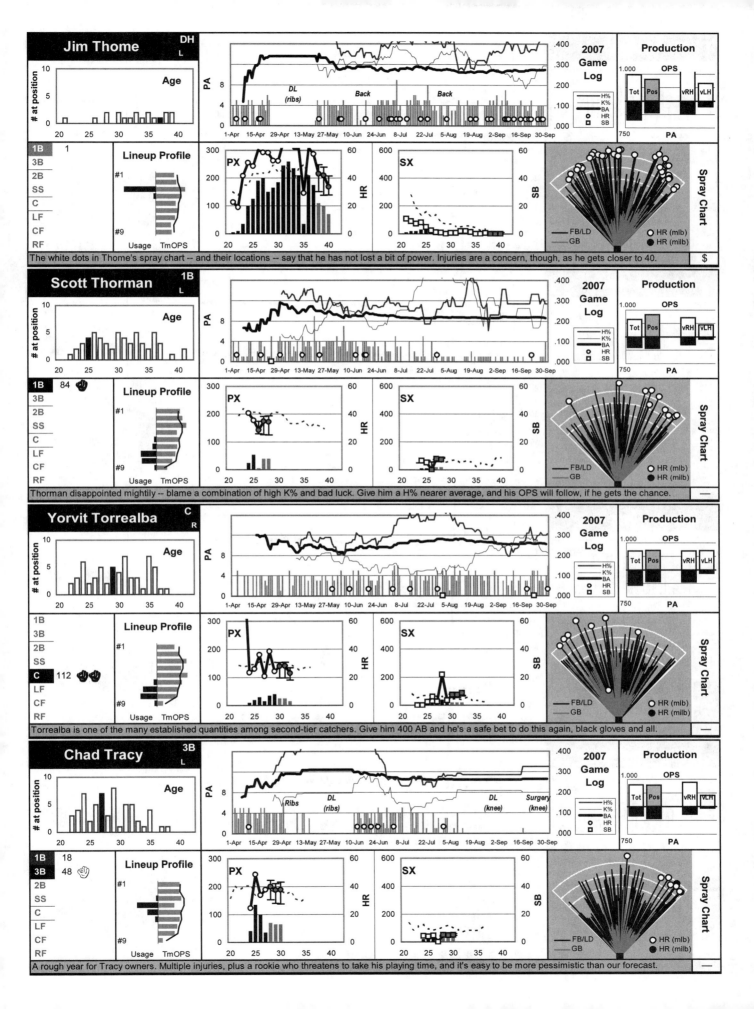

Jim Thome — DH / L

1B 1

Age | Lineup Profile | PX | SX | Spray Chart

2007 Game Log — H%, K%, BA, HR, SB

DL (ribs) — Back — Back

Production — OPS — Tot, Pos, vRH, vLH — PA

FB/LD, GB — HR (mlb), HR (milb)

The white dots in Thome's spray chart -- and their locations -- say that he has not lost a bit of power. Injuries are a concern, though, as he gets closer to 40.   **$**

Scott Thorman — 1B / L

1B 84

Age | Lineup Profile | PX | SX | Spray Chart

2007 Game Log — H%, K%, BA, HR, SB

Production — OPS — Tot, Pos, vRH, vLH — PA

FB/LD, GB — HR (mlb), HR (milb)

Thorman disappointed mightily -- blame a combination of high K% and bad luck. Give him a H% nearer average, and his OPS will follow, if he gets the chance.   **—**

Yorvit Torrealba — C / R

C 112

Age | Lineup Profile | PX | SX | Spray Chart

2007 Game Log — H%, K%, BA, HR, SB

Production — OPS — Tot, Pos, vRH, vLH — PA

FB/LD, GB — HR (mlb), HR (milb)

Torrealba is one of the many established quantities among second-tier catchers. Give him 400 AB and he's a safe bet to do this again, black gloves and all.   **—**

Chad Tracy — 3B / L

1B 18   **3B** 48

Age | Lineup Profile | PX | SX | Spray Chart

2007 Game Log — H%, K%, BA, HR, SB

Ribs — DL (ribs) — DL (knee) — Surgery (knee)

Production — OPS — Tot, Pos, vRH, vLH — PA

FB/LD, GB — HR (mlb), HR (milb)

A rough year for Tracy owners. Multiple injuries, plus a rookie who threatens to take his playing time, and it's easy to be more pessimistic than our forecast.   **—**

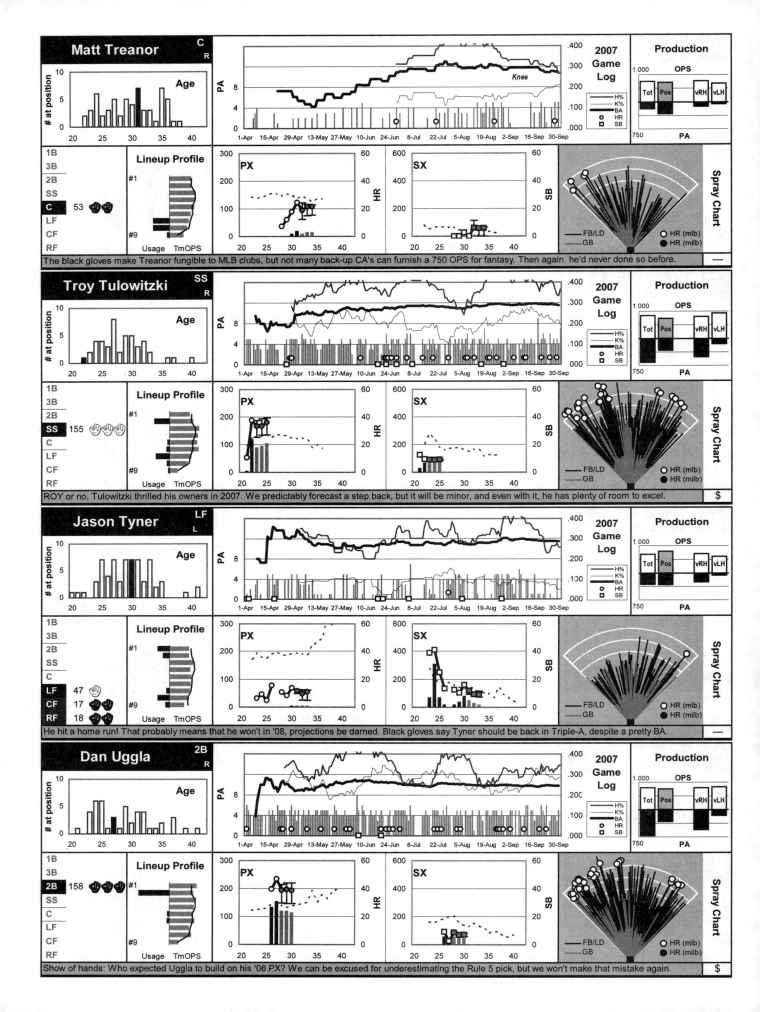

Matt Treanor C R

Age

2007 Game Log

Production — OPS

H% / K% / BA / HR / SB

Lineup Profile

C 53

PX | SX | Spray Chart

FB/LD / GB / HR (mlb) / HR (milb)

The black gloves make Treanor fungible to MLB clubs, but not many back-up CA's can furnish a 750 OPS for fantasy. Then again, he'd never done so before. —

Troy Tulowitzki SS R

Age

2007 Game Log

Production — OPS

Lineup Profile

SS 155

PX | SX | Spray Chart

ROY or no, Tulowitzki thrilled his owners in 2007. We predictably forecast a step back, but it will be minor, and even with it, he has plenty of room to excel. $

Jason Tyner LF L

Age

2007 Game Log

Production — OPS

Lineup Profile

LF 47
CF 17
RF 18

PX | SX | Spray Chart

He hit a home run! That probably means that he won't in '08, projections be darned. Black gloves say Tyner should be back in Triple-A, despite a pretty BA. —

Dan Uggla 2B R

Age

2007 Game Log

Production — OPS

Lineup Profile

2B 158

PX | SX | Spray Chart

Show of hands: Who expected Uggla to build on his '06 PX? We can be excused for underestimating the Rule 5 pick, but we won't make that mistake again. $

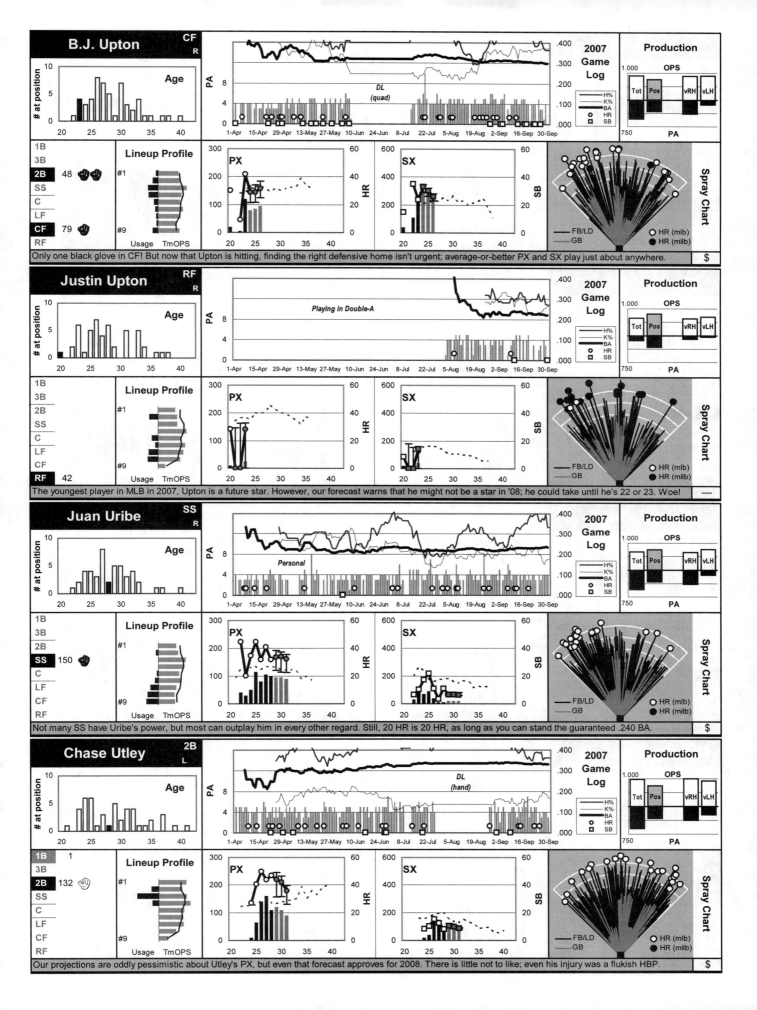

B.J. Upton — CF / R

at position / Age

2B 48 / CF 79

Lineup Profile — #1 ... #9 — Usage / TmOPS

PA / DL (quad)

2007 Game Log
- H%
- K%
- BA
- ○ HR
- □ SB

Production — OPS — Tot / Pos / vRH / vLH — 1.000 / 750 — PA

PX / HR — SX / SB

Spray Chart — FB/LD / GB — ○ HR (mlb) / ● HR (milb)

Only one black glove in CF! But now that Upton is hitting, finding the right defensive home isn't urgent; average-or-better PX and SX play just about anywhere. — $

Justin Upton — RF / R

at position / Age

RF 42

Lineup Profile — #1 ... #9 — Usage / TmOPS

PA / Playing in Double-A

2007 Game Log
- H%
- K%
- BA
- ○ HR
- □ SB

Production — OPS — Tot / Pos / vRH / vLH — 1.000 / 750 — PA

PX / HR — SX / SB

Spray Chart — FB/LD / GB — ○ HR (mlb) / ● HR (milb)

The youngest player in MLB in 2007, Upton is a future star. However, our forecast warns that he might not be a star in '08; he could take until he's 22 or 23. Woe! — —

Juan Uribe — SS / R

at position / Age

SS 150

Lineup Profile — #1 ... #9 — Usage / TmOPS

PA / Personal

2007 Game Log
- H%
- K%
- BA
- ○ HR
- □ SB

Production — OPS — Tot / Pos / vRH / vLH — 1.000 / 750 — PA

PX / HR — SX / SB

Spray Chart — FB/LD / GB — ○ HR (mlb) / ● HR (milb)

Not many SS have Uribe's power, but most can outplay him in every other regard. Still, 20 HR is 20 HR, as long as you can stand the guaranteed .240 BA. — $

Chase Utley — 2B / L

at position / Age

1B 1 / 2B 132

Lineup Profile — #1 ... #9 — Usage / TmOPS

PA / DL (hand)

2007 Game Log
- H%
- K%
- BA
- ○ HR
- □ SB

Production — OPS — Tot / Pos / vRH / vLH — 1.000 / 750 — PA

PX / HR — SX / SB

Spray Chart — FB/LD / GB — ○ HR (mlb) / ● HR (milb)

Our projections are oddly pessimistic about Utley's PX, but even that forecast approves for 2008. There is little not to like; even his injury was a flukish HBP. — $

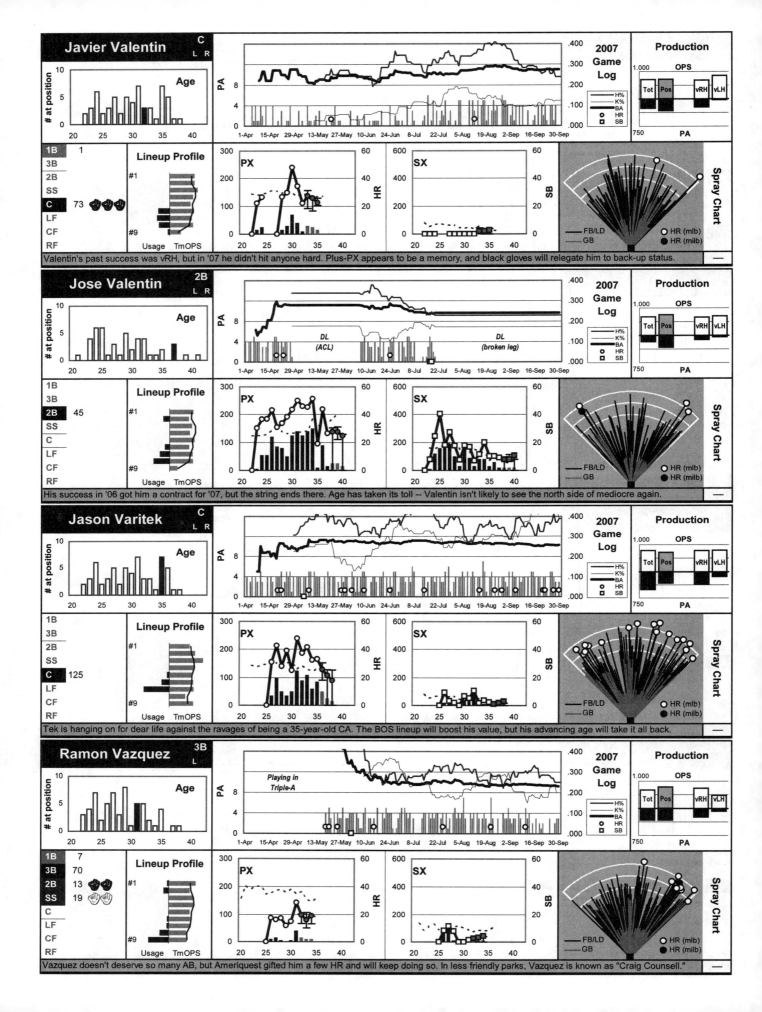

Javier Valentin — C / L R

at position · Age · 20 25 30 35 40

PA · 2007 Game Log · Production

1-Apr 15-Apr 29-Apr 13-May 27-May 10-Jun 24-Jun 8-Jul 22-Jul 5-Aug 19-Aug 2-Sep 16-Sep 30-Sep

.400 / .300 / .200 / .100 / .000

H% · K% · BA · HR · SB

OPS · 1.000 · Tot · Pos · vRH · vLH · 750 · PA

1B	1
3B	
2B	
SS	
C	73
LF	
CF	
RF	

Lineup Profile · #1 · #9 · Usage · TmOPS

PX · SX · Spray Chart

FB/LD · GB · HR (mlb) · HR (milb)

Valentin's past success was vRH, but in '07 he didn't hit anyone hard. Plus-PX appears to be a memory, and black gloves will relegate him to back-up status.

Jose Valentin — 2B / L R

at position · Age · 20 25 30 35 40

PA · 2007 Game Log · Production

DL (ACL) · DL (broken leg)

1-Apr 15-Apr 29-Apr 13-May 27-May 10-Jun 24-Jun 8-Jul 22-Jul 5-Aug 19-Aug 2-Sep 16-Sep 30-Sep

.400 / .300 / .200 / .100 / .000

H% · K% · BA · HR · SB

OPS · 1.000 · Tot · Pos · vRH · vLH · 750 · PA

1B	
3B	
2B	45
SS	
C	
LF	
CF	
RF	

Lineup Profile · #1 · #9 · Usage · TmOPS

PX · SX · Spray Chart

FB/LD · GB · HR (mlb) · HR (milb)

His success in '06 got him a contract for '07, but the string ends there. Age has taken its toll -- Valentin isn't likely to see the north side of mediocre again.

Jason Varitek — C / L R

at position · Age · 20 25 30 35 40

PA · 2007 Game Log · Production

1-Apr 15-Apr 29-Apr 13-May 27-May 10-Jun 24-Jun 8-Jul 22-Jul 5-Aug 19-Aug 2-Sep 16-Sep 30-Sep

.400 / .300 / .200 / .100 / .000

H% · K% · BA · HR · SB

OPS · 1.000 · Tot · Pos · vRH · vLH · 750 · PA

1B	
3B	
2B	
SS	
C	125
LF	
CF	
RF	

Lineup Profile · #1 · #9 · Usage · TmOPS

PX · SX · Spray Chart

FB/LD · GB · HR (mlb) · HR (milb)

Tek is hanging on for dear life against the ravages of being a 35-year-old CA. The BOS lineup will boost his value, but his advancing age will take it all back.

Ramon Vazquez — 3B / L

at position · Age · 20 25 30 35 40

PA · 2007 Game Log · Production

Playing in Triple-A

1-Apr 15-Apr 29-Apr 13-May 27-May 10-Jun 24-Jun 8-Jul 22-Jul 5-Aug 19-Aug 2-Sep 16-Sep 30-Sep

.400 / .300 / .200 / .100 / .000

H% · K% · BA · HR · SB

OPS · 1.000 · Tot · Pos · vRH · vLH · 750 · PA

1B	7
3B	70
2B	13
SS	19
C	
LF	
CF	
RF	

Lineup Profile · #1 · #9 · Usage · TmOPS

PX · SX · Spray Chart

FB/LD · GB · HR (mlb) · HR (milb)

Vazquez doesn't deserve so many AB, but Ameriquest gifted him a few HR and will keep doing so. In less friendly parks, Vazquez is known as "Craig Counsell."

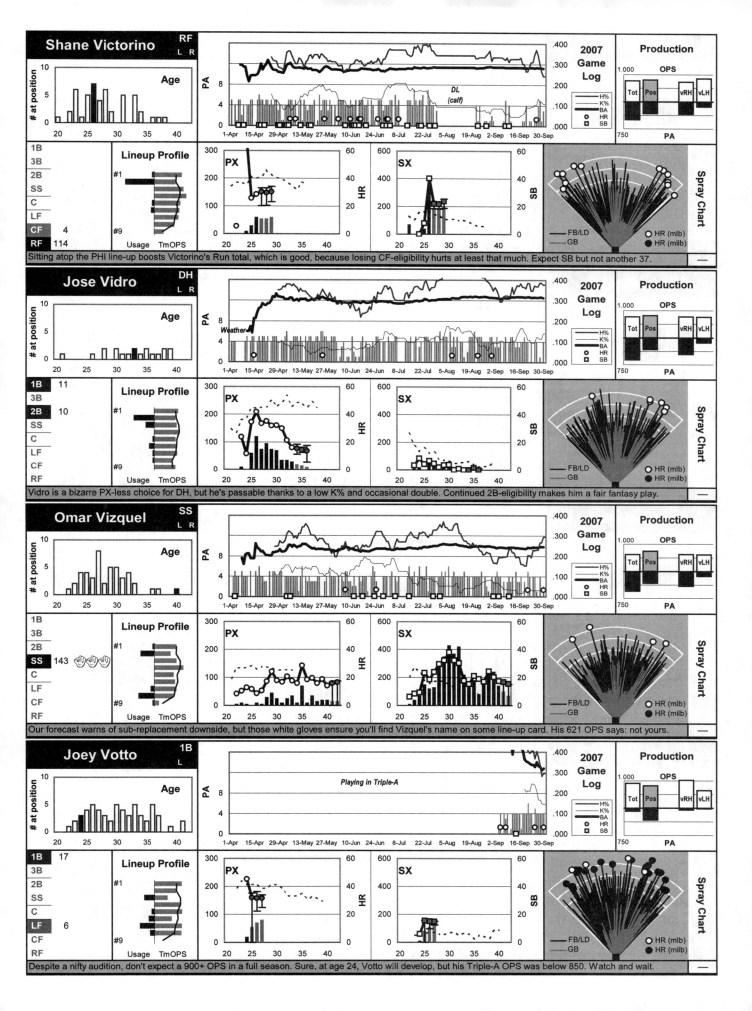

Shane Victorino — RF (L/R)

Age | **2007 Game Log** | **Production — OPS**

Positions: CF 4, RF 114

Lineup Profile (Usage / TmOPS), PX, SX, Spray Chart (FB/LD, GB; HR (mlb), HR (milb))

DL (calf)

Sitting atop the PHI line-up boosts Victorino's Run total, which is good, because losing CF-eligibility hurts at least that much. Expect SB but not another 37.

Jose Vidro — DH (L/R)

Age | **2007 Game Log** | **Production — OPS**

Positions: 1B 11, 2B 10

Weather

Vidro is a bizarre PX-less choice for DH, but he's passable thanks to a low K% and occasional double. Continued 2B-eligibility makes him a fair fantasy play.

Omar Vizquel — SS (L/R)

Age | **2007 Game Log** | **Production — OPS**

Positions: SS 143

Our forecast warns of sub-replacement downside, but those white gloves ensure you'll find Vizquel's name on some line-up card. His 621 OPS says: not yours.

Joey Votto — 1B (L)

Age | **2007 Game Log** | **Production — OPS**

Playing in Triple-A

Positions: 1B 17, LF 6

Despite a nifty audition, don't expect a 900+ OPS in a full season. Sure, at age 24, Votto will develop, but his Triple-A OPS was below 850. Watch and wait.

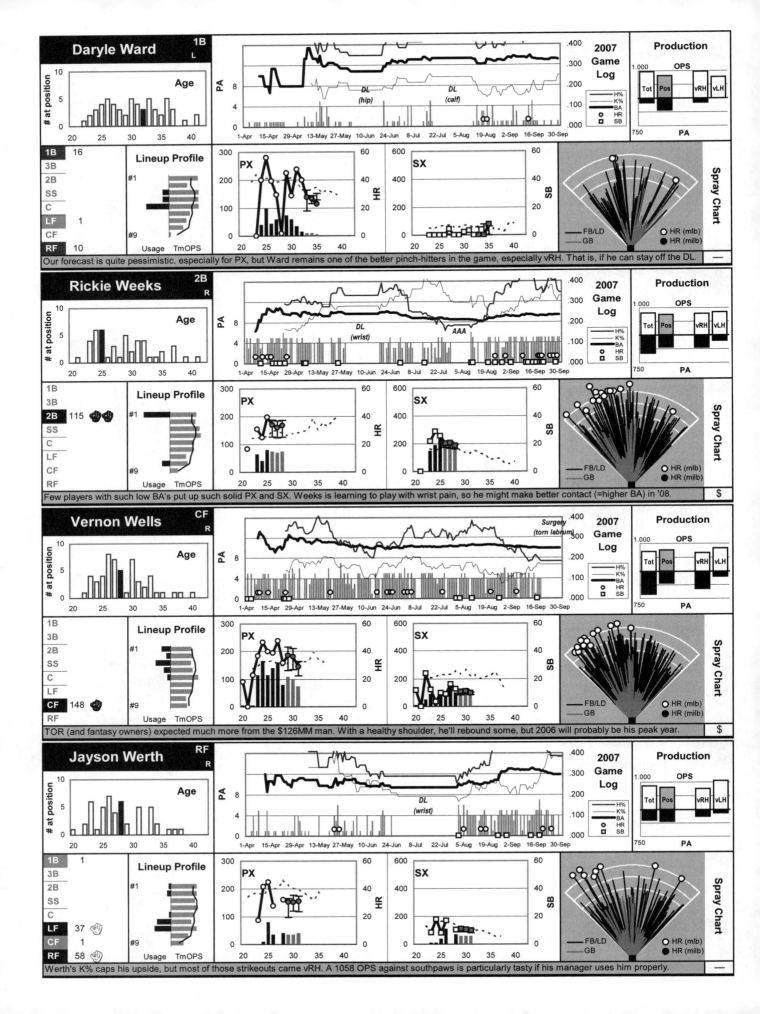

Daryle Ward 1B L

Age / # at position

PA — 2007 Game Log
H% / K% / BA / HR / SB

Production — OPS — Tot / Pos / vRH / vLH — PA

1B 16
3B
2B
SS
C
LF 1
CF
RF 10

Lineup Profile — #1 / #9 — Usage / TmOPS

PX — HR
SX — SB
FB/LD / GB — HR (mlb) / HR (milb) — Spray Chart

Our forecast is quite pessimistic, especially for PX, but Ward remains one of the better pinch-hitters in the game, especially vRH. That is, if he can stay off the DL. —

Rickie Weeks 2B R

Age / # at position

PA — 2007 Game Log — DL (wrist) / AAA
H% / K% / BA / HR / SB

Production — OPS — Tot / Pos / vRH / vLH — PA

1B
3B
2B 115
SS
C
LF
CF
RF

Lineup Profile — #1 / #9 — Usage / TmOPS

PX — HR
SX — SB
FB/LD / GB — HR (mlb) / HR (milb) — Spray Chart

Few players with such low BA's put up such solid PX and SX. Weeks is learning to play with wrist pain, so he might make better contact (=higher BA) in '08. $

Vernon Wells CF R

Age / # at position

PA — 2007 Game Log — Surgery (torn labrum)
H% / K% / BA / HR / SB

Production — OPS — Tot / Pos / vRH / vLH — PA

1B
3B
2B
SS
C
LF
CF 148
RF

Lineup Profile — #1 / #9 — Usage / TmOPS

PX — HR
SX — SB
FB/LD / GB — HR (mlb) / HR (milb) — Spray Chart

TOR (and fantasy owners) expected much more from the $126MM man. With a healthy shoulder, he'll rebound some, but 2006 will probably be his peak year. $

Jayson Werth RF R

Age / # at position

PA — 2007 Game Log — DL (wrist)
H% / K% / BA / HR / SB

Production — OPS — Tot / Pos / vRH / vLH — PA

1B 1
3B
2B
SS
C
LF 37
CF 1
RF 58

Lineup Profile — #1 / #9 — Usage / TmOPS

PX — HR
SX — SB
FB/LD / GB — HR (mlb) / HR (milb) — Spray Chart

Werth's K% caps his upside, but most of those strikeouts came vRH. A 1058 OPS against southpaws is particularly tasty if his manager uses him properly. —

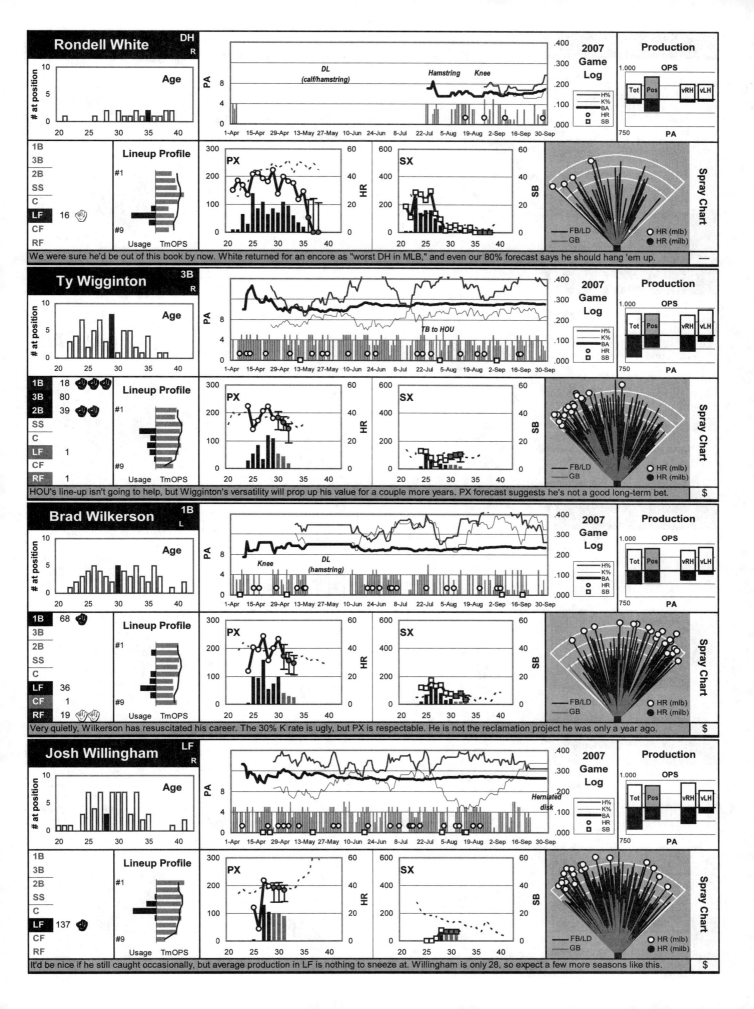

Rondell White — DH / R

2007 Game Log — DL (calf/hamstring), Hamstring, Knee

H% / K% / BA / HR / SB

Production — OPS: Tot, Pos, vRH, vLH — PA

LF 16

Lineup Profile — Usage / TmOPS — #1 / #9

PX / HR · SX / SB

Spray Chart — FB/LD / GB — HR (mlb) / HR (milb)

We were sure he'd be out of this book by now. White returned for an encore as "worst DH in MLB," and even our 80% forecast says he should hang 'em up. —

Ty Wigginton — 3B / R

2007 Game Log — TB to HOU

H% / K% / BA / HR / SB

Production — OPS: Tot, Pos, vRH, vLH — PA

1B 18
3B 80
2B 39
SS
C
LF 1
CF
RF 1

Lineup Profile — Usage / TmOPS — #1 / #9

PX / HR · SX / SB

Spray Chart — FB/LD / GB — HR (mlb) / HR (milb)

HOU's line-up isn't going to help, but Wigginton's versatility will prop up his value for a couple more years. PX forecast suggests he's not a good long-term bet. $

Brad Wilkerson — 1B / L

2007 Game Log — Knee, DL (hamstring)

H% / K% / BA / HR / SB

Production — OPS: Tot, Pos, vRH, vLH — PA

1B 68
3B
2B
SS
C
LF 36
CF 1
RF 19

Lineup Profile — Usage / TmOPS — #1 / #9

PX / HR · SX / SB

Spray Chart — FB/LD / GB — HR (mlb) / HR (milb)

Very quietly, Wilkerson has resuscitated his career. The 30% K rate is ugly, but PX is respectable. He is not the reclamation project he was only a year ago. $

Josh Willingham — LF / R

2007 Game Log — Herniated disk

H% / K% / BA / HR / SB

Production — OPS: Tot, Pos, vRH, vLH — PA

1B
3B
2B
SS
C
LF 137
CF
RF

Lineup Profile — Usage / TmOPS — #1 / #9

PX / HR · SX / SB

Spray Chart — FB/LD / GB — HR (mlb) / HR (milb)

It'd be nice if he still caught occasionally, but average production in LF is nothing to sneeze at. Willingham is only 28, so expect a few more seasons like this. $

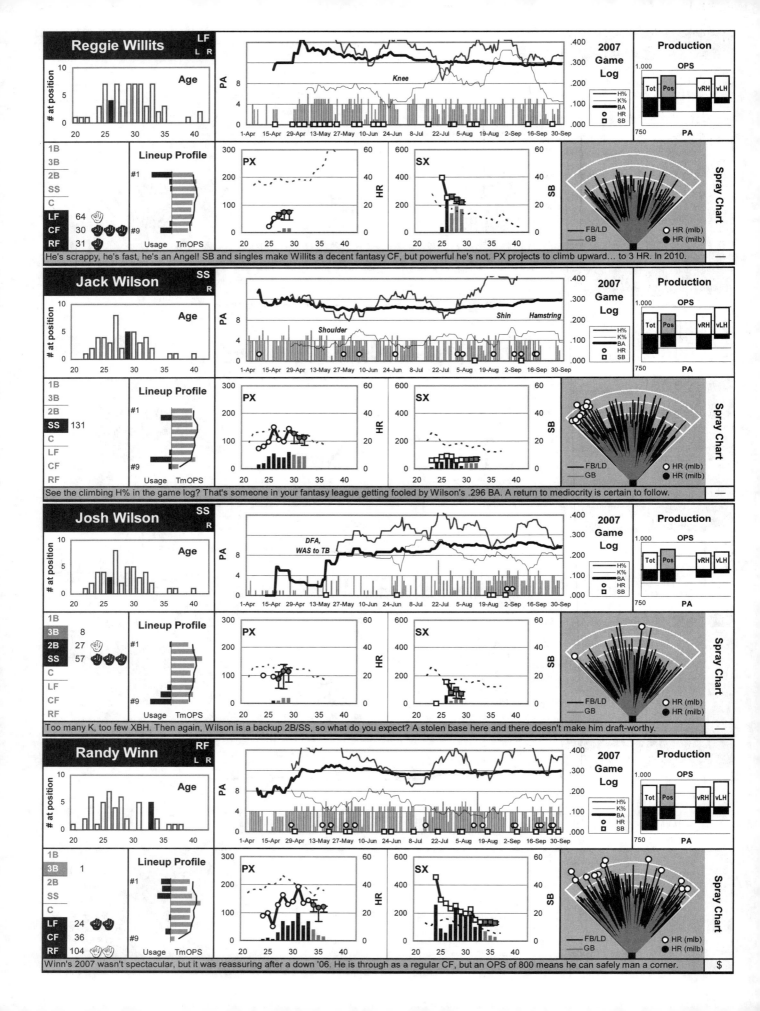

Reggie Willits — LF / L R

Age | **2007 Game Log** | **Production — OPS**

He's scrappy, he's fast, he's an Angel! SB and singles make Willits a decent fantasy CF, but powerful he's not. PX projects to climb upward... to 3 HR. In 2010. | —

Lineup Profile · Usage · TmOPS · PX · SX · Spray Chart

1B / 3B / 2B / SS / C / **LF 64** / **CF 30** / **RF 31**

Knee

Jack Wilson — SS / R

Age | **2007 Game Log** | **Production — OPS**

See the climbing H% in the game log? That's someone in your fantasy league getting fooled by Wilson's .296 BA. A return to mediocrity is certain to follow. | —

1B / 3B / 2B / **SS 131** / C / LF / CF / RF

Shoulder · Shin · Hamstring

Josh Wilson — SS / R

Age | **2007 Game Log** | **Production — OPS**

Too many K, too few XBH. Then again, Wilson is a backup 2B/SS, so what do you expect? A stolen base here and there doesn't make him draft-worthy. | —

1B / **3B 8** / **2B 27** / **SS 57** / C / LF / CF / RF

DFA, WAS to TB

Randy Winn — RF / L R

Age | **2007 Game Log** | **Production — OPS**

Winn's 2007 wasn't spectacular, but it was reassuring after a down '06. He is through as a regular CF, but an OPS of 800 means he can safely man a corner. | $

1B / **3B 1** / 2B / SS / C / **LF 24** / **CF 36** / **RF 104**

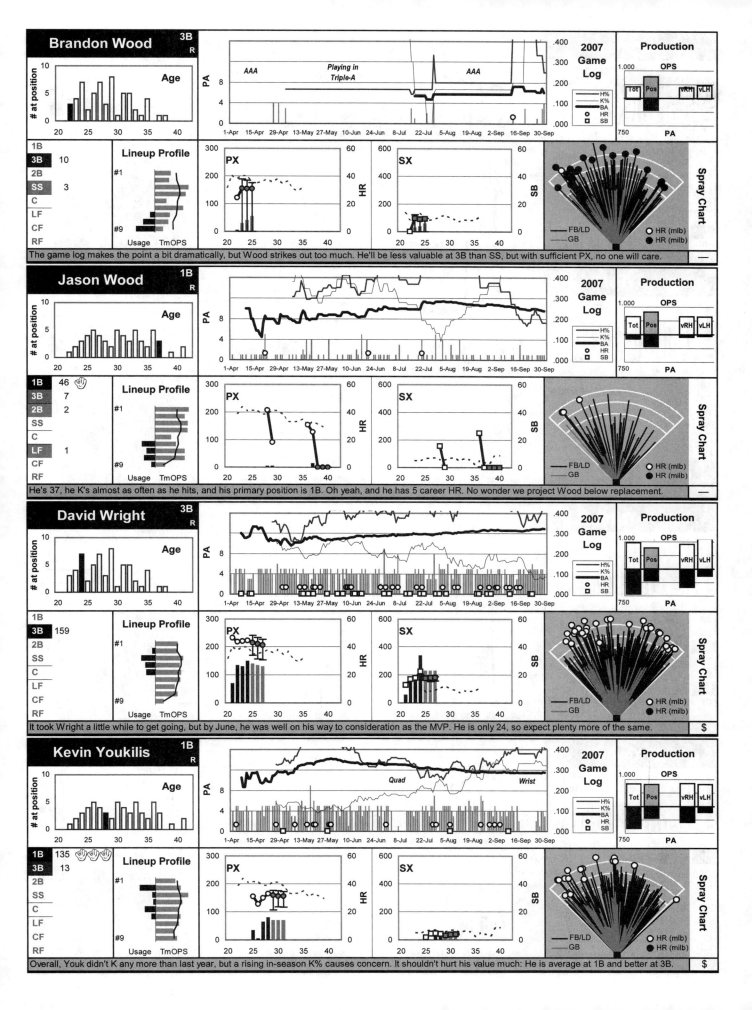

Brandon Wood — 3B / R

2007 Game Log

AAA — Playing in Triple-A — AAA

Production — OPS

Age

Lineup Profile — Usage / TmOPS

1B	
3B	10
2B	
SS	3
C	
LF	
CF	
RF	

PX · HR · SX · SB · Spray Chart

H% · K% · BA · HR · SB
FB/LD · GB · HR (mlb) · HR (milb)

The game log makes the point a bit dramatically, but Wood strikes out too much. He'll be less valuable at 3B than SS, but with sufficient PX, no one will care. — —

Jason Wood — 1B / R

2007 Game Log

Production — OPS

Age

Lineup Profile — Usage / TmOPS

1B	46
3B	7
2B	2
SS	
C	
LF	1
CF	
RF	

PX · HR · SX · SB · Spray Chart

H% · K% · BA · HR · SB
FB/LD · GB · HR (mlb) · HR (milb)

He's 37, he K's almost as often as he hits, and his primary position is 1B. Oh yeah, and he has 5 career HR. No wonder we project Wood below replacement. — —

David Wright — 3B / R

2007 Game Log

Production — OPS

Age

Lineup Profile — Usage / TmOPS

1B	
3B	159
2B	
SS	
C	
LF	
CF	
RF	

PX · HR · SX · SB · Spray Chart

H% · K% · BA · HR · SB
FB/LD · GB · HR (mlb) · HR (milb)

It took Wright a little while to get going, but by June, he was well on his way to consideration as the MVP. He is only 24, so expect plenty more of the same. — $

Kevin Youkilis — 1B / R

2007 Game Log

Quad — Wrist

Production — OPS

Age

Lineup Profile — Usage / TmOPS

1B	135
3B	13
2B	
SS	
C	
LF	
CF	
RF	

PX · HR · SX · SB · Spray Chart

H% · K% · BA · HR · SB
FB/LD · GB · HR (mlb) · HR (milb)

Overall, Youk didn't K any more than last year, but a rising in-season K% causes concern. It shouldn't hurt his value much: He is average at 1B and better at 3B. — $

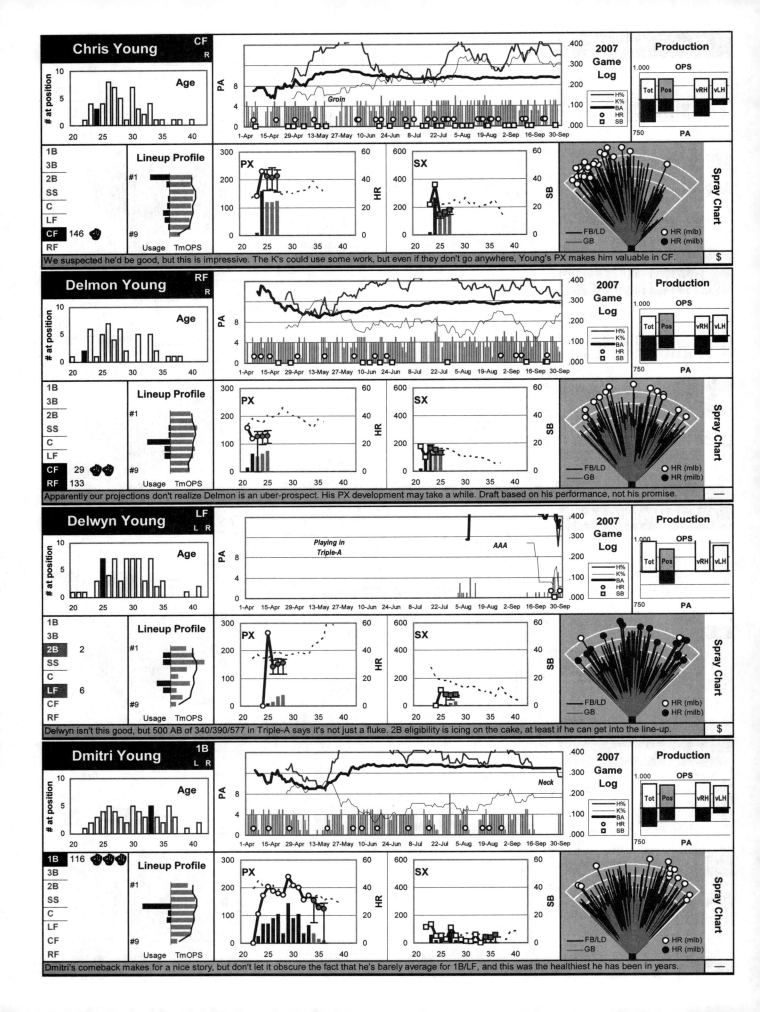

Chris Young CF
R

Age

at position

PA

Groin

2007 Game Log

H%
K%
BA
HR
SB

Production
OPS
1.000

Tot | Pos | vRH | vLH

750   PA

1B
3B
2B
SS
C
LF
CF 146
RF

Lineup Profile
#1

#9
Usage TmOPS

PX

HR

SX

SB

FB/LD
GB

HR (mlb)
HR (milb)

Spray Chart

We suspected he'd be good, but this is impressive. The K's could use some work, but even if they don't go anywhere, Young's PX makes him valuable in CF. $

Delmon Young RF
R

Age

at position

PA

2007 Game Log

H%
K%
BA
HR
SB

Production
OPS
1.000

Tot | Pos | vRH | vLH

750   PA

1B
3B
2B
SS
C
LF
CF 29
RF 133

Lineup Profile
#1

#9
Usage TmOPS

PX

HR

SX

SB

FB/LD
GB

HR (mlb)
HR (milb)

Spray Chart

Apparently our projections don't realize Delmon is an uber-prospect. His PX development may take a while. Draft based on his performance, not his promise. —

Delwyn Young LF
L R

Age

at position

PA

Playing in Triple-A   AAA

2007 Game Log

H%
K%
BA
HR
SB

Production
OPS
1.000

Tot | Pos | vRH | vLH

750   PA

1B
3B
2B 2
SS
C
LF 6
CF
RF

Lineup Profile
#1

#9
Usage TmOPS

PX

HR

SX

SB

FB/LD
GB

HR (mlb)
HR (milb)

Spray Chart

Delwyn isn't this good, but 500 AB of 340/390/577 in Triple-A says it's not just a fluke. 2B eligibility is icing on the cake, at least if he can get into the line-up. $

Dmitri Young 1B
L R

Age

at position

PA

Neck

2007 Game Log

H%
K%
BA
HR
SB

Production
OPS
1.000

Tot | Pos | vRH | vLH

750   PA

1B 116
3B
2B
SS
C
LF
CF
RF

Lineup Profile
#1

#9
Usage TmOPS

PX

HR

SX

SB

FB/LD
GB

HR (mlb)
HR (milb)

Spray Chart

Dmitri's comeback makes for a nice story, but don't let it obscure the fact that he's barely average for 1B/LF, and this was the healthiest he has been in years. —

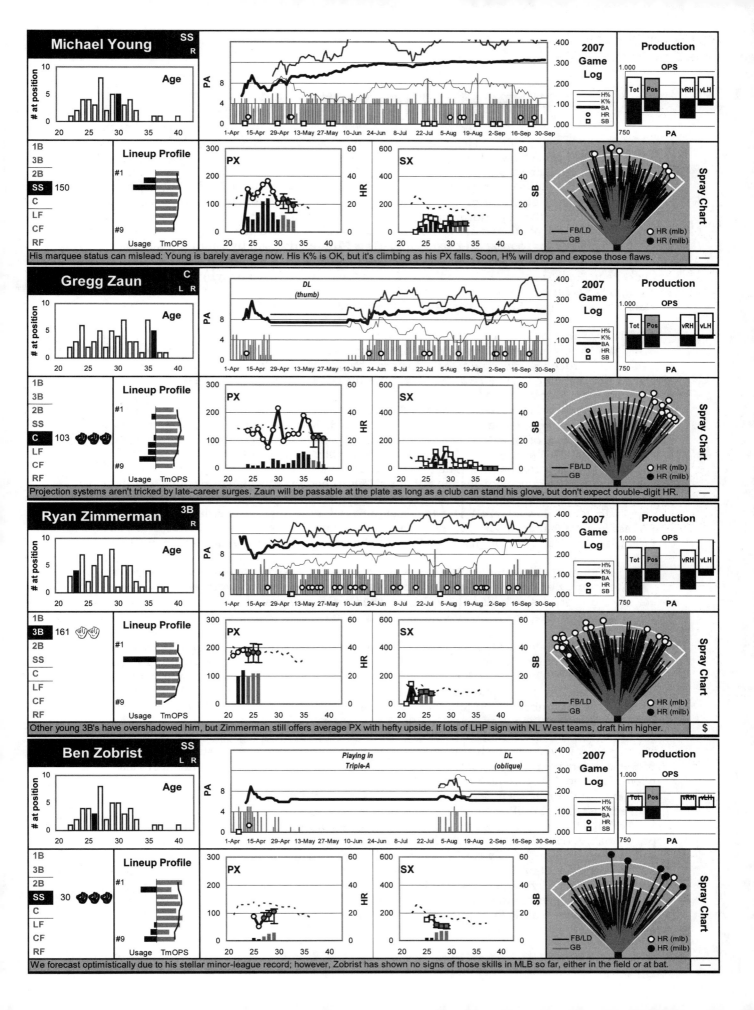

Michael Young SS R

His marquee status can mislead: Young is barely average now. His K% is OK, but it's climbing as his PX falls. Soon, H% will drop and expose those flaws. —

Gregg Zaun C L R

Projection systems aren't tricked by late-career surges. Zaun will be passable at the plate as long as a club can stand his glove, but don't expect double-digit HR. —

Ryan Zimmerman 3B R

Other young 3B's have overshadowed him, but Zimmerman still offers average PX with hefty upside. If lots of LHP sign with NL West teams, draft him higher. $

Ben Zobrist SS L R

We forecast optimistically due to his stellar minor-league record; however, Zobrist has shown no signs of those skills in MLB so far, either in the field or at bat. —

WORKING THE SEAM

By Jeff Sackmann

Another year, another projection system. Putting aside the issue of why the world needs another set of baseball forecasts, the more pressing question is: What sets our method apart from the others?

Before we get to that, we need to set the stage a bit. Our system, **MINER**, is based on the concept of regression. By "regression," we mean that players generally follow typical career trends, and that outlying performances in one season tend to return in the next season to some combination of the player's previously established skill level and the league average.

The baseline for regression-based forecasts is **Marcel**, devised by Tom Tango. Marcel uses three years of MLB data (with later data weighted more heavily); it regresses to the MLB average in those seasons (weighted according to the player's playing time); and it factors in aging trends. For such a simple approach, Marcel is remarkably accurate in forecasting rate stats such as BA and ERA. However, there is plenty to be gained by adding other variables.

The advance of MINER is that it doesn't pull those variables only from the majors. MINER, like Marcel, uses three years of data; however, we get three years of data for *all* players – even relative newcomers to the majors – by fleshing out that stretch with minor-league stats. Depending on the tenure of the player, we drill down as deep as Single-A.

Of course, for established players like Ryan Howard or Dontrelle Willis, minor-league data doesn't matter. Generally speaking, though, guys like them are the easiest to forecast. The tough players are those with less of a track record. What can a projection system that relies on three years of MLB data make of Ryan Braun, Phil Hughes, or, to take a more extreme case, Joey Votto? We think that MINER lets us speak with greater authority on these players.

Now, although it's cool to use minor-league data, these numbers don't predict big-league success as well as real major-league numbers. Minor-league equivalencies, which try to turn minor-league numbers into major-league counterparts, are useful, but they can be unreliable, especially for the low minors. So we took a slightly different tack: We weighted minor-league PA less heavily than major-league PA. And the weighting is lower for lower levels. Thus, a PA in Triple-A is 90% as meaningful as an ML PA, whereas a PA in Single-A is only about 40% so.

Another improvement of MINER over Marcel lies in its use of batted-ball data. If you're reading this book, you probably know that both hitters and pitchers tend to have batting averages on balls in play (BABIP) near the league average. Much higher or lower than that, and you're probably looking at a lucky or unlucky season, especially in the case of pitchers.

MINER goes a step further, by breaking down the rates for different types of batted balls. For instance, we know that line drives fall for hits as a much higher rate than do ground balls or fly balls. Thus, a batter who has a consistently high line-drive percentage could sustain an above-average hit rate. Similarly, a pitcher who is able to induce lots of ground balls or an unusually high number of pop-ups could manage to post a below-average BABIP (assuming that the underlying behavior is repeatable).

Let's look at Ryan Howard. His 50th-percentile MINER projection gives him a BABIP of .364 That figure is *way* above the league average. However, as noted above, a strong predictor of BABIP is line-drive percentage; this *is* a skill, and one that Howard has in abundance. Most players hit line drives about 20% of the time that they make contact, but Howard has put up LD% the last three years of 26.6%, 21.9%, and 24.3%. MINER rewards Howard by forecasting with a boost in his BABIP, which translates into higher OBP and SLG numbers as well.

Perhaps the most crucial batted-ball datum is the consideration, for pitchers, of home runs per fly ball. Although the best sluggers consistently turn more fly balls into circuit clouts (by simply hitting the ball really hard), pitchers tend to return to league average by this measure.

To take one notable example, 15% of Dontrelle Willis's fly balls cleared the wall in 2007. Not only is league average closer to 11%, but Dontrelle himself had previously allowed rates of 6.2% (itself unsustainably low) and 10.8%. Taking all these variables into account, MINER projects a return to a HR/FB of about 12.5%, which brings a more hype-worthy sub-4.50 ERA.

All the theory in the world does not mean a thing if we don't have the data to back it up. Thankfully, the store of historical batted-ball data is catching up to our understanding of its implications. MINER not only uses such granular information for major-leaguers, going back to 2005 – it also takes advantage of all of the same data for minor-leaguers.

This information greatly illuminates a player's output in the minors. Analysts have long been able to translate conventional minor-league stats like hits and runs to their major-league equivalents. For instance, Braun's 22 home runs between High-A and Double-A in 2006 are equal to about 15 major-league HR (and his SLG of .514 shrinks to a less awe-inspiring .344). The trick is knowing how much stock to put in the translations, given what we know about the tendencies of the underlying events. Park adjustments help to control for some of the wilder run environments, but, as with major-league stats, compensating for numbers like line-drive percentage, ground-ball rate, and homers per fly ball are also necessary pieces of the puzzle.

To look closer at Braun, a key question in creating a projection for him is whether (and to what extent) he can sustain his BABIP in the majors of .373. His low line-drive rate of 16.3% suggests that he can't, but that number is based on fewer than 500 plate appearances. We can boost the sample size by including Braun's minor-league numbers in 2005 and 2006. If we do that, the outlook remains bleak: Although nearly 22% of Braun's batted balls were line drives in '05 (in Rookie and Single-A), his LD% the next year was less than 14%. That's one of several reasons that MINER forecasts Braun's league-leading SLG to drop more than 130 points in '08.

Along with three years of data for the player, there is a fourth input: the league average. The weighting of the league data depends on how often the player played (and so how much data we have on him) in those three years. If the hitter has accumulated at least 600 plate appearance in each of the last three seasons, the weights are 5/4/3/2, where "5" is the most recent player season and "2" is the league average. If the hitter has more than 600 PA per year, the weight of the league average is less; if the player has more than 600 PA, the final weight is more. Because we treat minor-league PA as less telling than major-league PA, a player with a lot of recent time in the minors will be regressed more heavily to the major-league mean than will a player who has had the same amount of playing time in the majors

For Braun and the other hitters in this book, we give not one but three sets of projections: a median forecast plus 20th- and 80th-percentile forecasts (higher percentiles are better). For most hitters, the extreme downside (a debilitating injury) is more striking than is the extreme upside (a high hit rate and a streaky couple of weeks). Consequently, the 20th-percentile forecasts are generally more pessimistic than the 80th-percentile numbers are optimistic.

Some of the most pessimistic projections of all are for power stats for older players. All but the very best hitters start losing power in their early 30's, and some of those guys tank very fast. The median projections for older hitters might suggest a gentle decline, but their 20th-percentile numbers are often a warning signal, one that may persuade you to tilt your fantasy draft toward younger players, who have less downside risk in this area.

Aging is one of the key cogs in any projection system, so we looked at each type of skill separately. On average, hitters keep developing power until age 30, but speed-related skills start going downhill much earlier. Pitchers see different trends in K%, BB%, and HR%.

You will notice many players whose projected playing time hits zero at some point. As a player's quality of play drops, his manager will put him in the line-up less frequently. (There are exceptions – we are projecting only offensive skills for hitters, and batsmanship doesn't explain why Brad Ausmus is in the major leagues.) To address the relationship between performance and play, we reduce a player's PA or IP if he is projected below replacement level for his position. If he is far enough below (at least 100 points of OPS for hitters), then we forecast that he won't play at all. We treat pitchers a little differently – someone like Scott Elarton and Jason Simontacchi will always get another chance, so we reduce IP only as much as 80%. Everyone gets a spot start if they hang around Omaha long enough.

Finally, after going through the above process, we adjust each player's stats back to the park and league in which he ended the season. Depending on what happens in the offseason, you may have to do some additional tweaking. However, for the great many players who stay put, the projections in this book can go directly into your fantasy-draft preparations in March.

Jeff Sackmann is the curator of www.MinorLeagueSplits.com.

WHITE GLOVES, BLACK GLOVES

In fantasy baseball, the defensive prowess of a player generally does not rise even to the level of a secondary consideration. And it's true that we've never heard of a fantasy game that tracks "fielding outs" or "errors." Nevertheless, when you draft a hitter, you own not only his bat but also his glove. That is an important point, because many fantasy statistics *do* feed on playing time, and a player's defense is a key factor in how much playing time he logs.

Thus, for this edition of the GP, we decided to add a measure of a player's defense. As our base, we used the **Revised Zone Ratings** (RZR) compiled by Baseball Info Solutions. Revised Zone Rating is the percentage of balls hit into a fielder's zone that he converted into an out. (A "zone" is defined as the area of the field in which the average fielder at a position converted at least 50% of balls into outs.) Defensive success rates for 2007 are given to the right. (Standard RZR's exist for catchers, but we opted to use Caught Stealings per Stolen Base Attempts instead.)

However, it was not enough to present Range Factor alone – we also had to account for *chances*. In 2007, both Corey Patterson and Corey Hart had an above-average RZR at center field of .904, but Patterson recorded his rate in 270 chances versus 73 chances for Hart. Ideally, we would credit Patterson as the better center-fielder, since we have a larger sample by which to judge him.

To quantify this point, we turned to the *binomial distribution*. This formula gives the likelihood of a given number of successes in a set of N independent events that have two possible outcomes (as with a coin flip). In our case, a "success" is a defensive out.

Our null hypothesis is that a fielder has the average out rate. Using the binomial distribution, we then calculated the likelihood that a *genuinely* average fielder would have made the observed number of plays (or more) in the observed number of chances.

Defensive Success Rates for 2007 by Position	
1B	74.2%
2B	83.1%
3B	67.9%
SS	81.6%
LF	85.5%
CF	88.7%
RF	87.6%
CA	25.6%

Rate = (Plays Made)/(Balls in Zone) except at catcher, for which we use (Caught Stealings)/(Steal Attempts). Rates are for our pool of 456 hitters.

The result (subtracted from 1 so higher numbers are better) is Binomial Zone Rating, or **BINZ**. Like any probability, BINZ runs from 0 (impossible) to 1 (certain). The higher a fielder's BINZ, the more likely he is better than league-average. Note that we are dealing with probabilities, so even fielders who have inferior RZR's can be found to have *some* chance of being superior.

In our hitter profiles, we display BINZ as a number of gloves. Players can earn 1-3 gloves – *white gloves*, for good play, or *black gloves*, for bad play. To set the cut-offs, we first ranked our hitters by their BINZ at their *best* defensive position. We then decided that the top and bottom 5% of players merited three gloves (white or black), the next 10% got two gloves, and a further 20% got one. Thus, about 1/3 of hitters got at least one white glove at their best spot, 1/3 got at least one black glove, and 1/3 got nothing (again, at their *best* spot). As it happens, Corey Patterson had a .769 BINZ (good enough for a white glove) while Corey Hart had a .586.

We used the same thresholds to hand out gloves at secondary positions. To be eligible for any glove at a position, a player needed 20 chances in the associated zone. Note that we did not set different cut-offs for different positions because every fielder is ranked by BINZ, which already incorporates the league-average rate for a spot. Our method means that fielders have a harder time distinguishing themselves at spots with higher average out rates, but that's fair.

Player	Pos	N	RZR	Avg	BINZ
Pujols	1B	395	.843	.816	1.000
Vizquel	SS	235	.886	.742	1.000

Player	Pos	N	RZR	Avg	BINZ
Braun	3B	225	.564	.679	0.000
Dye	RF	305	.807	.876	0.000
Ramirez	LF	215	.684	.855	0.000

For 2007, two fielders with copious chances were deemed by BINZ to be positively above-average. Three others were regarded as positively *no better* than average. We list the stand-outs to the left.

This analysis is just a start – we didn't look at past seasons or tally plays (if any) *out* of a player's zone. Regardless, BINZ fulfills its job as a measure that uses both RZR and chances. And we like being able to speak of defensive skill as a probability. If you want to know which fielders shone in 2007, at the task that they were called to do, BINZ points the way.

TEAM DEFENSES

Here, we take BINZ – our method for reformulating RZR to reflect chances – and apply it to teams. As with players, teams can earn 1-3 gloves at a spot, either *white gloves* for good play or *black gloves* for bad play. Gloves are based on the combined chances and successes of eligible players. To make the ratings more meaningful for 2008, only players who ended the season with a team were eligible. Eligible players contributed at all the positions they played.

We used the same cut-off values to award gloves for positions as for players. For "Infield" and "Outfield," we adjusted the thresholds so that, as with players and positions, about 1/3 of teams got at least one white glove at each area, and 1/3 of teams got at least one black glove.

To calculate a rating for "Infield," we weighted the team's BINZ for the four infield spots (1B/2B/3B/SS) at a ratio of 1:2:2:2, which is the rough league-average proportion of chances at those spots. For "Outfield," we weighted BINZ for the three outfield spots (LF/CF/RF) by 3:4:3.

(Legend for the tables below: each cell contains a number of gloves — white gloves (outline) denote good play, black gloves (solid) denote bad play. "w" = white glove, "b" = black glove; the number of letters indicates the number of gloves.)

TEAM	1B	2B	3B	SS	Inf.	LF	CF	RF	Outf.
Baltimore	bb			ww	w			bb	b
Boston	ww		www	b	w	bbb			
New York	ww		b	bb	b		ww		www
Tampa Bay			bb	bbb	bb		bb	bb	bbb
Toronto	www	www	w	ww	www			w	
Chicago	b			b		b	ww	bbb	
Cleveland		bb	w	bb	b	bb	bb	w	bb
Detroit		w	ww	b	w	www	ww		bb
Kansas City	www	w	w	www	www	b	w		w
Minnesota		bb			b	www		bbb	
Los Angeles	w			b			bbb	bb	bb
Oakland		www	b		w	w		w	w
Seattle	bb		b		b		bb	b	b
Texas	b					w			

TEAM	1B	2B	3B	SS	Inf.	LF	CF	RF	Outf.
Atlanta		b	bb		b	www	w		ww
Florida	ww	www	www	ww	www		w		w
New York	ww	b		www		www	ww	w	www
Philadelphia	b			w		bb	bb	w	b
Washington	bbb	b	w	bb	b		ww	w	ww
Chicago		ww	ww	w	ww	w	ww		ww
Cincinnati	bbb	b	bb	ww		b	b	w	
Houston	b	bbb	b		bb	b	b	www	
Milwaukee	bb	ww	ww	b	bbb	w	ww		
Pittsburgh	w	b	bbb	w		b		b	bb
St. Louis	www	b	www	bbb		b	bb		bb
Arizona	b	bb	w	bb	bb	www		w	w
Colorado	www	ww	bb	ww	bb	www	b		
Los Angeles	bb		w				w		w
San Diego	b	www		ww	w	w			w
San Francisco	w	bb	www	www	ww		b		bb

203

TOWARD A NEW GAME SCORE

Among our many missions at *Heater Magazine* was coming up with a new Game Score for starting pitchers. We know of the system devised by Bill James which awards points for various events, but we hoped for a scheme with a more-direct connection to reality.

We had the idea that the most natural form of Game Score would be one that graded the starting pitcher in terms of his probability of getting the Win given his pitching performance. (Note that we could have taken the side of the pitcher's *team* and worked out *its* probability of winning the game that the pitcher started. We chose to keep the focus on the pitcher, in part because fantasy baseball puts a premium on identifying starters who can rack up Wins.)

Whereas James's equation counts runs allowed, we wanted to stick to isolated events that a pitcher controls. We decided to consider only the starter's strikeouts, walks, and home runs, along with the number of innings pitched; we ignored hits allowed, on the rationale that they are chiefly a function of hit balls allowed, which are themselves a function of strikeouts. For our output, we sought a figure that represented the probability that a starter who put up these stats would collect the win. This number would be our Game Score.

We gathered the pitching logs from 2004-06. Our intent was to run a regression of K, BB, HR, and IP vs. Wins. When seeking a probabilty, though, a normal linear regression isn't wise, in part because the resulting formula could yield a result that's smaller than 0 or larger than 1.

We had to turn to *logistic* regression. As with linear regression, logistic regression finds a relationship between input variables and an output variable. In logistic regression, though, the formula furnishes the *probability* of a value given the inputs, rather the value itself. (If you are curious, a logistic regression has the form $P = 1/(1 + e^{-(a+bX)})$, where P is the probability of the event under scrutiny, X is an input variable, and a and b are the parameters of the model.)

Before proceeding to the math, we looked at win probability by length of start. Not surprisingly, IP is a big factor in whether a pitcher gets a "W," in part because pitching *deeper* in a game is typically a mark of pitching *better*. (Note that, by MLB rules, a starter who goes less than 5 IP cannot get a win.)

With each out that passes, a manager must decide anew to sit his starter or not. We found four points at which a starter's win probability jumps: if the starter is still in the game at 6 IP, 7 IP, 7.2 IP, and 9 IP. In the graph to the right, the resulting tiers are indicated by shade. (The rate for 8.1 IP is high, but the sample size was small.)

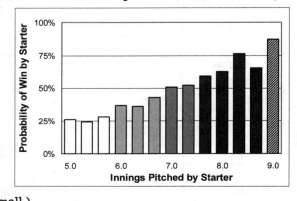

With five distinct tiers for IP, we decided to treat them differently and run a regression for each. The coefficients for K, BB, and HR are given along with the overall win probability by IP.

Winning Influences for Starters				
IP	pWin	K	BB	HR
5.0-5.2	26%	0.04	-0.09	-0.42
6.0-6.2	38%	0.05	-0.11	-0.41
7.0-7.1	51%	0.04	-0.16	-0.55
7.2-8.2	63%	NS	-0.11	-0.51
9.0	87%	NS	-0.50	-0.51

A starter's walk and homer totals are key in every regime. Homers are especially crucial – not surprising, since each such event scores at least one run for the opposition. In shorter starts, walks are twice as harmful to a starter's cause as strikeouts; in longer starts, their relative sway grows, perhaps because each added baserunner could spell the difference in a tight game, and also because walks hint at an overall lack of control by the starter. When a starter hits 7.2 IP, his strikeouts become irrelevant to his chances – lasting 7+ innings already implies that he allowed few hits.

You may be surprised that complete games generate wins at a rate of only 87%. Although surviving 9 IP suggests that a starter has *allowed* few runs, it's no guarantee that his team has *scored* any. Still, a starter can increase his odds. Our model gives its highest score of 92 for a start of 9 IP with no walks or home runs. In the big leagues in 2007, there were 21 such starts; all 21 starters got the Win. *Logistic Game Scores appear weekly in Heater Magazine.*

STAR MAPS

Here, we shine a light on the biggest over- and underachievers in pitchers in 2007. Each pitcher is a "star" with three characteristics. As with Historical Fortunes, our sky consists of *hit rate* (the rate at which balls in play fall for hits) along the wide axis, and *strand rate* (the rate at which baserunners don't become earned runs) along the tall axis. The coordinates of the star indicate the pitcher's hit & strand rates in 2007. The third characteristic of the star – its magnitude – marks the pitcher's skill, as measured by our GOG3.

Avoid dim stars in general but especially those in the upper left, where hit rate is favorably low and strand rate is favorably high. Most owners will ride these pitchers but they do so at good risk of flame-out, since hit rate is largely pitcher-independent while strand rate is more skill-fixed but still haphazard.

Conversely, track bright stars in the lower right, where hit rate is high and strand rate is low. These are talented pitchers who endured harsh luck in 2008. They could be hurt or surrounded by a poor cast, but they have the power to go nova.

STAR MAP: American League, Starting Pitchers

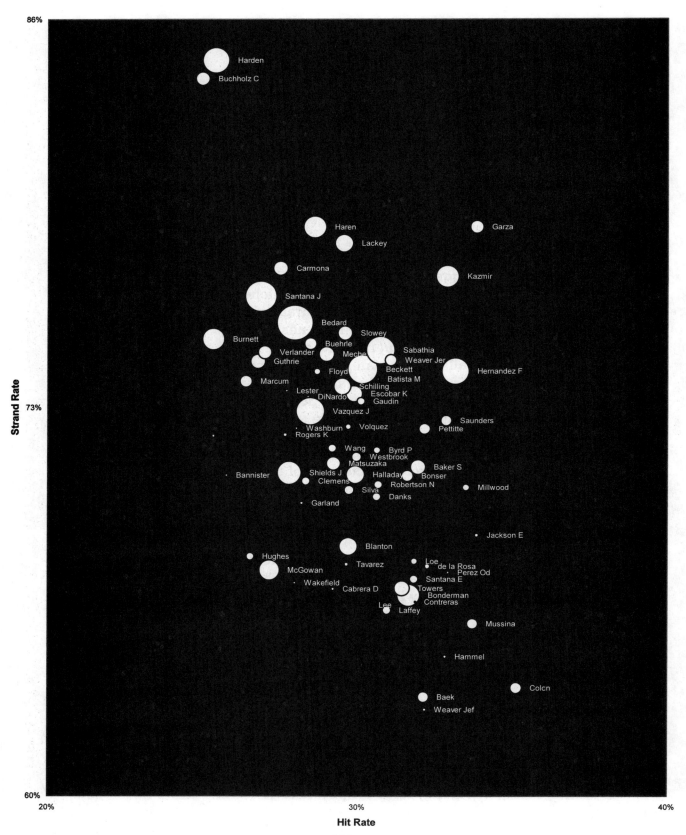

Strand Rate (y-axis: 60%, 73%, 86%)

Hit Rate (x-axis: 20%, 30%, 40%)

Harden, Buchholz C, Haren, Lackey, Garza, Carmona, Kazmir, Santana J, Bedard, Slowey, Burnett, Buehrle, Sabathia, Verlander, Meche, Weaver Jer, Guthrie, Beckett, Hernandez F, Floyd, Batista M, Marcum, Schilling, Lester, Escobar K, DiNardo, Gaudin, Vazquez J, Washburn, Volquez, Saunders, Rogers K, Pettitte, Wang, Byrd P, Westbrook, Matsuzaka, Baker S, Bannister, Shields J, Halladay, Bonser, Clemens, Robertson N, Millwood, Silva, Danks, Garland, Jackson E, Blanton, Hughes, Loe, de la Rosa, McGowan, Tavarez, Perez Od, Wakefield, Santana E, Cabrera D, Towers, Bonderman, Lee, Contreras, Laffey, Mussina, Hammel, Colcn, Baek, Weaver Jef

206

STAR MAP: American League, Relief Pitchers

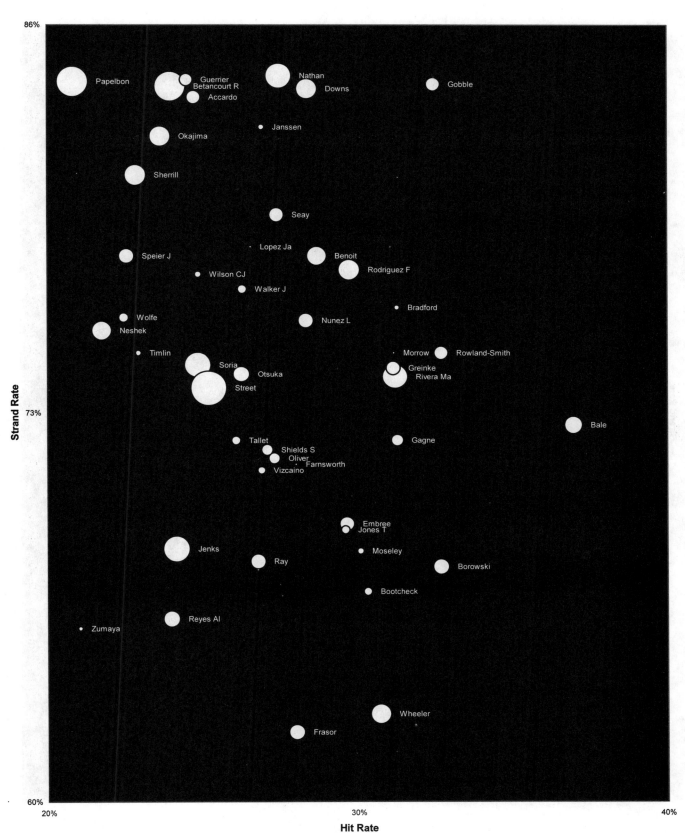

86%

Papelbon

Guerrier
Betancourt R
Accardo

Nathan
Downs

Gobble

Janssen

Okajima

Sherrill

Seay

Lopez Ja

Speier J

Benoit

Rodriguez F

Wilson CJ

Walker J

Bradford

Wolfe
Neshek

Nunez L

Timlin

Morrow

Rowland-Smith

Soria
Street

Otsuka

Greinke
Rivera Ma

Strand Rate

73%

Bale

Tallet

Gagne

Shields S
Oliver
Vizcaino

Farnsworth

Embree
Jones T

Jenks

Ray

Moseley

Borowski

Bootcheck

Reyes Al

Zumaya

Wheeler

Frasor

60%

20%   30%   40%

Hit Rate

207

STAR MAP: National League, Starting Pitchers

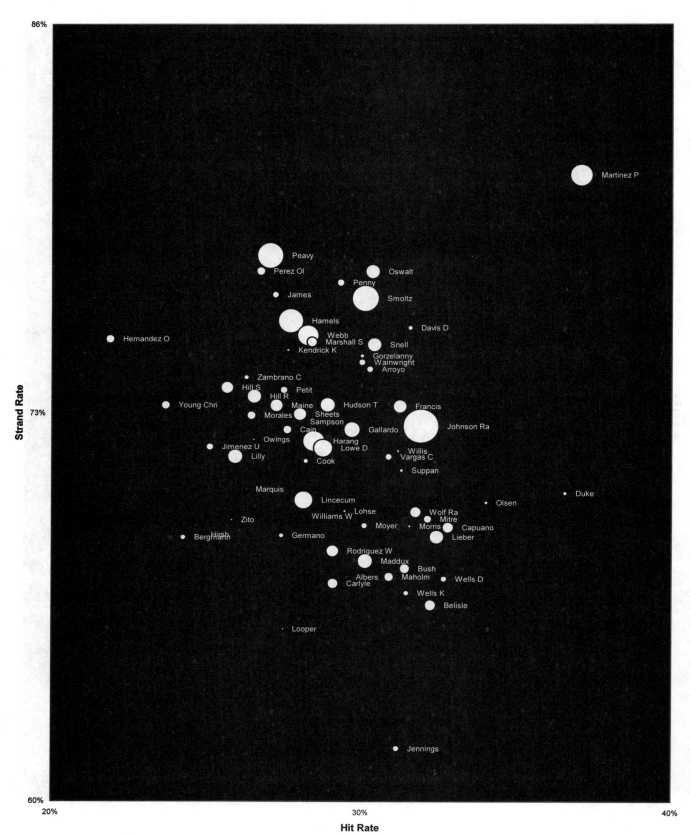

STAR MAP: National League, Relief Pitchers

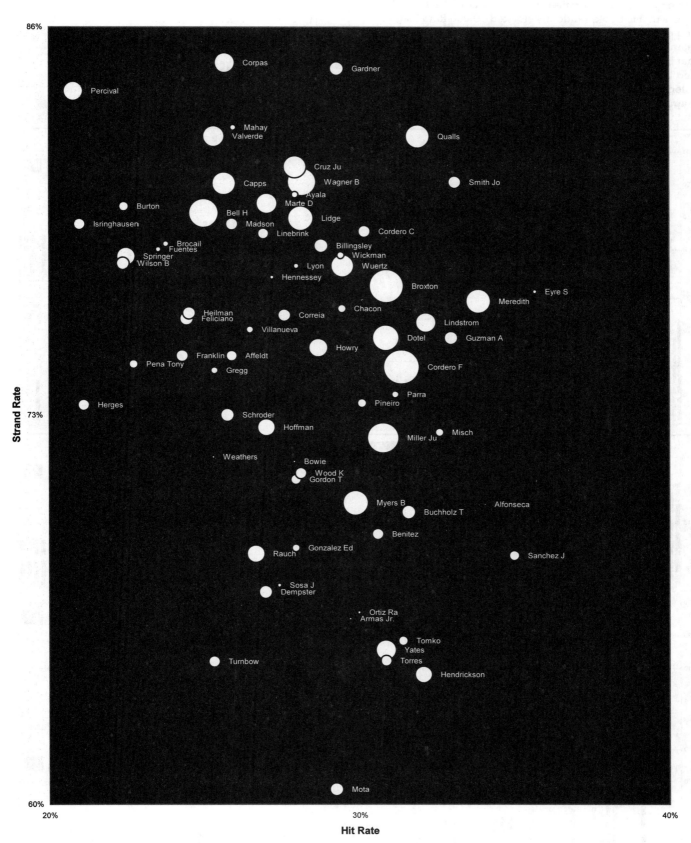

WOW FACTORS

WOW ("Weight on Winners") is a method of deriving fantasy values via simulation rather than calculation. We took all 456 hitters in this book, randomly stocked 10,000 Roto leagues, and counted how often each hitter appeared on the winning team. That rate is his WOW Factor. One benefit of WOW is that it treats players as they are – an indivisible bunch of stats tied to a position – rather than as 4 or 5 free-floating fantasy categories. The average WOW is 8 (that is, in a 12-team league, the average player has an 8% chance of winding up on the champion). A WOW of 12 is good, and 20 is amazing.

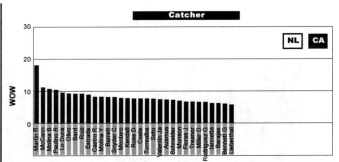

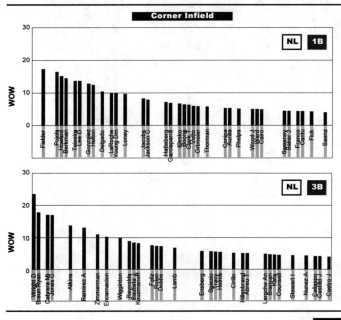

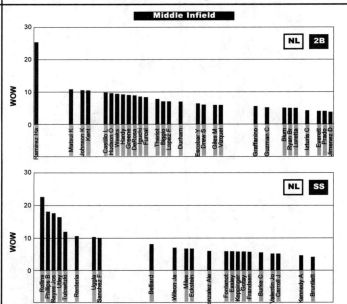

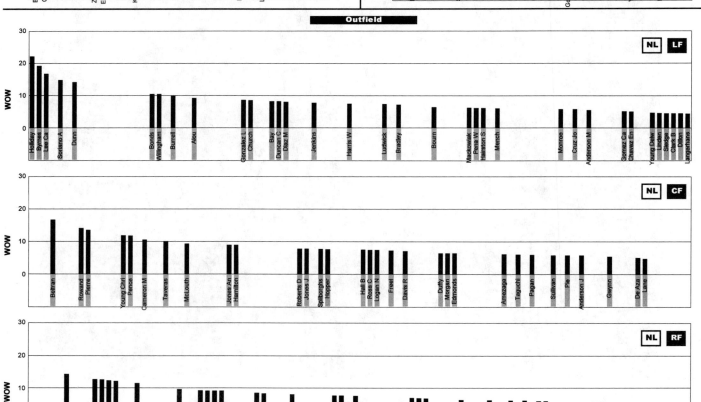

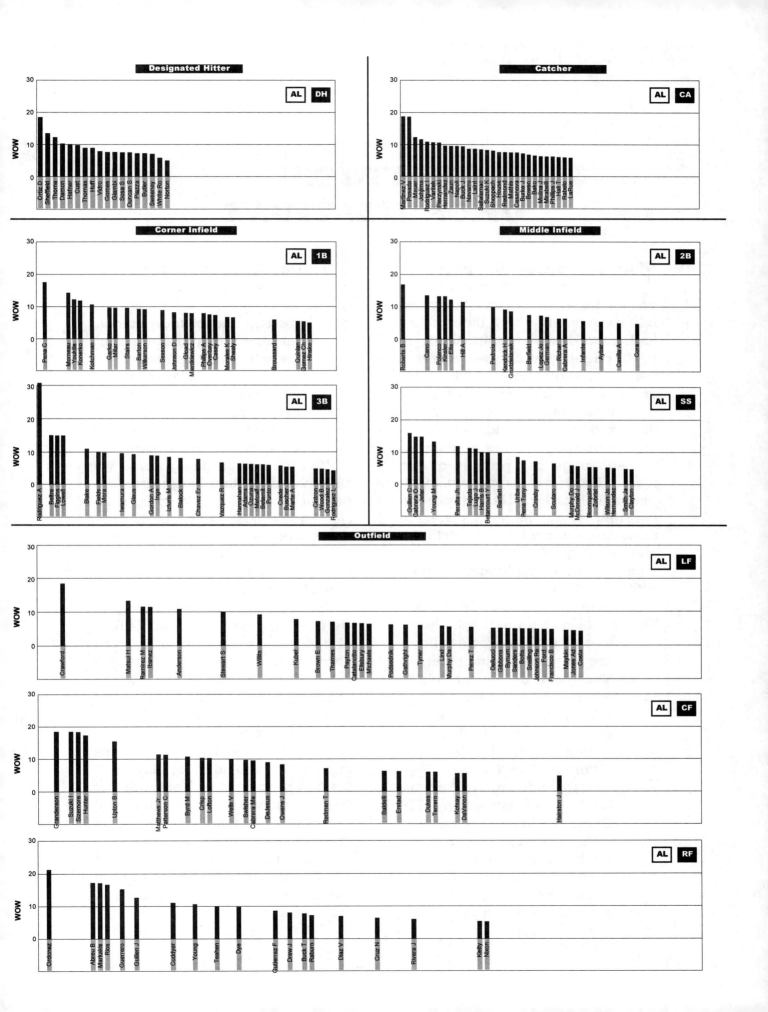

GRAPHICAL ORGANIZATIONS

In the preceding 200+ pages, we analyze the capabilities of *players*. Here, we survey the capabilities of *teams* – both their major- and minor-league components. In these pages, you can see where a team's strength lies, which teams are aging, which teams are forking over dollars (and what they are getting for their cash), and which ones have promising batches of rookies.

Each page has profiles of two teams; teams are presented in alphabetical order. The graphs on the right lay out the team's talent in three areas: the infield; the outfield; and pitching. (We lump designated hitters with the infield and catchers with the outfield.)

Players are indicated by circles. The circles have three properties:

- The **size** of the circle reflects the player's playing time.
- The **position** of the circle marries the player's age (along the bottom of the graph) and his level of play (along the side). We grade hitters by OPS (On-Base Percentage + Slugging Percentage), and pitchers by FIP ERA (Fielding-Independent ERA, an approximixation of the pitcher's expected ERA in front of a neutral fielding team, devised by noted researcher Tom Tango).

- The **shade** of the circle tells the caliber of the player at his position. Major-leaguers possess one of four shades; darker shades are superior. The white circles are minor-leaguers who played at the 95th percentile or better for their position in the MLE (minor-league equivalent) of the appropriate measure.

To the left of the graphs, we show the important long-term obligations of the club, including salaries for the next three years. Contracts are as November 1, 2007. (We left out a handful of smaller contracts that we could not pin down the details of.)

Finally, under the contract table, we give an overview of the caliber of the team's farm system compared to its 29 peers. Systems are rated in two facets: "Studs," which considers the number and talent of its minor-leaguers in the 90th percentile (or better) in quality of play in 2007, and "Depth," which weighs the number and talent of players in the 50th percentile or better. Below the overview are three numerical rankings of the team's caliber in its division, in its league, and overall.

The commentary is provided by Jeff Sackmann, who also supplied the minor-league data and devised the rankings.

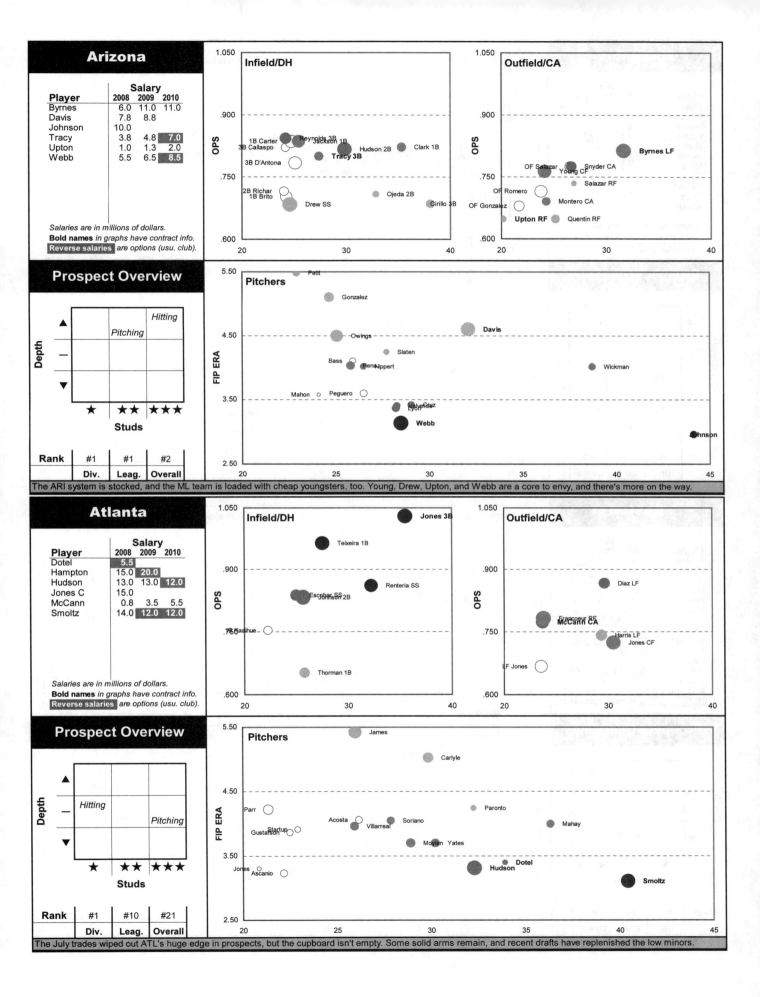

Arizona

Player	Salary 2008	2009	2010
Byrnes	6.0	11.0	11.0
Davis	7.8	8.8	
Johnson	10.0		
Tracy	3.8	4.8	7.0
Upton	1.0	1.3	2.0
Webb	5.5	6.5	8.5

Salaries are in millions of dollars.
Bold names *in graphs have contract info.*
Reverse salaries *are options (usu. club).*

Infield/DH
1B Carter, 3B Callaspo, Reynolds 3B, Jackson 1B, Hudson 2B, Clark 1B, 3B D'Antona, **Tracy 3B**, 2B Richar, 1B Brito, Drew SS, Ojeda 2B, Cirillo 3B

Outfield/CA
OF Salazar, Young CF, Snyder CA, **Byrnes LF**, Salazar RF, OF Romero, Montero CA, OF Gonzalez, **Upton RF**, Quentin RF

Pitchers
Petit, Gonzalez, Owings, Davis, Slaten, Bass, Pena, Nippert, Wickman, Mahon, Peguero, Valverde, Cruz, Lyon, **Webb**, Johnson

Prospect Overview

	Hitting
Pitching	

Depth / Studs ★ ★★ ★★★

Rank	#1	#1	#2
	Div.	Leag.	Overall

The ARI system is stocked, and the ML team is loaded with cheap youngsters, too. Young, Drew, Upton, and Webb are a core to envy, and there's more on the way.

Atlanta

Player	Salary 2008	2009	2010
Dotel	5.5		
Hampton	15.0	20.0	
Hudson	13.0	13.0	12.0
Jones C	15.0		
McCann	0.8	3.5	5.5
Smoltz	14.0	12.0	12.0

Salaries are in millions of dollars.
Bold names *in graphs have contract info.*
Reverse salaries *are options (usu. club).*

Infield/DH
Jones 3B, Teixeira 1B, Escobar SS, Johnson 2B, Renteria SS, 1B Kaaihue, Thorman 1B

Outfield/CA
Diaz LF, Francoeur RF, **McCann CA**, Harris LF, Jones CF, LF Jones

Pitchers
James, Carlyle, Parr, Paronto, Acosta, Villarreal, Soriano, Mahay, Gustafson, Startup, Moylan, Yates, Jones, Ascanio, **Hudson**, **Dotel**, **Smoltz**

Prospect Overview

Hitting	
	Pitching

Depth / Studs ★ ★★ ★★★

Rank	#1	#10	#21
	Div.	Leag.	Overall

The July trades wiped out ATL's huge edge in prospects, but the cupboard isn't empty. Some solid arms remain, and recent drafts have replenished the low minors.

Baltimore

Player	Salary 2008	2009	2010
Baez	4.5	5.5	
Bradford	3.5	3.5	
Gibbons	5.7	6.2	
Hernandez	7.5	8.0	8.5
Huff	8.0	8.0	
Millar	2.8		
Mora	8.0	8.0	
Payton	5.0		
Roberts	6.3	8.0	
Tejada	13.0	13.0	
Walker	4.5	4.5	

Salaries are in millions of dollars.
Bold names *in graphs have contract info.*
Reverse salaries *are options (usu. club).*

Prospect Overview

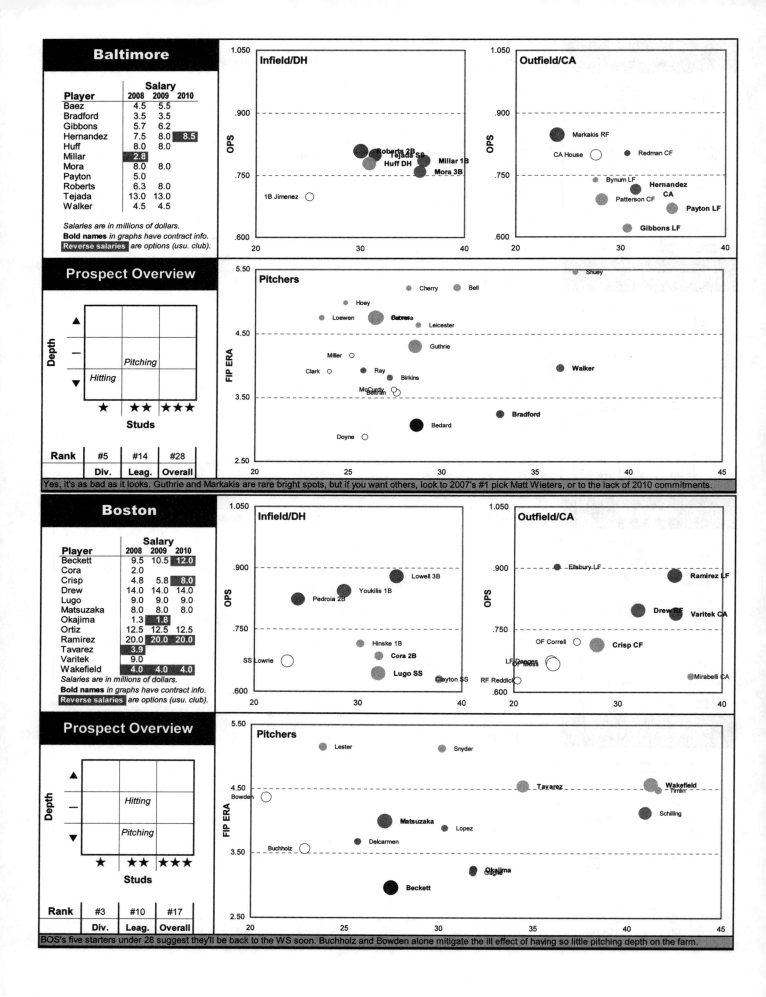

Infield/DH — OPS vs: Roberts 2B, Tejada SS, Huff DH, Millar 1B, Mora 3B, 1B Jimenez

Outfield/CA — Markakis RF, CA House, Redman CF, Bynum LF, Hernandez CA, Patterson CF, Payton LF, Gibbons LF

Pitchers — FIP ERA: Shuey, Cherry, Bell, Hoey, Loewen, Cabrera, Leicester, Guthrie, Miller, Clark, Ray, Birkins, McCurdy, Beltran, Walker, Doyne, Bedard, Bradford

Depth		
▲		
—		Pitching
▼	Hitting	
	★	★★ ★★★
		Studs

Rank	#5	#14	#28
	Div.	Leag.	Overall

Yes, it's as bad as it looks. Guthrie and Markakis are rare bright spots, but if you want others, look to 2007's #1 pick Matt Wieters, or to the lack of 2010 commitments.

Boston

Player	Salary 2008	2009	2010
Beckett	9.5	10.5	12.0
Cora	2.0		
Crisp	4.8	5.8	8.0
Drew	14.0	14.0	14.0
Lugo	9.0	9.0	9.0
Matsuzaka	8.0	8.0	8.0
Okajima	1.3	1.8	
Ortiz	12.5	12.5	12.5
Ramirez	20.0	20.0	20.0
Tavarez	3.9		
Varitek	9.0		
Wakefield	4.0	4.0	4.0

Salaries are in millions of dollars.
Bold names *in graphs have contract info.*
Reverse salaries *are options (usu. club).*

Infield/DH — Lowell 3B, Pedroia 2B, Youkilis 1B, Hinske 1B, Cora 2B, SS Lowrie, Lugo SS, Clayton SS

Outfield/CA — Ellsbury LF, Ramirez LF, Drew RF, Varitek CA, OF Correll, Crisp CF, LF Gagne, OF Moss, RF Reddick, Mirabelli CA

Pitchers — Lester, Snyder, Tavarez, Wakefield, Timlin, Bowden, Schilling, Matsuzaka, Lopez, Buchholz, Delcarmen, Okajima, Gagne, Beckett

Prospect Overview

Depth		
▲		
—	Hitting	
▼		Pitching
	★	★★ ★★★
		Studs

Rank	#3	#10	#17
	Div.	Leag.	Overall

BOS's five starters under 28 suggest they'll be back to the WS soon. Buchholz and Bowden alone mitigate the ill effect of having so little pitching depth on the farm.

Chicago (AL)

Player	Salary 2008	2009	2010
Buehrle	14.0	14.0	14.0
Contreras	10.0	10.0	
Dye	9.5	11.5	**12.0**
Garland	12.0		
Hall	1.8	**2.3**	
Konerko	12.0	12.0	12.0
MacDougal	2.0	2.7	**3.8**
Ozuna	1.1	**1.2**	
Pierzynski	6.3	6.3	
Thome	14.0	**13.0**	
Thornton	0.9	1.3	**2.3**
Uribe		**5.0**	
Vazquez	11.5	11.5	11.5

Bold names in graphs have contract info.
Reverse salaries are options (usu. club).

Prospect Overview

Rank	#3	#5	#8
	Div.	Leag.	Overall

Depth / Studs chart: Pitching, Hitting

$70MM in 2009 obligations is fearsome, but pitching holes can be filled from within. The problem is offense, especially as CF's Sweeney and Owens underwhelm.

Chicago (NL)

Player	Salary 2008	2009	2010
Blanco	2.8	**3.0**	
Dempster	5.5		
DeRosa	4.8	5.5	
Eyre	**3.8**		
Howry	4.0		
Jones	5.0		
Lee	13.0	13.0	13.0
Lilly	7.0	12.0	12.0
Marquis	6.4	9.9	
Ohman	1.6		
Ramirez	14.0	15.7	15.8
Trachsel	**4.8**		
Soriano	13.0	16.0	18.0
Ward	**1.2**		
Zambrano	15.0	17.8	17.9

Prospect Overview

Rank	#2	#6	#15
	Div.	Leag.	Overall

Depth / Studs chart: Hitting, Pitching

Patterson, Pie, and Soto drive the high prospect rank; however, to take advantage, Piniella will have to play them. There isn't room for many more $15MM players.

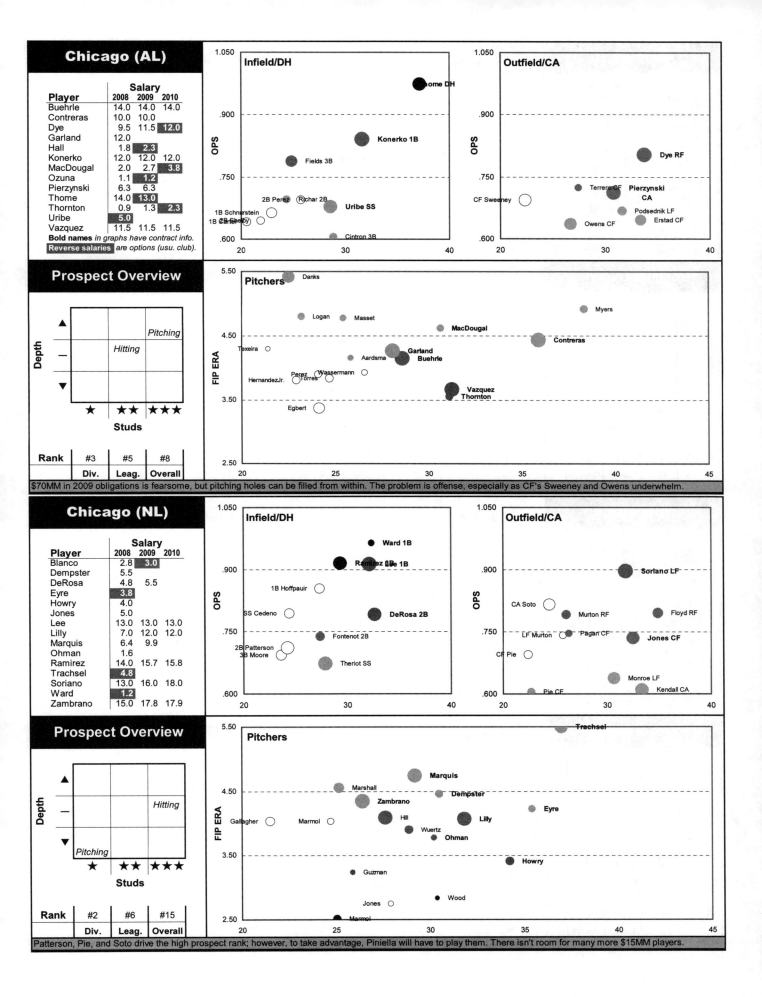

Cincinnati

Player	Salary 2008	2009	2010
Arroyo	4.0	9.5	11.0
Castro	1.0	1.1	
Coffey	0.9		
Dunn	13.0		
Freel	3.0	4.0	
Gonzalez	4.6	5.4	6.0
Griffey Jr.	12.5	16.5	
Harang	6.8	11.0	12.5
Hatteberg	1.9		
Ross	2.5	3.5	
Stanton	3.0	2.5	
Valentin	1.3		
Weathers	2.8		

Bold names in graphs have contract info.
Reverse salaries are options (usu. club).

Prospect Overview

Rank	#4	#9	#20
	Div.	Leag.	Overall

The low prospect ranking is a bit deceiving: Plenty of higher-rated teams would rather have Bailey, Votto, and Jay Bruce than a stable of B-minus RP's and 4th OF's.

Cleveland

Player	Salary 2008	2009	2010
Borowski	4.0		
Byrd	8.0		
Dellucci	3.8	4.0	
Fultz	1.5		
Hafner	8.1	11.5	11.5
Lee	3.8	5.8	8.0
Martinez	4.3	5.7	7.0
Michaels	2.2	2.6	
Peralta	2.3	3.4	4.6
Sabathia	9.0		
Sizemore	3.0	4.6	5.6
Westbrook	10.0	10.0	11.0

Salaries are in millions of dollars.
Bold names in graphs have contract info.
Reverse salaries are options (usu. club).

Prospect Overview

Rank	#1	#2	#4
	Div.	Leag.	Overall

CLE's supply of young pitching was a key part of their trip to the ALCS. And they're just the supporting cast -- Hafner, Martinez, and Sizemore are locked up for years.

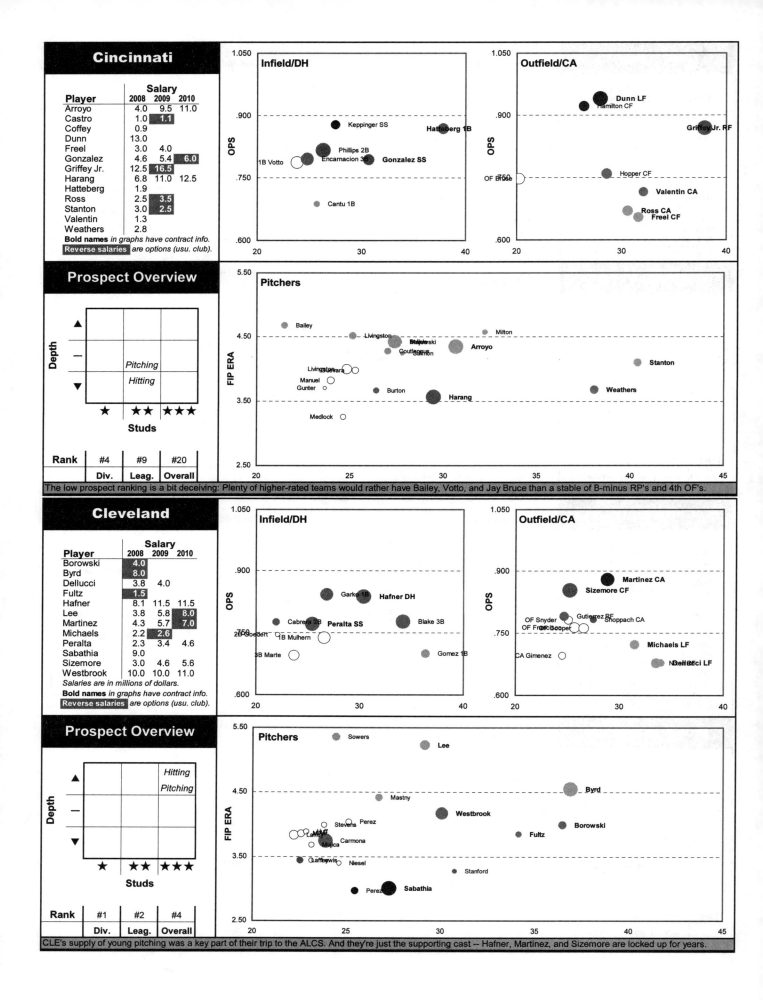

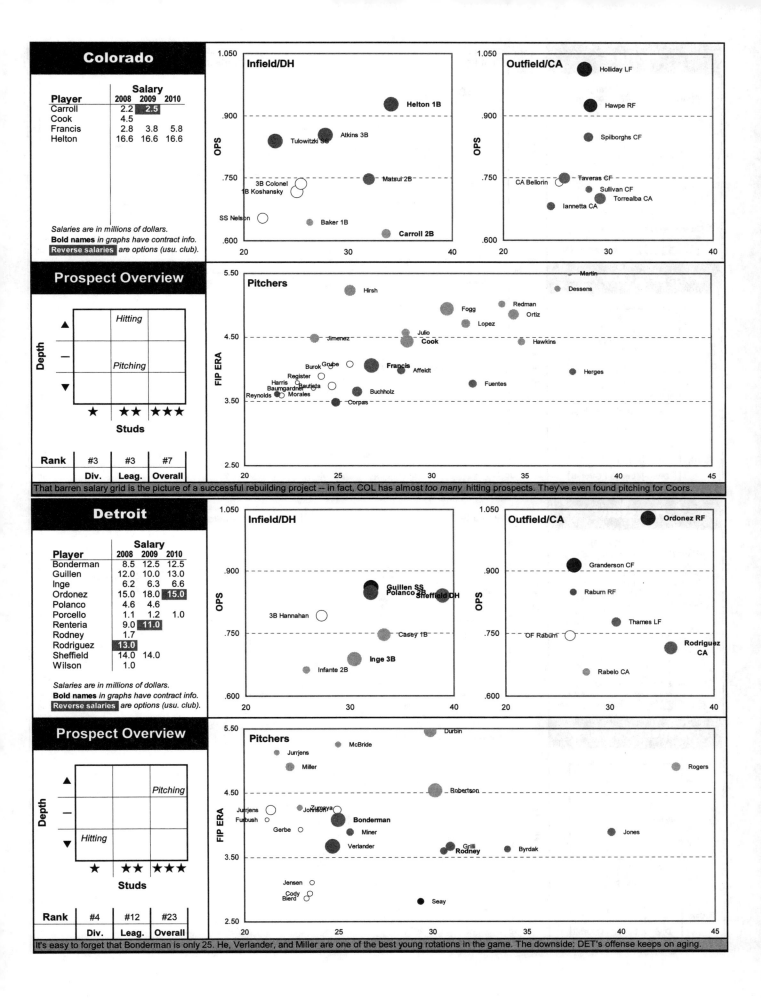

Colorado

Salary

Player	2008	2009	2010
Carroll	2.2	2.5	
Cook	4.5		
Francis	2.8	3.8	5.8
Helton	16.6	16.6	16.6

Salaries are in millions of dollars.
Bold names *in graphs have contract info.*
Reverse salaries *are options (usu. club).*

Prospect Overview

Depth / Hitting / Pitching / Studs

Rank	#3	#3	#7
	Div.	Leag.	Overall

That barren salary grid is the picture of a successful rebuilding project -- in fact, COL has almost *too many* hitting prospects. They've even found pitching for Coors.

Detroit

Salary

Player	2008	2009	2010
Bonderman	8.5	12.5	12.5
Guillen	12.0	10.0	13.0
Inge	6.2	6.3	6.6
Ordonez	15.0	18.0	15.0
Polanco	4.6	4.6	
Porcello	1.1	1.2	1.0
Renteria	9.0	11.0	
Rodney	1.7		
Rodriguez	13.0		
Sheffield	14.0	14.0	
Wilson	1.0		

Salaries are in millions of dollars.
Bold names *in graphs have contract info.*
Reverse salaries *are options (usu. club).*

Prospect Overview

Depth / Pitching / Hitting / Studs

Rank	#4	#12	#23
	Div.	Leag.	Overall

It's easy to forget that Bonderman is only 25. He, Verlander, and Miller are one of the best young rotations in the game. The downside: DET's offense keeps on aging.

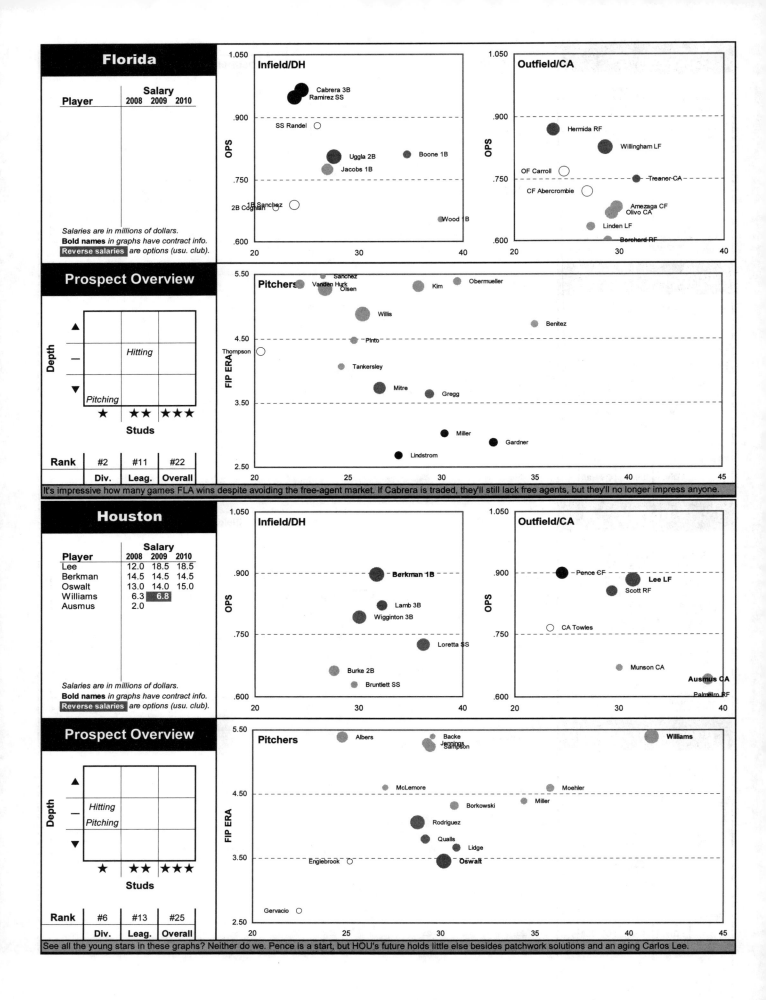

Florida

Player	Salary		
	2008	2009	2010

Salaries are in millions of dollars.
Bold names *in graphs have contract info.*
Reverse salaries *are options (usu. club).*

Infield/DH

Cabrera 3B
Ramirez SS
SS Randel
Uggla 2B
Jacobs 1B
Boone 1B
1B Sanchez
2B Coghlan
Wood 1B

Outfield/CA

Hermida RF
Willingham LF
OF Carroll
Treanor CA
CF Abercrombie
Amezaga CF
Olivo CA
Linden LF
Borchard RF

Prospect Overview

Depth — Hitting
Pitching
▲ ▼

★ ★★ ★★★
Studs

Rank	#2	#11	#22
	Div.	Leag.	Overall

Pitchers

Sanchez
Vanden Hurk
Olsen
Kim
Obermueller
Willis
Benitez
Pinto
Thompson
Tankersley
Mitre
Gregg
Miller
Gardner
Lindstrom

It's impressive how many games FLA wins despite avoiding the free-agent market. If Cabrera is traded, they'll still lack free agents, but they'll no longer impress anyone.

Houston

Player	Salary		
	2008	2009	2010
Lee	12.0	18.5	18.5
Berkman	14.5	14.5	14.5
Oswalt	13.0	14.0	15.0
Williams	6.3	6.8	
Ausmus	2.0		

Salaries are in millions of dollars.
Bold names *in graphs have contract info.*
Reverse salaries *are options (usu. club).*

Infield/DH

Berkman 1B
Lamb 3B
Wigginton 3B
Loretta SS
Burke 2B
Bruntlett SS

Outfield/CA

Pence CF
Lee LF
Scott RF
CA Towles
Munson CA
Ausmus CA
Palmeiro RF

Prospect Overview

Depth — Hitting
Pitching
▲ ▼

★ ★★ ★★★
Studs

Rank	#6	#13	#25
	Div.	Leag.	Overall

Pitchers

Albers
Backe
Jennings
Sampson
Williams
McLemore
Moehler
Borkowski
Miller
Rodriguez
Qualls
Lidge
Englebrook
Oswalt
Gervacio

See all the young stars in these graphs? Neither do we. Pence is a start, but HOU's future holds little else besides patchwork solutions and an aging Carlos Lee.

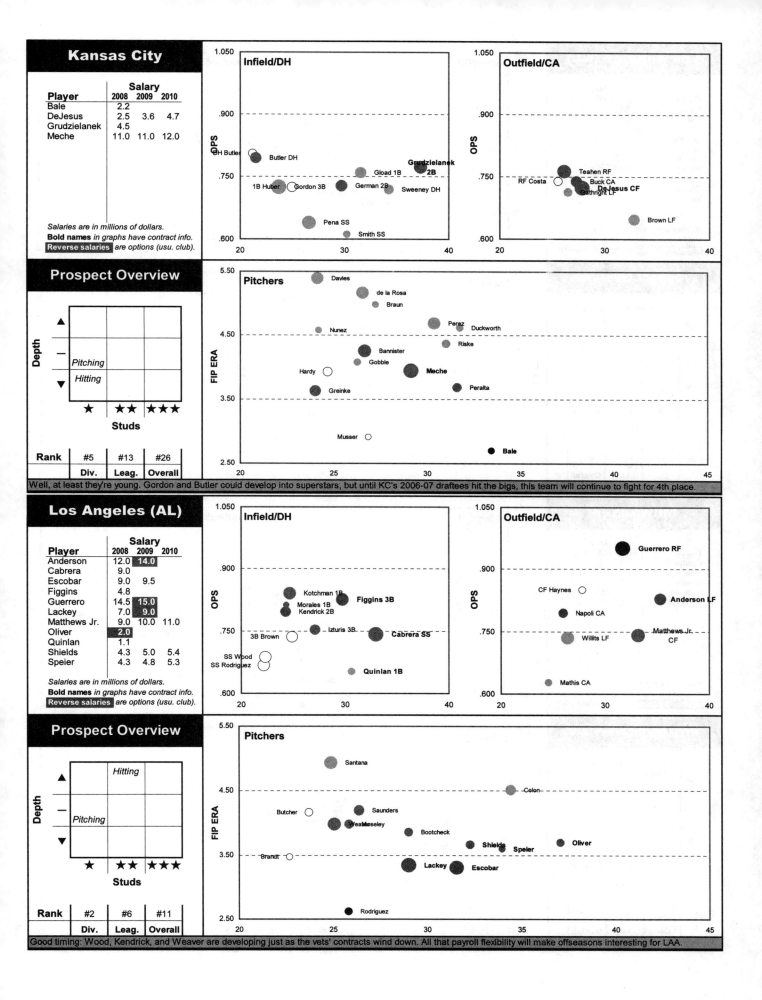

Kansas City

Salary

Player	2008	2009	2010
Bale	2.2		
DeJesus	2.5	3.6	4.7
Grudzielanek	4.5		
Meche	11.0	11.0	12.0

Salaries are in millions of dollars.
Bold names *in graphs have contract info.*
Reverse salaries *are options (usu. club).*

Prospect Overview

Depth ▲ — ▼
Pitching
Hitting
★ ★★ ★★★
Studs

Rank	#5	#13	#26
	Div.	Leag.	Overall

Infield/DH (OPS vs age)
- DH Butler
- Butler DH
- Gload 1B
- **Grudzielanek 2B**
- 1B Huber
- Gordon 3B
- German 2B
- Sweeney DH
- Pena SS
- Smith SS

Outfield/CA (OPS vs age)
- Teahen RF
- RF Costa
- Buck CA
- DeJesus CF
- Gathright LF
- Brown LF

Pitchers (FIP ERA vs age)
- Davies
- de la Rosa
- Braun
- Nunez
- Perez
- Duckworth
- Riske
- Bannister
- Gobble
- Hardy
- Meche
- Greinke
- Peralta
- Musser
- Bale

Well, at least they're young. Gordon and Butler could develop into superstars, but until KC's 2006-07 draftees hit the bigs, this team will continue to fight for 4th place.

Los Angeles (AL)

Salary

Player	2008	2009	2010
Anderson	12.0	14.0	
Cabrera	9.0		
Escobar	9.0	9.5	
Figgins	4.8		
Guerrero	14.5	15.0	
Lackey	7.0	9.0	
Matthews Jr.	9.0	10.0	11.0
Oliver	2.0		
Quinlan	1.1		
Shields	4.3	5.0	5.4
Speier	4.3	4.8	5.3

Salaries are in millions of dollars.
Bold names *in graphs have contract info.*
Reverse salaries *are options (usu. club).*

Prospect Overview

Depth ▲ — ▼
Hitting
Pitching
★ ★★ ★★★
Studs

Rank	#2	#6	#11
	Div.	Leag.	Overall

Infield/DH (OPS vs age)
- Kotchman 1B
- Morales 1B
- **Figgins 3B**
- Kendrick 2B
- Izturis 3B
- 3B Brown
- **Cabrera SS**
- SS Wood
- SS Rodriguez
- **Quinlan 1B**

Outfield/CA (OPS vs age)
- Guerrero RF
- CF Haynes
- **Anderson LF**
- Napoli CA
- Willits LF
- Matthews Jr. CF
- Mathis CA

Pitchers (FIP ERA vs age)
- Santana
- Colon
- Butcher
- Saunders
- Weaver
- Moseley
- Bootcheck
- **Shields**
- **Speier**
- Oliver
- Brandt
- **Lackey**
- **Escobar**
- Rodriguez

Good timing: Wood, Kendrick, and Weaver are developing just as the vets' contracts wind down. All that payroll flexibility will make offseasons interesting for LAA.

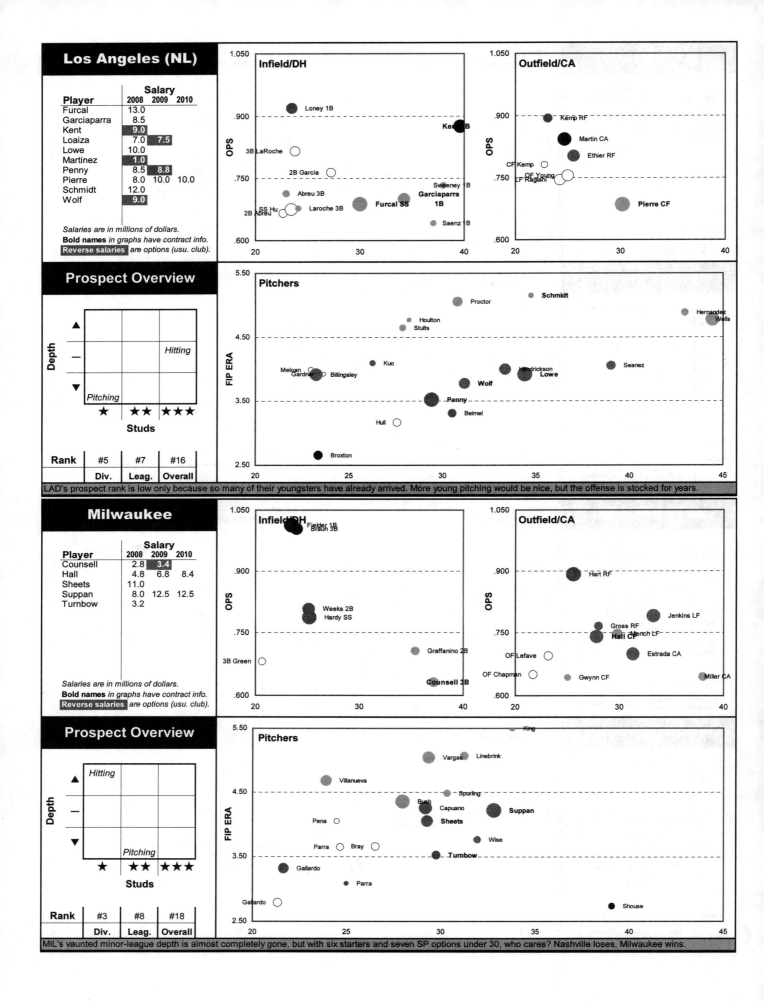

Los Angeles (NL)

Player	Salary 2008	2009	2010
Furcal	13.0		
Garciaparra	8.5		
Kent	9.0		
Loaiza	7.0	7.5	
Lowe	10.0		
Martinez	1.0		
Penny	8.5	8.8	
Pierre	8.0	10.0	10.0
Schmidt	12.0		
Wolf	9.0		

Salaries are in millions of dollars.
Bold names *in graphs have contract info.*
Reverse salaries *are options (usu. club).*

Prospect Overview

Rank	#5	#7	#16
	Div.	Leag.	Overall

LAD's prospect rank is low only because so many of their youngsters have already arrived. More young pitching would be nice, but the offense is stocked for years.

Milwaukee

Player	Salary 2008	2009	2010
Counsell	2.8	3.4	
Hall	4.8	6.8	8.4
Sheets	11.0		
Suppan	8.0	12.5	12.5
Turnbow	3.2		

Salaries are in millions of dollars.
Bold names *in graphs have contract info.*
Reverse salaries *are options (usu. club).*

Prospect Overview

Rank	#3	#8	#18
	Div.	Leag.	Overall

MIL's vaunted minor-league depth is almost completely gone, but with six starters and seven SP options under 30, who cares? Nashville loses, Milwaukee wins.

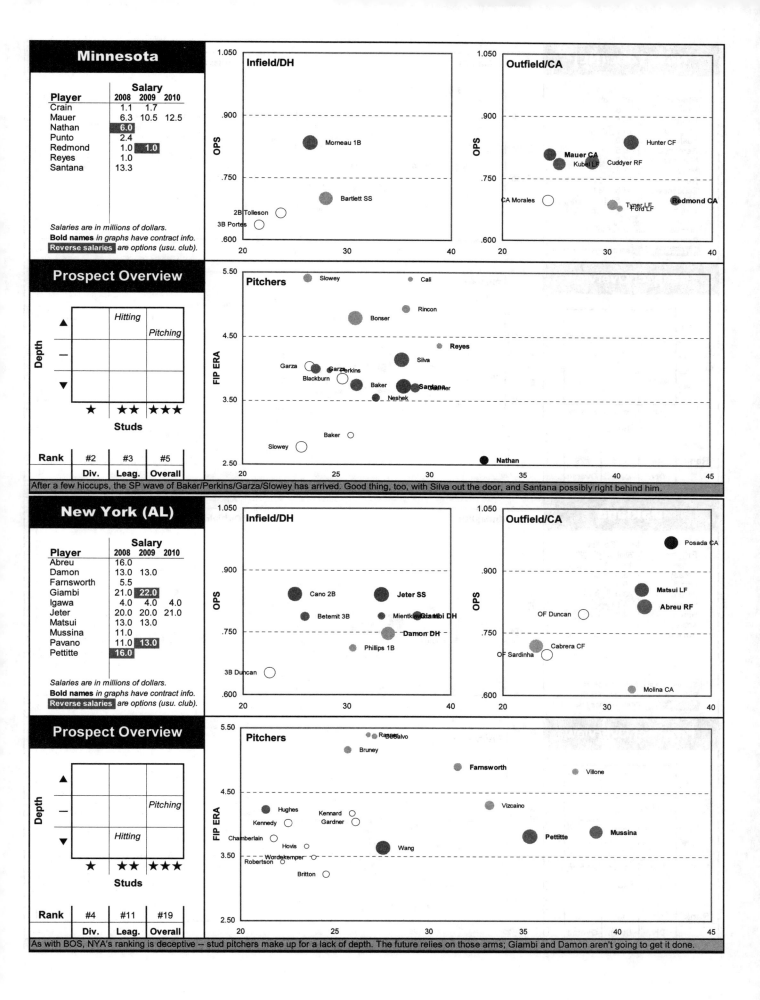

Minnesota

Player	Salary 2008	2009	2010
Crain	1.1	1.7	
Mauer	6.3	10.5	12.5
Nathan	6.0		
Punto	2.4		
Redmond	1.0	1.0	
Reyes	1.0		
Santana	13.3		

Salaries are in millions of dollars.
Bold names in graphs have contract info.
Reverse salaries are options (usu. club).

Infield/DH

Morneau 1B
Bartlett SS
2B Tolleson
3B Portes

Outfield/CA

Hunter CF
Mauer CA
Kubel LF
Cuddyer RF
CA Morales
Tyner LF
Ford LF
Redmond CA

Prospect Overview

Depth	Hitting	Pitching
▲		
—		
▼		
	★ ★★ ★★★	

Studs

Pitchers

Slowey
Cali
Rincon
Bonser
Reyes
Garza
Garza Perkins
Silva
Blackburn
Baker
Santana
Neshek
Baker
Slowey
Nathan

Rank	#2	#3	#5
	Div.	Leag.	Overall

After a few hiccups, the SP wave of Baker/Perkins/Garza/Slowey has arrived. Good thing, too, with Silva out the door, and Santana possibly right behind him.

New York (AL)

Player	Salary 2008	2009	2010
Abreu	16.0		
Damon	13.0	13.0	
Farnsworth	5.5		
Giambi	21.0	22.0	
Igawa	4.0	4.0	4.0
Jeter	20.0	20.0	21.0
Matsui	13.0	13.0	
Mussina	11.0		
Pavano	11.0	13.0	
Pettitte	16.0		

Salaries are in millions of dollars.
Bold names in graphs have contract info.
Reverse salaries are options (usu. club).

Infield/DH

Cano 2B
Jeter SS
Betemit 3B
Mientkiewicz Giambi DH
Damon DH
Phillips 1B
3B Duncan

Outfield/CA

Posada CA
Matsui LF
Abreu RF
OF Duncan
Cabrera CF
OF Sardinha
Molina CA

Prospect Overview

Depth		
▲		
—		Pitching
▼	Hitting	
	★ ★★ ★★★	

Studs

Pitchers

Ramirez DeSalvo
Bruney
Farnsworth
Villone
Hughes
Kennard
Vizcaino
Kennedy
Gardner
Chamberlain
Pettitte
Mussina
Hovis
Wang
Wordekemper
Robertson
Britton

Rank	#4	#11	#19
	Div.	Leag.	Overall

As with BOS, NYA's ranking is deceptive -- stud pitchers make up for a lack of depth. The future relies on those arms; Giambi and Damon aren't going to get it done.

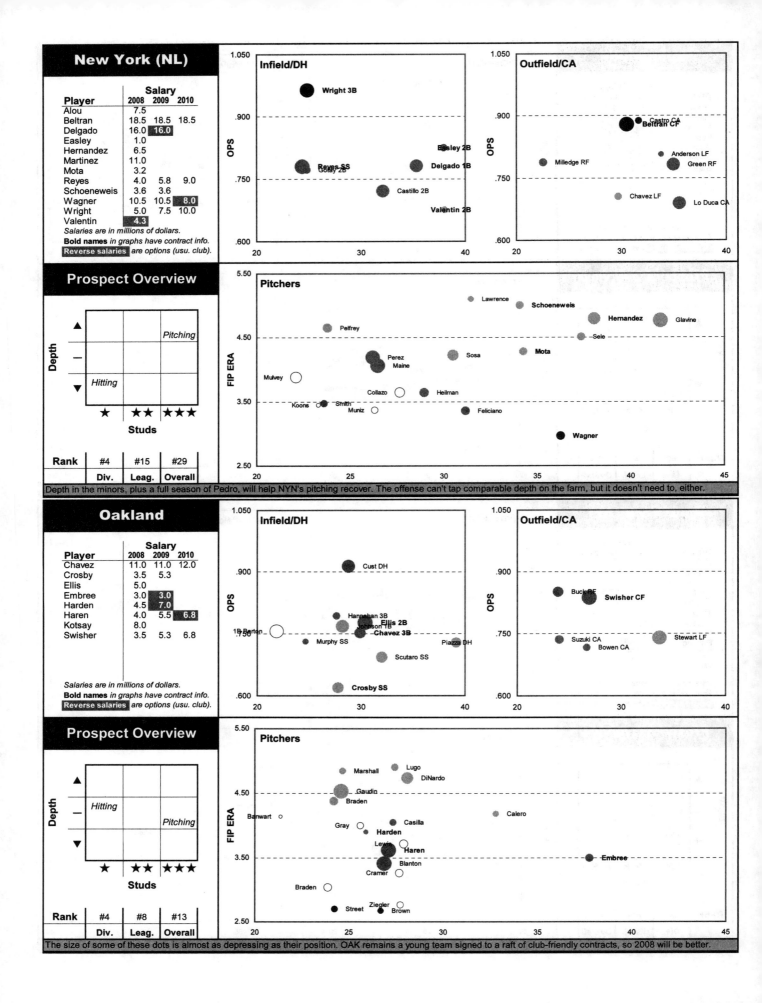

New York (NL)

Player	Salary 2008	2009	2010
Alou	7.5		
Beltran	18.5	18.5	18.5
Delgado	16.0	16.0	
Easley	1.0		
Hernandez	6.5		
Martinez	11.0		
Mota	3.2		
Reyes	4.0	5.8	9.0
Schoeneweis	3.6	3.6	
Wagner	10.5	10.5	8.0
Wright	5.0	7.5	10.0
Valentin		4.3	

Salaries are in millions of dollars.
Bold names *in graphs have contract info.*
Reverse salaries *are options (usu. club).*

Prospect Overview

Rank	#4	#15	#29
	Div.	Leag.	Overall

Depth in the minors, plus a full season of Pedro, will help NYN's pitching recover. The offense can't tap comparable depth on the farm, but it doesn't need to, either.

Oakland

Player	Salary 2008	2009	2010
Chavez	11.0	11.0	12.0
Crosby	3.5	5.3	
Ellis	5.0		
Embree	3.0	3.0	
Harden	4.5	7.0	
Haren	4.0	5.5	6.8
Kotsay	8.0		
Swisher	3.5	5.3	6.8

Salaries are in millions of dollars.
Bold names *in graphs have contract info.*
Reverse salaries *are options (usu. club).*

Prospect Overview

Rank	#4	#8	#13
	Div.	Leag.	Overall

The size of some of these dots is almost as depressing as their position. OAK remains a young team signed to a raft of club-friendly contracts, so 2008 will be better.

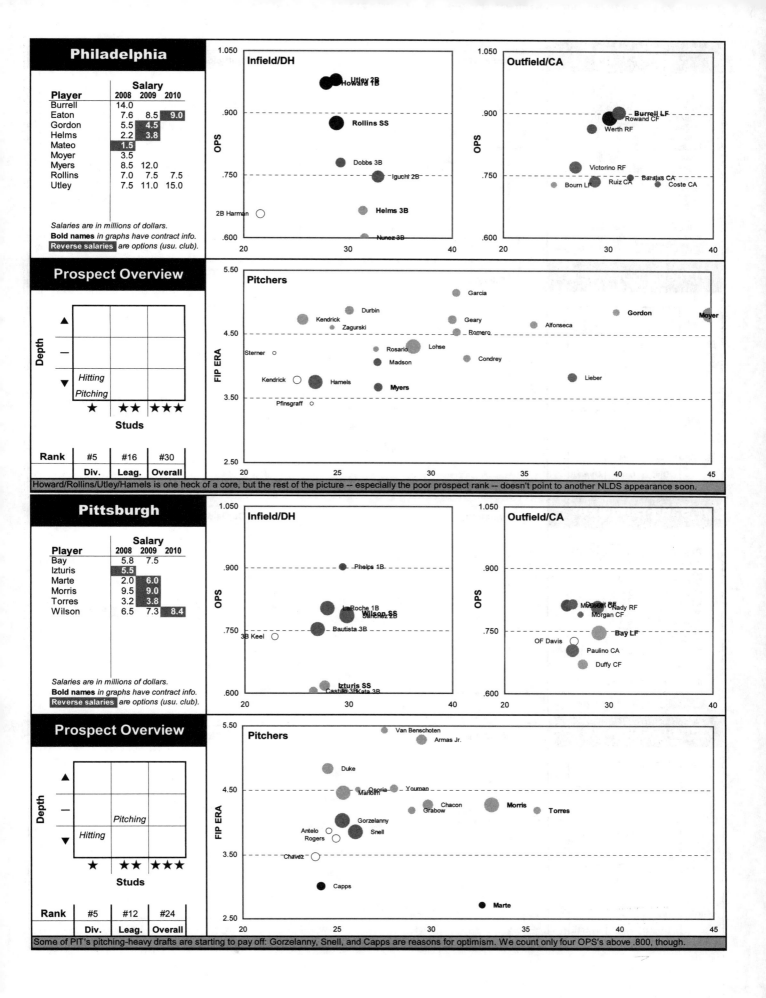

Philadelphia

Player	Salary		
	2008	2009	2010
Burrell	14.0		
Eaton	7.6	8.5	9.0
Gordon	5.5	4.5	
Helms	2.2	3.8	
Mateo	1.5		
Moyer	3.5		
Myers	8.5	12.0	
Rollins	7.0	7.5	7.5
Utley	7.5	11.0	15.0

Salaries are in millions of dollars.
Bold names *in graphs have contract info.*
Reverse salaries *are options (usu. club).*

Infield/DH

Utley 2B
Howard 1B
Rollins SS
Dobbs 3B
Iguchi 2B
2B Harman
Helms 3B
Nunez 3B

Outfield/CA

Burrell LF
Rowand CF
Werth RF
Victorino RF
Bourn LF
Barajas CA
Ruiz CA
Coste CA

Prospect Overview

Depth: ▲ — ▼
Hitting
Pitching
Studs: ★ ★★ ★★★

Rank	#5	#16	#30
	Div.	Leag.	Overall

Pitchers

Garcia
Durbin
Kendrick
Zagurski
Geary
Gordon
Moyer
Alfonseca
Romero
Sterner
Rosario
Lohse
Condrey
Madson
Kendrick
Lieber
Hamels
Myers
Pfinsgraff

Howard/Rollins/Utley/Hamels is one heck of a core, but the rest of the picture -- especially the poor prospect rank -- doesn't point to another NLDS appearance soon.

Pittsburgh

Player	Salary		
	2008	2009	2010
Bay	5.8	7.5	
Izturis	5.5		
Marte	2.0	6.0	
Morris	9.5	9.0	
Torres	3.2	3.8	
Wilson	6.5	7.3	8.4

Salaries are in millions of dollars.
Bold names *in graphs have contract info.*
Reverse salaries *are options (usu. club).*

Infield/DH

Phelps 1B
LaRoche 1B
Wilson SS
Sanchez 2B
Bautista 3B
3B Keel
Izturis SS
Castillo 3B Kata 3B

Outfield/CA

McLouth CF Grady RF
Morgan CF
Bay LF
OF Davis
Paulino CA
Duffy CF

Prospect Overview

Depth: ▲ — ▼
Pitching
Hitting
Studs: ★ ★★ ★★★

Rank	#5	#12	#24
	Div.	Leag.	Overall

Pitchers

Van Benschoten
Armas Jr.
Duke
Osoria
Youman
Maholm
Chacon
Morris
Grabow
Torres
Antelo
Gorzelanny
Rogers
Snell
Chavez
Capps
Marte

Some of PIT's pitching-heavy drafts are starting to pay off: Gorzelanny, Snell, and Capps are reasons for optimism. We count only four OPS's above .800, though.

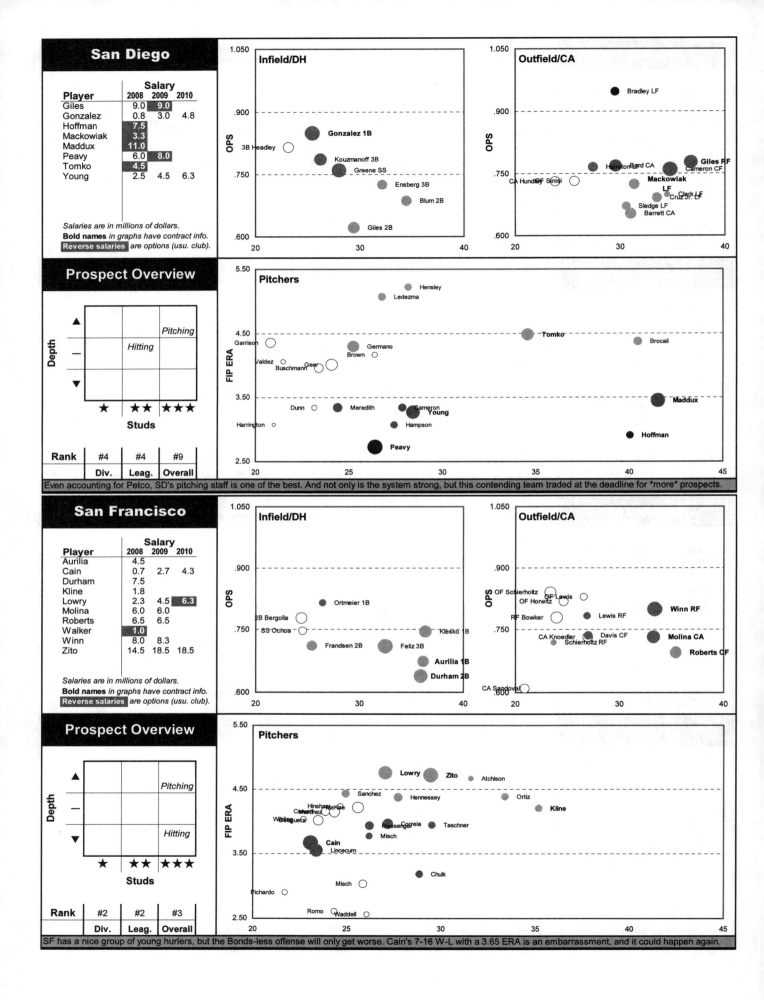

San Diego

Salary

Player	2008	2009	2010
Giles	9.0	9.0	
Gonzalez	0.8	3.0	4.8
Hoffman	7.5		
Mackowiak	3.3		
Maddux	11.0		
Peavy	6.0	8.0	
Tomko	4.5		
Young	2.5	4.5	6.3

Salaries are in millions of dollars.
Bold names *in graphs have contract info.*
Reverse salaries *are options (usu. club).*

Prospect Overview

Rank	#4	#4	#9
	Div.	Leag.	Overall

Depth: ▲ — ▼
Studs: ★ ★★ ★★★
Pitching / Hitting

Even accounting for Petco, SD's pitching staff is one of the best. And not only is the system strong, but this contending team traded at the deadline for *more* prospects.

San Francisco

Salary

Player	2008	2009	2010
Aurilia	4.5		
Cain	0.7	2.7	4.3
Durham	7.5		
Kline	1.8		
Lowry	2.3	4.5	6.3
Molina	6.0	6.0	
Roberts	6.5	6.5	
Walker	1.0		
Winn	8.0	8.3	
Zito	14.5	18.5	18.5

Salaries are in millions of dollars.
Bold names *in graphs have contract info.*
Reverse salaries *are options (usu. club).*

Prospect Overview

Rank	#2	#2	#3
	Div.	Leag.	Overall

Depth: ▲ — ▼
Studs: ★ ★★ ★★★
Pitching / Hitting

SF has a nice group of young hurlers, but the Bonds-less offense will only get worse. Cain's 7-16 W-L with a 3.65 ERA is an embarrassment, and it could happen again.

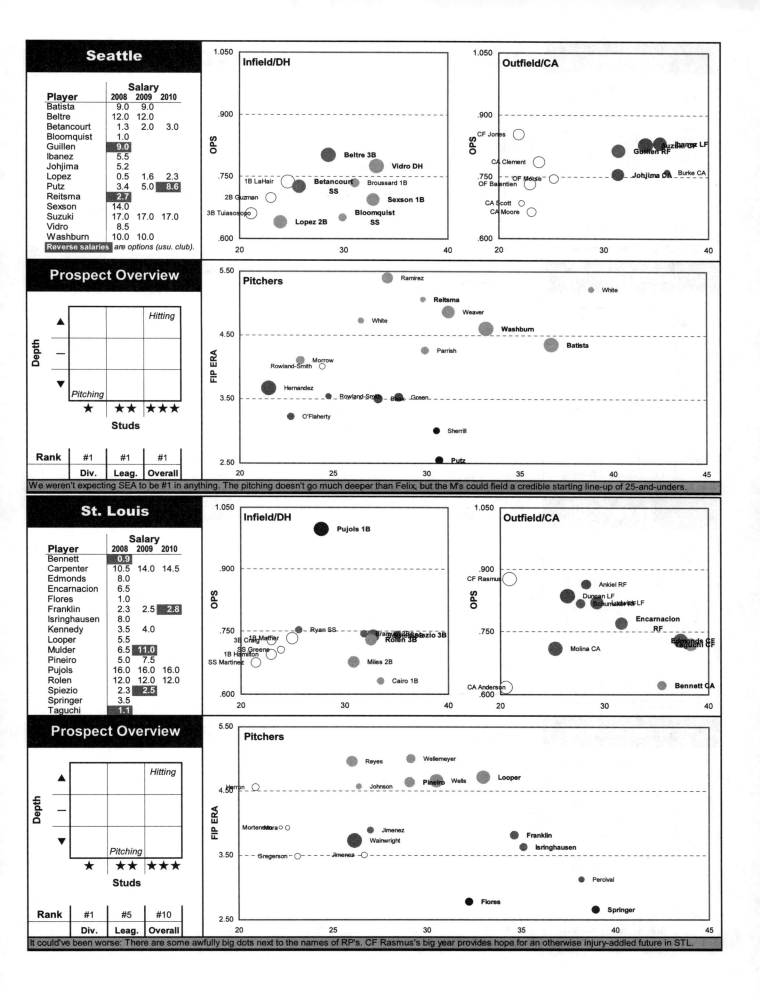

Seattle

Player	Salary 2008	2009	2010
Batista	9.0	9.0	
Beltre	12.0	12.0	
Betancourt	1.3	2.0	3.0
Bloomquist	1.0		
Guillen	9.0		
Ibanez	5.5		
Johjima	5.2		
Lopez	0.5	1.6	2.3
Putz	3.4	5.0	8.6
Reitsma	2.7		
Sexson	14.0		
Suzuki	17.0	17.0	17.0
Vidro	8.5		
Washburn	10.0	10.0	

Reverse salaries are options (usu. club).

Prospect Overview

Depth / Hitting / Pitching / Studs
★ ★★ ★★★

Rank	#1	#1	#1
	Div.	Leag.	Overall

Infield/DH — OPS
Beltre 3B, Vidro DH, 1B LaHair, Betancourt SS, Broussard 1B, 2B Guzman, 3B Tuiasosopo, Sexson 1B, Lopez 2B, Bloomquist SS

Outfield/CA — OPS
CF Jones, CA Clement, Suzuki RF, Ibanez LF, Guillen RF, OF Morse, OF Balentien, Johjima DH, Burke CA, CA Scott, CA Moore

Pitchers — FIP ERA
Ramirez, White, Reitsma, Weaver, White, Washburn, Parrish, Batista, Rowland-Smith, Morrow, Hernandez, Rowland-Smith, Baek, Green, O'Flaherty, Sherrill, Putz

We weren't expecting SEA to be #1 in anything. The pitching doesn't go much deeper than Felix, but the M's could field a credible starting line-up of 25-and-unders.

St. Louis

Player	Salary 2008	2009	2010
Bennett	0.9		
Carpenter	10.5	14.0	14.5
Edmonds	8.0		
Encarnacion	6.5		
Flores	1.0		
Franklin	2.3	2.5	2.8
Isringhausen	8.0		
Kennedy	3.5	4.0	
Looper	5.5		
Mulder	6.5	11.0	
Pineiro	5.0	7.5	
Pujols	16.0	16.0	16.0
Rolen	12.0	12.0	12.0
Spiezio	2.3	2.5	
Springer	3.5		
Taguchi	1.1		

Prospect Overview

Depth / Hitting / Pitching / Studs
★ ★★ ★★★

Rank	#1	#5	#10
	Div.	Leag.	Overall

Infield/DH — OPS
Pujols 1B, Ryan SS, 3B Craig, 1B Mather, SS Greene, 1B Hamilton, SS Martinez, Branyan 3B, Spiezio 3B, Rolen 3B, Miles 2B, Cairo 1B

Outfield/CA — OPS
CF Rasmus, Ankiel RF, Duncan LF, Schumaker RF, Ludwick LF, Encarnacion RF, Molina CA, Edmonds CF, Taguchi CF, CA Anderson, Bennett CA

Pitchers — FIP ERA
Reyes, Wellemeyer, Herron, Johnson, Pineiro, Wells, Looper, Mortensen, Mora, Jimenez, Franklin, Wainwright, Isringhausen, Gregerson, Jimenez, Percival, Flores, Springer

It could've been worse: There are some awfully big dots next to the names of RP's. CF Rasmus's big year provides hope for an otherwise injury-addled future in STL.

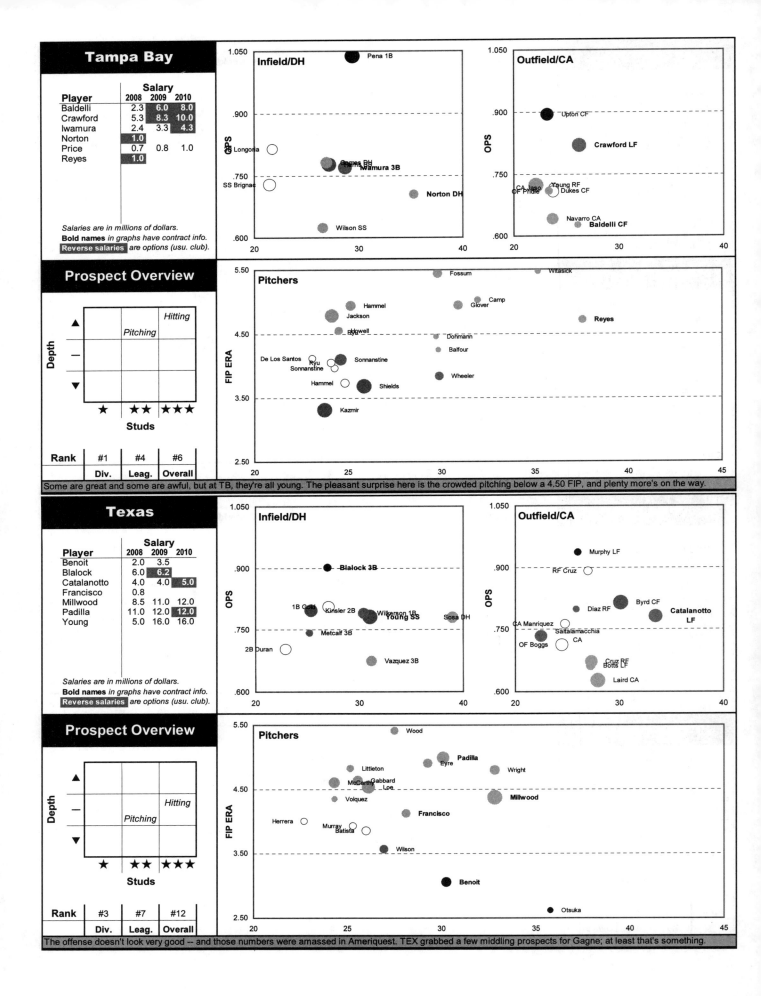

Tampa Bay

Infield/DH · **Outfield/CA**

Player	Salary		
	2008	2009	2010
Baldelli	2.3	6.0	8.0
Crawford	5.3	8.3	10.0
Iwamura	2.4	3.3	4.3
Norton	1.0		
Price	0.7	0.8	1.0
Reyes	1.0		

Salaries are in millions of dollars.
Bold names *in graphs have contract info.*
Reverse salaries *are options (usu. club).*

Prospect Overview

Depth — Pitching / Hitting
Studs — ★ ★★ ★★★

Rank	#1	#4	#6
	Div.	Leag.	Overall

Some are great and some are awful, but at TB, they're all young. The pleasant surprise here is the crowded pitching below a 4.50 FIP, and plenty more's on the way.

Texas

Infield/DH · **Outfield/CA**

Player	Salary		
	2008	2009	2010
Benoit	2.0	3.5	
Blalock	6.0	6.2	
Catalanotto	4.0	4.0	5.0
Francisco	0.8		
Millwood	8.5	11.0	12.0
Padilla	11.0	12.0	12.0
Young	5.0	16.0	16.0

Salaries are in millions of dollars.
Bold names *in graphs have contract info.*
Reverse salaries *are options (usu. club).*

Prospect Overview

Depth — Pitching / Hitting
Studs — ★ ★★ ★★★

Rank	#3	#7	#12
	Div.	Leag.	Overall

The offense doesn't look very good -- and those numbers were amassed in Ameriquest. TEX grabbed a few middling prospects for Gagne; at least that's something.

Toronto

Player	Salary 2008	2009	2010
Burnett	12.0	12.0	12.0
Glaus	12.8	11.3	
Halladay	10.0	14.3	15.8
McDonald	1.9	1.9	
Overbay	5.8	7.0	7.0
Ryan	10.0	10.0	10.0
Thomas	8.0	10.0	
Wells	0.5	1.5	12.5
Zaun	3.8	3.8	

Salaries are in millions of dollars.
Bold names in graphs have contract info.
Reverse salaries are options (usu. club).

Prospect Overview

Rank	#2	#9	#14
	Div.	Leag.	Overall

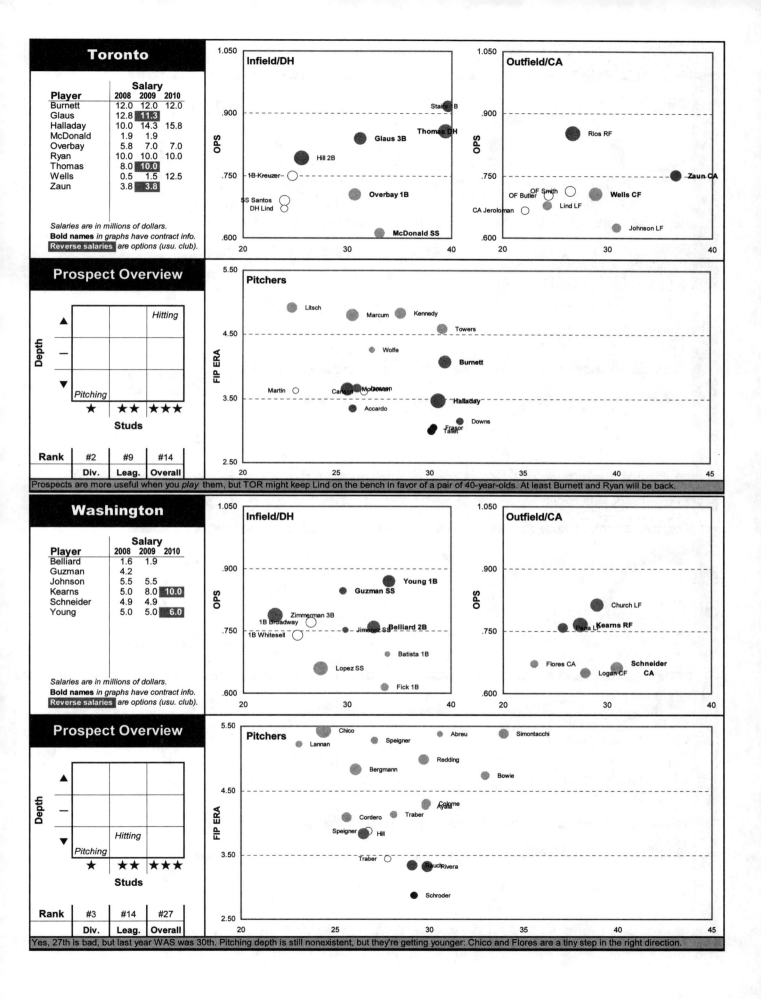

Infield/DH — OPS vs: Stairs 1B, Thomas DH, Glaus 3B, Hill 2B, 1B-Kreuzer, Overbay 1B, SS Santos, DH Lind, McDonald SS

Outfield/CA — OPS: Rios RF, Zaun CA, OF Butler, OF Smith, Lind LF, Wells CF, CA Jeroloman, Johnson LF

Pitchers — FIP ERA: Litsch, Marcum, Kennedy, Towers, Wolfe, Burnett, Martin, Carlson, McGowan, Halladay, Accardo, Frasor, Tallet, Downs

Prospects are more useful when you *play* them, but TOR might keep Lind on the bench in favor of a pair of 40-year-olds. At least Burnett and Ryan will be back.

Washington

Player	Salary 2008	2009	2010
Belliard	1.6	1.9	
Guzman	4.2		
Johnson	5.5	5.5	
Kearns	5.0	8.0	10.0
Schneider	4.9	4.9	
Young	5.0	5.0	6.0

Salaries are in millions of dollars.
Bold names in graphs have contract info.
Reverse salaries are options (usu. club).

Prospect Overview

Rank	#3	#14	#27
	Div.	Leag.	Overall

Infield/DH — OPS: Young 1B, Guzman SS, Zimmerman 3B, 1B Broadway, 1B Whitesell, Jimenez SS, Belliard 2B, Batista 1B, Lopez SS, Fick 1B

Outfield/CA — OPS: Church LF, Pena L, Kearns RF, Flores CA, Logan CF, Schneider CA

Pitchers — FIP ERA: Chico, Lannan, Speigner, Abreu, Simontacchi, Bergmann, Redding, Bowie, Cordero, Colome, Ayala, Traber, Speigner, Hill, Traber, Rauch, Rivera, Schroder

Yes, 27th is bad, but last year WAS was 30th. Pitching depth is still nonexistent, but they're getting younger: Chico and Flores are a tiny step in the right direction.

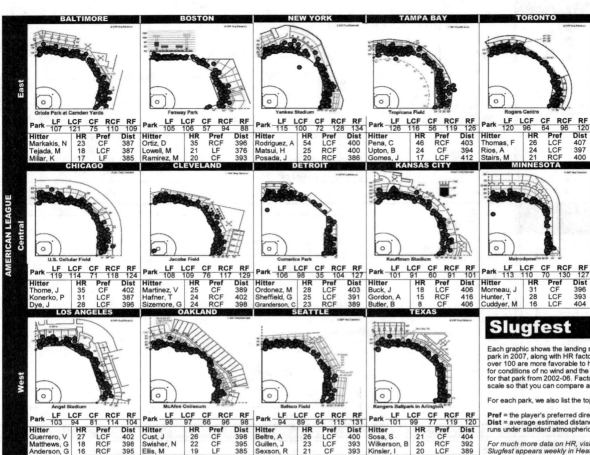

AMERICAN LEAGUE — East

BALTIMORE — Oriole Park at Camden Yards

Park	LF	LCF	CF	RCF	RF
	107	121	75	110	109

Hitter	HR	Pref	Dist
Markakis, N	23	CF	387
Tejada, M	18	LCF	387
Millar, K	17	LF	385

BOSTON — Fenway Park

Park	LF	LCF	CF	RCF	RF
	105	106	57	94	88

Hitter	HR	Pref	Dist
Ortiz, D	35	RCF	396
Lowell, M	21	LF	376
Ramirez, M	20	CF	393

NEW YORK — Yankee Stadium

Park	LF	LCF	CF	RCF	RF
	115	100	72	128	134

Hitter	HR	Pref	Dist
Rodriguez, A	54	CF	400
Matsui, H	25	RCF	400
Posada, J	20	RCF	386

TAMPA BAY — Tropicana Field

Park	LF	LCF	CF	RCF	RF
	126	116	56	119	128

Hitter	HR	Pref	Dist
Pena, C	46	RCF	403
Upton, B	24	CF	394
Gomes, J	17	LF	412

TORONTO — Rogers Centre

Park	LF	LCF	CF	RCF	RF
	120	96	64	96	120

Hitter	HR	Pref	Dist
Thomas, F	26	LCF	407
Rios, A	24	LCF	397
Stairs, M	21	RF	400

AMERICAN LEAGUE — Central

CHICAGO — U.S. Cellular Field

Park	LF	LCF	CF	RCF	RF
	119	114	71	118	124

Hitter	HR	Pref	Dist
Thome, J	35	CF	402
Konerko, P	31	LCF	387
Dye, J	28	LCF	396

CLEVELAND — Jacobs Field

Park	LF	LCF	CF	RCF	RF
	108	109	76	117	129

Hitter	HR	Pref	Dist
Martinez, V	25	CF	389
Hafner, T	24	RCF	402
Sizemore, G	24	RCF	398

DETROIT — Comerica Park

Park	LF	LCF	CF	RCF	RF
	106	98	35	104	127

Hitter	HR	Pref	Dist
Ordonez, M	28	LCF	403
Sheffield, G	25	LCF	391
Granderson, C	23	RCF	389

KANSAS CITY — Kauffman Stadium

Park	LF	LCF	CF	RCF	RF
	101	91	60	91	101

Hitter	HR	Pref	Dist
Buck, J	18	LCF	406
Gordon, A	15	RCF	416
Butler, B	8	CF	406

MINNESOTA — Metrodome

Park	LF	LCF	CF	RCF	RF
	113	110	70	130	127

Hitter	HR	Pref	Dist
Morneau, J	31	CF	396
Hunter, T	28	LCF	393
Cuddyer, M	16	LCF	404

AMERICAN LEAGUE — West

LOS ANGELES — Angel Stadium

Park	LF	LCF	CF	RCF	RF
	103	94	81	114	104

Hitter	HR	Pref	Dist
Guerrero, V	27	LCF	402
Matthews, G	18	RCF	398
Anderson, G	16	RCF	395

OAKLAND — McAfee Coliseum

Park	LF	LCF	CF	RCF	RF
	98	97	66	96	98

Hitter	HR	Pref	Dist
Cust, J	26	CF	398
Swisher, N	22	CF	395
Ellis, M	19	LF	385

SEATTLE — Safeco Field

Park	LF	LCF	CF	RCF	RF
	94	89	64	115	131

Hitter	HR	Pref	Dist
Beltre, A	26	LCF	400
Guillen, J	23	LCF	393
Sexson, R	21	CF	393

TEXAS — Rangers Ballpark in Arlington

Park	LF	LCF	CF	RCF	RF
	101	99	77	119	120

Hitter	HR	Pref	Dist
Sosa, S	21	CF	404
Wilkerson, B	20	RCF	392
Kinsler, I	20	LCF	389

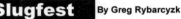

Slugfest
By Greg Rybarcyzk

Each graphic shows the landing spots of all home runs at that park in 2007, along with HR factors by direction. HR factors over 100 are more favorable to hitters. Factors are estimated for conditions of no wind and the average game temperature for that park from 2002-06. Factors are calculated on a single scale so that you can compare any direction to any other one.

For each park, we also list the top HR hitters for that team.

Pref = the player's preferred direction of his home runs.
Dist = average estimated distance of the player's home runs under standard atmospheric conditions.

For much more data on HR, visit www.HitTrackerOnline.com. Slugfest appears weekly in Heater Magazine.

NATIONAL LEAGUE — East

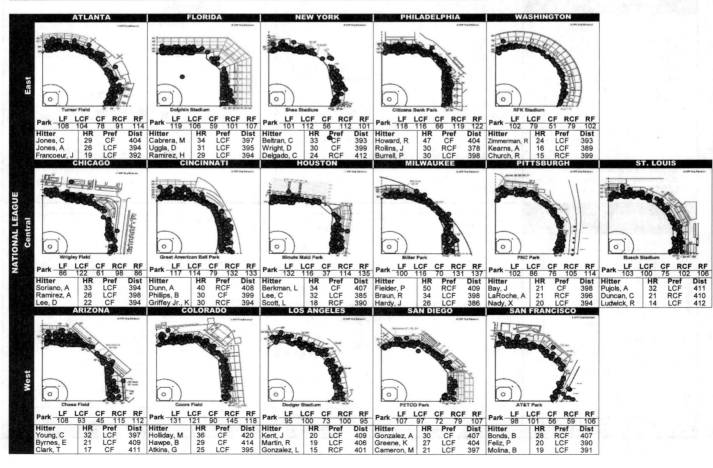

ATLANTA — Turner Field

Park	LF	LCF	CF	RCF	RF
	108	104	78	91	114

Hitter	HR	Pref	Dist
Jones, C	29	CF	404
Jones, A	26	LCF	394
Francoeur, J	19	LCF	392

FLORIDA — Dolphin Stadium

Park	LF	LCF	CF	RCF	RF
	119	106	59	101	107

Hitter	HR	Pref	Dist
Cabrera, M	34	LCF	397
Uggla, D	31	CF	395
Ramirez, H	29	LCF	394

NEW YORK — Shea Stadium

Park	LF	LCF	CF	RCF	RF
	101	112	56	112	101

Hitter	HR	Pref	Dist
Beltran, C	33	CF	393
Wright, D	30	CF	390
Delgado, C	24	RCF	412

PHILADELPHIA — Citizens Bank Park

Park	LF	LCF	CF	RCF	RF
	118	116	66	119	122

Hitter	HR	Pref	Dist
Howard, R	47	CF	404
Rollins, J	30	RCF	378
Burrell, P	30	LCF	398

WASHINGTON — RFK Stadium

Park	LF	LCF	CF	RCF	RF
	102	79	51	79	102

Hitter	HR	Pref	Dist
Zimmerman, R	24	LCF	393
Kearns, A	16	LCF	389
Church, R	15	RCF	399

NATIONAL LEAGUE — Central

CHICAGO — Wrigley Field

Park	LF	LCF	CF	RCF	RF
	86	122	61	98	86

Hitter	HR	Pref	Dist
Soriano, A	33	LCF	394
Ramirez, A	26	LCF	398
Lee, D	22	CF	394

CINCINNATI — Great American Ball Park

Park	LF	LCF	CF	RCF	RF
	117	114	79	132	133

Hitter	HR	Pref	Dist
Dunn, A	40	RCF	408
Phillips, B	30	CF	399
Griffey Jr., K	30	RCF	394

HOUSTON — Minute Maid Park

Park	LF	LCF	CF	RCF	RF
	132	116	37	114	135

Hitter	HR	Pref	Dist
Berkman, L	34	CF	407
Lee, C	32	LCF	385
Scott, L	18	RCF	390

MILWAUKEE — Miller Park

Park	LF	LCF	CF	RCF	RF
	100	116	70	114	137

Hitter	HR	Pref	Dist
Fielder, P	50	RCF	409
Braun, R	34	LCF	398
Hardy, J	26	LCF	386

PITTSBURGH — PNC Park

Park	LF	LCF	CF	RCF	RF
	102	86	76	105	114

Hitter	HR	Pref	Dist
Bay, J	21	CF	398
LaRoche, A	21	RCF	396
Nady, X	20	LCF	394

ST. LOUIS — Busch Stadium

Park	LF	LCF	CF	RCF	RF
	103	100	75	102	114

Hitter	HR	Pref	Dist
Pujols, A	32	LCF	411
Duncan, C	21	RCF	410
Ludwick, R	14	LCF	412

NATIONAL LEAGUE — West

ARIZONA — Chase Field

Park	LF	LCF	CF	RCF	RF
	108	93	45	115	112

Hitter	HR	Pref	Dist
Young, C	32	LCF	397
Byrnes, E	21	LCF	409
Clark, T	17	CF	411

COLORADO — Coors Field

Park	LF	LCF	CF	RCF	RF
	131	121	90	145	118

Hitter	HR	Pref	Dist
Holliday, M	36	CF	420
Hawpe, B	29	CF	414
Atkins, G	25	LCF	395

LOS ANGELES — Dodger Stadium

Park	LF	LCF	CF	RCF	RF
	95	100	73	100	95

Hitter	HR	Pref	Dist
Kent, J	20	LCF	409
Martin, R	19	LCF	406
Gonzalez, L	15	RCF	401

SAN DIEGO — PETCO Park

Park	LF	LCF	CF	RCF	RF
	107	97	72	79	107

Hitter	HR	Pref	Dist
Gonzalez, A	30	CF	407
Greene, K	27	LCF	404
Cameron, M	21	LCF	397

SAN FRANCISCO — AT&T Park

Park	LF	LCF	CF	RCF	RF
	98	101	56	59	106

Hitter	HR	Pref	Dist
Bonds, B	28	RCF	407
Feliz, P	20	LCF	390
Molina, B	19	LCF	391